A READER IN
CATHOLIC SOCIAL TEACHING

A Reader in
Catholic Social Teaching

From *Syllabus Errorum* to *Deus Caritas Est*

Edited and with a Preface by
Peter A. Kwasniewski, PH.D.

CLUNY MEDIA

CLUNY HARDCOVER EDITION, 2023

For information regarding this title
or any other Cluny Media publication,
please write to info@clunymedia.com, or to
Cluny Media, P.O. Box 1664, Providence, RI 02901

Translation of *Dignitatis Humanae* by Michael Pakaluk, Ph.D.
Used with permission and gratitude.

ISBN: 978-1949899153

Cover design by Clarke & Clarke
Cover image: Giovanni di Paolo, *Paradise*, 1445,
tempera and gold on canvas, transferred from wood
Courtesy of The Metropolitan Museum of Art, New York

Table of Contents

† ABRIDGED

PIUS XII (1939–1958)

SECOND VATICAN COUNCIL (1962–1965)

JOHN PAUL II (1978–2005)

CONGREGATION FOR THE DOCTRINE OF THE FAITH

BENEDICT XVI (2005–2013)

PREFACE

⁓

T his collection of major documentary sources for the social doctrine of the Catholic Church has been in the works for many years. Its remote origins go back to the academic year 1993–1994, when I had the opportunity to participate in extracurricular seminars at Thomas Aquinas College on many of the documents included here, which gave me a first unforgettable experience of the grandeur, critical force, coherence, and fertile adaptability of Catholic social teaching (CST). The collection has evolved over many years of teaching, culminating in a set of readings used for a senior theology course at Wyoming Catholic College, "Life in Christ," which begins with fundamental moral theology, moves into marriage and family as a natural and supernatural reality of the moral order, and then devotes the lion's share to political and economic matters. Experience has shown that this complex approach significantly enriches the conversation about social ethics and the reign of Christ in the world. To be most complete, one would need to include discussion of the priesthood and consecrated life, but as any collection must have its limits, this book does not contain any *ex professo* treatment of these.

If one wishes to become more than superficially acquainted with CST, there is simply no substitute for reading the original documents of the popes, who from Leo XIII onwards are the real masters in this area of moral theology. Their ideas, terminology, critiques, and counsels have left a permanent mark not only on Catholic thinking, as is to be expected, but perhaps more surprisingly on a wide variety of secular schools of thought and political institutions. There is always a need—especially now in the third millennium, when such deep shadows loom across the modern world—to return *ad fontes*, to drink from these pure papal streams, and not to allow mountains of secondary literature, most of it superficial or agenda-driven or both, to stand between us and the wisdom of the Church's magisterium.[1]

1.　See Stephen Sharkey's disconcerting study of the CST materials available today: "Unwrapping Our 'Best Kept Secret': A Critical Review of Some Best-Selling Textbooks in Catholic Social Teaching," in *The Catholic Social Science Review* IX (2004): 317–335.

i

I compiled this book because, in my opinion, there existed no introductory sourcebook that conveys the full breadth and depth of papal social teaching. Nearly everyone falls into the trap of equating CST with *Rerum Novarum* and its commemorative documents, as if economic issues such as labor-capital relations were the chief concern of this branch of moral theology. While it is true that the phrase "the social question" came to refer primarily to the condition of the working classes and to achieving justice in a world of drastically unequal property distribution, CST goes far beyond economics, as the great pope of the social question, Leo XIII, stated in 1901:

> We have designedly made mention here of virtue and religion. For, it is the opinion of some, and the error is already very common, that the social question is merely an economic one, whereas in point of fact it is, above all, a moral and religious matter, and for that reason must be settled by the principles of morality and according to the dictates of religion.[2]

Six years earlier he had written:

> This question cannot be regarded from one standpoint only. It is indeed concerned with external goods, but it is preeminently concerned with religion and morals. It is also directly connected with the civil constitution of the laws, so that in the last analysis, it has a broad reference to the rights and duties of all classes.[3]

But there is no need to multiply examples; one will see just by reading *Rerum Novarum* how its author refers to a host of earlier encyclicals in which he lays the broad and deep foundations upon which the analysis given in that encyclical rests. In fact, the subject-matter of CST is nothing less than the totality of man's social life, in all its dimensions—domestic, political, cultural, and, of course, economic. The available CST readers and textbooks take too much for granted, carve out too narrow a scope, and fail, in the end, to engage the questions that are most profound *and* most urgent.

The purpose of the present collection, then, is to facilitate a comprehensive one-semester (or preferably two-semester) introduction to CST that is faithful to the Church's own mind and heart by remaining anchored in her classic

---

2. *Graves de Communi*, 11.

3. *Permoti Nos*, 5.

documents. With the exception of a few texts that I scanned or typed in, the documents gathered here were originally downloaded either from the Vatican's website (www.vatican.va) or from "Papal Encyclicals Online" (www.papalen-cyclicals.net). Sadly, all the texts were stricken with the plague of typographi-cal errors and, at times, were missing entire phrases. Hundreds of corrections have thus been made to improve the quality of the text presented here, including re-translations of poorly-translated sentences.

If there is one drawback to using primary sources, it would have to be the sheer length of these documents: many are circa 15,000 words; some go beyond 20,000. To make this collection a realistic teaching tool, I abridged some of the longer documents, removing things purely circumstantial (such as mentions of meetings or congresses that have long since passed) and omitting paragraphs that merely repeat, without elaboration, what has been taught several times before, or that descend into details not so important for an introductory course. Any cuts that have been made are announced by the use of ellipses and brackets. As a result, someone who wishes to do further research could easily look up the other passages.

Headings, subdivisions, and paragraph or section numbers are present in some papal documents, absent in others. The only pattern one can see is that, over the passage of time, papal documents tend to provide ever more in the way of headings and divisions and are more generous in their use of formatting (prob-ably in step with the progress of publishing technology). In this book, paragraph numbers and headings have been added where they were lacking, for ease of study and reference. As with abridgments, so with formatting: a moment's glance at the official Latin text will indicate what (if anything) has been superimposed by a translator or an editor.

Concerning footnotes: all notes that simply cite sources—Scripture, Fathers, Doctors, Popes, etc.—are from the original documents and are to be consid-ered part of them. Historical or philosophical commentary, on the other hand, is usually the work of one or another editor of these documents. Such editorial additions are marked with brackets to set them apart from the content promul-gated by the authors. On account of ellipses and editorial notes, the numbering of the notes is often not identical to the numbering found in the official versions published in *Acta Leonis, Acta Sanctae Sedis*, or *Acta Apostolicae Sedis*. Hence, anyone who intends to do research or publishing in CST beyond the confines of this book would be well advised to have a look at the original (Latin) text and gather bearings from it. In general, I would encourage serious students of the Church's magisterium to get used to looking at important passages *in the Latin text* transmitted by publications of the Apostolic See. This is the *only* official text, the one that is promulgated and authoritative. The translations are approved in a generic way (they are allowed to be published), but they are not "promulgated," nor is there any guarantee of perfect fidelity to the original source. Indeed, regrettably, one encounters places where the meaning of the author has been poorly served in the translation, and this can have, at times, the effect of obscuring even the doctrinal content. As with any translation of any classic text, one should therefore be a "critical reader" and get used to working with the original texts if possible.

A word should be said about why certain documents are *not* found in this collection. My general policy was to select classic texts that articulate principles with great clarity and relative succinctness. Some later documents, such as those of Vatican II, tend to lack this clarity and succinctness. Moreover, recent materials tend to be better known than the classic sources to which they continually refer. For example, the content of *Gaudium et Spes* is largely a résumé and synthesis of the magisterium of Pius XII and John XXIII, while its most fruitful ideas were taken up and better developed by John Paul II. In like manner, the content of the Decree on the Apostolate of the Laity *Apostolicam Actuositatem* is not altogether novel but was anticipated in earlier papal encyclicals, most strikingly in Leo XIII's *Sapientiae Christianae* and in Pius XI's exhortations of the 1920s and 1930s. Hence, for the student who wants to enter most deeply into Vatican II's contribution to CST, there is no better way than to study the Council's roots in the magisterium of the preconciliar popes as well as the Council's reception and development in the magisterium of the postconciliar popes.

This collection does include the highly controversial Decree on Religious Liberty *Dignitatis Humanae* of the Second Vatican Council, over the interpretation of which more ink has been spilled than over that of any other in the Church's history. Regardless of where one stands on the hermeneutical spectrum, *Dignitatis Humanae* raises more questions than it answers. But as it forms an important moment in the arc of CST's consideration of freedom, rights, and the place of religion and objective morality in civil society and the international community, it cannot be avoided. Readers who wish to delve more deeply into whether or how it is compatible with traditional CST should look into the illuminating debate between Martin Rhonheimer and Thomas Pink. This book offers the reader a special advantage in Dr. Michael Pakaluk's superb new translation of *Dignitatis Humanae*, which hews far closer to the original Latin than the standard English translation people have been citing for decades. I am grateful to Dr. Pakaluk for his permission to include it in this collection of magisterial texts.

As an aid to teachers and students, a syllabus for a one-semester course on Catholic Social Teaching has been included after the Preface. I have taught from this syllabus (or ones quite like it) for many years and found the selection and pacing of readings to be excellent for college students. It could also be adopted for homeschool use and for self-study. The syllabus given herein is keyed only to documents contained in this book, and utilizes all of them. When I teach the course, I also add some documents prior to Pius IX's *Quanta Cura* for the sake of establishing historical context for the Church/State question: the *Epistle to Diognetus*; the *Edict of Milan*; excerpts from the *Codex Theodosianus*; Pope Gelasius I, *Duo Quippe Sunt*; Pope Boniface VIII, *Unam Sanctam*; John Locke's *Letter on Toleration*; excerpts from other French, English, American, and German Enlightenment authors. Prior to Leo XIII's *Testem Benevolentia* we read John Ireland's Introduction to *The Life of Father Hecker*. I would be happy to provide these texts upon request: professorkwasniewski@gmail.com. I would say, however, that a successful course could be taught exclusively from the texts in this book, even without these additional contextual readings.

May this collection assist its readers to come to an ever-greater appreciation of the nobility of man, made in God's image to rule and to keep the garden of the world; the lofty purpose of our freedom, which finds its origin and its fulfillment in loving surrender to the truth that sets us free; and the Kingship of Christ, our God and Savior, who took on our human nature to share with us His ever-blessed divinity.

~Peter A. Kwasniewski, Ph.D.
September 8, 2017
The Nativity of the Blessed Virgin Mary

SAMPLE SYLLABUS

—

The syllabus below furnishes one possible order in which to read all the documents contained in this book. It approaches the subject of Catholic Social Teaching by first laying the foundations of Christian moral action (via *Veritatis Splendor*); second, looking to marriage and the family as the most natural form of social life and the most basic "cell" of society; third, investigating society, state, and culture; fourth, focusing on specifically economic issues; and finally, reviewing the entire realm of morality from the vantage of the Kingship of Christ. Because the course is designed thematically while the book is ordered chronologically, the reading assignments jump from one part of the book to another, but, as mentioned, all of the book is utilized.

FOUNDATIONS OF MORAL THEOLOGY

1. John Paul II, *Veritatis Splendor*, Introduction and Chapter 1: pp. 318–40.
2. John Paul II, *Veritatis Splendor*, Chapter 2, nn. 28–53: pp. 340–61.
3. John Paul II, *Veritatis Splendor*, Chapter 2, cont'd, nn. 54–83: pp. 362–84.
4. John Paul II, *Veritatis Splendor*, Chapter 3 and Conclusion: pp. 384–411.

THE FAMILY

5. Pius XI, *Casti Connubii*, Parts I & II: pp. 166–94.
6. Pius XI, *Casti Connubii*, Part III; John Paul II, *Familiaris Consortio*†: pp. 194–205, 264–75.
7. John Paul II, *Gratissimam Sane*, Introduction and Part I: pp. 412–50.
8. John Paul II, *Gratissimam Sane*, Part II; *Evangelium Vitae*†: pp. 450–84.
9. Benedict XVI, *Deus Caritas Est*, Introduction & Part I: pp. 497–511.

---

† These documents are abridged.

SOCIETY, STATE, AND CULTURE

10. Benedict XVI, *Deus Caritas Est*, Part II & Conclusion: pp. 511–29.
11. Pius IX, *Quanta Cura* & *Syllabus Errorum*: pp. 1–19.
12. Leo XIII, *Diuturnum Illud*: pp. 20–31.
13. Leo XIII, *Immortale Dei*: pp. 32–51.
14. Leo XIII, *Libertas Praestantissimum*: pp. 52–71.
15. Leo XIII, *Sapientiae Christianae*: pp. 72–91.
16. Leo XIII, *Au Milieu des Sollicitudes* and *Longinqua Oceani*†: pp. 122–41.
17. Leo XIII, *Testem Benevolentiae*: pp. 142–51.
18. Pius XII, *Ci Riesce*: pp. 242–50.
19. Vatican II, *Dignitatis Humanae*: pp. 251–63.
20. Congregation for the Doctrine of the Faith, *On the Participation of Catholics in Political Life*: pp. 485–96.

ECONOMIC JUSTICE

21. Leo XIII, *Rerum Novarum*: pp. 92–121.
22. Pius XI, *Quadragesimo Anno*†: pp. 207–41.
23. John Paul II, *Centesimus Annus*†: pp. 276–317.

THE KINGSHIP OF CHRIST

24. Pius XI, *Quas Primas*: pp. 152–65.

QUANTA CURA

Condemning Current Errors

Encyclical Letter of Pope Pius IX,
promulgated December 8, 1864

To our Venerable Brethren, all Patriarchs, Primates, Archbishops, and Bishops
having Favor and Communion with the Holy See. Venerable Brethren, Health and
Apostolic Benediction.

With how great care and pastoral vigilance the Roman Pontiffs, Our predecessors, fulfilling the duty and office committed to them by the Lord Christ Himself in the person of most Blessed Peter, Prince of the Apostles, of feeding the lambs and the sheep, have never ceased sedulously to nourish the Lord's whole flock with words of faith and with salutary doctrine, and to guard it from poisoned pastures, is thoroughly known to all, and especially to you, venerable brethren. And truly the same, Our predecessors, asserters of justice, being especially anxious for the salvation of souls, had nothing ever more at heart than by their most wise letters and constitutions to unveil and condemn all those heresies and errors which, being adverse to our divine Faith, to the doctrine of the Catholic Church, to purity of morals, and to the eternal salvation of men, have frequently excited violent tempests, and have miserably afflicted both Church and State. For which cause the same Our predecessors, have, with apostolic fortitude, constantly resisted the nefarious enterprises of wicked men, who, like raging waves of the sea foaming out their own confusion, and promising liberty whereas they are the slaves of corruption, have striven by their deceptive opinions and most pernicious writings to raze the foundations of the Catholic religion and of civil society, to remove from among men all virtue and justice, to deprave persons, and especially inexperienced youth, to lead it into the snares of error, and at length to tear it from the bosom of the Catholic Church.

2. But now, as is already well known to you, venerable brethren, scarcely had we been elevated to this Chair of Peter (by the hidden counsel of divine Providence, certainly by no merit of our own), when, seeing with the greatest grief of Our soul a truly awful storm excited by so many evil opinions, and seeing

also the most grievous calamities never sufficiently to be deplored which overspread the Christian people from so many errors, and following the illustrious example of Our predecessors, We raised Our voice according to the duty of Our apostolic ministry, and in many published encyclical letters and allocutions delivered in consistory, and other apostolic letters, we condemned the chief errors of this most unhappy age, and we excited your admirable episcopal vigilance, and we again and again admonished and exhorted all sons of the Catholic Church, to us most dear, that they should altogether abhor and flee from the contagion of so dire a pestilence. And especially in our first encyclical letter written to you on 9 November 1846, and in two allocutions delivered by us in consistory, the one on 9 December 1854, and the other on 9 June 1862, we condemned the monstrous portents of opinion which prevail especially in this age, bringing with them the greatest loss of souls and detriment of civil society itself; which are grievously opposed also, not only to the Catholic Church and her salutary doctrine and venerable rights, but also to the eternal natural law engraved by God in all men's hearts, and to right reason; and from which almost all other errors have their origin.

3. But, although we have not omitted often to proscribe and reprobate the chief errors of this kind, yet the cause of the Catholic Church, and the salvation of souls entrusted to us by God, and the welfare of human society itself, altogether demand that we again stir up your pastoral solicitude to exterminate other evil opinions, which spring forth from the said errors as from a fountain. Which false and perverse opinions are on that ground the more to be detested, because they chiefly tend to this, that that salutary influence be impeded and even removed, which the Catholic Church, according to the institution and command of her divine Author, should freely exercise even to the end of the world—not only over private individuals, but over nations, peoples, and their sovereign princes; and tend also to take away that mutual fellowship and concord of counsels between Church and State which has ever proved itself propitious and salutary, both for religious and civil interests.[1]

For you well know, venerable brethren, that at this time men are found not a few who, applying to civil society the impious and absurd principle of "naturalism," as they call it, dare to teach that "the best constitution of public society and (also) civil progress altogether require that human society be conducted and governed without regard being had to religion any more than if it did not exist; or, at least, without any distinction being made between the true religion and false ones." And, against the doctrine of Scripture, of the Church, and of the

---

1. Gregory XVI, encyclical *Mirari vos*, August 15, 1832.

Holy Fathers, they do not hesitate to assert that "that is the best condition of civil society in which no duty is recognized, as attached to the civil power, of restraining by enacted penalties offenders against the Catholic religion, except so far as public peace may require." From which totally false idea of social government they do not fear to foster that erroneous opinion, most fatal in its effects on the Catholic Church and the salvation of souls, called by Our predecessor, Gregory XVI, an "insanity" [*deliramentum*], viz., that "liberty of conscience and worship is each man's personal right, which ought to be legally proclaimed and asserted in every rightly constituted society; and that a right resides in the citizens to an absolute liberty, which should be restrained by no authority whether ecclesiastical or civil, whereby they may be able openly and publicly to manifest and declare any of their ideas whatever, either by word of mouth, by the press, or in any other way." But, while they rashly affirm this, they do not think and consider that they are preaching "liberty of perdition"[2]; and that "if human arguments are always allowed free room for discussion, there will never be wanting men who will dare to resist truth, and to trust in the flowing speech of human wisdom; whereas we know, from the very teaching of our Lord Jesus Christ, how carefully Christian faith and wisdom should avoid this most injurious babbling."[3]

4. And, since where religion has been removed from civil society, and the doctrine and authority of divine revelation repudiated, the genuine notion itself of justice and human right is darkened and lost, and the place of true justice and legitimate right is supplied by material force, thence it appears why it is that some, utterly neglecting and disregarding the surest principles of sound reason, dare to proclaim that "the people's will, manifested by what is called public opinion or in some other way, constitutes a supreme law, free from all divine and human control; and that in the political order accomplished facts, from the very circumstance that they are accomplished, have the force of right." But who does not see and clearly perceive that human society, when set loose from the bonds of religion and true justice, can have, in truth, no other end than the purpose of obtaining and amassing wealth, and that society under such circumstances follows no other law in its actions, except the unchastened desire of ministering to its own pleasure and interests? For this reason, men of the kind pursue with bitter hatred the religious orders, although these have deserved extremely well of Christendom, civilization, and literature, and cry out that the same have no legitimate reason for being permitted to exist; and thus these evil men applaud the calumnies of heretics. For, as Pius VI, Our predecessor, taught most wisely,

---

2.   St. Augustine, *Epistle* 105 (166).
3.   St. Leo, *Epistle* 14 (133), sect. 2.

"the abolition of regulars is injurious to that state in which the evangelical counsels are openly professed; it is injurious to a method of life praised in the Church as agreeable to apostolic doctrine; it is injurious to the illustrious founders themselves, whom we venerate on our altars, who did not establish these societies but by God's inspiration."[4] And these wretches also impiously declare that permission should be refused to citizens and to the Church, "whereby they may openly give alms for the sake of Christian charity"; and that the law should be abrogated "whereby on certain fixed days servile works are prohibited because of God's worship"; and on the most deceptive pretext that the said permission and law are opposed to the principles of the best public economy. Moreover, not content with removing religion from public society, they wish to banish it also from private families. For, teaching and professing the most fatal error of communism and socialism, they assert that "domestic society or the family derives the whole principle of its existence from the civil law alone; and, consequently, that on civil law alone depend all rights of parents over their children, and especially that of providing for education." By which impious opinions and machinations these most deceitful men chiefly aim at this result, viz., that the salutary teaching and influence of the Catholic Church may be entirely banished from the instruction and education of youth, and that the tender and flexible minds of young men may be infected and depraved by every most pernicious error and vice. For all who have endeavored to throw into confusion things both sacred and secular, and to subvert the right order of society, and to abolish all rights, human and divine, have always (as we above hinted) devoted all their nefarious schemes, devices and efforts, to deceiving and depraving incautious youth and have placed all their hope in its corruption. For which reason they never cease by every wicked method to assail the clergy, both secular and regular, from whom (as the surest monuments of history conspicuously attest), so many great advantages have abundantly flowed to Christianity, civilization and literature, and to proclaim that "the clergy, as being hostile to the true and beneficial advance of science and civilization, should be removed from the whole charge and duty of instructing and educating youth."

5. Others meanwhile, reviving the wicked and so often condemned inventions of innovators, dare with signal impudence to subject to the will of the civil authority the supreme authority of the Church and of this Apostolic See given to her by Christ Himself, and to deny all those rights of the same Church and See which concern matters of the external order. For they are not ashamed of affirming "that the Church's laws do not bind in conscience unless when they

---

4. Epistle to Cardinal De la Rochefoucault, March 10, 1791.

are promulgated by the civil power; that acts and decrees of the Roman Pontiffs, referring to religion and the Church, need the civil power's sanction and appro- bation, or at least its consent; that the apostolic constitutions,[5] whereby secret societies are condemned (whether an oath of secrecy be or be not required in such societies), and whereby their frequenters and favorers are smitten with anathema, have no force in those regions of the world wherein associations of the kind are tolerated by the civil government; that the excommunication pronounced by the Council of Trent and by Roman Pontiffs against those who assail and usurp the Church's rights and possessions, rests on a confusion between the spiritual and temporal orders, and (is directed) to the pursuit of a purely secular good; that the Church can decree nothing which binds the conscience of the faithful in regard to their use of temporal things; that the Church has no right of restraining by temporal punishments those who violate her laws; that it is conformable to the principles of sacred theology and public law to assert and claim for the civil government a right of property in those goods which are possessed by the Church, by the religious orders, and by other pious establishments." Nor do they blush openly and publicly to profess the maxim and principle of heretics from which arise so many perverse opinions and errors. For they repeat that the "ecclesiastical power is not by divine right distinct from, and independent of, the civil power, and that such distinction and independence cannot be preserved without the civil power's essential rights being assailed and usurped by the Church." Nor can we pass over in silence the audacity of those who, not enduring sound doctrine, contend that "without sin and without any sacrifice of the Catholic profession assent and obedience may be refused to those judgments and decrees of the Apostolic See, whose object is declared to concern the Church's general good and her rights and discipline, so only it does not touch the dogmas of faith and morals." But no one can be found who does not clearly and distinctly see and understand how grievously this is opposed to the Catholic dogma of the full power given from God by Christ our Lord Himself to the Roman Pontiff of feeding, ruling and guiding the Universal Church.

6. Amidst, therefore, such great perversity of depraved opinions, we, well remembering our apostolic office, and very greatly solicitous for our most holy religion, for sound doctrine and the salvation of souls which is entrusted to us by God, and (solicitous also) for the welfare of human society itself, have thought it right again to raise up our apostolic voice. *Therefore, by our apostolic authority,*

---

5.   Clement XII, *In eminenti;* Benedict XIV, *Providas Romanorum;* Pius VII, *Ecclesiam;* Leo XII, *Quo graviora.*

6 — POPE PIUS IX

we reprobate, proscribe, and condemn all the singular and evil opinions and doctrines severally mentioned in this letter, and will and command that they be thoroughly held by all children of the Catholic Church as reprobated, proscribed and condemned.[6]

7. And besides these things, you know very well, venerable brethren, that in these times the haters of truth and justice and most bitter enemies of our religion, deceiving the people and maliciously lying, disseminate sundry and other impious doctrines by means of pestilential books, pamphlets and newspapers dispersed over the whole world. Nor are you ignorant also, that in this our age some men are found who, moved and excited by the spirit of Satan, have reached to that degree of impiety as not to shrink from denying our Ruler and Lord Jesus Christ, and from impugning His Divinity with wicked pertinacity. Here, however, we cannot but extol you, venerable brethren, with great and deserved praise, for not having failed to raise with all zeal your episcopal voice against impiety so great.

8. Therefore, in this our letter, we again most lovingly address you, who, having been called unto a part of our solicitude, are to us, among our grievous distresses, the greatest solace, joy and consolation, because of the admirable religion and piety wherein you excel, and because of that marvelous love, fidelity, and dutifulness, whereby bound as you are to us and to this Apostolic See in most harmonious affection, you strive strenuously and sedulously to fulfill your most weighty episcopal ministry. For from your signal pastoral zeal we expect that, taking up the sword of the spirit which is the word of God, and strengthened by the grace of our Lord Jesus Christ, you will, with redoubled care, each day more anxiously provide that the faithful entrusted to your charge "abstain from noxious verbiage, which Jesus Christ does not cultivate because it is not His Father's plantation."[7] Never cease also to inculcate on the said faithful that all true felicity flows abundantly upon man from our august religion and its doctrine and practice; and that happy is the people whose God is their Lord.[8] Teach that "kingdoms rest on the foundation of the Catholic Faith[9]; and that nothing is so deadly, so hastening to a fall, so exposed to all danger, (as that which exists) if, believing this alone to be sufficient for us that we receive free will at our birth, we seek nothing further from the Lord; that is, if forgetting our Creator we abjure his power that we may display our freedom."[10] And again do not fail to teach "that the royal power was given

---

6. [The Syllabus attached to this letter enucleates the main "opinions and doctrines" targeted.]

7. St. Ignatius, *To the Philadelphians*, 3.

8. Ps. 143.

9. St. Celestine, *Epistle 22* to Synod. Ephes.

10. St. Innocent I, *Epistle 29 ad Episc. conc. Carthag.*

not only for the governance of the world, but most of all for the protection of the Church"[11]; and that there is nothing which can be of greater advantage and glory to Princes and Kings than if, as another most wise and courageous predecessor of ours, St. Felix, instructed the Emperor Zeno, they "permit the Catholic Church to practice her laws, and allow no one to oppose her liberty. For it is certain that this mode of conduct is beneficial to their interests, viz., that where there is question concerning the causes of God, they study, according to His appointment, to subject the royal will to Christ's Priests, not to raise it above theirs."[12]

9. But if always, venerable brethren, now most of all amidst such great calamities both of the Church and of civil society, amidst so great a conspiracy against Catholic interests and this Apostolic See, and so great a mass of errors, it is altogether necessary to approach with confidence the throne of grace, that we may obtain mercy and find grace in timely aid. Wherefore, we have thought it well to excite the piety of all the faithful in order that, together with us and you, they may unceasingly pray and beseech the most merciful Father of light and pity with most fervent and humble prayers, and in the fullness of faith flee always to our Lord Jesus Christ, who redeemed us to God in His Blood, and earnestly and constantly supplicate His most sweet Heart, the victim of most burning love toward us, that He would draw all things to Himself by the bonds of His love, and that all men inflamed by His most holy love may walk worthily according to His Heart, pleasing God in all things, bearing fruit in every good work. But since without doubt men's prayers are more pleasing to God if they reach Him from minds free from all stain, therefore we have determined to open to Christ's faithful, with apostolic liberality, the Church's heavenly treasures committed to our charge, in order that the said faithful, being more earnestly enkindled to true piety, and cleansed through the sacrament of Penance from the defilement of their sins, may with greater confidence pour forth their prayers to God, and obtain His mercy and grace.

10. By these letters, therefore, in virtue of our apostolic authority, we concede to all and singular the faithful of the Catholic world, a Plenary Indulgence in the form of Jubilee, during the space of one month only for the whole coming year 1865, and not beyond, to be fixed by you, venerable brethren. [...]

11. "Let us implore," venerable brethren, "God's mercy from our inmost heart and with our whole mind; because He has Himself added, 'I will not remove my mercy from them.' Let us ask and we shall receive; and if there be delay and slowness in our receiving because we have gravely offended, let us knock, because to

---

11. St. Leo, *Epistle* 156 (125).

12. Pius VII, encyclical *Diu satis*, May 15, 1800.

him that knocketh it shall be opened, if only the door be knocked by our prayers, groans and tears, in which we must persist and persevere, and if the prayer be unanimous ... let each man pray to God, not for himself alone, but for all his brethren, as the Lord hath taught us to pray."[13] But in order that God may the more readily assent to the prayers and desires of ourselves, of you and of all the faithful, let us with all confidence employ as our advocate with Him the Immaculate and most holy Virgin Mary, Mother of God, who has slain all heresies throughout the world, and who, the most loving Mother of us all, "is all sweet ... and full of mercy ... shows herself to all as easily entreated; shows herself to all as most merciful; pities the necessities of all with a most large affection"[14]; and standing as a Queen at the right hand of her only-begotten Son, our Lord Jesus Christ, in gilded clothing, surrounded with variety, can obtain from Him whatever she will. Let us also seek the suffrages of the Most Blessed Peter, Prince of the Apostles, and of Paul, his Fellow-Apostle, and of all the Saints in Heaven, who having now become God's friends, have arrived at the heavenly kingdom, and being crowned bear their palms, and being secure of their own immortality are anxious for our salvation.

12. Lastly, imploring from our great heart for You from God the abundance of all heavenly gifts, we most lovingly impart the apostolic benediction from our inmost heart, a pledge of our signal love towards you, to yourselves, venerable brethren, and to all the clerics and lay faithful committed to your care.

Given at Rome, from St. Peter's, the eighth day of December, in the year 1864, the tenth from the dogmatic definition of the Immaculate Conception of the Virgin Mary, Mother of God. In the nineteenth year of Our pontificate.

✠ Pius IX

---

13. St. Cyprian, *Epist.* 11.

14. St. Bernard, Serm. *De duodecim praerogativis B. M. V. ex verbis Apocalyp.*

SYLLABUS ERRORUM

Eighty Condemned Propositions†

Promulgated jointly with QUANTA CURA

I. PANTHEISM, NATURALISM,
AND ABSOLUTE RATIONALISM

1. There exists no Supreme, all-wise, all-provident divine Being, distinct from the universe, and God is identical with the nature of things, and is, therefore, subject to changes. In effect, God is produced in man and in the world, and all things are God and have the very substance of God, and God is one and the same thing with the world, and, therefore, spirit with matter, necessity with liberty, good with evil, justice with injustice.—Allocution *Maxima quidem*, June 9, 1862.

2. All action of God upon man and the world is to be denied.—Ibid.

3. Human reason, without any reference whatsoever to God, is the sole arbiter of truth and falsehood, and of good and evil; it is law to itself, and suffices, by its natural force, to secure the welfare of men and of nations.—Ibid.

4. All the truths of religion proceed from the innate strength of human reason; hence reason is the ultimate standard by which man can and ought to arrive at the knowledge of all truths of every kind.—Ibid. and Encyclical *Qui pluribus*, Nov. 9, 1846, etc.

5. Divine revelation is imperfect, and therefore subject to a continual and indefinite progress, corresponding with the advancement of human reason.—Ibid.

---

†   [Each proposition encapsulates some error and cites the document in which Pius IX had expressly condemned it. To gather the meaning of the *Syllabus* it is necessary to preface each proposition with: "According to the teaching of the Church, it is *not* the case that…" or "It is false to hold that…"]

6. The faith of Christ is in opposition to human reason and divine revelation not only is not useful, but is even hurtful to the perfection of man.—Ibid.

7. The prophecies and miracles set forth and recorded in the Sacred Scriptures are the fiction of poets, and the mysteries of the Christian faith the result of philosophical investigations. In the books of the Old and the New Testament there are contained mythical inventions, and Jesus Christ is Himself a myth.

II. MODERATE RATIONALISM

8. As human reason is placed on a level with religion itself, so theological must be treated in the same manner as philosophical sciences.—Allocution *Singulari quadam*, Dec. 9, 1854.

9. All the dogmas of the Christian religion are indiscriminately the object of natural science or philosophy, and human reason, enlightened solely in an historical way, is able, by its own natural strength and principles, to attain to the true science of even the most abstruse dogmas; provided only that such dogmas be proposed to reason itself as its object.—Letters to the Archbishop of Munich, *Gravissimas inter*, Dec. 11, 1862, and *Tuas libenter*, Dec. 21, 1863.

10. As the philosopher is one thing, and philosophy another, so it is the right and duty of the philosopher to subject himself to the authority which he shall have proved to be true; but philosophy neither can nor ought to submit to any such authority.—Ibid., Dec. 11, 1862.

11. The Church not only ought never to pass judgment on philosophy, but ought to tolerate the errors of philosophy, leaving it to correct itself.—Ibid., Dec. 21, 1863.

12. The decrees of the Apostolic See and of the Roman congregations impede the true progress of science.—Ibid.

13. The method and principles by which the old scholastic doctors cultivated theology are no longer suitable to the demands of our times and to the progress of the sciences.—Ibid.

14. Philosophy is to be treated without taking any account of supernatural revelation.—Ibid.

III. INDIFFERENTISM, LATITUDINARIANISM

15. Every man is free to embrace and profess that religion which, guided by the light of reason, he shall consider true.—Allocution *Maxima quidem*, June 9, 1862; Damnatio *Multiplices inter*, June 10, 1851.

16. Man may, in the observance of any religion whatever, find the way of eternal salvation, and arrive at eternal salvation.—Encyclical *Qui pluribus*, Nov. 9, 1846.

17. Good hope at least is to be entertained of the eternal salvation of all those who are not at all in the true Church of Christ.—Encyclical *Quanto conficiamur*, Aug. 10, 1863, etc.

18. Protestantism is nothing more than another form of the same true Christian religion, in which form it is given to please God equally as in the Catholic Church.—Encyclical *Noscitis et nobiscum*, Dec. 8, 1849.

IV. SOCIALISM, COMMUNISM, SECRET SOCIETIES, BIBLICAL SOCIETIES, CLERICO-LIBERAL SOCIETIES

Pests of this kind are frequently reprobated in the severest terms in the Encyclical *Qui pluribus*, Nov. 9, 1846, Allocution *Quibus quantisque*, April 20, 1849, Encyclical *Noscitis et nobiscum*, Dec. 8, 1849, Allocution *Singulari quadam*, Dec. 9, 1854, Encyclical *Quanto conficiamur*, Aug. 10, 1863.

V. ERRORS CONCERNING THE CHURCH AND HER RIGHTS

19. The Church is not a true and perfect society, entirely free, nor is she endowed with proper and perpetual rights of her own, conferred upon her by her divine Founder; but it appertains to the civil power to define what are the rights of the Church, and the limits within which she may exercise those rights.—Allocution *Singulari quadam*, Dec. 9, 1854, etc.

20. The ecclesiastical power ought not to exercise its authority without the permission and assent of the civil government.—Allocution *Meminit unusquisque*, Sept. 30, 1861.

21. The Church has not the power of defining dogmatically that the religion of the Catholic Church is the only true religion.—Damnatio *Multiplices inter*, June 10, 1851.

22. The obligation by which Catholic teachers and authors are strictly bound is confined to those things only which are proposed to universal belief as dogmas of faith by the infallible judgment of the Church.—Letter to the Archbishop of Munich, *Tuas libenter*, Dec. 21, 1863.

23. Roman pontiffs and ecumenical councils have wandered outside the limits of their powers, have usurped the rights of princes, and have even erred in defining matters of faith and morals.—Damnatio *Multiplices inter*, June 10, 1851.

24. The Church has not the power of using force, nor has she any temporal power, direct or indirect.—Apostolic Letter *Ad Apostolicae*, Aug. 22, 1851.

25. Besides the power inherent in the episcopate, other temporal power has been attributed to it by the civil authority granted either explicitly or tacitly, which on that account is revocable by the civil authority whenever it thinks fit.—Ibid.

26. The Church has no innate and legitimate right of acquiring and possessing property.—Allocution *Nunquam fore*, Dec. 15, 1856; Encyclical *Incredibili*, Sept. 7, 1863.

27. The sacred ministers of the Church and the Roman pontiff are to be absolutely excluded from every charge and dominion over temporal affairs.—Allocution *Maxima quidem*, June 9, 1862.

28. It is not lawful for bishops to publish even letters Apostolic without the permission of Government.—Allocution *Nunquam fore*, Dec. 15, 1856.

29. Favors granted by the Roman pontiff ought to be considered null, unless they have been sought for through the civil government.—Ibid.

30. The immunity of the Church and of ecclesiastical persons derived its origin from civil law.—Damnatio *Multiplices inter*, June 10, 1851.

31. The ecclesiastical forum or tribunal for the temporal causes, whether civil or criminal, of clerics, ought by all means to be abolished, even without consulting and against the protest of the Holy See.—Allocution *Nunquam fore*, Dec. 15, 1856; Allocution *Acerbissimum*, Sept. 27, 1852.

32. The personal immunity by which clerics are exonerated from military conscription and service in the army may be abolished without violation either of natural right or equity. Its abolition is called for by civil progress, especially in a society framed on the model of a liberal government.—Letter to the Bishop of Monreale, *Singularis nobisque*, Sept. 29, 1864.

33. It does not appertain exclusively to the power of ecclesiastical jurisdiction by right, proper and innate, to direct the teaching of theological questions.—Letter to the Archbishop of Munich, *Tuas libenter*, Dec. 21, 1863.

34. The teaching of those who compare the Sovereign Pontiff to a prince, free and acting in the universal Church, is a doctrine which prevailed in the Middle Ages.—Apostolic Letter *Ad Apostolicae*, Aug. 22, 1851.

35. There is nothing to prevent the decree of a general council, or the act of all peoples, from transferring the supreme pontificate from the bishop and city of Rome to another bishop and another city.—Ibid.

36. The definition of a national council does not admit of any subsequent discussion, and the civil authority can assume this principle as the basis of its acts.—Ibid.

37. National churches, withdrawn from the authority of the Roman pontiff and altogether separated, can be established.—Allocution *Multis gravibusque*, Dec. 17, 1860.

38. The Roman pontiffs have, by their too arbitrary conduct, contributed to the division of the Church into Eastern and Western.—Apostolic Letter *Ad Apostolicae*, Aug. 22, 1851.

VI. ERRORS ABOUT CIVIL SOCIETY, CONSIDERED BOTH
IN ITSELF AND IN ITS RELATION TO THE CHURCH

39. The State, as being the origin and source of all rights, is endowed with a certain right not circumscribed by any limits.—Allocution *Maxima quidem*, June 9, 1862.

40. The teaching of the Catholic Church is hostile to the well-being and interests of society.—Encyclical *Qui pluribus*, Nov. 9, 1846; Allocution *Quibus quantisque*, April 20, 1849.

41. The civil government, even when in the hands of an infidel sovereign, has a right to an indirect negative power over religious affairs. It therefore possesses not only the right called that of *exsequatur*, but also that of appeal, called *appellatio ab abusu*.—Apostolic Letter *Ad Apostolicae*, Aug. 22, 1851.

42. In the case of conflicting laws enacted by the two powers, the civil law prevails.—Ibid.

43. The secular power has authority to rescind, declare and render null, solemn conventions, commonly called concordats, entered into with the Apostolic See, regarding the use of rights appertaining to ecclesiastical immunity, without the consent of the Apostolic See, and even in spite of its protest.—Allocution *Multis gravibusque*, Dec. 17, 1860; Allocution *In consistoriali*, Nov. 1, 1850.

44. The civil authority may interfere in matters relating to religion, morality and spiritual government: hence, it can pass judgment on the instructions issued for the guidance of consciences, conformably with their mission, by the pastors of the Church. Further, it has the right to make enactments regarding the administration of the divine sacraments, and the dispositions necessary for receiving them.—Allocutions *In consistoriali*, Nov. 1, 1850, and *Maxima quidem*, June 9, 1862.

45. The entire government of public schools in which the youth of a Christian State is educated, except (to a certain extent) in the case of episcopal seminaries, may and ought to appertain to the civil power, and belong to it so far that no other authority whatsoever shall be recognized as having any right to interfere in the discipline of the schools, the arrangement of the studies, the conferring of degrees, in the choice or approval of the teachers.—Allocutions *Quibus luctuosissimis*, Sept. 5, 1851, and *In consistoriali*, Nov. 1, 1850.

46. Moreover, even in ecclesiastical seminaries, the method of studies to be adopted is subject to the civil authority.—Allocution *Nunquam fore*, Dec. 15, 1856.

47. The best theory of civil society requires that popular schools open to children of every class of the people, and, generally, all public institutes intended for instruction in letters and philosophical sciences and for carrying on the education of youth, should be freed from all ecclesiastical authority, control and interference, and should be fully subjected to the civil and political power at the pleasure of the rulers, and according to the standard of the prevalent opinions of the age.—Epistle to the Archbishop of Freiburg, *Cum non sine*, July 14, 1864.

48. Catholics may approve of the system of educating youth unconnected with Catholic faith and the power of the Church, and which regards the knowledge of merely natural things, and only, or at least primarily, the ends of earthly social life.—Ibid.

49. The civil power may prevent the prelates of the Church and the faithful from communicating freely and mutually with the Roman pontiff.—Allocution *Maxima quidem*, June 9, 1862.

50. Lay authority possesses of itself the right of presenting bishops, and may require of them to undertake the administration of the diocese before they receive canonical institution, and the Letters Apostolic from the Holy See.—Allocution *Nunquam fore*, Dec. 15, 1856.

51. And, further, the lay government has the right of deposing bishops from their pastoral functions, and is not bound to obey the Roman pontiff in those things which relate to the institution of bishoprics and the appointment of bishops.—Allocutions *Acerbissimum*, Sept. 27, 1852, Damnatio *Multiplices inter*, June 10, 1851.

52. Government can, by its own right, alter the age prescribed by the Church for the religious profession of women and men; and may require of all religious orders to admit no person to take solemn vows without its permission.—Allocution *Nunquam fore*, Dec. 15, 1856.

53. The laws enacted for the protection of religious orders and regarding their rights and duties ought to be abolished; nay, more, civil government may lend its assistance to all who desire to renounce the obligation which they have

undertaken of a religious life, and to break their vows. Government may also suppress the said religious orders, as likewise collegiate churches and simple benefices, even those of advowson[15] and subject their property and revenues to the administration and pleasure of the civil power.—Allocutions *Acerbissimum,* Sept. 27, 1852; *Probe memineritis,* Jan. 22, 1855; *Cum saepe,* July 26, 1855.

54. Kings and princes are not only exempt from the jurisdiction of the Church, but are superior to the Church in deciding questions of jurisdiction.—Damnatio *Multiplices inter,* June 10, 1851.

55. The Church ought to be separated from the State, and the State from the Church.—Allocution *Acerbissimum,* Sept. 27, 1852.

VII. ERRORS CONCERNING NATURAL AND CHRISTIAN ETHICS

56. Moral laws do not stand in need of the divine sanction, and it is not at all necessary that human laws should be made conformable to the laws of nature and receive their power of binding from God.—Allocution *Maxima quidem,* June 9, 1862.

57. The science of philosophical things and morals and also civil laws may and ought to keep aloof from divine and ecclesiastical authority.—Ibid.

58. No other forces are to be recognized except those which reside in matter, and all the rectitude and excellence of morality ought to be placed in the accumulation and increase of riches by every possible means, and the gratification of pleasure.—Ibid.; Encyclical *Quanto conficiamur,* Aug. 10, 1863.

59. Right consists in the material fact. All human duties are an empty word, and all human facts have the force of right.—Allocution *Maxima quidem,* June 9, 1862.

60. Authority is nothing else but numbers and the sum total of material forces.—Ibid.

---

15. [*advowson:* "The 'patronage' of an ecclesiastical office or religious house; the right of presentation to a benefice or living" (OED).]

61. The injustice of an act when successful inflicts no injury on the sanctity of right.—Allocution *Jamdudum cernimus*, March 18, 1861.

62. The principle of non-intervention, as it is called, ought to be proclaimed and observed.—Allocution *Novos et ante*, Sept. 28, 1860.

63. It is lawful to refuse obedience to legitimate princes, and even to rebel against them.—Encyclical *Qui pluribus*, Nov. 9, 1864; Allocution *Quibusque vestrum*, Oct. 4, 1847; Encyclical *Noscitis et nobiscum*, Dec. 8, 1849; Apostolic Letter *Cum Catholica*.

64. The violation of any solemn oath, as well as any wicked and flagitious action repugnant to the eternal law, is not only not blamable but is altogether lawful and worthy of the highest praise when done through love of country.—Allocution *Quibus quantisque*, April 20, 1849.

VIII. ERRORS CONCERNING CHRISTIAN MARRIAGE

65. The doctrine that Christ has raised marriage to the dignity of a sacrament cannot be at all tolerated.—Apostolic Letter *Ad Apostolicae*, Aug. 22, 1851.

66. The sacrament of Marriage is only something accessory to the contract and separate from it, and the sacrament itself consists in the nuptial blessing alone.—Ibid.

67. By the law of nature, the marriage tie is not indissoluble, and in many cases divorce properly so called may be decreed by the civil authority.—Ibid.; Allocution *Acerbissimum*, Sept. 27, 1852.

68. The Church has not the power of establishing diriment impediments of marriage, but such a power belongs to the civil authority by which existing impediments are to be removed.—Damnatio *Multiplices inter*, June 10, 1851.

69. In the dark ages the Church began to establish diriment impediments, not by her own right, but by using a power borrowed from the State.—Apostolic Letter *Ad Apostolicae*, Aug. 22, 1851.

70. The canons of the Council of Trent, which anathematize those who dare to deny to the Church the right of establishing diriment impediments, either are not dogmatic or must be understood as referring to such borrowed power.—Ibid.

71. The form of solemnizing marriage prescribed by the Council of Trent, under pain of nullity, does not bind in cases where the civil law lays down another form, and declares that when this new form is used the marriage shall be valid.

72. Boniface VIII was the first who declared that the vow of chastity taken at ordination renders marriage void.—Ibid.

73. In force of a merely civil contract there may exist between Christians a real marriage, and it is false to say either that the marriage contract between Christians is always a sacrament, or that there is no contract if the sacrament be excluded.—Ibid.; Letter to the King of Sardinia, Sept. 9, 1852; Allocutions *Acerbissimum*, Sept. 27, 1852; *Multis gravibusque*, Dec. 17, 1860.

74. Matrimonial causes and espousals belong by their nature to civil tribunals.—Encyclical *Qui pluribus*, Nov. 9 1846; Damnatio *Multiplices inter*, June 10, 1851; Apostolic Letter *Ad Apostolicae*, Aug. 22, 1851; Allocution *Acerbissimum*, Sept. 27, 1852.

IX. ERRORS REGARDING THE CIVIL POWER OF THE SOVEREIGN PONTIFF

75. The children of the Christian and Catholic Church are divided amongst themselves about the compatibility of the temporal with the spiritual power.—Apostolic Letter *Ad Apostolicae*, Aug. 22, 1851.

76. The abolition of the temporal power of which the Apostolic See is possessed would contribute in the greatest degree to the liberty and prosperity of the Church.—Allocutions *Quibus quantisque*, April 20, 1849; *Si semper antea*, May 20, 1850.

X. ERRORS HAVING REFERENCE TO MODERN LIBERALISM

77. In the present day it is no longer expedient that the Catholic religion

should be held as the only religion of the State, to the exclusion of all other forms of worship.—Allocution *Nemo vestrum*, July 26, 1855.

78. Hence it has been wisely decided by law, in some Catholic countries, that persons coming to reside therein shall enjoy the public exercise of their own peculiar worship.—Allocution *Acerbissimum*, Sept. 27, 1852.

79. Moreover, it is false that the civil liberty of every form of worship, and the full power, given to all, of overtly and publicly manifesting any opinions whatsoever and thoughts, conduce more easily to corrupt the morals and minds of the people, and to propagate the pest of indifferentism.—Allocution *Nunquam fore*, Dec. 15, 1856.

80. The Roman Pontiff can, and ought to, reconcile himself to and come to terms with progress, liberalism, and modern civilization.—Allocution *Jamdudum cernimus*, March 18, 1861.

DIUTURNUM ILLUD

On the Origin of Civil Power

Encyclical Letter of Pope Leo XIII,
promulgated June 29, 1881

To the Patriarchs, Primates, Archbishops, and Bishops of the Catholic World in Grace and Communion with the Apostolic See.

T he long-continued and most bitter war waged against the divine authority of the Church has reached the culmination to which it was tending, the common danger, namely, of human society, and especially of the civil power on which the public safety chiefly reposes. In our own times most particularly this result is apparent. For popular passions now reject, with more boldness than formerly, every restraint of authority. So great is the license on all sides, so frequent are seditions and tumults, that not only is obedience often refused to those who rule States, but a sufficiently safe guarantee of security does not seem to have been left to them.

2. For a long time, indeed, pains have been taken to render rulers the object of contempt and hatred to the multitude. The flames of envy thus excited have at last burst forth, and attempts have been several times made, at very short intervals, on the life of sovereign princes, either by secret plots or by open attacks. The whole of Europe was lately filled with horror at the horrible murder of a most powerful emperor.[1] Whilst the minds of men are still filled with astonishment at the magnitude of the crime, abandoned men do not fear publicly to utter threats and intimidations against other European princes.

3. These perils to commonwealth, which are before Our eyes, fill Us with grave anxiety, when We behold the security of rulers and the tranquility of empires, together with the safety of nations, put in peril almost from hour to hour. Nevertheless, the divine power of the Christian religion has given birth to excellent principles of stability and order for the State, while at the same time it

---

1.   [An allusion to Alexander II (1818–1881), Emperor of Russia, a liberally minded sovereign and a great social reformer, who was murdered March 13, 1881, by a group of nihilists, in St. Petersburg.]

has penetrated into the customs and institutions of States. And of this power not the least nor last fruit is a just and wise proportion of mutual rights and duties in both princes and peoples. For in the precepts and example of Christ our Lord there is a wonderful force for restraining in their duty as much those who obey as those who rule; and for keeping between them that agreement which is most according to nature, and that concord of wills, so to speak, from which arises a course of administration tranquil and free from all disturbance. Wherefore, being, by the favor of God, entrusted with the government of the Catholic Church, and made guardian and interpreter of the doctrines of Christ, We judge that it belongs to Our jurisdiction, venerable brethren, publicly to set forth what Catholic truth demands of everyone in this sphere of duty; thus making clear also by what way and by what means measures may be taken for the public safety in so critical a state of affairs.

4. Although man, when excited by a certain arrogance and contumacy, has often striven to cast aside the reins of authority, he has never yet been able to arrive at the state of obeying no one. In every association and community of men, necessity itself compels that some should hold pre-eminence, lest society, deprived of a prince or head by which it is ruled, should come to dissolution and be prevented from attaining the end for which it was created and instituted. But, if it was not possible that political power should be removed from the midst of States, it is certain that men have used every art to take away its influence and to lessen its majesty, as was especially the case in the sixteenth century, when a fatal novelty of opinions infatuated many. Since that epoch, not only has the multitude striven after a liberty greater than is just, but it has seen fit to fashion the origin and construction of the civil society of men in accordance with its own will.

5. Indeed, very many men of more recent times, walking in the footsteps of those who in a former age assumed to themselves the name of philosophers,[2] say that all power comes from the people; so that those who exercise it in the State do so not as their own, but as delegated to them by the people, and that, by this rule, it can be revoked by the will of the very people by whom it was delegated. But from these, Catholics dissent, who affirm that the right to rule is from God, as from a natural and necessary principle.

6. It is of importance, however, to remark in this place that those who may be placed over the State may in certain cases be chosen by the will and decision of the multitude, without opposition to or impugning of the Catholic doctrine. And by this choice, in truth, the ruler is designated, but the rights of ruling are

---

2. [The title *philosophes* refers to a group of eighteenth-century French writers, especially Voltaire, d'Alembert, and Diderot, whose views are contained in the *Encyclopédie* (1751–1772).]

not thereby conferred. Nor is the authority delegated to him, but the person by whom it is to be exercised is determined upon.

7. There is no question here respecting forms of government, for there is no reason why the Church should not approve of the chief power being held by one man or by more, provided only it be just, and that it tend to the common advantage. Wherefore, so long as justice be respected, the people are not hindered from choosing for themselves that form of government which suits best either their own disposition, or the institutions and customs of their ancestors.

8. But, as regards political power, the Church rightly teaches that it comes from God, for it finds this clearly testified in the sacred Scriptures and in the monuments of antiquity; besides, no other doctrine can be conceived which is more agreeable to reason, or more in accord with the safety of both princes and peoples.

9. In truth, that the source of human power is in God the books of the Old Testament in very many places clearly establish. "By me kings reign ... by me princes rule, and the mighty decree justice."[3] And in another place: "Give ear you that rule the people ... for power is given you of the Lord and strength by the Most High."[4] The same thing is contained in the Book of Ecclesiasticus: "Over every nation He hath set a ruler."[5] These things, however, which they had learned of God, men were little by little untaught through heathen superstition, which even as it has corrupted the true aspect and often the very concept of things, so also it has corrupted the natural form and beauty of the chief power. Afterwards, when the Christian Gospel shed its light, vanity yielded to truth, and that noble and divine principle whence all authority flows began to shine forth. To the Roman governor, ostentatiously pretending that he had the power of releasing and of condemning, our Lord Jesus Christ answered: "Thou shouldst not have any power against me unless it were given thee from above."[6] And St. Augustine, in explaining this passage, says: "Let us learn what He said, which also He taught by His Apostle, that there is no power but from God."[7] The faithful voice of the Apostles, as an echo, repeats the doctrine and precepts of Jesus Christ. The teaching of Paul to the Romans, when subject to the authority of heathen princes, is lofty and full of gravity: "There is not power but from God," from which, as from its cause, he draws this conclusion: "The prince is the minister of God."[8]

---

3. Prov. 8:15–16.

4. Wisd. 6:3–4.

5. Ecclus. 7:14.

6. John 19:11.

7. Tract. 116 in Joan., n. 5 (PL 35, 1942).

8. Rom. 13:1–4.

10. The Fathers of the Church have taken great care to proclaim and propagate this very doctrine in which they had been instructed. "We do not attribute," says St. Augustine, "the power of giving government and empires to any but the true God."[9] On the same passage St. John Chrysostom says: "That there are kingdoms, and that some rule, while others are subject, and that none of these things is brought about by accident or rashly ... is, I say, a work of divine wisdom."[10] The same truth is testified by St. Gregory the Great, saying: "We confess that power is given from above to emperors and kings."[11] Verily the holy doctors have undertaken to illustrate also the same precepts by the natural light of reason in such a way that they must appear to be altogether right and true, even to those who follow reason for their sole guide.

11. And, indeed, nature, or rather God who is the Author of nature, wills that man should live in a civil society; and this is clearly shown both by the faculty of language, the greatest medium of intercourse, and by numerous innate desires of the mind, and the many necessary things, and things of great importance, which men isolated cannot procure, but which they can procure when joined and associated with others. But a society can neither exist nor be conceived in which there is no one to govern the wills of individuals, in such a way as to make, as it were, one will out of many, and to impel them rightly and orderly to the common good; therefore, God has willed that in a civil society there should be some to rule the multitude. And this also is a powerful argument, that those by whose authority the State is administered must be able so to compel the citizens to obedience that it is clearly a sin in the latter not to obey. But no man has in himself or of himself the power of constraining the free will of others by fetters of authority of this kind. This power resides solely in God, the Creator and Legislator of all things; and it is necessary that those who exercise it should do it as having received it from God. "There is one lawgiver and judge, who is able to destroy and deliver."[12] And this is clearly seen in every kind of power. That that which resides in priests comes from God is so acknowledged that among all nations they are recognized as, and called, the ministers of God. In like manner, the authority of fathers of families preserves a certain impressed image and form of the authority which is in God, "of whom all paternity in heaven and earth is named."[13] But in this way different kinds of authority have between them wonderful resemblances, since,

---

9. De civ. Dei 5, 21 (PL 41, 167).

10. In Epist. ad Rom., Homil. 23, n. 1 (PG 60, 615).

11. Epist. lib. II, epist. 61.

12. James 4:12.

13. Eph. 3:15.

whatever there is of government and authority, its origin is derived from one and the same Creator and Lord of the world, who is God.

12. Those who believe civil society to have risen from the free consent of men, looking for the origin of its authority from the same source, say that each individual has given up something of his right,[14] and that voluntarily every person has put himself into the power of the one man in whose person the whole of those rights has been centered. But it is a great error not to see, what is manifest, that men, as they are not a nomad race, have been created, without their own free will, for a natural community of life. It is plain, moreover, that the pact which they allege is openly a falsehood and a fiction, and that it has no authority to confer on political power such great force, dignity, and firmness as the safety of the State and the common good of the citizens require. Then only will the government have all those ornaments and guarantees, when it is understood to emanate from God as its august and most sacred source.

13. And it is impossible that any should be found not only more true but even more advantageous than this opinion. For the authority of the rulers of a State, if it be a certain communication of divine power, will by that very reason immediately acquire a dignity greater than human—not, indeed, that impious and most absurd dignity sometimes desired by heathen emperors when affecting divine honors, but a true and solid one received by a certain divine gift and benefaction. Whence it will behoove citizens to submit themselves and to be obedient to rulers, as to God, not so much through fear of punishment as through respect for their majesty; nor for the sake of pleasing, but through conscience, as doing their duty. And by this means authority will remain far more firmly seated in its place. For the citizens, perceiving the force of this duty, would necessarily avoid dishonesty and contumacy, because they must be persuaded that they who resist State authority resist the divine will; that they who refuse honor to rulers refuse it to God Himself.

14. This doctrine the Apostle Paul particularly inculcated on the Romans; to whom he wrote with so great authority and weight on the reverence to be entertained toward the higher powers, that it seems nothing could be prescribed more weightily: "Let every soul be subject to higher powers, for there is no power but from God, and those that are, are ordained of God. Therefore he that resisteth the power resisteth the ordinance of God, and they that resist purchase to themselves damnation ... wherefore be subject of necessity, not only for wrath, but

---

14. [An allusion to the doctrine of "social contract," developed by Thomas Hobbes, John Locke, Jean-Jacques Rousseau, and many other Enlightenment thinkers. In Rousseau's version of this doctrine, all political power comes to rulers from the people or the "general will."]

also for the sake of conscience."[15] And in agreement with this is the celebrated declaration of Peter, the Prince of the Apostles, on the same subject: "Be ye subject, therefore, to every human creature for God's sake; whether it be to the king as excelling, or to governors, as sent by him for the punishment of evildoers, and for the praise of the good, for so is the will of God."[16]

15. The one only reason which men have for not obeying is when anything is demanded of them which is openly repugnant to the natural or the divine law, for it is equally unlawful to command to do anything in which the law of nature or the will of God is violated. If, therefore, it should happen to anyone to be compelled to prefer one or the other, viz., to disregard either the commands of God or those of rulers, he must obey Jesus Christ, who commands us to "give to Caesar the things that are Caesar's, and to God the things that are God's,"[17] and must reply courageously after the example of the Apostles: "We ought to obey God rather than men."[18] And yet there is no reason why those who so behave themselves should be accused of refusing obedience; for, if the will of rulers is opposed to the will and the laws of God, they themselves exceed the bounds of their own power and pervert justice; nor can their authority then be valid, which, when there is no justice, is null.

16. But in order that justice may be retained in government it is of the highest importance that those who rule States should understand that political power was not created for the advantage of any private individual; and that the administration of the State must be carried on to the profit of those who have been committed to their care, not to the profit of those to whom it has been committed. Let princes take example from the Most High God, by whom authority is given to them; and, placing before themselves His model in governing the State, let them rule over the people with equity and faithfulness, and let them add to that severity which is necessary, a paternal charity. On this account they are warned in the oracles of the sacred Scriptures, that they will have themselves some day to render an account to the King of kings and Lord of lords; if they shall fail in their duty, that it will not be possible for them in any way to escape the severity of God: "The Most High will examine your work and search out your thoughts: because being ministers of his kingdom you have not judged rightly ... Horribly and speedily will he appear to you, for a most severe judgment shall be for them that bear rule. ... For God will not accept any man's person, neither will he stand

---

15. Rom. 13:1–2, 5.

16. 1 Peter 2:13, 15.

17. Matt. 22:21.

18. Acts 5:29.

in awe of any man's greatness; for he made the little and the great, and he hath equally care of all. But a greater punishment is ready for the more mighty."[19]

17. And if these precepts protect the State, all cause or desire for seditions is removed; the honor and security of rulers, the quiet and well-being of societies will be secure. The dignity also of the citizen is best provided for; for to them it has been permitted to retain even in obedience that greatness which conduces to the excellence of man. For they understand that, in the judgment of God, there is neither slave nor free man; that there is one Lord of all, rich "to all that call upon Him,"[20] but that they on this account submit to and obey their rulers, because these in a certain sort bring before them the image of God, "whom to serve is to reign."

18. But the Church has always so acted that the Christian form of civil government may not dwell [merely] in the minds of men, but that it may also be exhibited in the life and habits of nations. As long as there were at the helm of the States pagan emperors, who were prevented by superstition from rising to that form of imperial government which We have sketched, she studied how to instill into the minds of subjects, immediately on their embracing the Christian institutions, the teaching that they must be desirous of bringing their lives into conformity with them. Therefore, the pastors of souls, after the example of the Apostle Paul, were accustomed to teach the people with the utmost care and diligence "to be subject to princes and powers, to obey at a word,"[21] and to pray God for all men and particularly "for kings and all that are in a high station: for this is good and acceptable in the sight of God our Savior."[22] And the Christians of old left the most striking proofs of this; for, when they were harassed in a very unjust and cruel way by pagan emperors, they nevertheless at no time omitted to conduct themselves obediently and submissively, so that, in fact, they seemed to vie with each other: those in cruelty, and these in obedience.

19. This great modesty, this fixed determination to obey, was so well known that it could not be obscured by the calumny and malice of enemies. On this account, those who were going to plead in public before the emperors for any persons bearing the Christian name proved by this argument especially that it was unjust to enact laws against the Christians because they were in the sight of all men exemplary in their bearing according to the laws. Athenagoras thus confidently addresses Marcus Aurelius Antoninus and Lucius Aurelius Commodus,

---

19. Wisd. 6:4–6, 8–9.

20. Rom. 10:12.

21. Tit. 3:1.

22. 1 Tim. 2:1–3.

his son: "You allow us, who commit no evil, yea, who demean ourselves the most piously and justly of all toward God and likewise toward your government, to be driven about, plundered and exiled."[23] In like manner, Tertullian openly praises the Christians because they were the best and surest friends of all to the Empire: "The Christian is the enemy of no one, much less of the emperor, whom he knows to be appointed by God, and whom he must, therefore, of necessity love, reverence and honor, and wish to be preserved together with the whole Roman Empire."[24] Nor did he hesitate to affirm that, within the limits of the Empire, the number of enemies was wont to diminish just in proportion as the number of Christians increased.[25] There is also a remarkable testimony to the same point in the Epistle to Diognetus, which confirms the statement that the Christians at that period were not only in the habit of obeying the laws, but in every office they, of their own accord, did more, and more perfectly, than they were required to do by the laws. "Christians observe these things which have obtained the sanction of the law, and in the character of their lives they even go beyond the law."[26]

20. The case, indeed, was different when they were ordered by the edicts of emperors and the threats of praetors to abandon the Christian faith or in any way fail in their duty. At these times, undoubtedly, they preferred to displease men rather than God. Yet, even under these circumstances, they were so far from doing anything seditious or despising the imperial majesty that they took it on themselves only to profess themselves Christians, and declare that they would not in any way alter their faith. But they had no thought of resistance, calmly and joyfully they went to the torture of the rack, in so much that the magnitude of the torments gave place to their magnitude of mind. During the same period the force of Christian principles was observed in like manner in the army. For it was a mark of a Christian soldier to combine the greatest fortitude with the greatest attention to military discipline, and to add to nobility of mind immovable fidelity towards his prince. But, if anything dishonorable was required of him, as, for instance, to break the laws of God, or to turn his sword against innocent disciples of Christ, then, indeed, he refused to execute the orders, yet in such wise that he would rather retire from the army and die for his religion than oppose the public authority by means of sedition and tumult.

21. But afterward, when Christian rulers were at the head of States, the Church insisted much more on testifying and preaching how much sanctity was

---

23. *Legatio pro christianis* 1 (PG 6, 891B–894A).

24. *Apolog.*, 35.

25. *Apolog.*, 37 (PL 1, 526A).

26. *Ad Diogn.*, 10 (ed. H. I. Marrou, Paris, 1951, pp. 64–65).

inherent in the authority of rulers. Hence, when people thought of princedom, the image of a certain sacred majesty would present itself to their minds, by which they would be impelled to greater reverence and love of rulers. And on this account she wisely provides that kings should commence their reign with the celebration of solemn rites; which, in the Old Testament, was appointed by divine authority.[27]

22. But from the time when the civil society of men, raised from the ruins of the Roman Empire, gave hope of its future Christian greatness, the Roman Pontiffs, by the institution of the Holy Empire, consecrated the political power in a wonderful manner. Greatly, indeed, was the authority of rulers ennobled; and it is not to be doubted that what was then instituted would always have been a very great gain, both to ecclesiastical and civil society, if princes and peoples had ever looked to the same object as the Church. And, indeed, tranquility and a sufficient prosperity lasted so long as there was a friendly agreement between these two powers. If the people were turbulent, the Church was at once the mediator for peace. Recalling all to their duty, she subdued the more lawless passions partly by kindness and partly by authority. So, if, in ruling, princes erred in their government, she went to them and, putting before them the rights, needs, and lawful wants of their people, urged them to equity, mercy, and kindness. Whence it was often brought about that the dangers of civil wars and popular tumults were stayed.

23. On the other hand, the doctrines on political power invented by late writers have already produced great ills amongst men, and it is to be feared that they will cause the very greatest disasters to posterity. For an unwillingness to attribute the right of ruling to God, as its Author, is not less than a willingness to blot out the greatest splendor of political power and to destroy its force. And they who say that this power depends on the will of the people err in opinion first of all; then they place authority on too weak and unstable a foundation. For the popular passions, incited and goaded on by these opinions, will break out more insolently; and, with great harm to the common weal, descend headlong by an easy and smooth road to revolts and to open sedition. In truth, sudden uprisings and the boldest rebellions immediately followed in Germany the so-called Reformation,[28] the authors and leaders of which, by their new doctrines, attacked at the very foundation religious and civil authority; and this with so fearful an outburst of civil war and with such slaughter that there was

---

27. 1 Kings 9:16; 10:1; 16:13.

28. [Especially the Peasant Revolt and its repression by the German princes. Luther himself then had to stress the duty of the citizens to obey the civil power (see his treatise *On the Civil Power* of 1523).]

scarcely any place free from tumult and bloodshed. From this heresy there arose in the last century[29] a false philosophy—a new right as it is called, and a popular authority, together with an unbridled license which many regard as the only true liberty. Hence we have reached the limit of horrors, to wit, communism, socialism, nihilism, hideous deformities of the civil society of men and almost its ruin. And yet too many attempt to enlarge the scope of these evils, and under the pretext of helping the multitude, already have fanned no small flames of misery. The things we thus mention are neither unknown nor very remote from us.

24. This, indeed, is all the graver because rulers, in the midst of such threatening dangers, have no remedies sufficient to restore discipline and tranquility. They supply themselves with the power of laws, and think to coerce, by the severity of their punishment, those who disturb their governments. They are right to a certain extent, but yet should seriously consider that no power of punishment can be so great that it alone can preserve the State. For fear, as St. Thomas admirably teaches, "is a weak foundation; for those who are subdued by fear would, should an occasion arise in which they might hope for immunity, rise more eagerly against their rulers, in proportion to the previous extent of their restraint through fear." And besides, "from too great fear many fall into despair; and despair drives men to attempt boldly to gain what they desire."[30] That these things are so we see from experience. It is therefore necessary to seek a higher and more reliable reason for obedience, and to say explicitly that legal severity cannot be efficacious unless men are led on by duty, and moved by the salutary fear of God. But this is what religion can best ask of them, religion which by its power enters into the souls and bends the very wills of men causing them not only to render obedience to their rulers, but also to show their affection and good will, which is in every society of men the best guardian of safety.

25. For this reason the Roman Pontiffs are to be regarded as having greatly served the public good, for they have ever endeavored to break the turbulent and restless spirit of innovators, and have often warned men of the danger they are to civil society. In this respect we may worthily recall to mind the declaration of Clement VII to Ferdinand, King of Bohemia and Hungary: "In the cause of faith your own dignity and advantage and that of other rulers is included, since the faith cannot be shaken without your authority being brought down; which has been most clearly shown in several instances." In the same way the

---

29. [That is, in the eighteenth century, the heyday of the Enlightenment in its French, German, English, and American varieties.]

30. *De Regno* 1, 10.

supreme forethought and courage of Our predecessors have been shown, especially of Clement XI, Benedict XIV, and Leo XII,[31] who, when in their day the evil of vicious doctrine was more widely spreading and the boldness of the sects was becoming greater, endeavored by their authority to close the door against them. And We Ourselves have several times declared what great dangers are impending, and have pointed out the best ways of warding them off. To princes and other rulers of the State we have offered the protection of religion, and we have exhorted the people to make abundant use of the great benefits which the Church supplies. Our present object is to make rulers understand that this protection, which is stronger than any, is again offered to them; and We earnestly exhort them in our Lord to defend religion, and to consult the interest of their States by giving that liberty to the Church which cannot be taken away without injury and ruin to the commonwealth.

26. The Church of Christ, indeed, cannot be an object of suspicion to rulers, nor of hatred to the people; for it urges rulers to follow justice, and in nothing to decline from their duty; while at the same time it strengthens and in many ways supports their authority. All things that are of a civil nature the Church acknowledges and declares to be under the power and authority of the ruler; and in things whereof for different reasons the decision belongs both to the sacred and to the civil power, the Church wishes that there should be harmony between the two so that injurious contests may be avoided. As to what regards the people, the Church has been established for the salvation of all men and has ever loved them as a mother. For it is the Church which by the exercise of her charity has given gentleness to the minds of men, kindness to their manners, and justice to their laws. Never opposed to honest liberty, the Church has always detested a tyrant's rule. This custom which the Church has ever had of deserving well of mankind is notably expressed by St. Augustine when he says that "the Church teaches kings to study the welfare of their people, and people to submit to their kings, showing what is due to all: and that to all is due charity and to no one injustice."[32]

27. For these reasons, venerable brethren, your work will be most useful and salutary if you employ with us every industry and effort which God has given you in order to avert the dangers and evils of human society. Strive with all possible care to make men understand and show forth in their lives what the Catholic Church teaches on government and the duty of obedience. Let the people be frequently urged by your authority and teaching to fly from the forbidden sects, to abhor all conspiracy, to have nothing to do with sedition, and let them

---

31. Clement XI (1700–1721); Benedict XIV (1740–1758); Leo XII (1823–1829).
32. *De mor. eccl.* I, 30, 53 (PL 32, 1236).

understand that they who for God's sake obey their rulers render a reasonable service and a generous obedience. And as it is God "who gives safety to kings,"[33] and grants to the people "to rest in the beauty of peace and in the tabernacles of confidence and in wealthy repose,"[34] it is to Him that we must pray, beseeching Him to incline all minds to uprightness and truth, to calm angry passions, to restore the long-wished-for tranquility to the world.

28. That we may pray with greater hope, let us take as our intercessors and protectors of our welfare the Virgin Mary, the great Mother of God, the help of Christians, and protector of the human race; St. Joseph, her chaste spouse, in whose patronage the whole Church greatly trusts; and the Princes of the Apostles, Peter and Paul, the guardians and protectors of the Christian name.

Given at St. Peter's in Rome, the twenty-ninth day of June, 1881, the third year of Our pontificate.

✠ Leo XIII

---

33. Ps. 152:11.
34. Isa. 37:18.

IMMORTALE DEI

On the Christian Constitution of States

Encyclical Letter of Pope Leo XIII,
promulgated November 1, 1885

To Our Venerable Brethren the Patriarchs, Primates, Archbishops, Bishops, and other Ordinaries in Peace and Communion with the Apostolic See.

The Catholic Church, that imperishable handiwork of our all-merciful God, has for her immediate and natural purpose the saving of souls and securing our happiness in heaven. Yet, in regard to things temporal, she is the source of benefits as manifold and great as if the chief end of her existence were to ensure the prospering of our earthly life. And, indeed, wherever the Church has set her foot she has straightway changed the face of things, and has tempered the moral tone of the people with a new civilization and with virtues before unknown. All nations which have yielded to her sway have become eminent by their gentleness, their sense of justice, and the glory of their high deeds.

2. And yet a hackneyed reproach of old date is leveled against her, that the Church is opposed to the rightful aims of the civil government, and is wholly unable to afford help in spreading that welfare and progress which justly and naturally are sought after by every well-regulated State. From the very beginning Christians were harassed by slanderous accusations of this nature, and on that account were held up to hatred and execration, for being (so they were called) enemies of the Empire. The Christian religion was moreover commonly charged with being the cause of the calamities that so frequently befell the State, whereas, in very truth, just punishment was being awarded to guilty nations by an avenging God. This odious calumny, with most valid reason, nerved the genius and sharpened the pen of St. Augustine, who, notably in his treatise *The City of God*, set forth in so bright a light the worth of Christian wisdom in its relation to the commonwealth that he seems not merely to have pleaded the cause of the Christians of his day, but to have refuted for all future times impeachments so grossly contrary to truth. The wicked proneness, however, to levy like charges and accusations has not been lulled to rest. Many, indeed, are

they who have tried to work out a plan of civil society based on doctrines other than those approved by the Catholic Church. Nay, in these latter days a novel conception of law has begun here and there to gain increase and influence, the outcome, as it is maintained, of an age arrived at full stature, and the result of progressive liberty. But, though endeavors of various kinds have been ventured on, it is clear that no better mode has been devised for the building up and ruling of the State than that which is the necessary growth of the teachings of the Gospel. We deem it, therefore, of the highest moment, and a strict duty of Our apostolic office, to contrast with the lessons taught by Christ the novel theories now advanced touching the State. By this means We cherish hope that the bright shining of the truth may scatter the mists of error and doubt, so that one and all may see clearly the imperious law of life which they are bound to follow and obey.

3. It is not difficult to determine what would be the form and character of the State were it governed according to the principles of Christian philosophy. Man's natural instinct moves him to live in civil society, for he cannot, if dwelling apart, provide himself with the necessary requirements of life, nor procure the means of developing his mental and moral faculties. Hence, it is divinely ordained that he should lead his life—be it family, or civil—with his fellow men, amongst whom alone his several wants can be adequately supplied. But, as no society can hold together unless someone be over all, directing all to strive earnestly for the common good, every body politic must have a ruling authority, and this authority, no less than society itself, has its source in nature, and has, consequently, God for its Author. Hence, it follows that all public power must proceed from God. For God alone is the true and supreme Lord of the world. Everything, without exception, must be subject to Him, and must serve him, so that whosoever holds the right to govern holds it from one sole and single source, namely, God, the sovereign Ruler of all. "There is no power but from God."[1]

4. The right to rule is not necessarily, however, bound up with any special mode of government. It may take this or that form, provided only that it be of a nature to ensure the general welfare. But whatever be the nature of the government, rulers must ever bear in mind that God is the paramount ruler of the world, and must set Him before themselves as their exemplar and law in the administration of the State. For, in things visible God has fashioned secondary causes, in which His divine action can in some wise be discerned, leading up to the end to which the course of the world is ever tending. In like manner, in civil society, God has always willed that there should be a ruling authority, and that they who are

---

1. Rom. 13:1.

invested with it should reflect the divine power and providence in some measure over the human race.

5. They, therefore, who rule should rule with evenhanded justice, not as masters, but rather as fathers, for the rule of God over man is most just, and is tempered always with a father's kindness. Government should, moreover, be administered for the well-being of the citizens, because they who govern others possess authority solely for the welfare of the State. Furthermore, the civil power must not be subservient to the advantage of any one individual or of some few persons, inasmuch as it was established for the common good of all. But, if those who are in authority rule unjustly, if they govern overbearingly or arrogantly, and if their measures prove hurtful to the people, they must remember that the Almighty will one day bring them to account, the more strictly in proportion to the sacredness of their office and preeminence of their dignity. "The mighty shall be mightily tormented."[2] Then, truly, will the majesty of the law meet with the dutiful and willing homage of the people, when they are convinced that their rulers hold authority from God, and feel that it is a matter of justice and duty to obey them, and to show them reverence and fealty, united to a love not unlike that which children show their parents. "Let every soul be subject to higher powers."[3] To despise legitimate authority, in whomsoever vested, is unlawful, as a rebellion against the divine will, and whoever resists that, rushes willfully to destruction. "He that resisteth the power resisteth the ordinance of God, and they that resist, purchase to themselves damnation."[4] To cast aside obedience, and by popular violence to incite to revolt, is therefore treason, not against man only, but against God.

6. As a consequence, the State, constituted as it is, is clearly bound to act up to the manifold and weighty duties linking it to God, by the public profession of religion. Nature and reason, which command every individual devoutly to worship God in holiness, because we belong to Him and must return to Him, since from Him we came, bind also the civil community by a like law. For, men living together in society are under the power of God no less than individuals are, and society, no less than individuals, owes gratitude to God who gave it being and maintains it and whose ever-bounteous goodness enriches it with countless blessings. Since, then, no one is allowed to be remiss in the service due to God, and since the chief duty of all men is to cling to religion in both its teaching and practice—not such religion as they may have a preference for, but the religion

---

2. Wisd. 6:7.

3. Rom. 13:1.

4. Rom. 13:2.

which God enjoins, and which certain and most clear marks show to be the only one true religion—it is a public crime to act as though there were no God. So, too, is it a sin for the State not to have care for religion as a something beyond its scope, or as of no practical benefit; or out of many forms of religion to adopt that one which chimes in with the fancy; for we are bound absolutely to worship God in that way which He has shown to be His will. All who rule, therefore, should hold in honor the holy name of God, and one of their chief duties must be to favor religion, to protect it, to shield it under the credit and sanction of the laws, and neither to organize nor enact any measure that may compromise its safety. This is the bounden duty of rulers to the people over whom they rule. For one and all are we destined by our birth and adoption to enjoy, when this frail and fleeting life is ended, a supreme and final good in heaven, and to the attainment of this every endeavor should be directed. Since, then, upon this depends the full and perfect happiness of mankind, the securing of this end should be of all imaginable interests the most urgent. Hence, civil society, established for the common welfare, should not only safeguard the well-being of the community, but have also at heart the interests of its individual members, in such mode as not in any way to hinder, but in every manner to render as easy as may be, the possession of that highest and unchangeable good for which all should seek. Wherefore, for this purpose, care must especially be taken to preserve unharmed and unimpeded the religion whereof the practice is the link connecting man with God.

7. Now, it cannot be difficult to find out which is the true religion, if only it be sought with an earnest and unbiased mind; for proofs are abundant and striking. We have, for example, the fulfillment of prophecies, miracles in great numbers, the rapid spread of the faith in the midst of enemies and in face of overwhelming obstacles, the witness of the martyrs, and the like. From all these it is evident that the only true religion is the one established by Jesus Christ Himself, and which He committed to His Church to protect and to propagate.

8. For the Only-begotten Son of God established on earth a society which is called the Church, and to it He handed over the exalted and divine office which He had received from His Father, to be continued through the ages to come. "As the Father hath sent Me, I also send you."[5] "Behold I am with you all days, even to the consummation of the world."[6] Consequently, as Jesus Christ came into the world that men "might have life and have it more abundantly,"[7] so also has the Church for its aim and end the eternal salvation of souls, and hence it is so

5. John 20:21.

6. Matt. 28:20.

7. John 10:10.

constituted as to open wide its arms to all mankind, unhampered by any limit of either time or place. "Preach ye the Gospel to every creature."[8]

9. Over this mighty multitude God has Himself set rulers with power to govern, and He has willed that one should be the head of all, and the chief and unerring teacher of truth, to whom He has given "the keys of the kingdom of heaven."[9] "Feed My lambs, feed My sheep."[10] "I have prayed for thee that thy faith fail not."[11]

10. This society is made up of men, just as civil society is, and yet is supernatural and spiritual, on account of the end for which it was founded, and of the means by which it aims at attaining that end. Hence, it is distinguished and differs from civil society, and, what is of highest moment, it is a society chartered as of right divine, perfect in its nature and in its title, to possess in itself and by itself, through the will and loving kindness of its Founder, all needful provision for its maintenance and action. And just as the end at which the Church aims is by far the noblest of ends, so is its authority the most exalted of all authority, nor can it be looked upon as inferior to the civil power, or in any manner dependent upon it.

11. In very truth, Jesus Christ gave to His Apostles unrestrained authority in regard to things sacred, together with the genuine and most true power of making laws, as also with the twofold right of judging and of punishing, which flow from that power. "All power is given to Me in heaven and on earth: going therefore teach all nations ... teaching them to observe all things whatsoever I have commanded you."[12] And in another place: "If he will not hear them, tell the Church."[13] And again: "In readiness to revenge all disobedience."[14] And once more: "That ... I may not deal more severely according to the power which the Lord hath given me, unto edification and not unto destruction."[15] Hence, it is the Church, and not the State, that is to be man's guide to heaven. It is to the Church that God has assigned the charge of seeing to, and legislating for, all that concerns religion; of teaching all nations; of spreading the Christian faith as widely as possible; in short, of administering freely and without hindrance, in accordance with her own judgment, all matters that fall within her competence.

---

8. Mark 16:15.
9. Matt. 16:19.
10. John 21: 16–17.
11. Luke 22:32.
12. Matt. 28:18–20.
13. Matt. 18:12.
14. 2 Cor. 10:6.
15. 2 Cor. 13:10.

12. Now, this authority, perfect in itself, and plainly meant to be unfettered, so long assailed by a philosophy that truckles to the State, the Church has never ceased to claim for herself and openly to exercise. The Apostles themselves were the first to uphold it, when, being forbidden by the rulers of the synagogue to preach the Gospel, they courageously answered: "We must obey God rather than men."[16] This same authority the holy Fathers of the Church were always careful to maintain by weighty arguments, according as occasion arose, and the Roman Pontiffs have never shrunk from defending it with unbending constancy. Nay, more, princes and all invested with power to rule have themselves approved it, in theory alike and in practice. It cannot be called in question that in the making of treaties, in the transaction of business matters, in the sending and receiving of ambassadors, and in the interchange of other kinds of official dealings they have been wont to treat with the Church as with a supreme and legitimate power. And, assuredly, all ought to hold that it was not without a singular disposition of God's providence that this power of the Church was provided with a civil sovereignty as the surest safeguard of her independence.

13. The Almighty, therefore, has given the charge of the human race to two powers, the ecclesiastical and the civil, the one being set over divine, and the other over human, things. Each in its kind is supreme, each has fixed limits within which it is contained, limits which are defined by the nature and special object of the province of each, so that there is, we may say, an orbit traced out within which the action of each is brought into play by its own native right. But, inasmuch as each of these two powers has authority over the same subjects, and as it might come to pass that one and the same thing—related differently, but still remaining one and the same thing—might belong to the jurisdiction and determination of both, therefore God, who foresees all things, and who is the author of these two powers, has marked out the course of each in right correlation to the other. "For the powers that are, are ordained of God."[17] Were this not so, deplorable contentions and conflicts would often arise, and, not infrequently, men, like travelers at the meeting of two roads, would hesitate in anxiety and doubt, not knowing what course to follow. Two powers would be commanding contrary things, and it would be a dereliction of duty to disobey either of the two.

14. But it would be most repugnant to them to think thus of the wisdom and goodness of God. Even in physical things, albeit of a lower order, the Almighty has so combined the forces and springs of nature with tempered action and wondrous harmony that no one of them clashes with any other, and all of them

16. Acts 5:29.
17. Rom. 13:1.

most fitly and aptly work together for the great purpose of the universe. There must, accordingly, exist between these two powers a certain orderly connection, which may be compared to the union of the soul and body in man. The nature and scope of that connection can be determined only, as We have laid down, by having regard to the nature of each power, and by taking account of the relative excellence and nobleness of their purpose. One of the two has for its proximate and chief object the well-being of this mortal life; the other, the everlasting joys of heaven. Whatever, therefore, in things human is of a sacred character, whatever belongs either of its own nature or by reason of the end to which it is referred, to the salvation of souls, or to the worship of God, is subject to the power and judgment of the Church. Whatever is to be ranged under the civil and political order is rightly subject to the civil authority. Jesus Christ has Himself given command that what is Caesar's is to be rendered to Caesar, and that what belongs to God is to be rendered to God.

15. There are, nevertheless, occasions when another method of concord is available for the sake of peace and liberty: We mean when rulers of the State and the Roman Pontiff come to an understanding touching some special matter. At such times the Church gives signal proof of her motherly love by showing the greatest possible kindliness and indulgence.[18]

16. Such, then, as We have briefly pointed out, is the Christian organization of civil society; not rashly or fancifully shaped out, but educed from the highest and truest principles, confirmed by natural reason itself.

17. In such organization of the State there is nothing that can be thought to infringe upon the dignity of rulers, and nothing unbecoming them; nay, so far from degrading the sovereign power in its due rights, it adds to it permanence and luster. Indeed, when more fully pondered, this mutual coordination has a perfection in which all other forms of government are lacking, and from which excellent results would flow, were the several component parts to keep their place and duly discharge the office and work appointed for each. And, doubtless, in the constitution of the State such as We have described, divine and human things are equitably shared; the rights of citizens assured to them, and fenced round by divine, by natural, and by human law; the duties incumbent on each one being wisely marked out, and their fulfillment fittingly insured. In their uncertain and toilsome journey to the everlasting city all see that they have safe guides and helpers on their way, and are conscious that others have charge to protect their persons alike and their possessions, and to obtain or preserve for them everything

---

18. [Pope Leo XIII refers here to the "concordats" that the Apostolic See has co-signed with secular powers in the modern period.]

essential for their present life. Furthermore, domestic society acquires that firmness and solidity so needful to it from the holiness of marriage, one and indissoluble, wherein the rights and duties of husband and wife are controlled with wise justice and equity; due honor is assured to the woman; the authority of the husband is conformed to the pattern afforded by the authority of God; the power of the father is tempered by a due regard for the dignity of the mother and her offspring; and the best possible provision is made for the guardianship, welfare, and education of the children.

18. In political affairs, and all matters civil, the laws aim at securing the common good, and are not framed according to the delusive caprices and opinions of the mass of the people, but by truth and by justice; the ruling powers are invested with a sacredness more than human, and are withheld from deviating from the path of duty, and from overstepping the bounds of rightful authority; and the obedience is not the servitude of man to man, but submission to the will of God, exercising His sovereignty through the medium of men. Now, this being recognized as undeniable, it is felt that the high office of rulers should be held in respect; that public authority should be constantly and faithfully obeyed; that no act of sedition should be committed; and that the civic order of the commonwealth should be maintained as sacred.

19. So, also, as to the duties of each one toward his fellow men, mutual forbearance, kindliness, generosity are placed in the ascendant; the man who is at once a citizen and a Christian is not drawn aside by conflicting obligations; and, lastly, the abundant benefits with which the Christian religion, of its very nature, endows even the mortal life of man are acquired for the community and civil society. And this to such an extent that it may be said in sober truth: "The condition of the commonwealth depends on the religion with which God is worshipped; and between one and the other there exists an intimate and abiding connection."[19]

20. Admirably, according to his wont, does St. Augustine, in many passages, enlarge upon the nature of these advantages; but nowhere more markedly and to the point than when he addresses the Catholic Church in the following words: "Thou dost teach and train children with much tenderness, young men with much vigor, old men with much gentleness; as the age not of the body alone, but of the mind of each requires. Women thou dost subject to their husbands in chaste and faithful obedience, not for the gratifying of their lust, but for bringing forth children, and for having a share in the family concerns. Thou dost set husbands over their wives, not that they may play false to the weaker sex, but according to the requirements of sincere affection. Thou dost subject children to their parents in a

---

19. *Sacr. Imp. ad Cyrillum Alexand. et Episcopos metrop.*; cf. Labbeus, *Collect. Conc.*, Vol. 3.

kind of free service, and dost establish parents over their children with a benign rule ... Thou joinest together, not in society only, but in a sort of brotherhood, citizen with citizen, nation with nation, and the whole race of men, by reminding them of their common parentage. Thou teachest kings to look to the interests of their people, and dost admonish the people to be submissive to their kings. With all care dost thou teach all to whom honor is due, and affection, and reverence, and fear, consolation, and admonition and exhortation, and discipline, and reproach, and punishment. Thou showest that all these are not equally incumbent on all, but that charity is owing to all, and wrongdoing to none."[20] And in another place, blaming the false wisdom of certain time-serving philosophers, he observes: "Let those who say that the teaching of Christ is hurtful to the State produce such armies as the maxims of Jesus have enjoined soldiers to bring into being; such governors of provinces; such husbands and wives; such parents and children; such masters and servants; such kings; such judges, and such payers and collectors of tribute, as the Christian teaching instructs them to become, and then let them dare to say that such teaching is hurtful to the State. Nay, rather will they hesitate to admit that this discipline, if duly acted up to, is the very mainstay of the commonwealth?"[21]

21. There was once a time when States were governed by the philosophy of the Gospel. Then it was that the power and divine virtue of Christian wisdom had diffused itself throughout the laws, institutions, and morals of the people, permeating all ranks and relations of civil society. Then, too, the religion instituted by Jesus Christ, established firmly in befitting dignity, flourished everywhere, by the favor of princes and the legitimate protection of magistrates; and Church and State were happily united in concord and friendly interchange of good offices. The State, constituted in this wise, bore fruits important beyond all expectation, whose remembrance is still, and always will be, in renown, witnessed to as they are by countless proofs which can never be blotted out or ever obscured by any craft of any enemies. Christian Europe has subdued barbarous nations, and changed them from a savage to a civilized condition, from superstition to true worship. It victoriously rolled back the tide of Mohammedan conquest; retained the headship of civilization; stood forth in the front rank as the leader and teacher of all, in every branch of national culture; bestowed on the world the gift of true and many-sided liberty; and most wisely founded very numerous institutions for the solace of human suffering. And if we inquire how it was able to bring about so altered a condition of things, the answer is—beyond all question, in

---

20. *De moribus ecclesiae* I, cap. 30, n. 63 (PL 32, 1336).

21. *Epist. 138 ad Marcellinum*, cap. 2, n. 15 (PL 33, 532).

large measure, through religion, under whose auspices so many great undertakings were set on foot, through whose aid they were brought to completion.

22. A similar state of things would certainly have continued had the agreement of the two powers been lasting. More important results even might have been justly looked for, had obedience waited upon the authority, teaching, and counsels of the Church, and had this submission been specially marked by greater and more unswerving loyalty. For that should be regarded in the light of an ever-changeless law which Ivo of Chartres wrote to Pope Paschal II: "When kingdom and priesthood are at one, in complete accord, the world is well ruled, and the Church flourishes, and brings forth abundant fruit. But when they are at variance, not only smaller interests prosper not, but even things of greatest moment fall into deplorable decay."[22]

23. But that harmful and deplorable passion for innovation which was aroused in the sixteenth century threw first of all into confusion the Christian religion, and next, by natural sequence, invaded the precincts of philosophy, whence it spread amongst all classes of society. From this source, as from a fountainhead, burst forth all those later tenets of unbridled license which, in the midst of the terrible upheavals of the last century, were wildly conceived and boldly proclaimed as the principles and foundation of that new conception of law which was not merely previously unknown, but was at variance on many points with not only the Christian, but even the natural law.

24. Amongst these principles the main one lays down that as all men are alike by race and nature, so in like manner all are equal in the control of their life; that each one is so far his own master as to be in no sense under the rule of any other individual; that each is free to think on every subject just as he may choose, and to do whatever he may like to do; that no man has any right to rule over other men. In a society grounded upon such maxims all government is nothing more nor less than the will of the people, and the people, being under the power of itself alone, is alone its own ruler. It does choose, nevertheless, some to whose charge it may commit itself, but in such wise that it makes over to them not the right so much as the business of governing, to be exercised, however, in its name.

25. The authority of God is passed over in silence, just as if there were no God; or as if He cared nothing for human society; or as if men, whether in their individual capacity or bound together in social relations, owed nothing to God; or as if there could be a government of which the whole origin and power and authority did not reside in God Himself. Thus, as is evident, a State becomes nothing but a multitude which is its own master and ruler. And since the people

---

22. *Epist.* 238, to Pope Paschal II (PL 162, 246B).

is declared to contain within itself the spring-head of all rights and of all power, it follows that the State does not consider itself bound by any kind of duty toward God. Moreover, it believes that it is not obliged to make public profession of any religion; or to inquire which of the very many religions is the only one true; or to prefer one religion to all the rest; or to show to any form of religion special favor; but, on the contrary, is bound to grant equal rights to every creed, so that public order may not be disturbed by any particular form of religious belief.

26. And it is a part of this theory that all questions that concern religion are to be referred to private judgment; that everyone is to be free to follow whatever religion he prefers, or none at all if he disapprove of all. From this the following consequences logically flow: that the judgment of each one's conscience is independent of all law; that the most unrestrained opinions may be openly expressed as to the practice or omission of divine worship; and that everyone has unbounded license to think whatever he chooses and to publish abroad whatever he thinks.

27. Now, when the State rests on foundations like those just named—and for the time being they are greatly in favor—it readily appears into what and how unrightful a position the Church is driven. For, when the management of public business is in harmony with doctrines of such a kind, the Catholic religion is allowed a standing in civil society equal only, or inferior, to societies alien from it; no regard is paid to the laws of the Church, and she who, by the order and commission of Jesus Christ, has the duty of teaching all nations, finds herself forbidden to take any part in the instruction of the people. With reference to matters that are of twofold jurisdiction, they who administer the civil power lay down the law at their own will, and in matters that appertain to religion defiantly put aside the most sacred decrees of the Church. They claim jurisdiction over the marriages of Catholics, even over the bond as well as the unity and the indissolubility of matrimony. They lay hands on the goods of the clergy, contending that the Church cannot possess property. Lastly, they treat the Church with such arrogance that, rejecting entirely her title to the nature and rights of a perfect society, they hold that she differs in no respect from other societies in the State, and for this reason possesses no right nor any legal power of action, save that which she holds by the concession and favor of the government. If in any State the Church retains her own agreement publicly entered into by the two powers, men forthwith begin to cry out that matters affecting the Church must be separated from those of the State.

28. Their object in uttering this cry is to be able to violate unpunished their plighted faith, and in all things to have unchecked control. And as the Church, unable to abandon her chiefest and most sacred duties, cannot patiently put up

with this, and asks that the pledge given to her be fully and scrupulously acted up to, contentions frequently arise between the ecclesiastical and the civil power, of which the issue commonly is that the weaker power yields to the one which is stronger in human resources.

29. Accordingly, it has become the practice and determination under this condition of public polity (now so much admired by many) either to forbid the action of the Church altogether, or to keep her in check and bondage to the State. Public enactments are in great measure framed with this design. The drawing up of laws, the administration of State affairs, the godless education of youth, the spoliation and suppression of religious orders, the overthrow of the temporal power of the Roman Pontiff, all alike aim to this one end—to paralyze the action of Christian institutions, to cramp to the utmost the freedom of the Catholic Church, and to curtail her every single prerogative.

30. Now, natural reason itself proves convincingly that such concepts of the government of a State are wholly at variance with the truth. Nature itself bears witness that all power, of every kind, has its origin from God, who is its chief and most august source.

31. The sovereignty of the people, however, and this without any reference to God, is held to reside in the multitude; which is doubtless a doctrine exceedingly well calculated to flatter and to inflame many passions, but which lacks all reasonable proof, and all power of insuring public safety and preserving order. Indeed, from the prevalence of this teaching, things have come to such a pass that many hold as an axiom of civil jurisprudence that seditions may be rightfully fostered. For the opinion prevails that princes are nothing more than delegates chosen to carry out the will of the people; whence it necessarily follows that all things are as changeable as the will of the people, so that risk of public disturbance is ever hanging over our heads.

To hold, therefore, that there is no difference in matters of religion between forms that are unlike each other, and even contrary to each other, most clearly leads in the end to the rejection of all religion in both theory and practice. And this is the same thing as atheism, however it may differ from it in name. Men who really believe in the existence of God must, in order to be consistent with themselves and to avoid absurd conclusions, understand that differing modes of divine worship involving dissimilarity and conflict even on most important points cannot all be equally probable, equally good, and equally acceptable to God.

32. So, too, the liberty of thinking, and of publishing, whatsoever each one likes, without any hindrance, is not in itself an advantage over which society can wisely rejoice. On the contrary, it is the fountainhead and origin of many evils. Liberty is a power perfecting man, and hence should have truth and goodness for

its object. But the character of goodness and truth cannot be changed at option. These remain ever one and the same, and are no less unchangeable than nature itself. If the mind assents to false opinions, and the will chooses and follows after what is wrong, neither can attain its native fullness, but both must fall from their native dignity into an abyss of corruption. Whatever, therefore, is opposed to virtue and truth may not rightly be brought temptingly before the eye of man, much less sanctioned by the favor and protection of the law. A well-spent life is the only way to heaven, whither all are bound, and on this account the State is acting against the laws and dictates of nature whenever it permits the license of opinion and of action to lead minds astray from truth and souls away from the practice of virtue. To exclude the Church, founded by God Himself, from life, from laws, from the education of youth, from domestic society is a grave and fatal error. A State from which religion is banished can never be well regulated; and already perhaps more than is desirable is known of the nature and tendency of the so-called civil philosophy of life and morals. The Church of Christ is the true and sole teacher of virtue and guardian of morals. She it is who preserves in their purity the principles from which duties flow, and, by setting forth most urgent reasons for virtuous life, bids us not only to turn away from wicked deeds, but even to curb all movements of the mind that are opposed to reason, even though they be not carried out in action.

33. To wish the Church to be subject to the civil power in the exercise of her duty is a great folly and a sheer injustice. Whenever this is the case, order is disturbed, for things natural are put above things supernatural; the many benefits which the Church, if free to act, would confer on society are either prevented or at least lessened in number; and a way is prepared for enmities and contentions between the two powers, with how evil result to both the issue of events has taught us only too frequently.

34. Doctrines such as these, which cannot be approved by human reason, and most seriously affect the whole civil order, Our predecessors the Roman Pontiffs (well aware of what their apostolic office required of them) have never allowed to pass uncondemned. Thus, Gregory XVI in his encyclical letter *Mirari Vos*, dated August 15, 1832, inveighed with weighty words against the sophisms which even at his time were being publicly inculcated—namely, that no preference should be shown for any particular form of worship; that it is right for individuals to form their own personal judgments about religion; that each man's conscience is his sole and all-sufficing guide; and that it is lawful for every man to publish his own views, whatever they may be, and even to conspire against the State. On the question of the separation of Church and State the same Pontiff writes as follows: "Nor can We hope for happier results either for religion or for

the civil government from the wishes of those who desire that the Church be separated from the State, and the concord between the secular and ecclesiastical authority be dissolved. It is clear that these men, who yearn for a shameless liberty, live in dread of an agreement which has always been fraught with good, and advantageous alike to sacred and civil interests." To the like effect, also, as occasion presented itself, did Pius IX brand publicly many false opinions which were gaining ground, and afterwards ordered them to be condensed in summary form in order that in this sea of error Catholics might have a light which they might safely follow.[23]

35. From these pronouncements of the Popes it is evident that the origin of public power is to be sought for in God Himself and not in the multitude, and that it is repugnant to reason to allow free scope for sedition. Again, that it is not lawful for the State, any more than for the individual, either to disregard all religious duties or to hold in equal favor different kinds of religion; that the unrestrained freedom of thinking and of openly making known one's thoughts is not inherent in the rights of citizens, and is by no means to be reckoned worthy of favor and support. In like manner it is to be understood that the Church no less than the State itself is a society perfect in its own nature and its own right, and that those who exercise sovereignty ought not so to act as to compel the Church to become subservient or subject to them, or to hamper her liberty in the management of her own affairs, or to despoil her in any way of the other privileges conferred upon her by Jesus Christ. In matters, however, of mixed jurisdiction, it is in the highest degree consonant to nature, as also to the designs of God, that so far from one of the powers separating itself from the other, or still less coming into conflict with it, complete harmony, such as is suited to the end for which each power exists, should be preserved between them.

36. This, then, is the teaching of the Catholic Church concerning the constitution and government of the State. By the words and decrees just cited, if judged dispassionately, no one of the several forms of government is in itself condemned, inasmuch as none of them contains anything contrary to Catholic doctrine, and all of them are capable, if wisely and justly managed, to insure the welfare of the

---

23. [Pope Pius IX, encyclical *Quanta Cura* (Dec. 8, 1864) and *Syllabus Errorum*. It will suffice to recall a few of the condemned propositions: 19. The Church is not a true, perfect, and wholly independent society, possessing in its own unchanging rights conferred upon it by its divine Founder; but it is for the civil power to determine what are the rights of the Church, and the limits within which it may use them. 29. The State, as the origin and source of all rights, enjoys a right that is unlimited. 55. The Church must be separated from the State and the State from the Church. 79. It is untrue that the civil liberty of every form of worship, and the full power given to all of openly and publicly manifesting whatsoever opinions and thoughts, lead to the more ready corruption of the minds and morals of the people, and to the spread of the plague of religious indifference.]

State. Neither is it blameworthy in itself, in any manner, for the people to have a share, greater or less, in the government: for at certain times, and under certain laws, such participation may not only be of benefit to the citizens, but may even be of obligation. Nor is there any reason why anyone should accuse the Church of being wanting in gentleness of action or largeness of view, or of being opposed to real and lawful liberty. The Church, indeed, deems it unlawful to place the various forms of divine worship on the same footing as the true religion, but does not, on that account, condemn those rulers who, for the sake of securing some great good or of hindering some great evil, allow patiently custom or usage to be a kind of sanction for each kind of religion having its place in the State. And, in fact, the Church is wont to take earnest heed that no one shall be forced to embrace the Catholic faith against his will, for, as St. Augustine wisely reminds us, "Man cannot believe otherwise than of his own will."

37. In the same way the Church cannot approve of that liberty which begets a contempt of the most sacred laws of God, and casts off the obedience due to lawful authority, for this is not liberty so much as license, and is most correctly styled by St. Augustine the "liberty of self-ruin," and by the Apostle St. Peter the "cloak of malice."[24] Indeed, since it is opposed to reason, it is a true slavery, "for whosoever committeth sin is the slave of sin."[25] On the other hand, that liberty is truly genuine, and to be sought after, which in regard to the individual does not allow men to be the slaves of error and of passion, the worst of all masters; which, too, in public administration guides the citizens in wisdom and provides for them increased means of well-being; and which, further, protects the State from foreign interference.

38. This honorable liberty, alone worthy of human beings, the Church approves most highly and has never slackened her endeavor to preserve, strong and unchanged, among nations. And, in truth, whatever in the State is of chief avail for the common welfare; whatever has been usefully established to curb the license of rulers who are opposed to the true interests of the people, or to keep in check the leading authorities from unwarrantably interfering in municipal or family affairs; whatever tends to uphold the honor, manhood, and equal rights of individual citizens—of all these things, as the monuments of past ages bear witness, the Catholic Church has always been the originator, the promoter, or the guardian. Ever, therefore, consistent with herself, while on the one hand she rejects that exorbitant liberty which in individuals and in nations ends in license or in thralldom, on the other hand, she willingly and most gladly welcomes

24. 1 Peter 2:16.

25. John 8:34.

whatever improvements the age brings forth, if these really secure the prosperity of life here below, which is, as it were, a stage in the journey to the life that will know no ending.

39. Therefore, when it is said that the Church is hostile to modern political regimes and that she repudiates the discoveries of modern research, the charge is a ridiculous and groundless calumny. Wild opinions she does repudiate, wicked and seditious projects she does condemn, together with that attitude of mind which points to the beginning of a willful departure from God. But, as all truth must necessarily proceed from God, the Church recognizes in all truth that is reached by research a trace of the divine intelligence. And as all truth in the natural order is powerless to destroy belief in the teachings of revelation, but can do much to confirm it, and as every newly discovered truth may serve to further the knowledge or the praise of God, it follows that whatsoever spreads the range of knowledge will always be willingly and even joyfully welcomed by the Church. She will always encourage and promote, as she does in other branches of knowledge, all study occupied with the investigation of nature. In these pursuits, should the human intellect discover anything not known before, the Church makes no opposition. She never objects to search being made for things that minister to the refinements and comforts of life. So far, indeed, from opposing these she is now, as she ever has been, hostile alone to indolence and sloth, and earnestly wishes that the talents of men may bear more and more abundant fruit by cultivation and exercise. Moreover, she gives encouragement to every kind of art and handicraft, and through her influence, directing all strivings after progress toward virtue and salvation, she labors to prevent man's intellect and industry from turning him away from God and from heavenly things.

40. All this, though so reasonable and full of counsel, finds little favor nowadays when States not only refuse to conform to the rules of Christian wisdom, but seem even anxious to recede from them further and further on each successive day. Nevertheless, since truth when brought to light is wont, of its own nature, to spread itself far and wide, and gradually take possession of the minds of men, We, moved by the great and holy duty of Our apostolic mission to all nations, speak, as We are bound to do, with freedom. Our eyes are not closed to the spirit of the times. We repudiate not the assured and useful improvements of our age, but devoutly wish affairs of State to take a safer course than they are now taking, and to rest on a more firm foundation without injury to the true freedom of the people; for the best parent and guardian of liberty amongst men is truth. "The truth shall make you free."[26]

---

26. John 8:32.

41. If in the difficult times in which Our lot is cast, Catholics will give ear to Us, as it behooves them to do, they will readily see what are the duties of each one in matters of opinion as well as action. As regards opinion, whatever the Roman Pontiffs have hitherto taught, or shall hereafter teach, must be held with a firm grasp of mind, and, so often as occasion requires, must be openly professed.

42. Especially with reference to the so-called "liberties" which are so greatly coveted in these days, all must stand by the judgment of the Apostolic See, and have the same mind. Let no man be deceived by the honest outward appearance of these liberties, but let each one reflect whence these have had their origin, and by what efforts they are everywhere upheld and promoted. Experience has made Us well acquainted with their results to the State, since everywhere they have borne fruits which the good and wise bitterly deplore. If there really exist anywhere, or if we in imagination conceive, a State, waging wanton and tyrannical war against Christianity, and if we compare with it the modern form of government just described, this latter may seem the more endurable of the two. Yet, undoubtedly, the principles on which such a government is grounded are, as We have said, of a nature which no one can approve.

43. Secondly, action may relate to private and domestic matters, or to matters public. As to private affairs, the first duty is to conform life and conduct to the Gospel precepts, and to refuse to shrink from this duty when Christian virtue demands some sacrifice slightly more difficult to make. All, moreover, are bound to love the Church as their common mother, to obey her laws, promote her honor, defend her rights, and to endeavor to make her respected and loved by those over whom they have authority. It is also of great moment to the public welfare to take a prudent part in the business of municipal administration, and to endeavor above all to introduce effectual measures, so that, as becomes a Christian people, public provision may be made for the instruction of youth in religion and true morality. Upon these things the well-being of every State greatly depends.

44. Furthermore, it is in general fitting and salutary that Catholics should extend their efforts beyond this restricted sphere, and give their attention to national politics. We say "in general" because these Our precepts are addressed to all nations. However, it may in some places be true that, for most urgent and just reasons, it is by no means expedient for Catholics to engage in public affairs or to take an active part in politics. Nevertheless, as We have laid down, to take no share in public matters would be as wrong as to have no concern for, or to bestow no labor upon, the common good, and the more so because Catholics are admonished, by the very doctrines which they profess, to be upright and faithful in the discharge of duty, while, if they hold aloof, men whose principles offer but small guarantee for the welfare of the State will the more readily seize

the reins of government. This would tend also to the injury of the Christian religion, forasmuch as those would come into power who are badly disposed toward the Church, and those who are willing to befriend her would be deprived of all influence.

45. It follows clearly, therefore, that Catholics have just reasons for taking part in the conduct of public affairs. For in so doing they assume not nor should they assume the responsibility of approving what is blameworthy in the actual methods of government, but seek to turn these very methods, so far as is possible, to the genuine and true public good, and to use their best endeavors at the same time to infuse, as it were, into all the veins of the State the healthy sap and blood of Christian wisdom and virtue. The morals and ambitions of the heathens differed widely from those of the Gospel, yet Christians were to be seen living undefiled everywhere in the midst of pagan superstition, and, while always true to themselves, coming to the front boldly wherever an opening was presented. Models of loyalty to their rulers, submissive, so far as was permitted, to the sovereign power, they shed around them on every side a halo of sanctity; they strove to be helpful to their brethren, and to attract others to the wisdom of Jesus Christ, yet were bravely ready to withdraw from public life, nay, even to lay down their life, if they could not without loss of virtue retain honors, dignities, and offices. For this reason, Christian ways and manners speedily found their way not only into private houses but into the camp, the senate, and even into the imperial palaces. "We are but of yesterday," wrote Tertullian, "yet we swarm in all your institutions, we crowd your cities, islands, villages, towns, assemblies, the army itself, your wards and corporations, the palace, the senate, and the law courts."[27] So that the Christian faith, when once it became lawful to make public profession of the Gospel, appeared in most of the cities of Europe, not like an infant crying in its cradle, but already grown up and full of vigor.

46. In these Our days it is well to revive these examples of Our forefathers. First and foremost, it is the duty of all Catholics worthy of the name and wishful to be known as most loving children of the Church, to reject without swerving whatever is inconsistent with so fair a title; to make use of popular institutions, so far as can honestly be done, for the advancement of truth and righteousness; to strive that liberty of action shall not transgress the bounds marked out by nature and the law of God; to endeavor to bring back all civil society to the pattern and form of Christianity which We have described. It is barely possible to lay down any fixed method by which such purposes are to be attained, because the means adopted must suit places and times widely differing from

---

27. *Apolog.*, 27 (PL 1, 525).

one another. Nevertheless, above all things, unity of aim must be preserved, and similarity must be sought after in all plans of action. Both these objects will be carried into effect without fail if all will follow the guidance of the Apostolic See as their rule of life and obey the bishops whom the Holy Spirit has placed to rule the Church of God.[28] The defense of Catholicism, indeed, necessarily demands that in the profession of doctrines taught by the Church all shall be of one mind and all steadfast in believing; and care must be taken never to connive, in any way, at false opinions, never to withstand them less strenuously than truth allows. In mere matters of opinion it is permissible to discuss things with moderation, with a desire of searching into the truth, without unjust suspicion or angry recriminations.

47. Hence, lest concord be broken by rash charges, let this be understood by all, that the integrity of Catholic faith cannot be reconciled with opinions verging on naturalism or rationalism, the essence of which is utterly to do away with Christian institutions and to install in society the supremacy of man to the exclusion of God. Further, it is unlawful to follow one line of conduct in private life and another in public, respecting privately the authority of the Church, but publicly rejecting it; for this would amount to joining together good and evil, and to putting man in conflict with himself; whereas he ought always to be consistent, and never in the least point nor in any condition of life to swerve from Christian virtue.

48. But in matters merely political, as, for instance, the best form of government, and this or that system of administration, a difference of opinion is lawful. Those, therefore, whose piety is in other respects known, and whose minds are ready to accept in all obedience the decrees of the Apostolic See, cannot in justice be accounted as bad men because they disagree as to subjects We have mentioned; and still graver wrong will be done them, if—as We have more than once perceived with regret—they are accused of violating, or of wavering in, the Catholic faith.

49. Let this be well borne in mind by all who are in the habit of publishing their opinions, and above all by journalists. In the endeavor to secure interests of the highest order there is no room for intestine strife or party rivalries; since all should aim with one mind and purpose to make safe that which is the common object of all—the maintenance of religion and of the State. If, therefore, there have hitherto been dissensions, let them henceforth be gladly buried in oblivion. If rash or injurious acts have been committed, whoever may have been at fault, let mutual charity make amends, and let the past be redeemed by

---

28. Acts 20:28.

a special submission of all to the Apostolic See. In this way Catholics will attain two most excellent results: they will become helpers to the Church in preserving and propagating Christian wisdom, and they will confer the greatest benefit on civil society, the safety of which is exceedingly imperiled by evil teachings and bad passions.

50. This, venerable brethren, is what We have thought it Our duty to expound to all nations of the Catholic world touching the Christian constitution of States and the duties of individual citizens. It behooves Us now with earnest prayer to implore the protection of heaven, beseeching God, who alone can enlighten the minds of men and move their will, to bring about those happy ends for which We yearn and strive, for His greater glory and the general salvation of mankind. As a happy augury of the divine benefits, and in token of Our paternal benevolence, to you, venerable brothers, and to the clergy and to the whole people committed to your charge and vigilance, We grant lovingly in the Lord the apostolic benediction.

Given at St. Peter's in Rome, the first day of November, 1885, the seventh year of Our pontificate.

✠ Leo XIII

LIBERTAS PRAESTANTISSIMUM

On the Nature of Human Liberty

Encyclical Letter of Pope Leo XIII,
promulgated June 20, 1888

To the Patriarchs, Primates, Archbishops, and Bishops of the Catholic World in Grace and Communion with the Apostolic See.

L iberty, the highest of natural endowments, being the portion only of intellectual or rational natures, confers on man this dignity—that he is "in the hand of his counsel"[1] and has power over his actions. But the manner in which such dignity is exercised is of the greatest moment, inasmuch as on the use that is made of liberty the highest good and the greatest evil alike depend. Man, indeed, is free to obey his reason, to seek moral good, and to strive unswervingly after his last end. Yet he is free also to turn aside to all other things; and, in pursuing the empty semblance of good, to disturb rightful order and to fall headlong into the destruction which he has voluntarily chosen. The Redeemer of mankind, Jesus Christ, having restored and exalted the original dignity of nature, vouchsafed special assistance to the will of man; and by the gifts of His grace here, and the promise of heavenly bliss hereafter, He raised it to a nobler state. In like manner, this great gift of nature has ever been, and always will be, deservingly cherished by the Catholic Church, for to her alone has been committed the charge of handing down to all ages the benefits purchased for us by Jesus Christ. Yet there are many who imagine that the Church is hostile to human liberty. Having a false and absurd notion as to what liberty is, either they pervert the very idea of freedom, or they extend it at their pleasure to many things in respect of which man cannot rightly be regarded as free.

2. We have on other occasions, and especially in Our encyclical letter *Immortale Dei,*[2] in treating of the so-called modern liberties, distinguished between their good and evil elements; and We have shown that whatsoever is good in those

---

1. Ecclus.15:14.
2. See nn. 37–38.

liberties is as ancient as truth itself, and that the Church has always most willingly approved and practiced that good: but whatsoever has been added as new is, to tell the plain truth, of a vitiated kind, the fruit of the disorders of the age, and of an insatiate longing after novelties. Seeing, however, that many cling so obstinately to their own opinion in this matter as to imagine these modern liberties, cankered as they are, to be the greatest glory of our age, and the very basis of civil life, without which no perfect government can be conceived, We feel it a pressing duty, for the sake of the common good, to treat separately of this subject.

3. It is with moral liberty, whether in individuals or in communities, that We proceed at once to deal. But, first of all, it will be well to speak briefly of natural liberty; for, though it is distinct and separate from moral liberty, natural freedom is the fountainhead from which liberty of whatsoever kind flows, *sua vi suaque sponte.* The unanimous consent and judgment of men, which is the trusty voice of nature, recognizes this natural liberty in those only who are endowed with intelligence or reason; and it is by his use of this that man is rightly regarded as responsible for his actions. For, while other animate creatures follow their senses, seeking good and avoiding evil only by instinct, man has reason to guide him in each and every act of his life. Reason sees that whatever things that are held to be good upon earth may exist or may not, and discerning that none of them are of necessity for us, it leaves the will free to choose what it pleases. But man can judge of this contingency, as We say, only because he has a soul that is simple, spiritual, and intellectual—a soul, therefore, which is not produced by matter, and does not depend on matter for its existence; but which is created immediately by God, and, far surpassing the condition of things material, has a life and action of its own—so that, knowing the unchangeable and necessary reasons of what is true and good, it sees that no particular kind of good is necessary to us. When, therefore, it is established that man's soul is immortal and endowed with reason and not bound up with things material, the foundation of natural liberty is at once most firmly laid.

4. As the Catholic Church declares in the strongest terms the simplicity, spirituality, and immortality of the soul, so with unequaled constancy and publicity she ever also asserts its freedom. These truths she has always taught, and has sustained them as a dogma of faith, and whensoever heretics or innovators have attacked the liberty of man, the Church has defended it and protected this noble possession from destruction. History bears witness to the energy with which she met the fury of the Manicheans and others like them; and the earnestness with which in later years she defended human liberty at the Council of Trent, and against the followers of Jansenius, is known to all. At no time, and in no place, has she held truce with fatalism.

5. Liberty, then, as We have said, belongs only to those who have the gift of reason or intelligence. Considered as to its nature, it is the faculty of choosing means fitted for the end proposed, for he is master of his actions who can choose one thing out of many. Now, since everything chosen as a means is viewed as good or useful, and since good, as such, is the proper object of our desire, it follows that freedom of choice is a property of the will, or, rather, is identical with the will in so far as it has in its action the faculty of choice. But the will cannot proceed to act until it is enlightened by the knowledge possessed by the intellect. In other words, the good wished by the will is necessarily good in so far as it is known by the intellect; and this the more, because in all voluntary acts choice is subsequent to a judgment upon the truth of the good presented, declaring to which good preference should be given. No sensible man can doubt that judgment is an act of reason, not of the will. The end, or object, both of the rational will and of its liberty is that good only which is in conformity with reason.

6. Since, however, both these faculties are imperfect, it is possible, as is often seen, that the reason should propose something which is not really good, but which has the appearance of good, and that the will should choose accordingly. For, as the possibility of error, and actual error, are defects of the mind and attest its imperfection, so the pursuit of what has a false appearance of good, though a proof of our freedom, just as a disease is a proof of our vitality, implies defect in human liberty. The will also, simply because of its dependence on the reason, no sooner desires anything contrary thereto than it abuses its freedom of choice and corrupts its very essence. Thus it is that the infinitely perfect God, although supremely free, nevertheless cannot choose evil, because of the supremacy of His intellect and His essential goodness; neither can the angels and saints, who enjoy the beatific vision. St. Augustine and others urged most admirably against the Pelagians that, if the possibility of deflection from good belonged to the essence or perfection of liberty, then God, Jesus Christ, and the angels and saints, who have not this power, would have no liberty at all, or would have less liberty than man has in his state of pilgrimage and imperfection. This subject is often discussed by the Angelic Doctor in his demonstration that the possibility of sinning is not freedom, but slavery. It will suffice to quote his subtle commentary on the words of our Lord: "Whosoever committeth sin is the slave of sin."[3] "Everything," he says, "is that which belongs to it naturally. When, therefore, it acts through a power outside itself, it does not act of itself, but through another, that is, as a slave. But man is by nature rational. When, therefore, he acts according to reason, he acts of himself and according to his free will; and this is liberty.

---

3. John 8:34.

Whereas, when he sins, he acts in opposition to reason, is moved by another, and is the victim of foreign misapprehensions. Therefore, 'Whosoever committeth sin is the slave of sin.'"[4] Even the heathen philosophers clearly recognized this truth, especially they who held that the wise man alone is free; and by the term "wise man" was meant, as is well known, the man trained to live in accordance with his nature, that is, in justice and virtue.

7. Such, then, being the condition of human liberty, it necessarily stands in need of light and strength to direct its actions to good and to restrain them from evil. Without this, the freedom of our will would be our ruin. First of all, there must be law; that is, a fixed rule of teaching what is to be done and what is to be left undone. This rule cannot affect the lower animals in any true sense, since they act of necessity, following their natural instinct, and cannot of themselves act in any other way. On the other hand, as was said above, he who is free can either act or not act, can do this or do that, as he pleases, because his judgment precedes his choice. And his judgment not only decides what is right or wrong of its own nature, but also what is practically good and therefore to be chosen, and what is practically evil and therefore to be avoided. In other words, reason prescribes to the will what it should seek after or shun, with a view to the eventual attainment of man's last end, for the sake of which all his actions ought to be performed. This ordination of reason is called law. In man's free will, therefore, or in the moral necessity of our voluntary acts being in accordance with reason, lies the very root of the necessity of law. Nothing more foolish can be uttered or conceived than the notion that, because man is free by nature, he is therefore exempt from law. Were this the case, it would follow that to become free we must be deprived of reason; whereas the truth is that we are bound to submit to law precisely because we are free by our very nature. For, law is the guide of man's actions; it turns him toward good by its rewards, and deters him from evil by its punishments.

8. Foremost in this office comes the natural law, which is written and engraved in the mind of every man; and this is nothing but our reason, commanding us to do right and forbidding sin. Nevertheless, all prescriptions of human reason can have force of law only inasmuch as they are the voice and the interpreters of some higher power on which our reason and liberty necessarily depend. For, since the force of law consists in the imposing of obligations and the granting of rights, authority is the one and only foundation of all law—the power, that is, of fixing duties and defining rights, as also of assigning the necessary sanctions of reward and chastisement to each and all of its commands. But all this, clearly, cannot be found in man, if, as his own supreme legislator, he is to be the rule of his own

---

4. Thomas Aquinas, *On the Gospel of St. John*, ch. viii, lect. 4, n. 3.

actions. It follows, therefore, that the law of nature is the same thing as the eternal law, implanted in rational creatures, and inclining them to their right action and end; and can be nothing else but the eternal reason of God, the Creator and Ruler of all the world. To this rule of action and restraint of evil God has vouchsafed to give special and most suitable aids for strengthening and ordering the human will. The first and most excellent of these is the power of His divine grace, whereby the mind can be enlightened and the will wholesomely invigorated and moved to the constant pursuit of moral good, so that the use of our inborn liberty becomes at once less difficult and less dangerous. Not that the divine assistance hinders in any way the free movement of our will; just the contrary, for grace works inwardly in man and in harmony with his natural inclinations, since it flows from the very Creator of his mind and will, by whom all things are moved in conformity with their nature. As the Angelic Doctor points out, it is because divine grace comes from the Author of nature that it is so admirably adapted to be the safeguard of all natures, and to maintain the character, efficiency, and operations of each.

9. What has been said of the liberty of individuals is no less applicable to them when considered as bound together in civil society. For that which reason and the natural law do for individuals, the same does human law, promulgated for their good, for the citizens of States. Of the laws enacted by men, some are concerned with what is good or bad by its very nature; and they command men to follow after what is right and to shun what is wrong, adding at the same time a suitable sanction. But such laws by no means derive their origin from civil society, because, just as civil society did not create human nature, so neither can it be said to be the author of the good which befits human nature, or of the evil which is contrary to it. Laws come before men live together in society, and have their origin in the natural, and consequently in the eternal, law. The precepts, therefore, of the natural law, contained bodily in the laws of men, have not merely the force of human law, but they possess that higher and more august sanction which belongs to the law of nature and the eternal law. And within the sphere of this kind of laws the duty of the civil legislator is, mainly, to keep the community in obedience by the adoption of a common discipline and by putting restraint upon refractory and viciously inclined men, so that, deterred from evil, they may turn to what is good, or at any rate may avoid causing trouble and disturbance to the State. Now, there are other enactments of the civil authority, which do not follow directly, but somewhat remotely, from the natural law, and decide many points which the law of nature treats only in a general and indefinite way. For instance, though nature commands all to contribute to the public peace and prosperity, whatever belongs to the manner, and circumstances, and conditions under

which such service is to be rendered must be determined by the wisdom of men and not by nature herself. It is in the constitution of these particular rules of life, suggested by reason and prudence, and put forth by competent authority, that human law, properly so called, consists, binding all citizens to work together for the attainment of the common end proposed to the community, and forbidding them to depart from this end, and, in so far as human law is in conformity with the dictates of nature, leading to what is good, and deterring from evil.

10. From this it is manifest that the eternal law of God is the sole standard and rule of human liberty, not only in each individual man, but also in the community and civil society which men constitute when united. Therefore, the true liberty of human society does not consist in every man doing what he pleases, for this would simply end in turmoil and confusion, and bring on the overthrow of the State; but rather in this, that through the injunctions of the civil law all may more easily conform to the prescriptions of the eternal law. Likewise, the liberty of those who are in authority does not consist in the power to lay unreasonable and capricious commands upon their subjects, which would equally be criminal and would lead to the ruin of the commonwealth; but the binding force of human laws is in this, that they are to be regarded as applications of the eternal law, and incapable of sanctioning anything which is not contained in the eternal law, as in the principle of all law. Thus, St. Augustine most wisely says: "I think that you can see, at the same time, that there is nothing just and lawful in that temporal law, unless what men have gathered from this eternal law."[5] If, then, by anyone in authority, something be sanctioned out of conformity with the principles of right reason, and consequently hurtful to the commonwealth, such an enactment can have no binding force of law, as being no rule of justice, but certain to lead men away from that good which is the very end of civil society.

11. Therefore, the nature of human liberty, however it be considered, whether in individuals or in society, whether in those who command or in those who obey, supposes the necessity of obedience to some supreme and eternal law, which is no other than the authority of God, commanding good and forbidding evil. And, so far from this most just authority of God over men diminishing, or even destroying their liberty, it protects and perfects it, for the real perfection of all creatures is found in the prosecution and attainment of their respective ends; but the supreme end to which human liberty must aspire is God.

12. These precepts of the truest and highest teaching, made known to us by the light of reason itself, the Church, instructed by the example and doctrine of her divine Author, has ever propagated and asserted; for she has ever made

---

5.   *De libero arbitrio*, lib. 1, cap. 6, n. 15 (PL 32, 1229).

them the measure of her office and of her teaching to the Christian nations. As to morals, the laws of the Gospel not only immeasurably surpass the wisdom of the heathen, but are an invitation and an introduction to a state of holiness unknown to the ancients; and, bringing man nearer to God, they make him at once the possessor of a more perfect liberty. Thus, the powerful influence of the Church has ever been manifested in the custody and protection of the civil and political liberty of the people. The enumeration of its merits in this respect does not belong to our present purpose. It is sufficient to recall the fact that slavery, that old reproach of the heathen nations, was mainly abolished by the beneficent efforts of the Church. The impartiality of law and the true brotherhood of man were first asserted by Jesus Christ; and His apostles re-echoed His voice when they declared that in future there was to be neither Jew, nor Gentile, nor barbarian, nor Scythian, but all were brothers in Christ. So powerful, so conspicuous, in this respect is the influence of the Church that experience abundantly testifies how savage customs are no longer possible in any land where she has once set her foot; but that gentleness speedily takes the place of cruelty, and the light of truth quickly dispels the darkness of barbarism. Nor has the Church been less lavish in the benefits she has conferred on civilized nations in every age, either by resisting the tyranny of the wicked, or by protecting the innocent and helpless from injury, or, finally, by using her influence in the support of any form of government which commended itself to the citizens at home, because of its justice, or was feared by their enemies without, because of its power.

13. Moreover, the highest duty is to respect authority, and obediently to submit to just law; and by this the members of a community are effectually protected from the wrong-doing of evil men. Lawful power is from God, "and whosoever resisteth authority resisteth the ordinance of God"[6]; wherefore, obedience is greatly ennobled when subjected to an authority which is the most just and supreme of all. But where the power to command is wanting, or where a law is enacted contrary to reason, or to the eternal law, or to some ordinance of God, obedience is unlawful, lest, while obeying man, we become disobedient to God. Thus, an effectual barrier being opposed to tyranny, the authority in the State will not have all its own way, but the interests and rights of all will be safeguarded—the rights of individuals, of domestic society, and of all the members of the commonwealth; all being free to live according to law and right reason; and in this, as We have shown, true liberty really consists.

14. If when men discuss the question of liberty they were careful to grasp its true and legitimate meaning, such as reason and reasoning have just explained,

6.   Rom.13:2.

they would never venture to affix such a calumny on the Church as to assert that she is the foe of individual and public liberty. But many there are who follow in the footsteps of Lucifer, and adopt as their own his rebellious cry, "I will not serve"; and consequently substitute for true liberty what is sheer and most foolish license. Such, for instance, are the men belonging to that widely spread and powerful organization, who, usurping the name of liberty, style themselves liberals.

15. What naturalists or rationalists aim at in philosophy, that the supporters of liberalism, carrying out the principles laid down by naturalism, are attempting in the domain of morality and politics. The fundamental doctrine of rationalism is the supremacy of the human reason, which, refusing due submission to the divine and eternal reason, proclaims its own independence, and constitutes itself the supreme principle and source and judge of truth. Hence, these followers of liberalism deny the existence of any divine authority to which obedience is due, and proclaim that every man is the law to himself; from which arises that ethical system which they style independent morality, and which, under the guise of liberty, exonerates man from any obedience to the commands of God, and substitutes a boundless license. The end of all this it is not difficult to foresee, especially when society is in question. For, when once man is firmly persuaded that he is subject to no one, it follows that the efficient cause of the unity of civil society is not to be sought in any principle external to man, or superior to him, but simply in the free will of individuals; that the authority in the State comes from the people only; and that, just as every man's individual reason is his only rule of life, so the collective reason of the community should be the supreme guide in the management of all public affairs. Hence the doctrine of the supremacy of the greater number, and that all right and all duty reside in the majority. But, from what has been said, it is clear that all this is in contradiction to reason. To refuse any bond of union between man and civil society, on the one hand, and God the Creator and consequently the supreme Law-giver, on the other, is plainly repugnant to the nature, not only of man, but of all created things; for, of necessity, all effects must in some proper way be connected with their cause; and it belongs to the perfection of every nature to contain itself within that sphere and grade which the order of nature has assigned to it, namely, that the lower should be subject and obedient to the higher.

16. Moreover, besides this, a doctrine of such character is most hurtful both to individuals and to the State. For, once ascribe to human reason the only authority to decide what is true and what is good, and the real distinction between good and evil is destroyed; honor and dishonor differ not in their nature, but in the opinion and judgment of each one; pleasure is the measure of what is lawful; and,

given a code of morality which can have little or no power to restrain or quiet the unruly propensities of man, a way is naturally opened to universal corruption. With reference also to public affairs: authority is severed from the true and natural principle whence it derives all its efficacy for the common good; and the law determining what it is right to do and avoid doing is at the mercy of a majority. Now, this is simply a road leading straight to tyranny. The empire of God over man and civil society once repudiated, it follows that religion, as a public institution, can have no claim to exist, and that everything that belongs to religion will be treated with complete indifference. Furthermore, with ambitious designs on sovereignty, tumult and sedition will be common amongst the people; and when duty and conscience cease to appeal to them, there will be nothing to hold them back but force, which of itself alone is powerless to keep their covetousness in check. Of this we have almost daily evidence in the conflict with socialists and members of other seditious societies, who labor unceasingly to bring about revolution. It is for those, then, who are capable of forming a just estimate of things to decide whether such doctrines promote that true liberty which alone is worthy of man, or rather, pervert and destroy it.

17. There are, indeed, some adherents of liberalism who do not subscribe to these opinions, which we have seen to be fearful in their enormity, openly opposed to the truth, and the cause of most terrible evils. Indeed, very many amongst them, compelled by the force of truth, do not hesitate to admit that such liberty is vicious, nay, is simple license, whenever intemperate in its claims, to the neglect of truth and justice; and therefore they would have liberty ruled and directed by right reason, and consequently subject to the natural law and to the divine eternal law. But here they think they may stop, holding that man as a free being is bound by no law of God except such as He makes known to us through our natural reason. In this they are plainly inconsistent. For if—as they must admit, and no one can rightly deny—the will of the divine Law-giver is to be obeyed, because every man is under the power of God, and tends toward Him as his end, it follows that no one can assign limits to His legislative authority without failing in the obedience which is due. Indeed, if the human mind be so presumptuous as to define the nature and extent of God's rights and its own duties, reverence for the divine law will be apparent rather than real, and arbitrary judgment will prevail over the authority and providence of God. Man must, therefore, take his standard of a loyal and religious life from the eternal law; and from all and every one of those laws which God, in His infinite wisdom and power, has been pleased to enact, and to make known to us by such clear and unmistakable signs as to leave no room for doubt. And the more so because laws of this kind have the same origin, the same author, as the eternal law, are

absolutely in accordance with right reason, and perfect the natural law. These laws it is that embody the government of God, who graciously guides and directs the intellect and the will of man lest these fall into error. Let, then, that continue to remain in a holy and inviolable union which neither can nor should be separated; and in all things—for this is the dictate of right reason itself—let God be dutifully and obediently served.

18. There are others, somewhat more moderate though not more consistent, who affirm that the morality of individuals is to be guided by the divine law, but not the morality of the State, for that in public affairs the commands of God may be passed over, and may be entirely disregarded in the framing of laws. Hence follows the fatal theory of the need of separation between Church and State. But the absurdity of such a position is manifest. Nature herself proclaims the necessity of the State providing means and opportunities whereby the community may be enabled to live properly, that is to say, according to the laws of God. For, since God is the source of all goodness and justice, it is absolutely ridiculous that the State should pay no attention to these laws or render them abortive by contrary enactments. Besides, those who are in authority owe it to the commonwealth not only to provide for its external well-being and the conveniences of life, but still more to consult the welfare of men's souls in the wisdom of their legislation. But, for the increase of such benefits, nothing more suitable can be conceived than the laws which have God for their author; and, therefore, they who in their government of the State take no account of these laws abuse political power by causing it to deviate from its proper end and from what nature itself prescribes. And, what is still more important, and what We have more than once pointed out, although the civil authority has not the same proximate end as the spiritual, nor proceeds on the same lines, nevertheless in the exercise of their separate powers they must occasionally meet. For their subjects are the same, and not infrequently they deal with the same objects, though in different ways. Whenever this occurs, since a state of conflict is absurd and manifestly repugnant to the most wise ordinance of God, there must necessarily exist some order or mode of procedure to remove the occasions of difference and contention, and to secure harmony in all things. This harmony has been not inaptly compared to that which exists between the body and the soul for the well-being of both one and the other, the separation of which brings irremediable harm to the body, since it extinguishes its very life.

19. To make this more evident, the growth of liberty ascribed to our age must be considered apart in its various details. And, first, let us examine that liberty in individuals which is so opposed to the virtue of religion, namely, the liberty of worship, as it is called. This is based on the principle that every man is free to profess as he may choose any religion or none.

20. But, assuredly, of all the duties which man has to fulfill, that, without doubt, is the chiefest and holiest which commands him to worship God with devotion and piety. This follows of necessity from the truth that we are ever in the power of God, are ever guided by His will and providence, and, having come forth from Him, must return to Him. Add to which, no true virtue can exist without religion, for moral virtue is concerned with those things which lead to God as man's supreme and ultimate good; and therefore religion, which (as St. Thomas says) "performs those actions which are directly and immediately ordained for the divine honor,"[7] rules and tempers all virtues. And if it be asked which of the many conflicting religions it is necessary to adopt, reason and the natural law unhesitatingly tell us to practice that one which God enjoins, and which men can easily recognize by certain exterior notes, whereby divine Providence has willed that it should be distinguished, because, in a matter of such moment, the most terrible loss would be the consequence of error. Wherefore, when a liberty such as We have described is offered to man, the power is given him to pervert or abandon with impunity the most sacred of duties, and to exchange the unchangeable good for evil; which, as We have said, is no liberty, but its degradation, and the abject submission of the soul to sin.

21. This kind of liberty, if considered in relation to the State, clearly implies that there is no reason why the State should offer any homage to God, or should desire any public recognition of Him; that no one form of worship is to be preferred to another, but that all stand on an equal footing, no account being taken of the religion of the people, even if they profess the Catholic faith. But, to justify this, it must needs be taken as true that the State has no duties toward God, or that such duties, if they exist, can be abandoned with impunity, both of which assertions are manifestly false. For it cannot be doubted but that, by the will of God, men are united in civil society; whether its component parts be considered; or its form, which implies authority; or the object of its existence; or the abundance of the vast services which it renders to man. God it is who has made man for society, and has placed him in the company of others like himself, so that what was wanting to his nature, and beyond his attainment if left to his own resources, he might obtain by association with others. Wherefore, civil society must acknowledge God as its Founder and Parent, and must obey and reverence His power and authority. Justice therefore forbids, and reason itself forbids, the State to be godless; or to adopt a line of action which would end in godlessness—namely, to treat the various religions (as they call them) alike, and to bestow upon them promiscuously equal rights and privileges. Since, then,

---

7. *Summa Theologiae* II-II, q. 81, a. 6, corp.

the profession of one religion is necessary in the State, that religion must be professed which alone is true, and which can be recognized without difficulty, especially in Catholic States, because the marks of truth are, as it were, engraved upon it. This religion, therefore, the rulers of the State must preserve and protect, if they would provide—as they should do—with prudence and usefulness for the good of the community. For public authority exists for the welfare of those whom it governs; and, although its proximate end is to lead men to the prosperity found in this life, yet, in so doing, it ought not to diminish, but rather to increase, man's capability of attaining to the supreme good in which his everlasting happiness consists: which never can be attained if religion be disregarded.

22. All this, however, We have explained more fully elsewhere. We now only wish to add the remark that liberty of so false a nature is greatly hurtful to the true liberty of both rulers and their subjects. Religion, of its essence, is wonderfully helpful to the State. For, since it derives the prime origin of all power directly from God Himself, with grave authority it charges rulers to be mindful of their duty, to govern without injustice or severity, to rule their people kindly and with almost paternal charity; it admonishes subjects to be obedient to lawful authority, as to the ministers of God; and it binds them to their rulers, not merely by obedience, but by reverence and affection, forbidding all seditions and venturesome enterprises calculated to disturb public order and tranquility, and cause greater restrictions to be put upon the liberty of the people. We need not mention how greatly religion conduces to pure morals, and pure morals to liberty. Reason shows, and history confirms the fact, that the higher the morality of States, the greater are the liberty and wealth and power which they enjoy.

23. We must now consider briefly liberty of speech, and liberty of the press. It is hardly necessary to say that there can be no such right as this, if it be not used in moderation, and if it pass beyond the bounds and end of all true liberty. For right is a moral power which—as We have before said and must again and again repeat—it is absurd to suppose that nature has accorded indifferently to truth and falsehood, to justice and injustice. Men have a right freely and prudently to propagate throughout the State whatever things are true and honorable, so that as many as possible may possess them; but lying opinions, than which no mental plague is greater, and vices which corrupt the heart and moral life should be diligently repressed by public authority, lest they insidiously work the ruin of the State. The excesses of an unbridled intellect, which unfailingly end in the oppression of the untutored multitude, are no less rightly controlled by the authority of the law than are the injuries inflicted by violence upon the weak. And this all the more surely, because by far the greater part of the community is either absolutely unable, or able only with great difficulty, to escape from illusions and deceitful

subtleties, especially such as flatter the passions. If unbridled license of speech and of writing be granted to all, nothing will remain sacred and inviolate; even the highest and truest mandates of nature, justly held to be the common and noblest heritage of the human race, will not be spared. Thus, truth being gradually obscured by darkness, pernicious and manifold error, as too often happens, will easily prevail. Thus, too, license will gain what liberty loses; for liberty will ever be more free and secure in proportion as license is kept in fuller restraint. In regard, however, to all matter of opinion which God leaves to man's free discussion, full liberty of thought and of speech is naturally within the right of everyone; for such liberty never leads men to suppress the truth, but often to discover it and make it known.

24. A like judgment must be passed upon what is called liberty of teaching. There can be no doubt that truth alone should imbue the minds of men, for in it are found the well-being, the end, and the perfection of every intelligent nature; and therefore nothing but truth should be taught both to the ignorant and to the educated, so as to bring knowledge to those who have it not, and to preserve it in those who possess it. For this reason it is plainly the duty of all who teach to banish error from the mind, and by sure safeguards to close the entry to all false convictions. From this it follows, as is evident, that the liberty of which We have been speaking is greatly opposed to reason, and tends absolutely to pervert men's minds, in as much as it claims for itself the right of teaching whatever it pleases—a liberty which the State cannot grant without failing in its duty. And the more so because the authority of teachers has great weight with their hearers, who can rarely decide for themselves as to the truth or falsehood of the instruction given to them.

25. Wherefore, this liberty, also, in order that it may deserve the name, must be kept within certain limits, lest the office of teaching be turned with impunity into an instrument of corruption. Now, truth, which should be the only subject matter of those who teach, is of two kinds: natural and supernatural. Of natural truths, such as the principles of nature and whatever is derived from them immediately by our reason, there is a kind of common patrimony in the human race. On this, as on a firm basis, morality, justice, religion, and the very bonds of human society rest: and to allow people to go unharmed who violate or destroy it would be most impious, most foolish, and most inhuman.

26. But with no less religious care must we preserve that great and sacred treasure of the truths which God Himself has taught us. By many and convincing arguments, often used by defenders of Christianity, certain leading truths have been laid down: namely, that some things have been revealed by God; that the Only-begotten Son of God was made flesh, to bear witness to the truth; that a

perfect society was founded by Him—the Church, namely, of which He is the head, and with which He has promised to abide till the end of the world. To this society He entrusted all the truths which He had taught, in order that it might keep and guard them and with lawful authority explain them; and at the same time He commanded all nations to hear the voice of the Church, as if it were His own, threatening those who would not hear it with everlasting perdition. Thus, it is manifest that man's best and surest teacher is God, the Source and Principle of all truth; and the Only-begotten Son, who is in the bosom of the Father, the Way, the Truth, and the Life, the true Light which enlightens every man, and to whose teaching all must submit: "And they shall all be taught of God."[8]

27. In faith and in the teaching of morality, God Himself made the Church a partaker of His divine authority, and through His heavenly gift she cannot be deceived. She is therefore the greatest and most reliable teacher of mankind, and in her swells an inviolable right to teach them. Sustained by the truth received from her divine Founder, the Church has ever sought to fulfill holily the mission entrusted to her by God; unconquered by the difficulties on all sides surrounding her, she has never ceased to assert her liberty of teaching, and in this way the wretched superstition of paganism being dispelled, the wide world was renewed unto Christian wisdom. Now, reason itself clearly teaches that the truths of divine revelation and those of nature cannot really be opposed to one another, and that whatever is at variance with them must necessarily be false. Therefore, the divine teaching of the Church, so far from being an obstacle to the pursuit of learning and the progress of science, or in any way retarding the advance of civilization, in reality brings to them the sure guidance of shining light. And for the same reason it is of no small advantage for the perfecting of human liberty, since our Savior Jesus Christ has said that by truth is man made free: "You shall know the truth, and the truth shall make you free."[9]

Therefore, there is no reason why genuine liberty should grow indignant, or true science feel aggrieved, at having to bear the just and necessary restraint of laws by which, in the judgment of the Church and of reason itself, human teaching has to be controlled.

28. The Church, indeed—as facts have everywhere proved—looks chiefly and above all to the defense of the Christian faith, while careful at the same time to foster and promote every kind of human learning. For learning is in itself good, and praiseworthy, and desirable; and further, all erudition which is the outgrowth of sound reason, and in conformity with the truth of things, serves

8. John 6:45.
9. John 8:32.

not a little to confirm what we believe on the authority of God. The Church, truly, to our great benefit, has carefully preserved the monuments of ancient wisdom; has opened everywhere homes of science, and has urged on intellectual progress by fostering most diligently the arts by which the culture of our age is so much advanced. Lastly, we must not forget that a vast field lies freely open to man's industry and genius, containing all those things which have no necessary connection with Christian faith and morals, or as to which the Church, exercising no authority, leaves the judgment of the learned free and unconstrained.

29. From all this may be understood the nature and character of that liberty which the followers of liberalism so eagerly advocate and proclaim. On the one hand, they demand for themselves and for the State a license which opens the way to every perversity of opinion; and on the other, they hamper the Church in diverse ways, restricting her liberty within narrowest limits, although from her teaching not only is there nothing to be feared, but in every respect very much to be gained.

30. Another liberty is widely advocated, namely, liberty of conscience. If by this is meant that everyone may, as he chooses, worship God or not, it is sufficiently refuted by the arguments already adduced. But it may also be taken to mean that every man in the State may follow the will of God and, from a consciousness of duty and free from every obstacle, obey His commands. This, indeed, is true liberty, a liberty worthy of the sons of God, which nobly maintains the dignity of man and is stronger than all violence or wrong—a liberty which the Church has always desired and held most dear. This is the kind of liberty the Apostles claimed for themselves with intrepid constancy, which the apologists of Christianity confirmed by their writings, and which the martyrs in vast numbers consecrated by their blood. And deservedly so; for this Christian liberty bears witness to the absolute and most just dominion of God over man, and to the chief and supreme duty of man toward God. It has nothing in common with a seditious and rebellious mind; and in no tittle derogates from obedience to public authority; for the right to command and to require obedience exists only so far as it is in accordance with the authority of God, and is within the measure that He has laid down. But when anything is commanded which is plainly at variance with the will of God, there is a wide departure from this divinely-constituted order, and at the same time a direct conflict with divine authority; therefore, it is right not to obey.

31. By the patrons of liberalism, however, who make the State absolute and omnipotent, and proclaim that man should live altogether independently of God, the liberty of which We speak, which goes hand in hand with virtue and religion, is not admitted; and whatever is done for its preservation is accounted an injury and an offense against the State. Indeed, if what they say were really true, there

would be no tyranny, no matter how monstrous, which we should not be bound to endure and submit to.

32. The Church most earnestly desires that the Christian teaching, of which We have given an outline, should penetrate every rank of society in reality and in practice; for it would be of the greatest efficacy in healing the evils of our day, which are neither few nor slight, and are the offspring in great part of the false liberty which is so much extolled, and in which the seeds of safety and glory were supposed to be contained. The hope has been disappointed by the result. The fruit, instead of being sweet and wholesome, has proved cankered and bitter. If, then, a remedy is desired, let it be sought for in a restoration of sound doctrine, from which alone the preservation of order and, as a consequence, the defense of true liberty can be confidently expected.

33. Yet, with the discernment of a true mother, the Church weighs the great burden of human weakness, and well knows the course down which the minds and actions of men are in this our age being borne. For this reason, while not conceding any right to anything save what is true and honest, she does not forbid public authority to tolerate what is at variance with truth and justice, for the sake of avoiding some greater evil, or of obtaining or preserving some greater good. God Himself in His providence, though infinitely good and powerful, permits evil to exist in the world, partly that greater good may not be impeded, and partly that greater evil may not ensue. In the government of States it is not forbidden to imitate the Ruler of the world; and, as the authority of man is powerless to prevent every evil, it has (as St. Augustine says) to overlook and leave unpunished many things which are punished, and rightly, by divine Providence.[10] But if, in such circumstances, for the sake of the common good (and this is the only legitimate reason), human law may or even should tolerate evil, it may not and should not approve or desire evil for its own sake; for evil of itself, being a privation of good, is opposed to the common welfare which every legislator is bound to desire and defend to the best of his ability. In this, human law must endeavor to imitate God, who, as St. Thomas teaches, in allowing evil to exist in the world, "neither wills evil to be done, nor wills it not to be done, but wills only to permit it to be done; and this is good."[11] This saying of the Angelic Doctor contains briefly the whole doctrine of the permission of evil.

34. But, to judge aright, we must acknowledge that, the more a State is driven to tolerate evil, the further is it from perfection; and that the tolerance of evil which is dictated by political prudence should be strictly confined to the

10. *De libero arbitrio*, lib. 1, cap. 6, n. 14 (PL 32, 1228).

11. *Summa Theologiae* I, q. 19, a. 9, ad 3.

limits which its justifying cause, the public welfare, requires. Wherefore, if such tolerance would be injurious to the public welfare, and entail greater evils on the State, it would not be lawful; for in such case the motive of good is wanting. And although in the extraordinary condition of these times the Church usually acquiesces in certain modern liberties, not because she prefers them in themselves, but because she judges it expedient to permit them, she would in happier times exercise her own liberty; and, by persuasion, exhortation, and entreaty would endeavor, as she is bound, to fulfill the duty assigned to her by God of providing for the eternal salvation of mankind. One thing, however, remains always true— that the liberty which is claimed for all to do all things is not, as We have often said, of itself desirable, inasmuch as it is contrary to reason that error and truth should have equal rights.

35. And as to tolerance, it is surprising how far removed from the equity and prudence of the Church are those who profess what is called liberalism. For, in allowing that boundless license of which We have spoken, they exceed all limits, and end at last by making no apparent distinction between truth and error, honesty and dishonesty. And because the Church, the pillar and ground of truth, and the unerring teacher of morals, is forced utterly to reprobate and condemn tolerance of such an abandoned and criminal character, they calumniate her as being wanting in patience and gentleness, and thus fail to see that, in so doing, they impute to her as a fault what is in reality a matter for commendation. But, in spite of all this show of tolerance, it very often happens that, while they profess themselves ready to lavish liberty on all in the greatest profusion, they are utterly intolerant toward the Catholic Church, by refusing to allow her the liberty of being herself free.

36. And now to reduce for clearness' sake to its principal heads all that has been set forth with its immediate conclusions: man, by a necessity of his nature, is wholly subject to the most faithful and ever enduring power of God; and, as a consequence, any liberty, except that which consists in submission to God and in subjection to His will, is unintelligible. To deny the existence of this authority in God, or to refuse to submit to it, means to act, not as a free man, but as one who treasonably abuses his liberty; and in such a disposition of mind the chief and deadly vice of liberalism essentially consists. The form, however, of the sin is manifold; for in more ways and degrees than one can the will depart from the obedience which is due to God or to those who share the divine power.

37. For, to reject the supreme authority to God, and to cast off all obedience to Him in public matters, or even in private and domestic affairs, is the greatest perversion of liberty and the worst kind of liberalism; and what We have said must be understood to apply to this alone in its fullest sense.

38. Next comes the system of those who admit indeed the duty of submitting to God, the Creator and Ruler of the world, inasmuch as all nature is dependent on His will, but who boldly reject all laws of faith and morals which are above natural reason, but are revealed by the authority of God; or who at least impudently assert that there is no reason why regard should be paid to these laws, at any rate publicly, by the State. How mistaken these men also are, and how inconsistent, we have seen above. From this teaching, as from its source and principle, flows that fatal principle of the separation of Church and State; whereas it is, on the contrary, clear that the two powers, though dissimilar in functions and unequal in degree, ought nevertheless to live in concord, by harmony in their action and the faithful discharge of their respective duties.

39. But this teaching is understood in two ways. Many wish the State to be separated from the Church wholly and entirely, so that with regard to every right of human society, in institutions, customs, and laws, the offices of State, and the education of youth, they would pay no more regard to the Church than if she did not exist; and, at most, would allow the citizens individually to attend to their religion in private if so minded. Against such as these, all the arguments by which We disprove the principle of separation of Church and State are conclusive; with this super-added, that it is absurd the citizen should respect the Church, while the State may hold her in contempt.

40. Others oppose not the existence of the Church, nor indeed could they; yet they despoil her of the nature and rights of a perfect society, and maintain that it does not belong to her to legislate, to judge, or to punish, but only to exhort, to advise, and to rule her subjects in accordance with their own consent and will. By such opinion they pervert the nature of this divine society, and attenuate and narrow its authority, its office of teacher, and its whole efficiency; and at the same time they aggrandize the power of the civil government to such extent as to subject the Church of God to the empire and sway of the State, like any voluntary association of citizens. To refute completely such teaching, the arguments often used by the defenders of Christianity, and set forth by Us, especially in the encyclical letter *Immortale Dei*,[12] are of great avail; for by those arguments it is proved that, by a divine provision, all the rights which essentially belong to a society that is legitimate, supreme, and perfect in all its parts exist in the Church.

41. Lastly, there remain those who, while they do not approve the separation of Church and State, think nevertheless that the Church ought to adapt herself to the times and conform to what is required by the modern system of government. Such an opinion is sound, if it is to be understood of some equitable adjustment

12. See nn. 8–11.

consistent with truth and justice; in so far, namely, that the Church, in the hope of some great good, may show herself indulgent, and may conform to the times in so far as her sacred office permits. But it is not so in regard to practices and doctrines which a perversion of morals and a warped judgment have unlawfully introduced. Religion, truth, and justice must ever be maintained; and, as God has entrusted these great and sacred matters to the care of the Church, she can never be so unfaithful to her office as to dissemble in regard to what is false or unjust, or to connive at what is hurtful to religion.

42. From what has been said it follows that it is quite unlawful to demand, to defend, or to grant unconditional freedom of thought, of speech, or writing, or of worship, as if these were so many rights given by nature to man. For, if nature had really granted them, it would be lawful to refuse obedience to God, and there would be no restraint on human liberty. It likewise follows that freedom in these things may be tolerated wherever there is just cause, but only with such moderation as will prevent its degenerating into license and excess. And, where such liberties are in use, men should employ them in doing good, and should estimate them as the Church does; for liberty is to be regarded as legitimate in so far only as it affords greater facility for doing good, but no farther.

43. Whenever there exists, or there is reason to fear, an unjust oppression of the people on the one hand, or a deprivation of the liberty of the Church on the other, it is lawful to seek for such a change of government as will bring about due liberty of action. In such case, an excessive and vicious liberty is not sought, but only some relief, for the common welfare, in order that, while license for evil is allowed by the State, the power of doing good may not be hindered.

44. Again, it is not of itself wrong to prefer a democratic form of government, if only the Catholic doctrine be maintained as to the origin and exercise of power. Of the various forms of government, the Church does not reject any that are fitted to procure the welfare of the subject; she wishes only—and this nature itself requires—that they should be constituted without involving wrong to anyone, and especially without violating the rights of the Church.

45. Unless it be otherwise determined, by reason of some exceptional condition of things, it is expedient to take part in the administration of public affairs. And the Church approves of every one devoting his services to the common good, and doing all that he can for the defense, preservation, and prosperity of his country.

46. Neither does the Church condemn those who, if it can be done without violation of justice, wish to make their country independent of any foreign or despotic power. Nor does she blame those who wish to assign to the State the power of self-government, and to its citizens the greatest possible measure of

prosperity. The Church has always most faithfully fostered civil liberty, and this was seen especially in Italy, in the municipal prosperity, and wealth, and glory which were obtained at a time when the salutary power of the Church had spread, without opposition, to all parts of the State.

47. These things, venerable brothers, which under the guidance of faith and reason, in the discharge of Our apostolic office, We have now delivered to you, We hope, especially by your cooperation with Us, will be useful unto very many. In lowliness of heart We raise Our eyes in supplication to God, and earnestly beseech Him to shed mercifully the light of His wisdom and of His counsel upon men, so that, strengthened by these heavenly gifts, they may in matters of such moment discern what is true, and may afterwards, in public and private at all times and with unshaken constancy, live in accordance with the truth. As a pledge of these heavenly gifts, and in witness of Our good will to you, venerable brothers, and to the clergy and people committed to each of you, We most lovingly grant in the Lord the apostolic benediction.

Given at St. Peter's in Rome, the twentieth day of June, 1888, the tenth year of Our pontificate.

✠ Leo XIII

SAPIENTIAE CHRISTIANAE

On the Duties of Christians as Citizens

Encyclical Letter of Pope Leo XIII,
promulgated January 10, 1890

To the Patriarchs, Primates, Archbishops, and Bishops of the Catholic World in
Grace and Communion with the Apostolic See.

From day to day it becomes more and more evident how needful it is
that the principles of Christian wisdom should ever be borne in mind,
and that the life, the morals, and the institutions of nations should be
wholly conformed to them. For, when these principles have been disregarded,
evils so vast have accrued that no right-minded man can face the trials of the
time being without grave anxiety or consider the future without alarm. Progress,
not inconsiderable indeed, has been made towards securing the well-being of
the body and of material things, but the material world, with the possession
of wealth, power, and resources, although it may well procure comforts and
increase the enjoyment of life, is incapable of satisfying our soul created for
higher and more glorious things. To contemplate God, and to tend to Him, is
the supreme law of the life of man. For we were created in the divine image and
likeness, and are impelled, by our very nature, to the enjoyment of our Creator. But not by bodily motion or effort do we make advance toward God, but
through acts of the soul, that is, through knowledge and love. For, indeed, God
is the first and supreme truth, and the mind alone feeds on truth. God is perfect
holiness and the sovereign good, to which only the will can desire and attain,
when virtue is its guide.

2. But what applies to individual men applies equally to society—domestic
alike and civil. Nature did not form society in order that man should seek in it his
last end, but in order that in it and through it he should find suitable aids whereby
to attain to his own perfection. If, then, a political government strives after external advantages only, and the achievement of a cultured and prosperous life; if, in
administering public affairs, it is wont to put God aside, and show no solicitude
for the upholding of moral law, it deflects woefully from its right course and from

the injunctions of nature; nor should it be accounted as a society or a community of men, but only as the deceitful imitation or appearance of a society.

3. As to what We have called the goods of the soul, which consist chiefly in the practice of the true religion and in the unswerving observance of the Christian precepts, We see them daily losing esteem among men, by reason either of forgetfulness or disregard, in such wise that all that is gained for the well-being of the body seems to be lost for that of the soul. A striking proof of the lessening and weakening of the Christian faith is seen in the insults too often done to the Catholic Church, openly and publicly—insults, indeed, which an age cherishing religion would not have tolerated. For these reasons, an incredible multitude of men is in danger of not achieving salvation; and even nations and empires themselves cannot long remain unharmed, since, when Christian institutions and morality decline, the main foundation of human society goes together with them. Force alone will remain to preserve public tranquility and order. But force is very feeble when the bulwark of religion has been removed, and, being more apt to beget slavery than obedience, it bears within itself the seeds of ever-increasing troubles. The present century has encountered memorable disasters, and it is not certain that some equally terrible are not impending. The very times in which we live are warning us to seek remedies there where alone they are to be found—namely, by re-establishing in the family circle and throughout the whole range of society the doctrines and practices of the Christian religion. In this lies the sole means of freeing us from the ills now weighing us down, of forestalling the dangers now threatening the world. For the accomplishment of this end, venerable brethren, We must bring to bear all the activity and diligence that lie within Our power. Although we have already, under other circumstances, and whenever occasion required, treated of these matters, We deem it expedient in this letter to define more in detail the duties of Catholics, inasmuch as these would, if strictly observed, wonderfully contribute to the good of the commonwealth. We have fallen upon times when a violent and well-nigh daily battle is being fought about matters of highest moment, a battle in which it is hard not to be sometimes deceived, not to go astray and, for many, not to lose heart. It behooves us, venerable brethren, to warn, instruct, and exhort each of the faithful with an earnestness befitting the occasion: that none may abandon the way of truth.[1]

4. It cannot be doubted that duties more numerous and of greater moment devolve on Catholics than upon such as are either not sufficiently enlightened in relation to the Catholic faith, or who are entirely unacquainted with its doctrines. Considering that forthwith upon salvation being brought out for mankind, Jesus

---

1. Tobias 1:2.

Christ laid upon His Apostles the injunction to "preach the Gospel to every creature," He imposed, it is evident, upon all men the duty of learning thoroughly and believing what they were taught. This duty is intimately bound up with the gaining of eternal salvation: "He that believeth and is baptized shall be saved; but he that believeth not, shall be condemned."[2] But the man who has embraced the Christian faith, as in duty bound, is by that very fact a subject of the Church as one of the children born of her, and becomes a member of that greatest and holiest body, which it is the special charge of the Roman Pontiff to rule with supreme power, under its invisible head, Jesus Christ.

5. Now, if the natural law enjoins us to love devotedly and to defend the country in which we had birth, and in which we were brought up, so that every good citizen hesitates not to face death for his native land, very much more is it the urgent duty of Christians to be ever quickened by like feelings toward the Church. For the Church is the holy City of the living God, born of God Himself, and by Him built up and established. Upon this earth, indeed, she accomplishes her pilgrimage, but by instructing and guiding men she summons them to eternal happiness. We are bound, then, to love dearly the country whence we have received the means of enjoyment this mortal life affords, but we have a much more urgent obligation to love, with ardent love, the Church to which we owe the life of the soul, a life that will endure forever. For fitting it is to prefer the good of the soul to the well-being of the body, inasmuch as duties toward God are of a far more hallowed character than those toward men.

6. Moreover, if we would judge aright, the supernatural love for the Church and the natural love of our own country proceed from the same eternal principle, since God Himself is their Author and originating Cause. Consequently, it follows that between the duties they respectively enjoin, neither can come into collision with the other. We can, certainly, and should love ourselves, bear ourselves kindly toward our fellow men, nourish affection for the State and the governing powers; but at the same time we can and must cherish toward the Church a feeling of filial piety, and love God with the deepest love of which we are capable. The order of precedence of these duties is, however, at times, either under stress of public calamities, or through the perverse will of men, inverted. For, instances occur where the State seems to require from men as subjects one thing, and religion, from men as Christians, quite another; and this in reality without any other ground, than that the rulers of the State either hold the sacred power of the Church of no account, or endeavor to subject it to their own will. Hence arises a conflict, and an occasion, through such conflict, of virtue being put

---

2. Mark 16:16.

to the proof. The two powers are confronted and urge their behests in a contrary sense; to obey both is wholly impossible. No man can serve two masters,[3] for to please the one amounts to contemning the other.

7. As to which should be preferred no one ought to balance for an instant. It is a high crime indeed to withdraw allegiance from God in order to please men, an act of consummate wickedness to break the laws of Jesus Christ, in order to yield obedience to earthly rulers, or, under pretext of keeping the civil law, to ignore the rights of the Church; "we ought to obey God rather than men."[4] This answer, which of old Peter and the other Apostles were accustomed to give the civil authorities who enjoined unrighteous things, we must, in like circumstances, give always and without hesitation. No better citizen is there, whether in time of peace or war, than the Christian who is mindful of his duty; but such a one should be ready to suffer all things, even death itself, rather than abandon the cause of God or of the Church.

8. Hence, they who blame, and call by the name of sedition, this steadfast-ness of attitude in the choice of duty have not rightly apprehended the force and nature of true law. We are speaking of matters widely known, and which We have before now more than once fully explained. Law is of its very essence a mandate of right reason, proclaimed by a properly constituted authority, for the common good. But true and legitimate authority is void of sanction, unless it proceed from God, the supreme Ruler and Lord of all. The Almighty alone can commit power to a man over his fellow men[5]; nor may that be accounted as right reason which is in disaccord with truth and with divine reason; nor that held to be true good which is repugnant to the supreme and unchangeable good, or that wrests aside and draws away the wills of men from the charity of God.

9. Hallowed, therefore, in the minds of Christians is the very idea of public authority, in which they recognize some likeness and symbol as it were of the divine Majesty, even when it is exercised by one unworthy. A just and due rever-ence to the laws abides in them, not from force and threats, but from a conscious-ness of duty; "for God hath not given us the spirit of fear."[6]

10. But, if the laws of the State are manifestly at variance with the divine law, containing enactments hurtful to the Church, or conveying injunctions adverse to the duties imposed by religion, or if they violate in the person of the supreme

---

3. Matt. 6:24.

4. Acts 5:29.

5. [Note the importance of this statement, establishing as it does that the only conceivable origin of political authority is divine.]

6. 2 Tim. 1:7.

Pontiff the authority of Jesus Christ, then, truly, to resist becomes a positive duty, to obey, a crime; a crime, moreover, combined with misdemeanor against the State itself, inasmuch as every offense leveled against religion is also a sin against the State. Here anew it becomes evident how unjust is the reproach of sedition; for the obedience due to rulers and legislators is not refused, but there is a deviation from their will in those precepts only which they have no power to enjoin. Commands that are issued adversely to the honor due to God, and hence are beyond the scope of justice, must be looked upon as anything rather than laws. You are fully aware, venerable brothers, that this is the very contention of the Apostle St. Paul, who, in writing to Titus, after reminding Christians that they are "to be subject to princes and powers, and to obey at a word," at once adds: "And to be ready to every good work."[7] Thereby he openly declares that, if laws of men contain injunctions contrary to the eternal law of God, it is right not to obey them. In like manner, the Prince of the Apostles gave this courageous and sublime answer to those who would have deprived him of the liberty of preaching the Gospel: "If it be just in the sight of God to hear you rather than God, judge ye, for we cannot but speak the things which we have seen and heard."[8]

11. Wherefore, to love both countries, that of earth below and that of heaven above, yet in such mode that the love of our heavenly surpass the love of our earthly home, and that human laws be never set above the divine law, is the essential duty of Christians, and the fountainhead, so to say, from which all other duties spring. The Redeemer of mankind of Himself has said: "For this was I born, and for this came I into the world, that I should give testimony to the truth."[9] In like manner: "I am come to cast fire upon earth, and would that it were already enkindled!"[10] In the knowledge of this truth, which constitutes the highest perfection of the mind; in divine charity which, in like manner, completes the will, all Christian life and liberty abide. This noble patrimony of truth and charity entrusted by Jesus Christ to the Church she defends and maintains ever with untiring endeavor and watchfulness.

12. But with what bitterness and in how many guises war has been waged against the Church it would be ill-timed now to urge. From the fact that it has been vouchsafed to human reason to snatch from nature, through the investigations of science, many of her treasured secrets and to apply them befittingly to the diverse requirements of life, men have become possessed with so arrogant a

---

7. Titus 3:1.
8. Acts 4:19–20.
9. John 18:37.
10. Luke 12:49.

sense of their own powers as already to consider themselves able to banish from social life the authority and empire of God. Led away by this delusion, they make over to human nature the dominion of which they think God has been despoiled; from nature, they maintain, we must seek the principle and rule of all truth; from nature, they aver, alone spring, and to it should be referred, all the duties that religious feeling prompts. Hence, they deny all revelation from on high, and all fealty due to the Christian teaching of morals as well as all obedience to the Church, and they go so far as to deny her power of making laws and exercising every other kind of right, even disallowing the Church any place among the civil institutions of the commonweal. These men aspire unjustly, and with their might strive, to gain control over public affairs and lay hands on the rudder of the State, in order that the legislation may the more easily be adapted to these principles, and the morals of the people influenced in accordance with them. Whence it comes to pass that in many countries Catholicism is either openly assailed or else secretly interfered with, full impunity being granted to the most pernicious doctrines, while the public profession of Christian truth is shackled oftentimes with manifold constraints.

13. Under such evil circumstances therefore, each one is bound in conscience to watch over himself, taking all means possible to preserve the faith inviolate in the depths of his soul, avoiding all risks, and arming himself on all occasions, especially against the various specious sophisms rife among non-believers. In order to safeguard this virtue of faith in its integrity, We declare it to be very profitable and consistent with the requirements of the time, that each one, according to the measure of his capacity and intelligence, should make a deep study of Christian doctrine, and imbue his mind with as perfect a knowledge as may be of those matters that are interwoven with religion and lie within the range of reason. And as it is necessary that faith should not only abide untarnished in the soul, but should grow with ever painstaking increase, the suppliant and humble entreaty of the apostles ought constantly to be addressed to God: "Increase our faith."[11]

14. But in this same matter, touching Christian faith, there are other duties whose exact and religious observance, necessary at all times in the interests of eternal salvation, become more especially so in these our days. Amid such reckless and widespread folly of opinion, it is, as We have said, the office of the Church to undertake the defense of truth and uproot errors from the mind, and this charge has to be at all times sacredly observed by her, seeing that the honor of God and the salvation of men are confided to her keeping. But, when necessity compels, not those only who are invested with power of rule are bound to

---

11. Luke 17:5.

safeguard the integrity of faith, but, as St. Thomas maintains: "Each one is under obligation to show forth his faith, either to instruct and encourage others of the faithful, or to repel the attacks of unbelievers."[12] To recoil before an enemy, or to keep silence when from all sides such clamors are raised against truth, is the part of a man either devoid of character or who entertains doubt as to the truth of what he professes to believe. In both cases such mode of behaving is base and is insulting to God, and both are incompatible with the salvation of mankind. This kind of conduct is profitable only to the enemies of the faith, for nothing emboldens the wicked so greatly as the lack of courage on the part of the good. Moreover, want of vigor on the part of Christians is so much the more blameworthy, as not seldom little would be needed on their part to bring to naught false charges and refute erroneous opinions, and by always exerting themselves more strenuously they might reckon upon being successful. After all, no one can be prevented from putting forth that strength of soul which is the characteristic of true Christians, and very frequently by such display of courage our enemies lose heart and their designs are thwarted. Christians are, moreover, born for combat, whereof the greater the vehemence, the more assured, God aiding, the triumph: "Have confidence; I have overcome the world."[13] Nor is there any ground for alleging that Jesus Christ, the Guardian and Champion of the Church, needs not in any manner the help of men. Power certainly is not wanting to Him, but in His loving kindness He would assign to us a share in obtaining and applying the fruits of salvation procured through His grace.

15. The chief elements of this duty consist in professing openly and unflinchingly the Catholic doctrine, and in propagating it to the utmost of our power. For, as is often said, with the greatest truth, there is nothing so hurtful to Christian wisdom as that it should not be known, since it possesses, when loyally received, inherent power to drive away error. So soon as Catholic truth is apprehended by a simple and unprejudiced soul, reason yields assent. Now, faith, as a virtue, is a great boon of divine grace and goodness; nevertheless, the objects themselves to which faith is to be applied are scarcely known in any other way than through the hearing. "How shall they believe Him of whom they have not heard? and how shall they hear without a preacher? Faith then cometh by hearing, and hearing by the word of Christ."[14] Since, then, faith is necessary for salvation, it follows that the word of Christ must be preached. The office, indeed, of preaching, that is, of teaching, lies by divine right in the province of the pastors, namely, of the bishops

---

12. *Summa Theologiae* II-II, q. 3, a. 2, ad 2.

13. John 16:33.

14. Rom. 10:14, 17.

whom "the Holy Spirit has placed to rule the Church of God."[15] It belongs, above all, to the Roman Pontiff, vicar of Jesus Christ, established as head of the universal Church, teacher of all that pertains to morals and faith.

16. No one, however, must entertain the notion that private individuals are prevented from taking some active part in this duty of teaching, especially those on whom God has bestowed gifts of mind with the strong wish of rendering themselves useful. These, so often as circumstances demand, may take upon themselves, not, indeed, the office of the pastor, but the task of communicating to others what they have themselves received, becoming, as it were, living echoes of their masters in the faith. Such co-operation on the part of the laity has seemed to the Fathers of the [First] Vatican Council so opportune and fruitful of good that they thought well to invite it. "All faithful Christians, but those chiefly who are in a prominent position, or engaged in teaching, we entreat, by the compassion of Jesus Christ, and enjoin by the authority of the same God and Savior, that they bring aid to ward off and eliminate these errors from holy Church, and contribute their zealous help in spreading abroad the light of undefiled faith."[16] Let each one, therefore, bear in mind that he both can and should, so far as may be, preach the Catholic faith by the authority of his example, and by open and constant profession of the obligations it imposes. In respect, consequently, to the duties that bind us to God and the Church, it should be borne earnestly in mind that in propagating Christian truth and warding off errors the zeal of the laity should, as far as possible, be brought actively into play.

17. The faithful would not, however, so completely and advantageously satisfy these duties as is fitting they should were they to enter the field as isolated champions of the faith. Jesus Christ, indeed, has clearly intimated that the hostility and hatred of men, which He first and foremost experienced, would be shown in like degree toward the work founded by Him, so that many would be barred from profiting by the salvation for which all are indebted to His loving kindness. Wherefore, He willed not only to train disciples in His doctrine, but to unite them into one society, and closely conjoin them in one body, "which is the Church,"[17] whereof He would be the head. The life of Jesus Christ pervades, therefore, the entire framework of this body, cherishes and nourishes its every member, uniting each with each, and making all work together to the same end, albeit the action of each be not the same.[18] Hence it follows that not only is the Church a perfect

---

15. Acts 20:28.

16. Constitution *Dei Filius*, at end.

17. Col. 1:24.

18. Cf. Rom. 12:4–5.

society far excelling every other, but it is enjoined by her Founder that for the salvation of mankind she is to contend "as an army drawn up in battle array."[19] The organization and constitution of Christian society can in no wise be changed, neither can any one of its members live as he may choose, nor elect that mode of fighting which best pleases him. For, in effect, he scatters and gathers not who gathers not with the Church and with Jesus Christ, and all who fight not jointly with him and with the Church are in very truth contending against God.[20]

18. To bring about such a union of minds and uniformity of action—not without reason so greatly feared by the enemies of Catholicism—the main point is that a perfect harmony of opinion should prevail; in which intent we find Paul the Apostle exhorting the Corinthians with earnest zeal and solemn weight of words: "Now I beseech you, brethren, by the name of our Lord Jesus Christ, that you all speak the same thing, and that there be no schisms among you: but that you be perfectly in the same mind, and in the same judgment."[21]

19. The wisdom of this precept is readily apprehended. In truth, thought is the principle of action, and hence there cannot exist agreement of will, or similarity of action, if people all think differently one from the other.

20. In the case of those who profess to take reason as their sole guide, there would hardly be found, if, indeed, there ever could be found, unity of doctrine. Indeed, the art of knowing things as they really are is exceedingly difficult; moreover, the mind of man is by nature feeble and drawn this way and that by a variety of opinions, and not seldom led astray by impressions coming from without; and, furthermore, the influence of the passions oftentimes takes away, or certainly at least diminishes, the capacity for grasping the truth. On this account, in controlling State affairs means are often used to keep those together by force who cannot agree in their way of thinking.

21. It happens far otherwise with Christians; they receive their rule of faith from the Church, by whose authority and under whose guidance they are conscious that they have beyond question attained to truth. Consequently, as the Church is one, because Jesus Christ is one, so throughout the whole Christian world there is, and ought to be, but one doctrine: "One Lord, one faith"[22]; "but having the same spirit of faith,"[23] they possess the saving principle whence proceed spontaneously one and the same will in all, and one and the same tenor of action.

19. Song 6:9.

20. Cf. Luke 11:22.

21. 1 Cor. 1:10.

22. Eph. 4:5.

23. 2 Cor. 4:13.

22. Now, as the Apostle Paul urges, this unanimity ought to be perfect. Christian faith reposes not on human but on divine authority, for what God has revealed "we believe not on account of the intrinsic evidence of the truth perceived by the natural light of our reason, but on account of the authority of God revealing, who cannot be deceived nor Himself deceive."[24] It follows as a consequence that whatever things are manifestly revealed by God we must receive with a similar and equal assent. To refuse to believe any one of them is equivalent to rejecting them all, for those at once destroy the very groundwork of faith who deny that God has spoken to men, or who bring into doubt His infinite truth and wisdom. To determine, however, which are the doctrines divinely revealed belongs to the teaching Church, to whom God has entrusted the safekeeping and interpretation of His utterances. But the supreme teacher in the Church is the Roman Pontiff. Union of minds, therefore, requires, together with a perfect accord in the one faith, complete submission and obedience of will to the Church and to the Roman Pontiff, as to God Himself. This obedience should, however, be perfect, because it is enjoined by faith itself, and has this in common with faith, that it cannot be given in shreds; nay, were it not absolute and perfect in every particular, it might wear the name of obedience, but its essence would disappear. Christian usage attaches such value to this perfection of obedience that it has been, and will ever be, accounted the distinguishing mark by which we are able to recognize Catholics. Admirably does the following passage from St. Thomas Aquinas set before us the right view: "The formal object of faith is primary truth, as it is shown forth in the holy Scriptures, and in the teaching of the Church, which proceeds from the fountainhead of truth. It follows, therefore, that he who does not adhere, as to an infallible divine rule, to the teaching of the Church, which proceeds from the primary truth manifested in the holy Scriptures, possesses not the habit of faith; but matters of faith he holds otherwise than by true faith. Now, it is evident that he who clings to the doctrines of the Church as to an infallible rule yields his assent to everything the Church teaches; but otherwise, if with reference to what the Church teaches he holds what he likes but does not hold what he does not like, he adheres not to the teaching of the Church as to an infallible rule, but to his own will."[25]

23. "The faith of the whole Church should be one, according to the precept (1 Cor. 1:10): 'Let all speak the same thing, and let there be no schisms among you'; and this cannot be observed save on condition that questions which arise touching faith should be determined by him who presides over the whole

---

24. Constitution *Dei Filius*, cap. 3.

25. *Summa Theologiae* II-II, q. 5, a. 3.

Church, whose sentence must consequently be accepted without wavering. And hence to the sole authority of the supreme Pontiff does it pertain to publish a new revision of the symbol, as also to decree all other matters that concern the universal Church."[26]

24. In defining the limits of the obedience owed to the pastors of souls, but most of all to the authority of the Roman Pontiff, it must not be supposed that it is only to be yielded in relation to dogmas of which the obstinate denial cannot be disjoined from the crime of heresy. Nay, further, it is not enough sincerely and firmly to assent to doctrines which, though not defined by any solemn pronouncement of the Church, are by her proposed to belief, as divinely revealed, in her common and universal teaching, and which the [First] Vatican Council declared are to be believed "with Catholic and divine faith."[27] But this likewise must be reckoned amongst the duties of Christians, that they allow themselves to be ruled and directed by the authority and leadership of bishops, and, above all, of the Apostolic See. And how fitting it is that this should be so anyone can easily perceive. For the things contained in the divine oracles have reference to God in part, and in part to man, and to whatever is necessary for the attainment of his eternal salvation. Now, both these, that is to say, what we are bound to believe and what we are obliged to do, are laid down, as we have stated, by the Church using her divine right, and in the Church by the supreme Pontiff. Wherefore it belongs to the Pope to judge authoritatively what things the sacred oracles contain, as well as what doctrines are in harmony, and what in disagreement, with them; and also, for the same reason, to show forth what things are to be accepted as right, and what to be rejected as worthless; what it is necessary to do and what to avoid doing, in order to attain eternal salvation. For, otherwise, there would be no sure interpreter of the commands of God, nor would there be any safe guide showing man the way he should live.

25. In addition to what has been laid down, it is necessary to enter more fully into the nature of the Church. She is not an association of Christians brought together by chance, but is a divinely established and admirably constituted society, having for its direct and proximate purpose to lead the world to peace and holiness. And since the Church alone has, through the grace of God, received the means necessary to realize such end, she has her fixed laws, special spheres of action, and a certain method, fixed and conformable to her nature, of governing Christian peoples. But the exercise of such governing power is difficult, and leaves room for numberless conflicts, inasmuch as the Church rules peoples

---

26. *Summa Theologiae* II-II, q. 1, a. 10.

27. Constit. *De fide catholica*, cap. 3, De fide.

scattered through every portion of the earth, differing in race and customs, who, living under the sway of the laws of their respective countries, owe obedience alike to the civil and religious authorities. The duties enjoined are incumbent on the same persons, as already stated, and between them there exists neither contradiction nor confusion; for some of these duties have relation to the prosperity of the State, others refer to the general good of the Church, and both have as their object to train men to perfection.

26. The tracing out of these rights and duties being thus set forth, it is plainly evident that the governing powers are wholly free to carry out the business of the State; and this not only not against the wish of the Church, but manifestly with her co-operation, inasmuch as she strongly urges to the practice of piety, which implies right feeling towards God, and by that very fact inspires a right-mindedness toward the rulers in the State. The spiritual power, however, has a far loftier purpose, the Church directing her aim to govern the minds of men in the defending of the "kingdom of God and His justice,"[28] a task she is wholly bent upon accomplishing.

27. No one can, however, without risk to faith, foster any doubt as to the Church alone having been invested with such power of governing souls as to exclude altogether the civil authority. In truth, it was not to Caesar but to Peter that Jesus Christ entrusted the keys of the kingdom of Heaven. From this doctrine touching the relations of politics and religion originate important consequences which we cannot pass over in silence.

28. A notable difference exists between every kind of civil rule and that of the kingdom of Christ. If this latter bear a certain likeness and character to a civil kingdom, it is distinguished from it by its origin, principle, and essence. The Church, therefore, possesses the right to exist and to protect herself by institutions and laws in accordance with her nature. And since she is not only a perfect society in herself, but superior to every other society of human growth, she resolutely refuses, promoted alike by right and by duty, to link herself to any mere party and to subject herself to the fleeting exigencies of politics. On like grounds, the Church, the guardian always of her own right and most observant of that of others, holds that it is not her province to decide which is the best amongst many diverse forms of government and the civil institutions of Christian States, and amid the various kinds of State rule she does not disapprove of any, provided the respect due to religion and the observance of good morals be upheld. By such standard of conduct should the thoughts and mode of acting of every Catholic be directed.

---

28. Matt. 6:33.

29. There is no doubt that in the sphere of politics ample matter may exist for legitimate difference of opinion, and that, the single reserve being made of the rights of justice and truth, all may strive to bring into actual working the ideas believed likely to be more conducive than others to the general welfare. But to attempt to involve the Church in party strife, and seek to bring her support to bear against those who take opposite views is only worthy of partisans. Religion should, on the contrary, be accounted by everyone as holy and inviolate; nay, in the public order itself of States—which cannot be severed from the laws influencing morals and from religious duties—it is always urgent, and indeed the main preoccupation, to take thought how best to consult the interests of Catholicism. Wherever these appear by reason of the efforts of adversaries to be in danger, all differences of opinion among Catholics should forthwith cease, so that, like thoughts and counsels prevailing, they may hasten to the aid of religion, the general and supreme good, to which all else should be referred. We think it well to treat this matter somewhat more in detail.

30. The Church alike and the State, doubtless, both possess individual sovereignty; hence, in the carrying out of public affairs, neither obeys the other within the limits to which each is restricted by its constitution. It does not hence follow, however, that Church and State are in any manner severed, and still less antagonistic. Nature, in fact, has given us not only physical existence, but moral life likewise. Hence, from the tranquility of public order, which is the immediate purpose of civil society, man expects to derive his well-being, and still more the sheltering care necessary to his moral life, which consists exclusively in the knowledge and practice of virtue. He wishes, moreover, at the same time, as in duty bound, to find in the Church the aids necessary to his religious perfection, in the knowledge and practice of the true religion; of that religion which is the queen of virtues, because in binding these to God it completes them all and perfects them. Therefore, they who are engaged in framing constitutions and in enacting laws should bear in mind the moral and religious nature of man, and take care to help him, but in a right and orderly way, to gain perfection, neither enjoining nor forbidding anything save what is reasonably consistent with civil as well as with religious requirements. On this very account, the Church cannot stand by, indifferent as to the import and significance of laws enacted by the State; not insofar, indeed, as they refer to the State, but in so far as, passing beyond their due limits, they trench upon the rights of the Church.

31. From God has the duty been assigned to the Church not only to interpose resistance, if at any time the State rule should run counter to religion, but, further, to make a strong endeavor that the power of the Gospel may pervade the law and institutions of the nations. And inasmuch as the destiny of the State

depends mainly on the disposition of those who are at the head of affairs, it follows that the Church cannot give countenance or favor to those whom she knows to be imbued with a spirit of hostility to her; who refuse openly to respect her rights; who make it their aim and purpose to tear asunder the alliance that should, by the very nature of things, connect the interests of religion with those of the State. On the contrary, she is (as she is bound to be) the upholder of those who are themselves imbued with the right way of thinking as to the relations between Church and State, and who strive to make them work in perfect accord for the common good. These precepts contain the abiding principle by which every Catholic should shape his conduct in regard to public life. In short, where the Church does not forbid taking part in public affairs, it is fit and proper to give support to men of acknowledged worth, and who pledge themselves to deserve well in the Catholic cause, and on no account may it be allowed to prefer to them any such individuals as are hostile to religion.

32. Whence it appears how urgent is the duty to maintain perfect union of minds, especially at these our times, when the Christian name is assailed with designs so concerted and subtle. All who have it at heart to attach themselves earnestly to the Church, which is "the pillar and ground of the truth,"[29] will easily steer clear of masters who are "lying and promising them liberty, when they themselves are slaves of corruption."[30] Nay, more, having made themselves sharers in the divine virtue which resides in the Church, they will triumph over the craft of their adversaries by wisdom, and over their violence by courage. This is not now the time and place to inquire whether and how far the inertness and internal dissensions of Catholics have contributed to the present condition of things; but it is certain at least that the perverse-minded would exhibit less boldness, and would not have brought about such an accumulation of ills, if the "faith that worketh by charity"[31] had been generally more energetic and lively in the souls of men, and had there not been so universal a drifting away from the divinely established rule of morality throughout Christianity. May at least the lessons afforded by the memory of the past have the good result of leading to a wiser mode of acting in the future.

33. As to those who mean to take part in public affairs, they should avoid with the very utmost care two criminal excesses: so-called prudence and false courage. Some there are, indeed, who maintain that it is not opportune boldly to attack evil-doing in its might and when in the ascendant, lest, as they say, opposition

---

29.   1 Tim. 3:15.

30.   2 Peter 2:1, 19.

31.   Gal. 5:6.

should exasperate minds already hostile. These make it a matter of guesswork as to whether they are for the Church or against her, since on the one hand they give themselves out as professing the Catholic faith, and yet wish that the Church should allow certain opinions, at variance with her teaching, to be spread abroad with impunity. They moan over the loss of faith and the perversion of morals, yet trouble themselves not to bring any remedy; nay, not seldom, even add to the intensity of the mischief through too much forbearance or harmful dissembling. These same individuals would not have anyone entertain a doubt as to their good will towards the Holy See; yet they have always a something by way of reproach against the supreme Pontiff.

34. The prudence of men of this cast is of that kind which is termed by the Apostle Paul "wisdom of the flesh" and "death" of the soul, "because it is not subject to the law of God, neither can it be."[32] Nothing is less calculated to amend such ills than prudence of this kind. For the enemies of the Church have for their object—and they hesitate not to proclaim it, and many among them boast of it—to destroy outright, if possible, the Catholic religion, which is alone the true religion. With such a purpose in hand they shrink from nothing, for they are fully conscious that the more faint-hearted those who withstand them become, the more easy will it be to work out their wicked will. Therefore, they who cherish the "prudence of the flesh" and who pretend to be unaware that every Christian ought to be a valiant soldier of Christ; they who would fain obtain the rewards owing to conquerors, while they are leading the lives of cowards, untouched in the fight, are so far from thwarting the onward march of the evil-disposed that, on the contrary, they even help it forward.

35. On the other hand, not a few, impelled by a false zeal, or—what is more blameworthy still—affecting sentiments which their conduct belies, take upon themselves to act a part which does not belong to them. They would fain see the Church's mode of action influenced by their ideas and their judgment to such an extent that everything done otherwise they take ill or accept with repugnance. Some, yet again, expend their energies in fruitless contention, being worthy of blame equally with the former. To act in such manner is not to follow lawful authority but to forestall it, and, unauthorized, assume the duties of the spiritual rulers, to the great detriment of the order which God established in His Church to be observed forever, and which He does not permit to be violated with impunity by anyone, whoever he may be.

36. Honor, then, to those who shrink not from entering the arena as often as need calls, believing and being convinced that the violence of injustice will be

---

32. Cf. Rom. 8:6–7.

brought to an end and finally give way to the sanctity of right and religion! They truly seem invested with the dignity of time-honored virtue, since they are struggling to defend religion, and chiefly against the faction banded together to attack Christianity with extreme daring and without tiring, and to pursue with incessant hostility the sovereign Pontiff, fallen into their power. But men of this high character maintain without wavering the love of obedience, nor are they wont to undertake anything upon their own authority. Now, since a like resolve to obey, combined with constancy and sturdy courage, is needful, so that whatever trials the pressure of events may bring about, they may be "deficient in nothing,"[33] We greatly desire to fix deep in the minds of each one that which Paul calls the "wisdom of the spirit,"[34] for in controlling human actions this wisdom follows the excellent rule of moderation, with the happy result that no one either timidly despairs through lack of courage or presumes overmuch from lack of prudence. There is, however, a difference between the political prudence that relates to the general good and that which concerns the good of individuals. This latter is shown forth in the case of private persons who obey the prompting of right reason in the direction of their own conduct; while the former is the characteristic of those who are set over others, and chiefly of rulers of the State, whose duty it is to exercise the power of command, so that the political prudence of private individuals would seem to consist wholly in carrying out faithfully the orders issued by lawful authority.[35]

37. The like disposition and the same order should prevail in the Christian society by so much the more that the political prudence of the Pontiff embraces diverse and multiform things, for it is his charge not only to rule the Church, but generally so to regulate the actions of Christian citizens that these may be in apt conformity to their hope of gaining eternal salvation. Whence it is clear that, in addition to the complete accordance of thought and deed, the faithful should follow the practical political wisdom of the ecclesiastical authority. Now, the

---

33. James 1:4.

34. Rom. 8:6.

35. "Prudence proceeds from reason, and to reason it specially pertains to guide and govern. Whence it follows that, in so much as any one takes part in the control and government of affairs, in so far ought he to be gifted with reason and prudence. But it is evident that the subject, so far as subject, and the servant ought neither to control nor govern, but rather to be controlled and governed. Prudence, then, is not the special virtue of the servant, so far as servant, nor of the subject, so far as subject. But because any man, on account of his character of a reasonable being, may have some share in the government on account of the rational choice which he exercises, it is fitting that in such proportion he should possess the virtue of prudence. Whence it manifestly results that prudence exists in the ruler as the art of building exists in the architect, whereas prudence exists in the subject as the art of building exists in the hand of the workman employed in the construction." *Summa Theologiae* II-II, q. 47, a. 12, corp. Aquinas refers to Aristotle, *Ethic. Nic.* VI, ch. 8 (1141b21–29).

administration of Christian affairs immediately under the Roman Pontiff appertains to the bishops, who, although they attain not to the summit of pontifical
power, are nevertheless truly princes in the ecclesiastical hierarchy; and as each
one of them administers a particular Church, they are "as master-workers ... in
the spiritual edifice,"[36] and they have members of the clergy to share their duties
and carry out their decisions. Everyone has to regulate his mode of conduct
according to this constitution of the Church, which it is not in the power of any
man to change. Consequently, just as in the exercise of their episcopal authority
the bishops ought to be united with the Apostolic See, so should the members of
the clergy and the laity live in close union with their bishops. Among the prelates,
indeed, one or other there may be affording scope to criticism either in regard to
personal conduct or in reference to opinions by him entertained about points of
doctrine; but no private person may arrogate to himself the office of judge which
Christ our Lord has bestowed on that one alone whom He placed in charge of
His lambs and of His sheep. Let everyone bear in mind that most wise teaching
of Gregory the Great: "Subjects should be admonished not rashly to judge their
prelates, even if they chance to see them acting in a blameworthy manner, lest,
justly reproving what is wrong, they be led by pride into greater wrong. They are
to be warned against the danger of setting themselves up in audacious opposition to the superiors whose shortcomings they may notice. Should, therefore, the
superiors really have committed grievous sins, their inferiors, penetrated with
the fear of God, ought not to refuse them respectful submission. The actions of
superiors should not be smitten by the sword of the word, even when they are
rightly judged to have deserved censure."[37]

38. However, all endeavors will avail but little unless our life be regulated
conformably with the discipline of the Christian virtues. Let us call to mind what
holy Scripture records concerning the Jewish nation: "As long as they sinned not
in the sight of their God, it was well with them: for their God hateth iniquity.
And ... when they had revolted from the way that God had given them to walk
therein, they were destroyed in battles by many nations."[38] Now, the nation of
the Jews bore an inchoate semblance to the Christian people, and the vicissitudes of their history in olden times have often foreshadowed the truth that was
to come, saving that God in His goodness has enriched and loaded us with far
greater benefits, and on this account the sins of Christians are much greater, and
bear the stamp of more shameful and criminal ingratitude.

---

36. Thomas Aquinas, *Quaest. Quodl.* I, q. 7, a. 2, corp.

37. *Regula pastoralis*, Part 3, ch. 4 (PL 77, 55).

38. Judith 5:21–22.

39. The Church, it is certain, at no time and in no particular is deserted by God; hence, there is no reason why she should be alarmed at the wickedness of men; but in the case of nations falling away from Christian virtue there is not a like ground of assurance, "for sin maketh nations miserable."[39] If every bygone age has experienced the force of this truth, wherefore should not our own? There are, in truth, very many signs which proclaim that just punishments are already menacing, and the condition of modern States tends to confirm this belief, since we perceive many of them in sad plight from intestine disorders, and not one entirely exempt. But, should those leagued together in wickedness hurry onward in the road they have boldly chosen, should they increase in influence and power in proportion as they make headway in their evil purposes and crafty schemes, there will be ground to fear lest the very foundations nature has laid for States to rest upon be utterly destroyed. Nor can such misgivings be removed by any mere human effort, especially as a vast number of men, having rejected the Christian faith, are on that account justly incurring the penalty of their pride, since blinded by their passions they search in vain for truth, laying hold on the false for the true, and thinking themselves wise when they call "evil good, and good evil," and "put darkness in the place of light, and light in the place of darkness."[40] It is therefore necessary that God come to the rescue, and that, mindful of His mercy, He turn an eye of compassion on human society.

40. Hence, We renew the urgent entreaty We have already made, to redouble zeal and perseverance, when addressing humble supplications to our merciful God, so that the virtues whereby a Christian life is perfected may be reawakened. It is, however, urgent before all, that charity, which is the main foundation of the Christian life, and apart from which the other virtues exist not or remain barren, should be quickened and maintained. Therefore is it that the Apostle Paul, after having exhorted the Colossians to flee all vice and cultivate all virtue, adds: "Above all things, have charity, which is the bond of perfection."[41] Yea, truly, charity is the bond of perfection, for it binds intimately to God those whom it has embraced and, with loving tenderness, causes them to draw their life from God, to act with God, to refer all to God. The love of God should not, however, be severed from the love of our neighbor, since men have a share in the infinite goodness of God and bear in themselves the impress of His image and likeness. "This commandment we have from God, that he who loveth God, love also his brother."[42] "If any

---

39. Prov. 14:34.

40. Isa. 5:20.

41. Col. 3: 14.

42. 1 John 4:21.

man say I love God, and he hateth his brother, he is a liar."[43] And this commandment concerning charity its divine proclaimer styled new, not in the sense that
a previous law, or even nature itself, had not enjoined that men should love one
another, but because the Christian precept of loving each other in that manner
was truly new, and quite unheard of in the memory of man. For, that love with
which Jesus Christ is beloved by His Father and with which He Himself loves men,
He obtained for His disciples and followers that they might be of one heart and of
one mind in Him by charity, as He Himself and His Father are one by their nature.

41. No one is unaware how deeply and from the very beginning the import
of that precept has been implanted in the breast of Christians, and what abundant fruits of concord, mutual benevolence, piety, patience, and fortitude it has
produced. Why, then, should we not devote ourselves to imitate the examples set
by our fathers? The very times in which we live should afford sufficient motives
for the practice of charity. Since impious men are bent on giving fresh impulse to
their hatred against Jesus Christ, Christians should be quickened anew in piety;
and charity, which is the inspirer of lofty deeds, should be imbued with new life.
Let dissensions therefore, if there be any, wholly cease; let those strifes which
waste the strength of those engaged in the fight, without any advantage resulting
to religion, be scattered to the winds; let all minds be united in faith and all hearts
in charity, so that, as it behooves, life may be spent in the practice of the love of
God and the love of men.

42. This is a suitable moment for us to exhort especially heads of families to
govern their households according to these precepts, and to be solicitous without failing for the right training of their children. The family may be regarded as
the cradle of civil society, and it is in great measure within the circle of family life
that the destiny of the States is fostered. Whence it is that they who would break
away from Christian discipline are working to corrupt family life, and to destroy it
utterly, root and branch. From such an unholy purpose they allow not themselves
to be turned aside by the reflection that it cannot, even in any degree, be carried
out without inflicting cruel outrage on the parents. These hold from nature their
right of training the children to whom they have given birth, with the obligation
super-added of shaping and directing the education of their little ones to the end
for which God vouchsafed the privilege of transmitting the gift of life. It is, then,
incumbent on parents to strain every nerve to ward off such an outrage, and to
strive manfully to have and to hold exclusive authority to direct the education
of their offspring, as is fitting, in a Christian manner, and first and foremost to
keep them away from schools where there is risk of their drinking in the poison of

43. 1 John 4:20.

impiety. Where the right education of youth is concerned, no amount of trouble or labor can be undertaken, howsoever great, but that even greater still may not be called for. In this regard, indeed, there are to be found in many countries Catholics worthy of general admiration, who incur considerable outlay and bestow much zeal in founding schools for the education of youth. It is highly desirable that such noble example may be generously followed, where time and circumstances demand; yet all should be intimately persuaded that the minds of children are most influenced by the training they receive at home. If in their early years they find within the walls of their homes the rule of an upright life and the discipline of Christian virtues, the future welfare of society will in great measure be guaranteed.

43. And now We seem to have touched upon those matters which Catholics ought chiefly nowadays to follow, or mainly to avoid. It rests with you, venerable brothers, to take measures that Our voice may reach everywhere, and that one and all may understand how urgent it is to reduce to practice the teachings set forth in this Our letter. The observance of these duties cannot be troublesome or onerous, for the yoke of Jesus Christ is sweet, and His burden is light. If anything, however, appear too difficult of accomplishment, you will afford aid by the authority of your example, so that each one of the faithful may make more strenuous endeavor, and display a soul unconquered by difficulties. Bring it home to their minds, as We have Ourselves oftentimes conveyed the warning, that matters of the highest moment and worthy of all honor are at stake, for the safeguarding of which every most toilsome effort should be readily endured; and that a sublime reward is in store for the labors of a Christian life. On the other hand, to refrain from doing battle for Jesus Christ amounts to fighting against Him; He Himself assures us "He will deny before His Father in heaven those who shall have refused to confess Him on earth."[44] As for Ourselves and you all, never assuredly, so long as life lasts, shall We allow Our authority, Our counsels, and Our solicitude to be in any wise lacking in the conflict. Nor is it to be doubted but that special aid of the great God will be vouchsafed, so long as the struggle endures, to the flock alike and to the pastors.

Sustained by this confidence, as a pledge of heavenly gifts, and of Our loving kindness in the Lord to you, venerable brothers, to your clergy and to all your people, We accord the apostolic benediction.

Given at St. Peter's in Rome, the tenth day of January, 1890, the twelfth year of Our pontificate.

✠ LEO XIII

---

44. Luke 9:26.

RERUM NOVARUM

On Capital and Labor

Encyclical Letter of Pope Leo XIII,
promulgated May 15, 1891

To Our Venerable Brethren the Patriarchs, Primates, Archbishops, Bishops, and other Ordinaries of Places having Peace and Communion with the Apostolic See.

I. INTRODUCTION: THE PROBLEM OF THE WORKER

That the spirit of revolutionary change, which has long been disturbing the nations of the world, should have passed beyond the sphere of politics and made its influence felt in the cognate sphere of practical economics is not surprising. The elements of the conflict now raging are unmistakable, in the vast expansion of industrial pursuits and the marvelous discoveries of science; in the changed relations between masters and workmen; in the enormous fortunes of some few individuals, and the utter poverty of the masses; in the increased self-reliance and closer mutual combination of the working classes; as also, finally, in the prevailing moral degeneracy. The momentous gravity of the state of things now obtaining fills every mind with painful apprehension; wise men are discussing it; practical men are proposing schemes; popular meetings, legislatures, and rulers of nations are all busied with it—actually there is no question which has taken a deeper hold on the public mind.

2. Therefore, venerable brethren, as on former occasions when it seemed opportune to refute false teaching, We have addressed you in the interests of the Church and of the common weal, and have issued letters bearing on political power, human liberty, the Christian constitution of the State,[1] and like matters, so have We thought it expedient now to speak on the condition of the working classes.[2] It

---

1. [I.e., *Diuturnum Illud, Libertas Praestantissimum,* and *Immortale Dei.*]
2. [The title sometimes given to this encyclical, "On the Condition of the Working Classes," is therefore justified. A few lines after this sentence, the Pope gives a more comprehensive definition of the subject of *Rerum Novarum.* Internal headings are editorial additions.]

is a subject on which We have already touched more than once, incidentally. But in the present letter, the responsibility of the apostolic office urges Us to treat the question of set purpose and in detail, in order that no misapprehension may exist as to the principles which truth and justice dictate for its settlement. The discussion is not easy, nor is it void of danger. It is no easy matter to define the relative rights and mutual duties of the rich and of the poor, of capital and of labor. And the danger lies in this, that crafty agitators are intent on making use of these differences of opinion to pervert men's judgments and to stir up the people to revolt.

3. In any case we clearly see, and on this there is general agreement, that some opportune remedy must be found quickly for the misery and wretchedness pressing so unjustly on the majority of the working class: for the ancient workingmen's guilds were abolished in the last century, and no other protective organization took their place. Public institutions and the laws set aside the ancient religion. Hence, by degrees it has come to pass that working men have been surrendered, isolated and helpless, to the hard-heartedness of employers and the greed of unchecked competition. The mischief has been increased by rapacious usury, which, although more than once condemned by the Church, is nevertheless, under a different guise, but with like injustice, still practiced by covetous and grasping men. To this must be added that the hiring of labor and the conduct of trade are concentrated in the hands of comparatively few; so that a small number of very rich men have been able to lay upon the teeming masses of the laboring poor a yoke little better than that of slavery itself.

II. RESPONSE TO SOCIALISM'S ATTEMPTED SOLUTION

The individual's right to private property

4. To remedy these wrongs the socialists, working on the poor man's envy of the rich, are striving to do away with private property, and contend that individual possessions should become the common property of all, to be administered by the State or by municipal bodies. They hold that by thus transferring property from private individuals to the community, the present mischievous state of things will be set to rights, inasmuch as each citizen will then get his fair share of whatever there is to enjoy. But their contentions are so clearly powerless to end the controversy that were they carried into effect the working man himself would be among the first to suffer. They are, moreover, emphatically unjust, for they would rob the lawful possessor, distort the functions of the State, and create utter confusion in the community.

5. It is surely undeniable that, when a man engages in remunerative labor, the impelling reason and motive of his work is to obtain property, and thereafter to hold it as his very own. If one man hires out to another his strength or skill, he does so for the purpose of receiving in return what is necessary for the satisfaction of his needs; he therefore expressly intends to acquire a right full and real, not only to the remuneration, but also to the disposal of such remuneration, just as he pleases. Thus, if he lives sparingly, saves money, and, for greater security, invests his savings in land, the land, in such case, is only his wages under another form; and, consequently, a working man's little estate thus purchased should be as completely at his full disposal as are the wages he receives for his labor. But it is precisely in such power of disposal that ownership obtains, whether the property consist of land or chattels. Socialists, therefore, by endeavoring to transfer the possessions of individuals to the community at large, strike at the interests of every wage-earner, since they would deprive him of the liberty of disposing of his wages, and thereby of all hope and possibility of increasing his resources and of bettering his condition in life.

6. What is of far greater moment, however, is the fact that the remedy they propose is manifestly against justice. For, every man has by nature the right to possess property as his own. This is one of the chief points of distinction between man and the animal creation, for the brute has no power of self-direction, but is governed by two main instincts, which keep his powers on the alert, impel him to develop them in a fitting manner, and stimulate and determine him to action without any power of choice. One of these instincts is self-preservation, the other the propagation of the species. Both can attain their purpose by means of things which lie within range; beyond their verge the brute creation cannot go, for they are moved to action by their senses only, and in the special direction which these suggest. But with man it is wholly different. He possesses, on the one hand, the full perfection of the animal being, and hence enjoys at least as much as the rest of the animal kind, the fruition of things material. But animal nature, however perfect, is far from representing the human being in its completeness, and is in truth but humanity's humble handmaid, made to serve and to obey. It is the mind, or reason, which is the predominant element in us who are human creatures; it is this which renders a human being human, and distinguishes him essentially from the brute. And on this very account—that man alone among the animal creation is endowed with reason—it must be within his right to possess things not merely for temporary and momentary use, as other living things do, but to have and to hold them in stable and permanent possession; he must have not only things that perish in the use, but those also which, though they have been reduced into use, continue for further use in after time.

7. This becomes still more clearly evident if man's nature be considered a little more deeply. For man, fathoming by his faculty of reason matters without number, linking the future with the present, and being master of his own acts, guides his ways under the eternal law and the power of God, whose providence governs all things. Wherefore, it is in his power to exercise his choice not only as to matters that regard his present welfare, but also about those which he deems may be for his advantage in time yet to come. Hence, man not only should possess the fruits of the earth, but also the very soil, inasmuch as from the produce of the earth he has to lay by provision for the future. Man's needs do not die out, but forever recur; although satisfied today, they demand fresh supplies for tomorrow. Nature accordingly must have given to man a source that is stable and remaining always with him, from which he might look to draw continual supplies. And this stable condition of things he finds solely in the earth and its fruits. There is no need to bring in the State. Man precedes the State, and possesses, prior to the formation of any State, the right of providing for the substance of his body.

8. The fact that God has given the earth for the use and enjoyment of the whole human race can in no way be a bar to the owning of private property. For God has granted the earth to mankind in general, not in the sense that all without distinction can deal with it as they like, but rather that no part of it was assigned to any one in particular, and that the limits of private possession have been left to be fixed by man's own industry, and by the laws of individual races. Moreover, the earth, even though apportioned among private owners, ceases not thereby to minister to the needs of all, inasmuch as there is not one who does not sustain life from what the land produces. Those who do not possess the soil contribute their labor; hence, it may truly be said that all human subsistence is derived either from labor on one's own land, or from some toil, some calling, which is paid for either in the produce of the land itself, or in that which is exchanged for what the land brings forth.

9. Here, again, we have further proof that private ownership is in accordance with the law of nature. Truly, that which is required for the preservation of life, and for life's well-being, is produced in great abundance from the soil, but not until man has brought it into cultivation and expended upon it his solicitude and skill. Now, when man thus turns the activity of his mind and the strength of his body toward procuring the fruits of nature, by such act he makes his own that portion of nature's field which he cultivates—that portion on which he leaves, as it were, the impress of his personality; and it cannot but be just that he should possess that portion as his very own, and have a right to hold it without anyone being justified in violating that right.

10. So strong and convincing are these arguments that it seems amazing that some should now be setting up anew certain obsolete opinions in opposition to what is here laid down. They assert that it is right for private persons to have the use of the soil and its various fruits, but that it is unjust for anyone to possess outright either the land on which he has built or the estate which he has brought under cultivation. But those who deny these rights do not perceive that they are defrauding man of what his own labor has produced. For the soil which is tilled and cultivated with toil and skill utterly changes its condition; it was wild before, now it is fruitful; was barren, but now brings forth in abundance. That which has thus altered and improved the land becomes so truly part of itself as to be in great measure indistinguishable and inseparable from it. Is it just that the fruit of a man's own sweat and labor should be possessed and enjoyed by anyone else? As effects follow their cause, so is it just and right that the results of labor should belong to those who have bestowed their labor.

11. With reason, then, the common opinion of mankind, little affected by the few dissentients who have contended for the opposite view, has found in the careful study of nature, and in the laws of nature, the foundations of the division of property, and the practice of all ages has consecrated the principle of private ownership, as being pre-eminently in conformity with human nature, and as conducing in the most unmistakable manner to the peace and tranquility of human existence. The same principle is confirmed and enforced by the civil laws—laws which, so long as they are just, derive from the law of nature their binding force. The authority of the divine law adds its sanction, forbidding us in severest terms even to covet that which is another's: "Thou shalt not covet thy neighbor's wife; nor his house, nor his field, nor his man-servant, nor his maid-servant, nor his ox, nor his ass, nor anything that is his."[3]

The family's right to private property

12. The rights here spoken of, belonging to each individual man, are seen in much stronger light when considered in relation to man's social and domestic obligations. In choosing a state of life, it is indisputable that all are at full liberty to follow the counsel of Jesus Christ as to observing virginity, or to bind themselves by the marriage tie. No human law can abolish the natural and original right of marriage, nor in any way limit the chief and principal purpose of marriage ordained by God's authority from the beginning: "Increase and multiply."[4] Hence

3.   Deut. 5:21.
4.   Gen. 1:28.

we have the family, the "society" of a man's house—a society very small, one must admit, but none the less a true society, and one older than any State. Consequently, it has rights and duties peculiar to itself which are quite independent of the State.

13. That right to property, therefore, which has been proved to belong naturally to individual persons, must in like manner belong to a man in his capacity of head of a family; nay, that right is all the stronger in proportion as the human person receives a wider extension in the family group. It is a most sacred law of nature that a father should provide food and all necessaries for those whom he has begotten; and, similarly, it is natural that he should wish that his children, who carry on, so to speak, and continue his personality, should be by him provided with all that is needful to enable them to keep themselves decently from want and misery amid the uncertainties of this mortal life. Now, in no other way can a father effect this except by the ownership of productive property, which he can transmit to his children by inheritance. A family, no less than a State, is, as We have said, a true society, governed by an authority peculiar to itself, that is to say, by the authority of the father. Provided, therefore, the limits which are prescribed by the very purposes for which it exists be not transgressed, the family has at least equal rights with the State in the choice and pursuit of the things needful to its preservation and its just liberty. We say, "at least equal rights"; for, inasmuch as the domestic household is antecedent, as well in idea as in fact, to the gathering of men into a community, the family must necessarily have rights and duties which are prior to those of the community, and founded more immediately in nature. If the citizens, if the families on entering into association and fellowship, were to experience hindrance in a commonwealth instead of help, and were to find their rights attacked instead of being upheld, society would rightly be an object of detestation rather than of desire.

14. The contention, then, that the civil government should at its option intrude into and exercise intimate control over the family and the household is a great and pernicious error. True, if a family finds itself in exceeding distress, utterly deprived of the counsel of friends, and without any prospect of extricating itself, it is right that extreme necessity be met by public aid, since each family is a part of the commonwealth. In like manner, if within the precincts of the household there occur grave disturbance of mutual rights, public authority should intervene to force each party to yield to the other its proper due; for this is not to deprive citizens of their rights, but justly and properly to safeguard and strengthen them.

But the rulers of the commonwealth must go no further; here, nature bids them stop. Paternal authority can be neither abolished nor absorbed by the State; for it has the same source as human life itself. "The child belongs to the father," and is, as it were, the continuation of the father's personality; and speaking strictly, the child takes its place in civil society, not of its own right, but in its quality as member of the family in which it is born. And for the very reason that "the child belongs to the father" it is, as St. Thomas Aquinas says, "before it attains the use of free will, under the power and the charge of its parents."[5] The socialists, therefore, in setting aside the parent and setting up a State supervision, act against natural justice, and destroy the structure of the home.

15. And in addition to injustice, it is only too evident what an upset and disturbance there would be in all classes, and to how intolerable and hateful a slavery citizens would be subjected. The door would be thrown open to envy, to mutual invective, and to discord; the sources of wealth themselves would run dry, for no one would have any interest in exerting his talents or his industry; and that ideal equality about which they entertain pleasant dreams would be in reality the leveling down of all to a like condition of misery and degradation. Hence, it is clear that the main tenet of socialism, community of goods, must be utterly rejected, since it only injures those whom it would seem meant to benefit, is directly contrary to the natural rights of mankind, and would introduce confusion and disorder into the commonweal. The first and most fundamental principle, therefore, if one would undertake to alleviate the condition of the masses, must be the inviolability of private property. This being established, we proceed to show where the remedy sought for must be found.

III. HOW THE CHURCH ADDRESSES THE PROBLEM

False messianism will not work

16. We approach the subject with confidence, and in the exercise of the rights which manifestly appertain to Us, for no practical solution of this question will be found apart from the intervention of religion and of the Church. It is We who are the chief guardian of religion and the chief dispenser of what pertains to the Church; and by keeping silence we would seem to neglect the duty incumbent on us. Doubtless, this most serious question demands the attention and the efforts of others besides ourselves—to wit, of the rulers of States, of employers of labor, of the wealthy, indeed of the working classes themselves, for whom We are pleading. But We affirm without hesitation that all the striving of men will be vain if they leave out the Church. It is the Church that insists, on the authority of the Gospel, upon those teachings whereby the conflict can be brought to an

---

5. *Summa Theologiae* II-II, q. 10, a. 12.

end, or rendered, at least, far less bitter; the Church uses her efforts not only to enlighten the mind, but to direct by her precepts the life and conduct of each and all; the Church improves and betters the condition of the working man by means of numerous organizations; does her best to enlist the services of all classes in discussing and endeavoring to further in the most practical way the interests of the working classes; and considers that for this purpose recourse should be had, in due measure and degree, to the intervention of the law and of State authority.

17. It must be first of all recognized that the condition of things inherent in human affairs must be borne with, for it is impossible to reduce civil society to one dead level. Socialists may in that intent do their utmost, but all striving against nature is in vain. There naturally exist among mankind manifold differences of the most important kind; people differ in capacity, skill, health, strength; and unequal fortune is a necessary result of unequal condition. Such inequality is far from being disadvantageous either to individuals or to the community. Social and public life can only be maintained by means of various kinds of capacity for business and the playing of many parts; and each man, as a rule, chooses the part which suits his own peculiar domestic condition. As regards bodily labor, even had man never fallen from the state of innocence, he would not have remained wholly idle; but that which would then have been his free choice and his delight became afterwards compulsory, and the painful expiation for his disobedience. "Cursed be the earth in thy work; in thy labor thou shalt eat of it all the days of thy life."[6]

18. In like manner, the other pains and hardships of life will have no end or cessation on earth; for the consequences of sin are bitter and hard to bear, and they must accompany man so long as life lasts. To suffer and to endure, therefore, is the lot of humanity; let them strive as they may, no strength and no artifice will ever succeed in banishing from human life the ills and troubles which beset it. If any there are who pretend differently—who hold out to a hard-pressed people the boon of freedom from pain and trouble, an undisturbed repose, and constant enjoyment—they delude the people and impose upon them, and their lying promises will only one day bring forth evils worse than the present. Nothing is more useful than to look upon the world as it really is, and at the same time to seek elsewhere, as We have said, for the solace to its troubles.

Natural considerations of riches and poverty

19. The great mistake made in regard to the matter now under consideration is to take up with the notion that class is naturally hostile to class, and that the

---

6. Gen. 3:17.

wealthy and the working men are intended by nature to live in mutual conflict. So irrational and so false is this view that the direct contrary is the truth. Just as the symmetry of the human frame is the result of the suitable arrangement of the different parts of the body, so in a State is it ordained by nature that these two classes should dwell in harmony and agreement, so as to maintain the balance of the body politic. Each needs the other: capital cannot do without labor, nor labor without capital. Mutual agreement results in the beauty of good order, while perpetual conflict necessarily produces confusion and savage barbarity. Now, in preventing such strife as this, and in uprooting it, the efficacy of Christian institutions is marvelous and manifold. First of all, there is no intermediary more powerful than religion (whereof the Church is the interpreter and guardian) in drawing the rich and the working class together, by reminding each of its duties to the other, and especially of the obligations of justice.

20. Of these duties, the following bind the proletarian and the worker: fully and faithfully to perform the work which has been freely and equitably agreed upon; never to injure the property, nor to outrage the person, of an employer; never to resort to violence in defending their own cause, nor to engage in riot or disorder; and to have nothing to do with men of evil principles, who work upon the people with artful promises of great results, and excite foolish hopes which usually end in useless regrets and grievous loss.

The following duties bind the wealthy owner and the employer: not to look upon their workers as their bondsmen, but to respect in every man his dignity as a person ennobled by Christian character. They are reminded that, according to natural reason and Christian philosophy, working for gain is creditable, not shameful, to a man, since it enables him to earn an honorable livelihood; but to misuse men as though they were things in the pursuit of gain, or to value them solely for their physical powers—that is truly shameful and inhuman. Again justice demands that, in dealing with the working man, religion and the good of his soul must be kept in mind. Hence, the employer is bound to see that the worker has time for his religious duties; that he be not exposed to corrupting influences and dangerous occasions; and that he be not led away to neglect his home and family, or to squander his earnings. Furthermore, the employer must never tax his work people beyond their strength, or employ them in work unsuited to their sex and age. His great and principal duty is to give everyone what is just. Doubtless, before deciding whether wages are fair, many things have to be considered; but wealthy owners and all masters of labor should be mindful of this—that to exercise pressure upon the indigent and the destitute for the sake of gain, and to gather one's profit out of the need of another, is condemned by all laws, human and divine. To defraud anyone of wages that are his due is a great crime which cries to the avenging anger of Heaven. "Behold, the hire of the laborers ... which by fraud has been kept back by you, crieth; and the cry of them hath entered into the ears of the Lord of Sabaoth."[7] Lastly, the rich must religiously refrain from cutting down the workmen's earnings, whether by force, by fraud, or by usurious dealing; and with all the greater reason because the laboring man is, as a rule, weak and unprotected, and because his slender means should in proportion to their scantiness be accounted sacred. Were these precepts carefully obeyed and followed out, would they not be sufficient of themselves to keep under all strife and all its causes?

Supernatural considerations of riches and poverty

21. But the Church, with Jesus Christ as her Master and Guide, aims higher still. She lays down precepts yet more perfect, and tries to bind class to class in friendliness and good feeling. The things of earth cannot be understood or valued aright without taking into consideration the life to come, the life that will know no death. Exclude the idea of futurity, and forthwith the very notion of what is good and right would perish; nay, the whole scheme of the universe would become a dark and unfathomable mystery. The great truth which we learn from nature herself is also the grand Christian dogma on which religion rests as on its foundation—that, when we have given up this present life, then shall we really begin to live. God has not created us for the perishable and transitory things of earth, but for things heavenly and everlasting; He has given us this world as a place of exile, and not as our abiding place. As for riches and the other things which men call good and desirable, whether we have them in abundance, or are lacking in them—so far as eternal happiness is concerned—it makes no difference; the only important thing is to use them aright. Jesus Christ, when He redeemed us with plentiful redemption, took not away the pains and sorrows which in such large proportion are woven together in the web of our mortal life. He transformed them into motives of virtue and occasions of merit; and no man can hope for eternal reward unless he follow in the blood-stained footprints of his Savior. "If we suffer with Him, we shall also reign with Him."[8] Christ's labors and sufferings, accepted of His own free will, have marvelously sweetened all suffering and all labor. And not only by His example, but by His grace and by the hope held forth of everlasting recompense, has He made pain and grief more easy to endure; "for that which is at present momentary and light

---

7.　James 5:4.

8.　2 Tim. 2:12.

of our tribulation, worketh for us above measure exceedingly an eternal weight of glory."[9]

22. Therefore, those whom fortune favors are warned that riches do not bring freedom from sorrow and are of no avail for eternal happiness, but rather are obstacles[10]; that the rich should tremble at the threatenings of Jesus Christ—threatenings so unwonted in the mouth of our Lord[11]—and that a most strict account must be given to the Supreme Judge for all we possess. The chief and most excellent rule for the right use of money is one the heathen philosophers hinted at, but which the Church has traced out clearly, and has not only made known to men's minds, but has impressed upon their lives. It rests on the principle that it is one thing to have a right to the possession of money and another to have a right to use money as one wills. Private ownership, as we have seen, is the natural right of man, and to exercise that right, especially as members of society, is not only lawful, but absolutely necessary. "It is lawful," says St. Thomas Aquinas, "for a man to hold private property; and it is also necessary for the carrying on of human existence."[12] But if the question be asked: How must one's possessions be used?—the Church replies without hesitation in the words of the same holy Doctor: "Man should not consider his material possessions as his own, but as common to all, so as to share them without hesitation when others are in need. Whence the apostle saith, 'Command the rich of this world ... to offer with no stint, to apportion largely.'"[13]

True, no one is commanded to distribute to others that which is required for his own needs and those of his household; nor even to give away what is reasonably required to keep up becomingly his condition in life, "for no one ought to live other than becomingly."[14] But, when what necessity demands has been supplied, and one's standing fairly taken thought for, it becomes a duty to give to the indigent out of what remains over. "Of that which remaineth, give alms."[15] It is a duty, not of justice (save in extreme cases), but of Christian charity—a duty not enforced by human law. But the laws and judgments of men must yield place to the laws and judgments of Christ the true God, who in many ways urges on His followers the practice of almsgiving—"It is more blessed to give than to

9. 2 Cor. 4:17.

10. Matt. 19:23–24.

11. Luke 6:24–25.

12. *Summa Theologiae* II-II, q. 66, a. 2.

13. Ibid.

14. *Summa Theologiae* II-II, q. 32, a. 6.

15. Luke 11:41.

receive"[16]; and who will count a kindness done or refused to the poor as done or refused to Himself—"As long as you did it to one of My least brethren you did it to Me."[17] To sum up, then, what has been said: Whoever has received from the divine bounty a large share of temporal blessings, whether they be external and material, or gifts of the mind, has received them for the purpose of using them for the perfecting of his own nature, and, at the same time, that he may employ them, as the steward of God's providence, for the benefit of others. "He that hath a talent," said St. Gregory the Great, "let him see that he hide it not; he that hath abundance, let him quicken himself to mercy and generosity; he that hath art and skill, let him do his best to share the use and the utility thereof with his neighbor."[18]

23. As for those who possess not the gifts of fortune, they are taught by the Church that in God's sight poverty is no disgrace, and that there is nothing to be ashamed of in earning their bread by labor. This is enforced by what we see in Christ Himself, who, "whereas He was rich, for our sakes became poor"[19]; and who, being the Son of God, and God Himself, chose to seem and to be considered the son of a carpenter—nay, did not disdain to spend a great part of His life as a carpenter Himself. "Is not this the carpenter, the son of Mary?"[20]

24. From contemplation of this divine Model, it is more easy to understand that the true worth and nobility of man lie in his moral qualities, that is, in virtue; that virtue is, moreover, the common inheritance of men, equally within the reach of high and low, rich and poor; and that virtue, and virtue alone, wherever found, will be followed by the rewards of everlasting happiness. Nay, God Himself seems to incline rather to those who suffer misfortune; for Jesus Christ calls the poor "blessed"[21]; He lovingly invites those in labor and grief to come to Him for solace[22]; and He displays the tenderest charity toward the lowly and the oppressed. These reflections cannot fail to keep down the pride of the well-to-do, and to give heart to the unfortunate; to move the former to be generous and the latter to be moderate in their desires. Thus, the separation which pride would set up tends to disappear, nor will it be difficult to make rich and poor join hands in friendly concord.

---

16. Acts 20:35.

17. Matt. 25:40.

18. *Hom. in Evang.*, 9, n. 7 (PL 76, 1109B).

19. 2 Cor. 8:9.

20. Mark 6:3.

21. Matt. 5:3.

22. Matt. 11:28.

25. But, if Christian precepts prevail, the respective classes will not only be united in the bonds of friendship, but also in those of brotherly love. For they will understand and feel that all men are children of the same common Father, who is God; that all have alike the same last end, which is God Himself, who alone can make either men or angels absolutely and perfectly happy; that each and all are redeemed and made sons of God, by Jesus Christ, "the first-born among many brethren"; that the blessings of nature and the gifts of grace belong to the whole human race in common, and that from none except the unworthy is withheld the inheritance of the kingdom of Heaven. "If sons, heirs also; heirs indeed of God, and co-heirs with Christ."[23] Such is the scheme of duties and of rights which is shown forth to the world by the Gospel. Would it not seem that, were society penetrated with ideas like these, strife must quickly cease?

The Church's history in dealing with this question

26. But the Church, not content with pointing out the remedy, also applies it. For the Church does her utmost to teach and to train men, and to educate them and by the intermediary of her bishops and clergy diffuses her salutary teachings far and wide. She strives to influence the mind and the heart so that all may willingly yield themselves to be formed and guided by the commandments of God. It is precisely in this fundamental and momentous matter, on which everything depends, that the Church possesses a power peculiarly her own. The instruments which she employs are given to her by Jesus Christ Himself for the very purpose of reaching the hearts of men, and derive their efficiency from God. They alone can reach the innermost heart and conscience, and bring men to act from a motive of duty, to control their passions and appetites, to love God and their fellow men with a love that is outstanding and of the highest degree and to break down courageously every barrier which blocks the way to virtue.

27. On this subject we need but recall for one moment the examples recorded in history. Of these facts there cannot be any shadow of doubt: for instance, that civil society was renovated in every part by Christian institutions; that in the strength of that renewal the human race was lifted up to better things—nay, that it was brought back from death to life, and to so excellent a life that nothing more perfect had been known before, or will come to be known in the ages that have yet to be. Of this beneficent transformation Jesus Christ was at once the first cause and the final end; as from Him all came, so to Him was all to be brought back. For, when the human race, by the light of the Gospel message, came to

---

23. Rom. 8:17.

know the grand mystery of the Incarnation of the Word and the redemption of man, at once the life of Jesus Christ, God and Man, pervaded every race and nation, and interpenetrated them with His faith, His precepts, and His laws. And if human society is to be healed now, in no other way can it be healed save by a return to Christian life and Christian institutions. When a society is perishing, the wholesome advice to give to those who would restore it is to call it to the principles from which it sprang; for the purpose and perfection of an association is to aim at and to attain that for which it is formed, and its efforts should be put in motion and inspired by the end and object which originally gave it being. Hence, to fall away from its primal constitution implies disease; to go back to it, recovery. And this may be asserted with utmost truth both of the whole body of the commonwealth and of that class of its citizens—by far the great majority— who get their living by their labor.

28. Neither must it be supposed that the solicitude of the Church is so preoccupied with the spiritual concerns of her children as to neglect their temporal and earthly interests. Her desire is that the poor, for example, should rise above poverty and wretchedness, and better their condition in life; and for this she makes a strong endeavor. By the fact that she calls men to virtue and forms them to its practice she promotes this in no slight degree. Christian morality, when adequately and completely practiced, leads of itself to temporal prosperity, for it merits the blessing of that God who is the source of all blessings; it powerfully restrains the greed of possession and the thirst for pleasure—twin plagues, which too often make a man who is void of self-restraint miserable in the midst of abundance[24]; it makes men supply for the lack of means through economy, teaching them to be content with frugal living, and further, keeping them out of the reach of those vices which devour not small incomes merely, but large fortunes, and dissipate many a goodly inheritance.

29. The Church, moreover, intervenes directly in behalf of the poor, by setting on foot and maintaining many associations which she knows to be efficient for the relief of poverty. Herein, again, she has always succeeded so well as to have even extorted the praise of her enemies. Such was the ardor of brotherly love among the earliest Christians that numbers of those who were in better circumstances despoiled themselves of their possessions in order to relieve their brethren; whence "neither was there anyone needy among them."[25] To the order of deacons, instituted in that very intent, was committed by the Apostles the charge of the daily doles; and the Apostle Paul, though burdened with the

---

24. 1 Tim. 6:10.

25. Acts 4:34.

solicitude of all the churches, hesitated not to undertake laborious journeys in order to carry the alms of the faithful to the poorer Christians. Tertullian calls these contributions, given voluntarily by Christians in their assemblies, deposits of piety, because, to cite his own words, they were employed "in feeding the needy, in burying them, in support of youths and maidens destitute of means and deprived of their parents, in the care of the aged, and the relief of the shipwrecked."[26]

30. Thus, by degrees, came into existence the patrimony which the Church has guarded with religious care as the inheritance of the poor. Nay, in order to spare them the shame of begging, the Church has provided aid for the needy. The common Mother of rich and poor has aroused everywhere the heroism of charity, and has established congregations of religious and many other useful institutions for help and mercy, so that hardly any kind of suffering could exist which was not afforded relief. At the present day many there are who, like the heathen of old, seek to blame and condemn the Church for such eminent charity. They would substitute in its stead a system of relief organized by the State. But no human expedients will ever make up for the devotedness and self-sacrifice of Christian charity. Charity, as a virtue, pertains to the Church; for virtue it is not, unless it be drawn from the Most Sacred Heart of Jesus Christ; and whosoever turns his back on the Church cannot be near to Christ.

IV. HOW THE STATE CAN ADDRESS THE PROBLEM

General principles

31. It cannot, however, be doubted that to attain the purpose we are treating of, not only the Church, but all human agencies, must concur. All who are concerned in the matter should be of one mind and according to their ability act together. It is with this, as with the Providence that governs the world; the results of causes do not usually take place save where all the causes cooperate. It is sufficient, therefore, to inquire what part the State should play in the work of remedy and relief.

32. By the State we here understand, not the particular form of government prevailing in this or that nation, but the State as rightly apprehended; that is to say, any government conformable in its institutions to right reason and natural law, and to those dictates of the divine wisdom which we have expounded in the

---

26. *Apologia secunda*, 39 (PL I, 533A).

encyclical on the Christian constitution of the State.[27] The foremost duty, therefore, of the rulers of the State should be to make sure that the laws and institutions, the general character and administration of the commonwealth, shall be such as of themselves to realize public well-being and private prosperity. This is the proper scope of wise statesmanship and is the work of the rulers. Now a State chiefly prospers and thrives through moral rule, well-regulated family life, respect for religion and justice, the moderation and fair imposing of public taxes, the progress of the arts and of trade, the abundant yield of the land—through everything, in fact, which makes the citizens better and happier. Hereby, then, it lies in the power of a ruler to benefit every class in the State, and amongst the rest to promote to the utmost the interests of the poor; and this in virtue of his office, and without being open to suspicion of undue interference—since it is the province of the commonwealth to serve the common good. And the more that is done for the benefit of the working classes by the general laws of the country, the less need will there be to seek for special means to relieve them.

33. There is another and deeper consideration which must not be lost sight of. As regards the State, the interests of all, whether high or low, are equal. The members of the working classes are citizens by nature and by the same right as the rich; they are real parts, living the life which makes up, through the family, the body of the commonwealth; and it need hardly be said that they are in every city very largely in the majority. It would be irrational to neglect one portion of the citizens and favor another, and therefore the public administration must duly and solicitously provide for the welfare and the comfort of the working classes; otherwise, that law of justice will be violated which ordains that each man shall have his due. To cite the wise words of St. Thomas Aquinas: "As the part and the whole are in a certain sense identical, so that which belongs to the whole in a sense belongs to the part."[28] Among the many and grave duties of rulers who would do their best for the people, the first and chief is to act with strict justice—with that justice which is called distributive—toward each and every class alike.

34. But although all citizens, without exception, can and ought to contribute to that common good in which individuals share so advantageously to themselves, yet it should not be supposed that all can contribute in the like way and to the same extent. No matter what changes may occur in forms of government, there will ever be differences and inequalities of condition in the State. Society cannot exist or be conceived of without them. Some there must be who devote themselves to the work of the commonwealth, who make the laws or administer

---

27. [Viz., *Immortale Dei.*]

28. *Summa Theologiae* II-II, q. 61, a. 1, ad 2.

justice, or whose advice and authority govern the nation in times of peace, and defend it in war. Such men clearly occupy the foremost place in the State, and should be held in highest estimation, for their work concerns most nearly and effectively the general interests of the community. Those who labor at a trade or calling do not promote the general welfare in such measure as this, but they benefit the nation, if less directly, in a most important manner. We have insisted, it is true, that, since the end of society is to make men better, the chief good that society can possess is virtue. Nevertheless, it is the business of a well consti-tuted body politic to see to the provision of those material and external helps "the use of which is necessary to virtuous action."[29] Now, for the provision of such commodities, the labor of the working class—the exercise of their skill, and the employment of their strength, in the cultivation of the land, and in the work-shops of trade—is especially responsible and quite indispensable. Indeed, their co-operation is in this respect so important that it may be truly said that it is only by the labor of working men that States grow rich. Justice, therefore, demands that the interests of the working classes should be carefully watched over by the administration, so that they who contribute so largely to the advantage of the community may themselves share in the benefits which they create—that being housed, clothed, and fit in body, they may find their life less hard and more endur-able. It follows that whatever shall appear to prove conducive to the well-being of those who work should obtain favorable consideration. There is no fear that solicitude of this kind will be harmful to any interest; on the contrary, it will be to the advantage of all, for it cannot but be good for the commonwealth to shield from misery those on whom it so largely depends for the things that it needs.

35. We have said that the State must not absorb the individual or the family; both should be allowed free and untrammeled action so far as is consistent with the common good and the interest of others. Rulers should, neverthe-less, anxiously safeguard the community and all its members; the community, because the conservation thereof is so emphatically the business of the supreme power, that the safety of the commonwealth is not only the first law, but it is a government's whole reason of existence; and the members, because both philos-ophy and the Gospel concur in laying down that the object of the government of the State should be, not the advantage of the ruler, but the benefit of those over whom he is placed. As the power to rule comes from God, and is, as it were, a participation in His, the highest of all sovereignties, it should be exercised as the power of God is exercised—with a fatherly solicitude which not only guides the whole, but reaches also individuals.

---

29. Thomas Aquinas, *De Regno* I, cap. 15.

36. Whenever the general interest or any particular class suffers or is threatened with harm which can in no other way be met or prevented, the public authority must step in to deal with it. Now, it is to the interest of the community, as well as of the individual, that peace and good order should be maintained; that all things should be carried on in accordance with God's laws and those of nature; that the discipline of family life should be observed and that religion should be obeyed; that a high standard of morality should prevail, both in public and private life; that justice should be held sacred and that no one should injure another with impunity; that the members of the commonwealth should grow up to man's estate strong and robust, and capable, if need be, of guarding and defending their country. If by a strike of workers or concerted interruption of work there should be imminent danger of disturbance to the public peace; or if circumstances were such as that among the working class the ties of family life were relaxed; if religion were found to suffer through the workers not having time and opportunity afforded them to practice its duties; if in workshops and factories there were danger to morals through the mixing of the sexes or from other harmful occasions of evil; or if employers laid burdens upon their workmen which were unjust, or degraded them with conditions repugnant to their dignity as human beings; finally, if health were endangered by excessive labor, or by work unsuited to sex or age—in such cases, there can be no question but that, within certain limits, it would be right to invoke the aid and authority of the law. The limits must be determined by the nature of the occasion which calls for the law's interference—the principle being that the law must not undertake more, nor proceed further, than is required for the remedy of the evil or the removal of the mischief.

37. Rights must be religiously respected wherever they exist, and it is the duty of the public authority to prevent and to punish injury, and to protect everyone in the possession of his own. Still, when there is question of defending the rights of individuals, the poor and badly off have a claim to special consideration. The richer class have many ways of shielding themselves, and stand less in need of help from the State; whereas the mass of the poor have no resources of their own to fall back upon, and must chiefly depend upon the assistance of the State. And it is for this reason that wage-earners, since they mostly belong to the mass of the needy, should be specially cared for and protected by the government.

38. Here, however, it is expedient to bring under special notice certain matters of moment. First of all, there is the duty of safeguarding private property by legal enactment and protection. Most of all it is essential, where the passion of greed is so strong, to keep the populace within the line of duty; for, if all may justly strive to better their condition, neither justice nor the common good allows any

individual to seize upon that which belongs to another, or, under the futile and shallow pretext of equality, to lay violent hands on other people's possessions. Most true it is that by far the larger part of the workers prefer to better themselves by honest labor rather than by doing any wrong to others. But there are not a few who are imbued with evil principles and eager for revolutionary change, whose main purpose is to stir up disorder and incite their fellows to acts of violence. The authority of the law should intervene to put restraint upon such firebrands, to save the working classes from being led astray by their maneuvers, and to protect lawful owners from spoliation.

39. When workers have recourse to a strike and become voluntarily idle, it is frequently because the hours of labor are too long, or the work too hard, or because they consider their wages insufficient. The grave inconvenience of this not uncommon occurrence should be obviated by public remedial measures; for such paralyzing of labor not only affects the masters and their work people alike, but is extremely injurious to trade and to the general interests of the public; moreover, on such occasions, violence and disorder are generally not far distant, and thus it frequently happens that the public peace is imperiled. The laws should forestall and prevent such troubles from arising; they should lend their influence and authority to the removal in good time of the causes which lead to conflicts between employers and employed.

40. The working man, too, has interests in which he should be protected by the State; and first of all, there are the interests of his soul. Life on earth, however good and desirable in itself, is not the final purpose for which man is created; it is only the way and the means to that attainment of truth and that love of goodness in which the full life of the soul consists. It is the soul which is made after the image and likeness of God; it is in the soul that the sovereignty resides in virtue of which man is commanded to rule the creatures below him and to use all the earth and the ocean for his profit and advantage. "Fill the earth and subdue it; and rule over the fishes of the sea, and the fowls of the air, and all living creatures that move upon the earth."[30] In this respect all men are equal; there is here no difference between rich and poor, master and servant, ruler and ruled, "for the same is Lord over all."[31] No man may with impunity outrage that human dignity which God Himself treats with great reverence, nor stand in the way of that higher life which is the preparation of the eternal life of heaven. Nay, more; no man has in this matter power over himself. To consent to any treatment which is calculated to defeat the end and purpose of his being is beyond his right; he cannot give up

---

30. Gen. 1:28.

31. Rom. 10:12.

his soul to servitude, for it is not man's own rights which are here in question, but the rights of God, the most sacred and inviolable of rights.

Particular laws the State should enforce

41. From this follows the obligation of the cessation from work and labor on Sundays and certain holy days. The rest from labor is not to be understood as mere giving way to idleness; much less must it be an occasion for spending money and for vicious indulgence, as many would have it to be; but it should be rest from labor, hallowed by religion. Rest (combined with religious observances) disposes man to forget for a while the business of his everyday life, to turn his thoughts to things heavenly, and to the worship which he so strictly owes to the eternal Godhead. It is this, above all, which is the reason and motive of Sunday rest; a rest sanctioned by God's great law of the Ancient Covenant—"Remember thou keep holy the Sabbath day,"[32] and taught to the world by His own mysterious "rest" after the creation of man: "He rested on the seventh day from all His work which He had done."[33]

42. If we turn now to things external and material, the first thing of all to secure is to save unfortunate working people from the cruelty of men of greed, who use human beings as mere instruments for money-making. It is neither just nor human so to grind men down with excessive labor as to stupefy their minds and wear out their bodies. Man's powers, like his general nature, are limited, and beyond these limits he cannot go. His strength is developed and increased by use and exercise, but only on condition of due intermission and proper rest. Daily labor, therefore, should be so regulated as not to be protracted over longer hours than strength admits. How many and how long the intervals of rest should be must depend on the nature of the work, on circumstances of time and place, and on the health and strength of the workman. Those who work in mines and quarries, and extract coal, stone and metals from the bowels of the earth, should have shorter hours in proportion as their labor is more severe and trying to health. Then, again, the season of the year should be taken into account; for not infrequently a kind of labor is easy at one time which at another is intolerable or exceedingly difficult. Finally, work which is quite suitable for a strong man cannot rightly be required from a woman or a child. And, in regard to children, great care should be taken not to place them in workshops and factories until their bodies and minds are sufficiently developed. For, just as very rough weather destroys the

---

32. Exod. 20:8.
33. Gen. 2:2.

buds of spring, so does too early an experience of life's hard toil blight the young promise of a child's faculties, and render any true education impossible. Women, again, are not suited for certain occupations; a woman is by nature fitted for home-work, and it is that which is best adapted at once to preserve her modesty and to promote the good bringing up of children and the well-being of the family. As a general principle it may be laid down that a workman ought to have leisure and rest proportionate to the wear and tear of his strength, for waste of strength must be repaired by cessation from hard work.

In all agreements between masters and work people there is always the condition expressed or understood that there should be allowed proper rest for soul and body. To agree in any other sense would be against what is right and just; for it can never be just or right to require on the one side, or to promise on the other, the giving up of those duties which a man owes to his God and to himself.

43. We now approach a subject of great importance, and one in respect of which, if extremes are to be avoided, right notions are absolutely necessary. Wages, as we are told, are regulated by free consent, and therefore the employer, when he pays what was agreed upon, has done his part and seemingly is not called upon to do anything beyond. The only way, it is said, in which injustice might occur would be if the master refused to pay the whole of the wages, or if the workman should not complete the work undertaken; in such cases the public authority should intervene, to see that each obtains his due, but not under any other circumstances.

44. To this kind of argument a fair-minded man will not easily or entirely assent; it is not complete, for there are important considerations which it leaves out of account altogether. To labor is to exert oneself for the sake of procuring what is necessary for the various purposes of life, and chief of all for self-preservation. "In the sweat of thy face thou shalt eat bread."[34] Hence, a man's labor necessarily bears two notes or characters. First of all, it is personal, inasmuch as the force which acts is bound up with the personality and is the exclusive property of him who acts, and, further, was given to him for his advantage. Secondly, man's labor is necessary; for without the result of labor a man cannot live, and self-preservation is a law of nature, which it is wrong to disobey. Now, were we to consider labor merely in so far as it is personal, doubtless it would be within the workman's right to accept any rate of wages whatsoever; for in the same way as he is free to work or not, so is he free to accept a small wage or even none at all. But our conclusion must be very different if, together with the personal element in a man's work, we consider the fact that work is also necessary for him to live:

---

34. Gen. 3:19.

these two aspects of his work are separable in thought, but not in reality. The preservation of life is the bounden duty of one and all, and to be wanting therein is a crime. It necessarily follows that each one has a natural right to procure what is required in order to live, and the poor can procure that in no other way than by what they can earn through their work.

45. Let the working man and the employer make free agreements, and in particular let them agree freely as to the wages; nevertheless, there underlies a dictate of natural justice more imperious and ancient than any bargain between man and man, namely, that wages ought not to be insufficient to support a frugal and well behaved wage-earner. If through necessity or fear of a worse evil the workman accept harder conditions because an employer or contractor will afford him no better, he is made the victim of force and injustice. In these and similar questions, however—such as, for example, the hours of labor in different trades, the sanitary precautions to be observed in factories and workshops, etc.—in order to supersede undue interference on the part of the State, especially as circumstances, times, and localities differ so widely, it is advisable that recourse be had to societies or boards such as We shall mention presently, or to some other mode of safeguarding the interests of the wage-earners; the State being appealed to, should circumstances require, for its sanction and protection.

46. If a workman's wages be sufficient to enable him comfortably to support himself, his wife, and his children, he will find it easy, if he be a sensible man, to practice thrift, and he will not fail, by cutting down expenses, to put by some little savings and thus secure a modest source of income. Nature itself would urge him to this. We have seen that this great labor question cannot be solved save by assuming as a principle that private ownership must be held sacred and inviolable. The law, therefore, should favor ownership, and its policy should be to induce as many as possible of the people to become owners.

47. Many excellent results will follow from this; and, first of all, property will certainly become more equitably divided. For, the result of civil change and revolution has been to divide cities into two classes separated by a wide chasm. On the one side there is the party which holds power because it holds wealth; which has in its grasp the whole of labor and trade; which manipulates for its own benefit and its own purposes all the sources of supply, and which is not without influence even in the administration of the commonwealth. On the other side there is the needy and powerless multitude, sick and sore in spirit and ever ready for disturbance. If working people can be encouraged to look forward to obtaining a share in the land, the consequence will be that the gulf between vast wealth and sheer poverty will be bridged over, and the respective classes will be brought nearer to one another. A further consequence will result in the great

abundance of the fruits of the earth. Men always work harder and more readily when they work on that which belongs to them; nay, they learn to love the
very soil that yields in response to the labor of their hands, not only food to eat,
but an abundance of good things for themselves and those that are dear to them.
That such a spirit of willing labor would add to the produce of the earth and to
the wealth of the community is self-evident. And a third advantage would spring
from this: men would cling to the country in which they were born, for no one
would exchange his country for a foreign land if his own afforded him the means
of living a decent and happy life. These three important benefits, however, can be
reckoned on only provided that a man's means be not drained and exhausted by
excessive taxation. The right to possess private property is derived from nature,
not from man; and the State has the right to control its use in the interests of
the public good alone, but by no means to absorb it altogether. The State would
therefore be unjust and cruel if under the name of taxation it were to deprive the
private owner of more than is fair.

V. HOW WORKERS THEMSELVES
CAN ADDRESS THE PROBLEM

Workers' associations have a right to exist

48. In the last place, employers and workmen may of themselves effect much,
in the matter We are treating, by means of such associations and organizations as
afford opportune aid to those who are in distress, and which draw the two classes
more closely together. Among these may be enumerated societies for mutual help;
various benevolent foundations established by private persons to provide for the
workman, and for his widow or his orphans, in case of sudden calamity, in sickness,
and in the event of death; and institutions for the welfare of boys and girls, young
people, and those more advanced in years.

49. The most important of all are workingmen's unions, for these virtually
include all the rest. History attests what excellent results were brought about
by the artificers' guilds of olden times. They were the means of affording not
only many advantages to the workmen, but in no small degree of promoting
the advancement of art, as numerous monuments remain to bear witness. Such
unions should be suited to the requirements of this our age—an age of wider
education, of different habits, and of far more numerous requirements in daily
life. It is gratifying to know that there are actually in existence not a few associations of this nature, consisting either of workmen alone, or of workmen and

employers together, but it were greatly to be desired that they should become more numerous and more efficient. We have spoken of them more than once, yet it will be well to explain here how notably they are needed, to show that they exist of their own right, and what should be their organization and their mode of action.

50. The consciousness of his own weakness urges man to call in aid from without. We read in the pages of Holy Writ: "It is better that two should be together than one; for they have the advantage of their society. If one fall he shall be supported by the other. Woe to him that is alone, for when he falleth he hath none to lift him up."[35] And further: "A brother that is helped by his brother is like a strong city."[36] It is this natural impulse which binds men together in civil society; and it is likewise this which leads them to join together in associations which are, it is true, lesser and not independent societies, but, nevertheless, real societies.

51. These lesser societies and the larger society differ in many respects, because their immediate purpose and aim are different. Civil society exists for the common good, and hence is concerned with the interests of all in general, albeit with individual interests also in their due place and degree. It is therefore called a public society, because by its agency, as St. Thomas Aquinas says, "men establish relations in common with one another in the setting up of a common-wealth."[37] But societies which are formed in the bosom of the commonwealth are styled private, and rightly so, since their immediate purpose is the private advantage of the associates. "Now, a private society," says St. Thomas again, "is one which is formed for the purpose of carrying out private objects; as when two or three enter into partnership with the view of trading in common."[38] Private societies, then, although they exist within the body politic, and are severally part of the commonwealth, cannot nevertheless be absolutely, and as such, prohibited by public authority. For, to enter into a "society" of this kind is the natural right of man; and the State has for its office to protect natural rights, not to destroy them; and, if it forbid its citizens to form associations, it contradicts the very princi-ple of its own existence, for both they and it exist in virtue of the like principle, namely, the natural tendency of man to dwell in society.

52. There are occasions, doubtless, when it is fitting that the law should inter-vene to prevent certain associations, as when men join together for purposes

---

35. Eccles. 4:9–10.

36. Prov. 18:19.

37. *Contra impugnantes Dei cultum et religionem*, Part 2, ch. 8.

38. Ibid.

which are evidently bad, unlawful, or dangerous to the State. In such cases, public authority may justly forbid the formation of such associations, and may dissolve them if they already exist. But every precaution should be taken not to violate the rights of individuals and not to impose unreasonable regulations under pretense of public benefit. For laws only bind when they are in accordance with right reason, and, hence, with the eternal law of God.[39]

53. And here we are reminded of the confraternities, societies, and religious orders which have arisen by the Church's authority and the piety of Christian men. The annals of every nation down to our own days bear witness to what they have accomplished for the human race. It is indisputable that on grounds of reason alone such associations, being perfectly blameless in their objects, possess the sanction of the law of nature. In their religious aspect they claim rightly to be responsible to the Church alone. The rulers of the State accordingly have no rights over them, nor can they claim any share in their control; on the contrary, it is the duty of the State to respect and cherish them, and, if need be, to defend them from attack. It is notorious that a very different course has been followed, more especially in our own times. In many places the State authorities have laid violent hands on these communities, and committed manifold injustice against them; it has placed them under control of the civil law, taken away their rights as corporate bodies, and despoiled them of their property. In such property the Church had her rights, each member of the body had his or her rights, and there were also the rights of those who had founded or endowed these communities for a definite purpose, and, furthermore, of those for whose benefit and assistance they had their being. Therefore We cannot refrain from complaining of such spoliation as unjust and fraught with evil results; and with all the more reason do We complain because, at the very time when the law proclaims that association is free to all, We see that Catholic societies, however peaceful and useful, are hampered in every way, whereas the utmost liberty is conceded to individuals whose purposes are at once hurtful to religion and dangerous to the commonwealth.

54. Associations of every kind, and especially those of working men, are now far more common than heretofore. As regards many of these there is no need at present to inquire whence they spring, what are their objects, or what the means they employ. Now, there is a good deal of evidence in favor of the opinion that many of these societies are in the hands of secret leaders, and are

---

39. "Human law is law only by virtue of its accordance with right reason; and thus it is manifest that it flows from the eternal law. And in so far as it deviates from right reason it is called an unjust law; in such case it is no law at all, but rather a species of violence" (*Summa Theologiae* I-II, q. 93, a. 3, ad 2).

managed on principles ill-according with Christianity and the public well-being; and that they do their utmost to get within their grasp the whole field of labor, and force working men either to join them or to starve. Under these circumstances Christian working men must do one of two things: either join associations in which their religion will be exposed to peril, or form associations among themselves and unite their forces so as to shake off courageously the yoke of so unrighteous and intolerable an oppression. No one who does not wish to expose man's chief good to extreme risk will for a moment hesitate to say that the second alternative should by all means be adopted.

55. Those Catholics are worthy of all praise—and they are not a few—who, understanding what the times require, have striven, by various undertakings and endeavors, to better the condition of the working class by rightful means. They have taken up the cause of the working man, and have spared no efforts to better the condition both of families and individuals; to infuse a spirit of equity into the mutual relations of employers and employed; to keep before the eyes of both classes the precepts of duty and the laws of the Gospel—that Gospel which, by inculcating self-restraint, keeps men within the bounds of moderation, and tends to establish harmony among the divergent interests and the various classes which compose the body politic. It is with such ends in view that we see men of eminence, meeting together for discussion, for the promotion of concerted action, and for practical work. Others, again, strive to unite working men of various grades into associations, help them with their advice and means, and enable them to obtain fitting and profitable employment. The bishops, on their part, bestow their ready goodwill and support; and with their approval and guidance many members of the clergy, both secular and regular, labor assiduously in behalf of the spiritual interest of the members of such associations. And there are not wanting Catholics blessed with affluence, who have, as it were, cast in their lot with the wage-earners, and who have spent large sums in founding and widely spreading benefit and insurance societies, by means of which the working man may without difficulty acquire through his labor not only many present advantages, but also the certainty of honorable support in days to come. How greatly such manifold and earnest activity has benefited the community at large is too well known to require Us to dwell upon it. We find therein grounds for most cheering hope in the future, provided always that the associations We have described continue to grow and spread, and are well and wisely administered. The State should watch over these societies of citizens banded together in accordance with their rights, but it should not thrust itself into their peculiar concerns and their organization, for things move and live by the spirit inspiring them, and may be killed by the rough grasp of a hand from without.

How to form good workers' associations

56. In order that an association may be carried on with unity of purpose and harmony of action, its administration and government should be firm and wise. All such societies, being free to exist, have the further right to adopt such rules and organization as may best conduce to the attainment of their respective objects. We do not judge it possible to enter into minute particulars touching the subject of organization; this must depend on national character, on practice and experience, on the nature and aim of the work to be done, on the scope of the various trades and employments, and on other circumstances of fact and of time—all of which should be carefully considered.

57. To sum up, then, We may lay it down as a general and lasting law that working men's associations should be so organized and governed as to furnish the best and most suitable means for attaining what is aimed at, that is to say, for helping each individual member to better his condition to the utmost in body, soul, and property. It is clear that they must pay special and chief attention to the duties of religion and morality, and that social betterment should have this chiefly in view; otherwise they would lose wholly their special character, and end by becoming little better than those societies which take no account whatever of religion. What advantage can it be to a working man to obtain by means of a society material well-being, if he endangers his soul for lack of spiritual food? "What doth it profit a man, if he gain the whole world and suffer the loss of his soul?"[40] This, as our Lord teaches, is the mark or character that distinguishes the Christian from the heathen. "After all these things do the heathen seek ... Seek ye first the Kingdom of God and His justice: and all these things shall be added unto you."[41] Let our associations, then, look first and before all things to God; let religious instruction have therein the foremost place, each one being carefully taught what is his duty to God, what he has to believe, what to hope for, and how he is to work out his salvation; and let all be warned and strengthened with special care against wrong principles and false teaching. Let the working man be urged and led to the worship of God, to the earnest practice of religion, and, among other things, to the keeping holy of Sundays and holy days. Let him learn to reverence and love holy Church, the common Mother of us all; and hence to obey the precepts of the Church, and to frequent the sacraments, since they are the means ordained by God for obtaining forgiveness of sin and for leading a holy life.

40. Matt. 16:26.

41. Matt. 6:32–33.

58. The foundations of the organization being thus laid in religion, We next proceed to make clear the relations of the members one to another, in order that they may live together in concord and go forward prosperously and with good results. The offices and charges of the society should be apportioned for the good of the society itself, and in such mode that difference in degree or standing should not interfere with unanimity and good-will. It is most important that office-bearers be appointed with due prudence and discretion, and each one's charge carefully mapped out, in order that no members may suffer harm. The common funds must be administered with strict honesty, in such a way that a member may receive assistance in proportion to his necessities. The rights and duties of the employers, as compared with the rights and duties of the employed, ought to be the subject of careful consideration. Should it happen that either a master or a workman believes himself injured, nothing would be more desirable than that a committee should be appointed, composed of reliable and capable members of the association, whose duty would be, conformably with the rules of the association, to settle the dispute. Among the several purposes of a society, one should be to try to arrange for a continuous supply of work at all times and seasons; as well as to create a fund out of which the members may be effectually helped in their needs, not only in the cases of accident, but also in sickness, old age, and distress.

59. Such rules and regulations, if willingly obeyed by all, will sufficiently ensure the well-being of the less well-to-do; whilst such mutual associations among Catholics are certain to be productive in no small degree of prosperity to the State. It is not rash to conjecture the future from the past. Age gives way to age, but the events of one century are wonderfully like those of another, for they are directed by the providence of God, who overrules the course of history in accordance with His purposes in creating the race of man. We are told that it was cast as a reproach on the Christians in the early ages of the Church that the greater number among them had to live by begging or by labor. Yet, destitute though they were of wealth and influence, they ended by winning over to their side the favor of the rich and the good-will of the powerful. They showed themselves industrious, hard-working, assiduous, and peaceful, ruled by justice, and, above all, bound together in brotherly love. In presence of such mode of life and such example, prejudice gave way, the tongue of malevolence was silenced, and the lying legends of ancient superstition little by little yielded to Christian truth.

60. At the time being, the condition of the working classes is the pressing question of the hour, and nothing can be of higher interest to all classes of the State than that it should be rightly and reasonably settled. But it will be easy for Christian working men to solve it aright if they will form associations, choose

wise guides, and follow on the path which with so much advantage to themselves and the common weal was trodden by their fathers before them. Prejudice, it is true, is mighty, and so is the greed of money; but if the sense of what is just and rightful be not deliberately stifled, their fellow citizens are sure to be won over to a kindly feeling towards men whom they see to be in earnest as regards their work and who prefer so unmistakably right dealing to mere lucre, and the sacredness of duty to every other consideration.

61. And further great advantage would result from the state of things We are describing; there would exist so much more ground for hope, and likelihood, even, of recalling to a sense of their duty those working men who have either given up their faith altogether, or whose lives are at variance with its precepts. Such men feel in most cases that they have been fooled by empty promises and deceived by false pretexts. They cannot but perceive that their grasping employers too often treat them with great inhumanity and hardly care for them outside the profit their labor brings; and if they belong to any union, it is probably one in which there exists, instead of charity and love, that intestine strife which ever accompanies poverty when unresigned and unsustained by religion. Broken in spirit and worn down in body, how many of them would gladly free themselves from such galling bondage! But human respect, or the dread of starvation, makes them tremble to take the step. To such as these Catholic associations are of incalculable service, by helping them out of their difficulties, inviting them to companionship and receiving the returning wanderers to a haven where they may securely find repose.

VI. CONCLUSION

62. We have now laid before you, venerable brethren, both who are the persons and what are the means whereby this most arduous question must be solved. Everyone should put his hand to the work which falls to his share, and that at once and straightway, lest the evil which is already so great become through delay absolutely beyond remedy. Those who rule the commonwealths should avail themselves of the laws and institutions of the country; masters and wealthy owners must be mindful of their duty; the working class, whose interests are at stake, should make every lawful and proper effort; and since religion alone, as We said at the beginning, can avail to destroy the evil at its root, all men should stand persuaded that the main thing needful is to re-establish Christian morals, apart from which all the plans and devices of the wisest will prove of little avail.

63. In regard to the Church, her cooperation will never be found lacking, be the time or the occasion what it may; and she will intervene with all the greater effect in proportion as her liberty of action is the more unfettered. Let this be carefully taken to heart by those whose office it is to safeguard the public welfare. Every minister of holy religion must bring to the struggle the full energy of his mind and all his power of endurance. Moved by your authority, venerable brethren, and quickened by your example, they should never cease to urge upon men of every class, upon the high-placed as well as the lowly, the Gospel doctrines of Christian life; by every means in their power they must strive to secure the good of the people; and above all must earnestly cherish in themselves, and try to arouse in others, charity, the mistress and the queen of virtues. For, the happy results we all long for must be chiefly brought about by the plenteous outpouring of charity; of that true Christian charity which is the fulfilling of the whole Gospel law, which is always ready to sacrifice itself for others' sake, and is man's surest antidote against worldly pride and immoderate love of self; that charity whose office is described and whose Godlike features are outlined by the Apostle St. Paul in these words: "Charity is patient, is kind, ... seeketh not her own, ... suffereth all things, ... endureth all things."[42]

64. On each of you, venerable brethren, and on your clergy and people, as an earnest of God's mercy and a mark of Our affection, we lovingly in the Lord bestow the apostolic benediction.

Given at St. Peter's in Rome, the fifteenth day of May, 1891, the fourteenth year of Our pontificate.

✠ Leo XIII

---

42. 1 Cor. 13:4–7.

AU MILIEU DES SOLLICITUDES

On Church and State in France

Encyclical Letter of Pope Leo XIII,
promulgated February 16, 1892

To Our Venerable Brothers, the Archbishops, Bishops, Clergy, and Faithful of France.

Amid the cares of the universal Church We have many times, in the course of Our pontificate, been pleased to testify Our affection for France and her noble people, and in one of Our encyclicals,[1] still within the memory of all, We endeavored solemnly to express the innermost feelings of Our soul on this subject. It is precisely this affection that has caused Us to watch with deep interest and then to revolve in Our mind the succession of events, sometimes sad, sometimes consoling, which, of late years, has taken place in your midst.

2. Again, at present, when contemplating the depths of the vast conspiracy that certain men have formed for the annihilation of Christianity in France and the animosity with which they pursue the realization of their design, trampling underfoot the most elementary notions of liberty and justice for the sentiment of the greater part of the nation, and of respect for the inalienable rights of the Catholic Church, how can We but be stricken with deepest grief? And when We behold, one after another, the dire consequences of these sinful attacks which conspire to ruin morals, religion, and even political interests (wisely understood), how can We express the bitterness that overwhelms Us and the apprehensions that beset Us?

3. On the other hand, We feel greatly consoled when We see this same French people increasing its zeal and affection for the Holy See in proportion as that See is abandoned—We should rather say warred with upon earth. Moved by deeply religious and patriotic sentiments, representatives of all the social classes have repeatedly come to Us from France, happy to aid the Church in her incessant needs and eager to ask us for light and counsel, so as to be sure that amid present tribulations they would in nowise deviate from the teachings of the head

---

1. [*Nobilissima Gallorum Gens* of 1884.]

of the faithful. And We, in Our turn, either in writing or by word of mouth, have openly told Our sons what they had a right to demand of their Father, and, far from discouraging them, we have strongly exhorted them to increase their love and efforts in defense of the Catholic faith and likewise of their native land: two duties of paramount importance, and from which, in this life, no man can exempt himself.

4. Now We deem it opportune, nay, even necessary, once again to raise Our voice entreating still more earnestly, We shall not say Catholics only, but all upright and intelligent Frenchmen, utterly to disregard all seeds of political strife in order to devote their efforts solely to the pacification of their country. All understand the value of this pacification; all continue to desire it more and more. And We who crave it more than anyone, since We represent on earth the God of peace, urge by this present letter all righteous souls, all generous hearts, to assist Us in making it stable and fruitful.

Religion and Country

5. First of all, let us take as a starting point a well-known truth admitted by all men of good sense and loudly proclaimed by the history of all peoples; namely, that religion, and religion only, can create the social bond; that it alone maintains the peace of a nation on a solid foundation. When different families, without giving up the rights and duties of domestic society, unite under the inspiration of nature, in order to constitute themselves members of another larger family circle called civil society, their object is not only to find therein the means of providing for their material welfare, but, above all, to draw thence the boon of moral improvement. Otherwise society would rise but little above the level of an aggregation of beings devoid of reason, and whose whole life would consist in the satisfaction of sensual instincts. Moreover, without this moral improvement it would be difficult to demonstrate that civil society was an advantage rather than a detriment to man, as man.

6. Now, morality, in man, by the mere fact that it should establish harmony among so many dissimilar rights and duties, since it enters as an element into every human act, necessarily supposes God, and with God, religion, that sacred bond whose privilege is to unite, anteriorly to all other bonds, man to God. Indeed, the idea of morality signifies, above all, an order of dependence in regard to truth which is the light of the mind; in regard to good which is the object of the will; and without truth and good there is no morality worthy of the name. And what is the principal and essential truth, that from which all truth is derived? It is God. What, therefore, is the supreme good from which all other good proceeds?

God. Finally, who is the creator and guardian of our reason, our will, our whole being, as well as the end of our life? God; always God. Since, therefore, religion is the interior and exterior expression of the dependence which, in justice, we owe to God, there follows a grave obligation. All citizens are bound to unite in maintaining in the nation true religious sentiment, and to defend it in case of need, if ever, despite the protestations of nature and of history, an atheistical school should set about banishing God from society, thereby surely annihilating the moral sense even in the depths of the human conscience. Among men who have not lost all notion of integrity there can exist no difference of opinion on this point.

7. In French Catholics the religious sentiment should be even deeper and more universal because they have the happiness of belonging to the true religion. If, indeed, religious beliefs were, always and everywhere, given as a basis of the morality of human actions and the existence of all well-ordained society, it is evident that the Catholic religion, by the mere fact that it is the true Church of Jesus Christ, possesses, more than any other, the efficacy required for the regulation of life in society and in the individual. Would you have a brilliant example of this? France herself furnishes the same. In proportion as France progressed in the Christian faith she was seen to rise gradually to the moral greatness which she attained as a political and military power. To the natural generosity of her heart Christian charity came and added an abundant source of new energy; her wonderful activity received still greater impetus from contact with the light that guides and is the pledge of constancy, the Christian faith, which, by the hand of France, traced such glorious pages in the history of mankind. And even today does not her faith continue to add new glories to those of the past? We behold France, inexhaustible in her genius and resources, multiplying works of charity at home; we admire her enterprises in foreign lands where, by means of her gold and the labors of her missionaries who work even at the price of their blood, she simultaneously propagates her own renown and the benefits of the Catholic religion. No Frenchman, whatever his convictions in other respects, would dare to renounce glory such as this, for to do so would be to deny his native land.

8. Now the history of a nation reveals in an incontestable way the generating and preserving element of its moral greatness, and should this element ever be missing, neither a superabundance of gold nor even force of arms could save it from moral decadence and perhaps death. Who then but understands that for all Frenchmen professing the Catholic religion the great anxiety should be to insure its preservation, and that with all the more devotedness since in their midst, sects are making Christianity an object of implacable hostility. Therefore, on this ground, they can afford neither indolence of action nor party divisions; the one

would bespeak cowardice unworthy of a Christian, the other would bring about disastrous weakness.

9. And now, before going any further, We must indicate a craftily circulated calumny making most odious imputations against Catholics, and even against the Holy See itself. It is maintained that that vigor of action inculcated in Catholics for the defense of their faith has for a secret motive much less the safeguarding of their religious interests than the ambition of securing to the Church political domination over the State. Truly this is the revival of a very ancient calumny, as its invention belongs to the first enemies of Christianity. Was it not first of all formulated against the adorable person of the Redeemer? Yes, when He illuminated souls by His preaching and alleviated the corporal or spiritual sufferings of the unfortunate with the treasures of His divine bounty, he was accused of having political ends in view. "We have found this man perverting our nation, and forbidding to give tribute to Caesar, and saying that he is Christ, the king ..."[2] "If thou release this man, thou are not Caesar's friend. For whosoever maketh himself a king, speaketh against Caesar. ... We have no king but Caesar."[3]

10. It was these threatening calumnies which drew from Pilate the sentence of death against Him whom he had repeatedly declared innocent. And the authors of these lies, or of others of equal strength, omitted nothing that would aid their emissaries in propagating them far and wide; and thus did St. Justin, martyr, rebuke the Jews of his time: "Far from repenting when you had learned of His resurrection from the dead, you sent to Jerusalem shrewdly chosen men to announce that a heresy and an impious sect had been started by a certain seducer called Jesus of Galilee."[4]

11. In so audaciously defaming Christianity its enemies knew well what they did; their plan was to raise against its propagation a formidable adversary, the Roman Empire. The calumny made headway; and in their credulity the pagans called the first Christians "useless creatures, dangerous citizens, factionists, enemies of the Empire and the Emperors."[5] But in vain did the apologists of Christianity by their writings, and Christians by their splendid conduct, endeavor to demonstrate the absurdity and criminality of these qualifications: they were not heeded. Their very name was equivalent to a declaration of war; and Christians, by the mere fact of their being such, and for no other reason, were forced to choose between apostasy and martyrdom, being allowed no

2. Luke 23:2.
3. John 19:12–15.
4. *Dialog. cum Tryphone.*
5. Tertull. *In Apolog.*; Minutius Felix, *In Octavio.*

alternative. During the following centuries the same grievances and the same severity prevailed to a greater or less extent, whenever governments were unreasonably jealous of their power and maliciously disposed against the Church. They never failed to call public attention to the pretended encroachment of the Church upon the State, in order to furnish the State with some apparent right to violently attack the Catholic religion.

12. We have expressly recalled some features of the past that Catholics might not be dismayed by the present. Substantially the struggle is ever the same: Jesus Christ is always exposed to the contradictions of the world, and the same means are always used by modern enemies of Christianity, means old in principle and scarcely modified in form; but the same means of defense are also clearly indicated to Christians of the present day by our apologists, our doctors and our martyrs. What they have done it is incumbent upon us to do in our turn. Let us therefore place above all else the glory of God and of His Church; let us work for her with an assiduity at once constant and effective, and leave all care of success to Jesus Christ, who tells us: "In the world you shall have distress: but have confidence, I have overcome the world."[6]

Forms of Government and Their Mutability

13. To attain this We have already remarked that a great union is necessary, and if it is to be realized, it is indispensable that all preoccupation capable of diminishing its strength and efficacy must be abandoned. Here We intend alluding principally to the political differences among the French in regard to the actual republic—a question We would treat with the clearness which the gravity of the subject demands, beginning with the principles and descending thence to practical results.

14. Various political governments have succeeded one another in France during the last century, each having its own distinctive form: the Empire, the Monarchy, and the Republic. By giving one's self up to abstractions, one could at length conclude which is the best of these forms, considered in themselves; and in all truth it may be affirmed that each of them is good, provided it lead straight to its end—that is to say, to the common good for which social authority is constituted; and finally, it may be added that, from a relative point of view, such and such a form of government may be preferable because of being better adapted to the character and customs of such or such a nation. In this order of speculative ideas, Catholics, like all other citizens, are free to prefer one form of government

6.　John 16:33.

to another precisely because no one of these social forms is, in itself, opposed to the principles of sound reason nor to the maxims of Christian doctrine. What amply justifies the wisdom of the Church is that in her relations with political powers she makes abstraction of the forms which differentiate them and treats with them concerning the great religious interests of nations, knowing that hers is the duty to undertake their tutelage above all other interests. Our preceding encyclicals have already exposed these principles, but it was nevertheless necessary to recall them for the development of the subject which occupies us today.

15. In descending from the domain of abstractions to that of facts, we must beware of denying the principles just established: they remain fixed. However, becoming incarnated in facts, they are clothed with a contingent character, determined by the center in which their application is produced. Otherwise said, if every political form is good by itself and may be applied to the government of nations, the fact still remains that political power is not found in all nations under the same form; each has its own. This form springs from a combination of historical or national, though always human, circumstances which, in a nation, give rise to its traditional and even fundamental laws, and by these is determined the particular form of government, the basis of transmission of supreme power.

16. It would be useless to recall that all individuals are bound to accept these governments and not to attempt their overthrow or a change in their form. Hence it is that the Church, the guardian of the truest and highest idea of political sovereignty, since she has derived it from God, has always condemned men who rebelled against legitimate authority and disapproved their doctrines—and that, too, at the very time when the custodians of power used it against her, thereby depriving themselves of the strongest support given their authority and of efficacious means of obtaining from the people obedience to their laws. And apropos of this subject, We cannot lay too great stress upon the precepts given to the first Christians by the Prince of the apostles in the midst of persecutions: "Honor all men: love the brotherhood: fear God: honor the king"[7]; and those of St. Paul: "I desire, therefore, first of all, that supplications, prayers, intercessions, and thanksgivings be made for all men: for kings and for all who are in high station, that we may lead a quiet and peaceable life, in all piety and chastity. For this is good and acceptable in the sight of God, our Savior."[8]

17. However, here it must be carefully observed that whatever be the form of civil power in a nation, it cannot be considered so definitive as to have the right to remain immutable, even though such were the intention of those who, in

---

7.   1 Pet. 2:17.

8.   1 Tim. 2:1–3.

the beginning, determined it. Only the Church of Jesus Christ has been able to preserve, and surely will preserve unto the consummation of time, her form of government. Founded by Him who was, who is, and who will be forever,[9] she has received from Him, since her very origin, all that she requires for the pursuing of her divine mission across the changeable ocean of human affairs. And, far from wishing to transform her essential constitution, she has not the power even to relinquish the conditions of true liberty and sovereign independence with which Providence has endowed her in the general interest of souls. But, in regard to purely human societies, it is an oft-repeated historical fact that time, that great transformer of all things here below, operates great changes in their political institutions. On some occasions it limits itself to modifying something in the form of the established government; or, again, it will go so far as to substitute other forms for the primitive ones—forms totally different, even as regards the mode of transmitting sovereign power.

18. And how are these political changes of which We speak produced? They sometimes follow in the wake of violent crises, too often of a bloody character, in the midst of which preexisting governments totally disappear; then anarchy holds sway, and soon public order is shaken to its very foundations and finally overthrown. From that time onward a social need obtrudes itself upon the nation; it must provide for itself without delay. Is it not its privilege—or, better still, its duty—to defend itself against a state of affairs troubling it so deeply, and to re-establish public peace in the tranquility of order? Now, this social need justifies the creation and the existence of new governments, whatever form they take; since, in the hypothesis wherein we reason, these new governments are a requisite to public order, all public order being impossible without a government. Thence it follows that, in similar junctures, all the novelty is limited to the political form of civil power, or to its mode of transmission; it in no wise affects the power considered in itself. This continues to be immutable and worthy of respect, as, considered in its nature, it is constituted to provide for the common good, the supreme end which gives human society its origin. To put it otherwise, in all hypotheses, civil power, considered as such, is from God, always from God: "For there is no power but from God."[10]

19. Consequently, when new governments representing this immutable power are constituted, their acceptance is not only permissible but even obligatory, being imposed by the need of the social good which has made and which upholds them. This is all the more imperative because an insurrection stirs up

9.   Heb. 13:8.
10.   Rom. 13:1.

hatred among citizens, provokes civil war, and may throw a nation into chaos and anarchy, and this great duty of respect and dependence will endure as long as the exigencies of the common good shall demand it, since this good is, after God, the first and last law in society.

20. Thus the wisdom of the Church explains itself in the maintenance of her relations with the numerous governments which have succeeded one another in France in less than a century, each change causing violent shocks. Such a line of conduct would be the surest and most salutary for all Frenchmen in their civil relations with the Republic, which is the actual government of their nation. Far be it from them to encourage the political dissensions which divide them; all their efforts should be combined to preserve and elevate the moral greatness of their native land.

Distinction between Political Power and Legislation

21. But a difficulty presents itself. "This Republic," it is said, "is animated by such anti-Christian sentiments that honest men, Catholics particularly, could not conscientiously accept it." This, more than anything else, has given rise to dissensions, and in fact aggravated them. These regrettable differences would have been avoided if the very considerable distinction between constituted power and legislation had been carefully kept in view. In so much does legislation differ from political power and its form, that under a system of government most excellent in form legislation could be detestable; while quite the opposite under a regime most imperfect in form, might be found excellent legislation. It were an easy task to prove this truth, history in hand, but what would be the use? All are convinced of it. And who is in a better position to know it than the Church—she who has striven to maintain habitual relations with all political governments? Assuredly she, better than any other power, could tell the consolation or sorrow occasioned her by the laws of the various governments by which nations have been ruled from the Roman Empire down to the present.

22. If the distinction just established has its major importance, it is likewise manifestly reasonable: Legislation is the work of men invested with power, and who, in fact, govern the nation; therefore it follows that, practically, the quality of the laws depends more upon the quality of these men than upon the power. The laws will be good or bad accordingly as the minds of the legislators are imbued with good or bad principles, and as they allow themselves to be guided by political prudence or by passion.

23. That several years ago different important acts of legislation in France proceeded from a tendency hostile to religion, and therefore to the interests of

the nation, is admitted by all, and unfortunately confirmed by the evidence of facts. We Ourselves, in obedience to a sacred duty, made earnest appeals to him who was then at the head of the Republic, but these tendencies continued to exist; the evil grew, and it was not surprising that the members of the French Episcopate chosen by the Holy Spirit to rule over their respective illustrious churches should even quite recently have considered it an obligation publicly to express their grief concerning the condition of affairs in France in regard to the Catholic religion. Poor France! God alone can measure the abyss of evil into which she will sink if this legislation, instead of improving, will stubbornly continue in a course which must end in plucking from the minds and hearts of Frenchmen the religion which has made them so great.

24. And here is precisely the ground on which, political dissensions aside, upright men should unite as one to combat, by all lawful and honest means, these progressive abuses of legislation. The respect due to constituted power cannot prohibit this: unlimited respect and obedience cannot be yielded to all legislative measures, of no matter what kind, enacted by this same power. Let it not be forgotten that law is a precept ordained according to reason and promulgated for the good of the community by those who, for this end, have been entrusted with power. Accordingly, such points in legislation as are hostile to religion and to God should never be approved; to the contrary, it is a duty to disapprove them. It was this that St. Augustine, the great Bishop of Hippo, brought out so strongly in his eloquent reasoning: "Sometimes the powerful ones of earth are good and fear God; at other times they fear Him not. Julian was an emperor unfaithful to God, an apostate, a pervert, an idolater. Christian soldiers served this faithless emperor, but as soon as there was question of the cause of Jesus Christ they recognized only Him who was in heaven. Julian commanded them to honor idols and offer them incense, but they put God above the prince. However, when he made them form into ranks and march against a hostile nation, they obeyed instantly. They distinguished the eternal from the temporal master and still in view of the eternal Master they submitted to such a temporal master."[11]

25. We know that, by a lamentable abuse of his reason, and still more so of his will, the atheist denies these principles. But, in a word, atheism is so monstrous an error that it could never, be it said to the honor of humanity, annihilate in it the consciousness of God's claims and substitute them with idolatry of the State.

26. The principles which should regulate our conduct towards God and towards human governments being thus defined, no unprejudiced man can censure French Catholics if, sparing themselves neither fatigue nor sacrifice, they

---

11. *Enarrat. in Psalm.* CXXIV, n. 7, fin.

labor to preserve a condition essential to their country's salvation, one which embodies so many glorious traditions registered by history, and which every Frenchmen is in duty bound not to forget.

The Concordat, and Separation of Church and State

27. Before closing Our letter, We wish to touch upon two points bearing an affinity to each other and which, because so closely connected with religious interests, have stirred up some division among Catholics. One of them is the Concordat, which for so many years has facilitated in France the harmony between the government of the Church and that of the State. On the observance of this solemn, bi-lateral compact, always faithfully kept by the Holy See, the enemies of the Catholic religion do not themselves agree. The more violent among them desire its abolition, that the State may be entirely free to molest the Church of Jesus Christ. On the contrary, others, being more astute, wish, or rather claim to wish, the preservation of the Concordat: not because they agree that the State should fulfill toward the Church the subscribed engagements, but solely that the State may be benefited by the concessions made by the Church; as if one could, at will, separate engagements entered into from concessions obtained, when both of these things form a substantial part of one whole. For them the Concordat would amount to no more than a chain forged to fetter the liberty of the Church, that holy liberty to which she has a divine and inalienable right. Of these two opinions which will prevail? We know not. We desired to recall them only to recommend Catholics not to provoke a secession by interfering in a matter with which it is the business of the Holy See to deal.

28. We shall not hold to the same language on another point, concerning the principle of the separation of the State and Church, which is equivalent to the separation of human legislation from Christian and divine legislation. We do not care to interrupt Ourselves here in order to demonstrate the absurdity of such a separation; each one will understand for himself. As soon as the State refuses to give to God what belongs to God, by a necessary consequence it refuses to give to citizens that to which, as men, they have a right; as, whether agreeable or not to accept, it cannot be denied that man's rights spring from his duty toward God. Whence it follows that the State, by missing in this connection the principal object of its institution, finally becomes false to itself by denying that which is the reason of its own existence. These superior truths are so clearly proclaimed by the voice of even natural reason, that they force themselves upon all who are not blinded by the violence of passion; therefore Catholics cannot be too careful in defending themselves against such a separation. In fact, to wish that the State

would separate itself from the Church would be to wish, by a logical sequence, that the Church be reduced to the liberty of living according to the law common to all citizens. It is true that in certain countries this state of affairs exists. It is a condition which, if it have numerous and serious inconveniences, also offers some advantages—above all when, by a fortunate inconsistency, the legislator is inspired by Christian principles—and, though these advantages cannot justify the false principle of separation nor authorize its defense, they nevertheless render worthy of toleration a situation which, practically, might be worse.

29. But in France, a nation Catholic in her traditions and by the present faith of the great majority of her sons, the Church should not be placed in the precarious position to which she must submit among other peoples; and the better that Catholics understand the aim of the enemies who desire this separation, the less will they favor it. To these enemies, and they say it clearly enough, this separation means that political legislation be entirely independent of religious legislation; nay, more, that [the temporal] power be absolutely indifferent to the interests of Christian society, that is to say, of the Church; in fact, that it deny her very existence. But they make a reservation formulated thus: As soon as the Church, utilizing the resources which common law accords to the least among Frenchmen, will, by redoubling her native activity, cause her work to prosper, then the State intervening, can and will put French Catholics outside the common law itself. In a word: the ideal of these men would be a return to paganism: the State would recognize the Church only when it would be pleased to persecute her.

30. We have explained, venerable brethren, in an abridged though clear way, some if not all the points upon which French Catholics and all intelligent men should be at peace and unity, so as to remedy, in so far as still remains possible, the evils with which France is afflicted, and to elevate its moral greatness. The points in question are: religion and country, political power and legislation, the conduct to be observed in regard to this power and legislation, the Concordat, the separation of Church and State. We cherish the hope and the confidence that the elucidation of these points will dissipate the prejudices of many honest, well-meaning men, facilitate the pacification of minds, and thereby cement the union of all Catholics for the sustaining of the great cause of Christ, who loves the Franks.

31. How consoling to Our heart to encourage you all in this way and to behold you all responding with docility to Our appeal! You, venerable brethren, by your authority and with the enlightened zeal for Church and Fatherland which so distinguishes you, will give able support to this peace-making work. We delight in the hope that those who are in power will appreciate Our words, which aim at the happiness and prosperity of France.

32. Meanwhile, as a pledge of Our paternal affection, we bestow upon you, venerable brethren, upon your clergy and also upon all the Catholics of France, the apostolic blessing.

Given at Rome, the sixteenth day of February, 1892, in the fourteenth year of Our pontificate.

✠ LEO XIII

LONGINQUA OCEANI

On Catholicism in the United States of America

Encyclical Letter of Pope Leo XIII,
promulgated January 6, 1895

To the Archbishops and Bishops of the United States.

We traverse in spirit and thought the wide expanse of ocean; and although We have at other times addressed you in writing—chiefly when We directed encyclical letters to the bishops of the Catholic world[1]—yet have We now resolved to speak to you separately, trusting that We shall be, God willing, of some assistance to the Catholic cause amongst you. To this We apply Ourselves with the utmost zeal and care, because We highly esteem and love exceedingly the young and vigorous American nation, in which We plainly discern latent forces for the advancement alike of civilization and of Christianity.

2. Not long ago, when your whole nation, as was fitting, celebrated, with grateful recollection and every manifestation of joy, the completion of the fourth century since the discovery of America, We, too, commemorated together with you that most auspicious event, sharing in your rejoicings with equal good-will. Nor were We on that occasion content with offering prayers at a distance for your welfare and greatness. It was Our wish to be in some manner present with you in your festivities. Hence We cheerfully sent one who should represent Our person. Not without good reason did We take part in your celebration. For when America was, as yet, but a new-born babe, uttering in its cradle its first feeble cries, the Church took it to her bosom and motherly embrace. Columbus, as We have elsewhere expressly shown,[2] sought, as the primary fruit of his voyages and labors, to open a pathway for the Christian faith into new lands and new seas. Keeping this thought constantly in view, his first solicitude, wherever he disembarked,

---

1. [Pope Leo XIII is referring to a whole string of encyclicals; he mentions them later by name.]
2. [In the encyclical *Quarto Abeunte Saeculo* of July 16, 1892, to the bishops of Spain, Italy, and the countries of North and South America.]

was to plant upon the shore the sacred emblem of the Cross. Wherefore, like as the Ark of Noah, surmounting the overflowing waters, bore the seed of Israel together with the remnants of the human race, even thus did the barks launched by Columbus upon the ocean carry into regions beyond the seas as well the seeds of mighty States as the principles of the Catholic religion.

3. This is not the place to give a detailed account of what thereupon ensued. Very rapidly did the light of the Gospel shine upon the savage tribes discovered by the Ligurian. For it is sufficiently well known how many of the children of Francis, as well as of Dominic and of Loyola, were accustomed during the two following centuries to voyage thither for this purpose; how they cared for the colonies brought over from Europe; but primarily and chiefly how they converted the natives from superstition to Christianity, sealing their labors in many instances with the testimony of their blood. The names newly given to so many of your towns and rivers and mountains and lakes teach and clearly witness how deeply your beginnings were marked with the footprints of the Catholic Church.

4. Nor, perchance, did the fact which We now recall take place without some design of divine Providence. Precisely at the epoch when the American colonies, having, with Catholic aid, achieved liberty and independence, coalesced into a constitutional Republic, the ecclesiastical hierarchy was happily established amongst you; and at the very time when the popular suffrage placed the great Washington at the helm of the Republic, the first bishop was set by apostolic authority over the American Church. The well-known friendship and familiar interaction which subsisted between these two men seems to be an evidence that the United States ought to be conjoined in concord and amity with the Catholic Church. And not without cause; for without morality the State cannot endure—a truth which that illustrious citizen of yours, whom We have just mentioned, with a keenness of insight worthy of his genius and statesmanship perceived and proclaimed. But the best and strongest support of morality is religion. She, by her very nature, guards and defends all the principles on which duties are founded, and setting before us the motives most powerful to influence us, commands us to live virtuously and forbids us to transgress. Now what is the Church other than a legitimate society, founded by the will and ordinance of Jesus Christ for the preservation of morality and the defense of religion? For this reason have We repeatedly endeavored, from the summit of the pontifical dignity, to inculcate that the Church, whilst directly and immediately aiming at the salvation of souls and the beatitude which is to be attained in heaven, is yet, even in the order of temporal things, the fountain of blessings so numerous and great that they could not have been greater or more numerous had the original purpose of her institution been the pursuit of happiness during the life which is spent on earth.

5. That your Republic is progressing and developing by giant strides is plain for all to see; and this holds good in religious matters also. For even as your cities, in the course of one century, have made a marvelous increase in wealth and power, so do we behold the Church, from scant and slender beginnings, grown with rapidity to be great and exceedingly flourishing. Now if, on the one hand, the increased riches and resources of your cities are justly attributed to the talents and active industry of the American people, on the other hand, the prosperous condition of Catholicity must be ascribed, first indeed, to the virtue, the ability, and the prudence of the bishops and clergy; but in no slight measure also, to the faith and generosity of the Catholic laity. Thus, while the different classes exerted their best energies, you were enabled to erect unnumbered religious and useful institutions, sacred edifices, schools for the instruction of youth, colleges for the higher branches, homes for the poor, hospitals for the sick, and convents and monasteries. As for what more closely touches spiritual interests, which are based upon the exercise of Christian virtues, many facts have been brought to Our notice, whereby We are animated with hope and filled with joy, namely, that the numbers of the secular and regular clergy are steadily augmenting, that pious sodalities and confraternities are held in esteem, that the Catholic parochial schools, the Sunday-schools for imparting Christian doctrine, and summer schools are in a flourishing condition; moreover, associations for mutual aid, for the relief of the indigent, for the promotion of temperate living, add to all this the many evidences of popular piety.

6. The main factor, no doubt, in bringing things into this happy state were the ordinances and decrees of your synods, especially of those which in more recent times were convened and confirmed by the authority of the Apostolic See. But, moreover (a fact which it gives pleasure to acknowledge), thanks are due to the equity of the laws which obtain in America and to the customs of the well-ordered Republic. For the Church amongst you, unopposed by the Constitution and government of your nation, fettered by no hostile legislation, protected against violence by the common laws and the impartiality of the tribunals, is free to live and act without hindrance. Yet, though all this is true, it would be very erroneous to draw the conclusion that in America is to be sought the type of the most desirable status of the Church, or that it would be universally lawful or expedient for State and Church to be, as in America, dissevered and divorced. The fact that Catholicity with you is in good condition, nay, is even enjoying a prosperous growth, is by all means to be attributed to the fecundity with which God has endowed His Church, in virtue of which, unless men or circumstances interfere, she spontaneously expands and propagates herself; but she would bring forth more abundant fruits if, in addition to liberty, she enjoyed the favor of the laws and the patronage of the public authority.

7. For Our part We have left nothing undone, as far as circumstances permitted, to preserve and more solidly establish amongst you the Catholic religion. With this intent, We have, as you are well aware, turned Our attention to two special objects: first, the advancement of learning; second, a perfecting of methods in the management of Church affairs. There already, indeed, existed several distinguished universities. We, however, thought it advisable that there should be one founded by authority of the Apostolic See and endowed by Us with all suitable powers, in which Catholic professors might instruct those devoted to the pursuit of learning. The design was to begin with philosophy and theology, adding, as means and circumstances would allow, the remaining branches, those particularly which the present age has introduced or perfected. An education cannot be deemed complete which takes no notice of modern sciences. It is obvious that in the existing keen competition of talents, and the widespread and, in itself, noble and praiseworthy passion for knowledge, Catholics ought to be not followers but leaders. It is necessary, therefore, that they should cultivate every refinement of learning, and zealously train their minds to the discovery of truth and the investigation, so far as it is possible, of the entire domain of nature. This in every age has been the desire of the Church; upon the enlargement of the boundaries of the sciences has she been wont to bestow all possible labor and energy. By a letter, therefore, dated the seventh day of March, in the year of Our Lord 1889, directed to you, venerable brethren, We established at Washington, your capital city, esteemed by a majority of you a very proper seat for the higher studies, a university for the instruction of young men desirous of pursuing advanced courses.[3] In announcing this matter to Our venerable brethren, the cardinals of the Holy Roman Church, in consistory, We expressed the wish that it should be regarded as the fixed law of the university to unite erudition and learning with soundness of faith and to imbue its students not less with religion than with scientific culture. […]

11. […] By this action,[4] as We have elsewhere intimated, We have wished, first of all, to certify that, in Our judgment and affection, America occupies the same place and rights as other States, be they ever so mighty and imperial. In addition to this We had in mind to draw more closely the bonds of duty and friendship which connect you and so many thousands of Catholics with the Apostolic See. In fact, the mass of the Catholics understood how salutary Our action was destined to be; they saw, moreover, that it accorded with the usage and policy of the Apostolic See. For it has been, from earliest antiquity, the

---

3. [Namely, The Catholic University of America in Washington, D.C., whose principal administrative building, McMahon Hall, contains in the foyer a magnificent statue of Leo XIII.]

4. [The pope is now speaking about his establishment of an Apostolic Legation to the United States.]

custom of the Roman Pontiffs in the exercise of the divinely bestowed gift of the primacy in the administration of the Church of Christ to send forth legates to Christian nations and peoples. And they did this, not by an adventitious but an inherent right. For "the Roman Pontiff, upon whom Christ has conferred ordinary and immediate jurisdiction, as well over all and singular churches, as over all and singular pastors and faithful,"[5] since he cannot personally visit the different regions and thus exercise the pastoral office over the flock entrusted to him, finds it necessary from time to time, in the discharge of the ministry imposed on him, to despatch legates into different parts of the world, according as the need arises; who, supplying his place, "may correct errors, make the rough ways plain, and administer to the people confided to their care increased means of salvation."[6]

[...] 13. Another consideration claims our earnest attention. All intelligent men are agreed, and We Ourselves have with pleasure intimated it above, that America seems destined for greater things. Now, it is Our wish that the Catholic Church should not only share in, but help to bring about, this prospective greatness. We deem it right and proper that she should, by availing herself of the opportunities daily presented to her, keep equal step with the Republic in the march of improvement, at the same time striving to the utmost, by her virtue and her institutions, to aid in the rapid growth of the States. Now, she will attain both these objects the more easily and abundantly, in proportion to the degree in which the future shall find her constitution perfected. But what is the meaning of the legation of which we are speaking, or what is its ultimate aim except to bring it about that the constitution of the Church shall be strengthened, her discipline better fortified? Wherefore, We ardently desire that this truth should sink day by day more deeply into the minds of Catholics—namely, that they can in no better way safeguard their own individual interests and the common good than by yielding a hearty submission and obedience to the Church. Your faithful people, however, are scarcely in need of exhortation on this point; for they are accustomed to adhere to the institutions of Catholicity with willing souls and a constancy worthy of all praise.

14. To one matter of the first importance and fraught with the greatest blessings it is a pleasure at this place to refer, on account of the holy firmness in principle and practice respecting it which, as a rule, rightly prevails amongst you; We mean the Christian dogma of the unity and indissolubility of marriage; which supplies the firmest bond of safety not merely to the family but to society at large. Not a few of your citizens, even of those who dissent from us in other doctrines, terrified

---

5. Con. Vat., Sess. iv., c. 3.

6. Cap. *Un. Extrav. Comm. De Consuet.*, 1. 1.

by the licentiousness of divorce, admire and approve in this regard the Catholic teaching and the Catholic customs. They are led to this judgment not less by love of country than by the wisdom of the doctrine. For difficult it is to imagine a more deadly pest to the community than the wish to declare dissoluble a bond which the law of God has made perpetual and inseverable. Divorce "is the fruitful cause of mutable marriage contracts; it diminishes mutual affection; it supplies a pernicious stimulus to unfaithfulness; it is injurious to the care and education of children; it gives occasion to the breaking up of domestic society; it scatters the seeds of discord among families; it lessens and degrades the dignity of women, who incur the danger of being abandoned once they have subserved the lust of their husbands. And since nothing tends so effectually as the corruption of morals to ruin families and undermine the strength of kingdoms, it may easily be perceived that divorce is especially hostile to the prosperity of families and States."[7]

15. As regards civil affairs, experience has shown how important it is that the citizens should be upright and virtuous. In a free State, unless justice be generally cultivated, unless the people be repeatedly and diligently urged to observe the precepts and laws of the Gospel, liberty itself may be pernicious. Let those of the clergy, therefore, who are occupied with the instruction of the multitude, treat plainly this topic of the duties of citizens, so that all may understand and feel the necessity, in political life, of conscientiousness, self-restraint, and integrity; for that cannot be lawful in public which is unlawful in private affairs. On this whole subject there are to be found, as you know, in the encyclical letters written by Us from time to time in the course of Our pontificate, many things which Catholics should attend to and observe. In these writings and expositions We have treated of human liberty, of the chief Christian duties, of civil government, and of the Christian constitution of States,[8] drawing Our principles as well from the teaching of the Gospels as from reason. They, then, who wish to be good citizens and discharge their duties faithfully may readily learn from Our letters the ideal of an upright life. In like manner, let the priests be persistent in keeping before the minds of the people the enactments of the Third Council of Baltimore, particularly those which inculcate the virtue of temperance, the frequent use of the sacraments, and the observance of the just laws and institutions of the Republic.

17. [...] The scenes of violence and riot which you witnessed last year in your own country sufficiently admonish you that America too is threatened with the audacity and ferocity of the enemies of public order. The state of the times, therefore, bids Catholics to labor for the tranquility of the commonwealth, and

---

7. Pope Leo XIII, *Arcanum*.

8. [Viz., *Libertas Praestantissimum, Sapientiae Christianae, Diuturnum Illud, Immortale Dei*.]

for this purpose to obey the laws, abhor violence, and seek no more than equity or justice permits.

18. Towards these objects much may be contributed by those who have devoted themselves to writing, and in particular by those who are engaged on the daily press. We are aware that already there labor in this field many men of skill and experience, whose diligence demands words of praise rather than of encouragement. Nevertheless, since the thirst for reading and knowledge is so vehement and widespread amongst you, and since, according to circumstances, it can be productive either of good or evil, every effort should be made to increase the number of intelligent and well-disposed writers who take religion for their guide and virtue for their constant companion. And this seems all the more necessary in America, on account of the familiar contact and intimacy between Catholics and those who are estranged from the Catholic name, a condition of things which certainly exacts from our people great circumspection and more than ordinary firmness. It is necessary to instruct, admonish, strengthen and urge them on to the pursuit of virtue and to the faithful observance, amid so many occasions of stumbling, of their duties towards the Church. It is, of course, the proper function of the clergy to devote their care and energies to this great work; but the age and the country require that journalists should be equally zealous in this same cause and labor in it to the full extent of their powers. Let them, however, seriously reflect that their writings, if not positively prejudicial to religion, will surely be of slight service to it unless in concord of minds they all seek the same end. They who desire to be of real service to the Church, and with their pens heartily to defend the Catholic cause, should carry on the conflict with perfect unanimity, and, as it were, with serried ranks, for they rather inflict than repel war if they waste their strength by discord. In like manner their work, instead of being profitable and fruitful, becomes injurious and disastrous whenever they presume to call before their tribunal the decisions and acts of bishops, and, casting off due reverence, cavil and find fault; not perceiving how great a disturbance of order, how many evils are thereby produced. Let them, then, be mindful of their duty, and not overstep the proper limits of moderation. The bishops, placed in the lofty position of authority, are to be obeyed, and suitable honor befitting the magnitude and sanctity of their office should be paid them. Now, this reverence, "which it is lawful to no one to neglect," should of necessity be eminently conspicuous and exemplary in Catholic journalists. For journals, naturally circulating far and wide, come daily into the hands of everybody, and exert no small influence upon the opinions and morals of the multitude.[9] [...]

---

9.   Cf. Ep. Cognita Nobis ad Archiepp. et Epp. Provinciarum, Taurinen, Mediolanen, et Vercellen, 25 Jan. 1882.

20. Our thoughts now turn to those who dissent from us in matters of Christian faith; and who shall deny that, with not a few of them, dissent is a matter rather of inheritance than of will? How solicitous We are of their salvation, with what ardor of soul We wish that they should be at length restored to the embrace of the Church, the common mother of all, Our apostolic epistle *Praeclara Gratulationis* has in very recent times declared. Nor are we destitute of all hope; for He is present and hath a care whom all things obey and who laid down His life that He might "gather in one the children of God who were dispersed."[10]

21. Surely we ought not to desert them nor leave them to their fancies; but with mildness and charity draw them to us, using every means of persuasion to induce them to examine closely every part of the Catholic doctrine, and to free themselves from preconceived notions. In this matter, if the first place belongs to the bishops and clergy, the second belongs to the laity, who have it in their power to aid the apostolic efforts of the clergy by the probity of their morals and the integrity of their lives. Great is the force of example, particularly with those who are earnestly seeking the truth, and who, from a certain inborn virtuous disposition, are striving to live an honorable and upright life, to which class very many of your fellow-citizens belong. If the spectacle of Christian virtues exerted the powerful influence over the heathens blinded, as they were, by inveterate superstition, which the records of history attest, shall we think it powerless to eradicate error in the case of those who have been initiated into the Christian religion?

22. Finally, We cannot pass over in silence those whose long-continued unhappy lot implores and demands succor from men of apostolic zeal; We refer to the Indians and the negroes who are to be found within the confines of America, the greatest portion of whom have not yet dispelled the darkness of superstition. How wide a field for cultivation! How great a multitude of human beings to be made partakers of the blessing derived through Jesus Christ!

23. Meanwhile, as a presage of heavenly graces and a testimony of Our benevolence, We most lovingly in the Lord impart to you, venerable brethren, and to your clergy and people, Our apostolic benediction.

Given at Rome, at St. Peter's, on the feast of the Epiphany, the sixth day of January, 1895, in the seventeenth year of Our pontificate.

✠ Leo XIII

---

10. John 11:52.

TESTEM BENEVOLENTIAE

Concerning "Americanism"

Encyclical Letter of Pope Leo XIII, promulgated January 22, 1899

To Our beloved son, James Cardinal Gibbons, Cardinal of Saint Mary beyond the Tiber, Archbishop of Baltimore: beloved son, health and apostolic blessing.

We send to you by this letter a renewed expression of that good will which we have not failed during the course of our pontificate to manifest frequently to you and to your colleagues in the episcopate and to the whole American people, availing ourselves of every opportunity offered us by the progress of your Church or whatever you have done for safeguarding and promoting Catholic interests. Moreover, we have often considered and admired the noble gifts of your nation which enable the American people to be alive to every good work which promotes the good of humanity and the splendor of civilization. Although this letter is not intended, as preceding ones, to repeat the words of praise so often spoken, but rather to call attention to some things to be avoided and corrected; still because it is conceived in that same spirit of apostolic charity which has inspired all our letters, we shall expect that you will take it as another proof of our love; the more so because it is intended to suppress certain contentions which have arisen lately among you to the detriment of the peace of many souls.

Adaptation to the "Spirit of the Age"

2. It is known to you, beloved son, that the biography of Isaac Thomas Hecker,[1] especially through the action of those who undertook to translate or

---

1. [Father Hecker (1819–1888) was an American Redemptorist who, with Pope Pius IX's consent, founded the Missionary Priests of St. Paul the Apostle, commonly known as the Paulists, in New York City in 1858. He was active throughout the United States as a preacher and lecturer who aimed at the conversion of Protestants to Catholicism. Fairly or not, he was seen, especially in Europe, as a model not only of courage and piety but also of an assertive self-initiative together with a

interpret it in a foreign language, has excited not a little controversy, on account of certain opinions brought forward concerning the way of leading Christian life. We, therefore, on account of our apostolic office, having to guard the integrity of the faith and the security of the faithful, are desirous of writing to you more at length concerning this whole matter.

3. The underlying principle of these new opinions is that, in order the more easily to attract those who differ from her, the Church should shape her teachings more in accord with the spirit of the age and relax some of her ancient severity and make some concessions to new opinions. Many think that these concessions should be made not only in regard to ways of living, but even in regard to doctrines which belong to the deposit of the faith. They contend that it would be opportune, in order to gain those who differ from us, to omit certain points of her teaching which are of lesser importance, and to tone down the meaning which the Church has always attached to them. It does not need many words, beloved son, to prove the falsity of these ideas if the nature and origin of the doctrine which the Church proposes are recalled to mind. The [First] Vatican Council says concerning this point: "For the doctrine of faith which God has revealed has not been proposed, like a philosophical invention to be perfected by human ingenuity, but has been delivered as a divine deposit to the Spouse of Christ to be faithfully kept and infallibly declared. Hence that meaning of the sacred dogmas is perpetually to be retained which our Holy Mother, the Church, has once declared, nor is that meaning ever to be departed from under the pretense or pretext of a deeper comprehension of them."[2]

4. We cannot consider as altogether blameless the silence which purposely leads to the omission or neglect of some of the principles of Christian doctrine, for all the principles come from the same Author and Master, "the Only-begotten Son, Who is in the bosom of the Father."[3] They are adapted to all times and all nations, as is clearly seen from the words of our Lord to His apostles: "Going, therefore, teach all nations; teaching them to observe all things whatsoever I

love of modern times and modern liberties. This perspective enabled French Catholic republicanists to adopt Hecker as a kind of patron of their cause, a cause that met with severe opposition from more traditional Catholics and eventually elicited from Leo XIII the present letter, in which the Pope endeavors to weed out such heresies as may have sought refuge under Fr. Hecker's umbrella. While the extent to which the chastised views belonged to Fr. Hecker or to his American disciples remains a debated question, any reader well-versed in the contemporary situation of the Catholic Church will be able to perceive the profound insightfulness of Leo XIII's critical analysis, which has become, if anything, still more relevant in the period after the Second Vatican Council.]

2.   *Constitutio de Fide Catholica*, Chapter iv.

3.   John 1:18.

have commanded you, and behold, I am with you all days, even to the end of the world."[4] Concerning this point the Vatican Council says: "All those things are to be believed with divine and catholic faith which are contained in the Word of God, written or handed down, and which the Church, either by a solemn judgment or by her ordinary and universal Magisterium, proposes for belief as having been divinely revealed."[5] Let it be far from anyone's mind to suppress for any reason any doctrine that has been handed down. Such a policy would tend rather to separate Catholics from the Church than to bring in those who differ. There is nothing closer to our heart than to have those who are separated from the fold of Christ return to it, but in no other way than the way pointed out by Christ.

5. The rule of life laid down for Catholics is not of such a nature that it cannot accommodate itself to the exigencies of various times and places. The Church has, guided by her divine Master, a kind and merciful spirit, for which reason from the very beginning she has been what St. Paul said of himself: "I became all things to all men that I might save all."[6] History proves clearly that the Apostolic See, to which has been entrusted the mission not only of teaching but of governing the whole Church, has continued "in one and the same doctrine, one and the same sense, and one and the same judgment."[7] In regard to ways of living, however, she has been accustomed to so yield that, the divine principle of morals being kept intact, she has never neglected to accommodate herself to the character and genius of the nations which she embraces. Who can doubt that she will act in this same spirit again if the salvation of souls requires it? In this matter the Church must be the judge, not private men who are often deceived by the appearance of right. In this, all who wish to escape the blame of Our predecessor, Pius VI, must concur. He condemned as injurious to the Church and the Spirit of God who guides her the doctrine contained in Proposition 78 of the Synod of Pistoia, "that the discipline made and approved by the Church should be submitted to examination, as if the Church could frame a code of laws useless or heavier than human liberty can bear."[8]

---

4.   Matt. 28:19.

5.   *Const. de fide,* Chapter iii.

6.   1 Cor. 9:22.

7.   *Const. de fide,* Chapter iv.

8.   [The Synod of Pistoia was a diocesan synod held in 1786 under Bishop Scipione de' Ricci (1741–1810) and the patronage of Grand-duke Leopold with a view to a reform of the Tuscan Church along Enlightenment lines. Soon after the synod published its decisions, they were condemned by Pope Pius VI in the bull *Auctorem fidei* of August 28, 1794. In May 1805, de' Ricci himself signed an act of submission to the papal decision.]

A Call for Greater "Liberty"

6. But, beloved son, in this present matter of which we are speaking, there is even a greater danger and a more manifest opposition to Catholic doctrine and discipline in that opinion of the lovers of novelty, according to which they hold such liberty should be allowed in the Church, that her supervision and watchfulness being in some sense lessened, allowance be granted the faithful, each one to follow out more freely the leading of his own mind and the trend of his own proper activity. They are of opinion that such liberty has its counterpart in the newly given civil freedom which is now the right and the foundation of almost every secular State. In the encyclical letters concerning the constitution of States, addressed by us to the bishops of the whole Church,[9] we discussed this point at length; and there set forth the difference existing between the Church, which is a divine society, and all other social human organizations which depend simply on the free will and choice of men.

7. It is well, then, to direct attention particularly to the opinion which serves as the argument in behalf of this greater liberty sought for and recommended to Catholics. It is alleged that now that the Vatican decree on the infallible teaching authority of the Roman Pontiff has been proclaimed, nothing further on that score can give any worry; and, accordingly, since that has been safeguarded and put beyond question, a wider and freer field both for thought and action lies open to each one. But such reasoning is evidently faulty, since, if we are to come to any conclusion from the infallible teaching authority of the Church, it should rather be that no one should wish to depart from it, and moreover that the minds of all being leavened and directed thereby, greater security from private error would be enjoyed by all. And further, those who avail themselves of such a way of reasoning seem to depart seriously from the over-ruling wisdom of the Most High—which wisdom, since it was pleased to set forth by most solemn decision the authority and supreme teaching rights of this Apostolic See, willed that decision precisely in order to safeguard the minds of the Church's children from the dangers of these present times.

8. These dangers, viz., the confounding of license with liberty, the passion for discussing and pouring contempt upon any possible subject, the assumed right to hold whatever opinions one pleases upon any subject and to set them forth in print to the world, have so wrapped minds in darkness that there is now a greater need of the Church's teaching office than ever before, lest people become unmindful both of conscience and of duty. We, indeed, have no thought of

---

9.   [*Diuturnum Illud, Immortale Dei, Libertas Praestantissimum,* etc.]

rejecting everything that modern industry and study has produced; so far from it that we welcome to the patrimony of truth and to an ever-widening scope of public well-being whatsoever helps toward the progress of learning and virtue. Yet all this, to be of any solid benefit, nay, to have a real existence and growth, can only be on the condition of recognizing the wisdom and authority of the Church.

A New "Age of the Spirit"

9. Coming now to speak of the conclusions which have been deduced from the above opinions—and we readily believe there was no thought of wrong or guile among those who deduced them—yet the things themselves certainly merit some degree of suspicion. First, all external guidance is set aside for those souls who are striving after Christian perfection as being superfluous or indeed, not useful in any sense—the contention being that the Holy Spirit pours richer and more abundant graces than formerly upon the souls of the faithful, so that without human intervention He teaches and guides them by some hidden instinct of His own. Yet it is the sign of no small over-confidence to desire to measure and determine the mode of the divine communication to mankind, since it wholly depends upon His own good pleasure, and He is a most generous dispenser of his own gifts. "The Spirit breatheth whereso He listeth."[10] "And to each one of us grace is given according to the measure of the giving of Christ."[11] And shall anyone who recalls the history of the apostles, the faith of the nascent Church, the trials and deaths of the martyrs—and, above all, those olden times [of the Middle Ages], so fruitful in saints—dare to measure our age with these, or affirm that they received less of the divine outpouring from the Spirit of Holiness? Not to dwell upon this point, there is no one who calls in question the truth that the Holy Spirit does work by a secret descent into the souls of the just and that He stirs them alike by warnings and impulses, since unless this were the case all outward defense and authority would be unavailing. "For if any persuades himself that he can give assent to saving, that is, to gospel truth when proclaimed, without any illumination of the Holy Spirit, who gives unto all sweetness both to assent and to hold, such a one is deceived by a heretical spirit."[12]

10. Moreover, as experience shows, these monitions and impulses of the Holy Spirit are for the most part felt through the medium of the aid and light of an external teaching authority. To quote St. Augustine: "He (the Holy Spirit)

10. John 3:8.
11. Eph. 4:7.
12. Second Council of Orange, canon 7.

co-operates to the fruit gathered from the good trees, since He externally waters and cultivates them by the outward ministry of men, and yet of Himself bestows the inward increase."[13] This, indeed, belongs to the ordinary law of God's loving providence that as He has decreed that men for the most part shall be saved by the ministry also of men, so has He wished that those whom He calls to the higher planes of holiness should be led thereto by men; hence St. Chrysostom declares we are taught of God through the instrumentality of men.[14] Of this a striking example is given us in the very first days of the Church. For though Saul, intent upon blood and slaughter, had heard the voice of our Lord Himself and had asked, "What dost Thou wish me to do?"—yet he was bidden to enter Damascus and search for Ananias. "Enter the city and it shall be there told to thee what thou must do."[15]

11. Nor can we leave out of consideration the truth that those who are striving after perfection, since by that fact they walk in no beaten or well-known path, are the most liable to stray, and hence have greater need than others of a teacher and guide. Such guidance has ever obtained in the Church; it has been the universal teaching of those who throughout the ages have been eminent for wisdom and sanctity—and hence to reject it would be to commit oneself to a belief at once rash and dangerous.

Exaggeration of "Natural" and "Active" Virtues

12. A thorough consideration of this point, in the supposition that no exterior guide is granted such souls, will make us see the difficulty of locating or determining the direction and application of that more abundant influx of the Holy Spirit so greatly extolled by innovators. To practice virtue there is absolute need of the assistance of the Holy Spirit, yet we find those who are fond of novelty giving an unwarranted importance to the natural virtues, as though they better responded to the customs and necessities of the times and that having these as his outfit man becomes more ready to act and more strenuous in action. It is not easy to understand how persons possessed of Christian wisdom can either prefer natural to supernatural virtues or attribute to them a greater efficacy and fruitfulness. Can it be that nature conjoined with grace is weaker than when left to herself? Can it be that those men illustrious for sanctity, whom the Church distinguishes and openly pays homage to, were deficient, came short in the order of nature and its

---

13.   *De Gratia Christi*, chapter xix.

14.   *Homilia I in Inscrib. Altar.*

15.   Cf. Acts 9.

endowments, because they excelled in Christian strength? And although it be allowed at times to wonder at acts worthy of admiration which are the outcome of natural virtue, is there anyone at all endowed simply with an outfit of natural virtue? Is there anyone not tried by mental anxiety, and this in no light degree? Yet ever to master such, as also to preserve in its entirety the law of the natural order, requires an assistance from on high. These single notable acts to which we have alluded will frequently upon a closer investigation be found to exhibit the appearance rather than the reality of virtue. Grant that it is virtue, unless we would "run in vain"[16] and be unmindful of that eternal bliss which a good God in His mercy has destined for us, of what avail are natural virtues unless seconded by the gift of divine grace? Hence St. Augustine well says: "Wonderful is the strength, and swift the course, but outside the true path." For as the nature of man, owing to the primal fault, is inclined to evil and dishonor, yet by the help of grace is raised up, is borne along with a new greatness and strength, so, too, virtue, which is not the product of nature alone, but of grace also, is made fruitful unto everlasting life and takes on a more strong and abiding character.

13. This overesteem of natural virtue finds a method of expression in assuming to divide all virtues into [the categories of] active and passive, and it is alleged that whereas passive virtues found better place in past times, our age is to be characterized by the active. That such a division and distinction cannot be maintained is patent—for there is not, nor can there be, merely passive virtue. "Virtue," says St. Thomas Aquinas, "designates the perfection of some faculty, but the end of such a faculty is an act, and an act of virtue is naught else than the good use of free will," acting, that is to say, under the grace of God if the act be one of supernatural virtue. He alone could wish that some Christian virtues be adapted to certain times and different ones for other times who is unmindful of the Apostle's words: "That those whom He foreknew, He predestined to be made conformable to the image of His Son."[17] Christ is the teacher and the exemplar of all sanctity, and to His standard must all those conform who wish for eternal life. Nor does Christ know any change as the ages pass, "for He is yesterday and today and the same forever."[18] To the men of all ages was the precept given: "Learn of Me, because I am meek and humble of heart."[19] To every age has He been made manifest to us as obedient even unto death; in every age the Apostle's dictum has its force: "Those who are Christ's have crucified their flesh with its vices and

16. Cf. Gal. 2:2; Phil. 2:16.
17. Rom. 8:29.
18. Heb. 13:8.
19. Matt. 11:29.

concupiscences."[20] Would to God that more nowadays practiced these virtues in the degree of the saints of past times, who in humility, obedience and self-restraint were powerful "in word and in deed"[21]—to the great advantage not only of religion, but of the State and the public welfare.

14. From this disregard of the angelical virtues, erroneously styled passive, the step was a short one to a contempt of the religious life which has in some degree taken hold of minds. That such an evaluation is generally made by the upholders of new views, we infer from certain statements concerning the vows which religious orders take. They say vows are alien to the spirit of our times, in that they limit the bounds of human liberty; that they are more suitable to weak than to strong minds; that so far from making for human perfection and the good of human organization, they are hurtful to both. But that this opinion is as false as possible from the practice and the doctrine of the Church is clear, since she has always given the very highest approval to the religious method of life; nor without good cause, for those who under the divine call have freely embraced that state of life did not content themselves with the observance of precepts, but, going forward to the evangelical counsels, showed themselves ready and valiant soldiers of Christ. Shall we judge this to be a characteristic of weak minds, or shall we say that it is useless or hurtful to a more perfect state of life?

15. Those who so bind themselves by the vows of religion, far from having suffered a loss of liberty, enjoy that fuller and freer kind—that liberty, namely, by which Christ hath made us free. And this further view of theirs, namely, that the religious life is either entirely useless or of little service to the Church, besides being injurious to the religious orders, cannot be the opinion of anyone who has read the annals of the Church. Did not your country, the United States, derive the beginnings both of faith and of culture from the children of these religious families? to one of whom but very lately, a thing greatly to your praise, you have decreed that a statue be publicly erected. And even at the present time wherever the religious families are found, how speedy and yet how fruitful a harvest of good works do they not bring forth! How very many leave home and seek strange lands to impart the truth of the gospel and to widen the bounds of civilization; and this they do with the greatest cheerfulness amid manifold dangers! Out of their number not less, indeed, than from the rest of the clergy, the Christian world finds the preachers of God's word, the directors of conscience, the teachers of youth, and the Church itself the examples of all sanctity. Nor should any difference of praise be made between those who follow the active state of life and

---

20. Gal. 5:24.

21. Cf. Acts 7:22; Rom. 15:18.

those others who, charmed with solitude, give themselves to prayer and bodily mortification. And how much, indeed, of good report these have merited, and do merit, is known surely to all who do not forget that the "continual prayer of the just man"[22] avails to placate and to bring down the blessings of heaven when to such prayers bodily mortification is added.

16. But if there be those who prefer to form one body without the obligation of the vows, let them pursue such a course. It is not new in the Church, nor in any wise censurable. Let them be careful, however, not to set forth such a state [as being] above that of religious orders. But rather, since mankind are more disposed at the present time to indulge themselves in pleasures, let those be held in still greater esteem "who, having left all things, have followed Christ."[23]

Methods for Bringing Back Non-Catholics

17. Finally, not to delay too long, it is stated that the way and method hitherto in use among Catholics for bringing back those who have fallen away from the Church should be left aside and another one chosen, in which matter it will suffice to note that it is not the part of prudence to neglect that which antiquity in its long experience has approved and which is also taught by apostolic authority. The Scriptures teach us that it is the duty of all to be solicitous for the salvation of one's neighbor, according to the power and position of each. The faithful do this by religiously discharging the duties of their state of life, by the uprightness of their conduct, by their works of Christian charity and by earnest and continuous prayer to God. On the other hand, those who belong to the clergy should do this by an enlightened fulfillment of their preaching ministry, by the pomp and splendor of ceremonies, and especially by setting forth that sound form of doctrine which Saint Paul inculcated upon Titus and Timothy. But if, among the different ways of preaching the word of God, that one sometimes seems to be preferable which is directed to non-Catholics, not in churches but in some suitable place, in such wise that controversy is not sought but rather friendly conference, such a method is certainly without fault. But let those who undertake such ministry be set apart by the authority of the bishops and let them be men whose science and virtue have been previously ascertained. For we think that there are many in your country who are separated from Catholic truth more by ignorance than by ill-will, who might perchance more easily be drawn to the one fold of Christ if this truth be set forth to them in a friendly and familiar way.

---

22. James 5:16.

23. Cf. Matt. 19:27; Mark 10:28; Luke 18:28.

Concluding Remarks

18. From the foregoing it is manifest, beloved son, that we are not able to give approval to those views which, in their collective sense, are called by some "Americanism." Now, if by this name are to be understood certain endowments of mind which belong to the American people, just as other characteristics belong to various other nations, and if, moreover, by it is designated your political condition and the laws and customs by which you are governed, there is no reason to take exception to the name. But if this is to be so understood that the doctrines which have been adverted to above are not only indicated, but exalted, there can be no manner of doubt that our venerable brethren, the bishops of America, would be the first to repudiate and condemn it as being most injurious to themselves and to their country. For it would give rise to the suspicion that there are among you some who conceive and would have the Church in America to be different from what it is in the rest of the world.

19. But the true Church is one, as by unity of doctrine, so by unity of government, and she is catholic also. Since God has placed the center and foundation of unity in the chair of Blessed Peter, she is rightly called the Roman Church, for "where Peter is, there is the Church." Wherefore, if anybody wishes to be considered a real Catholic, he ought to be able to say from his heart the selfsame words which Jerome addressed to Pope Damasus: "I, acknowledging no other leader than Christ, am bound in fellowship with Your Holiness; that is, with the chair of Peter. I know that the Church was built upon him as its rock, and that whosoever gathereth not with you, scattereth."

20. We have thought it fitting, beloved son, in view of your high office, that this letter should be addressed specially to you. It will also be our care to see that copies are sent to the bishops of the United States, testifying again that love by which we embrace your whole country, a country which in past times has done so much for the cause of religion, and which will by the divine assistance continue to do still greater things. To you, and to all the faithful of America, we grant most lovingly, as a pledge of divine assistance, our apostolic benediction.

Given at Rome, from St. Peter's, the twenty-second day of January, 1899, and the twenty-first of our pontificate.

✠ Leo XIII

QUAS PRIMAS

On the Kingship of Christ

Encyclical Letter of Pope Pius XI,
promulgated December 11, 1925

To Our Venerable Brethren the Patriarchs, Primates, Archbishops, Bishops, and other Ordinaries in Peace and Communion with the Apostolic See. Venerable Brethren, Greetings and the Apostolic Benediction.

In the first encyclical letter which We addressed at the beginning of Our pontificate to the bishops of the universal Church [*Ubi Arcano Dei Consilio*], We referred to the chief causes of the difficulties under which mankind was laboring. And We remember saying that these manifold evils in the world were due to the fact that the majority of men had thrust Jesus Christ and his holy law out of their lives; that these had no place either in private affairs or in politics: and we said further, that as long as individuals and states refused to submit to the rule of our Savior, there would be no really hopeful prospect of a lasting peace among nations. Men must look for the peace of Christ in the Kingdom of Christ; and that We promised to do as far as lay in Our power. In the Kingdom *of Christ*, that is; it seemed to Us that peace could not be more effectually restored nor fixed upon a firmer basis than through the restoration of the Empire of Our Lord. We were led in the meantime to indulge the hope of a brighter future at the sight of a more widespread and keener interest evinced in Christ and his Church, the one Source of Salvation, a sign that men who had formerly spurned the rule of our Redeemer and had exiled themselves from his kingdom were preparing, and even hastening, to return to the duty of obedience.

2. The many notable and memorable events which have occurred during this Holy Year have given great honor and glory to Our Lord and King, the Founder of the Church.

3. At the Missionary Exhibition men have been deeply impressed in seeing the increasing zeal of the Church for the spread of the kingdom of her Spouse to the most far distant regions of the earth. They have seen how many countries have been won to the Catholic name through the unremitting labor and

self-sacrifice of missionaries, and the vastness of the regions which have yet to be subjected to the sweet and saving yoke of our King. All those who in the course of the Holy Year have thronged to this city under the leadership of their Bishops or priests had but one aim—namely, to expiate their sins—and at the tombs of the Apostles and in Our presence to promise loyalty to the rule of Christ.

4. A still further light of glory was shed upon his kingdom, when after due proof of their heroic virtue, We raised to the honors of the altar six confessors and virgins.[1] It was a great joy, a great consolation, that filled Our heart when in the majestic basilica of St. Peter Our decree was acclaimed by an immense multitude with the hymn of thanksgiving, *Tu Rex gloriae Christe*. We saw men and nations cut off from God, stirring up strife and discord and hurrying along the road to ruin and death, while the Church of God carries on her work of providing food for the spiritual life of men, nurturing and fostering generation after generation of men and women dedicated to Christ, faithful and subject to him in his earthly kingdom, called by him to eternal bliss in the kingdom of heaven.

5. Moreover, since this jubilee Year marks the sixteenth centenary of the Council of Nicaea, We commanded that event to be celebrated, and We have done so in the Vatican basilica. There is a special reason for this in that the Nicene Synod defined and proposed for Catholic belief the dogma of the consubstantiality of the Only-begotten with the Father, and added to the Creed the words "of whose kingdom there shall be no end," thereby affirming the kingly dignity of Christ.

6. Since this Holy Year therefore has provided more than one opportunity to enhance the glory of the kingdom of Christ, we deem it in keeping with our apostolic office to accede to the desire of many of the cardinals, bishops, and faithful, made known to Us both individually and collectively, by closing this Holy Year with the insertion into the sacred liturgy of a special feast of the Kingship of Our Lord Jesus Christ. This matter is so dear to Our heart, venerable brethren, that I would wish to address to you a few words concerning it. It will be for you later to explain in a manner suited to the understanding of the faithful what We are about to say concerning the Kingship of Christ, so that the annual feast which We shall decree may be attended with much fruit and produce beneficial results in the future.

7. It has long been a common custom to give to Christ the metaphorical title of "King," because of the high degree of perfection whereby he excels all creatures. So he is said to reign "in the hearts of men," both by reason of the keenness of his intellect and the extent of his knowledge, and also because he is very truth, and it

---

1. [Viz., St. John Mary Vianney, St. John Eudes, St. Madeleine Sophie Barat, St. Marie Madeline Postel, St. Peter Canisius, and St. Thérèse of Lisieux.]

is from him that truth must be obediently received by all mankind. He reigns, too, in the wills of men, for in him the human will was perfectly and entirely obedient to the Holy Will of God, and further by his grace and inspiration he so subjects our free-will as to incite us to the most noble endeavors. He is King of hearts, too, by reason of his "charity which exceedeth all knowledge."[2] And his mercy and kindness which draw all men to him, for never has it been known, nor will it ever be, that man be loved so much and so universally as Jesus Christ. But if we ponder this matter more deeply, we cannot but see that the title and the power of King belongs to Christ as man in the strict and proper sense too. For it is only as man that he may be said to have received from the Father "power and glory and a kingdom,"[3] since the Word of God, as consubstantial with the Father, has all things in common with him, and therefore has necessarily supreme and absolute dominion over all things created.

8. Do we not read throughout the Scriptures that Christ is the King? He it is that shall come out of Jacob to rule,[4] who has been set by the Father as king over Sion, his holy mount, and shall have the Gentiles for his inheritance, and the utmost parts of the earth for his possession.[5] In the nuptial hymn, where the future King of Israel is hailed as a most rich and powerful monarch, we read: "Thy throne, O God, is for ever and ever; the scepter of thy kingdom is a scepter of righteousness."[6] There are many similar passages, but there is one in which Christ is even more clearly indicated. Here it is foretold that his kingdom will have no limits, and will be enriched with justice and peace: "in his days shall justice spring up, and abundance of peace. ... And he shall rule from sea to sea, and from the river unto the ends of the earth."[7]

9. The testimony of the Prophets is even more abundant. That of Isaiah is well known: "For a child is born to us and a son is given to us, and the government is upon his shoulder, and his name shall be called Wonderful, Counselor, God the mighty, the Father of the world to come, the Prince of Peace. His empire shall be multiplied, and there shall be no end of peace. He shall sit upon the throne of David and upon his kingdom; to establish it and strengthen it with judgment and with justice, from henceforth and for ever."[8] With Isaiah the other Prophets are

---

2. Eph. 3:9.

3. Dan. 7:13–14.

4. Num. 24:19.

5. Ps. 2.

6. Ps. 44.

7. Ps. 71.

8. Isa. 9:6–7.

in agreement. So Jeremiah foretells the "just seed" that shall rise from the house of David—the Son of David that shall reign as king, "and shall be wise, and shall execute judgment and justice in the earth."[9] So, too, Daniel, who announces the kingdom that the God of heaven shall found, "that shall never be destroyed, and shall stand for ever."[10] And again he says: "I beheld, therefore, in the vision of the night, and, lo! one like the son of man came with the clouds of heaven. And he came even to the Ancient of Days: and they presented him before him. And he gave him power and glory and a kingdom: and all peoples, tribes, and tongues shall serve him. His power is an everlasting power that shall not be taken away, and his kingdom shall not be destroyed."[11] The prophecy of Zachary concerning the merciful King "riding upon an ass and upon a colt the foal of an ass" entering Jerusalem as "the just and savior," amid the acclamations of the multitude,[12] was recognized as fulfilled by the holy evangelists themselves.

10. This same doctrine of the Kingship of Christ which we have found in the Old Testament is even more clearly taught and confirmed in the New. The Archangel, announcing to the Virgin that she should bear a Son, says that "the Lord God shall give unto him the throne of David his father, and he shall reign in the house of Jacob for ever; and of his kingdom there shall be no end."[13]

11. Moreover, Christ himself speaks of his own kingly authority: in his last discourse, speaking of the rewards and punishments that will be the eternal lot of the just and the damned[14]; in his reply to the Roman magistrate, who asked him publicly whether he were a king or not[15]; after his resurrection, when giving to his Apostles the mission of teaching and baptizing all nations, he solemnly proclaimed that all power was given him in heaven and on earth.[16] These words can only be taken to indicate the greatness of his power, the infinite extent of his kingdom. What wonder, then, that he whom St. John calls the "prince of the kings of the earth"[17] appears in the Apostle's vision of the future as he who "hath on his garment and on his thigh written 'King of kings and Lord of lords!'"[18] It is

---

9.　Jer. 23:5.

10.　Dan. 2:44.

11.　Dan. 7:13–14.

12.　Zach. 9:9.

13.　Luke 1:32–33.

14.　Matt. 25:31–40.

15.　John 18:37.

16.　Matt. 28:18.

17.　Apoc. 1:5.

18.　Apoc. 19:16.

Christ whom the Father "hath appointed heir of all things"[19]; "for he must reign until at the end of the world he hath put all his enemies under the feet of God and the Father."[20]

12. It was surely right, then, in view of the common teaching of the sacred books, that the Catholic Church, which is the kingdom of Christ on earth, destined to be spread among all men and all nations, should with every token of veneration salute her Author and Founder in her annual liturgy as King and Lord, and as King of Kings. And, in fact, she used these titles, giving expression with wonderful variety of language to one and the same concept, both in ancient psalmody and in the sacramentaries. She uses them daily now in the prayers publicly offered to God, and in offering the Immaculate Victim. The perfect harmony of the Eastern liturgies with our own in this continual praise of Christ the King shows once more the truth of the axiom: *Legem credendi lex statuit supplicandi.* The rule of faith is indicated by the law of our worship.

13. The foundation of this power and dignity of Our Lord is rightly indicated by Cyril of Alexandria. "Christ," he says, "has dominion over all creatures, a dominion not seized by violence nor usurped, but his by essence and by nature."[21] His kingship is founded upon the ineffable hypostatic union. From this it follows not only that Christ is to be adored by angels and men, but that to him as man angels and men are subject, and must recognize his empire; by reason of the hypostatic union Christ has power over all creatures. But a thought that must give us even greater joy and consolation is this, that Christ is our King by acquired, as well as by natural right, for he is our Redeemer. Would that they who forget what they have cost their Savior might recall the words: "You were not redeemed with corruptible things, but with the precious blood of Christ, as of a lamb unspotted and undefiled."[22] We are no longer our own property, for Christ has purchased us "with a great price"[23]; our very bodies are the "members of Christ."[24]

14. Let Us explain briefly the nature and meaning of this lordship of Christ. It consists, We need scarcely say, in a threefold power which is essential to lordship. This is sufficiently clear from the scriptural testimony already adduced concerning the universal dominion of our Redeemer, and moreover it is a dogma

---

19. Heb. 1:2.
20. Cf. 1 Cor. 15:25.
21. *In Luc.* x.
22. 1 Pet. 1:18–19.
23. 1 Cor. 6:20.
24. 1 Cor. 6:15.

of faith that Jesus Christ was given to man, not only as our Redeemer, but also as a law-giver, to whom obedience is due.[25] Not only do the gospels tell us that he made laws, but they present him to us in the act of making them. Those who keep them show their love for their divine Master, and he promises that they shall remain in his love.[26] He claimed judicial power as received from his Father, when the Jews accused him of breaking the Sabbath by the miraculous cure of a sick man. "For neither doth the Father judge any man; but hath given all judgment to the Son."[27] In this power is included the right of rewarding and punishing all men living, for this right is inseparable from that of judging. Executive power, too, belongs to Christ, for all must obey his commands; none may escape them, nor the sanctions he has imposed.

15. This kingdom is spiritual and is concerned with spiritual things. That this is so the above quotations from Scripture amply prove, and Christ by his own action confirms it. On many occasions, when the Jews and even the Apostles wrongly supposed that the Messiah would restore the liberties and the kingdom of Israel, he repelled and denied such a suggestion. When the populace thronged around him in admiration and would have acclaimed him King, he shrank from the honor and sought safety in flight. Before the Roman magistrate he declared that his kingdom was not of this world. The gospels present this kingdom as one which men prepare to enter by penance, and cannot actually enter except by faith and by baptism, which, though an external rite, signifies and produces an interior regeneration. This kingdom is opposed to none other than to that of Satan and to the power of darkness. It demands of its subjects a spirit of detachment from riches and earthly things, and a spirit of gentleness. They must hunger and thirst after justice, and more than this, they must deny themselves and carry the cross.

16. Christ as our Redeemer purchased the Church at the price of his own blood; as priest he offered himself, and continues to offer himself as a victim for our sins. Is it not evident, then, that his kingly dignity partakes in a manner of both these offices?

17. It would be a grave error, on the other hand, to say that Christ has no authority whatever in civil affairs, since, by virtue of the absolute empire over all creatures committed to him by the Father, all things are in his power. Nevertheless, during his life on earth he refrained from the exercise of such authority, and although he himself disdained to possess or to care for earthly goods, he did not,

---

25. Conc. Trid. Sess. VI, can. 21.

26. John 14:15; 15:10.

27. John 5:22.

nor does he today, interfere with those who possess them: *Non eripit mortalia qui regna dat caelestia.*[28]

18. Thus the empire of our Redeemer embraces all men. To use the words of Our immortal predecessor, Pope Leo XIII: "His empire includes not only Catholic nations, not only baptized persons who, though of right belonging to the Church, have been led astray by error, or have been cut off from her by schism, but also all those who are outside the Christian faith; so that truly the whole of mankind is subject to the power of Jesus Christ."[29] Nor is there any difference in this matter between the individual and the family or the State; for all men, whether collectively or individually, are under the dominion of Christ. In him is the salvation of the individual, in him is the salvation of society. "Neither is there salvation in any other, for there is no other name under heaven given to men whereby we must be saved."[30] He is the author of happiness and true prosperity for every man and for every nation. "For a nation is happy when its citizens are happy. What else is a nation but a number of men living in concord?"[31] If, therefore, the rulers of nations wish to preserve their authority, to promote and increase the prosperity of their countries, they will not neglect the public duty of reverence and obedience to the rule of Christ. What We said at the beginning of Our pontificate concerning the decline of public authority, and the lack of respect for the same, is equally true at the present day. "With God and Jesus Christ," we said, "excluded from political life, with authority derived not from God but from man, the very basis of that authority has been taken away, because the chief reason of the distinction between ruler and subject has been eliminated. The result is that human society is tottering to its fall, because it has no longer a secure and solid foundation."[32]

19. When once men recognize, both in private and in public life, that Christ is King, society will at last receive the great blessings of real liberty, well-ordered discipline, peace and harmony. Our Lord's regal office invests the human authority of princes and rulers with a religious significance; it ennobles the citizen's duty of obedience. It is for this reason that St. Paul, while bidding wives revere Christ in their husbands, and slaves respect Christ in their masters, warns them to give obedience to them not as men, but as the vicegerents of Christ; for it is

---

28. Hymn for the Epiphany: "He who bestows a heavenly kingdom does not snatch away an earthly one."

29. *Annum Sacrum,* May 25, 1899.

30. Acts 4:12.

31. S. Augustine, *Ep. ad Macedonium,* c. iii.

32. Encyclical *Ubi Arcano Dei Consilio.*

not meet that men redeemed by Christ should serve their fellow-men. "You are bought with a price; be not made the bond-slaves of men."[33] If princes and magistrates duly elected are filled with the persuasion that they rule, not by their own right, but by the mandate and in the place of the divine King, they will exercise their authority piously and wisely, and they will make laws and administer them, having in view the common good and also the human dignity of their subjects. The result will be a stable peace and tranquility, for there will be no longer any cause of discontent. Men will see in their king or in their rulers men like themselves, perhaps unworthy or open to criticism, but they will not on that account refuse obedience if they see reflected in them the authority of Christ, God and Man. Peace and harmony, too, will result; for with the spread and the universal extent of the kingdom of Christ men will become more and more conscious of the link that binds them together, and thus many conflicts will be either prevented entirely or at least their bitterness will be diminished.

20. If the kingdom of Christ, then, receives, as it should, all nations under its sway, there seems no reason why we should despair of seeing that peace which the King of Peace came to bring on earth—he who came to reconcile all things, who came not to be ministered unto but to minister, who, though Lord of all, gave himself to us as a model of humility, and made humility, joined with the precept of charity, his principal law; who said also: "My yoke is sweet and my burden light." Oh, what happiness would be Ours if all men, individuals, families, and nations, would but let themselves be governed by Christ! "Then at length," to use the words addressed by Our predecessor, Pope Leo XIII, twenty-five years ago to the bishops of the universal Church, "then at length will many evils be cured; then will the law regain its former authority; peace with all its blessings be restored. Men will sheathe their swords and lay down their arms when all freely acknowledge and obey the authority of Christ, and every tongue confesses that the Lord Jesus Christ is in the glory of God the Father."[34]

21. That these blessings may be abundant and lasting in Christian society, it is necessary that the kingship of our Savior should be as widely as possible recognized and understood, and to this end nothing would serve better than the institution of a special feast in honor of the Kingship of Christ. For people are instructed in the truths of faith and brought to appreciate the inner joys of religion far more effectually by the annual celebration of our sacred mysteries than by any official pronouncement of the teaching of the Church. Such pronouncements usually reach only a few and the more learned among the faithful; feasts

---

33. 1 Cor. 7:23.

34. *Annum Sacrum*, May 25, 1899.

reach them all; the former speak but once, the latter speak every year—in fact, forever. The Church's teaching affects the mind primarily; her feasts affect both mind and heart, and have a salutary effect upon the whole of man's nature. Man is composed of body and soul, and he needs these external festivities so that the sacred rites, in all their beauty and variety, may stimulate him to drink more deeply of the fountain of God's teaching, that he may make it a part of himself, and use it with profit for his spiritual life.

22. History, in fact, tells us that in the course of ages these festivals have been instituted one after another according as the needs or the advantage of the people of Christ seemed to demand: as when they needed strength to face a common danger, when they were attacked by insidious heresies, when they needed to be urged to the pious consideration of some mystery of faith or of some divine blessing. Thus in the earliest days of the Christian era, when the people of Christ were suffering cruel persecution, the cult of the martyrs was begun in order, says St. Augustine, "that the feasts of the martyrs might incite men to martyrdom."[35] The liturgical honors paid to confessors, virgins and widows produced wonderful results in an increased zeal for virtue, necessary even in times of peace. But more fruitful still were the feasts instituted in honor of the Blessed Virgin. As a result of these men grew not only in their devotion to the Mother of God as an ever-present advocate, but also in their love of her as a mother bequeathed to them by their Redeemer. Not least among the blessings which have resulted from the public and legitimate honor paid to the Blessed Virgin and the saints is the perfect and perpetual immunity of the Church from error and heresy. We may well admire in this the admirable wisdom of the Providence of God, who, ever bringing good out of evil, has from time to time suffered the faith and piety of men to grow weak, and allowed Catholic truth to be attacked by false doctrines, but always with the result that truth has afterwards shone out with greater splendor, and that men's faith, aroused from its lethargy, has shown itself more vigorous than before.

23. The festivals that have been introduced into the liturgy in more recent years have had a similar origin, and have been attended with similar results. When reverence and devotion to the Blessed Sacrament had grown cold, the feast of Corpus Christi was instituted, so that by means of solemn processions and prayer of eight days' duration, men might be brought once more to render public homage to Christ. So, too, the feast of the Sacred Heart of Jesus was instituted at a time when men were oppressed by the sad and gloomy severity of Jansenism, which had made their hearts grow cold, and shut them out from the love of God and the hope of salvation.

---

35. *Sermo 47 de Sanctis.*

24. If We ordain that the whole Catholic world shall revere Christ as King, We shall minister to the need of the present day, and at the same time provide an excellent remedy for the plague which now infects society. We refer to the plague of anticlericalism, its errors and impious activities. This evil spirit, as you are well aware, venerable brethren, has not come into being in one day; it has long lurked beneath the surface. The empire of Christ over all nations was rejected. The right which the Church has from Christ himself, to teach mankind, to make laws, to govern peoples in all that pertains to their eternal salvation, that right was denied. Then gradually the religion of Christ came to be likened to false religions and to be placed ignominiously on the same level with them. It was then put under the power of the State and tolerated more or less at the whim of princes and rulers. Some men went even further, and wished to set up in the place of God's religion a natural religion consisting in some instinctive affection of the heart. There were even some nations who thought they could dispense with God, and that their religion should consist in impiety and the neglect of God. The rebellion of individuals and states against the authority of Christ has produced deplorable consequences. We lamented these in the encyclical *Ubi Arcano*; we lament them today: the seeds of discord sown far and wide; those bitter enmities and rivalries between nations, which still hinder so much the cause of peace; that insatiable greed which is so often hidden under a pretense of public spirit and patriotism, and gives rise to so many private quarrels; a blind and immoderate selfishness, making men seek nothing but their own comfort and advantage, and measure everything by these; no peace in the home, because men have forgotten or neglect their duty; the unity and stability of the family undermined; society, in a word, shaken to its foundations and on the way to ruin. We firmly hope, however, that the feast of the Kingship of Christ, which in future will be yearly observed, may hasten the return of society to our loving Savior. It would be the duty of Catholics to do all they can to bring about this happy result. Many of these, however, have neither the station in society nor the authority which should belong to those who bear the torch of truth. This state of things may perhaps be attributed to a certain slowness and timidity in good people, who are reluctant to engage in conflict or oppose but a weak resistance; thus the enemies of the Church become bolder in their attacks. But if the faithful were generally to understand that it behooves them ever to fight courageously under the banner of Christ their King, then, fired with apostolic zeal, they would strive to win over to their Lord those hearts that are bitter and estranged from him, and would valiantly defend his rights.

25. Moreover, the annual and universal celebration of the feast of the Kingship of Christ will draw attention to the evils which anticlericalism has brought upon society in drawing men away from Christ, and will also do much to remedy

them. While nations insult the beloved name of our Redeemer by suppressing all mention of it in their conferences and parliaments, we must all the more loudly proclaim his kingly dignity and power, all the more universally affirm his rights.

26. The way has been happily and providentially prepared for the celebration of this feast ever since the end of the last century. It is well known that this cult has been the subject of learned disquisitions in many books published in every part of the world, written in many different languages. The kingship and empire of Christ have been recognized in the pious custom, practiced by many families, of dedicating themselves to the Sacred Heart of Jesus; not only families have performed this act of dedication, but nations, too, and kingdoms. In fact, the whole of the human race was at the instance of Pope Leo XIII, in the Holy Year 1900, consecrated to the divine Heart. It should be remarked also that much has been done for the recognition of Christ's authority over society by the frequent Eucharistic Congresses which are held in our age. These give an opportunity to the people of each diocese, district or nation, and to the whole world, of coming together to venerate and adore Christ the King hidden under the sacramental species. Thus by sermons preached at meetings and in churches, by public adoration of the Blessed Sacrament exposed and by solemn processions, men unite in paying homage to Christ, whom God has given them for their King. It is by a divine inspiration that the people of Christ bring forth Jesus from his silent hiding-place in the Church, and carry him in triumph through the streets of the city, so that he whom men refused to receive when he came unto his own, may now receive in full his kingly rights.

27. For the fulfillment of the plan of which We have spoken, the Holy Year, which is now speeding to its close, offers the best possible opportunity. For during this year the God of mercy has raised the minds and hearts of the faithful to the consideration of heavenly blessings which are above all understanding, has either restored them once more to his grace, or inciting them anew to strive for higher gifts, has set their feet more firmly in the path of righteousness. Whether, therefore, We consider the many prayers that have been addressed to Us, or look to the events of the Jubilee Year just past, We have every reason to think that the desired moment has at length arrived for enjoining that Christ be venerated by a special feast as King of all mankind. In this year, as We said at the beginning of this letter, the divine King, truly wonderful in all his works, has been gloriously magnified, for another company of his soldiers has been added to the list of saints. In this year men have looked upon strange things and strange labors, from which they have understood and admired the victories won by missionaries in the work of spreading his kingdom. In this year, by solemnly celebrating the centenary of the Council of Nicaea, We have commemorated the definition of the divinity of the Word Incarnate, the foundation of Christ's empire over all men.

28. Therefore by Our apostolic authority We institute the Feast of the Kingship of Our Lord Jesus Christ to be observed yearly throughout the whole world on the last Sunday of the month of October—the Sunday, that is, which immediately precedes the Feast of All Saints. We further ordain that the dedication of mankind to the Sacred Heart of Jesus, which Our predecessor of saintly memory, Pope Pius X, commanded to be renewed yearly, be made annually on that day. This year, however, We desire that it be observed on the thirty-first day of the month, on which day We Ourselves shall celebrate pontifically in honor of the kingship of Christ, and shall command that the same dedication be performed in Our presence. It seems to Us that We cannot in a more fitting manner close this Holy Year, nor better signify Our gratitude and that of the whole of the Catholic world to Christ the immortal King of ages, for the blessings showered upon Us, upon the Church, and upon the Catholic world during this holy period.

29. It is not necessary, venerable brethren, that We should explain to you at any length why We have decreed that this feast of the Kingship of Christ should be observed in addition to those other feasts in which his kingly dignity is already signified and celebrated. It will suffice to remark that although in all the feasts of Our Lord the material object of worship is Christ, nevertheless their formal object is something quite distinct from his royal title and dignity. We have commanded its observance on a Sunday in order that not only the clergy may perform their duty by saying Mass and reciting the Office, but that the laity too, free from their daily tasks, may in a spirit of holy joy give ample testimony of their obedience and subjection to Christ. The last Sunday of October seemed the most convenient of all for this purpose, because it is at the end of the liturgical year, and thus the feast of the Kingship of Christ sets the crowning glory upon the mysteries of the life of Christ already commemorated during the year, and, before celebrating the triumph of all the Saints, we proclaim and extol the glory of him who triumphs in all the Saints and in all the elect. Make it your duty and your task, venerable brethren, to see that sermons are preached to the people in every parish to teach them the meaning and the importance of this feast, that they may so establish and arrange their life that it may be worthy of those who faithfully and zealously serve the rule of the divine King.[36]

---

36. [As we read here, the Feast of the Kingship of Christ was originally established on the last Sunday of October, on which it continues to be celebrated in communities that avail themselves of the traditional Latin Mass. Pope Pius XI's intention, as can be gleaned from n. 29, is to emphasize the glory of Christ *as terminus of His earthly mission*—a glory and mission *visible and perpetuated in history by the saints*. Hence the feast falls shortly before the Feast of All Saints, to emphasize that what Christ inaugurated in His own person before ascending in glory, the saints then instantiate and carry further in human society, culture, and nations. It is a feast primarily about celebrating Christ's ongoing kingship over all reality, *including this present world*, where the Church must fight for His recognition.

30. We would now, venerable brethren, in closing this letter, briefly enumerate the blessings which We hope and pray may accrue to the Church, to society, and to each one of the faithful, as a result of the public veneration of the Kingship of Christ.

31. When we pay honor to the princely dignity of Christ, men will doubtless be reminded that the Church, founded by Christ as a perfect society, has a natural and inalienable right to perfect freedom and immunity from the power of the State; and that in fulfilling the task committed to her by God of teaching, ruling, and guiding to eternal bliss those who belong to the kingdom of Christ, she cannot be subject to any external power. The State is bound to extend similar freedom to the orders and communities of religious of either sex, who give most valuable help to the bishops of the Church by laboring for the extension and the establishment of the kingdom of Christ. By their sacred vows they fight against the threefold concupiscence of the world; by making profession of a more perfect life they render the holiness which her divine Founder willed should be a mark and characteristic of his Church more striking and more conspicuous in the eyes of all.

32. Nations will be reminded by the annual celebration of this feast that not only private individuals but also rulers and princes are bound to give public honor and obedience to Christ. It will call to their minds the thought of the last judgment, wherein Christ, who has been cast out of public life, despised, neglected and ignored, will most severely avenge these insults; for his kingly dignity demands that the State should take account of the commandments of God and of Christian principles, both in making laws and in administering justice, and also in providing for the young a sound moral education.

33. The faithful, moreover, by meditating upon these truths, will gain much strength and courage, enabling them to form their lives after the true Christian ideal. If to Christ our Lord is given all power in heaven and on earth; if all men, purchased by his precious blood, are by a new right subjected to his dominion; if this power embraces all men, it must be clear that not one of our faculties is exempt from his empire. He must reign in our minds, which should assent with

---

In the reform of the liturgical calendar following the Second Vatican Council, the place of this feast was changed to the last Sunday of the Church year, so that one week later would fall the first Sunday of Advent. This placement emphasizes the eschatological dimension of Christ's kingship: the Kingdom of Jesus Christ, though begun in time, is here present "as in a mystery" (*Lumen Gentium*) and in a "crucified" way. This Kingdom will be perfected and fully manifested *only at the end of time*, with the Second Coming. Hence in the new calendar the feast serves as a summation of salvation history and a symbol of what we hope for ("expectantes ... adventum salvatoris nostri Jesu Christi," as the liturgy in the Ordinary Form proclaims after the Lord's Prayer).]

perfect submission and firm belief to revealed truths and to the doctrines of Christ. He must reign in our wills, which should obey the laws and precepts of God. He must reign in our hearts, which should spurn natural desires and love God above all things, and cleave to him alone. He must reign in our bodies and in our members, which should serve as instruments for the interior sanctification of our souls, or to use the words of the Apostle Paul, as instruments of justice unto God.[37] If all these truths are presented to the faithful for their consideration, they will prove a powerful incentive to perfection. It is Our fervent desire, venerable brethren, that those who are outside the fold [of the Church] may seek after and accept the sweet yoke of Christ, and that we, who by the mercy of God are of the household of the faith, may bear that yoke, not as a burden but with joy, with love, with devotion; that having lived our lives in accordance with the laws of God's kingdom, we may receive full measure of good fruit, and counted by Christ good and faithful servants, we may be rendered partakers of eternal bliss and glory with him in his heavenly kingdom.

34. Let this letter, venerable brethren, be a token to you of Our fatherly love as the Feast of the Nativity of Our Lord Jesus Christ draws near; and receive the apostolic benediction as a pledge of divine blessings, which with loving heart, We impart to you, venerable brethren, to your clergy, and to your people.

Given at St. Peter's Rome, on the eleventh day of the month of December, in the Holy Year 1925, the fourth of Our pontificate.

✠ Pius XI

---

37. Rom. 6:13.

CASTI CONNUBII[†]

On Christian Marriage

Encyclical Letter of Pope Pius XI,
promulgated December 31, 1930

Venerable Brethren and Beloved Children, Health and Apostolic Benediction.

How great is the dignity of chaste wedlock, venerable brethren, may be judged best from this, that Christ Our Lord, Son of the Eternal Father, having assumed the nature of fallen man, not only, with His loving desire of compassing the redemption of our race, ordained it in an especial manner as the principle and foundation of domestic society and therefore of all human intercourse, but also raised it to the rank of a true and great sacrament of the New Law, restored it to the original purity of its divine institution, and accordingly entrusted all its discipline and care to His spouse the Church.

2. In order, however, that amongst men of every nation and every age the desired fruits may be obtained from this renewal of matrimony, it is necessary, first of all, that men's minds be illuminated with the true doctrine of Christ regarding it; and secondly, that Christian spouses, the weakness of their wills strengthened by the internal grace of God, shape all their ways of thinking and of acting in conformity with that pure law of Christ so as to obtain true peace and happiness for themselves and for their families.

3. Yet not only do We, looking with paternal eye on the universal world from this Apostolic See as from a watchtower, but you, also, venerable brethren, see, and seeing deeply grieve with Us, that a great number of men, forgetful of that divine work of redemption, either entirely ignore or shamelessly deny the great sanctity of Christian wedlock, or relying on the false principles of a new and utterly perverse morality, too often trample it under foot. And since these most pernicious errors and depraved morals have begun to spread even amongst the faithful and are gradually gaining ground, in Our office as Christ's Vicar upon earth and Supreme Shepherd and Teacher We consider it Our duty to raise Our

---

†   [Section headings have been added by the editor for ease of reference.]

voice to keep the flock committed to Our care from poisoned pastures and, as far as in Us lies, to preserve it from harm.

4. We have decided therefore to speak to you, venerable brethren, and through you to the whole Church of Christ and indeed to the whole human race, on the nature and dignity of Christian marriage, on the advantages and benefits which accrue from it to the family and to human society itself, on the errors contrary to this most important point of the Gospel teaching, on the vices opposed to conjugal union, and lastly on the principal remedies to be applied. In so doing We follow the footsteps of Our predecessor, Leo XIII, of happy memory, whose Encyclical *Arcanum*,[1] published fifty years ago, We hereby confirm and make Our own, and while We wish to expound more fully certain points called for by the circumstances of our times, nevertheless We declare that, far from being obsolete, it retains its full force at the present day.

I. THE NATURE AND GOODS OF MARRIAGE

5. And to begin with that same encyclical, which is wholly concerned in vindicating the divine institution of matrimony, its sacramental dignity, and its perpetual stability, let it be repeated as an immutable and inviolable fundamental doctrine that matrimony was not instituted or restored by man but by God; not by man were the laws made to strengthen and confirm and elevate it but by God, the Author of nature, and by Christ Our Lord by Whom nature was redeemed, and hence these laws cannot be subject to any human decrees or to any contrary pact even of the spouses themselves. This is the doctrine of Holy Scripture[2]; this is the constant tradition of the Universal Church; this the solemn definition of the sacred Council of Trent, which declares and establishes from the words of Holy Scripture itself that God is the Author of the perpetual stability of the marriage bond, its unity and its firmness.[3]

6. Yet although matrimony is of its very nature of divine institution, the human will, too, enters into it and performs a most noble part. For each individual marriage, inasmuch as it is a conjugal union of a particular man and woman, arises only from the free consent of each of the spouses; and this free act of the will, by which each party hands over and accepts those rights proper to the

---

1.   Encycl. *Arcanum divinae sapientiae*, 10 Febr. 1880.
2.   Gen. 1:27–28; 2:22–23; Matt. 19:3ff.; Eph. 5:23ff.
3.   Conc. Trid., Sess. XXIV.

state of marriage,[4] is so necessary to constitute true marriage that it cannot be supplied by any human power.[5] This freedom, however, regards only the question whether the contracting parties really wish to enter upon matrimony or to marry this particular person; but the nature of matrimony is entirely independent of the free will of man, so that if one has once contracted matrimony he is thereby subject to its divinely made laws and its essential properties. For the Angelic Doctor, writing on conjugal honor and on the offspring which is the fruit of marriage, says: "These things are so contained in matrimony by the marriage pact itself that, if anything to the contrary were expressed in the consent which makes the marriage, it would not be a true marriage."[6]

7. By matrimony, therefore, the souls of the contracting parties are joined and knit together more directly and more intimately than are their bodies, and that not by any passing affection of sense or spirit, but by a deliberate and firm act of the will; and from this union of souls by God's decree, a sacred and inviolable bond arises. Hence the nature of this contract, which is proper and peculiar to it alone, makes it entirely different both from the union of animals entered into by the blind instinct of nature alone in which neither reason nor free will plays a part, and also from the haphazard unions of men, which are far removed from all true and honorable unions of will and enjoy none of the rights of family life.

8. From this it is clear that legitimately constituted authority has the right and therefore the duty to restrict, to prevent, and to punish those base unions which are opposed to reason and to nature; but since it is a matter which flows from human nature itself, no less certain is the teaching of Our predecessor, Leo XIII of happy memory:[7] "In choosing a state of life there is no doubt but that it is in the power and discretion of each one to prefer one or the other: either to embrace the counsel of virginity given by Jesus Christ, or to bind himself in the bonds of matrimony. To take away from man the natural and primeval right of marriage, to circumscribe in any way the principal ends of marriage laid down in the beginning by God Himself in the words 'Increase and multiply,'[8] is beyond the power of any human law."

9. Therefore the sacred partnership of true marriage is constituted both by the will of God and the will of man. From God comes the very institution of marriage, the ends for which it was instituted, the laws that govern it, the

---

4.   *Cod. iur. can.* [1917], c. 1081 & 2.

5.   *Cod. iur. can.,* c. 1081 & 2.

6.   *Summa Theologiae,* Supplem. XLIX, a. 3.

7.   Encycl. *Rerum novarum,* 15 May 1891.

8.   Gen. 1:28.

blessings that flow from it; while man, through generous surrender of his own person made to another for the whole span of life, becomes, with the help and cooperation of God, the author of each particular marriage, with the duties and blessings annexed thereto from divine institution.

The Goods (i.e., Blessings) of Marriage

10. Now when We come to explain, venerable brethren, what are the blessings that God has attached to true matrimony, and how great they are, there occur to Us the words of that illustrious Doctor of the Church whom We commemorated recently in Our encyclical *Ad salutem* on the occasion of the fifteenth centenary of his death:[9] "These," says St. Augustine, "are all the blessings of matrimony on account of which matrimony itself is a blessing: offspring, conjugal faith, and the sacrament [*proles, fides, sacramentum*]."[10] And how under these three heads is contained a splendid summary of the whole doctrine of Christian marriage, the holy Doctor himself expressly declares when he said: "By conjugal faith it is provided that there should be no carnal intercourse outside the marriage bond with another man or woman; with regard to offspring, that children should be begotten of love, tenderly cared for and educated in a religious atmosphere; finally, in its sacramental aspect, that the marriage bond should not be broken and that a husband or wife, if separated, should not be joined to another even for the sake of offspring. This we regard as the law of marriage by which the fruitfulness of nature is adorned and the evil of incontinence is restrained."[11]

The Blessing of Offspring

11. Thus amongst the blessings of marriage, the child holds the first place. And indeed the Creator of the human race Himself, Who in His goodness wishes to use men as His helpers in the propagation of life, taught this when, instituting marriage in Paradise, He said to our first parents, and through them to all future spouses: "Increase and multiply, and fill the earth."[12] As St. Augustine admirably deduces from the words of the holy Apostle Saint Paul to Timothy[13] when he says: "The Apostle himself is therefore a witness that marriage is for the sake of

---

9. Encycl. *Ad salutem*, 20 April 1930.

10. St. August., *De bono coniug.*, cap. 24, n. 32.

11. St. August., *De Gen. ad litt.*, lib. IX, cap. 7, n. 12.

12. Gen. 1:28.

generation: 'I wish,' he says, 'young girls to marry.' And, as if someone said to him, 'Why?,' he immediately adds: 'To bear children, to be mothers of families.'"[14]

12. How great a boon of God this is, and how great a blessing of matrimony is clear from a consideration of man's dignity and of his sublime end. For man surpasses all other visible creatures by the superiority of his rational nature alone. Besides, God wishes men to be born not only that they should live and fill the earth, but much more that they may be worshippers of God, that they may know Him and love Him and finally enjoy Him for ever in heaven; and this end, since man is raised by God in a marvelous way to the supernatural order, surpasses all that eye hath seen, and ear heard, and all that hath entered into the heart of man.[15] From which it is easily seen how great a gift of divine goodness and how remarkable a fruit of marriage are children born by the omnipotent power of God through the cooperation of those bound in wedlock.

13. But Christian parents must also understand that they are destined not only to propagate and preserve the human race on earth, indeed not only to educate any kind of worshippers of the true God, but children who are to become members of the Church of Christ, to raise up fellow-citizens of the Saints, and members of God's household,[16] that the worshippers of God and Our Savior may daily increase.

14. For although Christian spouses even if sanctified themselves cannot transmit sanctification to their progeny, nay, although the very natural process of generating life has become the way of death by which original sin is passed on to posterity, nevertheless, they share to some extent in the blessings of that primeval marriage of Paradise, since it is theirs to offer their offspring to the Church in order that by this most fruitful Mother of the children of God they may be regenerated through the laver of baptism unto supernatural justice and finally be made living members of Christ, partakers of immortal life, and heirs of that eternal glory to which we all aspire from our inmost heart.

15. If a true Christian mother weigh well these things, she will indeed understand with a sense of deep consolation that of her the words of Our Savior were spoken: "A woman ... when she hath brought forth the child remembereth no more the anguish, for joy that a man is born into the world"[17]; and proving herself superior to all the pains and cares and solicitudes of her maternal office

---

13. 1 Tim. 5:14.

14. St. August., *De bono coniug.*, cap. 24, n. 32.

15. 1 Cor. 2:9

16. Eph. 2:19.

17. John 16:21.

with a more just and holy joy than that of the Roman matron, the mother of the Gracchi, she will rejoice in the Lord, crowned as it were with the glory of her offspring. Both husband and wife, however, receiving these children with joy and gratitude from the hand of God, will regard them as a talent committed to their charge by God, not only to be employed for their own advantage or for that of an earthly commonwealth, but to be restored to God with interest on the day of reckoning.

16. The blessing of offspring, however, is not completed by the mere begetting of them, but something else must be added, namely the proper education of the offspring. For the most wise God would have failed to make sufficient provision for children that had been born, and so for the whole human race, if He had not given to those to whom He had entrusted the power and right to beget them, the power also and the right to educate them. For no one can fail to see that children are incapable of providing wholly for themselves, even in matters pertaining to their natural life, and much less in those pertaining to the supernatural, but require for many years to be helped, instructed, and educated by others. Now it is certain that both by the law of nature and of God this right and duty of educating their offspring belongs in the first place to those who began the work of nature by giving them birth, and they are indeed forbidden to leave unfinished this work and so expose it to certain ruin. But in matrimony provision has been made in the best possible way for this education of children that is so necessary, for, since the parents are bound together by an indissoluble bond, the care and mutual help of each is always at hand.

17. Since, however, We have spoken fully elsewhere on the Christian education of youth,[18] let Us sum it all up by quoting once more the words of St. Augustine: "As regards the offspring it is provided that they should be begotten lovingly and educated religiously,"[19] and this is also expressed succinctly in the Code of Canon Law: "The primary end of marriage is the procreation and the education of children."[20]

18. Nor must We omit to remark, in fine, that since the duty entrusted to parents for the good of their children is of such high dignity and of such great importance, every use of the faculty given by God for the procreation of new life is the right and the privilege of the married state alone, by the law of God and of nature, and must be confined absolutely within the sacred limits of that state.

18. Encycl. *Divini illius Magistri*, 31 Dec. 1929.

19. St. August., *De Gen. ad litt.*, lib. IX, cap. 7, n. 12.

20. *Cod. iur. can.* [1917], c. 1013, §1.

The Blessing of Fidelity

19. The second blessing of matrimony which We said was mentioned by St. Augustine is the blessing of conjugal honor which consists in the mutual fidelity of the spouses in fulfilling the marriage contract, so that what belongs to one of the parties by reason of this contract sanctioned by divine law, may not be denied to him or permitted to any third person; nor may there be conceded to one of the parties anything which, being contrary to the rights and laws of God and entirely opposed to matrimonial faith, can never be conceded.

20. Wherefore, conjugal faith, or honor, demands in the first place the complete unity of matrimony which the Creator Himself laid down in the beginning when He wished it to be not otherwise than between one man and one woman. And although afterwards this primeval law was relaxed to some extent by God, the Supreme Legislator, there is no doubt that the law of the Gospel fully restored that original and perfect unity, and abrogated all dispensations, as the words of Christ and the constant teaching and action of the Church show plainly. With reason, therefore, does the Sacred Council of Trent solemnly declare: "Christ Our Lord very clearly taught that in this bond two persons only are to be united and joined together when He said: 'Therefore they are no longer two, but one flesh.'"[21]

21. Nor did Christ Our Lord wish only to condemn any form of polygamy or polyandry, as they are called, whether successive or simultaneous, and every other external dishonorable act, but, in order that the sacred bonds of marriage may be guarded absolutely inviolate, He forbade also even willful thoughts and desires of such like things: "But I say to you, that whosoever shall look on a woman to lust after her hath already committed adultery with her in his heart."[22] Which words of Christ Our Lord cannot be annulled even by the consent of one of the partners of marriage, for they express a law of God and of nature which no will of man can break or bend.[23]

22. Nay, that mutual familiar association between the spouses themselves, if the blessing of conjugal faith is to shine with becoming splendor, must be distinguished by chastity, so that husband and wife bear themselves in all things in accord with the law of God and of nature, and endeavor always to follow the will of their most wise and holy Creator with the greatest reverence toward the work of God.

23. This conjugal faith, however, which is most aptly called by St. Augustine the "faith of chastity," blooms more freely, more beautifully and more nobly,

---

21. Conc. Trid., Sess. XXIV.

22. Matt. 5:28.

23. *Decr. S. Officii*, 2 March 1679, propos. 50.

when it is rooted in that more excellent soil, the love of husband and wife which pervades all the duties of married life and holds pride of place in Christian marriage. For matrimonial faith demands that husband and wife be joined in an especially holy and pure love, not as adulterers love each other, but as Christ loved the Church. This precept the Apostle laid down when he said: "Husbands, love your wives as Christ also loved the Church,"[24] that Church which of a truth He embraced with a boundless love not for the sake of His own advantage, but seeking only the good of His Spouse.[25] The love, then, of which We are speaking is not that based on the passing lust of the moment nor does it consist in pleasing words only, but in the deep attachment of the heart which is expressed in action, since love is proved by deeds.[26] This outward expression of love in the home demands not only mutual help but must go further; must have as its primary purpose that man and wife help each other day by day in forming and perfecting themselves in the interior life, so that through their partnership in life they may advance ever more and more in virtue, and above all that they may grow in true love toward God and their neighbor, on which indeed "dependeth the whole Law and the Prophets."[27] For all men of every condition, in whatever honorable walk of life they may be, can and ought to imitate that most perfect example of holiness placed before man by God, namely Christ Our Lord, and by God's grace to arrive at the summit of perfection, as is proved by the example set us of many saints.

24. This mutual molding of husband and wife, this determined effort to perfect each other, can in a very real sense, as the Roman Catechism teaches, be said to be the chief reason and purpose of matrimony, provided matrimony be looked at not in the restricted sense as instituted for the proper conception and education of the child, but more widely as the blending of life as a whole and the mutual interchange and sharing thereof.

25. By this same love it is necessary that all the other rights and duties of the marriage state be regulated, as the words of the Apostle—"Let the husband render the debt to the wife, and the wife also in like manner to the husband"[28]— express not only a law of justice but also one of charity.

26. Domestic society being confirmed, therefore, by this bond of love, there should flourish in it the "order of love," as St. Augustine calls it. This order

---

24. Eph. 5:25; Col. 3:19.

25. *Catech. Rom.*, II, cap. VIII, q. 24.

26. St. Gregory the Great, *Hom. XXX in Evang.* (John 14:23–31), n. 1.

27. Matt. 22:40.

28. 1 Cor. 7:3.

includes both the primacy of the husband with regard to the wife and children, and the ready subjection of the wife and her willing obedience, which the
Apostle commends in these words: "Let women be subject to their husbands as
to the Lord, because the husband is the head of the wife, and Christ is the head
of the Church."[29]

27. This subjection, however, does not deny or take away the liberty which
fully belongs to the woman both in view of her dignity as a human person, and
in view of her most noble office as wife and mother and companion; nor does it
bid her obey her husband's every request if not in harmony with right reason or
with the dignity due to a wife; nor, in fine, does it imply that the wife should be
put on a level with those persons who in law are called minors, to whom it is not
customary to allow free exercise of their rights on account of their lack of mature
judgment, or of their ignorance of human affairs. But it forbids that exaggerated
liberty which cares not for the good of the family; it forbids that in this body
which is the family, the heart be separated from the head to the great detriment of
the whole body and the proximate danger of ruin. For if the man is the head, the
woman is the heart, and as he occupies the chief place in ruling, so she may and
ought to claim for herself the chief place in love.

28. Again, this subjection of wife to husband in its degree and manner may
vary according to the different conditions of persons, place and time. In fact, if
the husband neglect his duty, it falls to the wife to take his place in directing the
family. But the structure of the family and its fundamental law, established and
confirmed by God, must always and everywhere be maintained intact.

29. With great wisdom Our predecessor Leo XIII, of happy memory, in the
encyclical on Christian marriage which We have already mentioned, speaking
of this order to be maintained between man and wife, teaches: "The man is the
ruler of the family, and the head of the woman; but because she is flesh of his
flesh and bone of his bone, let her be subject and obedient to the man, not as a
servant but as a companion, so that nothing be lacking of honor or of dignity in
the obedience which she pays. Let divine charity be the constant guide of their
mutual relations, both in him who rules and in her who obeys, since each bears
the image, the one of Christ, the other of the Church."[30]

30. These, then, are the elements which compose the blessing of conjugal
faith: unity, chastity, charity, honorable noble obedience, which are at the same
time an enumeration of the benefits which are bestowed on husband and wife in
their married state, benefits by which the peace, the dignity and the happiness of

---

29. Eph. 5:22–23.

30. Encycl. *Arcanum divinae sapientiae*, 10 Febr. 1880, n. 11.

matrimony are securely preserved and fostered. Wherefore it is not surprising that this conjugal faith has always been counted amongst the most priceless and special blessings of matrimony.

The Blessing of Sacrament

31. But this accumulation of benefits is completed and, as it were, crowned by that blessing of Christian marriage which in the words of St. Augustine we have called the sacrament, by which is denoted both the indissolubility of the bond and the raising and hallowing of the contract by Christ Himself, whereby He made it an efficacious sign of grace.

32. In the first place Christ Himself lays stress on the indissolubility and firmness of the marriage bond when He says: "What God hath joined together let no man put asunder,"[31] and: "Everyone that putteth away his wife and marrieth another committeth adultery, and he that marrieth her that is put away from her husband committeth adultery."[32]

33. And St. Augustine clearly places what he calls the blessing of matrimony in this indissolubility when he says: "In the sacrament it is provided that the marriage bond should not be broken, and that a husband or wife, if separated, should not be joined to another even for the sake of offspring."[33]

34. And this inviolable stability, although not in the same perfect measure in every case, belongs to every true marriage, for the word of the Lord: "What God hath joined together let no man put asunder," must of necessity include all true marriages without exception, since it was spoken of the marriage of our first parents, the prototype of every future marriage. Therefore although before Christ the sublimeness and the severity of the primeval law was so tempered that Moses permitted to the chosen people of God on account of the hardness of their hearts that a bill of divorce might be given in certain circumstances, nevertheless, Christ, by virtue of His supreme legislative power, revoked this concession of greater liberty and restored the primeval law in its integrity by those words which must never be forgotten, "What God hath joined together let no man put asunder." Wherefore, Our predecessor Pius VI of happy memory, writing to the bishop of Agria, most wisely said: "Hence it is clear that marriage even in the state of nature, and certainly long before it was raised to the dignity of a sacrament, was divinely instituted in such a way that it should carry with it a perpetual and indissoluble

---

31. Matt. 19:6.
32. Luke 16:18.
33. St. August., *De Gen. ad litt.*, lib. IX, cap. 7, n. 12.

bond which cannot therefore be dissolved by any civil law. Therefore although the sacramental element may be absent from a marriage as is the case among unbelievers, still in such a marriage, inasmuch as it is a true marriage, there must remain and indeed there does remain that perpetual bond which by divine right is so bound up with matrimony from its first institution that it is not subject to any civil power. And so, whatever marriage is said to be contracted, either it is so contracted that it is really a true marriage, in which case it carries with it that enduring bond which by divine right is inherent in every true marriage; or it is thought to be contracted without that perpetual bond, and in that case there is no marriage, but an illicit union opposed of its very nature to the divine law, which therefore cannot be entered into or maintained."[34]

35. And if this stability seems to be open to exception, however rare the exception may be, as in the case of certain natural marriages between unbelievers, or amongst Christians in the case of those marriages which though valid have not been consummated [*ratum tantum*], that exception does not depend on the will of men nor on that of any merely human power, but on divine law, of which the only guardian and interpreter is the Church of Christ. However, not even this power can ever affect for any cause whatsoever a Christian marriage which is valid and has been consummated [*ratum et consummatum*], for as it is plain that here the marriage contract has its full completion, so, by the will of God, there is also the greatest firmness and indissolubility which may not be destroyed by any human authority.

36. If we wish with all reverence to inquire into the intimate reason of this divine decree, venerable brethren, we shall easily see it in the mystical signification of Christian marriage which is fully and perfectly verified in consummated marriage between Christians. For, as the Apostle says in his Epistle to the Ephesians,[35] the marriage of Christians recalls that most perfect union which exists between Christ and the Church: "Sacramentum hoc magnum est, ego autem dico, in Christo et in ecclesia"—which union, as long as Christ shall live and the Church through Him, can never be dissolved by any separation. And this St. Augustine clearly declares in these words: "This is safeguarded in Christ and the Church, which, living with Christ who lives for ever may never be divorced from Him. The observance of this sacrament is such in the City of God ... that is, in the Church of Christ, that when for the sake of begetting children, women marry or are taken to wife, it is wrong to leave a wife that is sterile in order to take another by whom children may be had. Anyone doing this is guilty of adultery,

34. Pius VI, *Rescript. ad Episc. Agriens.*, 11 July 1789.

35. Eph. 5:32.

just as if he married another—guilty not by the law of the day, according to which when one's partner is put away another may be taken, which the Lord allowed in the law of Moses because of the hardness of the hearts of the people of Israel; but by the law of the Gospel."[36]

37. Indeed, how many and how important are the benefits which flow from the indissolubility of matrimony cannot escape anyone who gives even a brief consideration either to the good of the married parties and the offspring or to the welfare of human society. First of all, both husband and wife possess a positive guarantee of the endurance of this stability which that generous yielding of their persons and the intimate fellowship of their hearts by their nature strongly require, since true love never falls away.[37] Besides, a strong bulwark is set up in defense of a loyal chastity against incitements to infidelity, should any be encountered either from within or from without; any anxious fear lest in adversity or old age the other spouse would prove unfaithful is precluded and in its place there reigns a calm sense of security. Moreover, the dignity of both man and wife is maintained and mutual aid is most satisfactorily assured, while through the indissoluble bond, always enduring, the spouses are warned continuously that not for the sake of perishable things nor that they may serve their passions, but that they may procure one for the other high and lasting good have they entered into the nuptial partnership, to be dissolved only by death. In the training and education of children, which must extend over a period of many years, it plays a great part, since the grave and long enduring burdens of this office are best borne by the united efforts of the parents. Nor do lesser benefits accrue to human society as a whole. For experience has taught that unassailable stability in matrimony is a fruitful source of virtuous life and of habits of integrity. Where this order of things obtains, the happiness and well being of the nation is safely guarded; what the families and individuals are, so also is the State, for a body is determined by its parts. Wherefore, both for the private good of husband, wife and children, as likewise for the public good of human society, they indeed deserve well who strenuously defend the inviolable stability of matrimony.

38. But considering the benefits of the sacrament, besides the firmness and indissolubility, there are also much higher emoluments as the word "sacrament" itself very aptly indicates; for to Christians this is not a meaningless and empty name. Christ the Lord, the Institutor and Perfecter of the holy sacraments,[38] by raising the matrimony of His faithful to the dignity of a true sacrament of the

---

36. St. August., *De nupt. et concup.*, lib. I, cap. 10.

37. 1 Cor. 13:8.

38. Conc. Trid., Sess. XXIV.

New Law, made it a sign and source of that peculiar internal grace by which "it perfects natural love, confirms an indissoluble union, and sanctifies both man and wife."[39]

39. And since the valid matrimonial consent among the faithful was constituted by Christ as a sign of grace, the sacramental nature is so intimately bound up with Christian wedlock that there can be no true marriage between baptized persons "without it being by that very fact a sacrament."[40]

40. By the very fact, therefore, that the faithful with sincere mind give such consent, they open up for themselves a treasure of sacramental grace from which they draw supernatural power for the fulfilling of their rights and duties faithfully, holily, perseveringly even unto death. Hence this sacrament not only increases sanctifying grace, the permanent principle of the supernatural life, in those who, as the expression is, place no obstacle in its way, but also adds particular gifts, dispositions, seeds of grace, by elevating and perfecting the natural powers. By these gifts the parties are assisted not only in understanding, but in knowing intimately, in adhering to firmly, in willing effectively, and in successfully putting into practice, those things which pertain to the marriage state, its aims and duties, giving them (in fine) right to the actual assistance of grace, whensoever they need it for fulfilling the duties of their state.

41. Nevertheless, since it is a law of divine Providence in the supernatural order that men do not reap the full fruit of the sacraments which they receive after acquiring the use of reason unless they cooperate with grace, the grace of matrimony will remain for the most part an unused talent hidden in the field unless the parties exercise these supernatural powers and cultivate and develop the seeds of grace they have received. If, however, doing all that lies with their power, they cooperate diligently, they will be able with ease to bear the burdens of their state and to fulfill their duties. By such a sacrament they will be strengthened, sanctified and in a manner consecrated. For, as St. Augustine teaches, just as by baptism and holy orders a man is set aside and assisted either for the duties of Christian life or for the priestly office and is never deprived of their sacramental aid, almost in the same way (although not by a sacramental character), the faithful once joined by marriage ties can never be deprived of the help and the binding force of the sacrament. Indeed, as the holy Doctor adds, even those who commit adultery carry with them that sacred yoke, although in this case not as a title to the glory of grace but for the ignominy of their guilty action, "as the soul by apostasy, withdrawing as it were from marriage with Christ, even though it

---

39. Conc. Trid., Sess. XXIV.

40. Cod. iur. can., c. 1012.

may have lost its faith, does not lose the sacrament of Faith which it received at the laver of regeneration."[41]

42. These parties, let it be noted, not fettered but adorned by the golden bond of the sacrament, not hampered but assisted, should strive with all their might to the end that their wedlock, not only through the power and symbolism of the sacrament, but also through their spirit and manner of life, may be and remain always the living image of that most fruitful union of Christ with the Church, which is to be venerated as the sacred token of most perfect love.

43. All of these things, venerable brethren, you must consider carefully and ponder over with a lively faith if you would see in their true light the extraordinary benefits of matrimony—offspring, conjugal faith, and the sacrament. No one can fail to admire the divine Wisdom, Holiness and Goodness which, while respecting the dignity and happiness of husband and wife, has provided so bountifully for the conservation and propagation of the human race by a single chaste and sacred fellowship of nuptial union.

II. ERRORS AND EVILS UNDERMINING MARRIAGE

44. When we consider the great excellence of chaste wedlock, venerable brethren, it appears all the more regrettable that particularly in our day we should witness this divine institution often scorned and on every side degraded.

45. For now, alas, not secretly nor under cover, but openly, with all sense of shame put aside, now by word, again by writings, by theatrical productions of every kind, by romantic fiction, by amorous and frivolous novels, by cinematographs portraying in vivid scene, in addresses broadcast by radio telephony, in short by all the inventions of modern science, the sanctity of marriage is trampled upon and derided; divorce, adultery, all the basest vices either are extolled or at least are depicted in such colors as to appear to be free of all reproach and infamy. Books are not lacking which dare to pronounce themselves as scientific but which in truth are merely coated with a veneer of science in order that they may the more easily insinuate their ideas. The doctrines defended in these are offered for sale as the productions of modern genius, of that genius namely, which, anxious only for truth, is considered to have *emancipated* itself from all those old-fashioned and immature opinions of the ancients; and to the number of these antiquated opinions they relegate the traditional doctrine of Christian marriage.

41.   St. August., *De nupt. et concup.*, lib. I, cap. 10.

46. These thoughts are instilled into men of every class, rich and poor, masters and workers, lettered and unlettered, married and single, the godly and godless, old and young, but for these last, as easiest prey, the worst snares are laid.

47. Not all the sponsors of these new doctrines are carried to the extremes of unbridled lust; there are those who, striving as it were to ride a middle course, believe nevertheless that something should be conceded in our times as regards certain precepts of the divine and natural law. But these likewise, more or less wittingly, are emissaries of the great enemy who is ever seeking to sow cockle among the wheat.[42] We, therefore, whom the Father has appointed over His field, We who are bound by Our most holy office to take care lest the good seed be choked by the weeds, believe it fitting to apply to Ourselves the most grave words of the Holy Ghost with which the Apostle Paul exhorted his beloved Timothy: "Be thou vigilant ... Fulfill thy ministry ... Preach the word, be instant in season, out of season, reprove, entreat, rebuke in all patience and doctrine."[43]

48. And in order that the deceits of the enemy may be avoided, it is necessary first of all that they be laid bare; since much is to be gained by denouncing these fallacies for the sake of the unwary, even though We prefer not to name these iniquities "as becometh saints,"[44] yet for the welfare of souls We cannot remain altogether silent.

49. To begin at the very source of these evils, their basic principle lies in this, that matrimony is repeatedly declared to be not instituted by the Author of nature nor raised by Christ the Lord to the dignity of a true sacrament, but invented by man. Some confidently assert that they have found no evidence of the existence of matrimony in nature or in her laws, but regard it merely as the means of producing life and of gratifying in one way or another a vehement impulse; on the other hand, others recognize that certain beginnings or, as it were, seeds of true wedlock are found in the nature of man since, unless men were bound together by some form of permanent tie, the dignity of husband and wife or the natural end of propagating and rearing the offspring would not receive satisfactory provision. At the same time they maintain that in all beyond this germinal idea matrimony, through various concurrent causes, is invented solely by the mind of man, established solely by his will.

50. How grievously all these err and how shamelessly they leave the ways of honesty is already evident from what we have set forth here regarding the origin and nature of wedlock, its purposes and the good inherent in it. The evil of this

42. Matt. 13:25.
43. 2 Tim. 4:2–5.
44. Eph. 5:3.

teaching is plainly seen from the consequences which its advocates deduce from it, namely, that the laws, institutions and customs by which wedlock is governed, since they take their origin solely from the will of man, are subject entirely to him, hence can and must be founded, changed and abrogated according to human caprice and the shifting circumstances of human affairs; that the generative power which is grounded in nature itself is more sacred and has wider range than matrimony—hence it may be exercised both outside as well as within the confines of wedlock, and even where the purpose of matrimony be set aside, as though to suggest that the license of a base fornicating woman should enjoy the same rights as the chaste motherhood of a lawfully wedded wife.

51. Armed with these principles, some men go so far as to concoct new species of unions, suited, as they say, to the present temper of men and the times, which various new forms of matrimony they presume to label "temporary," "experimental," and "companionate." These offer all the indulgence of matrimony and its rights without, however, the indissoluble bond, and without offspring, unless later the parties alter their cohabitation into a matrimony in the full sense of the law.

52. Indeed there are some who desire and insist that these practices be legitimatized by the law or, at least, excused by their general acceptance among the people. They do not seem even to suspect that these proposals partake of nothing of the modern "culture" in which they glory so much, but are simply hateful abominations which beyond all question reduce our truly cultured nations to the barbarous standards of savage peoples.

Errors Regarding Offspring

53. And now, venerable brethren, we shall explain in detail the evils opposed to each of the benefits of matrimony. First consideration is due to the offspring, which many have the boldness to call the disagreeable burden of matrimony and which they say is to be carefully avoided by married people not through virtuous continence (which Christian law permits in matrimony when both parties consent) but by frustrating the marriage act. Some justify this criminal abuse on the ground that they are weary of children and wish to gratify their desires without their consequent burden. Others say that they cannot on the one hand remain continent nor on the other can they have children because of the difficulties whether on the part of the mother or on the part of family circumstances.

54. But no reason, however grave, may be put forward by which anything intrinsically against nature may become conformable to nature and morally good. Since, therefore, the conjugal act is destined primarily by nature for the begetting

of children, those who in exercising it deliberately frustrate its natural power and purpose sin against nature and commit a deed which is shameful and intrinsically vicious.

55. Small wonder, therefore, if Holy Scripture bears witness that the Divine Majesty regards with greatest detestation this horrible crime and at times has punished it with death. As St. Augustine notes, "Intercourse even with one's legitimate wife is unlawful and wicked where the conception of the offspring is prevented. Onan, the son of Judah, did this and the Lord killed him for it."[45]

56. Since, therefore, openly departing from the uninterrupted Christian tradition some recently have judged it possible solemnly to declare another doctrine regarding this question, the Catholic Church, to whom God has entrusted the defense of the integrity and purity of morals, standing upright in the midst of the moral ruin which surrounds her, in order that she may preserve the chastity of the nuptial union from being defiled by this foul stain, raises her voice in token of her divine ambassadorship and through Our mouth proclaims anew: any use whatsoever of matrimony exercised in such a way that the act is deliberately frustrated in its natural power to generate life is an offense against the law of God and of nature, and those who indulge in such are branded with the guilt of a grave sin.[46]

57. We admonish, therefore, priests who hear confessions and others who have the care of souls, in virtue of Our supreme authority and in Our solicitude for the salvation of souls, not to allow the faithful entrusted to them to err regarding this most grave law of God; much more, that they keep themselves immune from such false opinions, in no way conniving in them. If any confessor or pastor of souls, which may God forbid, lead the faithful entrusted to him into these errors or should at least confirm them by approval or by guilty silence, let him be mindful of the fact that he must render a strict account to God, the Supreme Judge, for the betrayal of his sacred trust, and let him take to himself the words of Christ: "They are blind and leaders of the blind: and if the blind lead the blind, both fall into the pit."[47]

---

45. St. August., *De coniug. adult.*, lib. II, n. 12. Gen. 38:8–10.

46. [The "some" to which the Pope refers at the start of this paragraph are the Anglican bishops who, at the Seventh Lambeth Conference in 1930, approved in a limited way the use of birth control. Prior to this decision, all mainstream Protestant denominations had assumed or defended the historic Christian teaching against contraception, but it was not long after Lambeth that Protestant denominations began to abandon this and many other traditional teachings in the area of sexual morality, which today are maintained either principally or even exclusively by the Catholic Church. The present paragraph anticipates the judgment given, with a fuller explanation, by Pope Paul VI in the encyclical letter *Humanae Vitae* of 1968.]

47. Matt. 15:14.

58. As regards the evil use of matrimony, to pass over the arguments which are shameful, not infrequently others that are false and exaggerated are put forward. Holy Mother Church very well understands and clearly appreciates all that is said regarding the health of the mother and the danger to her life. And who would not grieve to think of these things? Who is not filled with the greatest admiration when he sees a mother risking her life with heroic fortitude, that she may preserve the life of the offspring which she has conceived? God alone, all bountiful and all merciful as He is, can reward her for the fulfillment of the office allotted to her by nature, and will assuredly repay her in a measure full to overflowing.[48]

59. Holy Church knows well that not infrequently one of the parties is sinned against rather than sinning, when for a grave cause he or she reluctantly allows the perversion of the right order. In such a case, there is no sin, provided that, mindful of the law of charity, he or she does not neglect to seek to dissuade and to deter the partner from sin. Nor are those considered as acting against nature who in the married state use their right in the proper manner although on account of natural reasons either of time or of certain defects, new life cannot be brought forth. For in matrimony as well as in the use of the matrimonial rights there are also secondary ends, such as mutual aid, the cultivating of mutual love, and the quieting of concupiscence which husband and wife are not forbidden to consider so long as they are subordinated to the primary end and so long as the intrinsic nature of the act is preserved.

60. We are deeply touched by the sufferings of those parents who, in extreme want, experience great difficulty in rearing their children.

61. However, they should take care lest the calamitous state of their external affairs should be the occasion for a much more calamitous error. No difficulty can arise that justifies the putting aside of the law of God which forbids all acts intrinsically evil. There is no possible circumstance in which husband and wife cannot, strengthened by the grace of God, fulfill faithfully their duties and preserve in wedlock their chastity unspotted. This truth of Christian Faith is expressed by the teaching of the Council of Trent. "Let no one be so rash as to assert that which the Fathers of the Council have placed under anathema, namely, that there are precepts of God impossible for the just to observe. God does not ask the impossible, but by His commands, instructs you to do what you are able, and to pray for what you are not able that He may help you."[49]

62. This same doctrine was again solemnly repeated and confirmed by the Church in the condemnation of the Jansenist heresy which dared to utter this

48. Luke 6:38.
49. Conc. Trid., Sess. VI, cap. 11.

blasphemy against the goodness of God: "Some precepts of God are, when one considers the powers which man possesses, impossible of fulfillment even to the just who wish to keep the law and strive to do so; grace is lacking whereby these laws could be fulfilled."[50]

63. But another very grave crime is to be noted, venerable brethren, which regards the taking of the life of the offspring hidden in the mother's womb. Some wish it to be allowed and left to the will of the father or the mother; others say it is unlawful unless there are weighty reasons which they call by the name of medical, social, or eugenic "indication." Because this matter falls under the penal laws of the State by which the destruction of the offspring begotten but unborn is forbidden, these people demand that the "indication," which in one form or another they defend, be recognized as such by the public law and in no way penalized. There are those, moreover, who ask that the public authorities provide aid for these death-dealing operations, a thing which, sad to say, everyone knows is of very frequent occurrence in some places.

64. As to the "medical and therapeutic indication" to which, using their own words, we have made reference, venerable brethren, however much we may pity the mother whose health and even life is gravely imperiled in the performance of the duty allotted to her by nature, nevertheless what could ever be a sufficient reason for excusing in any way the direct murder of the innocent? This is precisely what we are dealing with here. Whether inflicted upon the mother or upon the child, it is against the precept of God and the law of nature: "Thou shalt not kill."[51] The life of each is equally sacred, and no one has the power, not even the public authority, to destroy it. It is of no use to appeal to the right of taking away life for here it is a question of the innocent, whereas that right has regard only to the guilty; nor is there here question of defense by bloodshed against an unjust aggressor (for who would call an innocent child an unjust aggressor?); again there is not question here of what is called the "law of extreme necessity" which could even extend to the direct killing of the innocent. Upright and skillful doctors strive most praiseworthily to guard and preserve the lives of both mother and child; on the contrary, those show themselves most unworthy of the noble medical profession who encompass the death of one or the other, through a pretense at practicing medicine or through motives of misguided pity.

65. All of which agrees with the stern words of the Bishop of Hippo in denouncing those wicked parents who seek to remain childless, and failing in this, are not ashamed to put their offspring to death: "Sometimes this lustful

50. Const. Apost. *Cum occasione*, 31 May 1653, prop. 1.
51. Exod. 20:13; cfr. Decr. S. Offic. 4 May 1897, 24 July 1895; 31 May 1884.

cruelty or cruel lust goes so far as to seek to procure a baneful sterility, and if this fails the fetus conceived in the womb is in one way or another smothered or evacuated, in the desire to destroy the offspring before it has life, or if it already lives in the womb, to kill it before it is born. If both man and woman are party to such practices they are not spouses at all; and if from the first they have carried on thus they have come together not for honest wedlock, but for impure gratification. If both are not party to these deeds, I make bold to say that either the one makes herself a mistress of the husband, or the other simply the paramour of his wife."[52]

66. What is asserted in favor of the social and eugenic "indication" may and must be accepted, provided lawful and upright methods are employed within the proper limits; but to wish to put forward reasons based upon them for the killing of the innocent is unthinkable and contrary to the divine precept promulgated in the words of the Apostle: Evil is not to be done that good may come of it.[53]

67. Those who hold the reins of government should not forget that it is the duty of public authority by appropriate laws and sanctions to defend the lives of the innocent, and this all the more so since those whose lives are endangered and assailed cannot defend themselves—among whom we must mention in the first place infants hidden in the mother's womb. And if the public magistrates not only do not defend them, but by their laws and ordinances betray them to death at the hands of doctors or of others, let them remember that God is the Judge and Avenger of innocent blood which cried from earth to Heaven.[54]

68. Finally, that pernicious practice must be condemned which closely touches upon the natural right of man to enter matrimony but affects also in a real way the welfare of the offspring. For there are some who, over-solicitous for the cause of eugenics, not only give salutary counsel for more certainly procuring the strength and health of the future child—which, indeed, is not contrary to right reason—but put eugenics before aims of a higher order, and by public authority wish to prevent from marrying all those whom, even though naturally fit for marriage, they consider, according to the norms and conjectures of their investigations, would, through hereditary transmission, bring forth defective offspring. And more, they wish to legislate to deprive these of that natural faculty by medical action despite their unwillingness; and this they do not propose as an infliction of grave punishment under the authority of the State for a crime committed, nor to prevent future crimes by guilty persons, but against every

---

52. St. August., *De nupt. et concupisc.*, cap. XV.

53. Rom. 3:8.

54. Gen. 4:10.

right and good they wish the civil authority to arrogate to itself a power over a faculty which it never had and can never legitimately possess.

69. Those who act in this way are at fault in losing sight of the fact that the family is more sacred than the State and that men are begotten not for the earth and for time, but for heaven and eternity. Although often these individuals are to be dissuaded from entering into matrimony, certainly it is wrong to brand men with the stigma of crime because they contract marriage, on the ground that, despite the fact that they are in every respect capable of matrimony, they will give birth only to defective children, even though they use all care and diligence.

70. Public magistrates have no direct power over the bodies of their subjects; therefore, where no crime has taken place and there is no cause present for grave punishment, they can never directly harm or tamper with the integrity of the body, either for reasons of eugenics or for any other reason. St. Thomas teaches this when inquiring whether human judges for the sake of preventing future evils can inflict punishment. He admits that the power indeed exists as regards certain other forms of evil, but justly and properly denies it as regards the maiming of the body. "No one who is guiltless may be punished by a human tribunal either by flogging to death, or by mutilation, or by beating."[55]

71. Furthermore, Christian doctrine establishes, and the light of human reason makes it most clear, that private individuals have no other power over the members of their bodies than that which pertains to their natural ends; and they are not free to destroy or mutilate their members, or in any other way render themselves unfit for their natural functions, except when no other provision can be made for the good of the whole body.

Errors Regarding Fidelity

72. We may now consider another class of errors concerning conjugal faith. Every sin committed as regards the offspring becomes in some way a sin against conjugal faith, since both these blessings are essentially connected. However, we must mention briefly the sources of error and vice corresponding to those virtues which are demanded by conjugal faith, namely the chaste honor existing between man and wife, the due subjection of wife to husband, and the true love which binds both parties together.

73. It follows therefore that they are destroying mutual fidelity, who think that the ideas and morality of our present time concerning a certain harmful and false friendship with a third party can be countenanced, and who teach

---

55. *Summa Theologiae* II-II, q. 108, a. 4, ad 2.

that a greater freedom of feeling and action in such external relations should be allowed to man and wife, particularly as many (so they consider) are possessed of an inborn sexual tendency which cannot be satisfied within the narrow limits of monogamous marriage. That rigid attitude which condemns all sensual affections and actions with a third party they imagine to be a narrowing of mind and heart, something obsolete, or an abject form of jealousy, and as a result they look upon whatever penal laws are passed by the State for the preserving of conjugal faith as void or to be abolished. Such unworthy and idle opinions are condemned by that noble instinct which is found in every chaste husband and wife, and even by the light of the testimony of nature alone—a testimony that is sanctioned and confirmed by the command of God: "Thou shalt not commit adultery,"[56] and the words of Christ: "Whosoever shall look on a woman to lust after her hath already committed adultery with her in his heart."[57] The force of this divine precept can never be weakened by any merely human custom, bad example or pretext of human progress, for just as it is the one and the same "Jesus Christ, yesterday and today and the same for ever,"[58] so it is the one and the same doctrine of Christ that abides and of which no one jot or tittle shall pass away till all is fulfilled.[59]

74. The same false teachers who try to dim the luster of conjugal faith and purity do not scruple to do away with the honorable and trusting obedience which the woman owes to the man. Many of them even go further and assert that such a subjection of one party to the other is unworthy of human dignity, that the rights of husband and wife are equal; wherefore, they boldly proclaim the emancipation of women has been or ought to be effected. This emancipation in their ideas must be threefold: in the ruling of the domestic society, in the administration of family affairs and in the rearing of the children. It must be social, economic, physiological:—physiological, that is to say, the woman is to be freed at her own good pleasure from the burdensome duties properly belonging to a wife as companion and mother (We have already said that this is not an emancipation but a crime); social, inasmuch as the wife being freed from the cares of children and family, should, to the neglect of these, be able to follow her own bent and devote herself to business and even public affairs; finally economic, whereby the woman even without the knowledge and against the wish of her husband may be at liberty to conduct and administer her own

56. Exod. 20:14.
57. Matt. 5:28.
58. Hebr. 13:8.
59. Matt. 5:18.

affairs, giving her attention chiefly to these rather than to children, husband and family.

75. This, however, is not the true emancipation of woman, nor that rational and exalted liberty which belongs to the noble office of a Christian woman and wife; it is rather the debasing of the womanly character and the dignity of motherhood, and indeed of the whole family, as a result of which the husband suffers the loss of his wife, the children of their mother, and the home and the whole family of an ever watchful guardian. More than this, this false liberty and unnatural equality with the husband is to the detriment of the woman herself, for if the woman descends from her truly regal throne to which she has been raised within the walls of the home by means of the Gospel, she will soon be reduced to the old state of slavery (if not in appearance, certainly in reality) and become, as amongst the pagans, the mere instrument of man.

76. This equality of rights which is so much exaggerated and distorted, must indeed be recognized in those rights which belong to the dignity of the human soul and which are proper to the marriage contract and inseparably bound up with wedlock. In such things undoubtedly both parties enjoy the same rights and are bound by the same obligations. In other things there must be a certain inequality and due accommodation, which is demanded by the good of the family and the right ordering and unity and stability of home life.

77. As, however, the social and economic conditions of the married woman must in some way be altered on account of changes in social relations, it is part of the office of the public authority to adapt the civil rights of the wife to modern needs and requirements, keeping in view what the natural disposition and temperament of the female sex, good morality, and the welfare of the family demand, and provided always that the essential order of the domestic society remain intact, founded as it is on something higher than human authority and wisdom, namely on the authority and wisdom of God, and so not changeable by public laws or at the pleasure of private individuals.

78. These enemies of marriage go further, however, when they substitute for that true and solid love, which is the basis of conjugal happiness, a certain vague compatibility of temperament. This they call sympathy and assert that, since it is the only bond by which husband and wife are linked together, when it ceases the marriage is completely dissolved. What else is this than to build a house upon sand?—a house that in the words of Christ would forthwith be shaken and collapse, as soon as it was exposed to the waves of adversity: "and the winds blew and they beat upon that house, and it fell, and great was the fall thereof."[60] On the

---

60. Matt. 7:27.

other hand, the house built upon a rock, that is to say on mutual conjugal chastity and strengthened by a deliberate and constant union of spirit, will not only never fall away but will never be shaken by adversity.

Errors Regarding Sacrament

79. We have so far, venerable brethren, shown the excellency of the first two blessings of Christian wedlock which the modern subverters of society are attacking. And now considering that the third blessing, which is that of the sacrament, far surpasses the other two, we should not be surprised to find that this, because of its outstanding excellence, is much more sharply attacked by the same people. They put forward in the first place that matrimony belongs entirely to the profane and purely civil sphere, that it is not to be committed to the religious society, the Church of Christ, but to civil society alone. They then add that the marriage contract is to be freed from any indissoluble bond, and that separation and divorce are not only to be tolerated but sanctioned by the law; from which it follows finally that, robbed of all its holiness, matrimony should be enumerated amongst the secular and civil institutions. The first point is contained in their contention that the civil act itself should stand for the marriage contract (civil matrimony, as it is called), while the religious act is to be considered a mere addition, or at most a concession to a too superstitious people. Moreover they want it to be no cause for reproach that marriages be contracted by Catholics with non-Catholics without any reference to religion or recourse to the ecclesiastical authorities. The second point which is but a consequence of the first is to be found in their excuse for complete divorce and in their praise and encouragement of those civil laws which favor the loosening of the bond itself. As the salient features of the religious character of all marriage and particularly of the sacramental marriage of Christians have been treated at length and supported by weighty arguments in the encyclical letters of Leo XIII, letters which We have frequently recalled to mind and expressly made our own, We refer you to them, repeating here only a few points.

80. Even by the light of reason alone and particularly if the ancient records of history are investigated, if the unwavering popular conscience is interrogated and the manners and institutions of all races examined, it is sufficiently obvious that there is a certain sacredness and religious character attaching even to the purely natural union of man and woman, "not something added by chance but innate, not imposed by men but involved in the nature of things," since it has "God for its author and has been even from the beginning a foreshadowing of

the Incarnation of the Word of God."[61] This sacredness of marriage which is intimately connected with religion and all that is holy, arises from the divine origin we have just mentioned, from its purpose which is the begetting and education of children for God, and the binding of man and wife to God through Christian love and mutual support; and finally it arises from the very nature of wedlock, whose institution is to be sought for in the farseeing Providence of God, whereby it is the means of transmitting life, thus making the parents the ministers, as it were, of the divine omnipotence. To this must be added that new element of dignity which comes from the sacrament, by which the Christian marriage is so ennobled and raised to such a level, that it appeared to the Apostle as a great sacrament, honorable in every way.[62]

81. This religious character of marriage, its sublime signification of grace and the union between Christ and the Church, evidently requires that those about to marry should show a holy reverence towards it, and zealously endeavor to make their marriage approach as nearly as possible to the archetype of Christ and the Church.

82. They, therefore, who rashly and heedlessly contract mixed marriages, from which the maternal love and providence of the Church dissuades her children for very sound reasons, fail conspicuously in this respect, sometimes with danger to their eternal salvation. This attitude of the Church to mixed marriages appears in many of her documents, all of which are summed up in the Code of Canon Law: "Everywhere and with the greatest strictness the Church forbids marriages between baptized persons, one of whom is a Catholic and the other a member of a schismatic or heretical sect; and if there is, added to this, the danger of the falling away of the Catholic party and the perversion of the children, such a marriage is forbidden also by the divine law."[63] If the Church occasionally on account of circumstances does not refuse to grant a dispensation from these strict laws (provided that the divine law remains intact and the dangers above mentioned are provided against by suitable safeguards), it is unlikely that the Catholic party will not suffer some detriment from such a marriage.

83. Whence it comes about not infrequently, as experience shows, that deplorable defections from religion occur among the offspring, or at least a headlong descent into that religious indifference which is closely allied to impiety. There is this also to be considered, that in these mixed marriages it becomes

---

61. Leo XIII, Encycl. *Arcanum*, 10 Febr. 1880, n. 19.

62. Eph. 5:32; Heb. 13:4.

63. *Cod. iur. can.*, c. 1060.

much more difficult to imitate by a lively conformity of spirit the mystery of which We have spoken, namely that close union between Christ and His Church.

84. Assuredly, also, will there be wanting that close union of spirit which as it is the sign and mark of the Church of Christ, so also should be the sign of Christian wedlock, its glory and adornment. For, where there exists diversity of mind, truth and feeling, the bond of union of mind and heart is wont to be broken, or at least weakened. From this comes the danger lest the love of man and wife grow cold and the peace and happiness of family life, resting as it does on the union of hearts, be destroyed. Many centuries ago indeed, the old Roman law had proclaimed: "Marriages are the union of male and female, a sharing of life and the communication of divine and human rights."[64] But especially, as We have pointed out, venerable brethren, the daily increasing facility of divorce is an obstacle to the restoration of marriage to that state of perfection which the divine Redeemer willed it should possess.

85. The advocates of the neo-paganism of today have learned nothing from the sad state of affairs, but instead, day by day, more and more vehemently, they continue by legislation to attack the indissolubility of the marriage bond, proclaiming that the lawfulness of divorce must be recognized, and that the antiquated laws should give place to a new and more humane legislation. Many and varied are the grounds put forward for divorce, some arising from the wickedness and the guilt of the persons concerned, others arising from the circumstances of the case; the former they describe as subjective, the latter as objective; in a word, whatever might make married life hard or unpleasant. They strive to prove their contentions regarding these grounds for the divorce legislation they would bring about, by various arguments. Thus, in the first place, they maintain that it is for the good of either party that the one who is innocent should have the right to separate from the guilty, or that the guilty should be withdrawn from a union which is unpleasing to him and against his will. In the second place, they argue, the good of the child demands this, for it will be deprived of a proper education or the natural fruits of it, and will too easily be affected by the discords and shortcomings of the parents, and drawn from the path of virtue. And thirdly the common good of society requires that these marriages should be completely dissolved, which are now incapable of producing their natural results, and that legal reparations should be allowed when crimes are to be feared as the result of the common habitation and interaction of the parties. This last, they say, must be admitted to avoid the crimes being committed purposely with a view to obtaining the desired sentence of divorce for which the judge can legally loose the marriage bond, as also to prevent

---

64. Modestinus, *in Dig.* (Lib. XXIII, II: *De ritu nuptiarum*), lib. I, Regularum.

192 — POPE PIUS XI

people from coming before the courts when it is obvious from the state of the case that they are lying and perjuring themselves—all of which brings the court and the lawful authority into contempt. Hence the civil laws, in their opinion, have to be reformed to meet these new requirements, to suit the changes of the times and the changes in men's opinions, civil institutions and customs. Each of these reasons is considered by them as conclusive, so that all taken together offer a clear proof of the necessity of granting divorce in certain cases.

86. Others, taking a step further, simply state that marriage, being a private contract, is, like other private contracts, to be left to the consent and good pleasure of both parties, and so can be dissolved for any reason whatsoever.

87. Opposed to all these reckless opinions, venerable brethren, stands the unalterable law of God, fully confirmed by Christ, a law that can never be deprived of its force by the decrees of men, the ideas of a people or the will of any legislator: "What God hath joined together, let no man put asunder."[65] And if any man, acting contrary to this law, shall have put asunder, his action is null and void, and the consequence remains, as Christ Himself has explicitly confirmed: "Everyone that putteth away his wife and marrieth another, committeth adultery: and he that marrieth her that is put away from her husband committeth adultery."[66] Moreover, these words refer to every kind of marriage, even that which is natural and legitimate only; for, as has already been observed, that indissolubility by which the loosening of the bond is once and for all removed from the whim of the parties and from every secular power, is a property of every true marriage.

88. Let that solemn pronouncement of the Council of Trent be recalled to mind in which, under the stigma of anathema, it condemned these errors: "If anyone should say that on account of heresy or the hardships of cohabitation or a deliberate abuse of one party by the other the marriage tie may be loosened, let him be anathema;"[67] and again: "If anyone should say that the Church errs in having taught or in teaching that, according to the teaching of the Gospel and the Apostles, the bond of marriage cannot be loosed because of the sin of adultery of either party; or that neither party, even though he be innocent, having given no cause for the sin of adultery, can contract another marriage during the lifetime of the other; and that he commits adultery who marries another after putting away his adulterous wife, and likewise that she commits adultery who puts away her husband and marries another: let him be anathema."[68]

---

65. Matt. 19:6.

66. Luke 16:18.

67. Conc. Trid., Sess. XXIV, cap. 5.

68. Conc. Trid., Sess. XXIV, cap. 7.

89. If therefore the Church has not erred and does not err in teaching this, and consequently it is certain that the bond of marriage cannot be loosed even on account of the sin of adultery, it is evident that all the other weaker excuses that can be, and are usually brought forward, are of no value whatsoever. And the objections brought against the firmness of the marriage bond are easily answered. For, in certain circumstances, imperfect separation of the parties is allowed, the bond not being severed. This separation, which the Church herself permits, and expressly mentions in her Canon Law in those canons which deal with the separation of the parties as to marital relationship and cohabitation, removes all the alleged inconveniences and dangers.[69] It will be for the sacred law and, to some extent, also the civil law, in so far as civil matters are affected, to lay down the grounds, the conditions, the method and precautions to be taken in a case of this kind in order to safeguard the education of the children and the well-being of the family, and to remove all those evils which threaten the married persons, the children and the State. Now all those arguments that are brought forward to prove the indissolubility of the marriage tie, arguments which have already been touched upon, can equally be applied to excluding not only the necessity of divorce, but even the power to grant it; while for all the advantages that can be put forward for the former, there can be adduced as many disadvantages and evils which are a formidable menace to the whole of human society.

90. To revert again to the expression of Our predecessor, it is hardly necessary to point out what an amount of good is involved in the absolute indissolubility of wedlock and what a train of evils follows upon divorce. Whenever the marriage bond remains intact, then we find marriages contracted with a sense of safety and security, while, when separations are considered and the dangers of divorce are present, the marriage contract itself becomes insecure, or at least gives ground for anxiety and surprises. On the one hand we see a wonderful strengthening of goodwill and cooperation in the daily life of husband and wife, while, on the other, both of these are miserably weakened by the presence of a facility for divorce. Here we have at a very opportune moment a source of help by which both parties are enabled to preserve their purity and loyalty; there we find harmful inducements to unfaithfulness. On this side we find the birth of children and their instruction and upbringing effectively promoted, many avenues of discord closed amongst families and relations, and the beginnings of rivalry and jealousy easily suppressed; on that, very great obstacles to the birth and rearing of children and their education, and many occasions of quarrels, and seeds of jealousy sown everywhere. Finally, but especially, the dignity and position of

---

69. *Cod. iur. can.*, c. 1128ff.

women in civil and domestic society is reinstated by the former; while by the latter it is shamefully lowered and the danger is incurred "of their being considered outcasts, slaves of the lust of men."[70]

91. To conclude with the important words of Leo XIII, since the destruction of family life "and the loss of national wealth is brought about more by the corruption of morals than by anything else, it is easily seen that divorce, which is born of the perverted morals of a people, and leads, as experience shows, to vicious habits in public and private life, is particularly opposed to the well-being of the family and of the State. The serious nature of these evils will be the more clearly recognized, when we remember that, once divorce has been allowed, there will be no sufficient means of keeping it in check within any definite bounds. Great is the force of example, greater still that of lust; and with such incitements it cannot but happen that divorce and its consequent setting loose of the passions should spread daily and attack the souls of many like a contagious disease or a river bursting its banks and flooding the land."[71]

92. Thus, as we read in the same letter, "unless things change, the human family and State have every reason to fear lest they should suffer absolute ruin."[72] All this was written fifty years ago, yet it is confirmed by the daily increasing corruption of morals and the unheard-of degradation of the family in those lands where Communism reigns unchecked.

III. PASTORAL REMEDIES

93. Thus far, venerable brethren, We have admired with due reverence what the all-wise Creator and Redeemer of the human race has ordained with regard to human marriage; at the same time we have expressed Our grief that such a pious ordinance of the divine Goodness should today, and on every side, be frustrated and trampled upon by the passions, errors and vices of men.

94. It is then fitting that, with all fatherly solicitude, We should turn Our mind to seek out suitable remedies whereby those most detestable abuses which We have mentioned may be removed, and everywhere marriage may again be revered. To this end, it behooves Us, above all else, to call to mind that firmly established principle, esteemed alike in sound philosophy and sacred theology: namely, that whatever things have deviated from their right order, cannot be brought back to

---

70. Leo XIII, Encycl. *Arcanum divinae sapientiae*, 10 Febr. 1880, n. 29.

71. Ibid.

72. Ibid.

that original state which is in harmony with their nature except by a return to the divine plan which, as the Angelic Doctor teaches,[73] is the exemplar of all right order.

95. Wherefore, Our predecessor of happy memory, Leo XIII, attacked the doctrine of the naturalists in these words: "It is a divinely appointed law that whatsoever things are constituted by God, the Author of nature, these we find the more useful and salutary, the more they remain in their natural state, unimpaired and unchanged; inasmuch as God, the Creator of all things, intimately knows what is suited to the constitution and the preservation of each, and by his will and mind has so ordained all this that each may duly achieve its purpose. But if the boldness and wickedness of men change and disturb this order of things so providentially disposed, then, indeed, things so wonderfully ordained will begin to be injurious, or will cease to be beneficial, either because, in the change, they have lost their power to benefit, or because God Himself is thus pleased to draw down chastisement on the pride and presumption of men."[74]

96. In order, therefore, to restore due order in this matter of marriage, it is necessary that all should bear in mind what is the divine plan and strive to conform to it.

97. Wherefore, since the chief obstacle to this study is the power of unbridled lust, which indeed is the most potent cause of sinning against the sacred laws of matrimony, and since man cannot hold in check his passions, unless he first subject himself to God, this must be his primary endeavor, in accordance with the plan divinely ordained. For it is a sacred ordinance that whoever shall have first subjected himself to God will, by the aid of divine grace, be glad to subject to himself his own passions and concupiscence; while he who is a rebel against God will, to his sorrow, experience within himself the violent rebellion of his worst passions.

98. And how wisely this has been decreed St. Augustine thus shows: "This indeed is fitting, that the lower be subject to the higher, so that he who would have subject to himself whatever is below him, should himself submit to whatever is above him. Acknowledge order, seek peace. Be thou subject to God, and thy flesh subject to thee. What more fitting! What more fair! Thou art subject to the higher and the lower is subject to thee. Do thou serve Him who made thee, so that that which was made for thee may serve thee. For we do not commend this order, namely, 'The flesh to thee and thou to God,' but 'Thou to God, and the flesh to thee.' If, however, thou despisest the subjection of thyself to God, thou shalt never bring about the subjection of the flesh to thyself. If thou dost

---

73. *Summa Theologiae* I-II, q. 91, aa. 1–2.

74. Encycl. *Arcanum divinae sapientiae*, n. 25.

not obey the Lord, thou shalt be tormented by thy servant."[75] This right ordering on the part of God's wisdom is mentioned by the holy Doctor of the Gentiles, inspired by the Holy Spirit, for in speaking of those ancient philosophers who refused to adore and reverence Him whom they knew to be the Creator of the universe, he says: "Wherefore God gave them up to the desires of their heart, unto uncleanness, to dishonor their own bodies among themselves;" and again: "For this same God delivered them up to shameful affections."[76] And St. James says: "God resisteth the proud and giveth grace to the humble,"[77] without which grace, as the same Doctor of the Gentiles reminds us, man cannot subdue the rebellion of his flesh.[78]

99. Consequently, as the onslaughts of these uncontrolled passions cannot in any way be lessened, unless the spirit first shows a humble compliance of duty and reverence towards its Maker, it is above all and before all needful that those who are joined in the bond of sacred wedlock should be wholly imbued with a profound and genuine sense of duty towards God, which will shape their whole lives, and fill their minds and wills with a very deep reverence for the majesty of God.

100. Quite fittingly, therefore, and quite in accordance with the defined norm of Christian sentiment, do those pastors of souls act who, to prevent married people from failing in the observance of God's law, urge them to perform their duty and exercise their religion so that they should give themselves to God, continually ask for His divine assistance, frequent the sacraments, and always nourish and preserve a loyal and thoroughly sincere devotion to God.

Combating Naturalism and Rationalism

101. They are greatly deceived who having underestimated or neglected these means which rise above nature, think that they can induce men by the use and discovery of the natural sciences, such as those of biology, the science of heredity, and the like, to curb their carnal desires. We do not say this in order to belittle those natural means which are not dishonest; for God is the Author of nature as well as of grace, and He has disposed the good things of both orders for the beneficial use of men. The faithful, therefore, can and ought to be assisted also by natural means. But they are mistaken who think that these means are able

---

75. St. August., *Enarrat.* in Ps. 143.

76. Rom. 1:24, 26.

77. James 4:6.

78. Rom. 7, 8.

to establish chastity in the nuptial union, or that they are more effective than supernatural grace.

102. This conformity of wedlock and moral conduct with the divine laws respective of marriage, without which its effective restoration cannot be brought about, supposes, however, that all can discern readily, with real certainty, and without any accompanying error, what those laws are. But everyone can see to how many fallacies an avenue would be opened up and how many errors would become mixed with the truth, if it were left solely to the light of reason of each to find it out, or if it were to be discovered by the private interpretation of the truth which is revealed. And if this is applicable to many other truths of the moral order, we must all the more pay attention to those things which appertain to marriage, where the inordinate desire for pleasure can attack frail human nature and easily deceive it and lead it astray; this is all the more true of the observance of the divine law, which demands sometimes hard and repeated sacrifices, for which, as experience points out, a weak man can find so many excuses for avoiding the fulfillment of the divine law.

103. On this account, in order that no falsification or corruption of the divine law but a true genuine knowledge of it may enlighten the minds of men and guide their conduct, it is necessary that a filial and humble obedience towards the Church should be combined with devotedness to God and the desire of submitting to Him. For Christ Himself made the Church the teacher of truth in those things also which concern the right regulation of moral conduct, even though some knowledge of the same is not beyond human reason. For just as God, in the case of the natural truths of religion and morals, added revelation to the light of reason so that what is right and true, "in the present state also of the human race, may be known readily, with real certainty, without any admixture of error,"[79] so for the same purpose he has constituted the Church the guardian and the teacher of the whole of the truth concerning religion and moral conduct; to her therefore should the faithful show obedience and subject their minds and hearts so as to be kept unharmed and free from error and moral corruption, and so that they shall not deprive themselves of that assistance given by God with such liberal bounty, they ought to show this due obedience not only when the Church defines something with solemn judgment, but also, in proper proportion, when by the constitutions and decrees of the Holy See, opinions are proscribed and condemned as dangerous or distorted.[80]

104. Wherefore, let the faithful also be on their guard against the overrated independence of private judgment and that false autonomy of human reason.

79. Conc. Vat., Sess. III, cap. 2.
80. Conc. Vat., Sess. III, cap. 4; *Cod. iur. can.*, c. 1324.

For it is quite foreign to everyone bearing the name of a Christian to trust his own mental powers with such pride as to agree only with those things which he can examine from their inner nature, and to imagine that the Church, sent by God to teach and guide all nations, is not conversant with present affairs and circumstances; or even that they must obey only in those matters which she has decreed by solemn definition as though her other decisions might be presumed to be false or putting forward insufficient motive for truth and honesty. Quite to the contrary, a characteristic of all true followers of Christ, lettered or unlettered, is to allow themselves to be guided and led in all things that touch upon faith or morals by the Holy Church of God through its Supreme Pastor the Roman Pontiff, who is himself guided by Jesus Christ Our Lord.

Importance of Instruction

105. Consequently, since everything must be referred to the law and mind of God, in order to bring about the universal and permanent restoration of marriage, it is indeed of the utmost importance that the faithful should be well instructed concerning matrimony; both by word of mouth and by the written word, not cursorily but often and fully, by means of plain and weighty arguments, so that these truths will strike the intellect and will be deeply engraved on their hearts. Let them know and attentively consider what great wisdom, holiness, and goodness God has shown the human race by instituting matrimony and by upholding it with sacred laws, and still more when He wonderfully raised it to the dignity of a sacrament, through which so bountiful a font of graces lies open to Christian spouses that they may have the strength to serve the noble ends of wedlock, for the welfare and salvation of themselves, their children, and the whole of civil society, and indeed of the whole human community.

106. Certainly, if the latter day subverters of marriage are entirely devoted to misleading the minds of men and corrupting their hearts, to making a mockery of matrimonial purity and extolling the filthiest of vices by means of books and pamphlets and other innumerable methods, much more ought you, venerable brethren, whom "the Holy Ghost has placed as bishops, to rule the Church of God, which He hath purchased with His own blood,"[81] to give yourselves wholly to this, that through yourselves and through the priests subject to you, and, moreover, through the laity welded together by Catholic Action, so much desired and recommended by Us, into a power of hierarchical apostolate, you may, by every fitting means, oppose error by truth, vice by the excellent dignity of chastity, the

---

81. Acts 20:28.

slavery of covetousness by the liberty of the sons of God,[82] that disastrous ease in obtaining divorce by an enduring love in the bond of marriage and by the inviolate pledge of fidelity given even to death.

107. Thus will it come to pass that the faithful will wholeheartedly thank God that they are bound together by His command and led by gentle compulsion to fly as far as possible from every kind of idolatry of the flesh and from the base slavery of the passions. They will, in a great measure, turn and be turned away from these abominable opinions which to the dishonor of man's dignity are now spread about in speech and in writing and collected under the title of "perfect marriage" and which indeed would make that perfect marriage nothing better than "depraved marriage," as it has been rightly and truly called.

108. Such wholesome instruction and religious training in regard to Christian marriage will be quite different from that exaggerated physiological education by means of which, in these times of ours, some reformers of married life make pretense of helping those joined in wedlock, laying much stress on these physiological matters, in which is learned rather the art of sinning in a subtle way than the virtue of living chastely.

109. So, venerable brethren, we make entirely Our own the words which Our predecessor of happy memory, Leo XIII, in his encyclical letter on Christian marriage addressed to the bishops of the whole world: "Take care not to spare your efforts and authority in bringing about that among the people committed to your guidance that doctrine may be preserved whole and unadulterated which Christ the Lord and the apostles, the interpreters of the divine will, have handed down, and which the Catholic Church herself has religiously preserved, and commanded to be observed by the faithful of every age."[83]

What Spouses Must Do

110. Even the very best instruction given by the Church, however, will not alone suffice to bring about once more conformity of marriage to the law of God; something more is needed in addition to the education of the mind, namely a steadfast determination of the will, on the part of husband and wife, to observe the sacred laws of God and of nature in regard to marriage. In fine, in spite of what others may wish to assert and spread abroad by word of mouth or in writing, let husband and wife resolve: to stand fast to the commandments of God in all things that matrimony demands; always to render to each other the assistance of

---

82. John 8:32ff.; Gal. 5: 13.

83. Encycl. *Arcanum divinae sapientiae*, n. 38.

mutual love; to preserve the honor of chastity; not to lay profane hands on the stable nature of the bond; to use the rights given them by marriage in a way that will be always Christian and sacred, more especially in the first years of wedlock, so that should there be need of continence afterwards, custom will have made it easier for each to preserve it. In order that they may make this firm resolution, keep it and put it into practice, an oft-repeated consideration of their state of life, and a diligent reflection on the sacrament they have received, will be of great assistance to them. Let them constantly keep in mind that they have been sanctified and strengthened for the duties and for the dignity of their state by a special sacrament, the efficacious power of which, although it does not impress a character, is undying. To this purpose we may ponder over the words full of real comfort of holy Cardinal Robert Bellarmine, who with other well-known theologians with devout conviction thus expresses himself: "The sacrament of matrimony can be regarded in two ways: first, in the making, and then in its permanent state. For it is a sacrament like to that of the Eucharist, which not only when it is being conferred, but also whilst it remains, is a sacrament; for as long as the married parties are alive, so long is their union a sacrament of Christ and the Church."[84]

111. Yet in order that the grace of this sacrament may produce its full fruit, there is need, as we have already pointed out, of the cooperation of the married parties; which consists in their striving to fulfill their duties to the best of their ability and with unwearied effort. For just as in the natural order men must apply the powers given them by God with their own toil and diligence that these may exercise their full vigor, failing which, no profit is gained, so also men must diligently and unceasingly use the powers given them by the grace which is laid up in the soul by this sacrament. Let not, then, those who are joined in matrimony neglect the grace of the sacrament which is in them[85]; for, in applying themselves to the careful observance, however laborious, of their duties they will find the power of that grace becoming more effectual as time goes on. And if ever they should feel themselves to be overburdened by the hardships of their condition of life, let them not lose courage, but rather let them regard in some measure as addressed to them that which St. Paul the Apostle wrote to his beloved disciple Timothy regarding the sacrament of holy orders when the disciple was dejected through hardship and insults: "I admonish thee that thou stir up the grace which is in thee by the imposition of my hands. For God hath not given us the spirit of fear; but of power, and of love, and of sobriety."[86]

---

84. St. Rob. Bellarmin., *De controversiis*, tom. III, *De Matr.*, controvers. II, cap. 6.

85. 1 Tim. 4:14.

86. 2 Tim. 1:6–7.

Due Preparation for Marriage

112. All these things, however, venerable brethren, depend in large measure on the due preparation, remote and proximate, of the parties for marriage. For it cannot be denied that the basis of a happy wedlock, and the ruin of an unhappy one, is prepared and set in the souls of boys and girls during the period of childhood and adolescence. There is danger that those who before marriage sought in all things what is theirs, who indulged even their impure desires, will be in the married state what they were before, that they will reap that which they have sown[87]; indeed, within the home there will be sadness, lamentation, mutual contempt, strifes, estrangements, weariness of common life, and, worst of all, such parties will find themselves left alone with their own unconquered passions.

113. Let, then, those who are about to enter on married life approach that state well disposed and well prepared, so that they will be able, as far as they can, to help each other in sustaining the vicissitudes of life, and yet more in attending to their eternal salvation and in forming the inner man unto the fullness of the age of Christ.[88] It will also help them, if they behave towards their cherished offspring as God wills: that is, that the father be truly a father, and the mother truly a mother; through their devout love and unwearying care, the home, though it suffer the want and hardship of this valley of tears, may become for the children in its own way a foretaste of that paradise of delight in which the Creator placed the first men of the human race. Thus will they be able to bring up their children as perfect men and perfect Christians; they will instill into them a sound understanding of the Catholic Church, and will give them such a disposition and love for their fatherland as duty and gratitude demand.

114. Consequently, both those who are now thinking of entering upon this sacred married state, as well as those who have the charge of educating Christian youth, should, with due regard to the future, prepare that which is good, obviate that which is bad, and recall those points about which We have already spoken in Our encyclical letter concerning education: "The inclinations of the will, if they are bad, must be repressed from childhood, but such as are good must be fostered, and the mind, particularly of children, should be imbued with doctrines which begin with God, while the heart should be strengthened with the aids of divine grace, in the absence of which no one can curb evil desires, nor can his discipline and formation be brought to complete perfection by the Church. For

---

87. Gal. 6:9.

88. Eph. 4:13.

Christ has provided her with heavenly doctrines and divine sacraments, that He might make her an effectual teacher of men."[89]

115. To the proximate preparation of a good married life belongs very specially the care in choosing a partner; on that depends a great deal whether the forthcoming marriage will be happy or not, since one may be to the other either a great help in leading a Christian life, or a great danger and hindrance. And so that they may not deplore for the rest of their lives the sorrows arising from an indiscreet marriage, those about to enter into wedlock should carefully deliberate in choosing the person with whom henceforward they must live continually: they should, in so deliberating, keep before their minds the thought first of God and of the true religion of Christ, then of themselves, of their partner, of the children to come, as also of human and civil society, for which wedlock is a fountainhead. Let them diligently pray for divine help, so that they make their choice in accordance with Christian prudence, not indeed led by the blind and unrestrained impulse of lust, nor by any desire of riches or other base influence, but by a true and noble love and by a sincere affection for the future partner; and then let them strive in their married life for those ends for which the [married] state was constituted by God. Lastly, let them not omit to ask the prudent advice of their parents with regard to the partner, and let them regard this advice in no light manner, in order that by their [i.e., the parents'] mature knowledge and experience of human affairs, they may guard against a disastrous choice, and, on the threshold of matrimony, may receive more abundantly the divine blessing of the fourth commandment: "Honor thy father and thy mother (which is the first commandment with a promise) that it may be well with thee and thou mayest be long-lived upon the earth."[90]

Material Goods and Support of the Family

116. Now since it is no rare thing to find that the perfect observance of God's commands and conjugal integrity encounter difficulties by reason of the fact that the man and wife are in straitened circumstances, their necessities must be relieved as far as possible.

117. And so, in the first place, every effort must be made to bring about that which Our predecessor Leo XIII, of happy memory, has already insisted upon,[91] namely, that in the State such economic and social methods should be adopted

---

89. Encycl. *Divini illius Magistri*, n. 59.

90. Eph. 6:2–3; Exod. 20:12.

91. Encycl. *Rerum novarum*, 15 May 1891.

as will enable every head of a family to earn as much as, according to his station in life, is necessary for himself, his wife, and for the rearing of his children, for "the laborer is worthy of his hire."[92] To deny this, or to make light of what is equitable, is a grave injustice and is placed among the greatest sins by Holy Scripture[93]; nor is it lawful to fix such a scanty wage as will be insufficient for the upkeep of the family in the circumstances in which it is placed.

118. Care, however, must be taken that the parties themselves, for a considerable time before entering upon married life, should strive to dispose of, or at least to diminish, the material obstacles in their way. The manner in which this may be done effectively and honestly must be pointed out by those who are experienced. Provision must be made also, in the case of those who are not self-supporting, for joint aid by private or public guilds.[94]

119. When these means which We have pointed out do not fulfill the needs, particularly of a larger or poorer family, Christian charity towards our neighbor absolutely demands that those things which are lacking to the needy should be provided; hence it is incumbent on the rich to help the poor, so that, having an abundance of this world's goods, they may not expend them fruitlessly or completely squander them, but employ them for the support and well-being of those who lack the necessities of life. They who give of their substance to Christ in the person of His poor will receive from the Lord a most bountiful reward when He shall come to judge the world; they who act to the contrary will pay the penalty.[95] Not in vain does the Apostle warn us: "He that hath the substance of this world and shall see his brother in need, and shall shut up his bowels from him: how doth the charity of God abide in him?"[96]

120. If, however, for this purpose, private resources do not suffice, it is the duty of the public authority to supply for the insufficient forces of individual effort, particularly in a matter which is of such importance to the common weal, touching as it does the maintenance of the family and married people. If families, particularly those in which there are many children, have not suitable dwellings; if the husband cannot find employment and means of livelihood; if the necessities of life cannot be purchased except at exorbitant prices; if even the mother of the family, to the great harm of the home, is compelled to go forth and seek a living by her own labor; if she, too, in the ordinary or even extraordinary labors of childbirth, is

---

92. Luke 10:7.

93. Deut. 24:14, 15.

94. Encycl. *Rerum novarum.*

95. Matt. 25:34ff.

96. 1 John 3:17.

deprived of proper food, medicine, and the assistance of a skilled physician, it is patent to all to what an extent married people may lose heart, and how home life and the observance of God's commands are rendered difficult for them; indeed it is obvious how great a peril can arise to the public security and to the welfare and very life of civil society itself when such men are reduced to that condition of desperation that, having nothing which they fear to lose, they are emboldened to hope for chance advantage from the upheaval of the State and of established order.

121. Wherefore, those who have the care of the State and of the public good cannot neglect the needs of married people and their families, without bringing great harm upon the State and on the common welfare. Hence, in making the laws and in disposing of public funds they must do their utmost to relieve the needs of the poor, considering such a task as one of the most important of their administrative duties.

122. We are sorry to note that not infrequently nowadays it happens that through a certain inversion of the true order of things, ready and bountiful assistance is provided for the unmarried mother and her illegitimate offspring (who, of course, must be helped in order to avoid a greater evil) which is denied to legitimate mothers or given sparingly or almost grudgingly.

Good Laws Concerning Marriage and Family

123. But not only in regard to temporal goods, venerable brethren, is it the concern of the public authority to make proper provision for matrimony and the family, but also in other things which concern the good of souls. Just laws must be made for the protection of chastity, for reciprocal conjugal aid, and for similar purposes, and these must be faithfully enforced, because, as history testifies, the prosperity of the State and the temporal happiness of its citizens cannot remain safe and sound where the foundation on which they are established, which is the moral order, is weakened and where the very fountainhead from which the State draws its life, namely, wedlock and the family, is obstructed by the vices of its citizens.

124. For the preservation of the moral order neither the laws and sanctions of the temporal power are sufficient, nor is the beauty of virtue and the expounding of its necessity. Religious authority must enter in to enlighten the mind, to direct the will, and to strengthen human frailty by the assistance of divine grace. Such an authority is found nowhere save in the Church instituted by Christ the Lord. Hence We earnestly exhort in the Lord all those who hold the reins of power that they establish and maintain firmly harmony and friendship with this Church of Christ so that through the united activity and energy of both powers the tremendous

evils, fruits of those wanton liberties which assail both marriage and the family and are a menace to both Church and State, may be effectively frustrated.

125. Governments can assist the Church greatly in the execution of its important office, if, in laying down their ordinances, they take account of what is prescribed by divine and ecclesiastical law, and if penalties are fixed for offenders. For as it is, there are those who think that whatever is permitted by the laws of the State, or at least is not punished by them, is allowed also in the moral order, and, because they neither fear God nor see any reason to fear the laws of man, they act even against their conscience, thus often bringing ruin upon themselves and upon many others. There will be no peril to or lessening of the rights and integrity of the State from its association with the Church. Such suspicion and fear is empty and groundless, as Leo XIII has already so clearly set forth: "It is generally agreed," he says, "that the Founder of the Church, Jesus Christ, wished the spiritual power to be distinct from the civil, and each to be free and unhampered in doing its own work, not forgetting, however, that it is expedient to both, and in the interest of everybody, that there be a harmonious relationship… If the civil power combines in a friendly manner with the spiritual power of the Church, it necessarily follows that both parties will greatly benefit. The dignity of the State will be enhanced, and with religion as its guide, there will never be a rule that is not just; while for the Church there will be at hand a safeguard and defense which will operate to the public good of the faithful."[97]

126. To bring forward a recent and clear example of what is meant, it has happened quite in consonance with right order and entirely according to the law of Christ, that in the solemn Convention happily entered into between the Holy See and the Kingdom of Italy, also in matrimonial affairs a peaceful settlement and friendly cooperation has been obtained, such as befitted the glorious history of the Italian people and its ancient and sacred traditions. These decrees are to be found in the Lateran Pact: "The Italian State, desirous of restoring to the institution of matrimony, which is the basis of the family, that dignity conformable to the traditions of its people, assigns as civil effects of the sacrament of matrimony all that is attributed to it in Canon Law."[98] To this fundamental norm are added further clauses in the common pact.

127. This might well be a striking example to all of how, even in this our own day (in which, sad to say, the absolute separation of the civil power from the Church, and indeed from every religion, is so often taught), the one supreme authority can be united and associated with the other without detriment to

97. Encycl. *Arcanum divinae sapientiae*, n. 36.

98. Concord., art. 34; *Act. Apost. Sed.*, XXI (1929), p. 290.

the rights and supreme power of either, thus protecting Christian parents from pernicious evils and menacing ruin.

128. All these things which, venerable brethren, prompted by Our past solicitude We put before you, We wish according to the norm of Christian prudence to be promulgated widely among all Our beloved children committed to your care as members of the great family of Christ, that all may be thoroughly acquainted with sound teaching concerning marriage, so that they may be ever on their guard against the dangers advocated by the teachers of error, and most of all, that "denying ungodliness and worldly desires, they may live soberly and justly and godly in this world, looking for the blessed hope and coming of the glory of the great God and our Savior Jesus Christ."[99]

129. May the Father, "of whom all paternity in heaven and earth is named,"[100] Who strengthens the weak and gives courage to the pusillanimous and fainthearted; and Christ our Lord and Redeemer, "the Institutor and Perfecter of the holy sacraments,"[101] Who desired marriage to be and made it the mystical image of His own ineffable union with the Church; and the Holy Ghost, Love of God, the Light of hearts and the Strength of the mind, grant that all will perceive, will admit with a ready will, and by the grace of God will put into practice, what We by this letter have expounded concerning the holy sacrament of matrimony, the wonderful law and will of God respecting it, the errors and impending dangers, and the remedies with which they can be counteracted, so that that fruitfulness dedicated to God will flourish again vigorously in Christian wedlock.

130. We most humbly pour forth Our earnest prayer at the throne of His grace, that God, the Author of all graces, the inspirer of all good desires and deeds,[102] may bring this about, and deign to give it bountifully according to the greatness of His liberality and omnipotence, and as a token of the abundant blessing of the same omnipotent God, We most lovingly grant to you, venerable brethren, and to the clergy and people committed to your watchful care, the apostolic benediction.

Given at Rome, in Saint Peter's, this thirty-first day of December, of the year 1930, the ninth of Our Pontificate.

✠ Pius XI

---

99. Tit. 2:12–13.

100. Eph. 3:15.

101. Conc. Trid., Sess. XXIV.

102. Phil. 2:13.

QUADRAGESIMO ANNO

On the Reconstruction of the Social Order

Encyclical Letter of Pope Pius XI,
promulgated May 15, 1931

To Our Venerable Brethren, the Patriarchs, Primates, Archbishops, Bishops and other Ordinaries in peace and communion with the Holy See, and likewise to all the faithful of the Catholic world, on reconstructing the social order and perfecting it conformably to the precepts of the Gospel, in commemoration of the fortieth anniversary of the encyclical Rerum Novarum. *Venerable Brethren and beloved children, health and apostolic benediction.*

F orty years have passed since Leo XIII's peerless encyclical, *Rerum Novarum,* first saw the light, and the whole Catholic world, filled with grateful recollection, is undertaking to commemorate it with befitting solemnity.

2. Other encyclicals of Our predecessor had in a way prepared the path for that outstanding document and proof of pastoral care: namely, those on the family and the holy sacrament of matrimony as the source of human society, *Arcanum*[1]; on the origin of civil authority, *Diuturnum,*[2] and that authority's proper relations with the Church, *Immortale Dei*[3]; on the chief duties of Christian citizens, *Sapientiae Christianae*[4]; against the tenets of socialism, *Quod Apostolici Muneris*[5]; against false teachings on human liberty, *Libertas*[6]; and others of the same nature, fully expressing the mind of Leo XIII. Yet the encyclical *Rerum Novarum,* compared with the rest, had this special distinction: that, at a time when it was most opportune and actually necessary to do so, it laid down for all

---

1. *Arcanum,* Feb. 10, 1880.
2. *Diuturnum Illud,* June 20, 1881.
3. *Immortale Dei,* Nov. 1, 1885.
4. *Sapientiae Christianae,* Jan. 10, 1890.
5. *Quod Apostolici Muneris,* Dec. 28, 1878.
6. *Libertas Praestantissimum,* June 20, 1888.

mankind the surest rules to solve aright that difficult problem of human relations called "the social question."

3. For toward the close of the nineteenth century, the new kind of economic life that had arisen and the new developments of industry had gone to the point in most countries that human society was clearly becoming divided more and more into two classes. One class, very small in number, was enjoying almost all the advantages which modern inventions so abundantly provided; the other, embracing the huge multitude of working people, oppressed by wretched poverty, was vainly seeking escape from the straits wherein it stood.

4. Quite agreeable, of course, was this state of things to those who, in their abundant riches, thought it the result of inevitable economic laws and accordingly, as if it were for charity to veil the violation of justice which lawmakers not only tolerated but at times sanctioned, wanted the whole care of supporting the poor committed to charity alone. The workers, on the other hand, crushed by their hard lot, were barely enduring it and were refusing longer to bend their necks beneath so galling a yoke; and some of them, carried away by the heat of evil counsel, were seeking the overturn of everything, while others, whom Christian training restrained from such evil designs, stood firm in the judgment that much in this had to be wholly and speedily changed.

5. The same feeling those many Catholics, both priests and laymen, shared, whom a truly wonderful charity had long spurred on to relieve the unmerited poverty of the non-owning workers, and who could in no way convince themselves that so enormous and unjust an inequality in the distribution of this world's goods truly conforms to the designs of the all-wise Creator.

6. Those men were without question sincerely seeking an immediate remedy for this lamentable disorganization of States and a secure safeguard against worse dangers. Yet such is the weakness of even the best of human minds that, now rejected as dangerous innovators, now hindered in the good work by their very associates advocating other courses of action, and, uncertain in the face of various opinions, they were at a loss which way to turn.

7. In such a sharp conflict of mind, therefore, while the question at issue was being argued this way and that, nor always with calmness, all eyes as often before turned to the Chair of Peter, to that sacred depository of all truth whence words of salvation pour forth to all the world. And to the feet of Christ's Vicar on earth were flocking in unaccustomed numbers men well versed in social questions, employers, and workers themselves, begging him with one voice to point out, finally, the safe road to them.

8. The wise Pontiff long weighed all this in his mind before God; he summoned the most experienced and learned to counsel; he pondered the issues

carefully and from every angle. At last, admonished "by the consciousness of His apostolic office"[7]—lest silence on his part might be regarded as failure in his duty[8]—he decided, in virtue of the divine teaching office entrusted to him, to address not only the whole Church of Christ but all mankind.

9. Therefore on the fifteenth day of May, 1891, that long-awaited voice thundered forth; neither daunted by the arduousness of the problem nor weakened by age but with vigorous energy, it taught the whole human family to strike out in the social question upon new paths.

10. You know, venerable brethren and beloved children, and understand full well the wonderful teaching which has made the encyclical *Rerum Novarum* illustrious forever. In this letter the Supreme Pastor, grieving that so large a portion of mankind should "live undeservedly in miserable and wretched conditions,"[9] took it upon himself with great courage to defend "the cause of the workers whom the present age had handed over, each alone and defenseless, to the inhumanity of employers and the unbridled greed of competitors."[10] He sought no help from either liberalism or socialism, for the one had proved that it was utterly unable to solve the social problem aright, and the other, proposing a remedy far worse than the evil itself, would have plunged human society into great dangers.

11. Since a problem was being treated "for which no satisfactory solution" is found "unless religion and the Church have been called upon to aid,"[11] the Pope, clearly exercising his right and correctly holding that the guardianship of religion and the stewardship over those things that are closely bound up with it had been entrusted especially to him and relying solely upon the unchangeable principles drawn from the treasury of right reason and divine revelation, confidently and as one having authority,[12] declared and proclaimed "the rights and duties within which the rich and the proletariat—those who furnish material things and those who furnish work—ought to be restricted in relation to each other,"[13] and what the Church, heads of States and the people themselves directly concerned ought to do.

---

7. *Rerum Novarum*, May 15, 1891, n. 2.

8. *Rerum Novarum*, cf. n. 16.

9. *Rerum Novarum*, cf. n. 3.

10. Ibid.

11. *Rerum Novarum*, n. 16.

12. Cf. Matt. 7:29.

13. *Rerum Novarum*, n. 2.

12. The apostolic voice did not thunder forth in vain. On the contrary, not only did the obedient children of the Church hearken to it with marveling admiration and hail it with the greatest applause, but many also who were wandering far from the truth, from the unity of the faith, and nearly all who since then either in private study or in enacting legislation have concerned themselves with the social and economic question.

13. Feeling themselves vindicated and defended by the supreme authority on earth, Christian workers received this encyclical with special joy. So, too, did all those noble-hearted men who, long solicitous for the improvement of the condition of the workers, had up to that time encountered almost nothing but indifference from many, and even rankling suspicion, if not open hostility, from some. Rightly, therefore, have all these groups constantly held the apostolic encyclical from that time in such high honor that to signify their gratitude they are wont, in various places and in various ways, to commemorate it every year.

14. In spite of such great agreement, however, there were some who were not a little disturbed; and so it happened that the teaching of Leo XIII, so noble and lofty and so utterly new to worldly ears, was held suspect by some, even among Catholics, and to certain ones it even gave offense. For it boldly attacked and overturned the idols of liberalism, ignored long-standing prejudices, and was in advance of its time beyond all expectation, so that the slow of heart disdained to study this new social philosophy and the timid feared to scale so lofty a height. There were some also who stood, indeed, in awe at its splendor, but regarded it as a kind of imaginary ideal of perfection more desirable than attainable.

15. venerable brethren and beloved children, as all everywhere and especially Catholic workers who are pouring from all sides into this Holy City, are celebrating with such enthusiasm the solemn commemoration of the fortieth anniversary of the encyclical *Rerum Novarum*, We deem it fitting on this occasion to recall the great benefits this encyclical has brought to the Catholic Church and to all human society; to defend the illustrious Master's doctrine on the social and economic question against certain doubts and to develop it more fully as to some points; and lastly, summoning to court the contemporary economic regime and passing judgment on socialism, to lay bare the root of the existing social confusion and at the same time point the only way to sound restoration: namely, the Christian reform of morals. All these matters which we undertake to treat will fall under three main headings, and this entire encyclical will be devoted to their development.

I. BENEFITS DUE TO THE ENCYCLICAL

16. To begin with the topic which we have proposed first to discuss, We cannot refrain, following the counsel of St. Ambrose[14] who says that "no duty is more important than that of returning thanks," from offering our fullest gratitude to Almighty God for the immense benefits that have come through Leo's encyclical to the Church and to human society. If indeed We should wish to review these benefits even cursorily, almost the whole history of the social question during the last forty years would have to be recalled to mind. These benefits can be reduced conveniently, however, to three main points, corresponding to the three kinds of help which Our predecessor ardently desired for the accomplishment of his great work of restoration.

17. In the first place Leo himself clearly stated what ought to be expected from the Church: "Manifestly it is the Church which draws from the Gospel the teachings through which the struggle can be entirely resolved, or, after its bitterness is removed, can certainly become more tempered. It is the Church, again, that strives not only to instruct the mind, but to regulate by her precepts the life and morals of individuals, and that ameliorates the condition of the workers through her numerous and beneficent institutions."[15]

18. The Church did not let these rich fountains lie quiescent in her bosom, but from them drew copiously for the common good of the longed-for peace. Leo himself and his successors, showing paternal charity and pastoral constancy always, in defense especially of the poor and the weak,[16] proclaimed and urged without ceasing again and again by voice and pen the teaching on the social and economic question which *Rerum Novarum* presented, and adapted it fittingly to the needs of time and of circumstance. [...]

23. Meanwhile, as Leo's teachings were being widely diffused in the minds of men, with learned investigations leading the way, they have come to be put into practice. In the first place, zealous efforts have been made, with active good will, to lift up that class which on account of the modern expansion of industry had increased to enormous numbers but not yet had obtained its rightful place or rank in human society and was, for that reason, all but neglected and despised—the

---

14. St. Ambrose, *De excessu fratris sui Satyri* 1, 44.

15. *Rerum Novarum*, n. 16.

16. Let it be sufficient to mention some of these only: Leo XIII's Apostolic Letter *Praeclara*, June 20, 1894, and Encyclical *Graves de Communi*, Jan. 18, 1901; Pius X's *Motu Proprio De Actione Populari Christiana*, Dec. 8, 1903; Benedict XV's Encyclical *Ad Beatissimi*, Nov. 1, 1914; Pius XI's Encyclical *Ubi Arcano*, Dec. 23, 1922, and Encyclical *Rite Expiatis*, Apr. 30, 1926.

workers, We mean—to whose improvement, to the great advantage of souls, the diocesan and regular clergy, though burdened with other pastoral duties, have under the leadership of the bishops devoted themselves. This constant work, undertaken to fill the workers' souls with the Christian spirit, helped much also to make them conscious of their true dignity and render them capable, by placing clearly before them the rights and duties of their class, of legitimately and happily advancing and even of becoming leaders of their fellows.

24. From that time on, fuller means of livelihood have been more securely obtained; for not only did works of beneficence and charity begin to multiply at the urging of the Pontiff, but there have also been established everywhere new and continuously expanding organizations in which workers, draftsmen, farmers and employees of every kind, with the counsel of the Church and frequently under the leadership of her priests, give and receive mutual help and support.

25. With regard to civil authority, Leo XIII, boldly breaking through the confines imposed by liberalism, fearlessly taught that government must not be thought a mere guardian of law and of good order, but rather must put forth every effort so that "through the entire scheme of laws and institutions ... both public and individual well-being may develop spontaneously out of the very structure and administration of the State."[17] Just freedom of action must, of course, be left both to individual citizens and to families, yet only on condition that the common good be preserved and wrong to any individual be abolished. The function of the rulers of the State, moreover, is to watch over the community and its parts; but in protecting private individuals in their rights, chief consideration ought to be given to the weak and the poor. "For the nation, as it were, of the rich is guarded by its own defenses and is in less need of governmental protection, whereas the suffering multitude, without the means to protect itself, relies especially on the protection of the State. Wherefore, since wage workers are numbered among the great mass of the needy, the State must include them under its special care and foresight."[18] [...]

28. A new branch of law, wholly unknown to the earlier time, has arisen from this continuous and unwearied labor to protect vigorously the sacred rights of the workers that flow from their dignity as men and as Christians. These laws undertake the protection of life, health, strength, family, homes, workshops, wages and labor hazards, in fine, everything which pertains to the condition of wage workers, with special concern for women and children. Even though these laws do not conform exactly everywhere and in all respects to Leo's recommendations,

---

17. *Rerum Novarum*, n. 32.

18. *Rerum Novarum*, n. 37.

still it is undeniable that much in them savors of *Rerum Novarum*, to which great credit must be given for whatever improvement has been achieved in the workers' condition.

29. Finally, the wise Pontiff showed that "employers and workers themselves can accomplish much in this matter, manifestly through those institutions by the help of which the poor are opportunely assisted and the two classes of society are brought closer to each other."[19] First place among these institutions, he declares, must be assigned to associations that embrace either workers alone or workers and employers together. He goes into considerable detail in explaining and commending these associations and expounds with a truly wonderful wisdom their nature, purpose, timeliness, rights, duties, and regulations. [...]

32. With respect to the founding of these societies, *Rerum Novarum* most fittingly declared that "workers' associations ought to be so constituted and so governed as to furnish the most suitable and most convenient means to attain the object proposed, which consists in this, that the individual members of the association secure, so far as is possible, an increase in the goods of body, of soul, and of property," yet it is clear that "moral and religious perfection ought to be regarded as their principal goal, and that their social organization as such ought above all to be directed completely by this goal."[20] For "when the regulations of associations are founded upon religion, the way is easy toward establishing the mutual relations of the members, so that peaceful living together and prosperity will result."[21]

33. To the founding of these associations the clergy and many of the laity devoted themselves everywhere with truly praiseworthy zeal, eager to bring Leo's program to full realization. Thus associations of this kind have molded truly Christian workers who, in combining harmoniously the diligent practice of their occupation with the salutary precepts of religion, protect effectively and resolutely their own temporal interests and rights, keeping a due respect for justice and a genuine desire to work together with other classes of society for the Christian renewal of all social life. [...]

39. All these benefits of Leo's encyclical, venerable brethren and beloved children, which We have outlined rather than fully described, are so numerous and of such import as to show plainly that this immortal document does not exhibit a merely fanciful, even if beautiful, ideal of human society. Rather did Our predecessor draw from the Gospel and, therefore, from an ever-living and life-giving fountain, teachings capable of greatly mitigating, if not immediately

19.   *Rerum Novarum*, n. 48.

20.   *Rerum Novarum*, n. 57.

21.   *Rerum Novarum*, n. 58.

terminating that deadly internal struggle which is rending the family of mankind. The rich fruits which the Church of Christ and the whole human race have, by God's favor, reaped therefrom unto salvation prove that some of this good seed, so lavishly sown forty years ago, fell on good ground. On the basis of the long period of experience, it cannot be rash to say that Leo's encyclical has proved itself the Magna Charta upon which all Christian activity in the social field ought to be based, as on a foundation. And those who would seem to hold in little esteem this papal encyclical and its commemoration either blaspheme what they know not, or understand nothing of what they are only superficially acquainted with, or if they do understand convict themselves formally of injustice and ingratitude.

40. Yet since in the course of these same years, certain doubts have arisen concerning either the correct meaning of some parts of Leo's encyclical or conclusions to be deduced therefrom, which doubts in turn have even among Catholics given rise to controversies that are not always peaceful; and since, furthermore, new needs and changed conditions of our age have made necessary a more precise application of Leo's teaching or even certain additions thereto, We most gladly seize this fitting occasion, in accord with Our apostolic office through which We are debtors to all,[22] to answer, so far as in Us lies, these doubts and these demands of the present day.

II. DEFENSE AND CLARIFICATION OF LEO'S TEACHING

41. Yet before proceeding to explain these matters, that principle which Leo XIII so clearly established must be laid down at the outset here, namely, that there resides in Us the right and duty to pronounce with supreme authority upon social and economic matters.[23] Certainly the Church was not given the commission to guide men to an only fleeting and perishable happiness but to that which is eternal. Indeed the Church holds that it is unlawful for her to mix without cause in these temporal concerns[24]; however, she can in no wise renounce the duty God entrusted to her to interpose her authority, not of course in matters of technique for which she is neither suitably equipped nor endowed by office, but in all things that are connected with the moral law. For as to these, the deposit of truth that God committed to Us and the grave duty of disseminating and interpreting the whole moral law, and of urging it in season and out of season, bring

22. Cf. Rom. 1:14.
23. Cf. *Rerum Novarum*, n. 16.
24. *Ubi Arcano Dei Consilio*, Dec. 23, 1922, n. 65.

under and subject to Our supreme jurisdiction not only the social order but economic activities themselves.

42. Even though economics and moral science employs each its own principles in its own sphere, it is, nevertheless, an error to say that the economic and moral orders are so distinct from and alien to each other that the former depends in no way on the latter. Certainly the laws of economics, as they are termed, being based on the very nature of material things and on the capacities of the human body and mind, determine the limits of what productive human effort cannot, and of what it can attain in the economic field and by what means. Yet it is reason itself that clearly shows, on the basis of the individual and social nature of things and of men, the purpose which God ordained for all economic life.

43. But it is only the moral law which, just as it commands us to seek our supreme and last end in the whole scheme of our activity, so likewise commands us to seek directly in each kind of activity those purposes which we know that nature, or rather God the Author of nature, established for that kind of action, and in orderly relationship to subordinate such immediate purposes to our supreme and last end. If we faithfully observe this law, then it will follow that the particular purposes, both individual and social, that are sought in the economic field will fall in their proper place in the universal order of purposes, and We, in ascending through them, as it were by steps, shall attain the final end of all things, that is God—to Himself and to us, the supreme and inexhaustible Good.

44. But to come down to particular points, We shall begin with ownership or the right of property. venerable brethren and beloved children, you know that Our predecessor of happy memory strongly defended the right of property against the tenets of the socialists of his time by showing that its abolition would result, not in the advantage of the working class, but in their extreme harm. Yet since there are some who calumniate the Supreme Pontiff, and the Church herself, as if she had taken and were still taking the part of the rich against the non-owning workers—certainly no accusation is more unjust than that—and since Catholics are at variance with one another concerning the true and exact mind of Leo, it has seemed best to vindicate this, that is, the Catholic teaching on this matter from calumnies and safeguard it from false interpretations.

45. First, then, let it be considered as certain and established that neither Leo nor those theologians who have taught under the guidance and authority of the Church have ever denied or questioned the twofold character of ownership, called usually individual or social according as it regards either separate persons or the common good. For they have always unanimously maintained that nature, rather the Creator Himself, has given man the right of private ownership not only that individuals may be able to provide for themselves and their families but also

that the goods which the Creator destined for the entire family of mankind may through this institution truly serve this purpose. All this can be achieved in no wise except through the maintenance of a certain and definite order.

46. Accordingly, twin rocks of shipwreck must be carefully avoided. For, as one is wrecked upon, or comes close to, what is known as "individualism" by denying or minimizing the social and public character of the right of property, so by rejecting or minimizing the private and individual character of this same right, one inevitably runs into "collectivism" or at least closely approaches its tenets. Unless this is kept in mind, one is swept from his course upon the shoals of that moral, juridical, and social modernism which We denounced in the encyclical issued at the beginning of Our pontificate.[25] And, in particular, let those realize this who, in their desire for innovation, do not scruple to reproach the Church with infamous calumnies, as if she had allowed to creep into the teachings of her theologians a pagan concept of ownership which must be completely replaced by another that they with amazing ignorance call "Christian."

47. In order to place definite limits on the controversies that have arisen over ownership and its inherent duties there must be first laid down as foundation a principle established by Leo XIII: The right of property is distinct from its use.[26] That justice called commutative commands sacred respect for the division of possessions and forbids invasion of others' rights through the exceeding of the limits of one's own property; but the duty of owners to use their property only in a right way does not come under this type of justice, but under other virtues, obligations of which "cannot be enforced by legal action."[27] Therefore, they are in error who assert that ownership and its right use are limited by the same boundaries; and it is much farther still from the truth to hold that a right to property is destroyed or lost by reason of abuse or non-use.

48. Those, therefore, are doing a work that is truly salutary and worthy of all praise who, while preserving harmony among themselves and the integrity of the traditional teaching of the Church, seek to define the inner nature of these duties and their limits whereby either the right of property itself or its use, that is, the exercise of ownership, is circumscribed by the necessities of social living. On the other hand, those who seek to restrict the individual character of ownership to such a degree that in fact they destroy it are mistaken and in error.

49. It follows from what We have termed the individual and at the same time social character of ownership, that men must consider in this matter not only their

---

25. Ibid., n. 61.

26. *Rerum Novarum*, n. 22.

27. Ibid.

own advantage but also the common good. To define these duties in detail when necessity requires and the natural law has not done so, is the function of those in charge of the State. Therefore, public authority, under the guiding light always of the natural and divine law, can determine more accurately upon consideration of the true requirements of the common good, what is permitted and what is not permitted to owners in the use of their property. Moreover, Leo XIII wisely taught "that God has left the limits of private possessions to be fixed by the industry of men and institutions of peoples."[28] That history proves ownership, like other elements of social life, to be not absolutely unchanging, We once declared as follows: "What diverse forms has property had, from that primitive form among rude and savage peoples, which may be observed in some places even in our time, to the form of possession in the patriarchal age; and so further to the various forms under tyranny (We are using the word tyranny in its classical sense); and then through the feudal and monarchial forms down to the various types which are to be found in more recent times."[29] That the State is not permitted to discharge its duty arbitrarily is, however, clear. The natural right itself both of owning goods privately and of passing them on by inheritance ought always to remain intact and inviolate, since this indeed is a right that the State cannot take away: "For man is older than the State,"[30] and also "domestic living together is prior both in thought and in fact to uniting into a polity."[31] Wherefore the wise Pontiff declared that it is grossly unjust for a State to exhaust private wealth through the weight of imposts and taxes. "For since the right of possessing goods privately has been conferred not by man's law, but by nature, public authority cannot abolish it, but can only control its exercise and bring it into conformity with the common weal."[32] Yet when the State brings private ownership into harmony with the needs of the common good, it does not commit a hostile act against private owners but rather does them a friendly service; for it thereby effectively prevents the private possession of goods, which the Author of nature in His most wise providence ordained for the support of human life, from causing intolerable evils and thus rushing to its own destruction; it does not destroy private possessions, but safeguards them; and it does not weaken private property rights, but strengthens them.

50. Furthermore, a person's superfluous income, that is, income which he does not need to sustain life fittingly and with dignity, is not left wholly to his

28. *Rerum Novarum*, n. 8.

29. Allocution to the Convention of Italian Catholic Action, May 16, 1926.

30. *Rerum Novarum*, n. 7.

31. *Rerum Novarum*, n. 13.

32. *Rerum Novarum*, n. 47.

own free determination. Rather the Sacred Scriptures and the Fathers of the Church constantly declare in the most explicit language that the rich are bound by a very grave precept to practice almsgiving, beneficence, and munificence.

51. Expending larger incomes so that opportunity for gainful work may be abundant, provided, however, that this work is applied to producing really useful goods, ought to be considered, as We deduce from the principles of the Angelic Doctor,[33] an outstanding exemplification of the virtue of munificence and one particularly suited to the needs of the times.

52. That ownership is originally acquired both by occupancy of a thing not owned by anyone and by labor, or, as is said, by specification, the tradition of all ages as well as the teaching of Our predecessor Leo clearly testifies. For, whatever some idly say to the contrary, no injury is done to any person when a thing is occupied that is available to all but belongs to no one; however, only that labor which a man performs in his own name and by virtue of which a new form or increase has been given to a thing grants him title to these fruits.

53. Far different is the nature of work that is hired out to others and expended on the property of others. To this indeed especially applies what Leo XIII says is "incontestable," namely, that "the wealth of nations originates from no other source than from the labor of workers."[34] For is it not plain that the enormous volume of goods that makes up human wealth is produced by and issues from the hands of the workers that either toil unaided or have their efficiency marvelously increased by being equipped with tools or machines? Everyone knows, too, that no nation has ever risen out of want and poverty to a better and nobler condition save by the enormous and combined toil of all the people, both those who manage work and those who carry out directions. But it is no less evident that, had not God the Creator of all things, in keeping with His goodness, first generously bestowed natural riches and resources—the wealth and forces of nature—such supreme efforts would have been idle and vain, indeed could never even have begun. For what else is work but to use or exercise the energies of mind and body on or through these very things? And in the application of natural resources to human use the law of nature, or rather God's will promulgated by it, demands that right order be observed. This order consists in this: that each thing have its proper owner. Hence it follows that unless a man is expending labor on his own property, the labor of one person and the property of another must be associated, for neither can produce anything without the other. Leo XIII certainly had this in mind when he wrote: "Neither capital can do without labor, nor labor without

---

33. Cf. *Summa Theologiae* II-II, q. 134.

34. *Rerum Novarum*, n. 34.

capital."[35] Wherefore it is wholly false to ascribe to property alone or to labor alone whatever has been obtained through the combined effort of both, and it is wholly unjust for either, denying the efficacy of the other, to arrogate to itself whatever has been produced.

54. Property, that is, "capital," has undoubtedly long been able to appropriate too much to itself. Whatever was produced, whatever returns accrued, capital claimed for itself, hardly leaving to the worker enough to restore and renew his strength. For the doctrine was preached that all accumulation of capital falls by an absolutely insuperable economic law to the rich, and that by the same law the workers are given over and bound to perpetual want, to the scantiest of livelihoods. It is true, indeed, that things have not always and everywhere corresponded with this sort of teaching of the so-called Manchesterian Liberals; yet it cannot be denied that economic social institutions have moved steadily in that direction. That these false ideas, these erroneous suppositions, have been vigorously assailed, and not by those alone who through them were being deprived of their innate right to obtain better conditions, will surprise no one.

55. And therefore, to the harassed workers there have come "intellectuals," as they are called, setting up in opposition to a fictitious law the equally fictitious moral principle that all products and profits, save only enough to repair and renew capital, belong by very right to the workers. This error, much more specious [i.e., superficially attractive] than that of certain of the socialists who hold that whatever serves to produce goods ought to be transferred to the State, or, as they say "socialized," is consequently all the more dangerous and the more apt to deceive the unwary. It is an alluring poison which many have eagerly drunk whom open socialism had not been able to deceive.

56. Unquestionably, so as not to close against themselves the road to justice and peace through these false tenets, both parties ought to have been forewarned by the wise words of Our predecessor: "However the earth may be apportioned among private owners, it does not cease to serve the common interests of all."[36] This same doctrine We ourselves also taught above in declaring that the division of goods which results from private ownership was established by nature itself in order that created things may serve the needs of mankind in fixed and stable order. Lest one wander from the straight path of truth, this is something that must be continually kept in mind.

57. But not every distribution among human beings of property and wealth is of a character to attain either completely or to a satisfactory degree of perfection

35. *Rerum Novarum*, n. 19.

36. *Rerum Novarum*, n. 8.

the end which God intends. Therefore, the riches that economic-social developments constantly increase ought to be so distributed among individual persons and classes that the common advantage of all, which Leo XIII had praised, will be safeguarded; in other words, that the common good of all society will be kept inviolate. By this law of social justice, one class is forbidden to exclude the other from sharing in the benefits. Hence the class of the wealthy violates this law no less, when, as if free from care on account of its wealth, it thinks it the right order of things for it to get everything and the worker nothing, than does the non-owning working class when, angered deeply at outraged justice and too ready to assert wrongly the one right it is conscious of, it demands for itself everything as if produced by its own hands, and attacks and seeks to abolish, therefore, all property and returns or incomes, of whatever kind they are or whatever the function they perform in human society, that have not been obtained by labor, and for no other reason save that they are of such a nature. And in this connection We must not pass over the unwarranted and unmerited appeal made by some to the Apostle when he said: "If any man will not work neither let him eat."[37] For the Apostle is passing judgment on those who are unwilling to work, although they can and ought to, and he admonishes us that we ought diligently to use our time and energies of body and mind, and not be a burden to others when we can provide for ourselves. But the Apostle in no wise teaches that labor is the sole title to a living or an income.[38]

58. To each, therefore, must be given his own share of goods, and the distribution of created goods—which, as every discerning person knows, is laboring today under the gravest evils due to the huge disparity between the few exceedingly rich and the unnumbered propertyless—must be effectively called back to and brought into conformity with the norms of the common good, that is, social justice.

59. The redemption[39] of the non-owning workers—this is the goal that Our predecessor declared must necessarily be sought. And the point is the more

---

37. 2 Thess. 3:10.

38. Cf. 2 Thess. 3:8–10.

39. [In this context, "redemption" is being used with its literal meaning as an economic term: to purchase or buy back someone from slavery or bankruptcy. The pope's threefold point is that (i) the poor *ought* to have property ("To each *must* be given his own share of goods," etc.), (ii) it has effectively been stolen from them by an unjust liberal social order, and (iii) they therefore need to be "redeemed" from their non-ownership, i.e., made full owners of real property. The argument of this and surrounding paragraphs is, in fact, an argument in favor of just redistribution, out of which emerged the proposals of the "distributist" (or "distributivist") movement. See Thomas Storck, "Capitalism and Distributism: Definitions and Contrasts," *Faith & Reason* 27 (2002): 157–94. This article, along with many other excellent articles on Catholic Social Teaching, may be accessed from www.thomasstorck.org.]

emphatically to be asserted and more insistently repeated because the commands of the Pontiff, salutary as they are, have not infrequently been consigned to oblivion either because they were deliberately suppressed by silence or thought impracticable although they both can and ought to be put into effect. And these commands have not lost their force and wisdom for our time because that "pauperism" which Leo XIII beheld in all its horror is less widespread. Certainly the condition of the workers has been improved and made more equitable especially in the more civilized and wealthy countries where the workers can no longer be considered universally overwhelmed with misery and lacking the necessities of life. But since manufacturing and industry have so rapidly pervaded and occupied countless regions, not only in the countries called new, but also in the realms of the Far East that have been civilized from antiquity, the number of the non-owning working poor has increased enormously and their groans cry to God from the earth. Added to them is the huge army of rural wage workers, pushed to the lowest level of existence and deprived of all hope of ever acquiring "some property in land,"[40] and, therefore, permanently bound to the status of non-owning worker unless suitable and effective remedies are applied.

60. Yet while it is true that the status of non-owning worker is to be carefully distinguished from pauperism, nevertheless the immense multitude of the non-owning workers on the one hand and the enormous riches of certain very wealthy men on the other establish an unanswerable argument that the riches which are so abundantly produced in our age of "industrialism," as it is called, are not rightly distributed and equitably made available to the various classes of the people.

61. Therefore, with all our strength and effort we must strive that at least in the future the abundant fruits of production will accrue equitably to those who are rich and will be distributed in ample sufficiency among the workers—not that these may become remiss in work, for man is born to labor as the bird to fly—but that they may increase their property by thrift, that they may bear, by wise management of this increase in property, the burdens of family life with greater ease and security, and that, emerging from the insecure lot in life in whose uncertainties non-owning workers are cast, they may be able not only to endure the vicissitudes of earthly existence but have also assurance that when their lives are ended they will provide in some measure for those they leave after them.

62. All these things which Our predecessor has not only suggested but clearly and openly proclaimed, We emphasize with renewed insistence in our present encyclical; and unless utmost efforts are made without delay to put them into

---

40. *Rerum Novarum*, n. 47.

effect, let no one persuade himself that public order, peace, and the tranquility of human society can be effectively defended against agitators of revolution.

63. As We have already indicated, following in the footsteps of Our predecessor, it will be impossible to put these principles into practice unless the non-owning workers through industry and thrift advance to the state of possessing some little property. But except from pay for work, from what source can a man who has nothing else but work from which to obtain food and the necessaries of life set anything aside for himself through practicing frugality? Let us, therefore, explaining and developing wherever necessary Leo XIII's teachings and precepts, take up this question of wages and salaries, which he called one "of very great importance."[41]

64. First of all, those who declare that a contract of hiring and being hired is unjust of its own nature, and hence a partnership-contract must take its place, are certainly in error and gravely misrepresent Our predecessor whose encyclical not only accepts working for wages or salaries but deals at some length with its regulation in accordance with the rules of justice.

65. We consider it more advisable, however, in the present condition of human society that, so far as is possible, the work-contract be somewhat modified by a partnership-contract, as is already being done in various ways and with no small advantage to workers and owners. Workers and other employees thus become sharers in ownership or management or participate in some fashion in the profits received.

66. The just amount of pay, however, must be calculated not on a single basis but on several, as Leo XIII already wisely declared in these words: "To establish a rule of pay in accord with justice, many factors must be taken into account."[42]

67. By this statement he plainly condemned the shallowness of those who think that this most difficult matter is easily solved by the application of a single rule or measure—and one quite false.

68. For they are greatly in error who do not hesitate to spread the principle that labor is worth and must be paid as much as its products are worth, and that consequently the one who hires out his labor has the right to demand all that is produced through his labor. How far this is from the truth is evident from that We have already explained in treating of property and labor.

69. It is obvious that, as in the case of ownership, so in the case of work, especially work hired out to others, there is a social aspect also to be considered in addition to the personal or individual aspect. For man's productive effort cannot

---

41. *Rerum Novarum*, n. 43.

42. *Rerum Novarum*, n. 20.

yield its fruits unless a truly social and organic body exists, unless a social and juridical order watches over the exercise of work, unless the various occupations, being interdependent, cooperate with and mutually complete one another, and, what is still more important, unless mind, material things, and work combine and form as it were a single whole. Therefore, where the social and individual nature of work is neglected, it will be impossible to evaluate work justly and pay it according to justice.

70. Conclusions of the greatest importance follow from this twofold character which nature has impressed on human work, and it is in accordance with these that wages ought to be regulated and established.

71. In the first place, the worker must be paid a wage sufficient to support him and his family.[43] That the rest of the family should also contribute to the common support, according to the capacity of each, is certainly right, as can be observed especially in the families of farmers, but also in the families of many craftsmen and small shopkeepers. But to abuse the years of childhood and the limited strength of women is grossly wrong. Mothers, concentrating on household duties, should work primarily in the home or in its immediate vicinity. It is an intolerable abuse, and to be abolished at all cost, for mothers on account of the father's low wage to be forced to engage in gainful occupations outside the home to the neglect of their proper cares and duties, especially the training of children. Every effort must therefore be made that fathers of families receive a wage large enough to meet ordinary family needs adequately. But if this cannot always be done under existing circumstances, social justice demands that changes be introduced as soon as possible whereby such a wage will be assured to every adult workingman. It will not be out of place here to render merited praise to all, who with a wise and useful purpose, have tried and tested various ways of adjusting the pay for work to family burdens in such a way that, as these increase, the former may be raised and indeed, if the contingency arises, there may be enough to meet extraordinary needs.

72. In determining the amount of the wage, the condition of a business and of the one carrying it on must also be taken into account; for it would be unjust to demand excessive wages which a business cannot stand without its ruin and consequent calamity to the workers. If, however, a business makes too little money, because of lack of energy or lack of initiative or because of indifference to technical and economic progress, that must not be regarded a just reason for reducing the compensation of the workers. But if the business in question is not making enough money to pay the workers an equitable wage because it is being

---

43. Cf. Encyclical, *Casti Connubii*, Dec. 31, 1930, n. 117.

crushed by unjust burdens or forced to sell its product at less than a just price, those who are thus the cause of the injury are guilty of grave wrong, for they deprive workers of their just wage and force them under the pinch of necessity to accept a wage less than fair.

73. Let, then, both workers and employers strive with united strength and counsel to overcome the difficulties and obstacles and let a wise provision on the part of public authority aid them in so salutary a work. If, however, matters come to an extreme crisis, it must be finally considered whether the business can continue or the workers are to be cared for in some other way. In such a situation, certainly most serious, a feeling of close relationship and a Christian concord of minds ought to prevail and function effectively among employers and workers.

74. Lastly, the amount of the pay must be adjusted to the public economic good. We have shown above how much it helps the common good for workers and other employees, by setting aside some part of their income which remains after necessary expenditures, to attain gradually to the possession of a moderate amount of wealth. But another point, scarcely less important, and especially vital in our times, must not be overlooked: namely, that the opportunity to work be provided to those who are able and willing to work. This opportunity depends largely on the wage and salary rate, which can help as long as it is kept within proper limits, but which on the other hand can be an obstacle if it exceeds these limits. For everyone knows that an excessive lowering of wages, or their increase beyond due measure, causes unemployment. This evil, indeed, especially as we see it prolonged and injuring so many during the years of Our pontificate, has plunged workers into misery and temptations, ruined the prosperity of nations, and put in jeopardy the public order, peace, and tranquility of the whole world. Hence it is contrary to social justice when, for the sake of personal gain and without regard for the common good, wages and salaries are excessively lowered or raised; and this same social justice demands that wages and salaries be so managed, through agreement of plans and wills, in so far as can be done, as to offer to the greatest possible number the opportunity of getting work and obtaining suitable means of livelihood.

75. A right proportion among wages and salaries also contributes directly to the same result; and with this is closely connected a right proportion in the prices at which the goods are sold that are produced by the various occupations, such as agriculture, manufacturing, and others. If all these relations are properly maintained, the various occupations will combine and coalesce into, as it were, a single body, and, like members of the body, mutually aid and complete one another. For then only will the social economy be rightly established and attain its purposes when all and each are supplied with all the goods that the wealth

and resources of nature, technical achievement, and the social organization of economic life can furnish. And these goods ought indeed to be enough both to meet the demands of necessity and decent comfort and to advance people to that happier and fuller condition of life which, when it is wisely cared for, is not only no hindrance to virtue but helps it greatly.[44]

76. What We have thus far stated regarding an equitable distribution of property and regarding just wages concerns individual persons and only indirectly touches social order, to the restoration of which according to the principles of sound philosophy and to its perfection according to the sublime precepts of the law of the Gospel, Our predecessor, Leo XIII, devoted all his thought and care.

77. Still, in order that what he so happily initiated may be solidly established, that what remains to be done may be accomplished, and that even more copious and richer benefits may accrue to the family of mankind, two things are especially necessary: reform of institutions and correction of morals.

78. When we speak of the reform of institutions, the State comes chiefly to mind, not as if universal well-being were to be expected from its activity, but because things have come to such a pass through the evil of what we have termed "individualism" that, following upon the overthrow and near extinction of that rich social life which was once highly developed through associations of various kinds, there remain virtually only individuals and the State. This is to the great harm of the State itself; for, with a structure of social governance lost, and with the taking over of all the burdens which the wrecked associations once bore, the State has been overwhelmed and crushed by almost infinite tasks and duties.

79. As history abundantly proves, it is true that on account of changed conditions many things which were done by small associations in former times cannot be done now save by large associations. Still, that most weighty principle, which cannot be set aside or changed, remains fixed and unshaken in social philosophy: Just as it is gravely wrong to take from individuals what they can accomplish by their own initiative and industry and give it to the community, so also it is an injustice and at the same time a grave evil and disturbance of right order to assign to a greater and higher association what lesser and subordinate organizations can do. For every social activity ought of its very nature to furnish help to the members of the body social, and never destroy and absorb them.

80. The supreme authority of the State ought, therefore, to let subordinate groups handle matters and concerns of lesser importance, which would otherwise dissipate its efforts greatly. Thereby the State will more freely, powerfully, and effectively do all those things that belong to it alone because it alone can do

---

44. Cf. St. Thomas, *De Regno* I, 15; *Rerum Novarum*, n. 34.

them: directing, watching, urging, restraining, as occasion requires and necessity demands. Therefore, those in power should be sure that the more perfectly a graduated order is kept among the various associations, in observance of the principle of "subsidiary function," the stronger social authority and effectiveness will be, the happier and more prosperous the condition of the State.

81. First and foremost, the State and every good citizen ought to look to and strive toward this end: that the conflict between the hostile classes be abolished and harmonious cooperation of the industries and professions be encouraged and promoted.

82. The social policy of the State, therefore, must devote itself to the re-establishment of the industries and professions. In actual fact, human society now, for the reason that it is founded on classes with divergent aims and hence opposed to one another and therefore inclined to enmity and strife, continues to be in a violent condition and is unstable and uncertain.

83. Labor, as Our predecessor explained well in his encyclical,[45] is not a mere commodity. On the contrary, the worker's human dignity in it must be recognized. It therefore cannot be bought and sold like a commodity. Nevertheless, as the situation now stands, hiring and offering for hire in the so-called labor market separate men into two divisions, as into battle lines, and the contest between these divisions turns the labor market itself almost into a battlefield where, face to face, the opposing lines struggle bitterly. Everyone understands that this grave evil which is plunging all human society to destruction must be remedied as soon as possible. But complete cure will not come until this opposition has been abolished and well-ordered members of the social body—industries and professions—are constituted in which men may have their place, not according to the position each has in the labor market but according to the respective social functions which each performs. For under nature's guidance it comes to pass that just as those who are joined together by nearness of habitation establish towns, so those who follow the same industry or profession—whether in the economic or other field—form guilds or associations, so that many are wont to consider these self-governing organizations, if not essential, at least natural to civil society.

84. Because order, as St. Thomas well explains,[46] is unity arising from the harmonious arrangement of many objects, a true, genuine social order demands that the various members of a society be united together by some strong bond. This unifying force is present not only in the producing of goods or the rendering of services—in which the employers and employees of an identical industry or

45. Cf. *Rerum Novarum*, n. 20.

46. St. Thomas, *Summa contra Gentiles*, III, 71.

profession collaborate jointly— but also in that common good, to achieve which all industries and professions together ought, each to the best of its ability, to cooperate amicably. And this unity will be the stronger and more effective, the more faithfully individuals and the industries and professions themselves strive to do their work and excel in it. [...]

88. Attention must be given also to another matter that is closely connected with the foregoing. Just as the unity of human society cannot be founded on an opposition of classes, so also the right ordering of economic life cannot be left to a free competition of forces. For from this source, as from a poisoned spring, have originated and spread all the errors of individualist economic teaching. Destroying through forgetfulness or ignorance the social and moral character of economic life, it held that economic life must be considered and treated as altogether free from and independent of public authority, because in the market, i.e., in the free struggle of competitors, it would have a principle of self-direction which governs it much more perfectly than would the intervention of any created intellect. But free competition, while justified and certainly useful provided it is kept within certain limits, clearly cannot direct economic life—a truth which the outcome of the application in practice of the tenets of this evil individualistic spirit has more than sufficiently demonstrated. Therefore, it is most necessary that economic life be again subjected to and governed by a true and effective directing principle. This function is one that the economic dictatorship which has recently displaced free competition can still less perform, since it is a headstrong power and a violent energy that, to benefit people, needs to be strongly curbed and wisely ruled. But it cannot curb and rule itself. Loftier and nobler principles—social justice and social charity—must, therefore, be sought whereby this dictatorship may be governed firmly and fully. Hence, the institutions themselves of peoples and, particularly those of all social life, ought to be penetrated with this justice, and it is most necessary that it be truly effective, that is, establish a juridical and social order which will, as it were, give form and shape to all economic life. Social charity, moreover, ought to be as the soul of this order, an order which public authority ought to be ever ready effectively to protect and defend. It will be able to do this the more easily as it rids itself of those burdens which, as We have stated above, are not properly its own.

89. Furthermore, since the various nations largely depend on one another in economic matters and need one another's help, they should strive with a united purpose and effort to promote by wisely conceived pacts and institutions a prosperous and happy international cooperation in economic life.

90. If the members of the body social are, as was said, reconstituted, and if the directing principle of economic-social life is restored, it will be possible to say

in a certain sense even of this body what the Apostle says of the Mystical Body of Christ: "The whole body (being closely joined and knit together through every joint of the system according to the functioning in due measure of each single part) derives its increase to the building up of itself in love."[47] [...]

97. That what We have taught about the reconstruction and perfection of social order can surely in no wise be brought to realization without the reform of morality, the very record of history clearly shows. For there was a social order once which, although indeed not perfect or in all respects ideal, nevertheless, met in a certain measure the requirements of right reason, considering the conditions and needs of the time. If that order has long since perished, that surely did not happen because the order could not have accommodated itself to changed conditions and needs by development and by a certain expansion, but rather because men, hardened by too much love of self, refused to open the order to the increasing masses as they should have done, or because, deceived by allurements of a false freedom and other errors, they became impatient of every authority and sought to reject every form of control.

98. There remains to Us, after again calling to judgment the economic system now in force and its most bitter accuser, socialism, and passing explicit and just sentence upon them, to search out more thoroughly the root of these many evils and to point out that the first and most necessary remedy is a reform of morals.

III. CHANGES SINCE LEO XIII

99. Important indeed have the changes been which both the economic system and socialism have undergone since Leo XIII's time.

100. That, in the first place, the whole aspect of economic life is vastly altered, is plain to all. You know, venerable brethren and beloved children, that the encyclical of Our predecessor of happy memory had in view chiefly that economic system, wherein, generally, some provide capital while others provide labor for a joint economic activity. And in a happy phrase he described it thus: "Neither capital can do without labor, nor labor without capital."[48]

101. With all his energy Leo XIII sought to adjust this economic system according to the norms of right order; hence, it is evident that this system is not to be condemned in itself. And surely it is not of its own nature vicious. But it does violate right order when capital hires workers, that is, the non-owning

---

47. Eph. 4:16.

48. *Rerum Novarum*, n. 19.

working class, with a view to and under such terms that it directs business and even the whole economic system according to its own will and advantage, scorning the human dignity of the workers, the social character of economic activity and social justice itself, and the common good.

102. Even today this is not, it is true, the only economic system in force everywhere; for there is another system also, which still embraces a huge mass of humanity, significant in numbers and importance, as for example, agriculture wherein the greater portion of mankind honorably and honestly procures its livelihood. This group, too, is being crushed with hardships and with difficulties, to which Our predecessor devotes attention in several places in his encyclical and which We Ourselves have touched upon more than once in Our present letter.

103. But, with the diffusion of modern industry throughout the whole world, the "capitalist" economic regime has spread everywhere to such a degree, particularly since the publication of Leo XIII's encyclical, that it has invaded and pervaded the economic and social life of even those outside its orbit and is unquestionably impressing on it its advantages, disadvantages and vices, and, in a sense, is giving it its own shape and form.

104. Accordingly, when directing Our special attention to the changes which the capitalist economic system has undergone since Leo's time, We have in mind the good not only of those who dwell in regions given over to "capital" and industry, but of all mankind.

105. In the first place, it is obvious that not only is wealth concentrated in our times but an immense power and despotic economic dictatorship is consolidated in the hands of a few, who often are not owners but only the trustees and managing directors of invested funds which they administer according to their own arbitrary will and pleasure.

106. This dictatorship is being most forcibly exercised by those who, since they hold the money and completely control it, control credit also and rule the lending of money. Hence they regulate the flow, so to speak, of the life-blood whereby the entire economic system lives, and have so firmly in their grasp the soul, as it were, of economic life that no one can breathe against their will.

107. This concentration of power and might, the characteristic mark, as it were, of contemporary economic life, is the fruit that the unlimited freedom of struggle among competitors has of its own nature produced, and which lets only the strongest survive; and this is often the same as saying, those who fight the most violently, those who give least heed to their conscience.

108. This accumulation of might and of power generates in turn three kinds of conflict. First, there is the struggle for economic supremacy itself; then there is the bitter fight to gain supremacy over the State in order to use in economic

struggles its resources and authority; finally there is conflict between States themselves, not only because countries employ their power and shape their policies to promote every economic advantage of their citizens, but also because they seek to decide political controversies that arise among nations through the use of their economic supremacy and strength.

109. The ultimate consequences of the individualist spirit in economic life are those which you yourselves, venerable brethren and beloved children, see and deplore: Free competition has destroyed itself; economic dictatorship has supplanted the free market; unbridled ambition for power has likewise succeeded greed for gain; all economic life has become tragically hard, inexorable, and cruel. To these are to be added the grave evils that have resulted from an intermingling and shameful confusion of the functions and duties of public authority with those of the economic sphere—such as, one of the worst, the virtual degradation of the majesty of the State, which although it ought to sit on high like a queen and supreme arbitress, free from all partiality and intent upon the one common good and justice, is become a slave, surrendered and delivered to the passions and greed of men. And as to international relations, two different streams have issued from the one fountainhead: On the one hand, economic nationalism or even economic imperialism; on the other, a no less deadly and accursed internationalism of finance or international imperialism whose country is where profit is.

110. In the second part of this encyclical where We have presented Our teaching, We have described the remedies for these great evils so explicitly that We consider it sufficient at this point to recall them briefly. Since the present system of economy is founded chiefly upon ownership and labor, the principles of right reason, that is, of Christian social philosophy, must be kept in mind regarding ownership and labor and their association together, and must be put into actual practice. First, so as to avoid the reefs of individualism and collectivism, the twofold character, that is individual and social, both of capital or ownership and of work or labor must be given due and rightful weight. Relations of one to the other must be made to conform to the laws of strictest justice—commutative justice, as it is called—with the support, however, of Christian charity. Free competition, kept within definite and due limits, and still more economic dictatorship, must be effectively brought under public authority in these matters which pertain to the latter's function. The public institutions themselves, of peoples, moreover, ought to make all human society conform to the needs of the common good; that is, to the norm of social justice. If this is done, that most important division of social life, namely, economic activity, cannot fail likewise to return to right and sound order.

111. Socialism, against which Our predecessor, Leo XIII, had especially to inveigh, has since his time changed no less profoundly than the form of economic life. For socialism, which could then be termed almost a single system and which maintained definite teachings reduced into one body of doctrine, has since then split chiefly into two sections, often opposing each other and even bitterly hostile, without either one however abandoning a position fundamentally contrary to Christian truth that was characteristic of socialism.

112. One section of socialism has undergone almost the same change that the capitalistic economic system, as We have explained above, has undergone. It has sunk into communism. Communism teaches and seeks two objectives: Unrelenting class warfare and absolute extermination of private ownership. Not secretly or by hidden methods does it do this, but publicly, openly, and by employing every and all means, even the most violent. To achieve these objectives there is nothing which it does not dare, nothing for which it has respect or reverence; and when it has come to power, it is incredible and portentous in its cruelty and inhumanity. The horrible slaughter and destruction through which it has laid waste vast regions of eastern Europe and Asia are the evidence; how much an enemy and how openly hostile it is to Holy Church and to God Himself is, alas, too well proved by facts and fully known to all. Although We, therefore, deem it superfluous to warn upright and faithful children of the Church regarding the impious and iniquitous character of communism, yet We cannot without deep sorrow contemplate the heedlessness of those who apparently make light of these impending dangers, and with sluggish inertia allow the widespread propagation of doctrine which seeks by violence and slaughter to destroy society altogether. All the more gravely to be condemned is the folly of those who neglect to remove or change the conditions that inflame the minds of peoples, and pave the way for the overthrow and destruction of society.

113. The other section, which has kept the name socialism, is surely more moderate. It not only professes the rejection of violence but modifies and tempers to some degree, if it does not reject entirely, the class struggle and the abolition of private ownership. One might say that, terrified by its own principles and by the conclusions drawn therefrom by communism, socialism inclines toward and in a certain measure approaches the truths which Christian tradition has always held sacred; for it cannot be denied that its demands at times come very near those that Christian reformers of society justly insist upon.

114. For if the class struggle abstains from enmities and mutual hatred, it gradually changes into an honest discussion of differences founded on a desire for justice, and if this is not that blessed social peace which we all seek, it can and ought to be the point of departure from which to move forward to the mutual

cooperation of the industries and professions. So also the war declared on private ownership, more and more abated, is being so restricted that now, finally, not the possession itself of the means of production is attacked but rather a kind of sovereignty over society which ownership has, contrary to all right, seized and usurped. For such sovereignty belongs in reality not to owners but to the public authority. If the foregoing happens, it can come even to the point that imperceptibly these ideas of the more moderate socialism will no longer differ from the desires and demands of those who are striving to remold human society on the basis of Christian principles. For certain kinds of property, it is rightly contended, ought to be reserved to the State since they carry with them a dominating power so great that they cannot without danger to the general welfare be entrusted to private individuals.

115. Such just demands and desire have nothing in them now which is inconsistent with Christian truth, and much less are they special to socialism. Those who work solely toward such ends have, therefore, no reason to become socialists.

116. Yet let no one think that all the socialist groups or factions that are not communist have, without exception, recovered their senses to this extent either in fact or in name. For the most part they do not reject the class struggle or the abolition of ownership, but only in some degree modify them. Now if these false principles are modified and to some extent erased from the program, the question arises, or rather is raised without warrant by some, whether the principles of Christian truth cannot perhaps be also modified to some degree and be tempered so as to meet socialism half-way and, as it were, by a middle course, come to agreement with it. There are some allured by the foolish hope that socialists in this way will be drawn to us. A vain hope! Those who want to be apostles among socialists ought to profess Christian truth whole and entire, openly and sincerely, and not connive at error in any way. If they truly wish to be heralds of the Gospel, let them above all strive to show to socialists that socialist claims, so far as they are just, are far more strongly supported by the principles of Christian faith and much more effectively promoted through the power of Christian charity.

117. But what if socialism has really been so tempered and modified as to the class struggle and private ownership that there is in it no longer anything to be censured on these points? Has it thereby renounced its contradictory nature to the Christian religion? This is the question that holds many minds in suspense. And numerous are the Catholics who, although they clearly understand that Christian principles can never be abandoned or diminished, seem to turn their eyes to the Holy See and earnestly beseech Us to decide whether this form of socialism has so far recovered from false doctrines that it can be accepted without the sacrifice of any Christian principle and in a certain sense be baptized. That

We, in keeping with Our fatherly solicitude, may answer their petitions, We make this pronouncement: Whether considered as a doctrine, or an historical fact, or a movement, socialism, if it remains truly socialism, even after it has yielded to truth and justice on the points which we have mentioned, cannot be reconciled with the teachings of the Catholic Church because its concept of society itself is utterly foreign to Christian truth.

118. For, according to Christian teaching, man, endowed with a social nature, is placed on this earth so that by leading a life in society and under an authority ordained of God[49] he may fully cultivate and develop all his faculties unto the praise and glory of his Creator; and that by faithfully fulfilling the duties of his craft or other calling he may obtain for himself temporal and at the same time eternal happiness. Socialism, on the other hand, wholly ignoring and indifferent to this sublime end of both man and society, affirms that human association has been instituted for the sake of material advantage alone.

119. Because of the fact that goods are produced more efficiently by a suitable division of labor than by the scattered efforts of individuals, socialists infer that economic activity, only the material ends of which enter into their thinking, ought of necessity to be carried on socially. Because of this necessity, they hold that men are obliged, with respect to the producing of goods, to surrender and subject themselves entirely to society. Indeed, possession of the greatest possible supply of things that serve the advantages of this life is considered of such great importance that the higher goods of man, liberty not excepted, must take a secondary place and even be sacrificed to the demands of the most efficient production of goods. This damage to human dignity, undergone in the "socialized" process of production, will be easily offset, they say, by the abundance of socially produced goods which will pour out in profusion to individuals to be used freely at their pleasure for comforts and cultural development. Society, therefore, as socialism conceives it, can on the one hand neither exist nor be thought of without an obviously excessive use of force; on the other hand, it fosters a liberty no less false, since there is no place in it for true social authority, which rests not on temporal and material advantages but descends from God alone, the Creator and last end of all things.[50]

120. If socialism, like all errors, contains some truth (which, moreover, the Supreme Pontiffs have never denied), it is based nevertheless on a theory of human society peculiar to itself and irreconcilable with true Christianity. Religious socialism, Christian socialism, are contradictory terms; no one can be at the same time a good Catholic and a true socialist. [...]

---

49. Cf. Rom. 13:1.

50. Cf. *Diuturnum Illud.*

125. It is certainly most lamentable, venerable brethren, that there have been, nay, that even now there are men who, although professing to be Catholics, are almost completely unmindful of that sublime law of justice and charity that binds us not only to render to everyone what is his but to succor brothers in need as Christ the Lord Himself,[51] and—what is worse—out of greed for gain do not scruple to exploit the workers. Even more, there are men who abuse religion itself, and under its name try to hide their unjust exactions in order to protect themselves from the manifestly just demands of the workers. The conduct of such We shall never cease to censure gravely. For they are the reason why the Church could, even though undeservedly, have the appearance of and be charged with taking the part of the rich and with being quite unmoved by the necessities and hardships of those who have been deprived, as it were, of their natural inheritance. The whole history of the Church plainly demonstrates that such appearances are unfounded and such charges unjust. The encyclical itself, whose anniversary we are celebrating, is clearest proof that it is the height of injustice to hurl these calumnies and reproaches at the Church and her teaching.

126. Although pained by the injustice and downcast in fatherly sorrow, it is so far from Our thought to repulse or to disown children who have been miserably deceived and have strayed so far from the truth and salvation that We cannot but invite them with all possible solicitude to return to the maternal bosom of the Church. May they lend ready ears to Our voice, may they return whence they have left, to the home that is truly their Father's, and may they stand firm there where their own place is, in the ranks of those who, zealously following the admonitions which Leo promulgated and We have solemnly repeated, are striving to restore society according to the mind of the Church on the firmly established basis of social justice and social charity. And let them be convinced that nowhere, even on earth, can they find full happiness save with Him who, being rich, became poor for our sakes that through His poverty we might become rich,[52] Who was poor and in labors from His youth, Who invited to Himself all that labor and are heavily burdened that He might refresh them fully in the love of His heart,[53] and Who, lastly, without any respect for persons will require more of them to whom more has been given[54] and "will render to everyone according to his conduct."[55]

---

51. Cf. James 2.
52. 2 Cor. 8:9.
53. Matt. 11:28.
54. Cf. Luke 12:48.
55. Matt. 16:27.

127. Yet, if we look into the matter more carefully and more thoroughly, we shall clearly perceive that, preceding this ardently desired social restoration, there must be a renewal of the Christian spirit, from which so many immersed in economic life have, far and wide, unhappily fallen away, lest all our efforts be wasted and our house be built not on a rock but on shifting sand.[56]

128. And so, venerable brethren and beloved sons, having surveyed the present economic system, We have found it laboring under the gravest of evils. We have also summoned communism and socialism again to judgment and have found all their forms, even the most modified, to wander far from the precepts of the Gospel.

129. "Wherefore," to use the words of Our predecessor, "if human society is to be healed, only a return to Christian life and institutions will heal it."[57] For this alone can provide effective remedy for that excessive care for passing things that is the origin of all vices; and this alone can draw away men's eyes, fascinated by and wholly fixed on the changing things of the world, and raise them toward Heaven. Who would deny that human society is in most urgent need of this cure now?

130. The minds of all, it is true, are affected almost solely by temporal upheavals, disasters, and calamities. But if we examine things critically with Christian eyes, as we should, what are all these compared with the loss of souls? Yet it is not rash by any means to say that the whole scheme of social and economic life is now such as to put in the way of vast numbers of mankind most serious obstacles which prevent them from caring for the one thing necessary; namely, their eternal salvation.

131. We, made Shepherd and Protector by the Prince of Shepherds, Who redeemed them by His Blood, of a truly innumerable flock, cannot hold back Our tears when contemplating this greatest of their dangers. Nay rather, fully mindful of Our pastoral office and with paternal solicitude, We are continually meditating on how We can help them; and We have summoned to Our aid the untiring zeal of others who are concerned on grounds of justice or charity. For what will it profit men to become expert in more wisely using their wealth, even to gaining the whole world, if thereby they suffer the loss of their souls?[58] What will it profit to teach them sound principles of economic life if in unbridled and sordid greed they let themselves be swept away by their passion for property, so that "hearing the commandments of the Lord they do all things contrary"?[59]

---

56. Cf. Matt. 7:24ff.

57. *Rerum Novarum*, n. 27.

58. Cf. Matt. 16:26.

59. Cf. Judg. 2:17.

132. The root and font of this defection in economic and social life from the Christian law, and of the consequent apostasy of great numbers of workers from the Catholic faith, are the disordered passions of the soul, the sad result of original sin which has so destroyed the wonderful harmony of man's faculties that, easily led astray by his evil desires, he is strongly incited to prefer the passing goods of this world to the lasting goods of Heaven. Hence arises that unquenchable thirst for riches and temporal goods, which has at all times impelled men to break God's laws and trample upon the rights of their neighbors, but which, on account of the present system of economic life, is laying far more numerous snares for human frailty. Since the instability of economic life, and especially of its structure, exacts of those engaged in it most intense and unceasing effort, some have become so hardened to the stings of conscience as to hold that they are allowed, in any manner whatsoever, to increase their profits and use means, fair or foul, to protect their hard-won wealth against sudden changes of fortune. The easy gains that a market unrestricted by any law opens to everybody attracts large numbers to buying and selling goods, and they, their one aim being to make quick profits with the least expenditure of work, raise or lower prices by their uncontrolled business dealings so rapidly according to their own caprice and greed that they nullify the wisest forecasts of producers. The laws passed to promote corporate business, while dividing and limiting the risk of business, have given occasion to the most sordid license. For We observe that consciences are little affected by this reduced obligation of accountability; that furthermore, by hiding under the shelter of a joint name, the worst of injustices and frauds are perpetrated; and that, too, directors of business companies, forgetful of their trust, betray the rights of those whose savings they have undertaken to administer. Lastly, We must not omit to mention those crafty men who, wholly unconcerned about any honest usefulness of their work, do not scruple to stimulate the baser human desires and, when they are aroused, use them for their own profit.

133. Strict and watchful moral restraint enforced vigorously by governmental authority could have banished these enormous evils and even forestalled them; this restraint, however, has too often been sadly lacking. For since the seeds of a new form of economy were bursting forth just when the principles of rationalism had been implanted and rooted in many minds, there quickly developed a body of economic teaching far removed from the true moral law, and, as a result, completely free rein was given to human passions.

134. Thus it came to pass that many, much more than ever before, were solely concerned with increasing their wealth by any means whatsoever, and that in seeking their own selfish interests before everything else they had no conscience about committing even the gravest of crimes against others. Those first entering

upon this broad way that leads to destruction[60] easily found numerous imitators of their iniquity by the example of their manifest success, by their insolent display of wealth, by their ridiculing the conscience of others, who, as they said, were troubled by silly scruples, or lastly by crushing more conscientious competitors.

135. With the rulers of economic life abandoning the right road, it was easy for the rank and file of workers everywhere to rush headlong also into the same chasm; and all the more so, because very many managements treated their workers like mere tools, with no concern at all for their souls, without indeed even the least thought of spiritual things. Truly the mind shudders at the thought of the grave dangers to which the morals of workers (particularly younger workers) and the modesty of girls and women are exposed in modern factories; when we recall how often the present economic scheme, and particularly the shameful housing conditions, create obstacles to the family bond and normal family life; when we remember how many obstacles are put in the way of the proper observance of Sundays and Holy Days; and when we reflect upon the universal weakening of that truly Christian sense through which even rude and unlettered men were wont to value higher things, and upon its substitution by the single preoccupation of getting in any way whatsoever one's daily bread. And thus bodily labor, which divine Providence decreed to be performed, even after original sin, for the good at once of man's body and soul, is being everywhere changed into an instrument of perversion; for dead matter comes forth from the factory ennobled, while men there are corrupted and degraded.

136. No genuine cure can be furnished for this lamentable ruin of souls, which, so long as it continues, will frustrate all efforts to regenerate society, unless men return openly and sincerely to the teaching of the Gospel, to the precepts of Him Who alone has the words of everlasting life,[61] words which will never pass away, even if heaven and earth will pass away.[62] All experts in social problems are seeking eagerly a structure so fashioned in accordance with the norms of reason that it can lead economic life back to sound and right order. But this order, which We Ourselves ardently long for and with all Our efforts promote, will be wholly defective and incomplete unless all the activities of men harmoniously unite to imitate and attain, in so far as it lies within human strength, the marvelous unity of the divine plan. We mean that perfect order which the Church with great force and power preaches and which right human reason itself demands, that all things be directed to God as the first and supreme end of all created activity, and

60. Cf. Matt. 7:13.

61. Cf. John 6:69.

62. Cf. Matt. 24:35.

that all created goods under God be considered as mere instruments to be used only in so far as they conduce to the attainment of the supreme end. Nor is it to be thought that gainful occupations are thereby belittled or judged less consonant with human dignity; on the contrary, we are taught to recognize in them with reverence the manifest will of the divine Creator Who placed man upon the earth to work it and use it in a multitude of ways for his needs. Those who are engaged in producing goods, therefore, are not forbidden to increase their fortune in a just and lawful manner; for it is only fair that he who renders service to the community and makes it richer should also, through the increased wealth of the community, be made richer himself according to his position, provided that all these things be sought with due respect for the laws of God and without impairing the rights of others and that they be employed in accordance with faith and right reason. If these principles are observed by everyone, everywhere, and always, not only the production and acquisition of goods but also the use of wealth, which now is seen to be so often contrary to right order, will be brought back soon within the bounds of equity and just distribution. The sordid love of wealth, which is the shame and great sin of our age, will be opposed in actual fact by the gentle yet effective law of Christian moderation which commands man to seek first the Kingdom of God and His justice, with the assurance that, by virtue of God's kindness and unfailing promise, temporal goods also, in so far as he has need of them, shall be given him besides.[63]

137. But in effecting all this, the law of charity, "which is the bond of perfection,"[64] must always take a leading role. How completely deceived, therefore, are those rash reformers who concern themselves with the enforcement of justice alone—and this, commutative justice—and in their pride reject the assistance of charity! Admittedly, no vicarious charity can substitute for justice which is due as an obligation and is wrongfully denied. Yet even supposing that everyone should finally receive all that is due him, the widest field for charity will always remain open. For justice alone can, if faithfully observed, remove the causes of social conflict but can never bring about union of minds and hearts. Indeed all the institutions for the establishment of peace and the promotion of mutual help among men, however perfect these may seem, have the principal foundation of their stability in the mutual bond of minds and hearts whereby the members are united with one another. If this bond is lacking, the best of regulations come to naught, as we have learned by too frequent experience. And so, then only will true cooperation be possible for a single common good when the constituent parts of society

63. Cf. Matt. 6:33.
64. Col. 3:14.

deeply feel themselves members of one great family and children of the same heavenly Father; nay, that they are one body in Christ, "but severally members one of another,"⁶⁵ so that "if one member suffers anything, all the members suffer with it."⁶⁶ For then the rich and others in positions of power will change their former indifference toward their poorer brothers into a solicitous and active love, listen with kindliness to their just demands, and freely forgive their possible mistakes and faults. And the workers, sincerely putting aside every feeling of hatred or envy which the promoters of social conflict so cunningly exploit, will not only accept without rancor the place in human society assigned them by divine Providence, but rather will hold it in esteem, knowing well that everyone according to his function and duty is toiling usefully and honorably for the common good and is following closely in the footsteps of Him Who, being in the form of God, willed to be a carpenter among men and to be known as the son of a carpenter.

138. Therefore, out of this new diffusion throughout the world of the spirit of the Gospel, which is the spirit of Christian moderation and universal charity, We are confident there will come that longed-for and full restoration of human society in Christ, and that "Peace of Christ in the Kingdom of Christ," to accomplish which, from the very beginning of Our pontificate, We firmly determined and resolved within Our heart to devote all Our care and all Our pastoral solicitude,⁶⁷ and toward this same highly important and most necessary end now, you also, venerable brethren, who with Us rule the Church of God under the mandate of the Holy Spirit,⁶⁸ are earnestly toiling with wholly praiseworthy zeal in all parts of the world, even in the regions of the holy missions to the infidels. Let well-merited acclamations of praise be bestowed upon you and at the same time upon all those, both clergy and laity, who, We rejoice to see, are daily participating and valiantly helping in this same great work, Our beloved sons engaged in Catholic Action, who with a singular zeal are undertaking with Us the solution of social problems in so far as by virtue of her divine institution this is proper to and devolves upon the Church. All these We urge in the Lord, again and again, to spare no labors and let no difficulties conquer them, but rather to become day by day more courageous and more valiant.⁶⁹ Arduous indeed is the task which We propose to them, for We know well that on both sides, both among the upper and the lower classes of society, there are many obstacles and barriers to be overcome.

65. Rom. 12:5.
66. 1 Cor. 12:26.
67. *Ubi Arcano.*
68. Cf. Act. 20:28.
69. Cf. Deut. 31:7.

Let them not, however, lose heart; to face bitter combats is a mark of Christians, and to endure grave labors to the end is a mark of them who, as good soldiers of Christ,[70] follow Him closely.

139. Relying therefore solely on the all-powerful aid of Him "Who wishes all men to be saved,"[71] let us strive with all our strength to help those unhappy souls who have turned from God and, drawing them away from the temporal cares in which they are too deeply immersed, let us teach them to aspire with confidence to the things that are eternal. Sometimes this will be achieved much more easily than seems possible at first sight to expect. For if wonderful spiritual forces lie hidden, like sparks beneath ashes, within the secret recesses of even the most abandoned man—certain proof that his soul is naturally Christian—how much the more in the hearts of those many upon many who have been led into error rather through ignorance or environment. […]

141. The present state of affairs, venerable brethren, clearly indicates the way in which We ought to proceed. For We are now confronted, as more than once before in the history of the Church, with a world that in large part has almost fallen back into paganism. That these whole classes of men may be brought back to Christ Whom they have denied, we must recruit and train, from among them themselves, auxiliary soldiers of the Church who know them well and their minds and wishes, and can reach their hearts with a tender brotherly love. The first and immediate apostles to the workers ought to be workers; the apostles to those who follow industry and trade ought to be from among them themselves.

142. It is chiefly your duty, venerable brethren, and of your clergy, to search diligently for these lay apostles both of workers and of employers, to select them with prudence, and to train and instruct them properly. A difficult task, certainly, is thus imposed on priests, and to meet it, all who are growing up as the hope of the Church, must be duly prepared by an intensive study of the social question. […]

144. Certainly there is the greatest need now of such valiant soldiers of Christ who will work with all their strength to keep the human family safe from the dire ruin into which it would be plunged were the teachings of the Gospel to be flouted, and that order of things permitted to prevail which tramples underfoot no less the laws of nature than those of God. The Church of Christ, built upon an unshakable rock, has nothing to fear for herself, as she knows for a certainty that the gates of hell shall never prevail against her.[72] Rather, she knows full well,

---

70. Cf. 2 Tim. 2:3.

71. 1 Tim. 2:4.

72. Cf. Matt. 16:18.

through the experience of many centuries, that she is wont to come forth from the most violent storms stronger than ever and adorned with new triumphs. Yet her maternal heart cannot but be moved by the countless evils with which so many thousands would be afflicted during storms of this kind, and above all by the consequent enormous injury to spiritual life which would work eternal ruin to so many souls redeemed by the Blood of Jesus Christ.

145. To ward off such great evils from human society nothing, therefore, is to be left untried; to this end may all our labors turn, to this all our energies, to this our fervent and unremitting prayers to God! For with the assistance of divine grace the fate of the human family rests in our hands. […]

Given at Rome, at Saint Peter's, the fifteenth day of May, in the year 1931, the tenth year of Our pontificate.

✠ Pius XI

CI RIESCE[†]

Discourse on Religious Tolerance

Pope Pius XII,
December 6, 1953

I t gives Us great satisfaction, beloved sons of the Union of Italian Catholic Jurists, to see you gathered round Us here and to bid you heartfelt welcome. In the beginning of October another congress of jurists, dealing with international penal law, gathered in Our summer residence. Your convention is national in character, but the subject it is treating, "The Nation and the International Community," touches again the relations between peoples and sovereign states. It is not by chance that congresses are multiplying for the study of international questions, be they scientific, economic, or political. The clear fact that relations between individuals of various nations and between nations themselves are growing in multiplicity and intensity makes daily more urgent a right ordering of international relations, both private and public; all the more so since this mutual drawing together is caused not only by vastly improved technological progress and by free choice but also by the more profound action of an intrinsic law of development. This movement, then, is not to be repressed but fostered and promoted.

I

2. In this work of expansion, communities of states and peoples, whether already existing or only a goal to be achieved, have naturally a special importance. They are communities in which sovereign states, that is to say, states which are subordinate to no other state, are united into a juridical community to attain definite juridical ends. It would give a false idea of these juridical communities to compare them to world empires of the past or of the present, in which different

---

† [Delivered to participants in the Fifth National Convention of the Union of Italian Catholic Jurists, the address *Ci Riesce* is arguably the most important magisterial treatment of religious freedom between the time of Leo XIII and the promulgation of *Dignitatis Humanae*, although certain paragraphs from John XXIII's encyclicals make a signal contribution as well. The paragraph numbers have been added for convenient reference.]

racial stocks, peoples, and states become fused, whether they want it or not, into a single conglomeration of states. In the present instance, however, states, remaining sovereign, freely unite into a juridical community.

3. In this connection, the history of the world, which shows a continuous succession of struggles for power, no doubt might make the establishment of a juridical community of free states seem almost utopian. The conflicts of the past have too often been motivated by a desire to subjugate other nations and to extend the range of one's own power, or by the necessity of defending one's liberty and one's own independent existence. This time, on the contrary, it is precisely the will to prevent threatening conflicts that urges men toward a supra-national juridical community. Utilitarian considerations, which certainly carry considerable weight, point toward the working out of peace; and finally, perhaps, it is precisely this mingling of men of different nations because of technological progress that has awakened the faith, implanted in the hearts and souls of individuals, in a higher community of men, willed by the Creator and rooted in the unity of their common origin, nature, and final destiny.

II

4. These and other similar considerations show that advance toward establishing a community of peoples does not look, as to a unique and ultimate norm, to the will of the states but rather to nature, to the Creator. The right to existence, the right to respect from others and to one's good name, the right to one's own culture and national character, the right to develop oneself, the right to demand observance of international treaties, and other like rights, are exigencies of the law of nations, dictated by nature itself. The positive law of different peoples, also indispensable in the community of states, has the office of defining more exactly the rights derived from nature and of adapting them to concrete circumstances, and also of making other provisions, directed, of course, toward the common good, on the basis of a positive agreement, which, once freely entered into, has binding force.

5. In this community of nations, then, every state becomes a part of the system of international law, and hence of natural law, which is both foundation and crown of the whole. Thus the individual nation no longer is—nor in fact was it ever—"sovereign," in the sense of being entirely without restrictions. "Sovereignty" in the true sense means self-rule and exclusive competence concerning what has to be done and how it is to be done in regard to the affairs of a definite territory, always within the framework of international law, without however becoming dependent on the juridical system of any other state. Every

state is immediately subject to international law. States which would lack this full-ness of power, or whose independence of the power of any other state would not be guaranteed by international law, would not be sovereign. But no state could complain about a limitation of its sovereignty if it were denied the power of acting arbitrarily and without regard for other states. Sovereignty is not a divinization of the state, or omnipotence of the state in the Hegelian sense, or after the manner of absolute juridical positivism.

III

6. There is no need to explain to you students of law how the setting up, maintenance, and operation of a real community of states, especially one that would embrace all peoples, give rise to many duties and problems, some of them extremely difficult and complicated, which cannot be solved by a simple yes or no answer. Such would be the question of race and origin, with their biological, psychological, and social consequences; the question of language; the question of family life, with its relations, varying according to nation, between husband and wife, parents, the larger family group; the question of the equality or equiv-alence of rights in what regards goods, contracts, and persons for the citizens of one sovereign state who either live for a short time in a foreign state or, retaining their own nationality, establish permanent residence there; the question of the right of immigration or of emigration, and other like questions.

7. The jurist, the statesman, the individual state, as well as the community of states should here take account of all the inborn inclinations of individuals and communities in their contracts and reciprocal relations, such as the tendency to adapt or to assimilate, often pushed even to an attempt to absorb; or contrariwise, the tendency to exclude and to destroy anything that appears incapable of assim-ilation; the tendency to expand, to embrace what is new, as on the contrary, the tendency to retreat and to segregate oneself; the tendency to give oneself entirely, forgetful of self, and its opposite, attachment to oneself, excluding any service of others; the lust for power, the yearning to keep others in subjection, and so on.

8. All these instincts, either of self-aggrandizement or of self-defense, have their roots in the natural dispositions of individuals, of peoples, of races, and of communities, and in their restrictions and limitations. One never finds in them everything that is good and just. God alone, the origin of all things, possesses within Himself, by reason of His infinity, all that is good.

9. From what We have said, it is easy to deduce the fundamental theoretical principle for dealing with these difficulties and tendencies: within the limits of the possible and lawful, to promote everything that facilitates union and makes

it more effective; to remove everything that disturbs it; to tolerate at times that which it is impossible to correct but which, on the other hand, must not be permitted to make shipwreck of the community, from which a higher good is hoped for. The difficulty rests in the application of this principle.

IV

10. In this connection, We wish to treat with you who are happy to profess yourselves Catholic jurists, concerning one of the questions which arises in a community of peoples, that is, the practical co-existence [*convivenza*] of Catholic with non-Catholic states.

11. Depending upon the religious belief of the great majority of citizens, or by reason of an explicit declaration of law, peoples and member states of the international community will be divided into those that are Christian, non-Christian, indifferent to religion or consciously without it, or even professedly atheist. The interests of religion and morality will require for the whole extent of the international community a well-defined rule, which will hold for all the territory of the individual sovereign member-states of the international community. According to probability and depending on circumstances, it can be foreseen that this ruling of positive law will be thus enunciated: within its own territory and for its own citizens, each state will regulate religious and moral affairs by its own laws. Nevertheless, throughout the whole territory of the international community of states, the citizens of every member-state will be allowed the exercise of their own beliefs and ethical and religious practices, insofar as these do not contravene the penal laws of the state in which they are residing.

12. For the jurist, the statesman, and the Catholic state arises here the question: can they give their consent to such a ruling when there is question of entering and remaining in an international community?

13. Now, in regard to religious and moral interests, a twofold question arises: the first deals with the objective truth and the obligation of conscience toward what is objectively true and good; the second deals with the practical attitude of the international community toward the individual sovereign state and the attitude of the individual state toward the international community in what regards religion and morality.

14. The first question can hardly be a matter for discussion and legal ruling between the individual states and the international community, especially in the case of a plurality of different religious beliefs within the international community. On the other hand, the second question can be of extreme importance and urgency.

V

15. Now to give the right answer to the second question. Above all, it must be clearly stated that no human authority, no state, no community of states, whatever be their religious character, can give a positive command or positive authorization to teach or to do that which would be contrary to religious truth or moral good. Such a command or such an authorization would have no obligatory power and would remain without effect. No authority may give such a command, because it is contrary to nature to oblige the spirit and the will of man to error and evil, or to consider one or the other as indifferent. Not even God could give such a positive command or positive authorization, because it would be in contradiction to His absolute truth and sanctity.

16. Another question, essentially different, is this: could the norm be established in a community of states—at least in certain circumstances—that the free exercise of a belief and of a religious or moral practice which possess validity in one of the member states, be not hindered throughout the entire territory of the community of nations by state laws or coercive measures? In other words, the question is raised whether in these circumstances *non impedire* or toleration is permissible, and whether, consequently, positive repression is not always a duty.

17. We have just adduced the authority of God. Could God, although it would be possible and easy for Him to repress error and moral deviation, in some cases choose the *non impedire* without contradicting His infinite perfection? Could it be that *in certain circumstances* He would not give men any mandate, would not impose any duty, and would not even communicate the right to impede or to repress what is erroneous and false? A look at things as they are gives an affirmative answer. Reality shows that error and sin are in the world in great measure. God reprobates them, but He permits them to exist. Hence the affirmation: "religious and moral error must always be impeded, when it is possible, because toleration of them is in itself immoral," is not valid *absolutely and unconditionally*.

18. Moreover, God has not given even to human authority such an absolute and universal command in matters of faith and morality. Such a command is unknown to the common convictions of mankind, to Christian conscience, to the sources of revelation, and to the practice of the Church. To omit here other Scriptural texts which are adduced in support of this argument, Christ in the parable of the cockle gives the following advice: let the cockle grow in the field of the world together with the good seed in view of the harvest (cf. Mt. 13:24–30). The duty of repressing moral and religious error cannot therefore be an ultimate norm of action. It must be subordinate to *higher and more general* norms, which *in*

some circumstances permit, and even perhaps seem to indicate as the better policy, toleration of error in order to promote a *greater good.*

19. Thus the two principles are clarified to which recourse must be had in concrete cases for the answer to the serious question concerning the attitude which the jurist, the statesman, and the sovereign Catholic state is to adopt in consideration of the community of nations in regard to a formula of religious and moral toleration as described above. First: that which does not correspond to truth or to the norm of morality objectively has no right to exist, to be spread, or to be activated. Secondly: failure to impede this with civil laws and coercive measures can nevertheless be justified in the interests of a higher and more general good.

20. Before all else the Catholic statesman must judge if this condition is verified in the concrete—this is the "question of fact." In his decision he will permit himself to be guided by weighing the dangerous consequences that stem from toleration against those from which the community of nations will be spared, if the formula of toleration be accepted. Moreover, he will be guided by the good which, according to a wise prognosis, can be derived from toleration for the international community as such, and indirectly for the member state. In that which concerns religion and morality he will also ask for the judgment of the Church. For her, only He to whom Christ has entrusted the guidance of His whole Church is competent to speak in the last instance on such vital questions, touching international life; that is, the Roman Pontiff.

VI

21. The institution of a community of nations, which today has been partly realized but which is striving to be established and consolidated upon a higher and more perfect level, is an ascent from the lower to the higher, that is, from a plurality of sovereign states to the greatest possible unity.

22. The Church of Christ has, in virtue of a mandate from her divine Founder, a similar universal mission. She must draw to herself and bind together in religious unity the men of all races and of all times. But here the process is in a certain sense the contrary: she descends from the higher to the lower. In the former case, the superior juridical unity of nations was and still is to be created. In the latter, the juridical community with its universal end, its constitution, its powers and those in whom these powers are invested are already established from the beginning, by the will and decree of Christ Himself. The duty of this universal community from the outset is to incorporate all men and all races (cf. Mt. 28:19) and thereby to bring them to the full truth and the grace of Jesus Christ.

23. The Church, in the fulfillment of this her mission, has always been faced and is still faced in large measure by the same problems which the functioning of a community of sovereign states must overcome; only she feels them more acutely, for she is obligated to the purpose of her mission, determined by her Founder Himself—a purpose which penetrates to the very depths of the spirit and heart of man. In this state of affairs conflicts are inevitable, and history shows that there have always been conflicts, there still are, and, according to the words of the Lord, there will be till the end of time.

24. For the Church with her mission has been, and is, confronted with men and nations of marvelous culture, with others of almost incredible lack of civilization, and with all possible intermediate degrees: diversity of extraction, of language, of philosophy, of religious belief, of national aspirations and characteristics; free peoples and enslaved peoples; peoples that have never belonged to the Church and peoples that have been separated from her communion.

25. The Church must live among them and with them; she can never declare before anyone that she is "not interested." The mandate imposed upon her by her divine Founder renders it impossible for her to follow a policy of non-interference or *laissez-faire*. She has the duty of teaching and educating in all the inflexibility of truth and goodness, and with this absolute obligation she must remain and work among men and nations that in mental outlook are completely different from each other.

26. Let Us return now, however, to the two propositions mentioned above: and in the first place to the one which denies unconditionally everything that is religiously false and morally wrong. With regard to this point there never has been, and there is not now, in the Church any vacillation or any compromise, either in theory or in practice. Her deportment has not changed in the course of history, nor can it change whenever or wherever, under the most diversified forms, she is confronted with the choice: either incense for idols or blood for Christ. The place where you are now present, Eternal Rome, with the remains of a greatness that was and with the glorious memories of its martyrs, is the most eloquent witness to the answer of the Church. Incense was not burned before the idols, and Christian blood flowed and consecrated the ground. But the temples of the gods lie in the cold devastation of ruins howsoever majestic; while at the tombs of the martyrs the faithful of all nations and all tongues fervently repeat the ancient Creed of the Apostles.

27. Concerning the second proposition, that is to say, concerning tolerance in determined circumstances—toleration even in cases in which one could [legitimately] proceed to [take steps of] repression—the Church, out of regard for those who in good conscience (though erroneous, but invincibly so) are of

different opinion, has been led to act and has acted with that tolerance, after she became the State Church under Constantine the Great and the other Christian emperors, [and she has done so] always for higher and more cogent motives. So she acts today, and also in the future she will be faced with the same necessity. In such individual cases the attitude of the Church is determined by what is demanded for safeguarding and considering the *bonum commune*—on the one hand, the common good of the Church and the State in individual states, and, on the other, the common good of the universal Church, the reign of God over the whole world. In considering the *pro* and *con* for resolving the "question of fact," as well as what concerns the final and supreme judge in these matters, no other norms are valid for the Church except the norms which We have just indicated for the Catholic jurist and statesman.

VII

28. The ideas We have set forth may also be useful for the Catholic jurist and statesman when, in their studies or in the exercise of their profession, they come in contact with the agreements (concordats, treaties, agreements, *modus vivendi*, etc.) which the Church (that is to say, for a long time now, the Apostolic See) has concluded and still concludes with sovereign states. The Concordats are for her an expression of the collaboration between the Church and the State. In principle, that is, in theory, she cannot approve complete separation of the two powers. The Concordats, therefore, must assure to the Church a stable condition in right and in fact in the State with which they are concluded, and must guarantee to her full independence in the fulfillment of her divine mission.

29. It is possible that the Church and the State proclaim in a Concordat their common religious conviction; but it may also happen that a Concordat have, together with other purposes, that of forestalling disputes with regard to questions of principle and of removing from the very beginning possible matters of conflict. When the Church has set her signature to a Concordat, it holds for everything contained therein. But, with the mutual acknowledgment of both high contracting parties, it may not hold in the same way for everything. It may signify an express approval, but it may also mean a simple tolerance, according to those two principles which are the norm for the co-existence [*convivenza*] of the Church and her faithful with the civil powers and with men of another belief.

30. This, beloved sons, is what We intended to treat of with you rather fully. For the rest, We are confident that the international community can banish every danger of war and establish peace, and, as far as the Church is concerned, can guarantee to her freedom of action everywhere, so that she may be able to

establish in the spirit and heart, in the thoughts and actions of men, the Kingdom of Him who is the Redeemer, the Lawgiver, the Judge, the Lord of the world, Jesus Christ, who rules as God over all things, blessed forever (Rom. 9:5).

31. While with Our paternal good wishes We follow your work for the greater good of nations and for the perfecting of international relations, from the fullness of Our heart We impart to you, as a pledge of the richest divine graces, the apostolic benediction.

✠ Pius XII

DIGNITATIS HUMANAE[†]

Declaration on the Right of the Person and of Communities to Social and Civil Freedom in Religious Matters

The Second Vatican Ecumenical Council, promulgated by Pope Paul VI on December 7, 1965

INTRODUCTION

Men in this age are becoming daily more aware of the dignity of the human person.[1] The number of those is growing who insist that men, in their actions, should enjoy and make use of their own counsel and responsible liberty, not forced by coercive means, but led in conscience by the recognition of a duty. Moreover, they demand that limits in law be placed on public authorities, so that the virtuous liberty of persons and of associations is not excessively restricted. This insistence on liberty in human society especially concerns goods of the human spirit, most fundamentally those which pertain to the free exercise in society of religion. This Vatican Council, taking careful note of these aspirations of the human spirit, and proposing to declare the extent to which these aspirations are in conformity with truth and justice, searches diligently the sacred tradition and doctrine of the Church, from which it brings forth new things which are, without exception, in harmony with the old.

Accordingly, this Sacred Council professes first of all that God Himself has made known to the human race a pathway by which, through serving Him, men can be made whole and completely happy in Christ. This single, true religion, we believe, subsists in the Catholic and apostolic Church, to which the Lord Jesus entrusted the responsibility of spreading this religion to all men without exception, when he told the Apostles, "Go, therefore, and make disciples of all nations, baptizing them in the name of the Father, and of the Son, and of the Holy Spirit,

---

† A new translation by Michael Pakaluk, Ph.D.

1. Cf. John XXIII, encycl. *Pacem in Terris*, April 11, 1963: AAS 55 (1963) p. 279; ibid., p. 265; Pius XII, Radio Message, Dec. 24, 1944: AAS 37 (1945), p. 14.

teaching them to observe all that I have commanded you" (Mt. 28:19–20). Indeed all men are bound, especially in matters which concern God and His Church, to seek the truth; to embrace it, when known by them; and to safeguard it.

This Sacred Council similarly professes that these obligations reach through to and bind the consciences of men. Nor is there any other way for truth to impose itself except by the force of truth itself, which penetrates sweetly and yet at the same time strongly into the human mind.

On the other hand, religious liberty involves an immunity from coercion in civil society, which men insist upon in carrying out their duty of giving honor to God. Religious liberty therefore leaves whole and entire the traditional Catholic teaching concerning the moral duty, owed by men and by societies, towards the true religion and the sole Church of Christ. But beyond that, this Sacred Council, in taking up the matter of religious liberty, intends to expound the teaching of recent Popes concerning the inviolable rights of the human person and the jurid-ical structure of society.

I. THE NATURE OF RELIGIOUS LIBERTY IN GENERAL

2. This Vatican Council declares that a human person has a right to religious liberty. This type of liberty consists in the fact that, within necessary limits, all men need to be immune from coercion, whether deriving from individuals, social groups, or any human authority, in any matter of religion, in such a way that no one is either forced to act against his conscience, or impeded from acting in accordance with his conscience, regardless of whether he is acting in private or in public, alone or in association with others.

Moreover, it declares that the right to religious liberty is, in truth, based on the very dignity of the human person, which is known both through the revealed Word of God and by reason itself.[2] This right of the human person to religious liberty should be recognized in the juridical structure of a society in such a way that it finds expression as a civil right.

All men without exception, on account of their dignity, because they are persons, that is to say, beings endowed with reason and freewill, and adorned with the gift of personal responsibility, are not only impelled by their own nature, but also bound by a moral obligation, to seek that truth which religion

---

2. Cf. John XXIII, encycl. *Pacem in Terris*, April 11, 1963: *AAS* 55 (1963), pp. 260–61; Pius XII, Ra-dio Message, Dec. 24, 1942: *AAS* 35 (1943), p. 19; Pius XI, encycl. *Mit Brennender Sorge*, March 14, 1937: *AAS* 29 (1937), p. 160; Leo XIII, encycl. *Libertas Praestantissimum*, June 20, 1888: *Acts of Leo XIII* 8 (1888), pp. 237–38.

most fundamentally is concerned with. They are moreover bound to embrace the truth once it is known, and to order their entire life according to the requirements of the truth. Men cannot satisfy this obligation, in a manner which befits their distinctive nature, unless they enjoy psychological liberty together with an immunity from external coercion. The right to religious liberty, therefore, is not based on any subjective disposition of a person, but rather in the very nature of a person. That is why the right to this immunity remains even in those who do not meet their obligation to seek the truth and embrace it, and why the exercise of this right cannot be impeded (assuming that, in that exercise, a just public order is maintained).

3. These conclusions appear in an even clearer light if one considers that the highest authority for human life is the divine law itself—eternal, objective, and universal—by which God, deliberating in His wisdom and love, orders, directs, and governs the whole world and the paths taken by the human community. God gives man the opportunity to be a sharer in this law of God, so that, as divine providence "orders things sweetly," man gives increasing recognition to unchangeable divine truth. That is why each person has a duty, and therefore also a right, of seeking the truth in matters of religion—in order that each person, through those means truly suited to him, might wisely form his own correct and true judgments of conscience.

Again, truth when sought after needs to be pursued in the manner which matches the dignity of the human person and his social nature, that is, through an inquiry which is liberal, aided by a teaching authority or course of instruction, and with the assistance of communication and dialogue, through which men propose to one another the truth they have found or believe they have found, so that they can help one another in the search for truth; again, truth once known needs to be adhered to firmly through a personal assent.

Indeed, man perceives and discerns the indications of the divine law through the medium of his own conscience, which he is obliged to follow faithfully in all of his actions, so that he might find his way to God, his final goal. Therefore, he must not be forced to act contrary to his conscience. But neither should he be hindered from acting in accordance with his conscience, especially in matters of religion. For the exercise of religion, of its very nature, consists most fundamentally in interior and free acts of the will, by which a man orders himself directly to God. Acts like that cannot be commanded or prohibited by any merely human authority.[3] Yet the social nature of man requires that man give external expression

---

3. Cf. John XXIII, encycl. *Pacem in Terris*, April 11, 1963: *AAS* 55 (1963), p. 270; Paul VI, Radio Message, Dec. 22, 1964: *AAS* 57 (1965), pp. 181–82.

to his interior acts of religion: since, when he communicates with others in some matter of religion, he professes his own religion in a communitarian manner. Therefore, an injury is done to the human person, and to the order established by God for men, if man is denied the free exercise of religion in society (assuming that, in that exercise, a just public order is maintained).

Besides, religious acts, by which men, whether privately or publicly, out of the convictions of their hearts, order themselves to God, by their nature transcend the earthly and temporal order of things. Therefore, civil authority, the specific end of which is care of the temporal common good, needs actually to recognize the religious life of citizens and encourage it. But civil authority must be said to be overstepping its specific limits, if it should presume to direct or impede religious acts.

4. The liberty, or immunity from coercion, in matters of religion, which pertains to persons considered individually, must be acknowledged to pertain also to persons acting in concert. After all, that there should be communities of a religious character is implied both by the social nature of man and by religion itself.

These communities, therefore, need an immunity under the law (assuming that, in their enjoyment of this immunity, the requirements of a just public order are not violated), so that they can conduct themselves in accordance with their own distinctive norms, render honor to the Supreme Divinity in public worship, aid their members in the practice of religious life and strengthen them with instruction, and promote those institutions in which their members work together to follow their own distinctive way of life in accordance with their religious principles.

Similarly religious communities have a right not to be hindered, either by legal measures or by the administrative actions of civil authorities, in selecting, educating, appointing, and transferring their own ministers, in communications with religious authorities or with communities at work in other parts of the world, in the construction of religious buildings, and, not least, in acquiring and enjoying appropriate goods.

Religious communities also have a right not to be hindered in teaching and bearing witness to their faith in public, whether in speech or in writing. However, in spreading religious faith, and in introducing religious practices, one should always abstain from every kind of action which smacks of coercion, or illicit persuasion, or persuasion which is less than upright, especially when one is dealing with the uneducated or persons in need. That sort of action should be regarded as an abuse of one's own right and as an attack on the rights of others.

Religious liberty additionally comes into play, in insuring that religious communities are not prohibited from freely demonstrating the special power of their teaching for the good ordering of society and for bringing life to human activity in its entirety.

Finally, the social nature of man, and the nature of religion itself, are the foundation for the right by which men, moved by their own particular religious sense, are able freely to hold meetings and to form educational, cultural, charitable and social associations.

5. Each family has the right freely to order its own domestic religious life under the guidance of the parents. It does so as a society which enjoys its own distinctive and primordial right. The parents in particular have a right to determine, in accordance with their own religious convictions, the nature of the religious instruction passed on to their children. Moreover, civil authorities must recognize the right of parents to select, with genuine liberty, schools or other means of education, nor should any unjust burdens be placed, directly or indirectly, upon this liberty of selection. Additionally, the rights of the parents are violated if their children are forced to attend classes which are at odds with the religious convictions of their parents, or if a single type of education is imposed, which entirely excludes religious formation.

6. Since the common good of society, which is the sum total of those conditions of social life by which men are able to pursue their perfection more fully and more expeditiously, consists above all in the rights and duties distinctive of the human person,[4] the care of the right to religious liberty falls in part upon citizens, in part upon social groups, in part upon civil authorities, and in part upon the Church and other religious communities, in the manner appropriate for each, depending upon the responsibility which each of these has for the common good.

To superintend and promote the inviolable rights of man is essentially bound up with the duties of any civil authority whatsoever.[5] It follows that each civil authority is bound, through just laws and through other appropriate measures, to undertake the effective superintendence of the religious liberty of all of its citizens, and to supply in abundance those conditions which foster a religious way of life, with the aim that its citizens might be well positioned to exercise the right and fulfill the responsibilities of religion, so that society might enjoy the goods of justice and peace, which originate in the faithfulness of men towards God and towards His holy will.[6]

---

4. Cf. John XXIII, encycl. *Mater et Magistra*, May 15, 1961: *AAS* 53 (1961), p. 417; John XXIII, encycl. *Pacem in Terris*, April 11, 1963: *AAS* 55 (1963), p. 273.

5. Cf. John XXIII, encycl. *Pacem in Terris*, April 11, 1963: *AAS* 55 (1963), pp. 273–74; Pius XII, Radio Message, June 1, 1941: *AAS* 33 (1941), p. 200.

6. Cf. Leo XIII, encycl. *Immortale Dei*, Nov. 1, 1885: *AAS* 18 (1885), p. 161.

If, in response to the particular circumstances of a people, special civil recognition is accorded, in the legal structure of the body politic, to one religious community, it is necessary that, at the same time, the right to liberty in matters of religion, of all citizens and all religious communities, be recognized and observed.

Finally, civil authority needs to insure that the equality of citizens before the law, which is a component of the common good of society, is never violated, either openly or in secret, because of considerations of religion, nor that there be any discrimination among citizens.

Whence it follows that a public authority commits an execrable crime, if by force, by fear, or by any other means, it imposes upon the citizens the profession or rejection of any religion, or if it impedes the citizens from joining or leaving any religious community. And how much more does it go against the will of God and against the sacred rights of the person and of the family of nations, when force is applied with the aim of destroying or suppressing religion simply!—whether this be throughout the human race in its entirety, or in some geographical region, or within some particular group.

7. Human society is the context in which the right to liberty in matters of religion is exercised. Hence, the use of this liberty is subject to identifiable governing norms.

In the use of any liberty, the moral principle of personal and social responsibility needs to be observed: individual men and social groups, when exercising the rights that belong to them, are obliged by the moral law to take into account the rights of others, their own duties toward others, and the common good of all—since we must act in accordance with justice and humanity in our dealings with everyone.

Again, since civil society has the right to protect itself against those abuses which can take place under the pretext of religious liberty, the task of providing that sort of protection pertains especially to civil authorities. Nevertheless this should not be carried out in an arbitrary way, or in such a way as to favor one party over another, but rather in accordance with those legal norms, conformable to the objective moral order, which are required (1) for the effective safeguarding of, and the peaceful settlement of conflicts among, the rights of all citizens, (2) for the adequate care of that honorable public peace which amounts to ordered life in common in true justice, and (3) for the required protection of public morality. All of these together form a basic part of the common good and fall under the definition of "public order."

Assuming these things are in place, the customary principle of the fullness of liberty in society should be upheld, according to which liberty should be recognized by men to the fullest extent possible and should not be restricted, except on the occasion when, and to the extent that, it is necessary to do so.

8. In our age for a variety of reasons men are subject to pressures and face the danger that they become shorn of the free decision-making that belongs to them. Yet also, on the other hand, there are not a few men who seem set on rejecting, under the appearance of liberty, any form of subordination, and who treat rightful obedience as a small matter.

For this reason, this Vatican Council exhorts everyone, especially those who have responsibility for the education of others, to take trouble to form men, who, precisely because they place themselves under a moral order, obey legitimate authority, and who are true lovers of liberty: men, to be sure, who by the decision-making that belongs to them will determine a matter in the light of truth; who will carry out their activities with a sense of responsibility; and who will endeavor to promote whatever is true and just, gladly cooperating with others in their own tasks.

Religious liberty therefore needs to be in the service of, and should be ordered to, this goal as well: namely, that men in the fulfillment of their own responsibilities comport themselves with greater responsibility in social life.

II. LIBERTY BY THE LIGHT OF REVELATION

9. These matters, which this Vatican Council declares about the right of man to religious liberty, have their foundation in the dignity of the person, the requirements of which have become more amply recognized by human reason from centuries of experience. Yet at the same time, this teaching about liberty has roots in divine Revelation—all the more reason, then, why Christians should keenly defend it.

Now, although Revelation does not explicitly affirm the right to immunity from external coercion in religious matters, still, (i) it makes evident the dignity of the human person in its complete fullness, (ii) it draws attention to the respect which Christ showed toward the liberty of man, in man's correspondence to the duty of believing the word of God, and (iii) it instructs us as regards the Spirit, which disciples of such a Master should recognize and follow in everything. In all these ways Revelation illuminates the general principles on which the doctrine of this Declaration of Religious Liberty is founded and in particular, that religious liberty is the perfect counterpart, in the context of human society, to the liberty of the act of Christian faith.

10. The very foremost among these principles of Catholic doctrine, contained

in the word of God, and constantly preached by the Fathers,[7] is that man, in the act of believing, must respond to God of his own accord. Therefore, no one who is reluctant should be forced into embracing the faith.[8] The reason is that the act of faith, of its very nature, is a free act—since man, who is redeemed by Christ the Savior, and called into the adoption of sons through Jesus Christ,[9] is not able to cling to God as He reveals Himself, except the Father should draw him,[10] and he, reasonably and freely, should surrender himself in obedience to God in faith. Therefore, it is entirely consonant with the inherent nature of faith that, in matters of religion, any type of external force on the part of men be excluded. The logic of religious liberty, then, makes no small contribution to encouraging that condition of things in which men are able easily to be invited to share in the Christian faith, to embrace it spontaneously, and to profess it eagerly in their entire way of life.

11. Indeed, God calls men to His service in spirit and in truth, and, as a result, men are bound in conscience—and yet they are not coerced. The reason is that God has regard for the dignity of the human person created by Him, which needs to be guided by his own counsel and needs to enjoy liberty. This regard is most apparent in Christ Jesus, in whom God made Himself and His ways perfectly clear. For Christ, who is our Master and Lord,[11] and at the same time meek and humble of heart,[12] attracted and invited disciples with patience.[13] When He used miracles to highlight and confirm His teaching, He did so in order to enliven and

---

7. Cf. Lactantius, *Divinarum Institutionum*, Book V, 19: CSEL 19, pp. 463–64, 465: PL 6, 614 and 616 (ch. 20); St. Ambrose, *Epistola ad Valentianum Imp.*, Letter 21: PL 16, 1005; St. Augustine, *Contra Litteras Petiliani*, Book II, ch. 83: CSEL 52, p. 112: PL 43, 315; cf. C. 23, q. 5, c. 33 (ed. Friedberg, col. 939); idem, Letter 23: PL 33, 98, idem, Letter 34: PL 33, 132; idem, Letter 35: PL 33, 135; St. Gregory the Great, *Epistola ad Virgilium et Theodorum Episcopos Massiliae Galliarum*, Register of Letters I, 45: MGH Ep. 1, p. 72: PL 77, 510–11 (Book I, Ep. 47); idem, *Epistola ad Johannem Episcopum Constantinopolitanum*, Register of Letters, III, 52: MGH Letter 1, p. 210: PL 77, 649 (Book III, Letter 53); cf. D. 45, c. 1 (ed. Friedberg, col. 160); Council of Toledo IV, c. 57: Mansi 10, 633; cf. D. 45, c. 5 (ed. Friedberg, col. 161–62); Clement III: X., V, 6, 9: ed. Friedberg, col. 774; Innocent III, *Epistola ad Arelatensem Archiepiscopum*, X., III, 42, 3: Friedberg, col. 646.

8. Cf. CIC, c. 1351; Pius XII, allocution to prelate auditors and other officials and administrators of the tribune of the Holy Roman Rota, Oct. 6, 1946: AAS 38 (1946), p. 394; Pius XII, encycl. *Mystici Corporis*, June 29, 1943: AAS (1943), p. 243.

9. Cf. Eph. 1:5.

10. Cf. John 6:44.

11. Cf. John 13:13.

12. Cf. Matt. 11:29.

13. Cf. Matt. 11:28–30; John 6:67–68.

confirm the faith of those who listened to His preaching, not to achieve some kind of coercive effect in them.[14]

To be sure, He decried lack of belief in his listeners. But He left vengeance to God on the Day of Judgment.[15] When He sent the Apostles into the world, He said to them, "he who believes and is baptized will be saved, and he who does not believe will be condemned" (Mk. 16:16). But knowing full well that weeds had been sown amidst the wheat, He gave the order that both should be left to grow until the harvest which is to take place at the end of time.[16] Not wanting to be a political Messiah or someone who rules by force,[17] He preferred to call Himself the "Son of Man" who has come "to serve and to give his own life as a ransom for many" (Mk. 10:45). He showed Himself the perfect Servant of God,[18] who "does not break the bruised reed nor extinguish the smoking flax" (Mt. 12:20). He recognized civil authority and its rights, commanding that tribute be given to Caesar. However, He gave clear warning that the higher rights of God are to be kept inviolate: "Render to Caesar the things that are Caesar's and to God the things that are God's" (Mt. 22:21). In the end, when He fulfilled the work of our redemption on the Cross, by which He won for us men salvation and true freedom, He brought His own revelation to perfect completion: for He bore witness to the truth,[19] while yet He declined to impose the truth by force on those who contradicted it. The reason is that His kingship is not enforced by violence from without.[20] Rather, it is established by one's testifying to the truth, and by the hearing of the truth, and it grows by the love by which Christ as exalted upon the Cross draws all men to Himself.[21]

The Apostles, instructed by both the word and the example of Christ, took the same approach. From the first beginnings of the Church, these followers of Christ labored strenuously with the aim that all men be converted to confess Christ as Lord, yet not by coercive action nor by measures unworthy of the Gospel, but most fundamentally by the power of the word of God.[22] With

---

14. Cf. Matt. 9:28–29; Mark 9:23–24; 6:5–6; Paul VI, encycl. *Ecclesiam Suam*, Aug. 6, 1964: *AAS* 56 (1964), pp. 642–43.

15. Cf. Matt. 11:20–24; Rom. 12:19–20; 2 Thess. 1:8.

16. Cf. Matt. 13:30 and 40–42.

17. Cf. Matt. 4:8–10; John 6:15.

18. Cf. Is. 42:1–4.

19. Cf. John 18:37.

20. Cf. Matt. 26:51–53; John 18:36.

21. Cf. John 12:32.

22. Cf. 1 Cor. 2:3–5; 1 Thess. 2:3–5.

courage they proclaimed to one and all the plan of God our Savior, "who wills that all men should be saved and come to the acknowledgment of the truth" (1 Tim. 2:4). However, they showed respect for those who were weak, even if they continued in error, demonstrating in this way how "each one of us is to render to God an account of himself" (Rom. 14:12)[23] and the degree to which each of us is obliged to obey his own conscience. Like Christ, the Apostles were always intent on bearing witness to the truth of God, daring with an abundance of audacity before the people and before princes to speak "the word of God with confidence" (Acts 4:31).[24] With a firm faith they held the Gospel truly to be of itself the power of God for salvation to everyone who has faith.[25] Therefore, casting aside "carnal weapons,"[26] and following the gentle and unassuming example set by Christ, they preached the word of God with complete confidence in the power of this divine word to destroy all authorities opposed to God[27] and to bring all men to the faith and obedience of Christ.[28] The Apostles recognized legitimate civil authority, just as their Master did: "For there is no power except from God," the Apostle teaches, and thereafter commands: "Let everyone be subject to higher authorities. ... He who resists authority resists God's ordinance" (Rom. 13:1–5).[29] At the same time, however, they were not afraid to contradict public authority when it set itself in opposition to the holy will of God: "It is necessary to obey God rather than men" (Acts 5:29).[30] This is the approach which has been taken by innumerable martyrs and other faithful throughout the ages and across the whole earth.

12. Therefore, the Church, faithful to the truth of the Gospel, follows the approach of Christ and the Apostles, when it recognizes and promotes the logic of religious liberty as in harmony with the dignity of man and the revelation of God. The Church has kept safe and handed down throughout the ages the teaching it received from the Master and from the Apostles. Even if, from the vicissitudes of the pilgrimage of human history, there has sometimes existed, in the life of the People of God, a manner of acting that was less in conformity with the spirit of the Gospel, or even opposed to it, nevertheless the doctrine of the Church that no one is to be forced into the faith has always stood firm.

---

23. Cf. Rom. 14:1–23; 1 Cor. 8:9–13; 10:23–33.
24. Cf. Eph. 6:19–20.
25. Cf. Rom. 1:16.
26. Cf. 2 Cor. 10:4; 1 Thess. 5:8–9.
27. Cf. Eph. 6:11–17.
28. Cf. 2 Cor. 10:3–5.
29. Cf. 1 Pet. 2:13–17.
30. Cf. Acts 4:19–20.

Thus the leaven of the Gospel has long been operative in the minds of men and has worked a significant effect, such that men in the course of time have recognized more widely the dignity which is distinctive of their own person, and the conviction has attained full maturity that, in political society, in matters of religion, an immunity from any kind of human coercion should be upheld.

13. Among the things that concern the good of the Church, and indeed the good of the earthly city, and which need to be always and everywhere upheld and defended against every injury, this certainly is preeminent, namely, that the Church should enjoy that degree of liberty which her care for the salvation of men requires.[31] The reason is that this liberty is a sacred liberty, with which the Only-Begotten Son endowed the Church, after purchasing this liberty with His own blood. This liberty is so very distinctive an attribute of the Church, that anyone who impugns it acts against the will of God. The liberty of the Church is the fundamental principle relevant to the relations between the Church and public authorities, and the whole civil order.

In human society, and in the face of any public authority, the Church claims by right a liberty for itself, as a spiritual authority, established by Christ, to which, by divine mandate, there falls the responsibility of going into the whole world and proclaiming the Gospel to every creature.[32] The Church likewise claims by right a liberty for herself, insofar as it is additionally an association of men, who each and together enjoy the right to live in civil society in accordance with the precepts of the Christian faith.[33]

It must be admitted that, when the logic of religious liberty goes beyond mere proclamation in words, or mere endorsement law, but in addition is applied in practice with sincerity, then the Church attains a certain stability, and a position of right and of fact, sufficient for the independence it needs to fulfil its divine mission. This independence in society is what church authorities have with greater and greater emphasis demanded by right.[34] At the same time, too, in such a case, the Christian faithful enjoy the same civil right as other men not to be hindered in living their life in accordance with their conscience. Therefore, one finds a harmonious agreement between the liberty of the Church,

31. Cf. Leo XIII, letter *Officio Sanctissimo*, Dec. 22, 1887: *AAS* 20 (1887), p. 269; Leo XIII, letter *Ex Litteris*, April 7, 1887: *AAS* 19 (1886), p. 465.

32. Cf. Mark 16:15; Matt. 28:18–20, Pius XII, encycl. *Summi Pontificatus*, Oct. 20, 1939: *AAS* 31 (1939), pp. 445–46.

33. Cf. Pius XI, letter *Firmissimam Constantiam*, March 28, 1937: *AAS* 29 (1937), p. 196.

34. Cf. Pius XII, allocution *Ci Riesce*, Dec. 6, 1953: *AAS* 45 (1953), p. 802.

and that religious liberty, pertaining to individual men without exception, and to communities, which requires recognition and endorsement as a right in the legal order.

14. The Catholic Church, to correspond to the divine command, "teach all nations" (Mt. 28:19–20), needs to work strenuously with urgent concern, "that the word of God be spread abroad and glorified" (2 Thes. 3:1).

Mindful of this, the Church implores its own children, first of all, that "supplications, prayers, petitions, acts of thanksgiving be made for all men. ... For this is good and agreeable in the sight of God our Savior, who wills that all men be saved and come to the knowledge of the truth" (1 Tim. 2:1–4).

Moreover, the Christian faithful in forming their consciences must pay careful attention to the holy and certain doctrine of the Church.[35] For by the will of Christ the Church is the teacher of the truth, and its office is to articulate and authentically teach that truth which is Christ Himself; and, at the same time, by its own authority, it declares and confirms the basic principles of the moral order, which flow from human nature itself. Furthermore, may Christians, walking in wisdom to meet those who are without, "in the Holy Spirit, in unaffected love, in the word of truth" (2 Cor. 6:6–7), be about their task of spreading the light of life with all confidence[36] and apostolic courage, even to the shedding of their blood.

Assuredly, each disciple is bound by a grave obligation toward Christ, his Master, each day to come to know more fully the truth received from Him, to proclaim it faithfully, and to defend it strenuously—on the assumption that means that are contrary to the spirit of the Gospel are excluded. At the same time, nonetheless, the charity of Christ urges him to deal with love, patience, and good judgment with men who continue in error or ignorance as concerns the faith.[37] What he must take into account are (i) his duties toward Christ the life-giving Word, which is to be proclaimed; (ii) the rights of the human person; and (iii) the measure of grace given by God through Christ to man, who is invited to accept and profess the faith of his own accord.

15. It holds true that men of the present time hope to be able freely to profess their religion whether in private or in public, and indeed religious liberty is now declared to be a civil right in most constitutions, and it is solemnly recognized in international documents.[38]

---

35. Cf. Pius XII, Radio Message, March 23, 1952: *AAS* 44 (1952), pp. 270–78.

36. Cf. Acts 4:29.

37. Cf. John XXIII, encycl. *Pacem in Terris*, April 11, 1963: *AAS* 55 (1963), pp. 299–300.

38. Cf. ibid., pp. 295–96.

And yet there is no lack of regimes in which, even if the liberty of religious worship is recognized in their constitution, nevertheless public authorities themselves strive to keep citizens from professing any religion, and they make life difficult and even dangerous for religious communities.

Greeting the first with joy as an auspicious sign of our times, while denouncing the other with sorrow as something to be deplored, this Sacred Council exhorts Catholics, and it implores men in general, to consider with utmost care how necessary religious liberty is, especially in the present condition of the human family. For it is obvious that all nations are day by day becoming more of a unity. Men diverse in culture and religion are joined together on closer grounds, and they are growing in their awareness of the personal responsibility of each. Accordingly, in order that peaceful relationships and harmonious agreement be established and strengthened, there is a need that religious liberty be everywhere protected with an effective legal safeguard, and that the highest duty and right, namely, of leading a religious life freely in society, be observed.

May the God and Father of all grant that the human family through diligently safeguarding the logic of religious liberty in society be brought by the grace of Christ and the power of the Holy Spirit to the sublime and everlasting "liberty in glory of the sons of God" (Rom. 8:21).

The entire text and all the points which have been set forth in this Declaration have pleased the fathers of the sacred Council. And we, by the apostolic authority given us by Christ, together with the venerable fathers, approve, appoint, and decree its contents in the Holy Spirit and order that what has been decided in the Council be promulgated to the glory of God.

✠ Paul, Bishop of the Catholic Church

(the signatures of the Council Fathers follow)

excerpts[†] from

FAMILIARIS CONSORTIO

On the Role of the Christian Family in the Modern World

*Apostolic Exhortation of Pope John Paul II,
promulgated November 22, 1981*

PART TWO
THE PLAN OF GOD FOR MARRIAGE AND THE FAMILY

Man, the Image of the God Who Is Love

God created man in His own image and likeness[1]: calling him to existence through love, He called him at the same time for love. God is love[2] and in Himself He lives a mystery of personal loving communion. Creating the human race in His own image and continually keeping it in being, God inscribed in the humanity of man and woman the vocation, and thus the capacity and responsibility, of love and communion.[3] Love is therefore the fundamental and innate vocation of every human being.

As an incarnate spirit, that is a soul which expresses itself in a body and a body informed by an immortal spirit, man is called to love in his unified totality. Love includes the human body, and the body is made a sharer in spiritual love.

Christian revelation recognizes two specific ways of realizing the vocation of the human person in its entirety, to love: marriage and virginity or celibacy. Either one is, in its own proper form, an actuation of the most profound truth of man, of his being "created in the image of God."

Consequently, sexuality, by means of which man and woman give themselves to one another through the acts which are proper and exclusive to spouses, is by

---

† [Because these pages present excerpts, footnote numbers do not match those of the original document.]

1. Cf. Gen. 1:26–27.

2. 1 John 4:8.

3. Cf. Second Vatican Council, *Gaudium et Spes*, 12.

no means something purely biological, but concerns the innermost being of the human person as such. It is realized in a truly human way only if it is an integral part of the love by which a man and a woman commit themselves totally to one another until death. The total physical self-giving would be a lie if it were not the sign and fruit of a total personal self-giving, in which the whole person, including the temporal dimension, is present: if the person were to withhold something or reserve the possibility of deciding otherwise in the future, by this very fact he or she would not be giving totally.

This totality which is required by conjugal love also corresponds to the demands of responsible fertility. This fertility is directed to the generation of a human being, and so by its nature it surpasses the purely biological order and involves a whole series of personal values. For the harmonious growth of these values a persevering and unified contribution by both parents is necessary.

The only "place" in which this self-giving in its whole truth is made possible is marriage, the covenant of conjugal love freely and consciously chosen, whereby man and woman accept the intimate community of life and love willed by God Himself[4] which only in this light manifests its true meaning. The institution of marriage is not an undue interference by society or authority, nor the extrinsic imposition of a form. Rather it is an interior requirement of the covenant of conjugal love which is publicly affirmed as unique and exclusive, in order to live in complete fidelity to the plan of God the Creator. A person's freedom, far from being restricted by this fidelity, is secured against every form of subjectivism or relativism and is made a sharer in creative Wisdom.

Marriage and Communion Between God and People

12. The communion of love between God and people, a fundamental part of the Revelation and faith experience of Israel, finds a meaningful expression in the marriage covenant which is established between a man and a woman.

For this reason the central word of Revelation, "God loves His people," is likewise proclaimed through the living and concrete word whereby a man and a woman express their conjugal love. Their bond of love becomes the image and the symbol of the covenant which unites God and His people.[5] And the same sin which can harm the conjugal covenant becomes an image of the infidelity of the people to their God: idolatry is prostitution,[6] infidelity is adultery, disobedience

---

4. Cf. ibid., 48.

5. Cf., e.g., Hos. 2:21; Jer. 3:6–13; Is. 54.

6. Ez. 16:25.

to the law is abandonment of the spousal love of the Lord. But the infidelity of Israel does not destroy the eternal fidelity of the Lord, and therefore the ever faithful love of God is put forward as the model of the faithful love which should exist between spouses.[7]

Jesus Christ, Bridegroom of the Church, and the Sacrament of Matrimony

13. The communion between God and His people finds its definitive fulfillment in Jesus Christ, the Bridegroom who loves and gives Himself as the Savior of humanity, uniting it to Himself as His body.

He reveals the original truth of marriage, the truth of the "beginning,"[8] and, freeing man from his hardness of heart, He makes man capable of realizing this truth in its entirety.

This revelation reaches its definitive fullness in the gift of love which the Word of God makes to humanity in assuming a human nature, and in the sacrifice which Jesus Christ makes of Himself on the Cross for His bride, the Church. In this sacrifice there is entirely revealed that plan which God has imprinted on the humanity of man and woman since their creation[9]; the marriage of baptized persons thus becomes a real symbol of that new and eternal covenant sanctioned in the blood of Christ. The Spirit which the Lord pours forth gives a new heart, and renders man and woman capable of loving one another as Christ has loved us. Conjugal love reaches that fullness to which it is interiorly ordained, conjugal charity, which is the proper and specific way in which the spouses participate in and are called to live the very charity of Christ who gave Himself on the Cross.

In a deservedly famous page, Tertullian has well expressed the greatness of this conjugal life in Christ and its beauty: "How can I ever express the happiness of the marriage that is joined together by the Church strengthened by an offering, sealed by a blessing, announced by angels and ratified by the Father? ... How wonderful the bond between two believers with a single hope, a single desire, a single observance, a single service! They are both brethren and both fellow-servants; there is no separation between them in spirit or flesh; in fact they are truly two in one flesh and where the flesh is one, one is the spirit."[10]

---

7. Cf. Hos. 3.
8. Cf. Gen. 2:24; Matt. 19:5.
9. Cf. Eph. 5:32–33.
10. Tertullian, *Ad Uxorem*, II, VIII, 6–8: CCL, I, 393.

Receiving and meditating faithfully on the word of God, the Church has solemnly taught and continues to teach that the marriage of the baptized is one of the seven sacraments of the New Covenant.[11]

Indeed, by means of baptism, man and woman are definitively placed within the new and eternal covenant, in the spousal covenant of Christ with the Church. And it is because of this indestructible insertion that the intimate community of conjugal life and love, founded by the Creator,[12] is elevated and assumed into the spousal charity of Christ, sustained and enriched by His redeeming power.

By virtue of the sacramentality of their marriage, spouses are bound to one another in the most profoundly indissoluble manner. Their belonging to each other is the real representation, by means of the sacramental sign, of the very relationship of Christ with the Church.

Spouses are therefore the permanent reminder to the Church of what happened on the Cross; they are for one another and for the children witnesses to the salvation in which the sacrament makes them sharers. Of this salvation event, marriage, like every sacrament, is a memorial, actuation and prophecy: "As a memorial, the sacrament gives them the grace and duty of commemorating the great works of God and of bearing witness to them before their children. As actuation, it gives them the grace and duty of putting into practice in the present, towards each other and their children, the demands of a love which forgives and redeems. As prophecy, it gives them the grace and duty of living and bearing witness to the hope of the future encounter with Christ."[13]

Like each of the seven sacraments, so also marriage is a real symbol of the event of salvation, but in its own way. "The spouses participate in it as spouses, together, as a couple, so that the first and immediate effect of marriage (*res et sacramentum*) is not supernatural grace itself, but the Christian conjugal bond, a typically Christian communion of two persons because it represents the mystery of Christ's incarnation and the mystery of His covenant. The content of participation in Christ's life is also specific: conjugal love involves a totality, in which all the elements of the person enter—appeal of the body and instinct, power of feeling and affectivity, aspiration of the spirit and of will. It aims at a deeply personal unity, the unity that, beyond union in one flesh, leads to forming one heart and soul; it demands indissolubility and faithfulness in definitive mutual giving; and

---

11. Cf. Council of Trent, Session XXIV, Canon 1: Mansi, *Sacrorum Conciliorum Nova et Amplissima Collectio*, 33, 149–50.

12. Cf. Second Vatican Council, *Gaudium et Spes*, 48.

13. John Paul II, Address to the delegates of the Centre de Liaison des Équipes de Recherche (Nov. 3, 1979), 3: *Insegnamenti* II, 2 (1979), 1038.

it is open to fertility (cf. *Humanae Vitae*, 9). In a word, it is a question of the normal characteristics of all natural conjugal love, but with a new significance which not only purifies and strengthens them, but raises them to the extent of making them the expression of specifically Christian values."[14]

Children, the Precious Gift of Marriage

14. According to the plan of God, marriage is the foundation of the wider community of the family, since the very institution of marriage and conjugal love are ordained to the procreation and education of children, in whom they find their crowning.[15]

In its most profound reality, love is essentially a gift; and conjugal love, while leading the spouses to the reciprocal "knowledge" which makes them "one flesh,"[16] does not end with the couple, because it makes them capable of the greatest possible gift, the gift by which they become cooperators with God for giving life to a new human person. Thus the couple, while giving themselves to one another, give not just themselves but also the reality of children, who are a living reflection of their love, a permanent sign of conjugal unity and a living and inseparable synthesis of their being a father and a mother.

When they become parents, spouses receive from God the gift of a new responsibility. Their parental love is called to become for the children the visible sign of the very love of God, "from whom every family in heaven and on earth is named."[17]

It must not be forgotten however that, even when procreation is not possible, conjugal life does not for this reason lose its value. Physical sterility in fact can be for spouses the occasion for other important services to the life of the human person, for example, adoption, various forms of educational work, and assistance to other families and to poor or handicapped children.

The Family, a Communion of Persons

15. In matrimony and in the family a complex of interpersonal relationships is set up—married life, fatherhood and motherhood, filiation and fraternity—through which each human person is introduced into the "human family" and into the "family of God," which is the Church.

---

14. Ibid., 4: *Insegnamenti* II, 2 (1979), 1032.

15. Cf. Second Vatican Council, *Gaudium et Spes*, 50.

16. Cf. Gen. 2:24.

17. Eph. 3:15.

Christian marriage and the Christian family build up the Church: for in the family the human person is not only brought into being and progressively introduced by means of education into the human community, but by means of the rebirth of baptism and education in the faith the child is also introduced into God's family, which is the Church.

The human family, disunited by sin, is reconstituted in its unity by the redemptive power of the death and resurrection of Christ.[18] Christian marriage, by participating in the salvific efficacy of this event, constitutes the natural setting in which the human person is introduced into the great family of the Church. The commandment to grow and multiply, given to man and woman in the beginning, in this way reaches its whole truth and full realization. The Church thus finds in the family, born from the sacrament, the cradle and the setting in which she can enter the human generations, and where these in their turn can enter the Church.

Marriage and Virginity or Celibacy

16. Virginity or celibacy for the sake of the Kingdom of God not only does not contradict the dignity of marriage but presupposes it and confirms it. Marriage and virginity or celibacy are two ways of expressing and living the one mystery of the covenant of God with His people. When marriage is not esteemed, neither can consecrated virginity or celibacy exist; when human sexuality is not regarded as a great value given by the Creator, the renunciation of it for the sake of the Kingdom of Heaven loses its meaning.

Rightly indeed does St. John Chrysostom say: "Whoever denigrates marriage also diminishes the glory of virginity. Whoever praises it makes virginity more admirable and resplendent. What appears good only in comparison with evil would not be particularly good. It is something better than what is admitted to be good that is the most excellent good."[19]

In virginity or celibacy, the human being is awaiting, also in a bodily way, the eschatological marriage of Christ with the Church, giving himself or herself completely to the Church in the hope that Christ may give Himself to the Church in the full truth of eternal life. The celibate person thus anticipates in his or her flesh the new world of the future resurrection.[20] By virtue of this witness, virginity or celibacy keeps alive in the Church a consciousness of the mystery of marriage and defends it from any reduction and impoverishment.

---

18. Cf. Second Vatican Council, *Gaudium et Spes*, 78.

19. St. John Chrysostom, *On Virginity*, X: PG 48:540.

20. Cf. Matt. 22:30.

Virginity or celibacy, by liberating the human heart in a unique way,[21] "so as to make it burn with greater love for God and all humanity,"[22] bears witness that the Kingdom of God and His justice is that pearl of great price which is preferred to every other value no matter how great, and hence must be sought as the only definitive value. It is for this reason that the Church, throughout her history, has always defended the superiority of this charism to that of marriage, by reason of the wholly singular link which it has with the Kingdom of God.[23]

In spite of having renounced physical fecundity, the celibate person becomes spiritually fruitful, the father and mother of many, cooperating in the realization of the family according to God's plan.

Christian couples therefore have the right to expect from celibate persons a good example and a witness of fidelity to their vocation until death. Just as fidelity at times becomes difficult for married people and requires sacrifice, mortification and self-denial, the same can happen to celibate persons, and their fidelity, even in the trials that may occur, should strengthen the fidelity of married couples.[24]

These reflections on virginity or celibacy can enlighten and help those who, for reasons independent of their own will, have been unable to marry and have then accepted their situation in a spirit of service. [...]

Faith as the Discovery and Admiring Awareness of God's Plan for the Family

51. As a sharer in the life and mission of the Church, which listens to the word of God with reverence and proclaims it confidently,[25] the Christian family fulfills its prophetic role by welcoming and announcing the word of God: it thus becomes more and more each day a believing and evangelizing community.

Christian spouses and parents are required to offer "the obedience of faith."[26] They are called upon to welcome the word of the Lord which reveals to them the marvelous news—the Good News—of their conjugal and family life sanctified and made a source of sanctity by Christ Himself. Only in faith can they discover and admire with joyful gratitude the dignity to which God has deigned to raise marriage and the family, making them a sign and meeting place of the

---

21. Cf. 1 Cor. 7:32–35.

22. Second Vatican Council, *Perfectae Caritatis*, 12.

23. Cf. Pius XII, Encyclical *Sacra Virginitas*, II: *AAS* 46 (1954), 174ff.

24. Cf. John Paul II, Letter *Novo Incipiente* (April 8, 1979), 9: *AAS* 71 (1979), 410–11.

25. Cf. Second Vatican Council, *Dei Verbum*, 1.

26. Rom. 16:26.

loving covenant between God and man, between Jesus Christ and His bride, the Church. [...]

This profession of faith demands that it be prolonged in the life of the married couple and of the family. God, who called the couple to marriage, continues to call them in marriage.[27] In and through the events, problems, difficulties and circumstances of everyday life, God comes to them, revealing and presenting the concrete "demands" of their sharing in the love of Christ for His Church in the particular family, social and ecclesial situation in which they find themselves. [...]

The Church's Sanctuary in the Home

55. The proclamation of the Gospel and its acceptance in faith reach their fullness in the celebration of the sacraments. The Church which is a believing and evangelizing community is also a priestly people invested with the dignity and sharing in the power of Christ the High Priest of the New and Eternal Covenant.[28]

The Christian family too is part of this priestly people which is the Church. By means of the sacrament of marriage, in which it is rooted and from which it draws its nourishment, the Christian family is continuously vivified by the Lord Jesus and called and engaged by Him in a dialogue with God through the sacraments, through the offering of one's life, and through prayer.

This is the priestly role which the Christian family can and ought to exercise in intimate communion with the whole Church, through the daily realities of married and family life. In this way the Christian family is called to be sanctified and to sanctify the ecclesial community and the world.

Marriage as a Sacrament of Mutual Sanctification and an Act of Worship

56. The sacrament of marriage is the specific source and original means of sanctification for Christian married couples and families. It takes up again and makes specific the sanctifying grace of baptism. By virtue of the mystery of the death and resurrection of Christ, of which the spouses are made part in a new way by marriage, conjugal love is purified and made holy: "This love the Lord has judged worthy of special gifts, healing, perfecting and exalting gifts of grace and of charity."[29]

---

27. Cf. Paul VI, *Humanae Vitae*, 25.

28. Cf. Second Vatican Council, *Lumen Gentium*, 10.

29. Second Vatican Council, *Gaudium et Spes*, 49.

The gift of Jesus Christ is not exhausted in the actual celebration of the sacrament of marriage, but rather accompanies the married couple throughout their lives. This fact is explicitly recalled by the Second Vatican Council when it says that Jesus Christ "abides with them so that, just as He loved the Church and handed Himself over on her behalf, the spouses may love each other with perpetual fidelity through mutual self-bestowal ... For this reason, Christian spouses have a special sacrament by which they are fortified and receive a kind of consecration in the duties and dignity of their state. By virtue of this sacrament, as spouses fulfill their conjugal and family obligations, they are penetrated with the Spirit of Christ, who fills their whole lives with faith, hope and charity. Thus they increasingly advance towards their own perfection, as well as towards their mutual sanctification, and hence contribute jointly to the glory of God."[30]

Christian spouses and parents are included in the universal call to sanctity. For them this call is specified by the sacrament they have celebrated and is carried out concretely in the realities proper to their conjugal and family life.[31] This gives rise to the grace and requirement of an authentic and profound conjugal and family spirituality that draws its inspiration from the themes of creation, covenant, cross, resurrection, and sign, which were stressed more than once by the Synod.

Christian marriage, like the other sacraments, "whose purpose is to sanctify people, to build up the body of Christ, and finally, to give worship to God,"[32] is in itself a liturgical action glorifying God in Jesus Christ and in the Church. By celebrating it, Christian spouses profess their gratitude to God for the sublime gift bestowed on them of being able to live in their married and family lives the very love of God for people and that of the Lord Jesus for the Church, His bride.

Just as husbands and wives receive from the sacrament the gift and responsibility of translating into daily living the sanctification bestowed on them, so the same sacrament confers on them the grace and moral obligation of transforming their whole lives into a "spiritual sacrifice."[33] What the Council says of the laity applies also to Christian spouses and parents, especially with regard to the earthly and temporal realities that characterize their lives: "As worshippers leading holy lives in every place, the laity consecrate the world itself to God."[34] [...]

---

30. Ibid., 48.

31. Cf. Second Vatican Council, *Lumen Gentium*, 41.

32. Second Vatican Council, *Sacrosanctum Concilium*, 59.

33. Cf. 1 Pet. 2:5; Second Vatican Council, *Lumen Gentium*, 34.

34. Second Vatican Council, *Lumen Gentium*, 34.

Liturgical Prayer and Private Prayer

61. There exists a deep and vital bond between the prayer of the Church and the prayer of the individual faithful, as has been clearly reaffirmed by the Second Vatican Council.[35] An important purpose of the prayer of the domestic Church is to serve as the natural introduction for the children to the liturgical prayer of the whole Church, both in the sense of preparing for it and of extending it into personal, family and social life. Hence the need for gradual participation by all the members of the Christian family in the celebration of the Eucharist, especially on Sundays and feast days, and of the other sacraments, particularly the sacraments of Christian initiation of the children. The directives of the Council opened up a new possibility for the Christian family when it listed the family among those groups to whom it recommends the recitation of the Divine Office in common.[36] Likewise, the Christian family will strive to celebrate at home, and in a way suited to the members, the times and feasts of the liturgical year.

As preparation for the worship celebrated in church, and as its prolongation in the home, the Christian family makes use of private prayer, which presents a great variety of forms. While this variety testifies to the extraordinary richness with which the Spirit vivifies Christian prayer, it serves also to meet the various needs and life situations of those who turn to the Lord in prayer. Apart from morning and evening prayers, certain forms of prayer are to be expressly encouraged, following the indications of the Synod Fathers, such as reading and meditating on the word of God, preparation for the reception of the sacraments, devotion and consecration to the Sacred Heart of Jesus, the various forms of veneration of the Blessed Virgin Mary, grace before and after meals, and observance of popular devotions.

While respecting the freedom of the children of God, the Church has always proposed certain practices of piety to the faithful with particular solicitude and insistence. Among these should be mentioned the recitation of the rosary: "We now desire, as a continuation of the thought of our predecessors, to recommend strongly the recitation of the family rosary ... There is no doubt that ... the rosary should be considered as one of the best and most efficacious prayers in common that the Christian family is invited to recite. We like to think, and sincerely hope, that when the family gathering becomes a time of prayer the rosary is a frequent and favored manner of praying."[37] In this

---

35. Cf. Second Vatican Council, *Sacrosanctum Concilium*, 12.

36. Cf. *Institutio Generalis de Liturgia Horarum*, 27.

37. Paul VI, Apostolic Exhortation *Marialis Cultus*, 52, 54: *AAS* 66 (1974), 160–61.

way authentic devotion to Mary, which finds expression in sincere love and generous imitation of the Blessed Virgin's interior spiritual attitude, constitutes a special instrument for nourishing loving communion in the family and for developing conjugal and family spirituality. For she who is the Mother of Christ and of the Church is in a special way the Mother of Christian families, of domestic Churches.

Prayer and Life

62. It should never be forgotten that prayer constitutes an essential part of Christian life, understood in its fullness and centrality. Indeed, prayer is an important part of our very humanity: it is "the first expression of man's inner truth, the first condition for authentic freedom of spirit."[38]

Far from being a form of escapism from everyday commitments, prayer constitutes the strongest incentive for the Christian family to assume and comply fully with all its responsibilities as the primary and fundamental cell of human society. Thus the Christian family's actual participation in the Church's life and mission is in direct proportion to the fidelity and intensity of the prayer with which it is united with the fruitful vine that is Christ the Lord.[39]

The fruitfulness of the Christian family in its specific service to human advancement, which of itself cannot but lead to the transformation of the world, derives from its living union with Christ, nourished by Liturgy, by self-oblation and by prayer.[40]

The New Commandment of Love

63. The Church, a prophetic, priestly and kingly people, is endowed with the mission of bringing all human beings to accept the word of God in faith, to celebrate and profess it in the sacraments and in prayer, and to give expression to it in the concrete realities of life in accordance with the gift and new commandment of love.

The law of Christian life is to be found not in a written code, but in the personal action of the Holy Spirit who inspires and guides the Christian. It is the

---

38. John Paul II, Address at the Mentorella Shrine (Oct. 29, 1978): *Insegnamenti*, I (1978), 78–79.

39. Cf. Second Vatican Council, *Apostolicam Actuositatem*, 4.

40. Cf. John Paul I, Address to the Bishops of the 12th Pastoral Region of the United States (Sept. 21, 1978): *AAS* 70 (1978), 767.

"law of the Spirit of life in Christ Jesus."[41] "God's love has been poured into our hearts through the Holy Spirit who has been given to us."[42]

This is true also for the Christian couple and family. Their guide and rule of life is the Spirit of Jesus poured into their hearts in the celebration of the sacrament of matrimony. In continuity with baptism in water and the Spirit, marriage sets forth anew the evangelical law of love, and with the gift of the Spirit engraves it more profoundly on the hearts of Christian husbands and wives. Their love, purified and saved, is a fruit of the Spirit acting in the hearts of believers and constituting, at the same time, the fundamental commandment of their moral life to be lived in responsible freedom.

Thus, the Christian family is inspired and guided by the new law of the Spirit and, in intimate communion with the Church, the kingly people, it is called to exercise its "service" of love towards God and towards fellow human beings. Just as Christ exercises His royal power by serving us,[43] so also the Christian finds the authentic meaning of his participation in the kingship of his Lord in sharing His spirit and practice of service to man. "Christ has communicated this power to his disciples that they might be established in royal freedom and that by self-denial and a holy life they might conquer the reign of sin in themselves (cf. Rom. 6:12). Further, He has shared this power so that by serving Him in their fellow human beings they might through humility and patience lead their brothers and sisters to that King whom to serve is to reign. For the Lord wishes to spread His kingdom by means of the laity also, a kingdom of truth and life, a kingdom of holiness and grace, a kingdom of justice, love and peace. In this kingdom, creation itself will be delivered out of its slavery to corruption and into the freedom of the glory of the children of God (cf. Rom. 8:21)."[44] [...]

✠ JOHN PAUL II

---

41. Rom. 8:2.

42. Rom. 5:5.

43. Cf. Mark 10:45.

44. Second Vatican Council, *Lumen Gentium*, 36.

excerpts† from

CENTESIMUS ANNUS

On the Hundredth Anniversary of Rerum Novarum

Encyclical Letter of Pope John Paul II, promulgated May 1, 1991

Venerable Brothers, Beloved Sons and Daughters, Health and the Apostolic Blessing!

T he hundredth year since the promulgation of the encyclical which begins with the words *Rerum Novarum*,[1] by my predecessor of venerable memory Pope Leo XIII, is an occasion of great importance for the present history of the Church and for my own pontificate. It is an encyclical that has the distinction of having been commemorated by solemn papal documents from its fortieth anniversary to its ninetieth. It may be said that its path through history has been marked by other documents which paid tribute to it and applied it to the circumstances of the day.[2]

In doing likewise for the hundredth anniversary, in response to requests from many bishops, Church institutions, and study centers, as well as business leaders and workers, both individually and as members of associations, I wish first and foremost to satisfy the debt of gratitude which the whole Church owes to this great Pope and his "immortal document."[3] I also mean to show that the vital energies rising from that root have not been spent with the passing of the years, but rather have increased even more. ...

---

† [Because these pages present excerpts, footnote numbers do not match those of the original document.]

1. Leo XIII, Encyclical Letter *Rerum Novarum* (May 15, 1891): *Leonis XIII P.M. Acta*, XI, Romae 1892, 97–144.

2. Pius XI, Encyclical Letter *Quadragesimo Anno* (May 15, 1931): *AAS* 23 (1931), 177–228; Pius XII, Radio Message of June 1, 1941: *AAS* 33 (1941), 195–205; John XXIII, Encyclical Letter *Mater et Magistra* (May 15, 1961): *AAS* 53 (1961), 401–64; Paul VI, Apostolic Epistle *Octogesima Adveniens* (May 14, 1971): *AAS* 63 (1971), 401–41.

3. Cf. Pius XI, Encyclical Letter *Quadragesimo Anno*, III: *AAS* 23 (1931), 228.

2. The present encyclical is part of these celebrations, which are meant to thank God—the origin of "every good endowment and every perfect gift" (Jas 1:17)—for having used a document published a century ago by the See of Peter to achieve so much good and to radiate so much light in the Church and in the world. Although the commemoration at hand is meant to honor *Rerum Novarum*, it also honors those encyclicals and other documents of my predecessors which have helped to make Pope Leo's encyclical present and alive in history, thus constituting what would come to be called the Church's "social doctrine," "social teaching" or even "social magisterium." The validity of this teaching has already been pointed out in two encyclicals published during my pontificate: *Laborem Exercens* on human work, and *Sollicitudo Rei Socialis* on current problems regarding the development of individuals and peoples.[4]

3. I now wish to propose a "rereading" of Pope Leo's encyclical by issuing an invitation to "look back" at the text itself in order to discover anew the richness of the fundamental principles which it formulated for dealing with the question of the condition of workers. But this is also an invitation to "look around" at the "new things" which surround us and in which we find ourselves caught up, very different from the "new things" which characterized the final decade of the last century. Finally, it is an invitation to "look to the future" at a time when we can already glimpse the third millennium of the Christian era, so filled with uncertainties but also with promises—uncertainties and promises which appeal to our imagination and creativity, and which reawaken our responsibility, as disciples of the "one teacher" (cf. Mt 23:8), to show the way, to proclaim the truth, and to communicate the life which is Christ (cf. Jn 14:6).

A rereading of this kind will not only confirm the permanent value of such teaching, but will also manifest the true meaning of the Church's Tradition which, being ever living and vital, builds upon the foundation laid by our fathers in the faith, and particularly upon what "the Apostles passed down to the Church"[5] in the name of Jesus Christ, who is her irreplaceable foundation (cf. 1 Cor 3:11). ...

The present encyclical seeks to show the fruitfulness of the principles enunciated by Leo XIII, which belong to the Church's doctrinal patrimony and, as such, involve the exercise of her teaching authority. But pastoral solicitude also prompts me to propose an analysis of some events of recent history. It goes without saying that part of the responsibility of pastors is to give careful consideration

---

4. Encyclical Letter *Laborem Exercens* (September 14, 1981): *AAS* 73 (1981), 577–647; Encyclical Letter *Sollicitudo Rei Socialis* (December 30, 1987): *AAS* 80 (1988), 513–86.

5. Cf. St. Irenaeus, *Adversus Haereses*, I, 10, 1; III, 4, 1: PG 7, 549f.; 855f.; S. Ch. 264, 154f.; 211, 44–46.

to current events in order to discern the new requirements of evangelization. However, such an analysis is not meant to pass definitive judgments, since this does not fall per se within the Magisterium's specific domain.

I. CHARACTERISTICS OF *RERUM NOVARUM*

4. Towards the end of the last century the Church found herself facing an historical process which had already been taking place for some time, but which was by then reaching a critical point. The determining factor in this process was a combination of radical changes which had taken place in the political, economic and social fields, and in the areas of science and technology, to say nothing of the wide influence of the prevailing ideologies. In the sphere of politics, the result of these changes was a new conception of society and of the State, and consequently of authority itself. A traditional society was passing away and another was beginning to be formed—one which brought the hope of new freedoms but also the threat of new forms of injustice and servitude.

In the sphere of economics, in which scientific discoveries and their practical application come together, new structures for the production of consumer goods had progressively taken shape. A new form of property had appeared—capital; and a new form of labor—labor for wages, characterized by high rates of production which lacked due regard for sex, age, or family situation, and were determined solely by efficiency, with a view to increasing profits.

In this way labor became a commodity to be freely bought and sold on the market, its price determined by the law of supply and demand, without taking into account the bare minimum required for the support of the individual and his family. Moreover, the worker was not even sure of being able to sell "his own commodity," continually threatened as he was by unemployment, which, in the absence of any kind of social security, meant the specter of death by starvation.

The result of this transformation was a society "divided into two classes, separated by a deep chasm."[6] This situation was linked to the marked change taking place in the political order already mentioned. Thus the prevailing political theory of the time sought to promote total economic freedom by appropriate laws, or, conversely, by a deliberate lack of any intervention. At the same time, another conception of property and economic life was beginning to appear in an organized and often violent form, one which implied a new political and social structure.

6. Leo XIII, Encyclical Letter *Rerum Novarum: Leonis XIII P.M. Acta*, XI, Romae 1892, 132.

At the height of this clash, when people finally began to realize fully the very grave injustice of social realities in many places and the danger of a revolution fanned by ideals which were then called "socialist," Pope Leo XIII intervened with a document which dealt in a systematic way with the "condition of the workers." The encyclical had been preceded by others devoted to teachings of a political character; still others would appear later.[7] Here, particular mention must be made of the encyclical *Libertas Praestantissimum*, which called attention to the essential bond between human freedom and truth, so that freedom which refused to be bound to the truth would fall into arbitrariness and end up submitting itself to the vilest of passions, to the point of self-destruction. Indeed, what is the origin of all the evils to which *Rerum Novarum* wished to respond, if not a kind of freedom which, in the area of economic and social activity, cuts itself off from the truth about humanity?

5. ... Here we find the first reflection for our times as suggested by the encyclical. In the face of a conflict which set man against man, almost as if they were "wolves," a conflict between the extremes of mere physical survival on the one side and opulence on the other, the Pope did not hesitate to intervene by virtue of his "apostolic office,"[8] that is, on the basis of the mission received from Jesus Christ himself to "feed his lambs and tend his sheep" (cf. Jn 21:15–17), and to "bind and loose" on earth for the kingdom of heaven (cf. Mt 16:19). The Pope's intention was certainly to restore peace, and the present-day reader cannot fail to note his severe condemnation, in no uncertain terms, of the class struggle.[9]

However, the Pope was very much aware that peace is built on the foundation of justice: what was essential to the encyclical was precisely its proclamation of the fundamental conditions for justice in the economic and social situation of the time.[10]

In this way, Pope Leo XIII, in the footsteps of his predecessors, created a lasting paradigm for the Church. The Church, in fact, has something to say about specific human situations, both individual and communal, national and international. She formulates a genuine doctrine for these situations, a corpus

---

7. Cf., e.g., Leo XIII, Encyclical Epistle *Arcanum Divinae Sapientiae* (February 10, 1880): *Leonis XIII P.M. Acta*, II, Romae 1882, 10–40; Encyclical Epistle *Diuturnum Illud* (June 29, 1881): *Leonis XIII P.M. Acta*, II, Romae 1882, 269–87; Encyclical Letter *Libertas Praestantissimum* (June 20, 1888): *Leonis XIII P.M. Acta*, VIII, Romae 1889, 212–46; Encyclical Epistle *Graves de communi* (January 18,1901): *Leonis XIII P.M. Acta*, XXI, Romae 1902, 3–20.

8. Encyclical Letter *Rerum Novarum*: *Leonis XIII P.M. Acta*, XI, Romae 1892, 98.

9. Cf. ibid., 109f.

10. Cf. ibid., description of working conditions; 44: anti-Christian workers' associations: 110f.; 136f.

which enables her to analyze social realities, to make judgments about them and to indicate directions to be taken for the just resolution of the problems involved.

In Pope Leo XIII's time such a concept of the Church's right and duty was far from being commonly admitted. Indeed, a twofold approach prevailed: one directed to this world and this life, to which faith ought to remain extraneous; the other directed towards a purely other-worldly salvation, which neither enlightens nor directs existence on earth. The Pope's approach in publishing *Rerum Novarum* gave the Church "citizenship status" as it were, amid the changing realities of public life, and this standing would be more fully confirmed later on. In effect, to teach and to spread her social doctrine pertains to the Church's evangelizing mission and is an essential part of the Christian message, since this doctrine points out the direct consequences of that message in the life of society and situates daily work and struggles for justice in the context of bearing witness to Christ the Savior. This doctrine is likewise a source of unity and peace in dealing with the conflicts which inevitably arise in social and economic life. Thus it is possible to meet these new situations without degrading the human person's transcendent dignity, either in oneself or in one's adversaries, and to direct those situations towards just solutions.

Today, at a distance of a hundred years, the validity of this approach affords me the opportunity to contribute to the development of Christian social doctrine. The "new evangelization," which the modern world urgently needs and which I have emphasized many times, must include among its essential elements a proclamation of the Church's social doctrine. As in the days of Pope Leo XIII, this doctrine is still suitable for indicating the right way to respond to the great challenges of today, when ideologies are being increasingly discredited. Now, as then, we need to repeat that there can be no genuine solution of the "social question" apart from the Gospel, and that the "new things" can find in the Gospel the context for their correct understanding and the proper moral perspective for judgment on them.

6. With the intention of shedding light on the conflict which had arisen between capital and labor, Pope Leo XIII affirmed the fundamental rights of workers. Indeed, the key to reading the encyclical is the dignity of the worker as such, and, for the same reason, the dignity of work, which is defined as follows: "to exert oneself for the sake of procuring what is necessary for the various purposes of life, and first of all for self-preservation."[11] The Pope describes work as "personal, inasmuch as the energy expended is bound up with the personality

11. Ibid.: 130; also 114f.

and is the exclusive property of him who acts, and, furthermore, was given to him for his advantage."[12] Work thus belongs to the vocation of every person; indeed, a human being expresses and fulfills himself by working. At the same time, work has a "social" dimension through its intimate relationship not only to the family, but also to the common good, since "it may truly be said that it is only by the labor of working men that states grow rich."[13] These are themes that I have taken up and developed in my encyclical *Laborem Exercens*.[14]

Another important principle is undoubtedly that of the right to "private property."[15] The amount of space devoted to this subject in the encyclical shows the importance attached to it. The Pope is well aware that private property is not an absolute value, nor does he fail to proclaim the necessary complementary principles, such as the universal destination of the earth's goods.[16]

On the other hand, it is certainly true that the type of private property which Leo XIII mainly considers is land ownership.[17] But this does not mean that the reasons adduced to safeguard private property or to affirm the right to possess the things necessary for one's personal development and the development of one's family, whatever the concrete form which that right may assume, are not still valid today. This is something which must be affirmed once more in the face of the changes we are witnessing in systems formerly dominated by collective ownership of the means of production, as well as in the face of the increasing instances of poverty or, more precisely, of hindrances to private ownership in many parts of the world, including those where systems predominate which are based on an affirmation of the right to private property. As a result of these changes and of the persistence of poverty, a deeper analysis of the problem is called for, an analysis which will be developed later in this document.

8. The Pope immediately adds another right which the worker has as a person. This is the right to a "just wage," which cannot be left to the "free consent of the parties, so that the employer, having paid what was agreed upon, has done his part and seemingly is not called upon to do anything further."[18] It was said at the time that the State does not have the power to intervene in the terms of these contracts, except to ensure the fulfillment of what had been explicitly agreed

---

12. Ibid.: 130.

13. Ibid.: 123.

14. Cf. Encyclical Letter *Laborem Exercens,* 1, 2, 6: *AAS* 73 (1981), 578–83; 589–92.

15. Cf. Encyclical Letter *Rerum Novarum: Leonis XIII P.M. Acta,* XI, Romae 1892, 99–107.

16. Cf. ibid., 102f.

17. Cf. ibid., 101–104.

18. Ibid., 129.

upon. This concept of relations between employers and employees, purely pragmatic and inspired by a thoroughgoing individualism, is severely censured in the
encyclical as contrary to the twofold nature of work as a personal and necessary
reality. For if work as something personal belongs to the sphere of the individual's free use of his own abilities and energy, as something necessary it is governed
by the grave obligation of every individual to ensure "the preservation of life."
"It necessarily follows," the Pope concludes, "that every individual has a natural
right to procure what is required to live; and the poor can procure that in no
other way than by what they can earn through their work."[19]

A workman's wages should be sufficient to enable him to support himself,
his wife, and his children. "If through necessity or fear of a worse evil the workman accepts harder conditions because an employer or contractor will afford no
better, he is made the victim of force and injustice."[20]

Would that these words, written at a time when what has been called "unbridled capitalism" was pressing forward, should not have to be repeated today with
the same severity. Unfortunately, even today one finds instances of contracts
between employers and employees which lack reference to the most elementary
justice regarding the employment of children or women, working hours, the
hygienic condition of the workplace and fair pay; and this is the case despite the
international declarations and conventions on the subject[21] and the internal laws
of states. The Pope attributed to the "public authority" the "strict duty" of providing properly for the welfare of the workers, because a failure to do so violates
justice; indeed, he did not hesitate to speak of "distributive justice."[22]

9. To these rights Pope Leo XIII adds another right regarding the condition
of the working class, one which I wish to mention because of its importance:
namely, the right to discharge freely one's religious duties. The Pope wished to
proclaim this right within the context of the other rights and duties of workers, notwithstanding the general opinion, even in his day, that such questions
pertained exclusively to an individual's private life. He affirms the need for
Sunday rest so that people may turn their thoughts to heavenly things and to the
worship which they owe to Almighty God.[23] No one can take away this human
right, which is based on a commandment; in the words of the Pope: "no man
may with impunity violate that human dignity which God himself treats with

19. Ibid., 130f.
20. Ibid., 131.
21. Cf. *Universal Declaration of Human Rights.*
22. Cf. Encyclical Letter *Rerum Novarum: Leonis XIII P.M. Acta*, XI, Romae 1892, 121–23.
23. Cf. ibid., 127.

great reverence," and consequently, the State must guarantee to the worker the exercise of this freedom.[24]

It would not be mistaken to see in this clear statement a springboard for the principle of the right to religious freedom, which was to become the subject of many solemn international declarations and conventions,[25] as well as of the Second Vatican Council's well-known declaration and of my own repeated teaching.[26] In this regard, one may ask whether existing laws and the practice of industrialized societies effectively ensure in our own day the exercise of this basic right to Sunday rest.

10. Another important aspect, which has many applications to our own day, is the concept of the relationship between the State and its citizens. *Rerum Novarum* criticizes two social and economic systems: socialism and liberalism. The opening section, in which the right to private property is reaffirmed, is devoted to socialism. Liberalism is not the subject of a special section, but it is worth noting that criticisms of it are raised in the treatment of the duties of the State.[27] The State cannot limit itself to "favoring one portion of the citizens," namely the rich and prosperous, nor can it "neglect the other," which clearly represents the majority of society. Otherwise, there would be a violation of that law of justice which ordains that every person should receive his due. "When there is question of defending the rights of individuals, the defenseless and the poor have a claim to special consideration. The richer class has many ways of shielding itself, and stands less in need of help from the State; whereas the mass of the poor have no resources of their own to fall back on, and must chiefly depend on the assistance of the State. It is for this reason that wage-earners, since they mostly belong to the latter class, should be specially cared for and protected by the government."[28]

These passages are relevant today, especially in the face of the new forms of poverty in the world, and also because they are affirmations which do not depend on a specific notion of the State or on a particular political theory. Leo XIII is repeating an elementary principle of sound political organization, namely, the more that individuals are defenseless within a given society, the more they

---

24. Ibid., 126f.

25. Cf. *Universal Declaration of Human Rights*; Declaration on the elimination of every form of intolerance and discrimination based on religion or convictions.

26. Second Vatican Ecumenical Council, Declaration on Religious Freedom *Dignitatis Humanae*; John Paul II, Letter to Heads of State (September 1, 1980): *AAS* 72 (1980), 1252–60; Message for the 1988 World Day of Peace (January 1, 1988): *AAS* 80 (1988), 278–86.

27. Cf. Encyclical Letter *Rerum Novarum*, 42: *Leonis XIII P.M. Acta*, XI, Romae 1892, 99–105; 130f.; 135.

28. Ibid.: 125.

require the care and concern of others, and in particular the intervention of governmental authority.

In this way what we nowadays call the principle of solidarity, the validity of which both in the internal order of each nation and in the international order I have discussed in the encyclical *Sollicitudo Rei Socialis,*[29] is clearly seen to be one of the fundamental principles of the Christian view of social and political organization. This principle is frequently stated by Pope Leo XIII, who uses the term "friendship," a concept already found in Greek philosophy. Pope Pius XI refers to it with the equally meaningful term "social charity." Pope Paul VI, expanding the concept to cover the many modern aspects of the social question, speaks of a "civilization of love."[30]

11. Rereading the encyclical in the light of contemporary realities enables us to appreciate the Church's constant concern for and dedication to categories of people who are especially beloved to the Lord Jesus. The contents of the text is an excellent testimony to the continuity within the Church of the so-called "preferential option for the poor," an option which I defined as a "special form of primacy in the exercise of Christian charity."[31] Pope Leo's encyclical on the "condition of the workers" is thus an encyclical on the poor and on the terrible conditions to which the new and often violent process of industrialization had reduced great multitudes of people. Today, in many parts of the world, similar processes of economic, social, and political transformation are creating the same evils.

If Pope Leo XIII calls upon the State to remedy the condition of the poor in accordance with justice, he does so because of his timely awareness that the State has the duty of watching over the common good and of ensuring that every sector of social life, not excluding the economic one, contributes to achieving that good, while respecting the rightful autonomy of each sector. This should not however lead us to think that Pope Leo expected the State to solve every social problem. On the contrary, he frequently insists on necessary limits to the State's intervention and on its instrumental character, inasmuch as the individual, the family and society are prior to the State, and inasmuch as the State exists in order to protect their rights and not stifle them.[32]

29. Cf. Encyclical Letter *Sollicitudo Rei Socialis,* 38–40: *AAS* 80 (1988), 564–69; cf. also John XXIII, Encyclical Letter *Mater et Magistra, AAS* 53 (1961), 407.

30. Cf. Leo XIII, Encyclical Letter *Rerum Novarum,* 42: 114–16; Pius XI, Encyclical Letter *Quadragesimo Anno,* III: *AAS* 23 (1931), 208; Paul VI, Homily for the Closing of the Holy Year (December 25, 1975): *AAS* 68 (1976), 145; Message for the 1977 World Day of Peace (January 1, 1977): *AAS* 68 (1976), 709.

31. Encyclical Letter *Sollicitudo Rei Socialis,* 42: *AAS* 80 (1988), 572.

32. Cf. Encyclical Letter *Rerum Novarum,* 42: 101f.; 104f.; 130f.; 136.

The relevance of these reflections for our own day is inescapable. It will be useful to return later to this important subject of the limits inherent in the nature of the State. For now, the points which have been emphasized (certainly not the only ones in the encyclical) are situated in continuity with the Church's social teaching, and in the light of a sound view of private property, work, the economic process, the reality of the State and, above all, of the person himself. Other themes will be mentioned later when we examine certain aspects of the contemporary situation. From this point forward it will be necessary to keep in mind that the main thread and, in a certain sense, the guiding principle of Pope Leo's encyclical, and of all of the Church's social doctrine, is a correct view of the human person and of the person's unique value, inasmuch as the human being "is the only creature on earth which God willed for itself."[33] God has imprinted his own image and likeness on human beings (cf. Gen 1:26), conferring upon them an incomparable dignity, as the encyclical frequently insists. In effect, beyond the rights which one acquires by one's own work, there exist rights which do not correspond to any work performed, but which flow from one's essential dignity as a person.

II. TOWARDS THE "NEW THINGS" OF TODAY

12. ... Pope Leo foresaw the negative consequences—political, social and economic—of the social order proposed by "socialism," which at that time was still only a social philosophy and not yet a fully structured movement. It may seem surprising that "socialism" appeared at the beginning of the Pope's critique of solutions to the "question of the working class" at a time when "socialism" was not yet in the form of a strong and powerful State, with all the resources which that implies, as was later to happen. However, he correctly judged the danger posed to the masses by the attractive presentation of this simple and radical solution to the "question of the working class" of the time—all the more so when one considers the terrible situation of injustice in which the working classes of the recently industrialized nations found themselves.

Two things must be emphasized here: first, the great clarity in perceiving, in all its harshness, the actual condition of the working class—men, women and children; secondly, equal clarity in recognizing the evil of a solution which, by appearing to reverse the positions of the poor and the rich, was in reality

---

33. Second Vatican Ecumenical Council, Pastoral Constitution on the Church in the Modern World *Gaudium et Spes*, 24.

detrimental to the very people whom it was meant to help. The remedy would prove worse than the sickness. By defining the nature of the socialism of his day as the suppression of private property, Leo XIII arrived at the crux of the problem.

His words deserve to be reread attentively: "To remedy these wrongs [the unjust distribution of wealth and the poverty of the workers], the socialists encourage the poor man's envy of the rich and strive to do away with private property, contending that individual possessions should become the common property of all ...; but their contentions are so clearly powerless to end the controversy that, were they carried into effect, the working man himself would be among the first to suffer. They are moreover emphatically unjust, for they would rob the lawful possessor, distort the functions of the State, and create utter confusion in the community."[34] The evils caused by the setting up of this type of socialism as a state system—what would later be called "Real Socialism"—could not be better expressed.

13. Continuing our reflections, and referring also to what has been said in the encyclicals *Laborem Exercens* and *Sollicitudo Rei Socialis*, we have to add that the fundamental error of socialism is anthropological in nature. Socialism considers the individual person simply as an element, a molecule within the social organism, so that the good of the individual is completely subordinated to the functioning of the socioeconomic mechanism. Socialism likewise maintains that the good of the individual can be realized without reference to his free choice, to the unique and exclusive responsibility which he exercises in the face of good or evil. Man is thus reduced to a series of social relationships, and the concept of the person as the autonomous subject of moral decision disappears, the very subject whose decisions build the social order. From this mistaken conception of the person there arise both a distortion of law, which defines the sphere of the exercise of freedom, and an opposition to private property. A person who is deprived of something he can call "his own," and of the possibility of earning a living through his own initiative, comes to depend on the social machine and on those who control it. This makes it much more difficult for him to recognize his dignity as a person, and hinders progress towards the building up of an authentic human community.

In contrast, from the Christian vision of the human person there necessarily follows a correct picture of society. According to *Rerum Novarum* and the whole social doctrine of the Church, the social nature of man is not completely fulfilled in the State, but is realized in various intermediary groups, beginning with the

34. Encyclical Letter *Rerum Novarum: Leonis XIII P.M. Acta*, XI, Romae 1892, 99.

family and including economic, social, political and cultural groups which stem from human nature itself and have their own autonomy, always with a view to the common good. This is what I have called the "subjectivity" of society which, together with the subjectivity of the individual, was cancelled out by "Real Socialism."[35]

If we then inquire as to the source of this mistaken concept of the nature of the person and the "subjectivity" of society, we must reply that its first cause is atheism. It is by responding to the call of God contained in the being of things that man becomes aware of his transcendent dignity. Every individual must give this response, which constitutes the apex of his humanity, and no social mechanism or collective subject can substitute for it. The denial of God deprives the person of his foundation, and consequently leads to a reorganization of the social order without reference to the person's dignity and responsibility.

The atheism of which we are speaking is also closely connected with the rationalism of the Enlightenment, which views human and social reality in a mechanistic way. Thus there is a denial of the supreme insight concerning man's true greatness, his transcendence in respect to earthly realities, the contradiction in his heart between the desire for the fullness of what is good and his own inability to attain it and, above all, the need for salvation which results from this situation. ...

15. *Rerum Novarum* is opposed to state control of the means of production, which would reduce every citizen to being a "cog" in the state machine. It is no less forceful in criticizing a concept of the State which completely excludes the economic sector from the State's range of interest and action. There is certainly a legitimate sphere of autonomy in economic life which the State should not enter. The State, however, has the task of determining the juridical framework within which economic affairs are to be conducted, and thus of safeguarding the prerequisites of a free economy, which presumes a certain equality between the parties, such that one party would not be so powerful as practically to reduce the other to subservience.[36]

[...] The State must contribute to the achievement of these goals both directly and indirectly. Indirectly and according to the principle of subsidiarity, by creating favorable conditions for the free exercise of economic activity, which will lead to abundant opportunities for employment and sources of wealth. Directly and according to the principle of solidarity, by defending the weakest, by placing certain limits on the autonomy of the parties who determine working

---

35. Cf. Encyclical Letter *Sollicitudo Rei Socialis*, 15, 28: *AAS* 80 (1988), 530; 548ff.

36. Cf. Encyclical Letter *Rerum Novarum*: *Leonis XIII P.M. Acta*, XI, Romae 1892, 121–25.

conditions, and by ensuring in every case the necessary minimum support for the unemployed worker.[37] [...]

17. Reading the encyclical within the context of Pope Leo's whole magisterium,[38] we see how it points essentially to the socioeconomic consequences of an error which has even greater implications. As has been mentioned, this error consists in an understanding of human freedom which detaches it from obedience to the truth, and consequently from the duty to respect the rights of others. The essence of freedom then becomes self-love carried to the point of contempt for God and neighbor, a self-love which leads to an unbridled affirmation of self-interest and which refuses to be limited by any demand of justice.[39]

This very error had extreme consequences in the tragic series of wars which ravaged Europe and the world between 1914 and 1945. Some of these resulted from militarism and exaggerated nationalism, and from related forms of totalitarianism; some derived from the class struggle; still others were civil wars or wars of an ideological nature. Without the terrible burden of hatred and resentment which had built up as a result of so many injustices both on the international level and within individual states, such cruel wars would not have been possible, in which great nations invested their energies and in which there was no hesitation to violate the most sacred human rights, with the extermination of entire peoples and social groups being planned and carried out. Here we recall the Jewish people in particular, whose terrible fate has become a symbol of the aberration of which man is capable when he turns against God.

However, it is only when hatred and injustice are sanctioned and organized by the ideologies based on them, rather than on the truth about the human person, that they take possession of entire nations and drive them to act.[40] *Rerum Novarum* opposed ideologies of hatred and showed how violence and resentment could be overcome by justice. May the memory of those terrible events

37. Cf. Encyclical Letter *Laborem Exercens*, 8: *AAS* 73 (1981), 594–98.

38. Cf. Encyclical Epistle *Arcanum Divinae Sapientiae* (February 10, 1880): *Leonis XIII P.M. Acta*, II, Romae 1882, 10–40; Encyclical Epistle *Diuturnum Illud* (June 29, 1881): *Leonis XIII P.M. Acta*, II, Romae 1882, 269–87; Encyclical Epistle *Immortale Dei* (November 1, 1885): *Leonis XIII P.M. Acta*, V, Romae 1886, 118–50; Encyclical Letter *Sapientiae Christianae* (January 10, 1890): *Leonis XIII P.M. Acta*, X, Romae 1891, 10–41; Encyclical Epistle *Quod Apostolici Muneris* (December 28, 1878): *Leonis XIII P.M. Acta*, 1, Romae 1881, 170–83; Encyclical Letter *Libertas Praestantissimum* (June 20, 1888): *Leonis XIII P.M. Acta*, VIII, Romae 1889, 212–46.

39. Cf. Leo XIII, Encyclical Letter *Libertas Praestantissimum*, 10: *Leonis XIII P.M. Acta*, VIII, Romae 1889, 224–26.

40. Cf. Message for the 1980 World Day of Peace: *AAS* 71 (1979), 1572–80.

guide the actions of everyone, particularly the leaders of nations in our own time, when other forms of injustice are fueling new hatreds and when new ideologies which exalt violence are appearing on the horizon. ...

19. ... Following the destruction caused by the war [Second World War], we see in some countries and under certain aspects a positive effort to rebuild a democratic society inspired by social justice, so as to deprive Communism of the revolutionary potential represented by masses of people subjected to exploitation and oppression. In general, such attempts endeavor to preserve free market mechanisms, ensuring, by means of a stable currency and the harmony of social relations, the conditions for steady and healthy economic growth in which people through their own work can build a better future for themselves and their families. At the same time, these attempts try to avoid making market mechanisms the only point of reference for social life, and they tend to subject them to public control which upholds the principle of the common destination of material goods. In this context, an abundance of work opportunities, a solid system of social security and professional training, the freedom to join trade unions and the effective action of unions, the assistance provided in cases of unemployment, the opportunities for democratic participation in the life of society—all these are meant to deliver work from the mere condition of "a commodity," and to guarantee its dignity.

Then there are the other social forces and ideological movements which oppose Marxism by setting up systems of "national security," aimed at controlling the whole of society in a systematic way, in order to make Marxist infiltration impossible. By emphasizing and increasing the power of the State, they wish to protect their people from Communism, but in doing so they run the grave risk of destroying the freedom and values of the person, the very things for whose sake it is necessary to oppose Communism.

Another kind of response, practical in nature, is represented by the affluent society or the consumer society. It seeks to defeat Marxism on the level of pure materialism by showing how a free market society can achieve a greater satisfaction of material human needs than Communism, while equally excluding spiritual values. In reality, while on the one hand it is true that this social model shows the failure of Marxism to contribute to a humane and better society, on the other hand, insofar as it denies an autonomous existence and value to morality, law, culture and religion, it agrees with Marxism, in the sense that it totally reduces man to the sphere of economics and the satisfaction of material needs. [...]

III. THE YEAR 1989

24. The second factor in the crisis [afflicting socialist and communist countries] was certainly the inefficiency of the economic system, which is not to be considered simply as a technical problem, but rather a consequence of the violation of the human rights to private initiative, to ownership of property and to freedom in the economic sector. To this must be added the cultural and national dimension: it is not possible to understand the human person on the basis of economics alone, nor to define the person simply on the basis of class membership. A human being is understood in a more complete way when situated within the sphere of culture through language, history, and the position one takes towards the fundamental events of life, such as birth, love, work and death. At the heart of every culture lies the attitude a person takes to the greatest mystery: the mystery of God. Different cultures are basically different ways of facing the question of the meaning of personal existence. When this question is eliminated, the culture and moral life of nations are corrupted. For this reason the struggle to defend work was spontaneously linked to the struggle for culture and for national rights.

But the true cause of the new developments was the spiritual void brought about by atheism, which deprived the younger generations of a sense of direction and in many cases led them, in the irrepressible search for personal identity and for the meaning of life, to rediscover the religious roots of their national cultures, and to rediscover the person of Christ himself as the existentially adequate response to the desire in every human heart for goodness, truth and life. This search was supported by the witness of those who, in difficult circumstances and under persecution, remained faithful to God. Marxism had promised to uproot the need for God from the human heart, but the results have shown that it is not possible to succeed in this without throwing the heart into turmoil.

25. ... Not only is it wrong from the ethical point of view to disregard human nature, which is made for freedom, but in practice it is impossible to do so. Where society is so organized as to reduce arbitrarily or even suppress the sphere in which freedom is legitimately exercised, the result is that the life of society becomes progressively disorganized and goes into decline.

Moreover, mankind, created for freedom, bears within itself the wound of original sin which constantly draws persons toward evil and puts them in need of redemption. Not only is this doctrine an integral part of Christian revelation; it also has great hermeneutical value insofar as it helps one to understand human reality. The human person tends towards good, but is also capable of evil. One can transcend one's immediate interest and still remain bound to it. The social order will be all the more stable the more it takes this fact into account and does not place in opposition personal interest and the interests of society as a whole, but rather seeks ways to bring them into fruitful harmony. In fact where self-interest is violently suppressed, it is replaced by a burdensome system of bureaucratic control which dries up the wellsprings of initiative and creativity. When people think they possess the secret of a perfect social organization which makes evil impossible, they also think that they can use any means, including violence and deceit, in order to bring that organization into being. Politics then becomes a "secular religion" which operates under the illusion of creating paradise in this world. But no political society—which possesses its own autonomy and laws[41]— can ever be confused with the Kingdom of God. The Gospel parable of the weeds among the wheat (cf. Mt 13:24–30; 36–43) teaches that it is for God alone to separate the subjects of the Kingdom from the subjects of the Evil One, and that this judgment will take place at the end of time. By presuming to anticipate judgment here and now, people put themselves in the place of God and set themselves against the patience of God.

Through Christ's sacrifice on the cross, the victory of the Kingdom of God has been achieved once and for all. Nevertheless, the Christian life involves a struggle against temptation and the forces of evil. Only at the end of history will the Lord return in glory for the final judgment (cf. Mt 25:31) with the establishment of a new heaven and a new earth (cf. 2 Pt 3:13; Rev 21:1); but as long as time lasts the struggle between good and evil continues even in the human heart itself.

What Sacred Scripture teaches us about the prospects of the Kingdom of God is not without consequences for the life of temporal societies, which, as the adjective indicates, belong to the realm of time, with all that this implies of imperfection and impermanence. The Kingdom of God, being in the world without being of the world, throws light on the order of human society, while the power of grace penetrates that order and gives it life. In this way the requirements of a society worthy of man are better perceived, deviations are corrected, the courage to work for what is good is reinforced. In union with all people of good will, Christians, especially the laity, are called to this task of imbuing human realities with the Gospel.[42]

26. ... The crisis of Marxism [i.e., the fact that it has largely collapsed] does not rid the world of the situations of injustice and oppression which Marxism

---

41. Cf. Second Vatican Ecumenical Council, Pastoral Constitution on the Church in the Modern World *Gaudium et Spes*, 36; 39.

42. Cf. Apostolic Exhortation *Christifideles Laici* (December 30, 1988), 32–44: *AAS* 81 (1989), 431–81.

itself exploited and on which it fed. To those who are searching today for a new and authentic theory and praxis of liberation, the Church offers not only her social doctrine and, in general, her teaching about the human person redeemed in Christ, but also her concrete commitment and material assistance in the struggle against marginalization and suffering.

In the recent past, the sincere desire to be on the side of the oppressed and not to be cut off from the course of history has led many believers to seek in various ways an impossible compromise between Marxism and Christianity. Moving beyond all that was short-lived in these attempts, present circumstances are leading to a reaffirmation of the positive value of an authentic theology of integral human liberation.[43] ...

29. Finally, development must not be understood solely in economic terms, but in a way that is fully human.[44] It is not only a question of raising all peoples to the level currently enjoyed by the richest countries, but rather of building up a more decent life through united labor, of concretely enhancing every individual's dignity and creativity, as well as his capacity to respond to his personal vocation, and thus to God's call. The apex of development is the exercise of the right and duty to seek God, to know him and to live in accordance with that knowledge.[45] In the totalitarian and authoritarian regimes, the principle that force predominates over reason was carried to the extreme. A person was compelled to submit to a conception of reality imposed on him by coercion, and not reached by virtue of his own reason and the exercise of his own freedom. This principle must be overturned and total recognition must be given to the rights of the human conscience, which is bound only to the truth, both natural and revealed. The recognition of these rights represents the primary foundation of every authentically free political order.[46] It is important to reaffirm this latter principle for several reasons:

a) because the old forms of totalitarianism and authoritarianism are not yet completely vanquished; indeed there is a risk that they will regain their strength. This demands renewed efforts of cooperation and solidarity between all countries;

b) because in the developed countries there is sometimes an excessive promotion of purely utilitarian values, with an appeal to the appetites and

43. Cf. Congregation for the Doctrine of the Faith, Instruction on Christian Freedom and Liberation *Libertatis Conscientia* (March 22, 1986): *AAS* 79 (1987), 554–99.

44. Cf. Encyclical Letter *Sollicitudo Rei Socialis*, 27–28: *AAS* 80 (1988), 547–50; Paul VI, Encyclical Letter *Populorum Progressio*, 43–44: *AAS* 59 (1967), 278f.

45. Cf. Encyclical Letter *Sollicitudo Rei Socialis*, 29–31: *AAS* 80 (1988), 550–56.

46. Cf. Helsinki Final Act and Vienna Accord; Leo XIII, Encyclical Letter *Libertas Praestantissimum*, 5: *Leonis XIII P.M. Acta*, VIII, Romae 1889, 215–17.

inclinations towards immediate gratification, making it difficult to recognize and respect the hierarchy of the true values of human existence;

c) because in some countries new forms of religious fundamentalism are emerging which covertly, or even openly, deny to citizens of faiths other than that of the majority the full exercise of their civil and religious rights, preventing them from taking part in the cultural process, and restricting both the Church's right to preach the Gospel and the rights of those who hear this preaching to accept it and to be converted to Christ. No authentic progress is possible without respect for the natural and fundamental right to know the truth and live according to that truth. The exercise and development of this right includes the right to discover and freely to accept Jesus Christ, who is humanity's true good.[47]

IV. PRIVATE PROPERTY AND THE UNIVERSAL DESTINATION OF GOODS

30. In *Rerum Novarum*, Leo XIII strongly affirmed the natural character of the right to private property, using various arguments against the socialism of his time.[48] This right, which is fundamental for the autonomy and development of the person, has always been defended by the Church up to our own day. At the same time, the Church teaches that the possession of material goods is not an absolute right, and that its limits are inscribed in its very nature as a human right.

While the Pope proclaimed the right to private ownership, he affirmed with equal clarity that the "use" of goods, while marked by freedom, is subordinated to their original common destination as created goods, as well as to the will of Jesus Christ as expressed in the Gospel. Pope Leo wrote: "those whom fortune favors are admonished ... that they should tremble at the warnings of Jesus Christ ... and that a most strict account must be given to the Supreme Judge for the use of all they possess"; and quoting Saint Thomas Aquinas, he added: "But if the question be asked, how must one's possessions be used?, the Church replies without hesitation that man should not consider his material possessions as his own, but as common to all," because "above the laws and judgments of men stands the law, the judgment of Christ."[49]

---

47. Cf. Encyclical Letter *Redemptoris Missio* (December 7, 1990), 7: *L'Osservatore Romano*, January 23, 1991.

48. Cf. Encyclical Letter *Rerum Novarum*: *Leonis XIII P.M. Acta*, XI, Romae 1892, 99–107; 131–33.

49. Ibid., 111–13f.

The Successors of Leo XIII have repeated this twofold affirmation: the necessity and therefore the legitimacy of private ownership, as well as the limits which are imposed on it.[50] The Second Vatican Council likewise clearly restated the traditional doctrine in words which bear repeating: "In making use of the exterior things we lawfully possess, we ought to regard them not just as our own but also as common, in the sense that they can profit not only the owners but others too"; and a little later we read: "Private property or some ownership of external goods affords each person the scope needed for personal and family autonomy, and should be regarded as an extension of human freedom. ... Of its nature private property also has a social function which is based on the law of the common purpose of goods."[51] I have returned to this same doctrine, first in my address to the Third Conference of the Latin American bishops at Puebla, and later in the encyclicals *Laborem Exercens* and *Sollicitudo Rei Socialis*.[52]

31. Rereading this teaching on the right to property and the common destination of material wealth as it applies to the present time, the question can be raised concerning the origin of the material goods which sustain human life, satisfy people's needs, and are an object of their rights.

The original source of all that is good is the very act of God, who created both the earth and mankind, and who gave the earth to mankind, so that we might have dominion over it by our work and enjoy its fruits (Gen 1:28). God gave the earth to the whole human race for the sustenance of all its members, without excluding or favoring anyone. This is the foundation of the universal destination of the earth's goods. The earth, by reason of its fruitfulness and its capacity to satisfy human needs, is God's first gift for the sustenance of human life. But the earth does not yield its fruits without a particular human response to God's gift, that is to say, without work. It is through work that we, using our intelligence and exercising our freedom, succeed in dominating the earth and making it a fitting home. In this way, one makes part of the earth one's own, precisely the part which one has acquired through work; this is the origin of individual property. Obviously, one also has the responsibility not to hinder others from having their

50. Cf. Pius XI, Encyclical Letter *Quadragesimo Anno*, II: *AAS* 23 (1931), 191; Pius XII, Radio Message on June 1, 1941: *AAS* 33 (1941), 199; John XXIII, Encyclical Letter *Mater et Magistra: AAS* 53 (1961), 428–29; Paul VI, Encyclical Letter *Populorum Progressio*, 22–24: *AAS* 59 (1967), 268f.

51. Second Vatican Ecumenical Council, Pastoral Constitution on the Church in the Modern World *Gaudium et Spes*, 69; 71.

52. Cf. Discourse to Latin American Bishops at Puebla (January 28, 1979), III, 4: *AAS* 71 (1979), 199–201; Encyclical Letter *Laborem Exercens*, 14: *AAS* 73 (1981), 612–16; Encyclical Letter *Sollicitudo Rei Socialis*, 42: *AAS* 80 (1988), 572–74.

own part of God's gift; indeed, one must cooperate with others so that together all can have dominion over the earth.

In history, these two factors—work and the land—are to be found at the beginning of every human society. However, they do not always stand in the same relationship to each other. At one time the natural fruitfulness of the earth appeared to be, and was in fact, the primary factor of wealth, while work was, as it were, the help and support for this fruitfulness. In our time, the role of human work is becoming increasingly important as the productive factor both of nonmaterial and of material wealth. Moreover, it is becoming clearer how a person's work is naturally interrelated with the work of others. More than ever, work is work with others and work for others: it is a matter of doing something for someone else. Work becomes ever more fruitful and productive to the extent that people become more knowledgeable of the productive potentialities of the earth and more profoundly cognizant of the needs of those for whom their work is done.

32. In our time, in particular, there exists another form of ownership which is becoming no less important than land: the possession of know-how, technology and skill. The wealth of the industrialized nations is based much more on this kind of ownership than on natural resources.

Mention has just been made of the fact that people work with each other, sharing in a "community of work" which embraces ever widening circles. A person who produces something other than for his own use generally does so in order that others may use it after they have paid a just price, mutually agreed upon through free bargaining. It is precisely the ability to foresee both the needs of others and the combinations of productive factors most adapted to satisfying those needs that constitutes another important source of wealth in modern society. Besides, many goods cannot be adequately produced through the work of an isolated individual; they require the cooperation of many people in working towards a common goal. Organizing such a productive effort, planning its duration in time, making sure that it corresponds in a positive way to the demands which it must satisfy, and taking the necessary risks—all this too is a source of wealth in today's society. In this way, the role of disciplined and creative human work and, as an essential part of that work, initiative and entrepreneurial ability becomes increasingly evident and decisive.[53]

This process, which throws practical light on a truth about the person which Christianity has constantly affirmed, should be viewed carefully and favorably. Indeed, besides the earth, mankind's principal resource is the person himself. His

---

53. Cf. Encyclical Letter *Sollicitudo Rei Socialis*, 15: *AAS* 80 (1988), 528–31.

intelligence enables him to discover the earth's productive potential and the many different ways in which human needs can be satisfied. It is his disciplined work in close collaboration with others that makes possible the creation of ever more extensive working communities which can be relied upon to transform natural and human environments. Important virtues are involved in this process, such as diligence, industriousness, prudence in undertaking reasonable risks, reliability and fidelity in interpersonal relationships, as well as courage in carrying out decisions which are difficult and painful but necessary, both for the overall working of a business and in meeting possible setbacks.

The modern business economy has positive aspects. Its basis is human freedom exercised in the economic field, just as it is exercised in many other fields. Economic activity is indeed but one sector in a great variety of human activities, and like every other sector, it includes the right to freedom, as well as the duty of making responsible use of freedom. But it is important to note that there are specific differences between the trends of modern society and those of the past, even the recent past. Whereas at one time the decisive factor of production was the land, and later capital—understood as a total complex of the instruments of production—today the decisive factor is increasingly the person, that is, one's knowledge, especially one's scientific knowledge, one's capacity for interrelated and compact organization, as well as one's ability to perceive the needs of others and to satisfy them.

33. However, the risks and problems connected with this kind of process should be pointed out. The fact is that many people, perhaps the majority today, do not have the means which would enable them to take their place in an effective and humanly dignified way within a productive system in which work is truly central. They have no possibility of acquiring the basic knowledge which would enable them to express their creativity and develop their potential. They have no way of entering the network of knowledge and intercommunication which would enable them to see their qualities appreciated and utilized. Thus, if not actually exploited, they are to a great extent marginalized; economic development takes place over their heads, so to speak, when it does not actually reduce the already narrow scope of their old subsistence economies. They are unable to compete against the goods which are produced in ways which are new and which properly respond to needs, needs which they had previously been accustomed to meeting through traditional forms of organization. Allured by the dazzle of an opulence which is beyond their reach, and at the same time driven by necessity, these people crowd the cities of the Third World where they are often without cultural roots, and where they are exposed to situations of violent uncertainty, without the possibility of becoming integrated. Their dignity is not acknowledged in any real way,

and sometimes there are even attempts to eliminate them from history through coercive forms of demographic control which are contrary to human dignity.

Many other people, while not completely marginalized, live in situations in which the struggle for a bare minimum is uppermost. These are situations in which the rules of the earliest period of capitalism still flourish in conditions of "ruthlessness" in no way inferior to the darkest moments of the first phase of industrialization. In other cases the land is still the central element in the economic process, but those who cultivate it are excluded from ownership and are reduced to a state of quasi-servitude.[54] In these cases, it is still possible today, as in the days of *Rerum Novarum*, to speak of inhuman exploitation. In spite of the great changes which have taken place in the more advanced societies, the human inadequacies of capitalism and the resulting domination of things over people are far from disappearing. In fact, for the poor, to the lack of material goods has been added a lack of knowledge and training which prevents them from escaping their state of humiliating subjection. ...

34. It would appear that, on the level of individual nations and of international relations, the free market is the most efficient instrument for utilizing resources and effectively responding to needs. But this is true only for those needs which are "solvent," insofar as they are endowed with purchasing power, and for those resources which are "marketable," insofar as they are capable of obtaining a satisfactory price. But there are many human needs which find no place on the market. It is a strict duty of justice and truth not to allow fundamental human needs to remain unsatisfied, and not to allow those burdened by such needs to perish. It is also necessary to help these needy people to acquire expertise, to enter the circle of exchange, and to develop their skills in order to make the best use of their capacities and resources. Even prior to the logic of a fair exchange of goods and the forms of justice appropriate to it, there exists something which is due to the person because he is a person, by reason of his lofty dignity. Inseparable from that required "something" is the possibility to survive and, at the same time, to make an active contribution to the common good of humanity. ...

35. ... In this sense, it is right to speak of a struggle against an economic system, if the latter is understood as a method of upholding the absolute predominance of capital, the possession of the means of production and of the land, in contrast to the free and personal nature of human work.[55] In the struggle against such a system, what is being proposed as an alternative is not the socialist system, which in fact turns out to be state capitalism, but rather a society of free work, of

---

54. Cf. Encyclical Letter *Laborem Exercens*, 21: *AAS* 73 (1981), 632–34.

55. Cf. ibid., 7: *AAS* 73 (1981), 592–94.

enterprise, and of participation. Such a society is not directed against the market, but demands that the market be appropriately controlled by the forces of society and by the State, so as to guarantee that the basic needs of the whole of society are satisfied.

The Church acknowledges the legitimate role of profit as an indication that a business is functioning well. When a firm makes a profit, this means that productive factors have been properly employed and corresponding human needs have been duly satisfied. But profitability is not the only indicator of a firm's condition. It is possible for the financial accounts to be in order, and yet for the people—who make up the firm's most valuable asset—to be humiliated and their dignity offended. Besides being morally inadmissible, this will eventually have negative repercussions on the firm's economic efficiency. In fact, the purpose of a business firm is not simply to make a profit, but is to be found in its very existence as a community of persons who in various ways are endeavoring to satisfy their basic needs, and who form a particular group at the service of the whole of society. Profit is a regulator of the life of a business, but it is not the only one; other human and moral factors must also be considered which, in the long term, are at least equally important for the life of a business.

We have seen that it is unacceptable to say that the defeat of so-called "Real Socialism" leaves capitalism as the only model of economic organization. ...

36. It would now be helpful to direct our attention to the specific problems and threats emerging within the more advanced economies and which are related to their particular characteristics. In earlier stages of development, people always lived under the weight of necessity. Their needs were few and were determined, to a degree, by the objective structures of their physical make-up. Economic activity was directed towards satisfying these needs. It is clear that today the problem is not only one of supplying people with a sufficient quantity of goods, but also of responding to a demand for quality: the quality of the goods to be produced and consumed, the quality of the services to be enjoyed, the quality of the environment and of life in general.

To call for an existence which is qualitatively more satisfying is of itself legitimate, but one cannot fail to draw attention to the new responsibilities and dangers connected with this phase of history. The manner in which new needs arise and are defined is always marked by a more or less appropriate concept of the human person and of the person's true good. A given culture reveals its overall understanding of life through the choices it makes in production and consumption. It is here that the phenomenon of consumerism arises. In singling out new needs and new means to meet them, one must be guided by a comprehensive picture of the person which respects all the dimensions of his being and which subordinates his material and instinctive dimensions to his interior and spiritual ones. If, on the contrary, a direct appeal is made to human instincts—while ignoring in various ways the reality of the person as intelligent and free—then consumer attitudes and lifestyles can be created which are objectively improper and often damaging to the person's physical and spiritual health. Of itself, an economic system does not possess criteria for correctly distinguishing new and higher forms of satisfying human needs from artificial new needs which hinder the formation of a mature personality. Thus a great deal of educational and cultural work is urgently needed, including the education of consumers in the responsible use of their power of choice, the formation of a strong sense of responsibility among producers and among people in the mass media in particular, as well as the necessary intervention by public authorities.

A striking example of artificial consumption contrary to the health and dignity of the human person, and certainly not easy to control, is the use of drugs. Widespread drug use is a sign of a serious malfunction in the social system; it also implies a materialistic and, in a certain sense, destructive "reading" of human needs. In this way the innovative capacity of a free economy is brought to a one-sided and inadequate conclusion. Drugs, as well as pornography and other forms of consumerism which exploit the frailty of the weak, tend to fill the resulting spiritual void.

It is not wrong to want to live better; what is wrong is a style of life which is presumed to be better when it is directed towards "having" rather than "being," and which wants to have more, not in order to be more but in order to spend life in enjoyment as an end in itself.[56] It is therefore necessary to create lifestyles in which the quest for truth, beauty, goodness, and communion with others for the sake of common growth are the factors which determine consumer choices, savings, and investments. In this regard, it is not a matter of the duty of charity alone, that is, the duty to give from one's "abundance," and sometimes even out of one's needs, in order to provide what is essential for the life of a poor person. I am referring to the fact that even the decision to invest in one place rather than another, in one productive sector rather than another, is always a moral and cultural choice. Given the utter necessity of certain economic conditions and of political stability, the decision to invest, that is, to offer people an opportunity to make good use of their own labor, is also determined by an attitude of human sympathy and trust in Providence, which reveal the human quality of the person making such decisions.

---

56. Cf. Second Vatican Ecumenical Council, Pastoral Constitution on the Church in the Modern World *Gaudium et Spes*, 35; Paul VI, Encyclical Letter *Populorum Progressio*, 19: loc. cit., 266f.

37. Equally worrying is the ecological question which accompanies the problem of consumerism and which is closely connected to it. In their desire to have and to enjoy rather than to be and to grow, people consume the resources of the earth and their own lives in an excessive and disordered way. At the root of the senseless destruction of the natural environment lies an anthropological error, which unfortunately is widespread in our day. Mankind, which discovers its capacity to transform and in a certain sense create the world through its own work, forgets that this is always based on God's prior and original gift of the things that are. People think that they can make arbitrary use of the earth, subjecting it without restraint to their wills, as though the earth did not have its own requisites and a prior God-given purpose, which human beings can indeed develop but must not betray. Instead of carrying out one's role as a cooperator with God in the work of creation, a person sets himself up in place of God and thus ends up provoking a rebellion on the part of nature, which is more tyrannized than governed by him.[57]

In all this, one notes first the poverty or narrowness of the human outlook, motivated as people are by a desire to possess things rather than to relate them to the truth, and lacking that disinterested, unselfish, and aesthetic attitude that is born of wonder in the presence of being and of the beauty which enables one to see in visible things the message of the invisible God who created them. In this regard, humanity today must be conscious of its duties and obligations towards future generations.

38. In addition to the irrational destruction of the natural environment, we must also mention the more serious destruction of the human environment, something which is by no means receiving the attention it deserves. Although people are rightly worried—though much less than they should be—about preserving the natural habitats of the various animal species threatened with extinction, because they realize that each of these species makes its particular contribution to the balance of nature in general, too little effort is made to safeguard the moral conditions for an authentic "human ecology." Not only has God given the earth to humanity, which must use it with respect for the original good purpose for which it was given, but man too is God's gift to man. A person must therefore respect the natural and moral structure with which he has been endowed. In this context, mention should be made of the serious problems of modern urbanization, of the need for urban planning which is concerned with how people are to live, and of the attention which should be given to a "social ecology" of work.

---

57. Cf. Encyclical Letter *Sollicitudo Rei Socialis*, 34: *AAS* 59 (1967), 559f.; Message for the 1990 World Day of Peace: *AAS* 82 (1990), 147–56.

The human person receives from God its essential dignity and with it the capacity to transcend every social order so as to move towards truth and goodness. But one is also conditioned by the social structure in which one lives, by the education one has received and by the environment. These elements can either help or hinder a person's living in accordance with the truth. The decisions which create a human environment can give rise to specific structures of sin which impede the full realization of those who are in any way oppressed by them. To destroy such structures and replace them with more authentic forms of living in community is a task which demands courage and patience.[58]

39. The first and fundamental structure for "human ecology" is the family, in which someone receives his first formative ideas about truth and goodness, and learns what it means to love and to be loved, and thus what it actually means to be a person. Here we mean the family founded on marriage, in which the mutual gift of self by husband and wife creates an environment in which children can be born and develop their potentialities, become aware of their dignity and prepare to face their unique and individual destiny. But it often happens that people are discouraged from creating the proper conditions for human reproduction and are led to consider themselves and their lives as a series of sensations to be experienced rather than as a work to be accomplished. The result is a lack of freedom, which causes a person to reject a commitment to enter into a stable relationship with another person and to bring children into the world, or which leads people to consider children as one of the many "things" which an individual can have or not have, according to taste, and which compete with other possibilities.

It is necessary to go back to seeing the family as the sanctuary of life. The family is indeed sacred: it is the place in which life—the gift of God—can be properly welcomed and protected against the many attacks to which it is exposed, and can develop in accordance with what constitutes authentic human growth. In the face of the so-called culture of death, the family is the heart of the culture of life.

Human ingenuity seems to be directed more towards limiting, suppressing or destroying the sources of life—including recourse to abortion, which unfortunately is so widespread in the world—than towards defending and opening up the possibilities of life. The encyclical *Sollicitudo Rei Socialis* denounced systematic anti-childbearing campaigns which, on the basis of a distorted view of the demographic problem and in a climate of "absolute lack of respect for the

---

58. Cf. Apostolic Exhortation *Reconciliatio et Poenitentia* (December 2,1984), 16: *AAS* 77 (1985), 213–17; Pius XI, Encyclical Letter *Quadragesimo Anno*, III: *AAS* 23 (1931), 219.

freedom of choice of the parties involved," often subject them "to intolerable pressures ... in order to force them to submit to this new form of oppression."[59] These policies are extending their field of action by the use of new techniques, to the point of poisoning the lives of millions of defenseless human beings, as if in a form of "chemical warfare."

These criticisms are directed not so much against an economic system as against an ethical and cultural system. The economy in fact is only one aspect and one dimension of the whole of human activity. If economic life is absolutized, if the production and consumption of goods become the center of social life and society's only value, not subject to any other value, the reason is to be found not so much in the economic system itself as in the fact that the entire socio-cultural system, by ignoring the ethical and religious dimension, has been weakened, and ends by limiting itself to the production of goods and services alone.[60]

All of this can be summed up by repeating once more that economic freedom is only one element of human freedom. When it becomes autonomous, when man is seen more as a producer or consumer of goods than as a subject who produces and consumes in order to live, then economic freedom loses its necessary relationship to the human person and ends up by alienating and oppressing him.[61]

40. It is the task of the State to provide for the defense and preservation of common goods such as the natural and human environments, which cannot be safeguarded simply by market forces. Just as in the time of primitive capitalism the State had the duty of defending the basic rights of workers, so now, with the new capitalism, the State and all of society have the duty of defending those collective goods which, among others, constitute the essential framework for the legitimate pursuit of personal goals on the part of each individual.

Here we find a new limit on the market: there are collective and qualitative needs which cannot be satisfied by market mechanisms. There are important human needs which escape its logic. There are goods which by their very nature cannot and must not be bought or sold. Certainly the mechanisms of the market offer secure advantages: they help to utilize resources better; they promote the exchange of products; above all they give central place to the person's desires and preferences, which, in a contract, meet the desires and preferences of another person. Nevertheless, these mechanisms carry the risk of an "idolatry" of the market, an idolatry which ignores the existence of goods which by their nature are not and cannot be mere commodities.

---

59. Encyclical Letter *Sollicitudo Rei Socialis*, 25: AAS 80 (1988), 544.

60. Cf. ibid., 34: AAS 80 (1988), 559f.

61. Cf. Encyclical Letter *Redemptor Hominis* (March 4, 1979), 15: AAS 71 (1979), 286–89.

41. Marxism criticized capitalist bourgeois societies, blaming them for the commercialization and alienation of human existence. This rebuke is of course based on a mistaken and inadequate idea of alienation, derived solely from the sphere of relationships of production and ownership, that is, giving them a materialistic foundation and moreover denying the legitimacy and positive value of market relationships even in their own sphere. Marxism thus ends up by affirming that only in a collective society can alienation be eliminated. However, the historical experience of socialist countries has sadly demonstrated that collectivism does not do away with alienation but rather increases it, adding to it a lack of basic necessities and economic inefficiency.

The historical experience of the West, for its part, shows that even if the Marxist analysis and its foundation of alienation are false, nevertheless alienation—and the loss of the authentic meaning of life—is a reality in Western societies too. This happens in consumerism, when people are ensnared in a web of false and superficial gratifications rather than being helped to experience their personhood in an authentic and concrete way. Alienation is found also in work, when it is organized so as to ensure maximum returns and profits with no concern whether the worker, through his own labor, grows or diminishes as a person, either through increased sharing in a genuinely supportive community or through increased isolation in a maze of relationships marked by destructive competitiveness and estrangement, in which he is considered only a means and not an end.

The concept of alienation needs to be led back to the Christian vision of reality, by recognizing in alienation a reversal of means and ends. When man does not recognize in himself and in others the value and grandeur of the human person, he effectively deprives himself of the possibility of benefitting from his humanity and of entering into that relationship of solidarity and communion with others for which God created him. Indeed, it is through the free gift of self that one truly finds oneself.[62] This gift is made possible by the human person's essential "capacity for transcendence." One cannot give oneself to a purely human plan for reality, to an abstract ideal or to a false utopia. As a person, one can give oneself to another person or to other persons, and ultimately to God, who is the author of our being and who alone can fully accept our gift.[63] A person is alienated if he refuses to transcend himself and to live the experience of self-giving and of the formation of an authentic human community oriented towards his final destiny, which is God. A society is alienated if its forms of social organization, production

---

62. Cf. Second Vatican Ecumenical Council, Pastoral Constitution on the Church in the Modern World *Gaudium et Spes*, 24.

63. Cf. ibid., 41.

and consumption make it more difficult to offer this gift of self and to establish this solidarity between people.

Exploitation, at least in the forms analyzed and described by Karl Marx, has been overcome in Western society. Alienation, however, has not been overcome as it exists in various forms of exploitation, when people use one another, and when they seek an ever more refined satisfaction of their individual and secondary needs, while ignoring the principal and authentic needs which ought to regulate the manner of satisfying the other ones too.[64] A person who is concerned solely or primarily with possessing and enjoying, who is no longer able to control his instincts and passions, or to subordinate them by obedience to the truth, cannot be free: obedience to the truth about God and mankind is the first condition of freedom, making it possible for a person to order his needs and desires and to choose the means of satisfying them according to a correct scale of values, so that the ownership of things may become an occasion of personal growth. This growth can be hindered as a result of manipulation by the means of mass communication, which impose fashions and trends of opinion through carefully orchestrated repetition, without it being possible to subject to critical scrutiny the premises on which these fashions and trends are based.

42. Returning now to the initial question: can it perhaps be said that, after the failure of Communism, capitalism is the victorious social system, and that capitalism should be the goal of the countries now making efforts to rebuild their economy and society? Is this the model which ought to be proposed to the countries of the Third World which are searching for the path to true economic and civil progress?

The answer is obviously complex. If by "capitalism" is meant an economic system which recognizes the fundamental and positive role of business, the market, private property and the resulting responsibility for the means of production, as well as free human creativity in the economic sector, then the answer is certainly in the affirmative, even though it would perhaps be more appropriate to speak of a "business economy," "market economy" or simply "free economy." But if by "capitalism" is meant a system in which freedom in the economic sector is not circumscribed within a strong juridical framework which places it at the service of human freedom in its totality and sees it as a particular aspect of that freedom, the core of which is ethical and religious, then the reply is certainly negative.

The Marxist solution has failed, but the realities of marginalization and exploitation remain in the world, especially the Third World, as does the reality

---

64. Cf. ibid., 26.

of human alienation, especially in the more advanced countries. Against these phenomena the Church strongly raises her voice. Vast multitudes are still living in conditions of great material and moral poverty. The collapse of the Communist system in so many countries certainly removes an obstacle to facing these problems in an appropriate and realistic way, but it is not enough to bring about their solution. Indeed, there is a risk that a radical capitalistic ideology could spread which refuses even to consider these problems, in the *a priori* belief that any attempt to solve them is doomed to failure, and which blindly entrusts their solution to the free development of market forces.

43. The Church has no models to present; models that are real and truly effective can only arise within the framework of different historical situations, through the efforts of all those who responsibly confront concrete problems in all their social, economic, political and cultural aspects, as these interact with one another.[65] For such a task the Church offers her social teaching as an indispensable and ideal orientation, a teaching which, as already mentioned, recognizes the positive value of the market and of enterprise, but which at the same time points out that these need to be oriented towards the common good. This teaching also recognizes the legitimacy of workers' efforts to obtain full respect for their dignity and to gain broader areas of participation in the life of industrial enterprises so that, while cooperating with others and under the direction of others, they can in a certain sense "work for themselves"[66] through the exercise of their intelligence and freedom.

The integral development of the human person through work does not impede but rather promotes the greater productivity and efficiency of work itself, even though it may weaken consolidated power structures. A business cannot be considered only as a "society of capital goods"; it is also a "society of persons" in which people participate in different ways and with specific responsibilities, whether they supply the necessary capital for the company's activities or take part in such activities through their labor. To achieve these goals there is still need for a broad associated workers' movement, directed towards the liberation and promotion of the whole person.

In the light of today's "new things," we have reread the relationship between individual or private property and the universal destination of material wealth. One fulfills oneself by using one's intelligence and freedom. In so doing a person

65. Cf. Second Vatican Ecumenical Council, Pastoral Constitution on the Church in the Modern World *Gaudium et Spes*, 36; Paul VI, Apostolic Epistle *Octogesima Adveniens*, 2–5: *AAS* 63 (1971), 402–5.

66. Cf. Encyclical Letter *Laborem Exercens*, 15: *AAS* 73 (1981), 616–18.

utilizes the things of this world as objects and instruments and makes them his own. The foundation of the right to private initiative and ownership is to be found in this activity. By means of his work a person commits himself, not only for his own sake but also for others and with others. Each person collaborates in the work of others and for their good. One works in order to provide for the needs of one's family, one's community, one's nation, and ultimately all humanity.[67] Moreover, a person collaborates in the work of his fellow employees, as well as in the work of suppliers and in the customers' use of goods, in a progressively expanding chain of solidarity. Ownership of the means of production, whether in industry or agriculture, is just and legitimate if it serves useful work. It becomes illegitimate, however, when it is not utilized or when it serves to impede the work of others, in an effort to gain a profit which is not the result of the overall expansion of work and the wealth of society, but rather is the result of curbing them or of illicit exploitation, speculation or the breaking of solidarity among working people.[68] Ownership of this kind has no justification, and represents an abuse in the sight of God and humanity.

The obligation to earn one's bread by the sweat of one's brow also presumes the right to do so. A society in which this right is systematically denied, in which economic policies do not allow workers to reach satisfactory levels of employment, cannot be justified from an ethical point of view, nor can that society attain social peace.[69] Just as the person fully realizes himself in the free gift of self, so too ownership morally justifies itself in the creation, at the proper time and in the proper way, of opportunities for work and human growth for all.

V. STATE AND CULTURE

44. Pope Leo XIII was aware of the need for a sound theory of the State in order to ensure the normal development of the human person's spiritual and temporal activities, both of which are indispensable.[70] For this reason, in one passage of *Rerum Novarum* he presents the organization of society according to the three powers—legislative, executive, and judicial—something which at the time represented a novelty in Church teaching.[71] Such an ordering reflects

---

67. Cf. ibid., 10: *AAS* 73 (1981), 600–602.

68. Ibid., 14: *AAS* 73 (1981), 612–16.

69. Cf. ibid., 18: *AAS* 73 (1981), 622–25.

70. Cf. Encyclical Letter *Rerum Novarum: Leonis XIII P.M. Acta*, XI, Romae 1892, 126–28.

71. Ibid., 121f.

a realistic vision of mankind's social nature, which calls for legislation capable of protecting the freedom of all. To that end, it is preferable that each power be balanced by other powers and by other spheres of responsibility which keep it within proper bounds. This is the principle of the "rule of law," in which the law is sovereign, and not the arbitrary will of individuals.

In modern times, this concept has been opposed by totalitarianism, which, in its Marxist-Leninist form, maintains that some people, by virtue of a deeper knowledge of the laws of the development of society, or through membership of a particular class or through contact with the deeper sources of the collective consciousness, are exempt from error and can therefore arrogate to themselves the exercise of absolute power. It must be added that totalitarianism arises out of a denial of truth in the objective sense.

If there is no transcendent truth, in obedience to which a person achieves his full identity, then there is no sure principle for guaranteeing just relations between people. Their self-interest as a class, group or nation would inevitably set them in opposition to one another. If one does not acknowledge transcendent truth, then the force of power takes over, and each person tends to make full use of the means at his disposal in order to impose his own interests or his own opinion, with no regard for the rights of others. People are then respected only to the extent that they can be exploited for selfish ends. Thus, the root of modern totalitarianism is to be found in the denial of the transcendent dignity of the human person who, as the visible image of the invisible God, is therefore by his very nature the subject of rights which no one may violate—no individual, group, class, nation or State. Not even the majority of a social body may violate these rights, by going against the minority, by isolating, oppressing, or exploiting it, or by attempting to annihilate it.[72]

45. The culture and praxis of totalitarianism also involve a rejection of the Church. The State or the party which claims to be able to lead history towards perfect goodness, and which sets itself above all values, cannot tolerate the affirmation of an objective criterion of good and evil beyond the will of those in power, since such a criterion, in given circumstances, could be used to judge their actions. This explains why totalitarianism attempts to destroy the Church, or at least to reduce her to submission, making her an instrument of its own ideological apparatus.[73]

---

72. Cf. Leo XIII, Encyclical Letter *Libertas Praestantissimum*: *Leonis XIII P.M. Acta*, VIII, Romae 1889, 224–26.

73. Cf. Second Vatican Ecumenical Council, Pastoral Constitution on the Church in the Modern World *Gaudium et Spes*, 76.

Furthermore, the totalitarian State tends to absorb within itself the nation, society, the family, religious groups and individuals themselves. In defending her own freedom, the Church is also defending the human person, who must obey God rather than men (cf. Acts 5:29), as well as defending the family, the various social organizations and nations—all of which enjoy their own spheres of autonomy and sovereignty.

46. The Church values the democratic system inasmuch as it ensures the participation of citizens in making political choices, guarantees to the governed the possibility both of electing and holding accountable those who govern them, and of replacing them through peaceful means when appropriate.[74] Thus she cannot encourage the formation of narrow ruling groups which usurp the power of the State for individual interests or for ideological ends.

Authentic democracy is possible only in a State ruled by law, and on the basis of a correct conception of the human person. It requires that the necessary conditions be present for the advancement both of the individual through education and formation in true ideals, and of the "subjectivity" of society through the creation of structures of participation and shared responsibility. Nowadays there is a tendency to claim that agnosticism and skeptical relativism are the philosophy and the basic attitude which correspond to democratic forms of political life. Those who are convinced that they know the truth and firmly adhere to it are considered unreliable from a democratic point of view, since they do not accept that truth is determined by the majority, or that it is subject to variation according to different political trends. It must be observed in this regard that if there is no ultimate truth to guide and direct political activity, then ideas and convictions can easily be manipulated for reasons of power. As history demonstrates, a democracy without values easily turns into open or thinly disguised totalitarianism.

Nor does the Church close her eyes to the danger of fanaticism or fundamentalism among those who, in the name of an ideology which purports to be scientific or religious, claim the right to impose on others their own concept of what is true and good. Christian truth is not of this kind. Since it is not an ideology, the Christian faith does not presume to imprison changing sociopolitical realities in a rigid schema, and it recognizes that human life is realized in history in conditions that are diverse and imperfect. Furthermore, in constantly reaffirming the transcendent dignity of the person, the Church's method is always that of respect for freedom.[75]

---

74. Cf. ibid., 29; Pius XII, Christmas Radio Message on December 24, 1944: *AAS* 37 (1945), 10–20.

75. Cf. Second Vatican Ecumenical Council, Declaration on Religious Freedom *Dignitatis Humanae.*

But freedom attains its full development only by accepting the truth. In a world without truth, freedom loses its foundation and people are exposed to the violence of passion and to manipulation, both open and hidden. The Christian upholds freedom and serves it, constantly offering to others the truth which he has known (cf. Jn 8:31–32), in accordance with the missionary nature of his vocation. While paying heed to every fragment of truth which he encounters in the life experience and in the culture of individuals and of nations, he will not fail to affirm in dialogue with others all that his faith and the correct use of reason have enabled him to understand.[76]

47. Following the collapse of Communist totalitarianism and of many other totalitarian and "national security" regimes, today we are witnessing a predominance, not without signs of opposition, of the democratic ideal, together with lively attention to and concern for human rights. But for this very reason it is necessary for peoples in the process of reforming their systems to give democracy an authentic and solid foundation through the explicit recognition of those rights.[77] Among the most important of these rights, mention must be made of the right to life, an integral part of which is the right of the child to develop in the mother's womb from the moment of conception; the right to live in a united family and in a moral environment conducive to the growth of the child's personality; the right to develop one's intelligence and freedom in seeking and knowing the truth; the right to share in the work which makes wise use of the earth's material resources, and to derive from that work the means to support oneself and one's dependents; and the right freely to establish a family, to have and to rear children through the responsible exercise of one's sexuality. In a certain sense, the source and synthesis of these rights is religious freedom, understood as the right to live in the truth of one's faith and in conformity with one's transcendent dignity as a person.[78]

Even in countries with democratic forms of government, these rights are not always fully respected. Here we are referring not only to the scandal of abortion, but also to different aspects of a crisis within democracies themselves, which seem at times to have lost the ability to make decisions aimed at the common good. Certain demands which arise within society are sometimes not examined in accordance with criteria of justice and morality, but rather on the basis of the

76. Cf. Encyclical Letter *Redemptoris Missio*, 11: *L'Osservatore Romano*, January 23, 1991.

77. Cf. Encyclical Letter *Redemptor Hominis*, 17: *AAS* 71 (1979), 270–72.

78. Cf. Message for the 1988 World Day of Peace: *AAS* 80 (1988), 1572–80; Message for the 1991 World Day of Peace: *L'Osservatore Romano*, December 19, 1990; Second Vatican Ecumenical Council, Declaration on Religious Freedom *Dignitatis Humanae*, 1–2.

electoral or financial power of the groups promoting them. With time, such distortions of political conduct create distrust and apathy, with a subsequent decline in the political participation and civic spirit of the general population, which feels abused and disillusioned. As a result, there is a growing inability to situate particular interests within the framework of a coherent vision of the common good. The latter is not simply the sum total of particular interests; rather it involves an assessment and integration of those interests on the basis of a balanced hierarchy of values; ultimately, it demands a correct understanding of the dignity and the rights of the person.[79]

The Church respects the legitimate autonomy of the democratic order and is not entitled to express preferences for this or that institutional or constitutional solution. Her contribution to the political order is precisely her vision of the dignity of the person revealed in all its fullness in the mystery of the Incarnate Word.[80]

48. These general observations also apply to the role of the State in the economic sector. Economic activity, especially the activity of a market economy, cannot be conducted in an institutional, juridical, or political vacuum. On the contrary, it presupposes sure guarantees of individual freedom and private property, as well as a stable currency and efficient public services. Hence the principal task of the State is to guarantee this security, so that those who work and produce can enjoy the fruits of their labors and thus feel encouraged to work efficiently and honestly. The absence of stability, together with the corruption of public officials and the spread of improper sources of growing rich and of easy profits deriving from illegal or purely speculative activities, constitutes one of the chief obstacles to development and to the economic order. ...

The State has the further right to intervene when particular monopolies create delays or obstacles to development. In addition to the tasks of harmonizing and guiding development, in exceptional circumstances the State can also exercise a substitute function, when social sectors or business systems are too weak or are just getting under way, and are not equal to the task at hand. Such supplementary interventions, which are justified by urgent reasons touching the common good, must be as brief as possible, so as to avoid removing permanently from society and business systems the functions which are properly theirs, and so as to avoid enlarging excessively the sphere of state intervention to the detriment of both economic and civil freedom.

79. Second Vatican Ecumenical Council, Pastoral Constitution on the Church in the Modern World *Gaudium et Spes*, 26.

80. Cf. ibid., 22.

In recent years the range of such intervention has vastly expanded, to the point of creating a new type of state, the so-called "Welfare State." This has happened in some countries in order to respond better to many needs and demands, by remedying forms of poverty and deprivation unworthy of the human person. However, excesses and abuses, especially in recent years, have provoked very harsh criticisms of the Welfare State, dubbed the "Social Assistance State." Malfunctions and defects in the Social Assistance State are the result of an inadequate understanding of the tasks proper to the State. Here again the principle of subsidiarity must be respected: a community of a higher order should not interfere in the internal life of a community of a lower order, depriving the latter of its functions, but rather should support it in case of need and help to coordinate its activity with the activities of the rest of society, always with a view to the common good.[81]

By intervening directly and depriving society of its responsibility, the Social Assistance State leads to a loss of human energies and an inordinate increase of public agencies, which are dominated more by bureaucratic ways of thinking than by concern for serving their clients, and which are accompanied by an enormous increase in spending. In fact, it would appear that needs are best understood and satisfied by people who are closest to them and who act as neighbors to those in need. It should be added that certain kinds of demands often call for a response which is not simply material but which is capable of perceiving the deeper human need. One thinks of the condition of refugees, immigrants, the elderly, the sick, and all those in circumstances which call for assistance, such as drug abusers: all these people can be helped effectively only by those who offer them genuine fraternal support, in addition to the necessary care.

49. ... In order to overcome today's widespread individualistic mentality, what is required is a concrete commitment to solidarity and charity, beginning in the family with the mutual support of husband and wife and the care which the different generations give to one another. In this sense the family too can be called a community of work and solidarity. It can happen, however, that when a family does decide to live up fully to its vocation, it finds itself without the necessary support from the State and without sufficient resources. It is urgent therefore to promote not only family policies, but also those social policies which have the family as their principal object, policies which assist the family by providing adequate resources and efficient means of support, both for bringing up children and for looking after the elderly, so as to avoid distancing the latter from the family unit and in order to strengthen relations between generations.[82]

---

81. Pius XI, Encyclical Letter *Quadragesimo Anno*, I: *AAS* 23 (1931), 184–86.

82. Cf. Apostolic Exhortation *Familiaris Consortio* (November 22, 1981), 45: *AAS* 74 (1982), 136f.

Apart from the family, other intermediate communities exercise primary functions and give life to specific networks of solidarity. These develop as real communities of persons and strengthen the social fabric, preventing society from becoming an anonymous and impersonal mass, as unfortunately often happens today. It is in interrelationships on many levels that a person lives, and that society becomes more "personalized." The individual today is often suffocated between two poles represented by the State and the marketplace. At times it seems as though he exists only as a producer and consumer of goods, or as an object of state administration. People lose sight of the fact that life in society has neither the market nor the State as its final purpose, since life itself has a unique value which the State and the market must serve. Man remains above all a being who seeks the truth and strives to live in that truth, deepening his understanding of it through a dialogue which involves past and future generations.[83] ...

51. All human activity takes place within a culture and interacts with culture. For an adequate formation of a culture, the involvement of the whole person is required, whereby one exercises one's creativity, intelligence, and knowledge of the world and of people. Furthermore, a person displays his capacity for self-control, personal sacrifice, solidarity and readiness to promote the common good. Thus the first and most important task is accomplished within the heart. The way in which one is involved in building one's own future depends on the understanding a person has of himself and of his own destiny. It is on this level that the Church's specific and decisive contribution to true culture is to be found. The Church promotes those aspects of human behavior which favor a true culture of peace, as opposed to models in which the individual is lost in the crowd, in which the role of one's initiative and freedom is neglected, and in which one's greatness is posited in the arts of conflict and war. The Church renders this service to human society by preaching the truth about the creation of the world, which God has placed in human hands so that people may make it fruitful and more perfect through their work; and by preaching the truth about the Redemption, whereby the Son of God has saved mankind and at the same time has united all people, making them responsible for one another. Sacred Scripture continually speaks to us of an active commitment to our neighbor and demands of us a shared responsibility for all of humanity. ...

52. [...] This is the culture which is hoped for, one which fosters trust in the human potential of the poor, and consequently in their ability to improve their condition through work or to make a positive contribution to economic prosperity. But to accomplish this, the poor—be they individuals or nations—need

83. Cf. Discourse to UNESCO (June 2, 1980): AAS 72 (1980), 735–52.

to be provided with realistic opportunities. Creating such conditions calls for a concerted worldwide effort to promote development, an effort which also involves sacrificing the positions of income and of power enjoyed by the more developed economies.[84]

This may mean making important changes in established lifestyles, in order to limit the waste of environmental and human resources, thus enabling every individual and all the peoples of the earth to have a sufficient share of those resources. In addition, the new material and spiritual resources must be utilized which are the result of the work and culture of peoples who today are on the margins of the international community, so as to obtain an overall human enrichment of the family of nations.

VI. MAN IS THE WAY OF THE CHURCH

53. [...] Her sole purpose [in articulating social doctrine] has been care and responsibility for the human person, who has been entrusted to her by Christ himself: for this person, who, as the Second Vatican Council recalls, is the only creature on earth which God willed for its own sake, and for which God has his plan, that is, a share in eternal salvation. We are not dealing here with humanity in the "abstract," but with the real, "concrete," "historical" person. We are dealing with each individual, since each one is included in the mystery of Redemption, and through this mystery Christ has united himself with each one forever.[85] It follows that the Church cannot abandon humanity, and that "this human person is the primary route that the Church must travel in fulfilling her mission ... the way traced out by Christ himself, the way that leads invariably through the mystery of the Incarnation and the Redemption."[86] [...]

54. Today, the Church's social doctrine focuses especially on the person as he is involved in a complex network of relationships within modern societies. The human sciences and philosophy are helpful for interpreting the person's central place within society and for enabling one to understand oneself better as a "social being." However, a person's true identity is only fully revealed to him through faith, and it is precisely from faith that the Church's social teaching begins. While drawing upon all the contributions made by the sciences and philosophy, her social teaching is aimed at helping everyone on the path of salvation.

---

84. Cf. Apostolic Exhortation *Familiaris Consortio*, 48: *AAS* 74 (1982), 139f.

85. Cf. Encyclical Letter *Redemptor Hominis*, 13: *AAS* 71 (1979), 283.

86. Ibid., 14: *AAS* 71 (1979), 284f.

The encyclical *Rerum Novarum* can be read as a valid contribution to socio-economic analysis at the end of the nineteenth century, but its specific value derives from the fact that it is a document of the Magisterium and is fully a part of the Church's evangelizing mission, together with many other documents of this nature. Thus the Church's social teaching is itself a valid instrument of evangelization. As such, it proclaims God and his mystery of salvation in Christ to every human being, and for that very reason reveals man to himself. In this light, and only in this light, does it concern itself with everything else: the human rights of the individual, and in particular of the "working class," the family and education, the duties of the State, the ordering of national and international society, economic life, culture, war and peace, and respect for life from the moment of conception until death.

55. The Church receives "the meaning of the person" from Divine Revelation. "In order to know man, authentic man, man in his fullness, one must know God," said Pope Paul VI, and he went on to quote Saint Catherine of Siena, who, in prayer, expressed the same idea: "In your nature, O eternal Godhead, I shall know my own nature."[87] Christian anthropology therefore is really a chapter of theology, and for this reason, the Church's social doctrine, by its concern for the person and by its interest in him and in the way he conducts himself in the world, "belongs to the field ... of theology and particularly of moral theology."[88]

The theological dimension is needed both for interpreting and solving present-day problems in human society. It is worth noting that this is true in contrast both to the "atheistic" solution, which deprives mankind of one of its basic dimensions, namely the spiritual one, and to permissive and consumerist solutions, which under various pretexts seek to convince man that he is free from every law and from God himself, thus imprisoning him within a selfishness which ultimately harms both him and others.

When the Church proclaims God's salvation to humanity, when she offers and communicates the life of God through the sacraments, when she gives direction to human life through the commandments of love of God and neighbor, she contributes to the enrichment of human dignity. But just as the Church can never abandon her religious and transcendent mission on behalf of mankind, so too she is aware that today her activity meets with particular difficulties and obstacles. That is why she devotes herself with ever new energies and methods to an evangelization which promotes the whole human being. Even on the eve of the

---

87. Paul VI, Homily at the Final Public Session of the Second Vatican Ecumenical Council (December 7, 1965): *AAS* 58 (1966), 58.

88. Encyclical Letter *Sollicitudo Rei Socialis*, 41: *AAS* 80 (1988), 571.

third millennium she continues to be "a sign and safeguard of the transcendence of the human person,"[89] as indeed she has always sought to be from the beginning of her existence, walking together with the human race through history. The encyclical *Rerum Novarum* itself is a significant sign of this. ...

57. As far as the Church is concerned, the social message of the Gospel must not be considered a theory, but above all else a basis and a motivation for action. Inspired by this message, some of the first Christians distributed their goods to the poor, bearing witness to the fact that, despite different social origins, it was possible for people to live together in peace and harmony. Through the power of the Gospel, down the centuries monks tilled the land, men and women religious founded hospitals and shelters for the poor, confraternities as well as individual men and women of all states of life devoted themselves to the needy and to those on the margins of society, convinced as they were that Christ's words "as you did it to one of the least of these my brethren, you did it to me" (Mt 25:40) were not intended to remain a pious wish, but were meant to become a concrete life commitment.

Today more than ever, the Church is aware that her social message will gain credibility more immediately from the witness of actions than as a result of its internal logic and consistency. This awareness is also a source of her preferential option for the poor, which is never exclusive or discriminatory towards other groups. This option is not limited to material poverty, since it is well known that there are many other forms of poverty, especially in modern society—not only economic but cultural and spiritual poverty as well. The Church's love for the poor, which is essential for her and a part of her constant tradition, impels her to give attention to a world in which poverty is threatening to assume massive proportions in spite of technological and economic progress. In the countries of the West, different forms of poverty are being experienced by groups which live on the margins of society, by the elderly and the sick, by the victims of consumerism, and even more immediately by so many refugees and migrants. In the developing countries, tragic crises loom on the horizon unless internationally coordinated measures are taken before it is too late.

58. Love for others, and in the first place love for the poor, in whom the Church sees Christ himself, is made concrete in the promotion of justice. Justice will never be fully attained unless people see in the poor person, who is asking for help in order to survive, not an annoyance or a burden, but an opportunity

89. Second Vatican Ecumenical Council, Pastoral Constitution on the Church in the Modern World *Gaudium et Spes*, 76; cf. John Paul II, Encyclical Letter *Redemptor Hominis*, 13: AAS 71 (1979), 283.

for showing kindness and a chance for greater enrichment. . . . For this to happen, it is not enough to draw on the surplus goods which in fact our world abundantly produces; it requires above all a change of lifestyles, of models of production and consumption, and of the established structures of power which today govern societies. Nor is it a matter of eliminating instruments of social organization which have proved useful, but rather of orienting them according to an adequate notion of the common good in relation to the whole human family. . . .

59. Therefore, in order that the demands of justice may be met, and attempts to achieve this goal may succeed, what is needed is the gift of grace, a gift which comes from God. Grace, in cooperation with human freedom, constitutes that mysterious presence of God in history which is Providence.

The newness which is experienced in following Christ demands to be communicated to other people in their concrete difficulties, struggles, problems, and challenges, so that these can then be illuminated and made more human in the light of faith. Faith not only helps people to find solutions; it makes even situations of suffering humanly bearable, so that in these situations people will not become lost or forget their dignity and vocation. . . .

61. At the beginning of industrialized society, it was "a yoke little better than that of slavery itself" which led my predecessor to speak out in defense of the human person. Over the past hundred years the Church has remained faithful to this duty. Indeed, she intervened in the turbulent period of class struggle after the First World War in order to defend people from economic exploitation and from the tyranny of the totalitarian systems. After the Second World War, she put the dignity of the person at the center of her social messages, insisting that material goods were meant for all, and that the social order ought to be free of oppression and based on a spirit of cooperation and solidarity. The Church has constantly repeated that the person and society need not only material goods but spiritual and religious values as well. Furthermore, as she has become more aware of the fact that too many people live, not in the prosperity of the Western world, but in the poverty of the developing countries amid conditions which are still "a yoke little better than that of slavery itself," she has felt and continues to feel obliged to denounce this fact with absolute clarity and frankness, although she knows that her call will not always win favor with everyone. . . .

62. . . . In concluding this encyclical I again give thanks to Almighty God, who has granted his Church the light and strength to accompany humanity on its earthly journey towards its eternal destiny. In the third millennium too, the Church will be faithful in making humanity's way her own, knowing that she does not walk alone, but with Christ her Lord. It is Christ who made man's way his own, and who guides him, even when he is unaware of it.

Mary, the Mother of the Redeemer, constantly remained beside Christ in his journey towards the human family and in its midst, and she goes before the Church on the pilgrimage of faith. May her maternal intercession accompany humanity towards the next millennium, in fidelity to him who "is the same yesterday and today and for ever" (cf. Heb 13 :8), Jesus Christ our Lord, in whose name I cordially impart my blessing to all.

Given in Rome, at Saint Peter's, on the first of May, the Memorial of Saint Joseph the Worker, in the year 1991, the thirteenth of my pontificate.

✠ JOHN PAUL II

VERITATIS SPLENDOR

Regarding Certain Fundamental Questions
of the Church's Moral Teaching

Encyclical Letter of Pope John Paul II,
promulgated August 6, 1993

Venerable Brothers in the Episcopate, Health and the Apostolic Blessing!

T he splendor of truth shines forth in all the works of the Creator and, in a special way, in man, created in the image and likeness of God (cf. *Gen* 1:26). Truth enlightens man's intelligence and shapes his freedom, leading him to know and love the Lord. Hence the Psalmist prays: "Let the light of your face shine on us, O Lord" (*Ps* 4:6).

INTRODUCTION

Jesus Christ, the true light that enlightens everyone

1. Called to salvation through faith in Jesus Christ, "the true light that enlightens every man" (*Jn* 1:9), people become "light in the Lord" and "children of light" (*Eph* 5:8), and are made holy by "obedience to the truth" (1 *Pet* 1:22).

This obedience is not always easy. As a result of that mysterious original sin, committed at the prompting of Satan, the one who is "a liar and the father of lies" (*Jn* 8:44), man is constantly tempted to turn his gaze away from the living and true God in order to direct it towards idols (cf. 1 *Thes* 1:9), exchanging "the truth about God for a lie" (*Rom* 1:25). Man's capacity to know the truth is also darkened, and his will to submit to it is weakened. Thus, giving himself over to relativism and skepticism (cf. *Jn* 18:38), he goes off in search of an illusory freedom apart from truth itself.

But no darkness of error or of sin can totally take away from man the light of God the Creator. In the depths of his heart there always remains a yearning for absolute truth and a thirst to attain full knowledge of it. This is eloquently proved by man's tireless search for knowledge in all fields. It is proved even more by his search for *the meaning of life*. The development of science and technology, this splendid testimony of the human capacity for understanding and for perseverance, does not free humanity from the obligation to ask the ultimate religious questions. Rather, it spurs us on to face the most painful and decisive of struggles, those of the heart and of the moral conscience.

2. No one can escape from the fundamental questions: *What must I do? How do I distinguish good from evil?* The answer is only possible thanks to the splendor of the truth which shines forth deep within the human spirit, as the Psalmist bears witness: "There are many who say: 'O that we might see some good! Let the light of your face shine on us, O Lord'" (*Ps* 4:6).

The light of God's face shines in all its beauty on the countenance of Jesus Christ, "the image of the invisible God" (*Col* 1:15), the "reflection of God's glory" (*Heb* 1:3), "full of grace and truth" (*Jn* 1:14). Christ is "the way, and the truth, and the life" (*Jn* 14:6). Consequently the decisive answer to every one of man's questions, his religious and moral questions in particular, is given by Jesus Christ, or rather is Jesus Christ himself, as the Second Vatican Council recalls: "In fact, *it is only in the mystery of the Word incarnate that light is shed on the mystery of man*. For Adam, the first man, was a figure of the future man, namely, of Christ the Lord. It is Christ, the last Adam, who fully discloses man to himself and unfolds his noble calling by revealing the mystery of the Father and the Father's love."[1]

Jesus Christ, the "light of the nations," shines upon the face of his Church, which he sends forth to the whole world to proclaim the Gospel to every creature (cf. *Mk* 16:15).[2] Hence the Church, as the People of God among the nations,[3] while attentive to the new challenges of history and to mankind's efforts to discover the meaning of life, offers to everyone the answer which comes from the truth about Jesus Christ and his Gospel. The Church remains deeply conscious of her "duty in every age of examining the signs of the times and interpreting them in the light of the Gospel, so that she can offer in a manner appropriate to each generation replies to the continual human questionings on the meaning of this life and the life to come and on how they are related."[4]

---

1. Pastoral Constitution on the Church in the Modern World *Gaudium et Spes*, 22.

2. Cf. Dogmatic Constitution on the Church *Lumen Gentium*, 1.

3. Cf. ibid., 9.

4. Second Vatican Ecumenical Council, Pastoral Constitution on the Church in the Modern World *Gaudium et Spes*, 4.

3. The Church's Pastors, in communion with the Successor of Peter, are close to the faithful in this effort; they guide and accompany them by their authoritative teaching, finding ever new ways of speaking with love and mercy not only to believers but to all people of good will. The Second Vatican Council remains an extraordinary witness of this attitude on the part of the Church which, as an "expert in humanity,"[5] places herself at the service of every individual and of the whole world.[6]

The Church knows that the issue of morality is one which deeply touches every person; it involves all people, even those who do not know Christ and his Gospel or God himself. She knows that it is precisely *on the path of the moral life that the way of salvation is open to all.* The Second Vatican Council clearly recalled this when it stated that "those who without any fault do not know anything about Christ or his Church, yet who search for God with a sincere heart and under the influence of grace, try to put into effect the will of God as known to them through the dictate of conscience ... can obtain eternal salvation." The Council added: "Nor does divine Providence deny the helps that are necessary for salvation to those who, through no fault of their own, have not yet attained to the express recognition of God, yet who strive, not without divine grace, to lead an upright life. For whatever goodness and truth is found in them is considered by the Church as a preparation for the Gospel and bestowed by him who enlightens all men that they may in the end have life."[7]

The purpose of the present Encyclical

4. At all times, but particularly in the last two centuries, the Popes, whether individually or together with the College of Bishops, have developed and proposed a moral teaching regarding the *many different spheres of human life.* In Christ's name and with his authority they have exhorted, passed judgment and explained. In their efforts on behalf of humanity, in fidelity to their mission, they have confirmed, supported and consoled. With the guarantee of assistance from the Spirit of truth they have contributed to a better understanding of moral demands in the areas of human sexuality, the family, and social, economic and political life. In the tradition of the Church and in the history of humanity,

---

5.   Paul VI, *Address* to the General Assembly of the United Nation (October 4, 1965), 1: *AAS* 57 (1965), 878; cf. Encyclical Letter *Populorum Progressio* (March 26,1967), 13: *AAS* 59 (1967), 263–64.

6.   Cf. Second Vatican Ecumenical Council, Pastoral Constitution on the Church in the Modern World *Gaudium et Spes,* 16.

7.   Dogmatic Constitution on the Church *Lumen Gentium,* 16.

their teaching represents a constant deepening of knowledge with regard to morality.[8]

Today, however, it seems *necessary to reflect on the whole of the Church's moral teaching,* with the precise goal of recalling certain fundamental truths of Catholic doctrine which, in the present circumstances, risk being distorted or denied. In fact, a new situation has come about *within the Christian community itself,* which has experienced the spread of numerous doubts and objections of a human and psychological, social and cultural, religious and even properly theological nature, with regard to the Church's moral teachings. It is no longer a matter of limited and occasional dissent, but of an overall and systematic calling into question of traditional moral doctrine, on the basis of certain anthropological and ethical presuppositions. At the root of these presuppositions is the more or less obvious influence of currents of thought which end by detaching human freedom from its essential and constitutive relationship to truth. Thus the traditional doctrine regarding the natural law, and the universality and the permanent validity of its precepts, is rejected; certain of the Church's moral teachings are found simply unacceptable; and the Magisterium itself is considered capable of intervening in matters of morality only in order to "exhort consciences" and to "propose values," in the light of which each individual will independently make his or her decisions and life choices.

In particular, note should be taken of the *lack of harmony between the traditional response of the Church and certain theological positions,* encountered even in Seminaries and in Faculties of Theology, *with regard to questions of the greatest importance* for the Church and for the life of faith of Christians, as well as for the life of society itself. In particular, the question is asked: do the commandments of God, which are written on the human heart and are part of the Covenant, really have the capacity to clarify the daily decisions of individuals and entire societies? Is it possible to obey God and thus love God and neighbor, without respecting these commandments in all circumstances? Also, an opinion is frequently heard which questions the intrinsic and unbreakable bond between faith and morality, as if membership in the Church and her internal unity were to be decided on the basis of faith alone, while in the sphere of morality a pluralism of opinions and of kinds of behavior could be tolerated, these being left to the judgment of the individual subjective conscience or to the diversity of social and cultural contexts.

---

8. Pius XII had already pointed out this doctrinal development: cf. *Radio Message* for the Fiftieth Anniversary of the Encyclical Letter *Rerum Novarum* of Leo XIII (June 1, 1941): *AAS* 33 (1941), 195–205. Also John XXIII, Encyclical Letter *Mater et Magistra* (May 15, 1961): *AAS* 53 (1961), 410–13.

5. Given these circumstances, which still exist, I came to the decision—as I announced in my Apostolic Letter *Spiritus Domini,* issued on 1 August 1987 on the second centenary of the death of Saint Alphonsus Maria de' Liguori— to write an encyclical with the aim of treating "more fully and more deeply the issues regarding the very foundations of moral theology,"[9] foundations which are being undermined by certain present day tendencies.

I address myself to you, Venerable Brothers in the Episcopate, who share with me the responsibility of safeguarding "sound teaching" (2 *Tim* 4:3), with the intention of *clearly setting forth certain aspects of doctrine which are of crucial importance in facing what is certainly a genuine crisis,* since the difficulties which it engenders have most serious implications for the moral life of the faithful and for communion in the Church, as well as for a just and fraternal social life.

If this encyclical, so long awaited, is being published only now, one of the reasons is that it seemed fitting for it to be preceded by the *Catechism of the Catholic Church,* which contains a complete and systematic exposition of Christian moral teaching. The *Catechism* presents the moral life of believers in its fundamental elements and in its many aspects as the life of the "children of God": "Recognizing in the faith their new dignity, Christians are called to lead henceforth a life 'worthy of the Gospel of Christ' (*Phil* 1:27). Through the sacraments and prayer they receive the grace of Christ and the gifts of his Spirit which make them capable of such a life."[10] Consequently, while referring back to the *Catechism* "as a sure and authentic reference text for teaching Catholic doctrine,"[11] the encyclical will limit itself to dealing with *certain fundamental questions regarding the Church's moral teaching,* taking the form of a necessary discernment about issues being debated by ethicists and moral theologians. The specific purpose of the present Encyclical is this: to set forth, with regard to the problems being discussed, the principles of a moral teaching based upon Sacred Scripture and the living apostolic Tradition,[12] and at the same time to shed light on the presuppositions and consequences of the dissent which that teaching has met.

---

9. Apostolic Letter *Spiritus Domini* (August 1, 1987): *AAS* 79 (1987), 1374.

10. *Catechism of the Catholic Church,* n. 1692.

11. Apostolic Constitution *Fidei Depositum* (October 11, 1992), 4.

12. Cf. Second Vatican Council, Dogmatic Constitution on Divine Revelation *Dei Verbum,* 10.

CHAPTER I

"TEACHER, WHAT GOOD MUST I DO...?" (*Mt 19:16*)

Christ and the answer to the question about morality

"Someone came to him..." (*Mt 19:16*)

6. *The dialogue of Jesus with the rich young man,* related in the nineteenth chapter of Saint Matthew's Gospel, can serve as a useful guide *for listening once more* in a lively and direct way to his moral teaching: "Then someone came to him and said, 'Teacher, what good must I do to have eternal life?' And he said to him, 'Why do you ask me about what is good? There is only one who is good. If you wish to enter into life, keep the commandments.' He said to him, 'Which ones?' And Jesus said, 'You shall not murder; You shall not commit adultery; You shall not steal; You shall not bear false witness; Honor your father and mother; also, You shall love your neighbor as yourself.' The young man said to him, 'I have kept all these; what do I still lack?' Jesus said to him, 'If you wish to be perfect, go, sell your possessions and give the money to the poor, and you will have treasure in heaven; then come, follow me'" (*Mt* 19:16–21).[13]

7. *"Then someone came to him ..."* In the young man, whom Matthew's Gospel does not name, we can recognize every person who, consciously or not, *approaches Christ the Redeemer of man and questions him about morality.* For the young man, the *question* is not so much about rules to be followed, but *about the full meaning of life.* This is in fact the aspiration at the heart of every human decision and action, the quiet searching and interior prompting which sets freedom in motion. This question is ultimately an appeal to the absolute Good which attracts us and beckons us; it is the echo of a call from God who is the origin and goal of man's life. Precisely in this perspective the Second Vatican Council called for a renewal of moral theology, so that its teaching would display the lofty vocation which the faithful have received in Christ,[14] the only response fully capable of satisfying the desire of the human heart.

In order to make this "encounter" with Christ possible, God willed his Church. Indeed, the Church "wishes to serve this single end: that each person may be able to find Christ, in order that Christ may walk with each person the path of life."[15]

---

13. Cf. Apostolic Epistle *Parati Semper* to the Young People of the World on the occasion of the International Year of Youth (March 31, 1985), 2–8: *AAS* 77 (1985), 581–600.

14. Cf. Decree on Priestly Formation *Optatam Totius*, 16.

15. Encyclical Letter *Redemptor Hominis* (March 4, 1979), 13: *AAS* 71 (1979), 282.

"Teacher, what good must I do to have eternal life?" (Mt 19:16)

8. The question which the rich young man puts to Jesus of Nazareth is one which rises from the depths of his heart. It is *an essential and unavoidable question for the life of every man,* for it is about the moral good which must be done, and about eternal life. The young man senses that there is a connection between moral good and the fulfillment of his own destiny. He is a devout Israelite, raised as it were in the shadow of the Law of the Lord. If he asks Jesus this question, we can presume that it is not because he is ignorant of the answer contained in the Law. It is more likely that the attractiveness of the person of Jesus had prompted within him new questions about moral good. He feels the need to draw near to the One who had begun his preaching with this new and decisive proclamation: "The time is fulfilled, and the Kingdom of God is at hand; repent, and believe in the Gospel" (*Mk* 1:15).

People today need to turn to Christ once again in order to receive from him the answer to their questions about what is good and what is evil. Christ is the Teacher, the Risen One who has life in himself and who is always present in his Church and in the world. It is he who opens up to the faithful the book of the Scriptures and, by fully revealing the Father's will, teaches the truth about moral action. At the source and summit of the economy of salvation, as the Alpha and the Omega of human history (cf. *Rev* 1:8; 21:6; 22:13), Christ sheds light on man's condition and his integral vocation. Consequently, "the man who wishes to understand himself thoroughly—and not just in accordance with immediate, partial, often superficial, and even illusory standards and measures of his being—must with his unrest, uncertainty and even his weakness and sinfulness, with his life and death, draw near to Christ. He must, so to speak, enter him with all his own self; he must 'appropriate' and assimilate the whole of the reality of the Incarnation and Redemption in order to find himself. If this profound process takes place within him, he then bears fruit not only of adoration of God but also of deeper wonder at himself."[16]

If we therefore wish to go to the heart of the Gospel's moral teaching and grasp its profound and unchanging content, we must carefully inquire into the meaning of the question asked by the rich young man in the Gospel and, even more, the meaning of Jesus' reply, allowing ourselves to be guided by him. Jesus, as a patient and sensitive teacher, answers the young man by taking him, as it were, by the hand, and leading him step by step to the full truth.

---

16. Ibid., 10: *AAS* 71 (1979), 274.

"There is only one who is good" (Mt 19:17)

9. Jesus says: "Why do you ask me about what is good? There is only one who is good. If you wish to enter into life, keep the commandments" (*Mt* 19:17). In the versions of the Evangelists Mark and Luke the question is phrased in this way: "Why do you call me good? No one is good but God alone" (*Mk* 10:18; cf. *Lk* 18:19).

Before answering the question, Jesus wishes the young man to have a clear idea of why he asked his question. The "Good Teacher" points out to him—and to all of us—that the answer to the question, "What good must I do to have eternal life?" can only be found by turning one's mind and heart to the "One" who is good: "No one is good but God alone" (*Mk* 10:18; cf. *Lk* 18:19). *Only God can answer the question about what is good, because he is the Good itself.*

To ask about the good, in fact, *ultimately means to turn towards God*, the fullness of goodness. Jesus shows that the young man's question is really a *religious question*, and that the goodness that attracts and at the same time obliges man has its source in God, and indeed is God himself. God alone is worthy of being loved "with all one's heart, and with all one's soul, and with all one's mind" (*Mt* 22:37). He is the source of man's happiness. Jesus brings the question about morally good action back to its religious foundations, to the acknowledgment of God, who alone is goodness, fullness of life, the final end of human activity, and perfect happiness.

10. The Church, instructed by the Teacher's words, believes that man, made in the image of the Creator, redeemed by the Blood of Christ and made holy by the presence of the Holy Spirit, has as the *ultimate purpose of his life to live "for the praise of God's glory"* (cf. *Eph* 1:12), striving to make each of his actions reflect the splendor of that glory. "Know, then, O beautiful soul, that you are *the image of God*," writes Saint Ambrose. "Know that you are *the glory of God* (1 *Cor* 11:7). Hear how you are his glory. The Prophet says: *Your knowledge has become too wonderful for me* (cf. *Ps.* 138:6, Vulg.). That is to say, in my work your majesty has become more wonderful; in the counsels of men your wisdom is exalted. When I consider myself, such as I am known to you in my secret thoughts and deepest emotions, the mysteries of your knowledge are disclosed to me. Know then, O man, your greatness, and be vigilant."[17]

What man is and what he must do becomes clear as soon as God reveals himself. The Decalogue is based on these words: "I am the Lord your God, who brought you out of the land of Egypt, out of the house of bondage" (*Ex* 20:2–3). In

---

17. *Exameron*, Dies VI, Sermo IX, 8, 50: CSEL 32, 24.

the "ten words" of the Covenant with Israel, and in the whole Law, God makes himself known and acknowledged as the One who "alone is good"; the One who despite man's sin remains the "model" for moral action, in accordance with his command, "You shall be holy; for I the Lord your God am holy" (*Lev* 19:2); as the One who, faithful to his love for man, gives him his Law (cf. *Ex* 19:9–24 and 20:18–21) in order to restore man's original and peaceful harmony with the Creator and with all creation, and, what is more, to draw him into his divine love: "I will walk among you, and will be your God, and you shall be my people" (*Lev* 26:12).

The moral life presents itself as the response due to the many gratuitous initiatives taken by God out of love for man. It is a response of love, according to the statement made in Deuteronomy about the fundamental commandment: "Hear, O Israel: The Lord our God is one Lord; and you shall love the Lord your God with all your heart, and with all your soul, and with all your might. And these words which I command you this day shall be upon your heart; and you shall teach them diligently to your children" (*Dt* 6:4–7). Thus the moral life, caught up in the gratuitousness of God's love, is called to reflect his glory: "For the one who loves God it is enough to be pleasing to the One whom he loves: for no greater reward should be sought than that love itself; charity in fact is of God in such a way that God himself is charity."[18]

11. The statement that "There is only one who is good" thus brings us back to the "first tablet" of the commandments, which calls us to acknowledge God as the one Lord of all and to worship him alone for his infinite holiness (cf. *Ex* 20:2–11). *The good is belonging to God, obeying him,* walking humbly with him in doing justice and in loving kindness (cf. *Mic* 6:8). *Acknowledging the Lord as God is the very core, the heart of the Law,* from which the particular precepts flow and towards which they are ordered. In the morality of the commandments the fact that the people of Israel belongs to the Lord is made evident, because God alone is the One who is good. Such is the witness of Sacred Scripture, imbued in every one of its pages with a lively perception of God's absolute holiness: "Holy, holy, holy is the Lord of hosts" (*Is* 6:3).

But if God alone is the Good, no human effort, not even the most rigorous observance of the commandments, succeeds in "fulfilling" the Law, that is, acknowledging the Lord as God and rendering him the worship due to him alone (cf. *Mt* 4:10). *This "fulfillment" can come only from a gift of God:* the offer of a share in the divine Goodness revealed and communicated in Jesus, the one whom the rich young man addresses with the words "Good Teacher" (*Mk* 10:17; *Lk* 18:18).

18. Saint Leo the Great, *Sermo XCII*, Chap. III: PL 54, 454.

What the young man now perhaps only dimly perceives will in the end be fully revealed by Jesus himself in the invitation: "Come, follow me" (*Mt* 19:21).

"If you wish to enter into life, keep the commandments" (*Mt 19:17*)

12. Only God can answer the question about the good, because he is the Good. But God has already given an answer to this question: he did so *by creating man and ordering him* with wisdom and love to his final end, through the law which is inscribed in his heart (cf. *Rom* 2:15), the "natural law." The latter "is nothing other than the light of understanding infused in us by God, whereby we understand what must be done and what must be avoided. God gave this light and this law to man at creation."[19] He also did so *in the history of Israel*, particularly in the "ten words," the *commandments of Sinai*, whereby he brought into existence the people of the Covenant (cf. *Ex* 24) and called them to be his "own possession among all peoples," "a holy nation" (*Ex* 19:5–6), which would radiate his holiness to all peoples (cf. *Wis* 18:4; *Ez* 20:41). The gift of the Decalogue was a promise and sign of the *New Covenant*, in which the law would be written in a new and definitive way upon the human heart (cf. *Jer* 31:31–34), replacing the law of sin which had disfigured that heart (cf. *Jer* 17:1). In those days, "a new heart" would be given, for in it would dwell "a new spirit," the Spirit of God (cf. *Ez* 36:24–28).[20]

Consequently, after making the important clarification: "There is only one who is good," Jesus tells the young man: "If you wish to enter into life, keep the commandments" (*Mt* 19:17). In this way, a close connection is made *between eternal life and obedience to God's commandments:* God's commandments show man the path of life and they lead to it. From the very lips of Jesus, the new Moses, man is once again given the commandments of the Decalogue. Jesus himself definitively confirms them and proposes them to us as the way and condition of salvation. *The commandments are linked to a promise.* In the Old Covenant the object of the promise was the possession of a land where the people would be able to live in freedom and in accordance with righteousness (cf. *Dt* 6:20–25). In the New Covenant the object of the promise is the "Kingdom of Heaven," as Jesus declares at the beginning of the "Sermon on the Mount"—a sermon which contains the fullest and most complete formulation of the New Law (cf. *Mt* 5–7), clearly linked to the Decalogue entrusted by God to Moses on Mount Sinai. This

---

19. Saint Thomas Aquinas, *In Duo Praecepta Caritatis et in Decem Legis Praecepta. Prologus: Opuscula Theologica,* II, n. 1129, ed. Taurinen (1954), 245; cf. *Summa Theologiae* I-II, q. 91, a. 2; *Catechism of the Catholic Church,* n. 1955.

20. Cf. Saint Maximus the Confessor, *Quaestiones ad Thalassium,* q. 64: PG 90, 723–28.

same reality of the Kingdom is referred to in the expression "eternal life," which is a participation in the very life of God. It is attained in its perfection only after death, but in faith it is even now a light of truth, a source of meaning for life, an inchoate share in the full following of Christ. Indeed, Jesus says to his disciples after speaking to the rich young man: "Every one who has left houses or brothers or sisters or father or mother or children or lands, for my name's sake, will receive a hundredfold and inherit eternal life" (*Mt* 19:29).

13. Jesus' answer is not enough for the young man, who continues by asking the Teacher about the commandments which must be kept: "He said to him, 'Which ones?'" (*Mt* 19:18). He asks what he must do in life in order to show that he acknowledges God's holiness. After directing the young man's gaze towards God, Jesus reminds him of the commandments of the Decalogue regarding one's neighbor: "Jesus said: 'You shall not murder; You shall not commit adultery; You shall not bear false witness; Honor your father and mother; also, You shall love your neighbor as yourself'" (*Mt* 19:18–19).

From the context of the conversation, and especially from a comparison of Matthew's text with the parallel passages in Mark and Luke, it is clear that Jesus does not intend to list each and every one of the commandments required in order to "enter into life," but rather wishes to draw the young man's attention to the *"centrality" of the Decalogue* with regard to every other precept, inasmuch as it is the interpretation of what the words "I am the Lord your God" mean for man. Nevertheless we cannot fail to notice which commandments of the Law the Lord recalls to the young man. They are some of the commandments belonging to the so-called "second tablet" of the Decalogue, the summary (cf. *Rom* 13: 8–10) and foundation of which is *the commandment of love of neighbor:* "You shall love your neighbor as yourself" (*Mt* 19:19; cf. *Mk* 12:31). In this commandment we find a precise expression of *the singular dignity of the human person,* "the only creature [on earth] that God has willed for its own sake."[21] The different commandments of the Decalogue are really only so many reflections of the one commandment about the good of the person, at the level of the many different goods which characterize his identity as a spiritual and bodily being in relationship with God, with his neighbor and with the material world. As we read in the *Catechism of the Catholic Church,* "the Ten Commandments are part of God's Revelation. At the same time, they teach us man's true humanity. They shed light on the essential duties, and so indirectly on the fundamental rights, inherent in the nature of the human person."[22]

---

21. Second Vatican Ecumenical Council, Pastoral Constitution on the Church in the Modern World *Gaudium et Spes,* 24.

22. *Catechism of the Catholic Church,* n. 2070.

The commandments of which Jesus reminds the young man are meant to safeguard *the good* of the person, the image of God, by protecting his *goods*. "You shall not murder; You shall not commit adultery; You shall not steal; You shall not bear false witness" are moral rules formulated in terms of prohibitions. These negative precepts express with particular force the ever urgent need to protect human life, the communion of persons in marriage, private property, truthfulness and people's good name.

The commandments thus represent the basic condition for love of neighbor; at the same time they are the proof of that love. They are the *first necessary step on the journey towards freedom*, its starting-point. "The beginning of freedom," Saint Augustine writes, "is to be free from crimes ... such as murder, adultery, fornication, theft, fraud, sacrilege and so forth. When once one is without these crimes (and every Christian should be without them), one begins to lift up one's head towards freedom. But this is only the beginning of freedom, not perfect freedom..."[23]

14. This certainly does not mean that Christ wishes to put the love of neighbor higher than, or even to set it apart from, the love of God. This is evident from his conversation with the teacher of the Law, who asked him a question very much like the one asked by the young man. Jesus refers him to *the two commandments of love of God and love of neighbor* (cf. *Lk* 10:25–27), and reminds him that only by observing them will he have eternal life: "Do this, and you will live" (*Lk* 10:28). Nonetheless it is significant that it is precisely the second of these commandments which arouses the curiosity of the teacher of the Law, who asks him: "And who is my neighbor?" (*Lk* 10:29). The Teacher replies with the parable of the Good Samaritan, which is critical for fully understanding the commandment of love of neighbor (cf. *Lk* 10:30–37).

These two commandments, on which "depend all the Law and the Prophets" (*Mt* 22:40), are profoundly connected and mutually related. *Their inseparable unity* is attested to by Christ in his words and by his very life: his mission culminates in the Cross of our Redemption (cf. *Jn* 3:14–15), the sign of his indivisible love for the Father and for humanity (cf. *Jn* 13:1).

Both the Old and the New Testaments explicitly affirm that *without love of neighbor*, made concrete in keeping the commandments, *genuine love for God is not possible*. Saint John makes the point with extraordinary forcefulness: "If anyone says, 'I love God', and hates his brother, he is a liar; for he who does not love his brother whom he has seen, cannot love God whom he has not seen" (*Jn* 4:20). The Evangelist echoes the moral preaching of Christ, expressed in a wonderful

---

23. *In Iohannis Evangelium Tractatus*, 41, 10: CCL 36, 363.

and unambiguous way in the parable of the Good Samaritan (cf. *Lk* 10:30–37) and in his words about the final judgment (cf. *Mt* 25:31–46).

15. In the "Sermon on the Mount," the *magna charta* of Gospel morality,[24] Jesus says: "Do not think that I have come to abolish the Law and the Prophets; I have come not to abolish them but to fulfill them" (*Mt* 5:17). Christ is the key to the Scriptures: "You search the Scriptures …; and it is they that bear witness to me" (*Jn* 5:39). Christ is the centre of the economy of salvation, the recapitulation of the Old and New Testaments, of the promises of the Law and of their fulfillment in the Gospel; he is the living and eternal link between the Old and the New Covenants. Commenting on Paul's statement that "Christ is the end of the law" (*Rom* 10:4), Saint Ambrose writes: "end not in the sense of a deficiency, but in the sense of the fullness of the Law: a fullness which is achieved in Christ (*plenitudo legis in Christo est*), since he came not to abolish the Law but to bring it to fulfillment. In the same way that there is an Old Testament, but all truth is in the New Testament, so it is for the Law: what was given through Moses is a figure of the true law. Therefore, the Mosaic Law is an image of the truth."[25]

Jesus brings God's commandments to fulfillment, particularly the commandment of love of neighbor, *by interiorizing their demands and by bringing out their fullest meaning.* Love of neighbor springs from *a loving heart* which, precisely because it loves, is ready to live out *the loftiest challenges.* Jesus shows that the commandments must not be understood as a minimum limit not to be gone beyond, but rather as a path involving a moral and spiritual journey towards perfection, at the heart of which is love (cf. *Col* 3:14). Thus the commandment "You shall not murder" becomes a call to an attentive love which protects and promotes the life of one's neighbor. The precept prohibiting adultery becomes an invitation to a pure way of looking at others, capable of respecting the spousal meaning of the body: "You have heard that it was said to the men of old, *'You shall not kill; and whoever kills shall be liable to judgment'. But I say to you* that every one who is angry with his brother shall be liable to judgment … You have heard that it was said, *'You shall not commit adultery'. But I say to you* that every one who looks at a woman lustfully has already committed adultery with her in his heart" (*Mt* 5:21–22, 27–28). *Jesus himself is the living "fulfillment" of the Law* inasmuch as he fulfils its authentic meaning by the total gift of himself: *he himself becomes a living and personal Law,* who invites people to follow him; through the Spirit, he

---

24. Cf. Saint Augustine, *De Sermone Domini in Monte*, I, 1, 1: CCL 35, 1–2.

25. *In Psalmum CXVIII Expositio*, Sermo 18, 37: PL 15, 1541; cf. Saint Chromatius of Aquileia, *Tractatus in Matthaeum*, XX, I, 1–4: CCL 9/A, 291–92.

gives the grace to share his own life and love and provides the strength to bear witness to that love in personal choices and actions (cf. *Jn* 13:34–35).

"If you wish to be perfect" (*Mt* 19:21)

16. The answer he receives about the commandments does not satisfy the young man, who asks Jesus a further question. "I have kept all these; *what do I still lack?*" (*Mt* 19:20). It is not easy to say with a clear conscience "I have kept all these," if one has any understanding of the real meaning of the demands contained in God's Law. And yet, even though he is able to make this reply, even though he has followed the moral ideal seriously and generously from childhood, the rich young man knows that he is still far from the goal: before the person of Jesus he realizes that he is still lacking something. It is his awareness of this insufficiency that Jesus addresses in his final answer. Conscious of *the young man's yearning for something greater, which would transcend a legalistic interpretation of the commandments*, the Good Teacher invites him to enter upon the path of perfection: "If you wish to be perfect, go, sell your possessions and give the money to the poor, and you will have treasure in heaven; then come, follow me" (*Mt* 19:21).

Like the earlier part of Jesus' answer, this part too must be read and interpreted in the context of the whole moral message of the Gospel, and in particular in the context of the Sermon on the Mount, the Beatitudes (cf. *Mt* 5:3–12), the first of which is precisely the Beatitude of the poor, the "poor in spirit" as Saint Matthew makes clear (*Mt* 5:3), the humble. In this sense it can be said that the Beatitudes are also relevant to the answer given by Jesus to the young man's question: "What good must I do to have eternal life?" Indeed, each of the Beatitudes promises, from a particular viewpoint, that very "good" which opens man up to eternal life, and indeed is eternal life.

The Beatitudes are not specifically concerned with certain particular rules of behavior. Rather, they speak of basic attitudes and dispositions in life and therefore they *do not coincide exactly with the commandments*. On the other hand, *there is no separation or opposition* between the Beatitudes and the commandments: both refer to the good, to eternal life. The Sermon on the Mount begins with the proclamation of the Beatitudes, but also refers to the commandments (cf. *Mt* 5:20–48). At the same time, the Sermon on the Mount demonstrates the openness of the commandments and their orientation towards the horizon of the perfection proper to the Beatitudes. These latter are above all *promises*, from which there also indirectly flow *normative indications* for the moral life. In their originality and profundity they are a sort of *self-portrait of Christ*, and for this very reason are *invitations to discipleship and to communion of life with Christ.*[26]

17. We do not know how clearly the young man in the Gospel understood the profound and challenging import of Jesus' first reply: "If you wish to enter into life, keep the commandments." But it is certain that the young man's commitment to respect all the moral demands of the commandments represents the absolutely essential ground in which the desire for perfection can take root and mature, the desire, that is, for the meaning of the commandments to be completely fulfilled in following Christ. Jesus' conversation with the young man helps us to grasp *the conditions for the moral growth of man, who has been called to perfection:* the young man, having observed all the commandments, shows that he is incapable of taking the next step by himself alone. To do so requires mature human freedom ("If you wish to be perfect") and God's gift of grace ("Come, follow me").

Perfection demands that maturity in self-giving to which human freedom is called. Jesus points out to the young man that the commandments are the first and indispensable condition for having eternal life; on the other hand, for the young man to give up all he possesses and to follow the Lord is presented as an invitation: "If you wish …" These words of Jesus reveal the particular dynamic of freedom's growth towards maturity, and at the same time *they bear witness to the fundamental relationship between freedom and divine law.* Human freedom and God's law are not in opposition; on the contrary, they appeal one to the other. The follower of Christ knows that his vocation is to freedom. "You were called to freedom, brethren" (*Gal* 5:13), proclaims the Apostle Paul with joy and pride. But he immediately adds: "only do not use your freedom as an opportunity for the flesh, but through love be servants of one another" (ibid.). The firmness with which the Apostle opposes those who believe that they are justified by the Law has nothing to do with man's "liberation" from precepts. On the contrary, the latter are at the service of the practice of love: "For he who loves his neighbor has fulfilled the Law. The commandments, *'You shall not commit adultery; You shall not murder; You shall not steal; You shall not covet,'* and any other commandment, are summed up in this sentence, *'You shall love your neighbor as yourself'"* (*Rom* 13:8–9). Saint Augustine, after speaking of the observance of the commandments as being a kind of incipient, imperfect freedom, goes on to say: "Why, someone will ask, is it not yet perfect? Because 'I see in my members another law at war with the law of my reason' … In part freedom, in part slavery: not yet complete freedom, not yet pure, not yet whole, because we are not yet in eternity. In part we retain our weakness and in part we have attained freedom. All our sins were destroyed

---

26. Cf. *Catechism of the Catholic Church,* n. 1717.

in baptism, but does it follow that no weakness remained after iniquity was destroyed? Had none remained, we would live without sin in this life. But who would dare to say this except someone who is proud, someone unworthy of the mercy of our deliverer? ... Therefore, since some weakness has remained in us, I dare to say that to the extent to which we serve God we are free, while to the extent that we follow the law of sin, we are still slaves."[27]

18. Those who live "by the flesh" experience God's law as a burden, and indeed as a denial or at least a restriction of their own freedom. On the other hand, those who are impelled by love and "walk by the Spirit" (*Gal* 5:16), and who desire to serve others, find in God's Law the fundamental and necessary way in which to practice love as something freely chosen and freely lived out. Indeed, they feel an interior urge—a genuine "necessity" and no longer a form of coercion—not to stop at the minimum demands of the Law, but to live them in their "fullness." This is a still uncertain and fragile journey as long as we are on earth, but it is one made possible by grace, which enables us to possess the full freedom of the children of God (cf. *Rom* 8:21) and thus to live our moral life in a way worthy of our sublime vocation as "sons in the Son."

This vocation to perfect love is not restricted to a small group of individuals. *The invitation*, "go, sell your possessions and give the money to the poor," and the promise "you will have treasure in heaven," *are meant for everyone*, because they bring out the full meaning of the commandment of love for neighbor, just as the invitation which follows, "Come, follow me," is the new, specific form of the commandment of love of God. Both the commandments and Jesus' invitation to the rich young man stand at the service of a single and indivisible charity, which spontaneously tends towards that perfection whose measure is God alone: "You, therefore, must be perfect, as your heavenly Father is perfect" (*Mt* 5:48). In the Gospel of Luke, Jesus makes even clearer the meaning of this perfection: "Be merciful, even as your Father is merciful" (*Lk* 6:36).

"Come, follow me" (Mt 19:21)

19. The way and at the same time the content of this perfection consist in the following of Jesus, *sequela Christi*, once one has given up one's own wealth and very self. This is precisely the conclusion of Jesus' conversation with the young man: "Come, follow me" (*Mt* 19:21). It is an invitation the marvelous grandeur of which will be fully perceived by the disciples after Christ's resurrection, when the Holy Spirit leads them to all truth (cf. *Jn* 16:13).

---

27. *In Iohannis Evangelium Tractatus*, 41, 10: CCL 36, 363.

It is Jesus himself who takes the initiative and calls people to follow him. His call is addressed first to those to whom he entrusts a particular mission, beginning with the Twelve; but it is also clear that every believer is called to be a follower of Christ (cf. *Acts* 6:1). *Following Christ is thus the essential and primordial foundation of Christian morality:* just as the people of Israel followed God who led them through the desert towards the Promised Land (cf. *Ex* 13:21), so every disciple must follow Jesus, towards whom he is drawn by the Father himself (cf. *Jn* 6:44).

This is not a matter only of disposing oneself to hear a teaching and obediently accepting a commandment. More radically, it involves *holding fast to the very person of Jesus,* partaking of his life and his destiny, sharing in his free and loving obedience to the will of the Father. By responding in faith and following the one who is Incarnate Wisdom, the disciple of Jesus truly becomes *a disciple of God* (cf. *Jn* 6:45). Jesus is indeed the light of the world, the light of life (cf. *Jn* 8:12). He is the shepherd who leads his sheep and feeds them (cf. *Jn* 10:11–16); he is the way, and the truth, and the life (cf. *Jn* 14:6). It is Jesus who leads to the Father, so much so that to see him, the Son, is to see the Father (cf. *Jn* 14:6–10). And thus to imitate the Son, "the image of the invisible God" (Col 1:15), means to imitate the Father.

20. *Jesus asks us to follow him and to imitate him along the path of love, a love which gives itself completely to the brethren out of love for God:* "This is my commandment, that you love one another as I have loved you" (*Jn* 15:12). The word "as" requires imitation of Jesus and of his love, of which the washing of feet is a sign: "If I then, your Lord and Teacher, have washed your feet, you also ought to wash one another's feet. For I have given you an example, that you should do as I have done to you" (Jn 13:14–15). Jesus' way of acting and his words, his deeds and his precepts constitute the moral rule of Christian life. Indeed, his actions, and in particular his Passion and Death on the Cross, are the living revelation of his love for the Father and for others. This is exactly the love that Jesus wishes to be imitated by all who follow him. It is *the "new" commandment:* "A new commandment I give to you, that you love one another; even as I have loved you, that you also love one another. By this all men will know that you are my disciples, if you have love for one another" (*Jn* 13:34–35).

The word "as" also indicates the *degree* of Jesus' love, and of the love with which his disciples are called to love one another. After saying: "This is my commandment, that you love one another as I have loved you" (*Jn* 15:12), Jesus continues with words which indicate the sacrificial gift of his life on the Cross, as the witness to a love "to the end" (*Jn* 13:1): "Greater love has no man than this, that a man lay down his life for his friends" (*Jn* 15:13).

As he calls the young man to follow him along the way of perfection, Jesus asks him to be perfect in the command of love, in "his" commandment: to become part of the unfolding of his complete giving, to imitate and rekindle the very love of the "Good" Teacher, the one who loved "to the end." This is what Jesus asks of everyone who wishes to follow him: "If any man would come after me, let him deny himself and take up his cross and follow me" (*Mt* 16:24).

21. *Following Christ* is not an outward imitation, since it touches man at the very depths of his being. Being a follower of Christ means *becoming conformed to him* who became a servant even to giving himself on the Cross (cf. *Phil* 2:5–8). Christ dwells by faith in the heart of the believer (cf. *Eph* 3:17), and thus the disciple is conformed to the Lord. This is the *effect of grace*, of the active presence of the Holy Spirit in us.

Having become one with Christ, the Christian *becomes a member of his Body, which is the Church* (cf. *Cor* 12:13, 27). By the work of the Spirit, baptism radically configures the faithful to Christ in the Paschal Mystery of death and resurrection; it "clothes him" in Christ (cf. *Gal* 3:27): "Let us rejoice and give thanks," exclaims Saint Augustine speaking to the baptized, "for we have become not only Christians, but Christ! ... Marvel and rejoice: we have become Christ!"[28] Having died to sin, those who are baptized receive new life (cf. *Rom* 6:3–11): alive for God in Christ Jesus, they are called to walk by the Spirit and to manifest the Spirit's fruits in their lives (cf. *Gal* 5:16–25). Sharing in the *Eucharist,* the sacrament of the New Covenant (cf. 1 *Cor* 11:23–29), is the culmination of our assimilation to Christ, the source of "eternal life" (cf. *Jn* 6:51–58), the source and power of that complete gift of self, which Jesus—according to the testimony handed on by Paul—commands us to commemorate in liturgy and in life: "As often as you eat this bread and drink the cup, you proclaim the Lord's death until he comes" (1 *Cor* 11:26).

"With God all things are possible" (Mt 19:26)

22. The conclusion of Jesus' conversation with the rich young man is very poignant: "When the young man heard this, he went away sorrowful, for he had many possessions" (*Mt* 19:22). Not only the rich man but the disciples themselves are taken aback by Jesus' call to discipleship, the demands of which transcend human aspirations and abilities: "When the disciples heard this, they were greatly astounded and said, 'Then who can be saved?'" (*Mt* 19:25). *But the Master refers them to God's power:* "With men this is impossible, but with God all things are possible" (*Mt* 19:26).

In the same chapter of Matthew's Gospel (19:3–10), Jesus, interpreting the Mosaic Law on marriage, rejects the right to divorce, appealing to a "beginning"

---

28. Ibid., 21, 8: *CCL* 36, 216.

more fundamental and more authoritative than the Law of Moses: God's original plan for mankind, a plan which man after sin has no longer been able to live up to: "For your hardness of heart Moses allowed you to divorce your wives, but from the beginning it was not so" (*Mt* 19:8). Jesus' appeal to the "beginning" dismays the disciples, who remark: "If such is the case of a man with his wife, it is not expedient to marry" (*Mt* 19:10). And Jesus, referring specifically to the charism of celibacy "for the Kingdom of Heaven" (*Mt* 19:12), but stating a general rule, indicates the new and surprising possibility opened up to man by God's grace. "He said to them: 'Not everyone can accept this saying, but only those to whom it is given'" (*Mt* 19:11).

To imitate and live out the love of Christ is not possible for man by his own strength alone. He becomes *capable of this love only by virtue of a gift received.* As the Lord Jesus receives the love of his Father, so he in turn freely communicates that love to his disciples: "As the Father has loved me, so have I loved you; abide in my love" (*Jn* 15:9). *Christ's gift is his Spirit,* whose first "fruit" (cf. *Gal* 5:22) is charity: "God's love has been poured into our hearts through the Holy Spirit which has been given to us" (*Rom* 5:5). Saint Augustine asks: "Does love bring about the keeping of the commandments, or does the keeping of the commandments bring about love?" And he answers: "But who can doubt that love comes first? For the one who does not love has no reason for keeping the commandments."[29]

23. "The law of the Spirit of life in Christ Jesus has set me free from the law of sin and death" (*Rom* 8:2). With these words the Apostle Paul invites us to consider in the perspective of the history of salvation, which reaches its fulfillment in Christ, *the relationship between the* (Old) *Law and grace* (the New Law). He recognizes the pedagogic function of the Law, which, by enabling sinful man to take stock of his own powerlessness and by stripping him of the presumption of his self-sufficiency, leads him to ask for and to receive "life in the Spirit." Only in this new life is it possible to carry out God's commandments. Indeed, it is through faith in Christ that we have been made righteous (cf. *Rom* 3:28): the "righteousness" which the Law demands, but is unable to give, is found by every believer to be revealed and granted by the Lord Jesus. Once again it is Saint Augustine who admirably sums up this Pauline dialectic of law and grace: "The law was given that grace might be sought; and grace was given, that the law might be fulfilled."[30]

Love and life according to the Gospel cannot be thought of first and foremost as a kind of precept, because what they demand is beyond man's abilities.

---

29. Ibid., 82, 3: CCL 36, 533.

30. *De Spiritu et Littera,* 19, 34: CSEL 60,187.

They are possible only as the result of a gift of God who heals, restores and transforms the human heart by his grace: "For the law was given through Moses; grace and truth came through Jesus Christ" (*Jn* 1:17). The promise of eternal life is thus linked to the gift of grace, and the gift of the Spirit which we have received is even now the "guarantee of our inheritance" (*Eph* 1:14).

24. And so we find revealed the authentic and original aspect of the commandment of love and of the perfection to which it is ordered: we are speaking of a *possibility opened up to man exclusively by grace*, by the gift of God, by his love. On the other hand, precisely the awareness of having received the gift, of possessing in Jesus Christ the love of God, generates and sustains *the free response* of a full love for God and the brethren, as the Apostle John insistently reminds us in his first Letter: "Beloved, let us love one another; for love is of God and knows God. He who does not love does not know God; for God is love ... Beloved, if God so loved us, we ought also to love one another ... We love, because he first loved us" (1 *Jn* 4:7–8, 11, 19).

This inseparable connection between the Lord's grace and human freedom, between gift and task, has been expressed in simple yet profound words by Saint Augustine in his prayer: *"Da quod iubes et iube quod vis"* (grant what you command and command what you will).[31]

The gift does not lessen but reinforces the moral demands of love: "This is his commandment, that we should believe in the name of his Son Jesus Christ and love one another just as he has commanded us" (1 *Jn* 3:32). One can "abide" in love only by keeping the commandments, as Jesus states: "If you keep my commandments, you will abide in my love, just as I have kept my Father's commandments and abide in his love" (*Jn* 15:10).

Going to the heart of the moral message of Jesus and the preaching of the Apostles, and summing up in a remarkable way the great tradition of the Fathers of the East and West, and of Saint Augustine in particular,[32] Saint Thomas was able to write that *the New Law is the grace of the Holy Spirit given through faith in Christ*.[33] The external precepts also mentioned in the Gospel dispose one for this grace or produce its effects in one's life. Indeed, the New Law is not content to say what must be done, but also gives the power to "do what is true" (cf. *Jn* 3:21). Saint John Chrysostom likewise observed that the New Law was promulgated at the descent of the Holy Spirit from heaven on the day of Pentecost, and that the Apostles "did not come down from the mountain carrying, like Moses, tablets

---

31. *Confessiones*, X, 29, 40: CCL 27, 176; cf. *De Gratia et Libero Arbitrio*, XV: PL 44, 899.

32. Cf. *De Spiritu et Littera*, 21, 36; 26, 46: CSEL 60, 189–90; 200–201.

33. Cf. *Summa Theologiae* I-II, q. 106, a. 1, conclusion and ad 2.

of stone in their hands; but they came down carrying the Holy Spirit in their hearts ... having become by his grace a living law, a living book."[34]

"Lo, I am with you always, to the close of the age" (Mt 28:20)

25. Jesus' conversation with the rich young man continues, in a sense, *in every period of history, including our own.* The question: "Teacher, what good must I do to have eternal life?" arises in the heart of every individual, and it is Christ alone who is capable of giving the full and definitive answer. The Teacher who expounds God's commandments, who invites others to follow him and gives the grace for a new life, is always present and at work in our midst, as he himself promised: "Lo, I am with you always, to the close of the age" (*Mt* 28:20). *Christ's relevance for people of all times is shown forth in his body, which is the Church.* For this reason the Lord promised his disciples the Holy Spirit, who would "bring to their remembrance" and teach them to understand his commandments (cf. *Jn* 14:26), and who would be the principle and constant source of a new life in the world (cf. *Jn* 3:5–8; *Rom* 8:1–13).

The moral prescriptions which God imparted in the Old Covenant, and which attained their perfection in the New and Eternal Covenant in the very person of the Son of God made man, must be *faithfully kept and continually put into practice* in the various different cultures throughout the course of history. The task of interpreting these prescriptions was entrusted by Jesus to the Apostles and to their successors, with the special assistance of the Spirit of truth: "He who hears you hears me" (*Lk* 10:16). By the light and the strength of this Spirit the Apostles carried out their mission of preaching the Gospel and of pointing out the "way" of the Lord (cf. *Acts* 18:25), teaching above all how to follow and imitate Christ: "For to me to live is Christ" (*Phil* 1:21).

26. In the *moral catechesis of the Apostles,* besides exhortations and directions connected to specific historical and cultural situations, we find an ethical teaching with precise rules of behavior. This is seen in their letters, which contain the interpretation, made under the guidance of the Holy Spirit, of the Lord's precepts as they are to be lived in different cultural circumstances (cf. *Rom* 12–15; 1 *Cor* 11–14; *Gal* 5–6; *Eph* 4–6; *Col* 3–4; 1 *Pet* and *Jas*). From the Church's beginnings, the Apostles, by virtue of their pastoral responsibility to preach the Gospel, *were vigilant over the right conduct of Christians,*[35] just as they were vigilant for the purity of the faith and the handing down of the divine gifts

---

34. *In Matthaeum,* Hom. I, 1: PG 57, 15.

35. Cf. Saint Irenaeus, *Adversus Haereses,* IV, 26, 2–5: SCh 100/2, 718–29.

in the sacraments.[36] The first Christians, coming both from the Jewish people and from the Gentiles, differed from the pagans not only in their faith and their liturgy but also in the witness of their moral conduct, which was inspired by the New Law.[37] The Church is in fact a communion both of faith and of life; her rule of life is "faith working through love" (*Gal* 5:6).

No damage must be done to the *harmony between faith and life: the unity of the Church* is damaged not only by Christians who reject or distort the truths of faith but also by those who disregard the moral obligations to which they are called by the Gospel (cf. 1 *Cor* 5:9–13). The Apostles decisively rejected any separation between the commitment of the heart and the actions which express or prove it (cf. 1 *Jn* 2:3–6). And ever since apostolic times the Church's Pastors have unambiguously condemned the behavior of those who fostered division by their teaching or by their actions.[38]

27. Within the unity of the Church, promoting and preserving the faith and the moral life is the task entrusted by Jesus to the Apostles (cf. *Mt* 28:19–20), a task which continues in the ministry of their successors. This is apparent from the *living Tradition*, whereby—as the Second Vatican Council teaches—"the Church, in her teaching, life and worship, perpetuates and hands on to every generation all that she is and all that she believes. This Tradition, which comes from the Apostles, progresses in the Church under the assistance of the Holy Spirit."[39] In the Holy Spirit, the Church receives and hands down the Scripture as the witness to the "great things" which God has done in history (cf. *Lk* 1:49); she professes by the lips of her Fathers and Doctors the truth of the Word made flesh, puts his precepts and love into practice in the lives of her Saints and in the sacrifice of her Martyrs, and celebrates her hope in him in the Liturgy. By this same Tradition Christians receive "the living voice of the Gospel,"[40] as the faithful expression of God's wisdom and will.

Within Tradition, *the authentic interpretation* of the Lord's law develops, with the help of the Holy Spirit. The same Spirit who is at the origin of the Revelation of Jesus' commandments and teachings guarantees that they will be reverently preserved, faithfully expounded and correctly applied in different times and places. This constant "putting into practice" of the commandments is the sign

36. Cf. Saint Justin, *Apologia*, I, 66: PG 6, 427–30.

37. Cf. 1 Pet. 2:12ff; cf. *Didache*, II, 2: *Patres Apostolici*, ed. F. X. Funk, I, 6–9; Clement of Alexandria, *Paedagogus*, I, 10; II, 10: PG 8, 355–64; 497–536; Tertullian, *Apologeticum*, IX, 8: *CSEL* 69, 24.

38. Cf. Saint Ignatius of Antioch, *Ad Magnesios*, VI, 1–2: *Patres Apostolici*, ed. F. X. Funk, I, 234–35; Saint Irenaeus, *Adversus Haereses*, IV, 33:1, 6, 7: SCh 100/2, 802–5; 814–15; 816–19.

39. Dogmatic Constitution on Divine Revelation *Dei Verbum*, 8.

40. Cf. ibid.

and fruit of a deeper insight into Revelation and of an understanding in the light of faith of new historical and cultural situations. Nevertheless, it can only confirm the permanent validity of Revelation and follow in the line of the interpretation given to it by the great Tradition of the Church's teaching and life, as witnessed by the teaching of the Fathers, the lives of the Saints, the Church's Liturgy and the teaching of the Magisterium.

In particular, as the Council affirms, *"the task of authentically interpreting the word of God, whether in its written form or in that of Tradition, has been entrusted only to those charged with the Church's living Magisterium, whose authority is exercised in the name of Jesus Christ."*[41] The Church, in her life and teaching, is thus revealed as "the pillar and bulwark of the truth" (1 *Tim* 3:15), including the truth regarding moral action. Indeed, "the Church has the right always and everywhere to proclaim moral principles, even in respect of the social order, and to make judgments about any human matter in so far as this is required by fundamental human rights or the salvation of souls."[42]

Precisely on the questions frequently debated in moral theology today and with regard to which new tendencies and theories have developed, the Magisterium, in fidelity to Jesus Christ and in continuity with the Church's tradition, senses more urgently the duty to offer its own discernment and teaching, in order to help man in his journey towards truth and freedom.

CHAPTER II
"DO NOT BE CONFORMED TO THIS WORLD" (*Rom 12:2*)

The Church and the discernment of certain tendencies in present-day moral theology

Teaching what befits sound doctrine (cf. Tit 2:1)

28. Our meditation on the dialogue between Jesus and the rich young man has enabled us to bring together the essential elements of Revelation in the Old and New Testament with regard to moral action. These are: *the subordination of man and his activity to God,* the One who "alone is good"; the *relationship* clearly indicated in the divine commandments, between *the moral good of human acts* and *eternal life; Christian discipleship,* which opens up before man the perspective

---

41. Ibid., 10.

42. *Code of Canon Law,* Canon 747, 2.

of perfect love; and finally the *gift of the Holy Spirit,* source and means of the moral life of the "new creation" (cf. 2 *Cor* 5:17).

In her reflection on morality, *the Church* has always kept in mind the words of Jesus to the rich young man. Indeed, Sacred Scripture remains the living and fruitful source of the Church's moral doctrine; as the Second Vatican Council recalled, the Gospel is "the source of all saving truth and moral teaching."[43] The Church has faithfully preserved what the word of God teaches, not only about truths which must be believed but also about moral action, action pleasing to God (cf. 1 *Thes* 4:1); she has achieved a *doctrinal development* analogous to that which has taken place in the realm of the truths of faith. Assisted by the Holy Spirit who leads her into all the truth (cf. Jn 16:13), the Church has not ceased, nor can she ever cease, to contemplate the "mystery of the Word Incarnate," in whom "light is shed on the mystery of man."[44]

29. The Church's moral reflection, always conducted in the light of Christ, the "Good Teacher," has also developed in the specific form of the theological science called *"moral theology,"* a science which accepts and examines Divine Revelation while at the same time responding to the demands of human reason. Moral theology is a reflection concerned with "morality," with the good and the evil of human acts and of the person who performs them; in this sense it is accessible to all people. But it is also "theology," inasmuch as it acknowledges that the origin and end of moral action are found in the One who "alone is good" and who, by giving himself to man in Christ, offers him the happiness of divine life.

The Second Vatican Council invited scholars to take *"special care for the renewal of moral theology,"* in such a way that "its scientific presentation, increasingly based on the teaching of Scripture, will cast light on the exalted vocation of the faithful in Christ and on their obligation to bear fruit in charity for the life of the world."[45] The Council also encouraged theologians, "while respecting the methods and requirements of theological science, to look for *a more appropriate way of communicating* doctrine to the people of their time; since there is a difference between the deposit or the truths of faith and the manner in which they are expressed, keeping the same meaning and the same judgment."[46] This led to a further invitation, one extended to all the faithful, but addressed to theologians in particular: "The faithful should live in the closest contact with others of their

43.　Dogmatic Constitution on Divine Revelation *Dei Verbum,* 7.

44.　Second Vatican Ecumenical Council, Pastoral Constitution on the Church in the Modem World *Gaudium et Spes,* 22.

45.　Decree on Priestly Formation *Optatam Totius,* 16.

46.　Pastoral Constitution on the Church in the Modern World *Gaudium et Spes,* 62.

time, and should work for a perfect understanding of their modes of thought and feelings as expressed in their culture."[47]

The work of many theologians who found support in the Council's encouragement has already borne fruit in interesting and helpful reflections about the truths of faith to be believed and applied in life, reflections offered in a form better suited to the sensitivities and questions of our contemporaries. The Church, and particularly the bishops, to whom Jesus Christ primarily entrusted the ministry of teaching, are deeply appreciative of this work, and encourage theologians to continue their efforts, inspired by that profound and authentic "fear of the Lord, which is the beginning of wisdom" (cf. *Prov* 1:7).

At the same time, however, within the context of the theological debates which followed the Council, there have developed *certain interpretations of Christian morality which are not consistent with "sound teaching"* (2 *Tim* 4:3). Certainly the Church's Magisterium does not intend to impose upon the faithful any particular theological system, still less a philosophical one. Nevertheless, in order to "reverently preserve and faithfully expound" the word of God,[48] the Magisterium has the duty to state that some trends of theological thinking and certain philosophical affirmations are incompatible with revealed truth.[49]

30. In addressing this encyclical to you, my brother bishops, it is my intention to state *the principles necessary for discerning what is contrary to "sound doctrine,"* drawing attention to those elements of the Church's moral teaching which today appear particularly exposed to error, ambiguity or neglect. Yet these are the very elements on which there depends "the answer to the obscure riddles of the human condition which today also, as in the past, profoundly disturb the human heart. What is man? What is the meaning and purpose of our life? What is good and what is sin? What origin and purpose do sufferings have? What is the way to attaining true happiness? What are death, judgment and retribution after death? Lastly, what is that final, unutterable mystery which embraces our lives and from which we take our origin and towards which we tend?"[50] These and other questions, such as: what is freedom and what is its relationship to the truth contained in God's law? what is the role of conscience in man's moral development? how do we determine, in accordance with the truth about the good, the specific rights and duties of the human

---

47. Ibid.

48. Cf. Second Vatican Ecumenical Council, Dogmatic Constitution on Divine Revelation *Dei Verbum*, 10.

49. Cf. First Vatican Ecumenical Council, Dogmatic Constitution on the Catholic Faith *Dei Filius*, ch. 4: *DS*, 3018.

50. Second Vatican Ecumenical Council, Declaration on the Relationship of the Church to Non-Christian Religions *Nostra Aetate*, 1.

person?—can all be summed up in the fundamental question which the young man in the Gospel put to Jesus: "Teacher, what good must I do to have eternal life?" Because the Church has been sent by Jesus to preach the Gospel and to "make disciples of all nations . . ., teaching them to observe all" that he has commanded (cf. *Mt* 28:19–20), *she today once more puts forward the Master's reply,* a reply that possesses a light and a power capable of answering even the most controversial and complex questions. This light and power also impel the Church constantly to carry out not only her dogmatic but also her moral reflection within an interdisciplinary context, which is especially necessary in facing new issues.[51]

It is in the same light and power that *the Church's Magisterium continues to carry out its task of discernment,* accepting and living out the admonition addressed by the Apostle Paul to Timothy: "I charge you in the presence of God and of Christ Jesus who is to judge the living and the dead, and by his appearing and his kingdom: preach the word, be urgent in season and out of season, convince, rebuke, and exhort, be unfailing in patience and in teaching. For the time will come when people will not endure sound teaching, but having itching ears they will accumulate for themselves teachers to suit their own likings, and will turn away from listening to the truth and wander into myths. As for you, always be steady, endure suffering, do the work of an evangelist, fulfill your ministry" (2 *Tim* 4:1–5; cf. *Tit* 1:10, 13–14).

"You will know the truth, and the truth will make you free" (Jn 8:32)

31. The human issues most frequently debated and differently resolved in contemporary moral reflection are all closely related, albeit in various ways, to a crucial issue: *human freedom.*

Certainly people today have a particularly strong sense of freedom. As the Council's Declaration on Religious Freedom *Dignitatis Humanae* had already observed, "the dignity of the human person is a concern of which people of our time are becoming increasingly more aware."[52] Hence the insistent demand that people be permitted to "enjoy the use of their own responsible judgment and freedom, and decide on their actions on grounds of duty and conscience, without external pressure or coercion."[53] In particular, the right to religious freedom

---

51. Cf. Second Vatican Ecumenical Council, Pastoral Constitution on the Church in the Modern World *Gaudium et Spes*, 43–44.

52. Declaration on Religious Freedom *Dignitatis Humanae*, 1, referring to John XXIII, Encyclical Letter *Pacem in Terris* (April 11, 1963): *AAS* 55 (1963), 279; ibid., 265, and to Pius XII, Radio Message (December 24, 1944): *AAS* 37 (1945), 14.

53. Declaration on Religious Freedom *Dignitatis Humanae*, 1.

and to respect for conscience on its journey towards the truth is increasingly perceived as the foundation of the cumulative rights of the person.[54]

This heightened sense of the dignity of the human person and of his or her uniqueness, and of the respect due to the journey of conscience, certainly represents one of the positive achievements of modern culture. This perception, authentic as it is, has been expressed in a number of more or less adequate ways, some of which however diverge from the truth about man as a creature and the image of God, and thus need to be corrected and purified in the light of faith.[55]

32. Certain currents of modern thought have gone so far as to *exalt freedom to such an extent that it becomes an absolute, which would then be the source of values.* This is the direction taken by doctrines which have lost the sense of the transcendent or which are explicitly atheist. The individual conscience is accorded the status of a supreme tribunal of moral judgment which hands down categorical and infallible decisions about good and evil. To the affirmation that one has a duty to follow one's conscience is unduly added the affirmation that one's moral judgment is true merely by the fact that it has its origin in the conscience. But in this way the inescapable claims of truth disappear, yielding their place to a criterion of sincerity, authenticity and "being at peace with oneself," so much so that some have come to adopt a radically subjectivistic conception of moral judgment.

As is immediately evident, *the crisis of truth* is not unconnected with this development. Once the idea of a universal truth about the good, knowable by human reason, is lost, inevitably the notion of conscience also changes. Conscience is no longer considered in its primordial reality as an act of a person's intelligence, the function of which is to apply the universal knowledge of the good in a specific situation and thus to express a judgment about the right conduct to be chosen here and now. Instead, there is a tendency to grant to the individual conscience the prerogative of independently determining the criteria of good and evil and then acting accordingly. Such an outlook is quite congenial to an individualist ethic, wherein each individual is faced with his own truth, different from the truth of others. Taken to its extreme consequences, this individualism leads to a denial of the very idea of human nature.

---

54. Cf. Encyclical Letter *Redemptor Hominis* (March 4, 1979), 17: *AAS* 71 (1979), 295–300; Address to those taking part in the Fifth International Colloquium of Juridical Studies (March 10, 1984), 4: *Insegnamenti* VII, 1 (1984), 656; Congregation for the Doctrine of the Faith, Instruction on Christian Freedom and Liberation *Libertatis Conscientia* (March 22, 1986), 19: *AAS* 79 (1987), 561.

55. Cf. Second Vatican Ecumenical Council, Pastoral Constitution on the Church in the Modern World *Gaudium et Spes*, 11.

These different notions are at the origin of currents of thought which posit a radical opposition between moral law and conscience, and between nature and freedom.

33. *Side by side* with its exaltation of freedom, yet oddly in contrast with it, *modern culture radically questions the very existence of this freedom.* A number of disciplines, grouped under the name of the "behavioral sciences," have rightly drawn attention to the many kinds of psychological and social conditioning which influence the exercise of human freedom. Knowledge of these conditionings and the study they have received represent important achievements which have found application in various areas, for example in pedagogy or the administration of justice. But some people, going beyond the conclusions which can be legitimately drawn from these observations, have come to question or even deny the very reality of human freedom.

Mention should also be made here of theories which misuse scientific research about the human person. Arguing from the great variety of customs, behavior patterns and institutions present in humanity, these theories end up, if not with an outright denial of universal human values, at least with a relativistic conception of morality.

34. "Teacher, what good must I do to have eternal life?" *The question of morality,* to which Christ provides the answer, *cannot prescind from the issue of freedom. Indeed, it considers that issue central,* for there can be no morality without freedom: "It is only in freedom that man can turn to what is good."[56] *But what sort of freedom?* The Council, considering our contemporaries who "highly regard" freedom and "assiduously pursue" it, but who "often cultivate it in wrong ways as a license to do anything they please, even evil," speaks of *"genuine" freedom:* "Genuine freedom is an outstanding manifestation of the divine image in man. For God willed to leave man 'in the power of his own counsel' (cf. *Sir* 15:14), so that he would seek his Creator of his own accord and would freely arrive at full and blessed perfection by cleaving to God."[57] Although each individual has a right to be respected in his own journey in search of the truth, there exists a prior moral obligation, and a grave one at that, to seek the truth and to adhere to it once it is known.[58] As Cardinal John Henry Newman, that outstanding defender

---

56. *Gaudium et Spes,* 17.

57. Ibid.

58. Cf. Second Vatican Ecumenical Council, Declaration on Religious Freedom *Dignitatis Humanae,* 2; cf. also Gregory XVI, Encyclical Epistle *Mirari Vos Arbitramur* (August 15, 1832): *Acta Gregorii Papae* XVI, I: 169–74; Pius IX, Encyclical Epistle *Quanta Cura* (December 8, 1864): *Pii IX P.M. Acta,* I.3: 687–700; Leo XIII, Encyclical Letter *Libertas Praestantissimum* (June 20, 1888): *Leonis XIII P.M. Acta,* VIII: 212–46.

of the rights of conscience, forcefully put it: "Conscience has rights because it has duties."[59]

Certain tendencies in contemporary moral theology, under the influence of the currents of subjectivism and individualism just mentioned, involve novel interpretations of the relationship of freedom to the moral law, human nature and conscience, and propose novel criteria for the moral evaluation of acts. Despite their variety, these tendencies are at one in lessening or even denying *the dependence of freedom on truth.*

If we wish to undertake a critical discernment of these tendencies—a discernment capable of acknowledging what is legitimate, useful and of value in them, while at the same time pointing out their ambiguities, dangers and errors—we must examine them in the light of the fundamental dependence of freedom upon truth, a dependence which has found its clearest and most authoritative expression in the words of Christ: "You will know the truth, and the truth will set you free" (*Jn* 8:32).

I. FREEDOM AND LAW

"Of the tree of the knowledge of good and evil you shall not eat" (Gen 2:17)

35. In the Book of Genesis we read: "The Lord God commanded the man, saying, 'You may eat freely of every tree of the garden; but of the tree of the knowledge of good and evil you shall not eat, for in the day that you eat of it you shall die'" (*Gen* 2:16–17).

With this imagery, revelation teaches that *the power to decide what is good and what is evil does not belong to man, but to God alone.* The man is certainly free, inasmuch as he can understand and accept God's commands. And he possesses an extremely far-reaching freedom, since he can eat "of every tree of the garden." But his freedom is not unlimited: it must halt before the "tree of the knowledge of good and evil," for it is called to accept the moral law given by God. In fact, human freedom finds its authentic and complete fulfillment precisely in the acceptance of that law. God, who alone is good, knows perfectly what is good for man, and by virtue of his very love proposes this good to man in the commandments.

God's law does not reduce, much less do away with human freedom; rather, it protects and promotes that freedom. In contrast, however, some present-day

---

59. *A Letter Addressed to His Grace the Duke of Norfolk: Certain Difficulties Felt by Anglicans in Catholic Teaching* (Uniform Edition: Longman, Green and Company, London, 1868–1881), 2:250.

cultural tendencies have given rise to several currents of thought in ethics which center upon *an alleged conflict between freedom and law.* These doctrines would grant to individuals or social groups the right *to determine what is good or evil.* Human freedom would thus be able to "create values" and would enjoy a primacy over truth, to the point that truth itself would be considered a creation of freedom. Freedom would thus lay claim to a *moral autonomy* which would actually amount to an *absolute sovereignty.*

36. The modern concern for the claims of autonomy has not failed to exercise an *influence* also *in the sphere of Catholic moral theology.* While the latter has certainly never attempted to set human freedom against the divine law or to question the existence of an ultimate religious foundation for moral norms, it has, nonetheless, been led to undertake a profound rethinking about the role of reason and of faith in identifying moral norms with reference to specific "innerworldly" kinds of behavior involving oneself, others and the material world.

It must be acknowledged that underlying this work of rethinking there are *certain positive concerns* which to a great extent belong to the best tradition of Catholic thought. In response to the encouragement of the Second Vatican Council,[60] there has been a desire to foster dialogue with modern culture, emphasizing the rational—and thus universally understandable and communicable—character of moral norms belonging to the sphere of the natural moral law.[61] There has also been an attempt to reaffirm the interior character of the ethical requirements deriving from that law, requirements which create an obligation for the will only because such an obligation was previously acknowledged by human reason and, concretely, by personal conscience.

Some people, however, disregarding the dependence of human reason on divine Wisdom and the need, given the present state of fallen nature, for divine revelation as an effective means for knowing moral truths, even those of the natural order,[62] have actually posited a *complete sovereignty of reason* in the domain of moral norms regarding the right ordering of life in this world. Such norms would constitute the boundaries for a merely "human" morality; they would be the expression of a law which man in an autonomous manner lays down for himself and which has its source exclusively in human reason. In no way could God be considered the Author of this law, except in the sense that human reason exercises its autonomy in setting down laws by virtue of a primordial and total mandate given to man by God. These trends of thought have led to a denial, in opposition

---

60. Cf. Pastoral Constitution on the Church in the Modern World *Gaudium et Spes,* 40 and 43.

61. Cf. *Summa Theologiae* I-II, q. 71, a. 6; see also ad 5.

62. Cf. Pius XII, Encyclical Letter *Humani Generis* (August 12, 1950): *AAS* 42 (1950), 561–62.

to Sacred Scripture (cf. *Mt* 15:3–6) and the Church's constant teaching, of the fact that the natural moral law has God as its author, and that man, by the use of reason, participates in the eternal law, which it is not for him to establish.

37. In their desire, however, to keep the moral life in a Christian context, certain moral theologians have introduced a sharp distinction, contrary to Catholic doctrine,[63] between an *ethical order*, which would be human in origin and of value for *this world* alone, and an *order of salvation*, for which only certain intentions and interior attitudes regarding God and neighbor would be significant. This has then led to an actual denial that there exists, in divine revelation, a specific and determined moral content, universally valid and permanent. The word of God would be limited to proposing an exhortation, a generic *paraenesis* [advice, exhortation], which the autonomous reason alone would then have the task of completing with normative directives which are truly "objective," that is, adapted to the concrete historical situation. Naturally, an autonomy conceived in this way also involves the denial of a specific doctrinal competence on the part of the Church and her Magisterium with regard to particular moral norms which deal with the so-called "human good." Such norms would not be part of the proper content of revelation, and would not in themselves be relevant for salvation.

No one can fail to see that such an interpretation of the autonomy of human reason involves positions incompatible with Catholic teaching.

In such a context it is absolutely necessary to clarify, in the light of the word of God and the living Tradition of the Church, the fundamental notions of human freedom and of the moral law, as well as their profound and intimate relationship. Only thus will it be possible to respond to the rightful claims of human reason in a way which accepts the valid elements present in certain currents of contemporary moral theology without compromising the Church's heritage of moral teaching with ideas derived from an erroneous concept of autonomy.

"God left man in the power of his own counsel" (*Sir 15:14*)

38. Taking up the words of Sirach, the Second Vatican Council explains the meaning of that "genuine freedom" which is "an outstanding manifestation of the divine image" in man: "God willed to leave man in the power of his own counsel, so that he would seek his Creator of his own accord and would freely arrive at full and blessed perfection by cleaving to God."[64] These words indicate the

---

63. Cf. Ecumenical Council of Trent, Sess. VI, Decree on Justification *Cum Hoc Tempore*, Canons 19–21: *DS*, 1569–71.

64. Pastoral Constitution on the Church in the Modern World *Gaudium et Spes*, 17.

wonderful depth of the *sharing in God's dominion* to which man has been called: they indicate that man's dominion extends in a certain sense over man himself. This has been a constantly recurring theme in theological reflection on human freedom, which is described as a form of kingship. For example, Saint Gregory of Nyssa writes: "The soul shows its royal and exalted character … in that it is free and self-governed, swayed autonomously by its own will. Of whom else can this be said, save a king? … Thus human nature, created to rule other creatures, was by its likeness to the King of the universe made as it were a living image, partaking with the Archetype both in dignity and in name."[65]

The exercise of dominion over the world represents a great and responsible task for man, one which involves his freedom in obedience to the Creator's command: "Fill the earth and subdue it" (*Gen* 1:28). In view of this, a rightful autonomy is due to every man, as well as to the human community, a fact to which the Council's Constitution *Gaudium et Spes* calls special attention. This is the autonomy of earthly realities, which means that "created things have their own laws and values which are to be gradually discovered, utilized and ordered by man."[66]

39. Not only the world, however, but also *man himself* has been *entrusted to his own care and responsibility.* God left man "in the power of his own counsel" (*Sir* 15:14), that he might seek his Creator and freely attain perfection. Attaining such perfection means *personally building up that perfection in himself.* Indeed, just as man in exercising his dominion over the world shapes it in accordance with his own intelligence and will, so too in performing morally good acts, man strengthens, develops and consolidates within himself his likeness to God.

Even so, the Council warns against a false concept of the autonomy of earthly realities, one which would maintain that "created things are not dependent on God and that man can use them without reference to their Creator."[67] With regard to man himself, such a concept of autonomy produces particularly baneful effects, and eventually leads to atheism: "Without its Creator the creature simply disappears … If God is ignored the creature itself is impoverished."[68]

40. The teaching of the Council emphasizes, on the one hand, *the role of human reason* in discovering and applying the moral law: the moral life calls for that creativity and originality typical of the person, the source and cause of his own deliberate acts. On the other hand, reason draws its own truth and authority

---

65. *De Hominis Opificio*, Chap. 4: PG 44, 135–36.

66. Pastoral Constitution on the Church in the Modern World *Gaudium et Spes*, 36.

67. Ibid.

68. Ibid.

from the eternal law, which is none other than divine wisdom itself.[69] At the heart of the moral life we thus find the principle of a "rightful autonomy"[70] of man, the personal subject of his actions. *The moral law has its origin in God and always finds its source in him:* at the same time, by virtue of natural reason, which derives from divine wisdom, it is *a properly human law.* Indeed, as we have seen, the natural law "is nothing other than the light of understanding infused in us by God, whereby we understand what must be done and what must be avoided. God gave this light and this law to man at creation."[71] The rightful autonomy of the practical reason means that man possesses in himself his own law, received from the Creator. Nevertheless, *the autonomy of reason cannot mean* that reason itself *creates values and moral norms.*[72] Were this autonomy to imply a denial of the participation of the practical reason in the wisdom of the divine Creator and Lawgiver, or were it to suggest a freedom which creates moral norms, on the basis of historical contingencies or the diversity of societies and cultures, this sort of alleged autonomy would contradict the Church's teaching on the truth about man.[73] It would be the death of true freedom: "But of the tree of the knowledge of good and evil you shall not eat, for in the day that you eat of it you shall die" (*Gen* 2:17).

41. Man's *genuine moral autonomy* in no way means the rejection but rather the acceptance of the moral law, of God's command: "The Lord God gave this command to the man ..." (*Gen* 2:16). *Human freedom and God's law meet and are called to intersect,* in the sense of man's free obedience to God and of God's completely gratuitous benevolence towards man. Hence obedience to God is not, as some would believe, a *heteronomy,* as if the moral life were subject to the will of something all-powerful, absolute, extraneous to man and intolerant of his freedom. If in fact a heteronomy of morality were to mean a denial of man's self-determination or the imposition of norms unrelated to his good, this would be in contradiction to the revelation of the Covenant and of the redemptive Incarnation. Such a heteronomy would be nothing but a form of alienation, contrary to divine wisdom and to the dignity of the human person.

---

69. Cf. *Summa Theologiae* I-II, q. 93, a. 3, ad 2, cited by John XXIII, Encyclical Letter *Pacem in Terris* (April 11, 1963): *AAS* 55 (1963), 271.

70. Second Vatican Ecumenical Council, Pastoral Constitution on the Church in the Modern World *Gaudium et Spes,* 41.

71. Saint Thomas Aquinas, *In Duo Praecepta Caritatis et in Decem Legis Praecepta. Prologus: Opuscula Theologica,* II, No. 1129, ed. Taurinen (1954), 245.

72. Cf. Address to a Group of Bishops from the United States on the occasion of their *ad Limina* Visit (October 15, 1988), 6: *Insegnamenti,* XI, 3 (1988), 1228.

73. Second Vatican Ecumenical Council, Pastoral Constitution on the Church in the Modern World *Gaudium et Spes,* 47.

Others speak, and rightly so, of *theonomy*, or *participated theonomy*, since man's free obedience to God's law effectively implies that human reason and human will participate in God's wisdom and providence. By forbidding man to "eat of the tree of the knowledge of good and evil," God makes it clear that man does not originally possess such "knowledge" as something properly his own, but only participates in it by the light of natural reason and of divine revelation, which manifest to him the requirements and the promptings of eternal wisdom. Law must therefore be considered an expression of divine wisdom: by submitting to the law, freedom submits to the truth of creation. Consequently one must acknowledge in the freedom of the human person the image and the nearness of God, who is present in all (cf. *Eph* 4:6). But one must likewise acknowledge the majesty of the God of the universe and revere the holiness of the law of God, who is infinitely transcendent: *Deus semper maior.*[74]

Blessed is the man who takes delight
in the law of the Lord (cf. Ps 1:1–2)

42. Patterned on God's freedom, man's freedom is not negated by his obedience to the divine law; indeed, only through this obedience does it abide in the truth and conform to human dignity. This is clearly stated by the Council: "Human dignity requires man to act through conscious and free choice, as motivated and prompted personally from within, and not through blind internal impulse or merely external pressure. Man achieves such dignity when he frees himself from all subservience to his feelings, and in a free choice of the good, pursues his own end by effectively and assiduously marshalling the appropriate means."[75]

In his journey towards God, the One who "alone is good," man must freely do good and avoid evil. But in order to accomplish this he must *be able to distinguish good from evil*. And this takes place above all *thanks to the light of natural reason*, the reflection in man of the splendor of God's countenance. Thus Saint Thomas, commenting on a verse of Psalm 4, writes: "After saying: *Offer right sacrifices* (*Ps* 4:5), as if some had then asked him what right works were, the Psalmist adds: *There are many who say: Who will make us see good?* And in reply to the question he says: *The light of your face, Lord, is signed upon us*, thereby implying that the light of natural reason whereby we discern good from evil, which is the function of the natural law, is nothing else but an imprint on us of the divine light."[76] It

---

74. Cf. Saint Augustine, *Enarratio in Psalmum LXII*, 16: CCL 39, 804.

75. Pastoral Constitution on the Church in the Modern World *Gaudium et Spes*, 17.

76. *Summa Theologiae* I-II, q. 91, a. 2.

also becomes clear why this law is called the natural law: it receives this name not because it refers to the nature of irrational beings but because the reason which promulgates it is proper to human nature.[77]

43. The Second Vatican Council points out that the "supreme rule of life is the divine law itself, the eternal, objective and universal law by which God out of his wisdom and love arranges, directs and governs the whole world and the paths of the human community. God has enabled man to share in this divine law, and hence man is able under the gentle guidance of God's providence increasingly to recognize the unchanging truth."[78]

The Council refers back to the classic teaching on *God's eternal law*. Saint Augustine defines this as "the reason or the will of God, who commands us to respect the natural order and forbids us to disturb it."[79] Saint Thomas identifies it with "the type of the divine wisdom as moving all things to their due end."[80] And God's wisdom is providence, a love which cares. God himself loves and cares, in the most literal and basic sense, for all creation (cf. *Wis* 7:22; 8:11). But God provides for man differently from the way in which he provides for beings which are not persons. He cares for man not "from without," through the laws of physical nature, but "from within," through reason, which, by its natural knowledge of God's eternal law, is consequently able to show man the right direction to take in his free actions.[81] In this way God calls man to participate in his own providence, since he desires to guide the world—not only the world of nature but also the world of human persons—through man himself, through man's reasonable and responsible care. The *natural law* enters here as the human expression of God's eternal law. Saint Thomas writes: "Among all others, the rational creature is subject to divine providence in the most excellent way, insofar as it partakes of a share of providence, being provident both for itself and for others. Thus it has a share of the Eternal Reason, whereby it has a natural inclination to its proper act and end. This participation of the eternal law in the rational creature is called natural law."[82]

44. The Church has often made reference to the Thomistic doctrine of natural law, including it in her own teaching on morality. Thus my venerable predecessor Leo XIII emphasized *the essential subordination of reason and human law to the Wisdom of God and to his law*. After stating that "the *natural law* is written and

---

77. Cf. *Catechism of the Catholic Church*, n. 1955.

78. Declaration on Religious Freedom *Dignitatis Humanae*, 3.

79. *Contra Faustum*, Bk. 22, Chap. 27: PL 42, 418.

80. *Summa Theologiae* I-II, q. 93, a. 1.

81. *Summa Theologiae* I-II, q. 90, a. 4, ad 1.

82. *Summa Theologiae* I-II, q. 91, a. 2.

engraved in the heart of each and every man, since it is none other than human reason itself which commands us to do good and counsels us not to sin," Leo XIII appealed to the "higher reason" of the divine Lawgiver: "But this prescription of human reason could not have the force of law unless it were the voice and the interpreter of some higher reason to which our spirit and our freedom must be subject." Indeed, the force of law consists in its authority to impose duties, to confer rights and to sanction certain behavior: "Now all of this, clearly, could not exist in man if, as his own supreme legislator, he gave himself the rule of his own actions." And he concluded: "It follows that the natural law is *itself the eternal law,* implanted in beings endowed with reason, and inclining them *towards their right action and end;* it is none other than the eternal reason of the Creator and Ruler of the universe."[83]

Man is able to recognize good and evil thanks to that discernment of good from evil which he himself carries out by his *reason, in particular by his reason enlightened by divine revelation and by faith,* through the law which God gave to the Chosen People, beginning with the commandments on Sinai. Israel was called to accept and to live out *God's law* as *a particular gift and sign of its election and of the divine Covenant,* and also as a pledge of God's blessing. Thus Moses could address the children of Israel and ask them: "What great nation is there that has a god so near to it as the Lord our God is to us, whenever we call upon him? And what great nation is there that has statutes and ordinances so righteous as all this law which I set before you this day?" (*Dt* 4:7–8). In the Psalms we encounter the sentiments of praise, gratitude and veneration which the Chosen People is called to show towards God's law, together with an exhortation to know it, ponder it and translate it into life. "Blessed is the man who walks not in the counsel of the wicked, nor stands in the way of sinners, nor sits in the seat of scoffers, but his delight is in the law of the Lord and on his law he meditates day and night" (*Ps* 1:1–2). "The law of the Lord is perfect, reviving the soul; the testimony of the Lord is sure, making wise the simple; the precepts of the Lord are right, rejoicing the heart; the commandment of the Lord is pure, enlightening the eyes" (*Ps* 18/19:8–9).

45. The Church gratefully accepts and lovingly preserves the entire deposit of revelation, treating it with religious respect and fulfilling her mission of authentically interpreting God's law in the light of the Gospel. In addition, the Church receives the gift of the New Law, which is the "fulfillment" of God's law in Jesus Christ and in his Spirit. This is an "interior" law (cf. *Jer* 31:31–33), "written not with ink but with the Spirit of the living God, not on tablets of stone but on tablets

---

83. Encyclical Letter *Libertas Praestantissimum* (June 20, 1888): *Leonis XIII P.M. Acta,* VIII (Romae, 1889), 219.

of human hearts" (2 *Cor* 3:3); a law of perfection and of freedom (cf. 2 *Cor* 3:17); "the law of the Spirit of life in Christ Jesus" (*Rom* 8:2). Saint Thomas writes that this law "can be called law in two ways. First, the law of the spirit is the Holy Spirit ... who, dwelling in the soul, not only teaches what it is necessary to do by enlightening the intellect on the things to be done, but also inclines the affections to act with uprightness ... Second, the law of the spirit can be called the proper effect of the Holy Spirit, and thus faith working through love (cf. *Gal* 5:6), which teaches inwardly about the things to be done ... and inclines the affections to act."[84]

Even if moral-theological reflection usually distinguishes between the positive or revealed law of God and the natural law, and, within the economy of salvation, between the "old" and the "new" law, it must not be forgotten that these and other useful distinctions always refer to that law whose author is the one and the same God and which is always meant for man. The different ways in which God, acting in history, cares for the world and for mankind are not mutually exclusive; on the contrary, they support each other and intersect. They have their origin and goal in the eternal, wise and loving counsel whereby God predestines men and women "to be conformed to the image of his Son" (*Rom* 8:29). God's plan poses no threat to man's genuine freedom; on the contrary, the acceptance of God's plan is the only way to affirm that freedom.

"What the law requires is written on their hearts" (Rom 2:15)

46. The alleged conflict between freedom and law is forcefully brought up once again today with regard to the natural law, and particularly with regard to nature. *Debates about nature and freedom* have always marked the history of moral reflection; they grew especially heated at the time of the Renaissance and the Reformation, as can be seen from the teaching of the Council of Trent.[85] Our own age is marked, though in a different sense, by a similar tension. The penchant for empirical observation, the procedures of scientific objectification, technological progress and certain forms of liberalism have led to these two terms being set in opposition, as if a dialectic, if not an absolute conflict, between freedom and nature were characteristic of the structure of human history. At other periods, it seemed that "nature" subjected man totally to its own dynamics and even its own unbreakable laws. Today too, the situation of the world of the senses within space and time, physio-chemical constants, bodily processes, psychological impulses and forms of social conditioning seem to many people the only really decisive

---

84. *In Epistulam ad Romanos*, c. VIII, lect. 1.

85. Cf. Sess. IV, Decree on Justification *Cum Hoc Tempore*, Chap. 1: *DS*, 1521.

factors of human reality. In this context even moral facts, despite their specificity, are frequently treated as if they were statistically verifiable data, patterns of behavior which can be subject to observation or explained exclusively in categories of psychosocial processes. As a result, *some ethicists*, professionally engaged in the study of human realities and behavior, can be tempted to take as the standard for their discipline and even for its operative norms the results of a statistical study of concrete human behavior patterns and the opinions about morality encountered in the majority of people.

Other moralists, however, in their concern to stress the importance of values, remain sensitive to the dignity of freedom, but they frequently conceive of freedom as somehow in opposition to or in conflict with material and biological nature, over which it must progressively assert itself. Here various approaches are at one in overlooking the created dimension of nature and in misunderstanding its integrity. *For some*, "nature" becomes reduced to raw material for human activity and for its power: thus nature needs to be profoundly transformed, and indeed overcome by freedom, inasmuch as it represents a limitation and denial of freedom. *For others*, it is in the untrammeled advancement of man's power, or of his freedom, that economic, cultural, social and even moral values are established: nature would thus come to mean everything found in man and the world apart from freedom. In such an understanding, nature would include in the first place the human body, its make-up and its processes: against this physical datum would be opposed whatever is "constructed," in other words "culture," seen as the product and result of freedom. Human nature, understood in this way, could be reduced to and treated as a readily available biological or social material. This ultimately means making freedom self-defining and a phenomenon creative of itself and its values. Indeed, when all is said and done man would not even have a nature; he would be his own personal life-project. Man would be nothing more than his own freedom!

47. In this context, *objections of physicalism and naturalism* have been leveled against the traditional conception of *the natural law*, which is accused of presenting as moral laws what are in themselves mere biological laws. Consequently, in too superficial a way, a permanent and unchanging character would be attributed to certain kinds of human behavior, and, on the basis of this, an attempt would be made to formulate universally valid moral norms. According to certain theologians, this kind of "biologistic or naturalistic argumentation" would even be present in certain documents of the Church's Magisterium, particularly those dealing with the area of sexual and conjugal ethics. It was, they maintain, on the basis of a naturalistic understanding of the sexual act that contraception, direct sterilization, autoeroticism, pre-marital sexual relations, homosexual relations

and artificial insemination were condemned as morally unacceptable. In the opinion of these same theologians, a morally negative evaluation of such acts fails to take into adequate consideration both man's character as a rational and free being and the cultural conditioning of all moral norms. In their view, man, as a rational being, not only can but actually *must freely determine the meaning* of his behavior. This process of "determining the meaning" would obviously have to take into account the many limitations of the human being, as existing in a body and in history. Furthermore, it would have to take into consideration the behavioral models and the meanings which the latter acquire in any given culture. Above all, it would have to respect the fundamental commandment of love of God and neighbor. Still, they continue, God made man as a rationally free being; he left him "in the power of his own counsel" and he expects him to shape his life in a personal and rational way. Love of neighbor would mean above all and even exclusively respect for his freedom to make his own decisions. The workings of typically human behavior, as well as the so-called "natural inclinations," would establish at the most—so they say—a general orientation towards correct behavior, but they cannot determine the moral assessment of individual human acts, so complex from the viewpoint of situations.

48. Faced with this theory, one has to consider carefully the correct relationship existing between freedom and human nature, and in particular *the place of the human body in questions of natural law.*

A freedom which claims to be absolute ends up treating the human body as a raw datum, devoid of any meaning and moral values until freedom has shaped it in accordance with its design. Consequently, human nature and the body appear as *presuppositions or preambles,* materially *necessary* for freedom to make its choice, yet extrinsic to the person, the subject and the human act. Their functions would not be able to constitute reference points for moral decisions, because the finalities of these inclinations would be merely *"physical"* goods, called by some "pre-moral." To refer to them, in order to find in them rational indications with regard to the order of morality, would be to expose oneself to the accusation of physicalism or biologism. In this way of thinking, the tension between freedom and a nature conceived of in a reductive way is resolved by a division within man himself.

This moral theory does not correspond to the truth about man and his freedom. It contradicts the *Church's teachings on the unity of the human person,* whose rational soul is *per se et essentialiter* the form of his body.[86] The spiritual and

---

86. Cf. Ecumenical Council of Vienne, Constitution *Fidei Catholicae*: DS, 902; Fifth Lateran Ecumenical Council, Bull *Apostolici Regiminis*: DS, 1440.

immortal soul is the principle of unity of the human being, whereby it exists as a whole—*corpore et anima unus*[87]—as a person. These definitions not only point out that the body, which has been promised the resurrection, will also share in glory. They also remind us that reason and free will are linked with all the bodily and sense faculties. *The person, including the body, is completely entrusted to himself, and it is in the unity of body and soul that the person is the subject of his own moral acts.* The person, by the light of reason and the support of virtue, discovers in the body the anticipatory signs, the expression and the promise of the gift of self, in conformity with the wise plan of the Creator. It is in the light of the dignity of the human person—a dignity which must be affirmed for its own sake—that reason grasps the specific moral value of certain goods towards which the person is naturally inclined. And since the human person cannot be reduced to a freedom which is self-designing, but entails a particular spiritual and bodily structure, the primordial moral requirement of loving and respecting the person as an end and never as a mere means also implies, by its very nature, respect for certain fundamental goods, without which one would fall into relativism and arbitrariness.

49. *A doctrine which dissociates the moral act from the bodily dimensions of its exercise is contrary to the teaching of Scripture and Tradition.* Such a doctrine revives, in new forms, certain ancient errors which have always been opposed by the Church, inasmuch as they reduce the human person to a "spiritual" and purely formal freedom. This reduction misunderstands the moral meaning of the body and of kinds of behavior involving it (cf. 1 *Cor* 6:19). Saint Paul declares that "the immoral, idolaters, adulterers, sexual perverts, thieves, the greedy, drunkards, revilers, robbers" are excluded from the Kingdom of God (cf. 1 *Cor* 6:9). This condemnation—repeated by the Council of Trent[88]—lists as "mortal sins" or "immoral practices" certain specific kinds of behavior the willful acceptance of which prevents believers from sharing in the inheritance promised to them. In fact, *body and soul are inseparable:* in the person, in the willing agent and in the deliberate act, *they stand or fall together.*

50. At this point the true meaning of the natural law can be understood: it refers to man's proper and primordial nature, the "nature of the human person,"[89]

---

87. Second Vatican Ecumenical Council, Pastoral Constitution on the Church in the Modern World *Gaudium et Spes*, 14.

88. Cf. Sess. VI, Decree on Justification *Cum Hoc Tempore*, Chap. 15: *DS*, 1544. The Post-Synodal Apostolic Exhortation on Reconciliation and Penance in the Mission of the Church Today cites other texts of the Old and New Testaments which condemn as mortal sins certain modes of conduct involving the body: cf. *Reconciliatio et Paenitentia* (December 2, 1984), 17: *AAS* 77 (1985), 218–23.

89. Second Vatican Ecumenical Council, Pastoral Constitution on the Church in the Modern World *Gaudium et Spes*, 51.

which is *the person himself in the unity of soul and body,* in the unity of his spiritual and biological inclinations and of all the other specific characteristics necessary for the pursuit of his end. "The natural moral law expresses and lays down the purposes, rights and duties which are based upon the bodily and spiritual nature of the human person. Therefore this law cannot be thought of as simply a set of norms on the biological level; rather it must be defined as the rational order whereby man is called by the Creator to direct and regulate his life and actions and in particular to make use of his own body."[90] To give an example, the origin and the foundation of the duty of absolute respect for human life are to be found in the dignity proper to the person and not simply in the natural inclination to preserve one's own physical life. Human life, even though it is a fundamental good of man, thus acquires a moral significance in reference to the good of the person, who must always be affirmed for his own sake. While it is always morally illicit to kill an innocent human being, it can be licit, praiseworthy or even imperative to give up one's own life (cf. *Jn* 15:13) out of love of neighbor or as a witness to the truth. Only in reference to the human person in his "unified totality," that is, as "a soul which expresses itself in a body and a body informed by an immortal spirit,"[91] can the specifically human meaning of the body be grasped. Indeed, natural inclinations take on moral relevance only insofar as they refer to the human person and his authentic fulfillment, a fulfillment which for that matter can take place always and only in human nature. By rejecting all manipulations of corporeity which alter its human meaning, the Church serves man and shows him the path of true love, the only path on which he can find the true God.

The natural law thus understood does not allow for any division between freedom and nature. Indeed, these two realities are harmoniously bound together, and each is intimately linked to the other.

"From the beginning it was not so" (*Mt 19:8*)

51. The alleged conflict between freedom and nature also has repercussions on the interpretation of certain specific aspects of the natural law, especially its *universality and immutability.* "Where then are these rules written," Saint Augustine wondered, "except in the book of that light which is called truth? From thence every just law is transcribed and transferred to the heart of the man who

---

90. Congregation for the Doctrine of the Faith, Instruction on Respect for Human Life in its Origin and on the Dignity of Procreation *Donum Vitae* (February 22, 1987), Introduction, 3: *AAS* 80 (1988), 74; cf. Paul VI, Encyclical Letter *Humanae Vitae* (July 25, 1968), 10: *AAS* 60 (1968), 487–88.

91. Apostolic Exhortation *Familiaris Consortio* (November 22, 1981), 11: *AAS* 74 (1982), 92.

works justice, not by wandering but by being, as it were, impressed upon it, just as the image from the ring passes over to the wax, and yet does not leave the ring."[92]

Precisely because of this "truth" *the natural law involves universality.* Inasmuch as it is inscribed in the rational nature of the person, it makes itself felt to all beings endowed with reason and living in history. In order to perfect himself in his specific order, the person must do good and avoid evil, be concerned for the transmission and preservation of life, refine and develop the riches of the material world, cultivate social life, seek truth, practice good and contemplate beauty.[93]

The separation which some have posited between the freedom of individuals and the nature which all have in common, as it emerges from certain philosophical theories which are highly influential in present-day culture, obscures the perception of the universality of the moral law on the part of reason. But inasmuch as the natural law expresses the dignity of the human person and lays the foundation for his fundamental rights and duties, it is universal in its precepts and its authority extends to all mankind. *This universality does not ignore the individuality of human beings,* nor is it opposed to the absolute uniqueness of each person. On the contrary, it embraces at its root each of the person's free acts, which are meant to bear witness to the universality of the true good. By submitting to the common law, our acts build up the true communion of persons and, by God's grace, practice charity, "which binds everything together in perfect harmony" (*Col* 3:14). When on the contrary they disregard the law, or even are merely ignorant of it, whether culpably or not, our acts damage the communion of persons, to the detriment of each.

52. It is right and just, always and for everyone, to serve God, to render him the worship which is his due and to honor one's parents as they deserve. Positive precepts such as these, which order us to perform certain actions and to cultivate certain dispositions, are universally binding; they are "unchanging."[94] They unite in the same common good all people of every period of history, created for "the same divine calling and destiny."[95] These universal and permanent laws

---

92. *De Trinitate,* XIV, 15, 21: *CCL* 50/A, 451.

93. Cf. *Summa Theologiae* I-II, q. 94, a. 2.

94. Cf. Second Vatican Ecumenical Council, Pastoral Constitution on the Church in the Modern World *Gaudium et Spes,* 10; Sacred Congregation for the Doctrine of the Faith, Declaration on Certain Questions Concerning Sexual Ethics *Persona Humana* (December 29,1975), 4: *AAS* 68 (1976, 80): "But in fact, divine revelation and, in its own proper order, philosophical wisdom, emphasize the authentic exigencies of human nature. They thereby necessarily manifest the existence of immutable laws inscribed in the constitutive elements of human nature and which are revealed to be identical in all beings endowed with reason."

95. Second Vatican Ecumenical Council, Pastoral Constitution on the Church in the Modern World *Gaudium et Spes,* 29.

correspond to things known by the practical reason and are applied to particular acts through the judgment of conscience. The acting subject personally assimilates the truth contained in the law. He appropriates this truth of his being and makes it his own by his acts and the corresponding virtues. The *negative precepts* of the natural law are universally valid. They oblige each and every individual, always and in every circumstance. It is a matter of prohibitions which forbid a given action *semper et pro semper,* without exception, because the choice of this kind of behavior is in no case compatible with the goodness of the will of the acting person, with his vocation to life with God and to communion with his neighbor. It is prohibited—to everyone and in every case—to violate these precepts. They oblige everyone, regardless of the cost, never to offend in anyone, beginning with oneself, the personal dignity common to all.

On the other hand, the fact that only the negative commandments oblige always and under all circumstances does not mean that in the moral life prohibitions are more important than the obligation to do good indicated by the positive commandments. The reason is this: the commandment of love of God and neighbor does not have in its dynamic any higher limit, but it does have a lower limit, beneath which the commandment is broken. Furthermore, what must be done in any given situation depends on the circumstances, not all of which can be foreseen; on the other hand there are kinds of behavior which can never, in any situation, be a proper response—a response which is in conformity with the dignity of the person. Finally, it is always possible that man, as the result of coercion or other circumstances, can be hindered from doing certain good actions; but he can never be hindered from not doing certain actions, especially if he is prepared to die rather than to do evil.

The Church has always taught that one may never choose kinds of behavior prohibited by the moral commandments expressed in negative form in the Old and New Testaments. As we have seen, Jesus himself reaffirms that these prohibitions allow no exceptions: "If you wish to enter into life, keep the commandments ... You shall not murder, You shall not commit adultery, You shall not steal, You shall not bear false witness" (*Mt* 19:17–18).

53. The great concern of our contemporaries for historicity and for culture has led some to call into question *the immutability of the natural law* itself, and thus the existence of "objective norms of morality"[96] valid for all people of the present and the future, as for those of the past. Is it ever possible, they ask, to consider as universally valid and always binding certain rational determinations established in the past, when no one knew the progress humanity would make in the future?

---

96. Cf. *Gaudium et Spes,* 16.

It must certainly be admitted that man always exists in a particular culture, but it must also be admitted that man is not exhaustively defined by that same culture. Moreover, the very progress of cultures demonstrates that there is something in man which transcends those cultures. This "something" is precisely human nature: this nature is itself the measure of culture and the condition ensuring that man does not become the prisoner of any of his cultures, but asserts his personal dignity by living in accordance with the profound truth of his being. To call into question the permanent structural elements of man which are connected with his own bodily dimension would not only conflict with common experience, but would render meaningless *Jesus' reference to the "beginning,"* precisely where the social and cultural context of the time had distorted the primordial meaning and the role of certain moral norms (cf. *Mt* 19:1–9). This is the reason why "the Church affirms that underlying so many changes there are some things which do not change and are *ultimately founded upon Christ,* who is the same yesterday and today and forever."[97] Christ is the "Beginning" who, having taken on human nature, definitively illumines it in its constitutive elements and in its dynamism of charity towards God and neighbor.[98]

Certainly there is a need to seek out and to discover *the most adequate formulation* for universal and permanent moral norms in the light of different cultural contexts, a formulation most capable of ceaselessly expressing their historical relevance, of making them understood and of authentically interpreting their truth. This truth of the moral law—like that of the "deposit of faith"—unfolds down the centuries: the norms expressing that truth remain valid in their substance, but must be specified and determined *"eodem sensu eademque sententia"*[99] in the light of historical circumstances by the Church's Magisterium, whose decision is preceded and accompanied by the work of interpretation and formulation characteristic of the reason of individual believers and of theological reflection.[100]

---

97. *Gaudium et Spes,* 10.

98. Cf. *Summa Theologiae* I-II, q. 108, a. 1. St. Thomas bases the fact that moral norms, even in the context of the New Law, are not merely formal in character but have a determined content, upon the assumption of human nature by the Word.

99. "with the same meaning and the same judgment": Saint Vincent of Lerins, *Commonitorium Primum,* c. 23: PL 50, 668.

100. The development of the Church's moral doctrine is similar to that of the doctrine of the faith (cf. First Vatican Ecumenical Council, Dogmatic Constitution on the Catholic Faith *Dei Filius,* Chap. 4: *DS,* 3020, and Canon 4: *DS,* 3024). The words spoken by John XXIII at the opening of the Second Vatican Council can also be applied to moral doctrine: "This certain and unchanging teaching (i.e., Christian doctrine in its completeness), to which the faithful owe obedience, needs to be more deeply understood and set forth in a way adapted to the needs of our time. Indeed, this deposit of the faith, the truths contained in our time-honored teaching, is one thing; the manner in which these truths are set forth (with their meaning preserved intact) is something else": *AAS* 54 (1962), 792; cf. *L'Osservatore Romano,* October 12, 1962, p. 2.

II. CONSCIENCE AND TRUTH

Man's sanctuary

54. The relationship between man's freedom and God's law is most deeply lived out in the "heart" of the person, in his moral conscience. As the Second Vatican Council observed: "In the depths of his conscience man detects a law which he does not impose on himself, but which holds him to obedience. Always summoning him to love good and avoid evil, the voice of conscience can when necessary speak to his heart more specifically: 'do this, shun that'. For man has in his heart a law written by God. To obey it is the very dignity of man; according to it he will be judged (cf. *Rom* 2:14–16)."[101]

The way in which one conceives the relationship between freedom and law is thus intimately bound up with one's understanding of the moral conscience. Here the cultural tendencies referred to above—in which freedom and law are set in opposition to each other and kept apart, and freedom is exalted almost to the point of idolatry—lead to a *"creative" understanding of moral conscience,* which diverges from the teaching of the Church's tradition and her Magisterium.

55. According to the opinion of some theologians, the function of conscience had been reduced, at least at a certain period in the past, to a simple application of general moral norms to individual cases in the life of the person. But those norms, they continue, cannot be expected to foresee and to respect all the individual concrete acts of the person in all their uniqueness and particularity. While such norms might somehow be useful for a correct *assessment* of the situation, they cannot replace the individual personal *decision* on how to act in particular cases. The critique already mentioned of the traditional understanding of human nature and of its importance for the moral life has even led certain authors to state that these norms are not so much a binding objective criterion for judgments of conscience, but a *general perspective* which helps man tentatively to put order into his personal and social life. These authors also stress the *complexity* typical of the phenomenon of conscience, a complexity profoundly related to the whole sphere of psychology and the emotions, and to the numerous influences exerted by the individual's social and cultural environment. On the other hand, they give maximum attention to the value of conscience, which the Council itself defined as "the sanctuary of man, where he is alone with God whose voice echoes within him."[102] This voice, it is said, leads man not so much to a meticulous observance

---

101. Pastoral Constitution on the Church in the Modern World *Gaudium et Spes,* 16.
102. Ibid.

of universal norms as to a creative and responsible acceptance of the personal tasks entrusted to him by God.

In their desire to emphasize the "creative" character of conscience, certain authors no longer call its actions "judgments" but "decisions": only by making these decisions "autonomously" would man be able to attain moral maturity. Some even hold that this process of maturing is inhibited by the excessively categorical position adopted by the Church's Magisterium in many moral questions; for them, the Church's interventions are the cause of unnecessary *conflicts of conscience.*

56. In order to justify these positions, some authors have proposed a kind of double status of moral truth. Beyond the doctrinal and abstract level, one would have to acknowledge the priority of a certain more concrete existential consideration. The latter, by taking account of circumstances and the situation, could legitimately be the basis of certain *exceptions to the general rule* and thus permit one to do in practice and in good conscience what is qualified as intrinsically evil by the moral law. A separation, or even an opposition, is thus established in some cases between the teaching of the precept, which is valid in general, and the norm of the individual conscience, which would in fact make the final decision about what is good and what is evil. On this basis, an attempt is made to legitimize so-called "pastoral" solutions contrary to the teaching of the Magisterium, and to justify a "creative" hermeneutic according to which the moral conscience is in no way obliged, in every case, by a particular negative precept.

No one can fail to realize that these approaches pose a challenge to the *very identity of the moral conscience* in relation to human freedom and God's law. Only the clarification made earlier with regard to the relationship, based on truth, between freedom and law makes possible a *discernment* concerning this "creative" understanding of conscience.

The judgment of conscience

57. The text of the Letter to the Romans which has helped us to grasp the essence of the natural law also indicates *the biblical understanding of conscience, especially in its specific connection with the law:* "When Gentiles who have not the law do by nature what the law requires, they are a law unto themselves, even though they do not have the law. They show that what the law requires is written on their hearts, while their conscience also bears witness and their conflicting thoughts accuse or perhaps excuse them" (*Rom* 2:14–15).

According to Saint Paul, conscience in a certain sense confronts man with the law, and thus becomes a *"witness" for man:* a witness of his own faithfulness or unfaithfulness with regard to the law, of his essential moral rectitude or iniquity. Conscience is the *only* witness, since what takes place in the heart of the person is hidden from the eyes of everyone outside. Conscience makes its witness known only to the person himself. And, in turn, only the person himself knows what his own response is to the voice of conscience.

58. The importance of this interior *dialogue of man with himself* can never be adequately appreciated. But it is also a *dialogue of man with God,* the author of the law, the primordial image and final end of man. Saint Bonaventure teaches that "conscience is like God's herald and messenger; it does not command things on its own authority, but commands them as coming from God's authority, like a herald when he proclaims the edict of the king. This is why conscience has binding force."[103] Thus it can be said that conscience bears witness to man's own rectitude or iniquity to man himself but, together with this and indeed even beforehand, conscience is *the witness of God himself,* whose voice and judgment penetrate the depths of man's soul, calling him *fortiter et suaviter* to obedience. "Moral conscience does not close man within an insurmountable and impenetrable solitude, but opens him to the call, to the voice of God. In this, and not in anything else, lies the entire mystery and the dignity of the moral conscience: in being the place, the sacred place where God speaks to man."[104]

59. Saint Paul does not merely acknowledge that conscience acts as a "witness"; he also reveals the way in which conscience performs that function. He speaks of "conflicting thoughts" which accuse or excuse the Gentiles with regard to their behavior (cf. *Rom* 2:15). The term "conflicting thoughts" clarifies the precise nature of conscience: it is a *moral judgment about man and his actions,* a judgment either of acquittal or of condemnation, according as human acts are in conformity or not with the law of God written on the heart. In the same text the Apostle clearly speaks of the judgment of actions, the judgment of their author and the moment when that judgment will be definitively rendered: "(This will take place) on that day when, according to my Gospel, God judges the secrets of men by Christ Jesus" (*Rom* 2:16).

The judgment of conscience is a *practical judgment,* a judgment which makes known what man must do or not do, or which assesses an act already performed by him. It is a judgment which applies to a concrete situation the rational conviction that one must love and do good and avoid evil. This first principle of practical reason is part of the natural law; indeed it constitutes the very foundation of the natural law, inasmuch as it expresses that primordial insight about good and

103. *In II Librum Sentent.,* dist. 39, a. 1, q. 3, conclusion; ed. Ad Claras Aquas, II, 907b.

104. Address (General Audience, August 17, 1983), 2: *Insegnamenti,* VI, 2 (1983), 256.

evil, that reflection of God's creative wisdom which, like an imperishable spark (*scintilla animae*), shines in the heart of every man. But whereas the natural law discloses the objective and universal demands of the moral good, conscience is the application of the law to a particular case; this application of the law thus becomes an inner dictate for the individual, a summons to do what is good in this particular situation. Conscience thus formulates *moral obligation* in the light of the natural law: it is the obligation to do what the individual, through the workings of his conscience, *knows* to be a good he is called to do *here and now*. The universality of the law and its obligation are acknowledged, not suppressed, once reason has established the law's application in concrete present circumstances. The judgment of conscience states "in an ultimate way" whether a certain particular kind of behavior is in conformity with the law; it formulates the proximate norm of the morality of a voluntary act, "applying the objective law to a particular case."[105]

60. Like the natural law itself and all practical knowledge, the judgment of conscience also has an imperative character: man must act in accordance with it. If man acts against this judgment or, in a case where he lacks certainty about the rightness and goodness of a determined act, still performs that act, he stands condemned by his own conscience, *the proximate norm of personal morality*. The dignity of this rational forum and the authority of its voice and judgments derive from the *truth* about moral good and evil, which it is called to listen to and to express. This truth is indicated by the "divine law," *the universal and objective norm of morality*. The judgment of conscience does not establish the law; rather it bears witness to the authority of the natural law and of the practical reason with reference to the supreme good, whose attractiveness the human person perceives and whose commandments he accepts. "Conscience is not an independent and exclusive capacity to decide what is good and what is evil. Rather there is profoundly imprinted upon it a principle of obedience vis-à-vis the objective norm which establishes and conditions the correspondence of its decisions with the commands and prohibitions which are at the basis of human behavior."[106]

61. The truth about moral good, as that truth is declared in the law of reason, is practically and concretely recognized by the judgment of conscience, which leads one to take responsibility for the good or the evil one has done. If man does evil, the just judgment of his conscience remains within him as a witness to the

---

105. Supreme Sacred Congregation of the Holy Office, Instruction on "Situation Ethics" *Contra Doctrinam* (February 2, 1956): *AAS* 48 (1956), 144.

106. Encyclical Letter *Dominum et Vivificantem* (May 18, 1986), 43: *AAS* 78 (1986), 859; cf. Second Vatican Ecumenical Council, Pastoral Constitution on the Church in the Modern World *Gaudium et Spes*, 16; Declaration on Religious Freedom *Dignitatis Humanae*, 3.

universal truth of the good, as well as to the malice of his particular choice. But the verdict of conscience remains in him also as a pledge of hope and mercy: while bearing witness to the evil he has done, it also reminds him of his need, with the help of God's grace, to ask forgiveness, to do good and to cultivate virtue constantly.

Consequently *in the practical judgment of conscience,* which imposes on the person the obligation to perform a given act, *the link between freedom and truth is made manifest.* Precisely for this reason conscience expresses itself in acts of "judgment" which reflect the truth about the good, and not in arbitrary "decisions." The maturity and responsibility of these judgments—and, when all is said and done, of the individual who is their subject—are not measured by the liberation of the conscience from objective truth, in favor of an alleged autonomy in personal decisions, but, on the contrary, by an insistent search for truth and by allowing oneself to be guided by that truth in one's actions.

Seeking what is true and good

62. Conscience, as the judgment of an act, is not exempt from the possibility of error. As the Council puts it, "not infrequently conscience can be mistaken as a result of invincible ignorance, although it does not on that account forfeit its dignity; but this cannot be said when a man shows little concern for seeking what is true and good, and conscience gradually becomes almost blind from being accustomed to sin."[107] In these brief words the Council sums up the doctrine which the Church down the centuries has developed with regard to the *erroneous conscience.* Certainly, in order to have a "good conscience" (1 *Tim* 1:5), man must seek the truth and must make judgments in accordance with that same truth. As the Apostle Paul says, the conscience must be "confirmed by the Holy Spirit" (cf. *Rom* 9:1); it must be "clear" (2 *Tim* 1:3); it must not "practice cunning and tamper with God's word," but "openly state the truth" (cf. 2 *Cor* 4:2). On the other hand, the Apostle also warns Christians: "Do not be conformed to this world but be transformed by the renewal of your mind, that you may prove what is the will of God, what is good and acceptable and perfect" (*Rom* 12:2).

Paul's admonition urges us to be watchful, warning us that in the judgments of our conscience the possibility of error is always present. Conscience *is not an infallible judge;* it can make mistakes. However, error of conscience can be the result of an *invincible ignorance,* an ignorance of which the subject is not aware

---

107. Second Vatican Ecumenical Council, Pastoral Constitution on the Church in the Modern World *Gaudium et Spes,* 16.

and which he is unable to overcome by himself. The Council reminds us that in cases where such invincible ignorance is not culpable, conscience does not lose its dignity, because even when it directs us to act in a way not in conformity with the objective moral order, it continues to speak in the name of that truth about the good which the subject is called to seek sincerely.

63. In any event, it is always from the truth that the dignity of conscience derives. In the case of the correct conscience, it is a question of the *objective truth* received by man; in the case of the erroneous conscience, it is a question of what man, mistakenly, *subjectively* considers to be true. It is never acceptable to confuse a "subjective" error about moral good with the "objective" truth rationally proposed to man in virtue of his end, or to make the moral value of an act performed with a true and correct conscience equivalent to the moral value of an act performed by following the judgment of an erroneous conscience.[108] It is possible that the evil done as the result of invincible ignorance or a non-culpable error of judgment may not be imputable to the agent; but even in this case it does not cease to be an evil, a disorder in relation to the truth about the good. Furthermore, a good act which is not recognized as such does not contribute to the moral growth of the person who performs it; it does not perfect him and it does not help to dispose him for the supreme good. Thus, before feeling easily justified in the name of our conscience, we should reflect on the words of the Psalm: "Who can discern his errors? Clear me from hidden faults" (*Ps* 19:12). There are faults which we fail to see but which nevertheless remain faults, because we have refused to walk towards the light (cf. *Jn* 9:39–41).

Conscience, as the ultimate concrete judgment, compromises its dignity when it is *culpably erroneous*, that is to say, "when man shows little concern for seeking what is true and good, and conscience gradually becomes almost blind from being accustomed to sin."[109] Jesus alludes to the danger of the conscience being deformed when he warns: "The eye is the lamp of the body. So if your eye is sound, your whole body will be full of light; but if your eye is not sound, your whole body will be full of darkness. If then the light in you is darkness, how great is the darkness!" (*Mt* 6:22–23).

64. The words of Jesus just quoted also represent a call to *form our conscience*, to make it the object of a continuous conversion to what is true and to what is good. In the same vein, Saint Paul exhorts us not to be conformed to the mentality of this world, but to be transformed by the renewal of our mind (cf. *Rom* 12:2).

---

108. Cf. Saint Thomas Aquinas, *De Veritate*, q. 17, a. 4.

109. Second Vatican Ecumenical Council, Pastoral Constitution on the Church in the Modern World *Gaudium et Spes*, 16.

It is the "heart" converted to the Lord and to the love of what is good which is really the source of *true* judgments of conscience. Indeed, in order to "prove what is the will of God, what is good and acceptable and perfect" (*Rom* 12:2), knowledge of God's law in general is certainly necessary, but it is not sufficient: what is essential is a sort of *"connaturality" between man and the true good*.[110] Such a connaturality is rooted in and develops through the virtuous attitudes of the individual himself: prudence and the other cardinal virtues, and even before these the theological virtues of faith, hope and charity. This is the meaning of Jesus' saying: "He who does what is true comes to the light" (*Jn* 3:21).

Christians have a great help for the formation of conscience *in the Church and her Magisterium*. As the Council affirms: "In forming their consciences the Christian faithful must give careful attention to the sacred and certain teaching of the Church. For the Catholic Church is by the will of Christ the teacher of truth. Her charge is to announce and teach authentically that truth which is Christ, and at the same time with her authority to declare and confirm the principles of the moral order which derive from human nature itself."[111] It follows that the authority of the Church, when she pronounces on moral questions, in no way undermines the freedom of conscience of Christians. This is so not only because freedom of conscience is never freedom "from" the truth but always and only freedom "in" the truth, but also because the Magisterium does not bring to the Christian conscience truths which are extraneous to it; rather it brings to light the truths which it ought already to possess, developing them from the starting point of the primordial act of faith. The Church puts herself always and only at the *service of conscience*, helping it to avoid being tossed to and fro by every wind of doctrine proposed by human deceit (cf. *Eph* 4:14), and helping it not to swerve from the truth about the good of man, but rather, especially in more difficult questions, to attain the truth with certainty and to abide in it.

III. FUNDAMENTAL CHOICE AND
SPECIFIC KINDS OF BEHAVIOR

*"Only do not use your freedom as
an opportunity for the flesh" (Gal 5:13)*

65. The heightened concern for freedom in our own day has led many students of the behavioral and the theological sciences to develop a more

---

110. Cf. *Summa Theologiae* II-II, q. 45, a. 2.

111. Declaration on Religious Freedom *Dignitatis Humanae*, 14.

penetrating analysis of its nature and of its dynamics. It has been rightly pointed out that freedom is not only the choice for one or another particular action; it is also, within that choice, a *decision about oneself* and a setting of one's own life for or against the Good, for or against the Truth, and ultimately for or against God. Emphasis has rightly been placed on the importance of certain choices which "shape" a person's entire moral life, and which serve as bounds within which other particular everyday choices can be situated and allowed to develop.

Some authors, however, have proposed an even more radical revision of the *relationship between person and acts*. They speak of a "fundamental freedom," deeper than and different from freedom of choice, which needs to be considered if human actions are to be correctly understood and evaluated. According to these authors, the *key role in the moral life* is to be attributed to a "fundamental option," brought about by that fundamental freedom whereby the person makes an over-all self-determination, not through a specific and conscious decision on the level of reflection, but in a "transcendental" and "athematic" way. *Particular acts* which flow from this option would constitute only partial and never definitive attempts to give it expression; they would only be its "signs" or symptoms. The immediate object of such acts would not be absolute Good (before which the freedom of the person would be expressed on a transcendental level), but particular (also termed "categorical") goods. In the opinion of some theologians, none of these goods, which by their nature are partial, could determine the freedom of man as a person in his totality, even though it is only by bringing them about or refusing to do so that man is able to express his own fundamental option.

A *distinction* thus comes to be introduced *between the fundamental option and deliberate choices of a concrete kind of behavior.* In some authors this division tends to become a *separation*, when they expressly limit moral "good" and "evil" to the transcendental dimension proper to the fundamental option, and describe as "right" or "wrong" the choices of particular "innerworldly" kinds of behavior: those, in other words, concerning man's relationship with himself, with others and with the material world. There thus appears to be established within human acting a clear disjunction between two levels of morality: on the one hand the order of good and evil, which is dependent on the will, and on the other hand specific kinds of behavior, which are judged to be morally right or wrong only on the basis of a technical calculation of the proportion between the "premoral" or "physical" goods and evils which actually result from the action. This is pushed to the point where a concrete kind of behavior, even one freely chosen, comes to be considered as a merely physical process, and not according to the criteria proper to a human act. The conclusion to which this eventually leads is that the properly moral assessment of the person is reserved to his fundamental option, prescinding in whole or in part from his choice of particular actions, of concrete kinds of behavior.

66. There is no doubt that Christian moral teaching, even in its Biblical roots, acknowledges the specific importance of a fundamental choice which qualifies the moral life and engages freedom on a radical level before God. It is a question of the decision of faith, of the *obedience of faith* (cf. *Rom* 16:26) "by which man makes a total and free self-commitment to God, offering 'the full submission of intellect and will to God as he reveals.'"[112] This faith, which works through love (cf. *Gal* 5:6), comes from the core of man, from his "heart" (cf. *Rom* 10:10), whence it is called to bear fruit in works (cf. *Mt* 12:33–35; *Lk* 6:43–45; *Rom* 8:5–10; *Gal* 5:22). In the Decalogue one finds, as an introduction to the various commandments, the basic clause: "I am the Lord your God …" (*Ex* 20:2), which, by impressing upon the numerous and varied particular prescriptions their primordial meaning, gives the morality of the Covenant its aspect of completeness, unity and profundity. Israel's fundamental decision, then, is about the fundamental commandment (cf. *Jos* 24:14–25; *Ex* 19:3–8; *Mic* 6:8). The morality of the New Covenant is similarly dominated by the fundamental call of Jesus to follow him—thus he also says to the young man: "If you wish to be perfect … then come, follow me" (*Mt* 19:21); to this call the disciple must respond with a radical decision and choice. The Gospel parables of the treasure and the pearl of great price, for which one sells all one's possessions, are eloquent and effective images of the radical and unconditional nature of the decision demanded by the Kingdom of God. The radical nature of the decision to follow Jesus is admirably expressed in his own words: "Whoever would save his life will lose it; and whoever loses his life for my sake and the Gospel's will save it" (*Mk* 8:35).

Jesus' call to "come, follow me" marks the greatest possible exaltation of human freedom, yet at the same time it witnesses to the truth and to the obligation of acts of faith and of decisions which can be described as involving a fundamental option. We find a similar exaltation of human freedom in the words of Saint Paul: "You were called to freedom, brethren" (*Gal* 5:13). But the Apostle immediately adds a grave warning: "Only do not use your freedom as an opportunity for the flesh." This warning echoes his earlier words: "For freedom Christ has set us free; stand fast therefore, and do not submit again to a yoke of slavery" (*Gal* 5:1). Paul encourages us to be watchful, because freedom is always threatened by slavery. And this is precisely the case when an act of faith—in the sense

---

112. Second Vatican Ecumenical Council, Dogmatic Constitution on Divine Revelation, *Dei Verbum*, 5; cf. First Vatican Ecumenical Council, Dogmatic Constitution on the Catholic Faith *Dei Filius*, Chap. 3: *DS*, 3008.

of a fundamental option—becomes separated from the choice of particular acts, as in the tendencies mentioned above.

67. These tendencies are therefore contrary to the teaching of Scripture itself, which sees the fundamental option as a genuine choice of freedom and links that choice profoundly to particular acts. By his fundamental choice, man is capable of giving his life direction and of progressing, with the help of grace, towards his end, following God's call. But this capacity is actually exercised in the particular choices of specific actions, through which man deliberately conforms himself to God's will, wisdom and law. It thus needs to be stated that *the so-called fundamental option, to the extent that it is distinct from a generic intention* and hence one not yet determined in such a way that freedom is obligated, *is always brought into play through conscious and free decisions*. Precisely for this reason, *it is revoked when man engages his freedom in conscious decisions to the contrary, with regard to morally grave matter.*

To separate the fundamental option from concrete kinds of behavior means to contradict the substantial integrity or personal unity of the moral agent in his body and in his soul. A fundamental option understood without explicit consideration of the potentialities which it puts into effect and the determinations which express it does not do justice to the rational finality immanent in man's acting and in each of his deliberate decisions. In point of fact, the morality of human acts is not deduced only from one's intention, orientation or fundamental option, understood as an intention devoid of a clearly determined binding content or as an intention with no corresponding positive effort to fulfill the different obligations of the moral life. Judgments about morality cannot be made without taking into consideration whether or not the deliberate choice of a specific kind of behavior is in conformity with the dignity and integral vocation of the human person. Every choice always implies a reference by the deliberate will to the goods and evils indicated by the natural law as goods to be pursued and evils to be avoided. In the case of the positive moral precepts, prudence always has the task of verifying that they apply in a specific situation, for example, in view of other duties which may be more important or urgent. But the negative moral precepts, those prohibiting certain concrete actions or kinds of behavior as intrinsically evil, do not allow for any legitimate exception. They do not leave room, in any morally acceptable way, for the "creativity" of any contrary determination whatsoever. Once the moral species of an action prohibited by a universal rule is concretely recognized, the only morally good act is that of obeying the moral law and of refraining from the action which it forbids.

68. Here an important pastoral consideration must be added. According to the logic of the positions mentioned above, an individual could, by virtue of a

fundamental option, remain faithful to God independently of whether or not certain of his choices and his acts are in conformity with specific moral norms or rules. By virtue of a primordial option for charity, that individual could continue to be morally good, persevere in God's grace and attain salvation, even if certain of his specific kinds of behavior were deliberately and gravely contrary to God's commandments as set forth by the Church.

In point of fact, man does not suffer perdition only by being unfaithful to that fundamental option whereby he has made "a free self-commitment to God."[113] With every freely committed mortal sin, he offends God as the giver of the law and as a result becomes guilty with regard to the entire law (cf. *Jas* 2:8–11); even if he perseveres in faith, he loses "sanctifying grace," "charity" and "eternal happiness."[114] As the Council of Trent teaches, "the grace of justification once received is lost not only by apostasy, by which faith itself is lost, but also by any other mortal sin."[115]

Mortal and venial sin

69. As we have just seen, reflection on the fundamental option has also led some theologians to undertake a basic revision of the traditional distinction between *mortal* sins and *venial* sins. They insist that the opposition to God's law which causes the loss of sanctifying grace—and eternal damnation, when one dies in such a state of sin—could only be the result of an act which engages the person in his totality: in other words, an act of fundamental option. According to these theologians, mortal sin, which separates man from God, only exists in the rejection of God, carried out at a level of freedom which is neither to be identified with an act of choice nor capable of becoming the object of conscious awareness. Consequently, they go on to say, it is difficult, at least psychologically, to accept the fact that a Christian, who wishes to remain united to Jesus Christ and to his Church, could so easily and repeatedly commit mortal sins, as the "matter" itself of his actions would sometimes indicate. Likewise, it would be hard to accept that man is able, in a brief lapse of time, to sever radically the bond of communion with God and afterwards be converted to him by sincere repentance. The

---

113. Second Vatican Ecumenical Council, Dogmatic Constitution on Divine Revelation *Dei Verbum*, 5. Cf. Sacred Congregation for the Doctrine of the Faith, Declaration on Certain Questions Concerning Sexual Ethics *Persona Humana* (December 29, 1975),10: *AAS* 68 (1976), 88–90.

114. Cf. Post-Synodal Apostolic Exhoration *Reconciliatio et Paenitentia* (December 2, 1984), 17; *AAS* 77 (1985), 218–23.

115. Sess. VI, Decree on Justification *Cum Hoc Tempore*, Chap. 15: *DS*, 1544; Canon 19: *DS*, 1569.

gravity of sin, they maintain, ought to be measured by the degree of engagement of the freedom of the person performing an act, rather than by the matter of that act.

70. The Post-Synodal Apostolic Exhortation *Reconciliatio et Paenitentia* reaffirmed the importance and permanent validity of the distinction between mortal and venial sins, in accordance with the Church's tradition. And the 1983 Synod of Bishops, from which that Exhortation emerged, "not only reaffirmed the teaching of the Council of Trent concerning the existence and nature of mortal and venial sins, but it also recalled that mortal sin is sin whose object is grave matter and which is also committed with full knowledge and deliberate consent."[116]

The statement of the Council of Trent does not only consider the "grave matter" of mortal sin; it also recalls that its necessary condition is "full awareness and deliberate consent." In any event, both in moral theology and in pastoral practice one is familiar with cases in which an act which is grave by reason of its matter does not constitute a mortal sin because of a lack of full awareness or deliberate consent on the part of the person performing it. Even so, "care will have to be taken not to reduce mortal sin to an act of *'fundamental option'*—as is commonly said today—against God," seen either as an explicit and formal rejection of God and neighbor or as an implicit and unconscious rejection of love. "For mortal sin exists also when a person knowingly and willingly, for whatever reason, chooses something gravely disordered. In fact, such a choice already includes contempt for the divine law, a rejection of God's love for humanity and the whole of creation: the person turns away from God and loses charity. Consequently, *the fundamental orientation can be radically changed by particular acts.* Clearly, situations can occur which are very complex and obscure from a psychological viewpoint, and which influence the sinner's subjective imputability. But from a consideration of the psychological sphere one cannot proceed to create a theological category, which is precisely what the 'fundamental option' is, understanding it in such a way that it objectively changes or casts doubt upon the traditional concept of mortal sin."[117]

The separation of fundamental option from deliberate choices of particular kinds of behavior, disordered in themselves or in their circumstances, which would not engage that option, thus involves a denial of Catholic doctrine on *mortal sin:* "With the whole tradition of the Church, we call mortal sin the act

---

116. Post-Synodal Apostolic Exhoration *Reconciliatio et Paenitentia* (December 2, 1984), 17: *AAS* 77 (1985), 221.

117. Ibid., 223.

by which man freely and consciously rejects God, his law, the covenant of love that God offers, preferring to turn in on himself or to some created and finite reality, something contrary to the divine will (*conversio ad creaturam*). This can occur in a direct and formal way, in the sins of idolatry, apostasy and atheism; or in an equivalent way, as in every act of disobedience to God's commandments in a grave matter."[118]

IV. THE MORAL ACT

Teleology and teleologism

71. The relationship between man's freedom and God's law, which has its intimate and living centre in the moral conscience, is manifested and realized in human acts. It is precisely through his acts that man attains perfection as man, as one who is called to seek his Creator of his own accord and freely to arrive at full and blessed perfection by cleaving to him.[119]

Human acts are moral acts because they express and determine the goodness or evil of the individual who performs them.[120] They do not produce a change merely in the state of affairs outside of man but, to the extent that they are deliberate choices, they give moral definition to the very person who performs them, determining his *profound spiritual traits*. This was perceptively noted by Saint Gregory of Nyssa: "All things subject to change and to becoming never remain constant, but continually pass from one state to another, for better or worse ... Now, human life is always subject to change; it needs to be born ever anew ... But here birth does not come about by a foreign intervention, as is the case with bodily beings ...; it is the result of a free choice. Thus we are in a certain way our own parents, creating ourselves as we will, by our decisions."[121]

72. The *morality of acts* is defined by the relationship of man's freedom with the authentic good. This good is established, as the eternal law, by Divine Wisdom which orders every being towards its end: this eternal law is known both by man's natural reason (hence it is "natural law"), and—in an integral and perfect way—by God's supernatural Revelation (hence it is called "divine law"). Acting is morally good when the choices of freedom are in conformity with man's

---

118. Ibid., 222.

119. Cf. Second Vatican Ecumenical Council, Pastoral Constitution on the Church in the Modern World *Gaudium et Spes*, 17.

120. Cf. *Summa Theologiae* I-II, q. 1, a. 3: "*Idem sunt actus morales et actus humani.*"

121. *De Vita Moysis*, II, 2–3: PG 44, 327–28.

true good and thus express the voluntary ordering of the person towards his ultimate end: God himself, the supreme good in whom man finds his full and perfect happiness. The first question in the young man's conversation with Jesus: "What good must I do to have eternal life?" (*Mt* 19:6) immediately brings out *the essential connection between the moral value of an act and man's final end.* Jesus, in his reply, confirms the young man's conviction: the performance of good acts, commanded by the One who "alone is good," constitutes the indispensable condition of and path to eternal blessedness: "If you wish to enter into life, keep the commandments" (*Mt* 19:17). Jesus' answer and his reference to the commandments also make it clear that the path to that end is marked by respect for the divine laws which safeguard human good. *Only the act in conformity with the good can be a path that leads to life.*

The rational ordering of the human act to the good in its truth and the voluntary pursuit of that good, known by reason, constitute morality. Hence human activity cannot be judged as morally good merely because it is a means for attaining one or another of its goals, or simply because the subject's intention is good.[122] Activity is morally good when it attests to and expresses the voluntary ordering of the person to his ultimate end and the conformity of a concrete action with the human good as it is acknowledged in its truth by reason. If the object of the concrete action is not in harmony with the true good of the person, the choice of that action makes our will and ourselves morally evil, thus putting us in conflict with our ultimate end, the supreme good, God himself.

73. The Christian, thanks to God's Revelation and to faith, is aware of the "newness" which characterizes the morality of his actions: these actions are called to show either consistency or inconsistency with that dignity and vocation which have been bestowed on him by grace. In Jesus Christ and in his Spirit, the Christian is a "new creation," a child of God; by his actions he shows his likeness or unlikeness to the image of the Son who is the first-born among many brethren (cf. *Rom* 8:29), he lives out his fidelity or infidelity to the gift of the Spirit, and he opens or closes himself to eternal life, to the communion of vision, love and happiness with God the Father, Son and Holy Spirit.[123] As Saint Cyril of Alexandria writes, Christ "forms us according to his image, in such a way that the traits of his divine nature shine forth in us through sanctification and justice and

---

122. Cf. *Summa Theologiae* II-II, q. 148, a. 3.

123. The Second Vatican Council, in the Pastoral Constitution on the Church in the Modern World, makes this clear: "This applies not only to Christians but to all men of good will in whose hearts grace is secretly at work. Since Christ died for all and since man's ultimate calling comes from God and is therefore a universal one, we are obliged to hold that the Holy Spirit offers to all the possibility of sharing in this paschal mystery in a manner known to God": *Gaudium et Spes*, 22.

the life which is good and in conformity with virtue ... The beauty of this image shines forth in us who are in Christ, when we show ourselves to be good in our works."[124]

Consequently the moral life has an essential *"teleological" character*, since it consists in the deliberate ordering of human acts to God, the supreme good and ultimate end (*telos*) of man. This is attested to once more by the question posed by the young man to Jesus: "What good must I do to have eternal life?" But this ordering to one's ultimate end is not something subjective, dependent solely upon one's intention. It presupposes that such acts are in themselves capable of being ordered to this end, insofar as they are in conformity with the authentic moral good of man, safeguarded by the commandments. This is what Jesus himself points out in his reply to the young man: "If you wish to enter into life, keep the commandments" (*Mt* 19:17).

Clearly such an ordering must be rational and free, conscious and deliberate, by virtue of which man is "responsible" for his actions and subject to the judgment of God, the just and good judge who, as the Apostle Paul reminds us, rewards good and punishes evil: "We must all appear before the judgment seat of Christ, so that each one may receive good or evil, according to what he has done in the body" (*2 Cor* 5:10).

74. But on what does the moral assessment of man's free acts depend? What is it that ensures this *ordering of human acts to God*? Is it the *intention* of the acting subject, the *circumstances*—and in particular the consequences—of his action, or the *object* itself of his act?

This is what is traditionally called the problem of the "sources of morality." Precisely with regard to this problem there have emerged in the last few decades new or newly-revived theological and cultural trends which call for careful discernment on the part of the Church's Magisterium.

Certain *ethical theories*, called *"teleological,"* claim to be concerned for the conformity of human acts with the ends pursued by the agent and with the values intended by him. The criteria for evaluating the moral rightness of an action are drawn from the *weighing of the non-moral or pre-moral goods* to be gained and the corresponding non-moral or pre-moral values to be respected. For some, concrete behavior would be right or wrong according to whether or not it is capable of producing a better state of affairs for all concerned. Right conduct would be the one capable of "maximizing" goods and "minimizing" evils.

---

124. *Tractatus ad Tiberium Diaconum sociosque*, II. *Responsiones ad Tiberium Diaconum sociosque*: Saint Cyril of Alexandria, *In Divi Johannis Evangelium*, vol. III, ed. Philip Edward Pusey, Brussels, Culture et Civilisation (1965), 590.

Many of the Catholic moralists who follow in this direction seek to distance themselves from utilitarianism and pragmatism, where the morality of human acts would be judged without any reference to the man's true ultimate end. They rightly recognize the need to find ever more consistent rational arguments in order to justify the requirements and to provide a foundation for the norms of the moral life. This kind of investigation is legitimate and necessary, since the moral order, as established by the natural law, is in principle accessible to human reason. Furthermore, such investigation is well-suited to meeting the demands of dialogue and cooperation with non-Catholics and non-believers, especially in pluralistic societies.

75. But as part of the effort to work out such a rational morality (for this reason it is sometimes called an "autonomous morality") there exist *false solutions, linked in particular to an inadequate understanding of the object of moral action. Some authors* do not take into sufficient consideration the fact that the will is involved in the concrete choices which it makes: these choices are a condition of its moral goodness and its being ordered to the ultimate end of the person. *Others* are inspired by a notion of freedom which prescinds from the actual conditions of its exercise, from its objective reference to the truth about the good, and from its determination through choices of concrete kinds of behavior. According to these theories, free will would neither be morally subjected to specific obligations nor shaped by its choices, while nonetheless still remaining responsible for its own acts and for their consequences. This *"teleologism,"* as a method for discovering the moral norm, can thus be called—according to terminology and approaches imported from different currents of thought—*"consequentialism"* or *"proportionalism."* The former claims to draw the criteria of the rightness of a given way of acting solely from a calculation of foreseeable consequences deriving from a given choice. The latter, by weighing the various values and goods being sought, focuses rather on the proportion acknowledged between the good and bad effects of that choice, with a view to the "greater good" or "lesser evil" actually possible in a particular situation.

The teleological ethical theories (proportionalism, consequentialism), while acknowledging that moral values are indicated by reason and by Revelation, maintain that it is never possible to formulate an absolute prohibition of particular kinds of behavior which would be in conflict, in every circumstance and in every culture, with those values. The acting subject would indeed be responsible for attaining the values pursued, but in two ways: the values or goods involved in a human act would be, from one viewpoint, *of the moral order* (in relation to properly moral values, such as love of God and neighbor, justice, etc.) and, from another viewpoint, *of the pre-moral order,* which some term non-moral, physical or ontic (in relation to the advantages and disadvantages accruing both to the agent and to all other persons possibly involved, such as, for example, health or its endangerment, physical integrity, life, death, loss of material goods, etc.). In a world where goodness is always mixed with evil, and every good effect linked to other evil effects, the morality of an act would be judged in two different ways: its moral "goodness" would be judged on the basis of the subject's intention in reference to moral goods, and its "rightness" on the basis of a consideration of its foreseeable effects or consequences and of their proportion. Consequently, concrete kinds of behavior could be described as "right" or "wrong," without it being thereby possible to judge as morally "good" or "bad" the will of the person choosing them. In this way, an act which, by contradicting a universal negative norm, directly violates goods considered as "pre-moral" could be qualified as morally acceptable if the intention of the subject is focused, in accordance with a "responsible" assessment of the goods involved in the concrete action, on the moral value judged to be decisive in the situation.

The evaluation of the consequences of the action, based on the proportion between the act and its effects and between the effects themselves, would regard only the pre-moral order. The moral specificity of acts, that is their goodness or evil, would be determined exclusively by the faithfulness of the person to the highest values of charity and prudence, without this faithfulness necessarily being incompatible with choices contrary to certain particular moral precepts. Even when grave matter is concerned, these precepts should be considered as operative norms which are always relative and open to exceptions.

In this view, deliberate consent to certain kinds of behavior declared illicit by traditional moral theology would not imply an objective moral evil.

The object of the deliberate act

76. These theories can gain a certain persuasive force from their affinity to the scientific mentality, which is rightly concerned with ordering technical and economic activities on the basis of a calculation of resources and profits, procedures and their effects. They seek to provide liberation from the constraints of a voluntaristic and arbitrary morality of obligation which would ultimately be dehumanizing.

Such theories however are not faithful to the Church's teaching, when they believe they can justify, as morally good, deliberate choices of kinds of behavior contrary to the commandments of the divine and natural law. These theories cannot claim to be grounded in the Catholic moral tradition. Although the latter did witness the development of a casuistry which tried to assess the best ways to achieve the good in certain concrete situations, it is nonetheless true that this casuistry concerned only cases in which the law was uncertain, and thus the absolute validity of negative moral precepts, which oblige without exception, was not called into question. The faithful are obliged to acknowledge and respect the specific moral precepts declared and taught by the Church in the name of God, the Creator and Lord.[125] When the Apostle Paul sums up the fulfillment of the law in the precept of love of neighbor as oneself (cf. *Rom* 13:8–10), he is not weakening the commandments but reinforcing them, since he is revealing their requirements and their gravity. *Love of God and of one's neighbor cannot be separated from the observance of the commandments of the Covenant* renewed in the blood of Jesus Christ and in the gift of the Spirit. It is an honor characteristic of Christians to obey God rather than men (cf. *Acts* 4:19; 5:29) and accept even martyrdom as a consequence, like the holy men and women of the Old and New Testaments, who are considered such because they gave their lives rather than perform this or that particular act contrary to faith or virtue.

77. In order to offer rational criteria for a right moral decision, the theories mentioned above take account of the intention and *consequences* of human action. Certainly there is need to take into account both the intention—as Jesus forcefully insisted in clear disagreement with the scribes and Pharisees, who prescribed in great detail certain outward practices without paying attention to the heart (cf. *Mk* 7:20–21; *Mt* 15:19)—and the goods obtained and the evils avoided as a result of a particular act. Responsibility demands as much. But the consideration of these consequences, and also of intentions, is not sufficient for judging the moral quality of a concrete choice. The weighing of the goods and evils foreseeable as the consequence of an action is not an adequate method for determining whether the choice of that concrete kind of behavior is "according to its species," or "in itself," morally good or bad, licit or illicit. The foreseeable consequences are part of those circumstances of the act, which, while capable of lessening the gravity of an evil act, nonetheless cannot alter its moral species.

Moreover, everyone recognizes the difficulty, or rather the impossibility, of evaluating all the good and evil consequences and effects—defined as pre-moral—of one's own acts: an exhaustive rational calculation is not possible. How then can one go about establishing proportions which depend on a measuring, the criteria of which remain obscure? How could an absolute obligation be justified on the basis of such debatable calculations?

125. Cf. Ecumenical Council of Trent, Session VI, Decree on Justification *Cum Hoc Tempore*, Canon 19: *DS*, 1569. See also: Clement XI, Constitution *Unigenitus Dei Filius* (September 8, 1713) against the Errors of Paschasius Quesnel, Nos. 53–56: *DS*, 2453–56.

78. *The morality of the human act depends primarily and fundamentally on the "object" rationally chosen by the deliberate will,* as is borne out by the insightful analysis, still valid today, made by Saint Thomas.[126] In order to be able to grasp the object of an act which specifies that act morally, it is therefore necessary to place oneself *in the perspective of the acting person.* The object of the act of willing is in fact a freely chosen kind of behavior. To the extent that it is in conformity with the order of reason, it is the cause of the goodness of the will; it perfects us morally, and disposes us to recognize our ultimate end in the perfect good, primordial love. By the object of a given moral act, then, one cannot mean a process or an event of the merely physical order, to be assessed on the basis of its ability to bring about a given state of affairs in the outside world. Rather, that object is the proximate end of a deliberate decision which determines the act of willing on the part of the acting person. Consequently, as the *Catechism of the Catholic Church* teaches, "there are certain specific kinds of behavior that are always wrong to choose, because choosing them involves a disorder of the will, that is, a moral evil."[127] And Saint Thomas observes that "it often happens that man acts with a good intention, but without spiritual gain, because he lacks a good will. Let us say that someone robs in order to feed the poor: in this case, even though the intention is good, the uprightness of the will is lacking. Consequently, no evil done with a good intention can be excused. 'There are those who say: And why not do evil that good may come? Their condemnation is just' (*Rom* 3:8)."[128]

The reason why a good intention is not itself sufficient, but a correct choice of actions is also needed, is that the human act depends on its object, whether that object is *capable or not of being ordered* to God, to the One who "alone is good," and thus brings about the perfection of the person. An act is therefore good, if its object is in conformity with the good of the person with respect to the goods morally relevant for him. Christian ethics, which pays particular attention to the moral object, does not refuse to consider the inner "teleology" of acting, inasmuch as it is directed to promoting the true good of the person; but it recognizes that it is really pursued only when the essential elements of human nature are respected. The human act, good according to its object, is also *capable of being ordered* to its ultimate end. That same act then attains its ultimate and decisive perfection when the will *actually does order* it to God through charity. As the Patron of moral theologians and confessors teaches: "It is not enough to do good

---

126. Cf. *Summa Theologiae* I-II, q. 18, a. 6.

127. *Catechism of the Catholic Church,* n. 1761.

128. *In Duo Praecepta Caritatis et in Decem Legis Praecepta. De Dilectione Dei: Opuscula Theologica,* II, No. 1168, ed. Taurinen (1954), 250.

works; they need to be done well. For our works to be good and perfect, they must be done for the sole purpose of pleasing God."[129]

"Intrinsic evil": it is not licit to do evil that good may come of it (cf. Rom 3:8)

79. *One must therefore reject the thesis,* characteristic of teleological and proportionalist theories, *which holds that it is impossible to qualify as morally evil according to its species—its "object"—the deliberate choice of certain kinds of behavior or specific acts, apart from a consideration of the intention for which the choice is made or the totality of the foreseeable consequences of that act for all persons concerned.*

The primary and decisive element for moral judgment is the object of the human act, which establishes whether it is *capable of being ordered to the good and to the ultimate end, which is God.* This capability is grasped by reason in the very being of man, considered in his integral truth, and therefore in his natural inclinations, his motivations and his finalities, which always have a spiritual dimension as well. It is precisely these which are the contents of the natural law and hence that ordered complex of "personal goods" which serve the "good of the person": the good which is the person himself and his perfection. These are the goods safeguarded by the commandments, which, according to Saint Thomas, contain the whole natural law.[130]

80. Reason attests that there are objects of the human act which are by their nature "incapable of being ordered" to God, because they radically contradict the good of the person made in his image. These are the acts which, in the Church's moral tradition, have been termed "intrinsically evil" (*intrinsece malum*): they are such *always and per se,* in other words, on account of their very object, and quite apart from the ulterior intentions of the one acting and the circumstances. Consequently, without in the least denying the influence on morality exercised by circumstances and especially by intentions, the Church teaches that "there exist acts which *per se* and in themselves, independently of circumstances, are always seriously wrong by reason of their object."[131] The

---

129. Saint Alphonsus Maria De Liguori, *Pratica di amar Gesù Cristo,* VII, 3.

130. Cf. *Summa Theologiae* I-II, q. 100, a. 1.

131. Post-Synodal Apostolic Exhortation *Reconciliatio et Paenitentia* (December 2, 1984), 17: *AAS* 77 (1985), 221; cf. Paul VI, *Address* to Members of the Congregation of the Most Holy Redeemer (September 1967): *AAS* 59 (1967), 962: "Far be it from Christians to be led to embrace another opinion, as if the Council taught that nowadays some things are permitted which the Church had previously declared intrinsically evil. Who does not see in this the rise of a depraved moral relativism, one that clearly endangers the Church's entire doctrinal heritage?"

Second Vatican Council itself, in discussing the respect due to the human person, gives a number of examples of such acts: "Whatever is hostile to life itself, such as any kind of homicide, genocide, abortion, euthanasia and voluntary suicide; whatever violates the integrity of the human person, such as mutilation, physical and mental torture and attempts to coerce the spirit; whatever is offensive to human dignity, such as subhuman living conditions, arbitrary imprisonment, deportation, slavery, prostitution and trafficking in women and children; degrading conditions of work which treat laborers as mere instruments of profit, and not as free responsible persons: all these and the like are a disgrace, and so long as they infect human civilization they contaminate those who inflict them more than those who suffer injustice, and they are a negation of the honor due to the Creator."[132]

With regard to intrinsically evil acts, and in reference to contraceptive practices whereby the conjugal act is intentionally rendered infertile, Pope Paul VI teaches: "Though it is true that sometimes it is lawful to tolerate a lesser moral evil in order to avoid a greater evil or in order to promote a greater good, it is never lawful, even for the gravest reasons, to do evil that good may come of it (cf. *Rom* 3:8)—in other words, to intend directly something which of its very nature contradicts the moral order, and which must therefore be judged unworthy of man, even though the intention is to protect or promote the welfare of an individual, of a family or of society in general."[133]

81. In teaching the existence of intrinsically evil acts, the Church accepts the teaching of Sacred Scripture. The Apostle Paul emphatically states: "Do not be deceived: neither the immoral, nor idolaters, nor adulterers, nor sexual perverts, nor thieves, nor the greedy, nor drunkards, nor revilers, nor robbers will inherit the Kingdom of God" (1 *Cor* 6:9–10).

If acts are intrinsically evil, a good intention or particular circumstances can diminish their evil, but they cannot remove it. They remain "irremediably" evil acts; *per se* and in themselves they are not capable of being ordered to God and to the good of the person. "As for acts which are themselves sins (*cum iam opera ipsa peccata sunt*)," Saint Augustine writes, "like theft, fornication, blasphemy, who would dare affirm that, by doing them for good motives (*causis bonis*), they would no longer be sins, or, what is even more absurd, that they would be sins that are justified?"[134]

---

132. Pastoral Constitution on the Church in the Modern World *Gaudium et Spes*, 27.

133. Encyclical Letter *Humanae Vitae* (July 25, 1968), 14: *AAS* 60 (1968), 490–91.

134. *Contra Mendacium*, VII, 18: *PL* 40, 528; cf. Saint Thomas Aquinas, *Quaestiones Quodlibetales*, IX, q. 7, a. 2; *Catechism of the Catholic Church*, nn. 1753–55.

Consequently, circumstances or intentions can never transform an act intrinsically evil by virtue of its object into an act "subjectively" good or defensible as a choice.

82. Furthermore, an intention is good when it has as its aim the true good of the person in view of his ultimate end. But acts whose object is "not capable of being ordered" to God and "unworthy of the human person" are always and in every case in conflict with that good. Consequently, respect for norms which prohibit such acts and oblige *semper et pro semper,* that is, without any exception, not only does not inhibit a good intention, but actually represents its basic expression.

The doctrine of the object as a source of morality represents an authentic explicitation of the Biblical morality of the Covenant and of the commandments, of charity and of the virtues. The moral quality of human acting is dependent on this fidelity to the commandments, as an expression of obedience and of love. For this reason—we repeat—the opinion must be rejected as erroneous which maintains that it is impossible to qualify as morally evil according to its species the deliberate choice of certain kinds of behavior or specific acts, without taking into account the intention for which the choice was made or the totality of the foreseeable consequences of that act for all persons concerned. Without the *rational determination of the morality of human acting* as stated above, it would be impossible to affirm the existence of an "objective moral order"[135] and to establish any particular norm the content of which would be binding without exception. This would be to the detriment of human fraternity and the truth about the good, and would be injurious to ecclesial communion as well.

83. As is evident, in the question of the morality of human acts, and in particular the question of whether there exist intrinsically evil acts, we find ourselves faced with *the question of man himself,* of his *truth* and of the moral consequences flowing from that truth. By acknowledging and teaching the existence of intrinsic evil in given human acts, the Church remains faithful to the integral truth about man; she thus respects and promotes man in his dignity and vocation. Consequently, she must reject the theories set forth above, which contradict this truth.

Dear Brothers in the Episcopate, we must not be content merely to warn the faithful about the errors and dangers of certain ethical theories. We must first of all show the inviting splendor of that truth which is Jesus Christ himself. In him, who is the Truth (cf. *Jn* 14:6), man can understand fully and live perfectly, through his good actions, his vocation to freedom in obedience to the divine law

---

135. Second Vatican Ecumenical Council, Declaration on Religious Freedom *Dignitatis Humanae,* 7.

summarized in the commandment of love of God and neighbor. And this is what takes place through the gift of the Holy Spirit, the Spirit of truth, of freedom and of love: in him we are enabled to interiorize the law, to receive it and to live it as the motivating force of true personal freedom: "the perfect law, the law of liberty" (*Jas* 1:25).

CHAPTER III
"LEST THE CROSS OF CHRIST BE EMPTIED OF ITS POWER"
(*1 Cor 1:17*)

Moral good for the life of the Church and of the world

"For freedom Christ has set us free" (Gal 5:1).

84. The *fundamental question* which the moral theories mentioned above pose in a particularly forceful way is that of the relationship of man's freedom to God's law; it is ultimately the question of the *relationship between freedom and truth*. According to Christian faith and the Church's teaching, "only the freedom which submits to the Truth leads the human person to his true good. The good of the person is to be in the Truth and to *do* the Truth."[136]

A comparison between the Church's teaching and today's social and cultural situation immediately makes clear the urgent need *for the Church herself to develop an intense pastoral effort precisely with regard to this fundamental question.* "This essential bond between Truth, the Good and Freedom has been largely lost sight of by present-day culture. As a result, helping man to rediscover it represents nowadays one of the specific requirements of the Church's mission, for the salvation of the world. Pilate's question: 'What is truth?' reflects the distressing perplexity of a man who often no longer knows *who he is, whence* he comes and *where* he is going. Hence we not infrequently witness the fearful plunging of the human person into situations of gradual self-destruction. According to some, it appears that one no longer need acknowledge the enduring absoluteness of any moral value. All around us we encounter contempt for human life after conception and before birth; the ongoing violation of basic rights of the person; the unjust destruction of goods minimally necessary for a human life. Indeed, something more serious has happened: man is no longer convinced that only in the

---

136. Address to those taking part in the International Congress of Moral Theology (April 10, 1986), 1: *Insegnamenti* IX, 1 (1986), 970.

truth can he find salvation. The saving power of the truth is contested, and freedom alone, uprooted from any objectivity, is left to decide by itself what is good and what is evil. This relativism becomes, in the field of theology, a lack of trust in the wisdom of God, who guides man with the moral law. Concrete situations are unfavorably contrasted with the precepts of the moral law, nor is it any longer maintained that, when all is said and done, the law of God is always the one true good of man."[137]

85. The discernment which the Church carries out with regard to these ethical theories is not simply limited to denouncing and refuting them. In a positive way, the Church seeks, with great love, to help all the faithful to form a moral conscience which will make judgments and lead to decisions in accordance with the truth, following the exhortation of the Apostle Paul: "Do not be conformed to this world but be transformed by the renewal of your mind, that you may prove what is the will of God, what is good and acceptable and perfect" (*Rom* 12:2). This effort by the Church finds its support—the "secret" of its educative power—not so much in doctrinal statements and pastoral appeals to vigilance, as in *constantly looking to the Lord Jesus*. Each day the Church looks to Christ with unfailing love, fully aware that the true and final answer to the problem of morality lies in him alone. In a particular way, it is *in the Crucified Christ* that *the Church finds the answer* to the question troubling so many people today: how can obedience to universal and unchanging moral norms respect the uniqueness and individuality of the person, and not represent a threat to his freedom and dignity? The Church makes her own the Apostle Paul's awareness of the mission he had received: "Christ ... sent me ... to preach the Gospel, and not with eloquent wisdom, lest the cross of Christ be emptied of its power. ... We preach Christ crucified, a stumbling block to Jews and folly to Gentiles, but to those who are called, both Jews and Greeks, Christ the power of God and the wisdom of God" (1 *Cor* 1:17, 23–24). *The Crucified Christ reveals the authentic meaning of freedom; he lives it fully in the total gift of himself* and calls his disciples to share in his freedom.

86. Rational reflection and daily experience demonstrate the weakness which marks man's freedom. That freedom is real but limited: its absolute and unconditional origin is not in itself, but in the life within which it is situated and which represents for it, at one and the same time, both a limitation and a possibility. Human freedom belongs to us as creatures; it is a freedom which is given as a gift, one to be received like a seed and to be cultivated responsibly. It is an essential part of that creaturely image which is the basis of the dignity of the person.

---

137. Address to those taking part in the International Congress of Moral Theology (April 10, 1986), 2: *Insegnamenti* IX, 1 (1986), 970–71.

Within that freedom there is an echo of the primordial vocation whereby the Creator calls man to the true Good, and even more, through Christ's revelation, to become his friend and to share his own divine life. It is at once inalienable self-possession and openness to all that exists, in passing beyond self to knowledge and love of the other.[138] Freedom then is rooted in the truth about man, and it is ultimately directed towards communion.

Reason and experience not only confirm the weakness of human freedom; they also confirm its tragic aspects. Man comes to realize that his freedom is in some mysterious way inclined to betray this openness to the True and the Good, and that all too often he actually prefers to choose finite, limited and ephemeral goods. What is more, within his errors and negative decisions, man glimpses the source of a deep rebellion, which leads him to reject the Truth and the Good in order to set himself up as an absolute principle unto himself: "You will be like God" (*Gen* 3:5). Consequently, *freedom itself needs to be set free. It is Christ who sets it free:* he "has set us free for freedom" (cf. *Gal* 5:1).

87. Christ reveals, first and foremost, that the frank and open acceptance of truth is the condition for authentic freedom: "You will know the truth, and the truth will set you free" (*Jn* 8:32).[139] This is truth which sets one free in the face of worldly power and which gives the strength to endure martyrdom. So it was with Jesus before Pilate: "For this I was born, and for this I have come into the world, to bear witness to the truth" (*Jn* 18:37). The true worshippers of God must thus worship him "in spirit and truth" (*Jn* 4:23): *in this worship they become free.* Worship of God and a relationship with truth are revealed in Jesus Christ as the deepest foundation of freedom.

Furthermore, Jesus reveals by his whole life, and not only by his words, that freedom is acquired in *love,* that is, in the *gift of self.* The one who says: "Greater love has no man than this, that a man lay down his life for his friends" (*Jn* 15:13), freely goes out to meet his Passion (cf. *Mt* 26:46), and in obedience to the Father gives his life on the Cross for all men (cf. *Phil* 2:6–11). Contemplation of Jesus Crucified is thus the highroad which the Church must tread every day if she wishes to understand the full meaning of freedom: the gift of self in *service to God and one's brethren.* Communion with the Crucified and Risen Lord is the never-ending source from which the Church draws unceasingly in order to live in freedom, to give of herself and to serve. Commenting on the verse in Psalm 100, "Serve the Lord with gladness," Saint Augustine says: "In the house of the Lord, slavery is

---

138. Cf. Second Vatican Ecumenical Council, Pastoral Constitution on the Church in the Modern World *Gaudium et Spes*, 24.

139. Cf. Encyclical Letter *Redemptor Hominis* (March 4, 1979), 12: *AAS* 71 (1979), 280–81.

free. It is free because it serves not out of necessity, but out of charity.... Charity should make you a servant, just as truth has made you free.... You are at once both a servant and free: a servant, because you have become such; free, because you are loved by God your Creator; indeed, you have also been enabled to love your Creator.... You are a servant of the Lord and you are a freedman of the Lord. Do not go looking for a liberation which will lead you far from the house of your liberator!"[140]

The Church, and each of her members, is thus called to share in the *munus regale* of the Crucified Christ (cf. *Jn* 12:32), to share in the grace and in the responsibility of the Son of man who came "not to be served but to serve, and to give his life as a ransom for many" (*Mt* 20:28).[141]

Jesus, then, is the living, personal summation of perfect freedom in total obedience to the will of God. His crucified flesh fully reveals the unbreakable bond between freedom and truth, just as his resurrection from the dead is the supreme exaltation of the fruitfulness and saving power of a freedom lived out in truth.

Walking in the light (cf. 1 Jn 1:7)

88. The attempt to set freedom in opposition to truth, and indeed to separate them radically, is the consequence, manifestation and consummation of *another more serious and destructive dichotomy, that which separates faith from morality.*

This separation represents one of the most acute pastoral concerns of the Church amid today's growing secularism, wherein many, indeed too many, people think and live "as if God did not exist." We are speaking of a mentality which affects, often in a profound, extensive and all-embracing way, even the attitudes and behavior of Christians, whose faith is weakened and loses its character as a new and original criterion for thinking and acting in personal, family and social life. In a widely dechristianized culture, the criteria employed by believers themselves in making judgments and decisions often appear extraneous or even contrary to those of the Gospel.

It is urgent then that Christians should rediscover *the newness of the faith and its power to judge* a prevalent and all-intrusive culture. As the Apostle Paul admonishes us: "Once you were darkness, but now you are light in the Lord; walk as children of the light (for the fruit of the light is found in all that is good

---

140. *Enarratio in Psalmum XCIX*, 7: CCL 39, 1397.

141. Cf. Second Vatican Ecumenical Council, Dogmatic Constitution on the Church *Lumen Gentium* 36; cf. Encyclical Letter *Redemptor Hominis* (March 4, 1979), 21: *AAS* 71 (1979), 316–17.

and right and true), and try to learn what is pleasing to the Lord. Take no part in the unfruitful works of darkness, but instead expose them ... Look carefully then how you walk, not as unwise men but as wise, making the most of the time, because the days are evil" (*Eph* 5:8–11, 15–16; cf. 1 *Thes* 5:4–8).

It is urgent to rediscover and to set forth once more the authentic reality of the Christian faith, which is not simply a set of propositions to be accepted with intellectual assent. Rather, faith is a lived knowledge of Christ, a living remembrance of his commandments, and a *truth to be lived out*. A word, in any event, is not truly received until it passes into action, until it is put into practice. Faith is a decision involving one's whole existence. It is an encounter, a dialogue, a communion of love and of life between the believer and Jesus Christ, the Way, and the Truth, and the Life (cf. *Jn* 14:6). It entails an act of trusting abandonment to Christ, which enables us to live as he lived (cf. *Gal* 2:20), in profound love of God and of our brothers and sisters.

89. Faith also possesses a moral content. It gives rise to and calls for a consistent life commitment; it entails and brings to perfection the acceptance and observance of God's commandments. As Saint John writes, "God is light and in him is no darkness at all. If we say we have fellowship with him while we walk in darkness, we lie and do not live according to the truth ... And by this we may be sure that we know him, if we keep his commandments. He who says 'I know him' but disobeys his commandments is a liar, and the truth is not in him; but whoever keeps his word, in him truly love for God is perfected. By this we may be sure that we are in him: he who says he abides in him ought to walk in the same way in which he walked" (1 *Jn* 1:5–6; 2:3–6).

Through the moral life, faith becomes "confession," not only before God but also before men: it becomes *witness*. "You are the light of the world," said Jesus; "a city set on a hill cannot be hid. Nor do men light a lamp and put it under a bushel, but on a stand, and it gives light to all in the house. Let your light so shine before men, that they may see your good works and give glory to your Father who is in heaven" (*Mt* 5:14–16). These works are above all those of charity (cf. *Mt* 25:31–46) and of the authentic freedom which is manifested and lived in the gift of self, *even to the total gift of self,* like that of Jesus, who on the Cross "loved the Church and gave himself up for her" (*Eph* 5:25). Christ's witness is the source, model and means for the witness of his disciples, who are called to walk on the same road: "If any man would come after me, let him deny himself and take up his cross daily and follow me" (*Lk* 9:23). Charity, in conformity with the radical demands of the Gospel, can lead the believer to the supreme witness of *martyrdom*. Once again this means imitating Jesus who died on the Cross: "Be imitators of God, as beloved children," Paul writes to the Christians of Ephesus, "and walk in love, as Christ loved us and gave himself up for us, a fragrant offering and sacrifice to God" (*Eph* 5:1–2).

Martyrdom, the exaltation of the inviolable holiness of God's law

90. The relationship between faith and morality shines forth with all its brilliance in the *unconditional respect due to the insistent demands of the personal dignity of every man,* demands protected by those moral norms which prohibit without exception actions which are intrinsically evil. The universality and the immutability of the moral norm make manifest and at the same time serve to protect the personal dignity and inviolability of man, on whose face is reflected the splendor of God (cf. *Gen* 9:5–6).

The unacceptability of "teleological," "consequentialist" and "proportionalist" ethical theories, which deny the existence of negative moral norms regarding specific kinds of behavior, norms which are valid without exception, is confirmed in a particularly eloquent way by Christian martyrdom, which has always accompanied and continues to accompany the life of the Church even today.

91. In the Old Testament we already find admirable witnesses of fidelity to the holy law of God even to the point of a voluntary acceptance of death. A prime example is the story of Susanna: in reply to the two unjust judges who threatened to have her condemned to death if she refused to yield to their sinful passion, she says: "I am hemmed in on every side. For if I do this thing, it is death for me; and if I do not, I shall not escape your hands. I choose not to do it and to fall into your hands, rather than to sin in the sight of the Lord!" (*Dan* 13:22–23). Susanna, preferring to "fall innocent" into the hands of the judges, bears witness not only to her faith and trust in God but also to her obedience to the truth and to the absoluteness of the moral order. By her readiness to die a martyr, she proclaims that it is not right to do what God's law qualifies as evil in order to draw some good from it. Susanna chose for herself the "better part": hers was a perfectly clear witness, without any compromise, to the truth about the good and to the God of Israel. By her acts, she revealed the holiness of God.

At the dawn of the New Testament, *John the Baptist,* unable to refrain from speaking of the law of the Lord and rejecting any compromise with evil, "gave his life in witness to truth and justice,"[142] and thus also became the forerunner of the Messiah in the way he died (cf. *Mk* 6:17–29). "The one who came to bear witness to the light and who deserved to be called by that same light, which is Christ, a burning and shining lamp, was cast into the darkness of prison … The one to

---

142. *Roman Missal,* Prayer for the Memorial of the Beheading of John the Baptist, August 29.

whom it was granted to baptize the Redeemer of the world was thus baptized in his own blood."[143]

In the New Testament we find many examples of *followers of Christ*, beginning with the deacon Stephen (cf. *Acts* 6:8–7:60) and the Apostle James (cf. *Acts* 12:1–2), who died as martyrs in order to profess their faith and their love for Christ, unwilling to deny him. In this they followed the Lord Jesus who "made the good confession" (1 *Tim* 6:13) before Caiaphas and Pilate, confirming the truth of his message at the cost of his life. Countless other martyrs accepted persecution and death rather than perform the idolatrous act of burning incense before the statue of the Emperor (cf. *Rev* 13:7–10). They even refused to feign such worship, thereby giving an example of the duty to refrain from performing even a single concrete act contrary to God's love and the witness of faith. Like Christ himself, they obediently trusted and handed over their lives to the Father, the one who could free them from death (cf. *Heb* 5:7).

The Church proposes the example of numerous Saints who bore witness to and defended moral truth even to the point of enduring martyrdom, or who preferred death to a single mortal sin. In raising them to the honor of the altars, the Church has canonized their witness and declared the truth of their judgment, according to which the love of God entails the obligation to respect his commandments, even in the most dire of circumstances, and the refusal to betray those commandments, even for the sake of saving one's own life.

92. Martyrdom, accepted as an affirmation of the inviolability of the moral order, bears splendid witness both to the holiness of God's law and to the inviolability of the personal dignity of man, created in God's image and likeness. This dignity may never be disparaged or called into question, even with good intentions, whatever the difficulties involved. Jesus warns us most sternly: "What does it profit a man, to gain the whole world and forfeit his life?" (*Mk* 8:36).

Martyrdom rejects as false and illusory whatever "human meaning" one might claim to attribute, even in "exceptional" conditions, to an act morally evil in itself. Indeed, it even more clearly unmasks the true face of such an act: *it is a violation of man's "humanity,"* in the one perpetrating it even before the one enduring it.[144] Hence martyrdom is also the exaltation of a person's perfect "humanity" and of true "life," as is attested by Saint Ignatius of Antioch, addressing the Christians of Rome, the place of his own martyrdom: "Have mercy on me, brethren: do not hold me back from living; do not wish that I die ... Let me

---

143. Saint Bede the Venerable, *Homeliarum Evangelii Libri*, II, 23: CCL 122, 556–57.

144. Cf. Second Vatican Ecumenical Council, Pastoral Constitution on the Church in the Modern World *Gaudium et Spes*, 27.

arrive at the pure light; once there *I will be truly a man.* Let me imitate the passion of my God."[145]

93. Finally, martyrdom is an *outstanding sign of the holiness of the Church.* Fidelity to God's holy law, witnessed to by death, is a solemn proclamation and missionary commitment *usque ad sanguinem,* so that the splendor of moral truth may be undimmed in the behavior and thinking of individuals and society. This witness makes an extraordinarily valuable contribution to warding off, in civil society and within the ecclesial communities themselves, a headlong plunge into the most dangerous crisis which can afflict man: the *confusion between good and evil,* which makes it impossible to build up and to preserve the moral order of individuals and communities. By their eloquent and attractive example of a life completely transfigured by the splendor of moral truth, the martyrs and, in general, all the Church's Saints, light up every period of history by reawakening its moral sense. By witnessing fully to the good, they are a living reproof to those who transgress the law (cf. *Wis* 2:12), and they make the words of the Prophet echo ever afresh: "Woe to those who call evil good and good evil, who put darkness for light and light for darkness, who put bitter for sweet and sweet for bitter!" (*Is* 5:20).

Although martyrdom represents the high point of the witness to moral truth, and one to which relatively few people are called, there is nonetheless a consistent witness which all Christians must daily be ready to make, even at the cost of suffering and grave sacrifice. Indeed, faced with the many difficulties which fidelity to the moral order can demand, even in the most ordinary circumstances, the Christian is called, with the grace of God invoked in prayer, to a sometimes heroic commitment. In this he or she is sustained by the virtue of fortitude, whereby—as Gregory the Great teaches—one can actually "love the difficulties of this world for the sake of eternal rewards."[146]

94. In this witness to the absoluteness of the moral good *Christians are not alone:* they are supported by the moral sense present in peoples and by the great religious and sapiential traditions of East and West, from which the interior and mysterious workings of God's Spirit are not absent. The words of the Latin poet Juvenal apply to all: "Consider it the greatest of crimes to prefer survival to honor and, out of love of physical life, to lose the very reason for living."[147] The voice of conscience has always clearly recalled that there are truths and moral values for which one must be prepared to give up one's life. In an individual's words and

---

145. *Ad Romanos,* VI, 2–3: Patres Apostolici, ed. F. X. Funk, I, 260–61.

146. *Moralia in Job,* VII, 21, 24: PL 75, 778: "*huius mundi aspera pro aeternis praemiis amore.*"

147. "*Summum crede nefas animam praeferre pudori et propter vitam vivendi perdere causas*": *Satirae,* VIII, 83–84.

above all in the sacrifice of his life for a moral value, the Church sees a single testimony to that truth which, already present in creation, shines forth in its fullness on the face of Christ. As Saint Justin put it, "the Stoics, at least in their teachings on ethics, demonstrated wisdom, thanks to the seed of the Word present in all peoples, and we know that those who followed their doctrines met with hatred and were killed."[148]

Universal and unchanging moral norms at the service of the person and of society

95. The Church's teaching, and in particular her firmness in defending the universal and permanent validity of the precepts prohibiting intrinsically evil acts, is not infrequently seen as the sign of an intolerable intransigence, particularly with regard to the enormously complex and conflict-filled situations present in the moral life of individuals and of society today; this intransigence is said to be in contrast with the Church's motherhood. The Church, one hears, is lacking in understanding and compassion. But the Church's motherhood can never in fact be separated from her teaching mission, which she must always carry out as the faithful Bride of Christ, who is the Truth in person. "As Teacher, she never tires of proclaiming the moral norm ... The Church is in no way the author or the arbiter of this norm. In obedience to the truth which is Christ, whose image is reflected in the nature and dignity of the human person, the Church interprets the moral norm and proposes it to all men of good will, without concealing its demands of radicalness and perfection."[149]

In fact, genuine understanding and compassion must mean love for the person, for his true good, for his authentic freedom. And this does not result, certainly, from concealing or weakening moral truth, but rather from proposing it in its most profound meaning as an outpouring of God's eternal Wisdom, which we have received in Christ, and as a service to man, to the growth of his freedom and to the attainment of his happiness.[150]

Still, a clear and forceful presentation of moral truth can never be separated from a profound and heartfelt respect, born of that patient and trusting love which man always needs along his moral journey, a journey frequently wearisome on account of difficulties, weakness and painful situations. The Church can never renounce the "the principle of truth and consistency, whereby she does

---

148. *Apologia* II, 8: PG 6, 457–58.

149. Apostolic Exhortation *Familiaris Consortio* (November 22, 1981), 33: *AAS* 74 (1982), 120.

150. Cf. Apostolic Exhortation *Familiaris Consortio* (November 22, 1981), 34: *AAS* 74 (1982), 123–25.

not agree to call good evil and evil good"[151]; she must always be careful not to break the bruised reed or to quench the dimly burning wick (cf. *Is* 42:3). As Paul VI wrote: "While it is an outstanding manifestation of charity towards souls to omit nothing from the saving doctrine of Christ, this must always be joined with tolerance and charity, as Christ himself showed by his conversations and dealings with men. Having come not to judge the world but to save it, he was uncompromisingly stern towards sin, but patient and rich in mercy towards sinners."[152]

96. The Church's firmness in defending the universal and unchanging moral norms is not demeaning at all. Its only purpose is to serve man's true freedom. Because there can be no freedom apart from or in opposition to the truth, the categorical—unyielding and uncompromising—defense of the absolutely essential demands of man's personal dignity must be considered the way and the condition for the very existence of freedom.

This service is directed to *every man,* considered in the uniqueness and singularity of his being and existence: only by obedience to universal moral norms does man find full confirmation of his personal uniqueness and the possibility of authentic moral growth. For this very reason, this service is also directed to *all mankind:* it is not only for individuals but also for the community, for society as such. These norms in fact represent the unshakable foundation and solid guarantee of a just and peaceful human coexistence, and hence of genuine democracy, which can come into being and develop only on the basis of the equality of all its members, who possess common rights and duties. *When it is a matter of the moral norms prohibiting intrinsic evil, there are no privileges or exceptions for anyone.* It makes no difference whether one is the master of the world or the "poorest of the poor" on the face of the earth. Before the demands of morality we are all absolutely equal.

97. In this way, moral norms, and primarily the negative ones, those prohibiting evil, manifest their *meaning and force, both personal and social.* By protecting the inviolable personal dignity of every human being they help to preserve the human social fabric and its proper and fruitful development. The commandments of the second table of the Decalogue in particular—those which Jesus quoted to the young man of the Gospel (cf. *Mt* 19:19)—constitute the indispensable rules of all social life.

These commandments are formulated in general terms. But the very fact that "the origin, the subject and the purpose of all social institutions is and should be

---

151. Post-Synodal Apostolic Exhortation *Reconciliatio et Paenitentia* (December 2, 1984), 34: *AAS* 77 (1985), 272.

152. Encyclical Letter *Humanae Vitae* (July 25, 1968), 29: *AAS* 60 (1968), 501.

the human person"[153] allows for them to be specified and made more explicit in a detailed code of behavior. The fundamental moral rules of social life thus entail *specific demands* to which both public authorities and citizens are required to pay heed. Even though intentions may sometimes be good, and circumstances frequently difficult, civil authorities and particular individuals never have authority to violate the fundamental and inalienable rights of the human person. In the end, only a morality which acknowledges certain norms as valid always and for everyone, with no exception, can guarantee the ethical foundation of social coexistence, both on the national and international levels.

Morality and the renewal of social and political life

98. In the face of serious forms of social and economic injustice and political corruption affecting entire peoples and nations, there is a growing reaction of indignation on the part of very many people whose fundamental human rights have been trampled upon and held in contempt, as well as an ever more widespread and acute sense of *the need for a radical* personal and social *renewal* capable of ensuring justice, solidarity, honesty and openness.

Certainly there is a long and difficult road ahead; bringing about such a renewal will require enormous effort, especially on account of the number and the gravity of the causes giving rise to and aggravating the situations of injustice present in the world today. But, as history and personal experience show, it is not difficult to discover at the bottom of these situations causes which are properly "cultural," linked to particular ways of looking at man, society and the world. Indeed, at the heart of the issue of culture we find the *moral sense,* which is in turn rooted and fulfilled in the *religious sense.*[154]

99. Only God, the Supreme Good, constitutes the unshakable foundation and essential condition of morality, and thus of the commandments, particularly those negative commandments which always and in every case prohibit behavior and actions incompatible with the personal dignity of every man. The Supreme Good and the moral good meet in *truth:* the truth of God, the Creator and Redeemer, and the truth of man, created and redeemed by him. Only upon this truth is it possible to construct a renewed society and to solve the complex and weighty problems affecting it, above all the problem of overcoming the various forms of totalitarianism, so as to make way for the authentic *freedom* of the

---

153. Second Vatican Ecumenical Council, Pastoral Constitution on the Church in the Modern World *Gaudium et Spes,* 25.

154. Cf. Encyclical Letter *Centesimus Annus* (May 1, 1991), 24: *AAS* 83 (1991), 821–22.

person. "Totalitarianism arises out of a denial of truth in the objective sense. If there is no transcendent truth, in obedience to which man achieves his full identity, then there is no sure principle for guaranteeing just relations between people. Their self-interest as a class, group or nation would inevitably set them in opposition to one another. If one does not acknowledge transcendent truth, then the force of power takes over, and each person tends to make full use of the means at his disposal in order to impose his own interests or his own opinion, with no regard for the rights of others ... Thus, the root of modern totalitarianism is to be found in the denial of the transcendent dignity of the human person who, as the visible image of the invisible God, is therefore by his very nature the subject of rights which no one may violate—no individual, group, class, nation or State. Not even the majority of a social body may violate these rights, by going against the minority, by isolating, oppressing, or exploiting it, or by attempting to annihilate it."[155]

Consequently, the inseparable connection between truth and freedom—which expresses the essential bond between God's wisdom and will—is extremely significant for the life of persons in the socio-economic and socio-political sphere. This is clearly seen in the Church's social teaching—which "belongs to the field ... of theology and particularly of moral theology"[156]—and from her presentation of commandments governing social, economic and political life, not only with regard to general attitudes but also to precise and specific kinds of behavior and concrete acts.

100. The *Catechism of the Catholic Church* affirms that "in economic matters, respect for human dignity requires the practice of the virtue of *temperance,* to moderate our attachment to the goods of this world; of the virtue of *justice,* to preserve our neighbor's rights and to render what is his or her due; and of *solidarity,* following the Golden Rule and in keeping with the generosity of the Lord, who 'though he was rich, yet for your sake ... became poor, so that by his poverty you might become rich' (2 *Cor* 8:9)."[157] The *Catechism* goes on to present a series of kinds of behavior and actions contrary to human dignity: theft, deliberate retention of goods lent or objects lost, business fraud (cf. *Dt* 25:13–16), unjust wages (cf. *Dt* 24:14–15), forcing up prices by trading on the ignorance or hardship of another (cf. *Am* 8:4–6), the misappropriation and private use of

---

155. Encyclical Letter *Centesimus Annus* (May 1, 1991), 44: *AAS* 83 (1991), 848–49; cf. Leo XIII, Encyclical Letter *Libertas Praestantissimum* (June 20, 1888), *Leonis XIII P.M. Acts,* VIII (Romae, 1889), 224–26.

156. Encyclical Letter *Sollicitudo Rei Socialis* (December 30, 1987), 41: *AAS* 80 (1988), 571.

157. *Catechism of the Catholic Church,* n. 2407.

the corporate property of an enterprise, work badly done, tax fraud, forgery of checks and invoices, excessive expenses, waste, etc.[158] It continues: "The seventh commandment prohibits actions or enterprises which for any reason—selfish or ideological, commercial or totalitarian—lead to the *enslavement of human beings*, disregard for their personal dignity, buying or selling or exchanging them like merchandise. Reducing persons by violence to use-value or a source of profit is a sin against their dignity as persons and their fundamental rights. Saint Paul set a Christian master right about treating his Christian slave 'no longer as a slave but ... as a brother ... in the Lord' (*Philem* 16)."[159]

101. In the political sphere, it must be noted that truthfulness in the relations between those governing and those governed, openness in public administration, impartiality in the service of the body politic, respect for the rights of political adversaries, safeguarding the rights of the accused against summary trials and convictions, the just and honest use of public funds, the rejection of equivocal or illicit means in order to gain, preserve or increase power at any cost—all these are principles which are primarily rooted in, and in fact derive their singular urgency from, the transcendent value of the person and the objective moral demands of the functioning of States.[160] When these principles are not observed, the very basis of political coexistence is weakened and the life of society itself is gradually jeopardized, threatened and doomed to decay (cf. *Ps* 14:3–4; *Rev* 18:2–3, 9–24). Today, when many countries have seen the fall of ideologies which bound politics to a totalitarian conception of the world— Marxism being the foremost of these—there is no less grave a danger that the fundamental rights of the human person will be denied and that the religious yearnings which arise in the heart of every human being will be absorbed once again into politics. This is *the risk of an alliance between democracy and ethical relativism,* which would remove any sure moral reference point from political and social life, and on a deeper level make the acknowledgement of truth impossible. Indeed, "if there is no ultimate truth to guide and direct political activity, then ideas and convictions can easily be manipulated for reasons of power. As history demonstrates, a democracy without values easily turns into open or thinly disguised totalitarianism."[161]

Thus, in every sphere of personal, family, social and political life, morality—founded upon truth and open in truth to authentic freedom—renders a

---

158. Cf. ibid., nn. 2408–13.

159. Ibid., n. 2414.

160. Cf. Encyclical Letter *Christifideles Laici* (December 30, 1988), 42: *AAS* 81 (1989), 472–76.

161. Encyclical Letter *Centesimus Annus* (May 1, 1991), 46: *AAS* 83 (1991), 850.

primordial, indispensable and immensely valuable service not only for the individual person and his growth in the good, but also for society and its genuine development.

Grace and obedience to God's law

102. Even in the most difficult situations man must respect the norm of morality so that he can be obedient to God's holy commandment and consistent with his own dignity as a person. Certainly, maintaining a harmony between freedom and truth occasionally demands uncommon sacrifices, and must be won at a high price: it can even involve martyrdom. But, as universal and daily experience demonstrates, man is tempted to break that harmony: "I do not do what I want, but I do the very thing I hate ... I do not do the good I want, but the evil I do not want" (Rom 7:15, 19).

What is the ultimate source of this inner division of man? His history of sin begins when he no longer acknowledges the Lord as his Creator and himself wishes to be the one who determines, with complete independence, what is good and what is evil. "You will be like God, knowing good and evil" (Gen 3:5): this was the first temptation, and it is echoed in all the other temptations to which man is more easily inclined to yield as a result of the original Fall.

But temptations can be overcome, sins can be avoided, because together with the commandments the Lord gives us the possibility of keeping them: "His eyes are on those who fear him, and he knows every deed of man. He has not commanded anyone to be ungodly, and he has not given anyone permission to sin" (Sir 15:19–20). Keeping God's law in particular situations can be difficult, extremely difficult, but it is never impossible. This is the constant teaching of the Church's tradition, and was expressed by the Council of Trent: "But no one, however much justified, ought to consider himself exempt from the observance of the commandments, nor should he employ that rash statement, forbidden by the Fathers under anathema, that the commandments of God are impossible of observance by one who is justified. For God does not command the impossible, but in commanding he admonishes you to do what you can and to pray for what you cannot, and he gives his aid to enable you. His commandments are not burdensome (cf. 1 Jn 5:3); his yoke is easy and his burden light (cf. Mt 11:30)."[162]

---

162. Sess. VI, Decree on Justification *Cum Hoc Tempore*, Chap. 11: DS, 1536; cf. Canon 18. DS, 1568. The celebrated text from Saint Augustine, which the Council cites, is found in *De Natura et Gratia*, 43, 40 (CSEL 60, 270).

103. Man always has before him the spiritual horizon of hope, thanks to the *help of divine grace* and with *the cooperation of human freedom.*

It is in the saving Cross of Jesus, in the gift of the Holy Spirit, in the sacraments which flow forth from the pierced side of the Redeemer (cf. *Jn* 19:34), that believers find the grace and the strength always to keep God's holy law, even amid the gravest of hardships. As Saint Andrew of Crete observes, the law itself "was enlivened by grace and made to serve it in a harmonious and fruitful combination. Each element preserved its characteristics without change or confusion. In a divine manner, he turned what could be burdensome and tyrannical into what is easy to bear and a source of freedom."[163]

Only in the mystery of Christ's Redemption do we discover the "concrete" possibilities of man. "It would be a very serious error to conclude ... that the Church's teaching is essentially only an 'ideal' which must then be adapted, proportioned, graduated to the so-called concrete possibilities of man, according to a 'balancing of the goods in question.' But what are the 'concrete possibilities of man'? And of *which* man are we speaking? Of man *dominated* by lust or of man *redeemed by Christ*? This is what is at stake: the *reality* of Christ's redemption. *Christ has redeemed us!* This means that he has given us the possibility of realizing *the entire* truth of our being; he has set our freedom free from the *domination* of concupiscence. And if redeemed man still sins, this is not due to an imperfection of Christ's redemptive act, but to man's will not to avail himself of the grace which flows from that act. God's command is of course proportioned to man's capabilities; but to the capabilities of the man to whom the Holy Spirit has been given; of the man who, though he has fallen into sin, can always obtain pardon and enjoy the presence of the Holy Spirit."[164]

104. In this context, appropriate allowance is made both for *God's mercy* towards the sinner who converts and for the *understanding of human weakness.* Such understanding never means compromising and falsifying the standard of good and evil in order to adapt it to particular circumstances. It is quite human for the sinner to acknowledge his weakness and to ask mercy for his failings; what is unacceptable is the attitude of one who makes his own weakness the criterion of the truth about the good, so that he can feel self-justified, without even the need to have recourse to God and his mercy. An attitude of this sort corrupts the morality of society as a whole, since it encourages doubt about the objectivity of the moral law in general and a rejection of the absoluteness of

---

163. *Oratio* I: PG 97, 805–6.

164. Address to those taking part in a course on "responsible parenthood" (March 1, 1984), 4: *Insegnamenti* VII, 1 (1984), 583.

moral prohibitions regarding specific human acts, and it ends up by confusing all judgments about values.

Instead, we should take to heart the *message of the Gospel parable of the Pharisee and the tax collector* (cf. *Lk* 18:9–14). The tax collector might possibly have had some justification for the sins he committed, such as to diminish his responsibility. But his prayer does not dwell on such justifications, but rather on his own unworthiness before God's infinite holiness: "God, be merciful to me a sinner!" (*Lk* 18:13). The Pharisee, on the other hand, is self-justified, finding some excuse for each of his failings. Here we encounter two different attitudes of the moral conscience of man in every age. The tax collector represents a "repentant" conscience, fully aware of the frailty of its own nature and seeing in its own failings, whatever their subjective justifications, a confirmation of its need for redemption. The Pharisee represents a "self-satisfied" conscience, under the illusion that it is able to observe the law without the help of grace and convinced that it does not need mercy.

105. All people must take great care not to allow themselves to be tainted by the attitude of the Pharisee, which would seek to eliminate awareness of one's own limits and of one's own sin. In our own day this attitude is expressed particularly in the attempt to adapt the moral norm to one's own capacities and personal interests, and even in the rejection of the very idea of a norm. Accepting, on the other hand, the "disproportion" between the law and human ability (that is, the capacity of the moral forces of man left to himself) kindles the desire for grace and prepares one to receive it. "Who will deliver me from this body of death?" asks the Apostle Paul. And in an outburst of joy and gratitude he replies: "Thanks be to God through Jesus Christ our Lord!" (*Rom* 7:24–25).

We find the same awareness in the following prayer of Saint Ambrose of Milan: "What then is man, if you do not visit him? Remember, Lord, that you have made me as one who is weak, that you formed me from dust. How can I stand, if you do not constantly look upon me, to strengthen this clay, so that my strength may proceed from your face? *When you hide your face, all grows weak* (*Ps* 104:29): if you turn to look at me, woe is me! You have nothing to see in me but the stain of my crimes; there is no gain either in being abandoned or in being seen, because when we are seen, we offend you. Still, we can imagine that God does not reject those he sees, because he purifies those upon whom he gazes. Before him burns a fire capable of consuming our guilt (cf. *Joel* 2:3)."[165]

165. *De Interpellatione David*, IV, 6, 22: CSEL 3212, 283–84.

Morality and new evangelization

106. Evangelization is the most powerful and stirring challenge which the Church has been called to face from her very beginning. Indeed, this challenge is posed not so much by the social and cultural milieux which she encounters in the course of history, as by the mandate of the Risen Christ, who defines the very reason for the Church's existence: "Go into all the world and preach the Gospel to the whole creation" (*Mk* 16:15).

At least for many peoples, however, the present time is instead marked by a formidable challenge to undertake a "new evangelization," a proclamation of the Gospel which is always new and always the bearer of new things, an evangelization which must be "new in its ardor, methods, and expression."[166] Dechristianization, which weighs heavily upon entire peoples and communities once rich in faith and Christian life, involves not only the loss of faith or in any event its becoming irrelevant for everyday life, but also, and of necessity, *a decline or obscuring of the moral sense*. This comes about both as a result of a loss of awareness of the originality of Gospel morality and as a result of an eclipse of fundamental principles and ethical values themselves. Today's widespread tendencies towards subjectivism, utilitarianism and relativism appear not merely as pragmatic attitudes or patterns of behavior, but rather as approaches having a basis in theory and claiming full cultural and social legitimacy.

107. *Evangelization*—and therefore the "new evangelization"—*also involves the proclamation and presentation of morality*. Jesus himself, even as he preached the Kingdom of God and its saving love, called people to faith and conversion (cf. *Mk* 1:15). And when Peter, with the other Apostles, proclaimed the resurrection of Jesus of Nazareth from the dead, he held out a new life to be lived, a "way" to be followed, for those who would be disciples of the Risen One (cf. *Acts* 2:37–41; 3:17–20).

Just as it does in proclaiming the truths of faith, and even more so in presenting the foundations and content of Christian morality, the new evangelization will show its authenticity and unleash all its missionary force when it is carried out through the gift not only of the word proclaimed but also of the word lived. In particular, *the life of holiness* which is resplendent in so many members of the People of God, humble and often unseen, constitutes the simplest and most attractive way to perceive at once the beauty of truth, the liberating force of God's love, and the value of unconditional fidelity to all the demands of the Lord's law, even in the most difficult situations. For this reason, the Church, as a wise teacher

---

166. Address to the Bishops of CELAM (March 9, 1983), III: *Insegnamenti*, VI, 1 (1983), 698.

of morality, has always invited believers to seek and to find in the Saints, and above all in the Virgin Mother of God "full of grace" and "all-holy," the model, the strength and the joy needed to live a life in accordance with God's commandments and the Beatitudes of the Gospel.

The lives of the saints, as a reflection of the goodness of God—the One who "alone is good"—constitute not only a genuine profession of faith and an incentive for sharing it with others, but also a glorification of God and his infinite holiness. The life of holiness thus brings to full expression and effectiveness the threefold and unitary *munus propheticum, sacerdotale et regale* which every Christian receives as a gift by being born again "of water and the Spirit" (*Jn* 3:5) in baptism. His moral life has the value of a "spiritual worship" (*Rom* 12:1; cf. *Phil* 3:3), flowing from and nourished by that inexhaustible source of holiness and glorification of God which is found in the sacraments, especially in the Eucharist: by sharing in the sacrifice of the Cross, the Christian partakes of Christ's self-giving love and is equipped and committed to live this same charity in all his thoughts and deeds. In the moral life the Christian's royal service is also made evident and effective: with the help of grace, the more one obeys the new law of the Holy Spirit, the more one grows in the freedom to which he or she is called by the service of truth, charity and justice.

108. At the heart of the new evangelization and of the new moral life which it proposes and awakens by its fruits of holiness and missionary zeal, there is *the Spirit of Christ*, the principle and strength of the fruitfulness of Holy Mother Church. As Pope Paul VI reminded us: "Evangelization will never be possible without the action of the Holy Spirit."[167] The Spirit of Jesus, received by the humble and docile heart of the believer, brings about the flourishing of Christian moral life and the witness of holiness amid the great variety of vocations, gifts, responsibilities, conditions and life situations. As Novatian once pointed out, here expressing the authentic faith of the Church, it is the Holy Spirit "who confirmed the hearts and minds of the disciples, who revealed the mysteries of the Gospel, who shed upon them the light of things divine. Strengthened by his gift, they did not fear either prisons or chains for the name of the Lord; indeed they even trampled upon the powers and torments of the world, armed and strengthened by him, having in themselves the gifts which this same Spirit bestows and directs like jewels to the Church, the Bride of Christ. It is in fact he who raises up prophets in the Church, instructs teachers, guides tongues, works wonders and healings, accomplishes miracles, grants the discernment of spirits, assigns governance, inspires counsels, distributes and harmonizes every other

---

167. Apostolic Exhortation *Evangelii Nuntiandi* (December 8, 1975), 75: *AAS* 68 (1976), 64.

charismatic gift. In this way he completes and perfects the Lord's Church every-where and in all things."[168]

In the living context of this new evangelization, aimed at generating and nourishing "the faith which works through love" (cf. *Gal* 5:6), and in relation to the work of the Holy Spirit, we can now understand the proper place which *continuing theological reflection about the moral life* holds in the Church, the community of believers. We can likewise speak of the mission and the responsi-bility proper to moral theologians.

The service of moral theologians

109. The whole Church is called to evangelization and to the witness of a life of faith, by the fact that she has been made a sharer in the *munus propheticum* of the Lord Jesus through the gift of his Spirit. Thanks to the permanent presence of the Spirit of truth in the Church (cf. *Jn* 14:16–17), "the universal body of the faithful who have received the anointing of the holy one (cf. 1 *Jn* 2:20, 27) cannot be mistaken in belief. It displays this particular quality through a supernatural sense of the faith in the whole people when, 'from the bishops to the last of the lay faithful,' it expresses the consensus of all in matters of faith and morals."[169]

In order to carry out her prophetic mission, the Church must constantly reawaken or "rekindle" her own life of faith (cf. 2 *Tim* 1:6), particularly through an ever deeper reflection, under the guidance of the Holy Spirit, upon the content of faith itself. *The "vocation" of the theologian in the Church* is specifically at the service of this "believing effort to understand the faith." As the Instruction *Donum Veritatis* teaches: "Among the vocations awakened by the Spirit in the Church is that of the theologian. His role is to pursue in a particular way an ever deeper understanding of the word of God found in the inspired Scriptures and handed on by the living Tradition of the Church. He does this in communion with the Magisterium, which has been charged with the responsibility of preserv-ing the deposit of faith. By its nature, faith appeals to reason because it reveals to man the truth of his destiny and the way to attain it. Revealed truth, to be sure, surpasses our telling. All our concepts fall short of its ultimately unfathomable grandeur (cf. *Eph* 3:19). Nonetheless, revealed truth beckons reason—God's gift fashioned for the assimilation of truth—to enter into its light and thereby come to understand in a certain measure what it has believed. Theological science responds to the invitation of truth as it seeks to understand the faith. It thereby

---

168. *De Trinitate*, XXIX, 9–10: CCL 4, 70.

169. Second Vatican Ecumenical Council, Dogmatic Constitution on the Church *Lumen Gentium*, 12.

aids the People of God in fulfilling the Apostle's command (cf. 1 *Pet* 3:15) to give an accounting for their hope to those who ask it."[170]

It is fundamental for defining the very identity of theology, and consequently for theology to carry out its proper mission, to recognize its *profound and vital connection with the Church, her mystery, her life and her mission:* "Theology is an ecclesial science because it grows in the Church and works in the Church ... It is a service to the Church and therefore ought to feel itself actively involved in the mission of the Church, particularly in its prophetic mission."[171] By its very nature and procedures, authentic theology can flourish and develop only through a committed and responsible participation in and "belonging" to the Church as a "community of faith." In turn, the fruits of theological research and deeper insight become a source of enrichment for the Church and her life of faith.

110. All that has been said about theology in general can and must also be said for *moral theology*, seen in its specific nature as a scientific reflection on the *Gospel as the gift and commandment of new life*, a reflection on the life which "professes the truth in love" (cf. *Eph* 4:15) and on the Church's life of holiness, in which there shines forth the truth about the good brought to its perfection. The Church's Magisterium intervenes not only in the sphere of faith, but also, and inseparably so, in the sphere of morals. It has the task of "discerning, by means of judgments normative for the consciences of believers, those acts which in themselves conform to the demands of faith and foster their expression in life and those which, on the contrary, because intrinsically evil, are incompatible with such demands."[172] In proclaiming the commandments of God and the charity of Christ, the Church's Magisterium also teaches the faithful specific particular precepts and requires that they consider them in conscience as morally binding. In addition, the Magisterium carries out an important work of vigilance, warning the faithful of the presence of possible errors, even merely implicit ones, when their consciences fail to acknowledge the correctness and the truth of the moral norms which the Magisterium teaches.

This is the point at which to consider the specific task of all those who by mandate of their legitimate Pastors teach moral theology in Seminaries and Faculties of Theology. They have the grave duty to instruct the faithful—especially future Pastors—about all those commandments and practical norms

---

170. Congregation for the Doctrine of the Faith, Instruction on the Ecclesial Vocation of the Theologian *Donum Veritatis* (May 24, 1990), 6: *AAS* 82 (1990), 1552.

171. *Address* to the Professors and Students of the Pontifical Gregorian University (December 15, 1979), 6: *Insegnamenti* 11, 2 (1979), 1424.

172. Congregation for the Doctrine of the Faith, Instruction on the Ecclesial Vocation of the Theologian *Donum Veritatis* (May 24, 1990), 16: *AAS* 82 (1990), 1557.

authoritatively declared by the Church.[173] While recognizing the possible limitations of the human arguments employed by the Magisterium, moral theologians are called to develop a deeper understanding of the reasons underlying its teachings and to expound the validity and obligatory nature of the precepts it proposes, demonstrating their connection with one another and their relation with man's ultimate end.[174] Moral theologians are to set forth the Church's teaching and to give, in the exercise of their ministry, the example of a loyal assent, both internal and external, to the Magisterium's teaching in the areas of both dogma and morality.[175] Working together in cooperation with the hierarchical Magisterium, theologians will be deeply concerned to clarify ever more fully the biblical foundations, the ethical significance and the anthropological concerns which underlie the moral doctrine and the vision of man set forth by the Church.

111. The service which moral theologians are called to provide at the present time is of the utmost importance, not only for the Church's life and mission, but also for human society and culture. Moral theologians have the task, in close and vital connection with biblical and dogmatic theology, to highlight through their scientific reflection "that dynamic aspect which will elicit the response that man must give to the divine call which comes in the process of his growth in love, within a community of salvation. In this way, moral theology will acquire an inner spiritual dimension in response to the need to develop fully the *imago Dei* present in man, and in response to the laws of spiritual development described by Christian ascetical and mystical theology."[176]

Certainly moral theology and its teaching are meeting with particular difficulty today. Because the Church's morality necessarily involves a *normative* dimension, moral theology cannot be reduced to a body of knowledge worked out purely in the context of the so-called *behavioral sciences*. The latter are concerned with the phenomenon of morality as a historical and social fact; moral theology, however, while needing to make use of the behavioral and natural sciences, does not rely on the results of formal empirical observation or phenomenological understanding alone. Indeed, the relevance of the behavioral sciences for moral theology must always be measured against the primordial question: *What is good or evil? What must be done to have eternal life?*

---

173. Cf. *Code of Canon Law*, Canons 252, 1; 659, 3.

174. Cf. First Vatican Ecumenical Council, Dogmatic Constitution on the Catholic Faith *Dei Filius*, Chap. 4: *DS*, 3016.

175. Cf. Paul VI, Encyclical Letter *Humanae Vitae* (July 25, 1968), 28: *AAS* 60 (1968), 501.

176. Sacred Congregation for Catholic Education, *The Theological Formation of Future Priests* (February 22, 1976), n. 100. See nn. 95–101, which present the prospects and conditions for a fruitful renewal of moral theology.

112. The moral theologian must therefore exercise careful discernment in the context of today's prevalently scientific and technical culture, exposed as it is to the dangers of relativism, pragmatism and positivism. From the theological viewpoint, moral principles are not dependent upon the historical moment in which they are discovered. Moreover, the fact that some believers act without following the teachings of the Magisterium, or erroneously consider as morally correct a kind of behavior declared by their Pastors as contrary to the law of God, cannot be a valid argument for rejecting the truth of the moral norms taught by the Church. The affirmation of moral principles is not within the competence of formal empirical methods. While not denying the validity of such methods, but at the same time not restricting its viewpoint to them, moral theology, faithful to the supernatural sense of the faith, takes into account first and foremost *the spiritual dimension of the human heart and its vocation to divine love.*

In fact, while the behavioral sciences, like all experimental sciences, develop an empirical and statistical concept of "normality," faith teaches that this normality itself bears the traces of a fall from man's original situation—in other words, it is affected by sin. Only Christian faith points out to man the way to return to "the beginning" (cf. *Mt* 19:8), a way which is often quite different from that of empirical normality. Hence the behavioral sciences, despite the great value of the information which they provide, cannot be considered decisive indications of moral norms. It is the Gospel which reveals the full truth about man and his moral journey, and thus enlightens and admonishes sinners; it proclaims to them God's mercy, which is constantly at work to preserve them both from despair at their inability fully to know and keep God's law and from the presumption that they can be saved without merit. God also reminds sinners of the joy of forgiveness, which alone grants the strength to see in the moral law a liberating truth, a grace-filled source of hope, a path of life.

113. Teaching moral doctrine involves the conscious acceptance of these intellectual, spiritual and pastoral responsibilities. Moral theologians, who have accepted the charge of teaching the Church's doctrine, thus have a grave duty to train the faithful to make this moral discernment, to be committed to the true good and to have confident recourse to God's grace.

While exchanges and conflicts of opinion may constitute normal expressions of public life in a representative democracy, moral teaching certainly cannot depend simply upon respect for a process: indeed, it is in no way established by following the rules and deliberative procedures typical of a democracy. *Dissent,* in the form of carefully orchestrated protests and polemics carried on in the media, *is opposed to ecclesial communion and to a correct understanding of the hierarchical constitution of the People of God.* Opposition to the teaching of the Church's

Pastors cannot be seen as a legitimate expression either of Christian freedom or of the diversity of the Spirit's gifts. When this happens, the Church's Pastors have the duty to act in conformity with their apostolic mission, insisting that *the right of the faithful* to receive Catholic doctrine in its purity and integrity must always be respected. "Never forgetting that he too is a member of the People of God, the theologian must be respectful of them, and be committed to offering them a teaching which in no way does harm to the doctrine of the faith."[177]

Our own responsibilities as Pastors

114. As the Second Vatican Council reminds us, responsibility for the faith and the life of faith of the People of God is particularly incumbent upon the Church's Pastors: "Among the principal tasks of bishops the preaching of the Gospel is pre-eminent. For the bishops are the heralds of the faith who bring new disciples to Christ. They are authentic teachers, that is, teachers endowed with the authority of Christ, who preach to the people entrusted to them the faith to be believed and put into practice; they illustrate this faith in the light of the Holy Spirit, drawing out of the treasury of Revelation things old and new (cf. *Mt* 13:52); they make it bear fruit and they vigilantly ward off errors that are threatening their flock (cf. 2 *Tim* 4:1–4)."[178]

It is our common duty, and even before that our common grace, as Pastors and bishops of the Church, to teach the faithful the things which lead them to God, just as the Lord Jesus did with the young man in the Gospel. Replying to the question: "What good must I do to have eternal life?," Jesus referred the young man to God, the Lord of creation and of the Covenant. He reminded him of the moral commandments already revealed in the Old Testament and he indicated their spirit and deepest meaning by inviting the young man to follow him in poverty, humility and love: "Come, follow me!" The truth of this teaching was sealed on the Cross in the Blood of Christ: in the Holy Spirit, it has become the new law of the Church and of every Christian.

This "answer" to the question about morality has been entrusted by Jesus Christ in a particular way to us, the Pastors of the Church; we have been called to make it the object of our preaching, in the fulfillment of our *munus propheticum*. At the same time, our responsibility as Pastors with regard to Christian moral

---

177. Congregation for the Doctrine of the Faith, Instruction on the Ecclesial Vocation of the Theologian *Donum Veritatis* (May 24, 1990), 11: AAS 82 (1990), 1554; cf. in particular nn. 32–39, devoted to the problem of dissent: *ibid., loc. cit.*, 1562–68.

178. Dogmatic Constitution on the Church *Lumen Gentium*, 25.

teaching must also be exercised as part of the *munus sacerdotale:* this happens when we dispense to the faithful the gifts of grace and sanctification as an effective means for obeying God's holy law, and when with our constant and confident prayers we support believers in their efforts to be faithful to the demands of the faith and to live in accordance with the Gospel (cf. *Col* 1:9–12). Especially today, Christian moral teaching must be one of the chief areas in which we exercise our pastoral vigilance, in carrying out our *munus regale.*

115. This is the first time, in fact, that the Magisterium of the Church has set forth in detail the fundamental elements of this teaching, and presented the principles for the pastoral discernment necessary in practical and cultural situations which are complex and even crucial.

In the light of Revelation and of the Church's constant teaching, especially that of the Second Vatican Council, I have briefly recalled the essential characteristics of freedom, as well as the fundamental values connected with the dignity of the person and the truth of his acts, so as to be able to discern in obedience to the moral law a grace and a sign of our adoption in the one Son (cf. *Eph* 1:4–6). Specifically, this encyclical has evaluated certain trends in moral theology today. I now pass this evaluation on to you, in obedience to the word of the Lord who entrusted to Peter the task of strengthening his brethren (cf. *Lk* 22:32), in order to clarify and aid our common discernment.

Each of us knows how important is the teaching which represents the central theme of this encyclical and which is today being restated with the authority of the Successor of Peter. Each of us can see the seriousness of what is involved, not only for individuals but also for the whole of society, with the *reaffirmation of the universality and immutability of the moral commandments,* particularly those which prohibit always and without exception *intrinsically evil acts.*

In acknowledging these commandments, Christian hearts and our pastoral charity listen to the call of the One who "first loved us" (*1 Jn* 4:19). God asks us to be holy as he is holy (cf. *Lev* 19:2), to be—in Christ—perfect as he is perfect (cf. *Mt* 5:48). The unwavering demands of that commandment are based upon God's infinitely merciful love (cf. *Lk* 6:36), and the purpose of that commandment is to lead us, by the grace of Christ, on the path of that fullness of life proper to the children of God.

116. We have the duty, as bishops, to *be vigilant that the word of God is faithfully taught.* My Brothers in the Episcopate, it is part of our pastoral ministry to see to it that this moral teaching is faithfully handed down and to have recourse to appropriate measures to ensure that the faithful are guarded from every doctrine and theory contrary to it. In carrying out this task we are all assisted by theologians; even so, theological opinions constitute neither the rule nor the

norm of our teaching. Its authority is derived, by the assistance of the Holy Spirit and in communion *cum Petro et sub Petro*, from our fidelity to the Catholic faith which comes from the Apostles. As bishops, we have the grave obligation to be *personally* vigilant that the "sound doctrine" (1 *Tim* 1:10) of faith and morals is taught in our Dioceses.

A particular responsibility is incumbent upon bishops with regard to *Catholic institutions.* Whether these are agencies for the pastoral care of the family or for social work, or institutions dedicated to teaching or health care, bishops can canonically erect and recognize these structures and delegate certain responsibilities to them. Nevertheless, bishops are never relieved of their own personal obligations. It falls to them, in communion with the Holy See, both to grant the title "Catholic" to Church-related schools,[179] universities,[180] health-care facilities and counseling services, and, in cases of a serious failure to live up to that title, to take it away.

117. In the heart of every Christian, in the inmost depths of each person, there is always an echo of the question which the young man in the Gospel once asked Jesus: "Teacher, what good must I do to have eternal life?" (*Mt* 19:16). Everyone, however, needs to address this question to the "Good Teacher," since he is the only one who can answer in the fullness of truth, in all situations, in the most varied of circumstances. And when Christians ask him the question which rises from their conscience, the Lord replies in the words of the New Covenant which have been entrusted to his Church. As the Apostle Paul said of himself, we have been sent "to preach the Gospel, and not with eloquent wisdom, lest the Cross of Christ be emptied of its power" (1 *Cor* 1:17). The Church's answer to man's question contains the wisdom and power of Christ Crucified, the Truth which gives of itself.

When people ask the Church the questions raised by their consciences, when the faithful in the Church turn to their bishops and Pastors, *the Church's reply contains the voice of Jesus Christ, the voice of the truth about good and evil.* In the words spoken by the Church there resounds, in people's inmost being, the voice of God who "alone is good" (cf. *Mt* 19:17), who alone "is love" (1 *Jn* 4:8, 16).

Through the *anointing of the Spirit* this gentle but challenging word becomes light and life for man. Again the Apostle Paul invites us to have confidence, because "our competence is from God, who has made us competent to be ministers of a new covenant, not in a written code but in the Spirit ... The Lord is the Spirit, and where the Spirit of the Lord is, there is freedom. And all of us, with

---

179. Cf. *Code of Canon Law*, Canon 803, 3.

180. Cf. *Code of Canon Law*, Canon 808.

unveiled faces, reflecting the glory of the Lord, are being changed into his likeness from one degree of glory to another; for this comes from the Lord, the Spirit" (2 *Cor* 3:5–6, 17–18).

CONCLUSION

Mary, Mother of Mercy

118. At the end of these considerations, let us entrust ourselves, the sufferings and the joys of our life, the moral life of believers and people of good will, and the research of moralists, to Mary, Mother of God and Mother of Mercy.

Mary is Mother of Mercy because her Son, Jesus Christ, was sent by the Father as the revelation of God's mercy (cf. *Jn* 3:16–18). Christ came not to condemn but to forgive, to show mercy (cf. *Mt* 9:13). And the greatest mercy of all is found in his being in our midst and calling us to meet him and to confess, with Peter, that he is "the Son of the living God" (*Mt* 16:16). No human sin can erase the mercy of God, or prevent him from unleashing all his triumphant power, if we only call upon him. Indeed, sin itself makes even more radiant the love of the Father who, in order to ransom a slave, sacrificed his Son:[181] his mercy towards us is Redemption. This mercy reaches its fullness in the gift of the Spirit who bestows new life and demands that it be lived. No matter how many and great the obstacles put in his way by human frailty and sin, the Spirit, who renews the face of the earth (cf. *Ps* 104:30), makes possible the miracle of the perfect accomplishment of the good. This renewal, which gives the ability to do what is good, noble, beautiful, pleasing to God and in conformity with his will, is in some way the flowering of the gift of mercy, which offers liberation from the slavery of evil and gives the strength to sin no more. Through the gift of new life, Jesus makes us sharers in his love and leads us to the Father in the Spirit.

119. Such is the consoling certainty of Christian faith, the source of its profound humanity and *extraordinary simplicity*. At times, in the discussions about new and complex moral problems, it can seem that Christian morality is in itself too demanding, difficult to understand and almost impossible to practice. This is untrue, since Christian morality consists, in the simplicity of the Gospel, in *following Jesus Christ*, in abandoning oneself to him, in letting oneself be transformed by his grace and renewed by his mercy, gifts which come to us in the living communion of his Church. Saint Augustine reminds us that "he who

---

181. *"O inaestimabilis dilectio caritatis: ut servum redimeres, Filium tradidisti!" Missale Romanum, In Resurrectione Domini, Praeconium Paschale.*

would live has a place to live, and has everything needed to live. Let him draw near, let him believe, let him become part of the body, that he may have life. Let him not shrink from the unity of the members."[182] By the light of the Holy Spirit, the living essence of Christian morality can be understood by everyone, even the least learned, but particularly those who are able to preserve an "undivided heart" (*Ps* 86:11). On the other hand, this evangelical simplicity does not exempt one from facing reality in its complexity; rather it can lead to a more genuine understanding of reality, inasmuch as following Christ will gradually bring out the distinctive character of authentic Christian morality, while providing the vital energy needed to carry it out. It is the task of the Church's Magisterium to see that the dynamic process of following Christ develops in an organic manner, without the falsification or obscuring of its moral demands, with all their consequences. The one who loves Christ keeps his commandments (cf. *Jn* 14:15).

120. Mary is also Mother of Mercy because it is to her that Jesus entrusts his Church and all humanity. At the foot of the Cross, when she accepts John as her son, when she asks, together with Christ, forgiveness from the Father for those who do not know what they do (cf. *Lk* 23:34), Mary experiences, in perfect docility to the Spirit, the richness and the universality of God's love, which opens her heart and enables it to embrace the entire human race. Thus Mary becomes Mother of each and every one of us, the Mother who obtains for us divine mercy.

Mary is the radiant sign and inviting model of the moral life. As Saint Ambrose put it, "The life of this one person can serve as a model for everyone,"[183] and while speaking specifically to virgins but within a context open to all, he affirmed: "The first stimulus to learning is the nobility of the teacher. Who can be more noble than the Mother of God? Who can be more glorious than the one chosen by Glory Itself?"[184] Mary lived and exercised her freedom precisely by giving herself to God and accepting God's gift within herself. Until the time of his birth, she sheltered in her womb the Son of God who became man; she raised him and enabled him to grow, and she accompanied him in that supreme act of freedom which is the complete sacrifice of his own life. By the gift of herself, Mary entered fully into the plan of God who gives himself to the world. By accepting and pondering in her heart events which she did not always understand (cf. *Lk* 2:19), she became the model of all those who hear the word of God and keep it (cf. *Lk* 11:28), and merited the title of "Seat of Wisdom." This Wisdom is Jesus Christ himself, the Eternal Word of God, who perfectly reveals and accomplishes

---

182. *In Iohannis Evangelium Tractatus*, 26, 13: CCL, 36, 266.

183. *De Virginibus*, Bk. II, Chap. II, 15: PL 16, 222.

184. Ibid., Bk. II, Chap. II, 7: PL 16, 220.

the will of the Father (cf. *Heb* 10:5–10). Mary invites everyone to accept this Wisdom. To us too she addresses the command she gave to the servants at Cana in Galilee during the marriage feast: "Do whatever he tells you" (*Jn* 2:5).

Mary shares our human condition, but in complete openness to the grace of God. Not having known sin, she is able to have compassion on every kind of weakness. She understands sinful man and loves him with a mother's love. Precisely for this reason she is on the side of truth and shares the Church's burden in recalling always and to everyone the demands of morality. Nor does she permit sinful man to be deceived by those who claim to love him by justifying his sin, for she knows that the sacrifice of Christ her Son would thus be emptied of its power. No absolution offered by beguiling doctrines, even in the areas of philosophy and theology, can make man truly happy: only the Cross and the glory of the Risen Christ can grant peace to his conscience and salvation to his life.

O Mary, Mother of Mercy,
watch over all people,
that the Cross of Christ
may not be emptied of its power,
that man may not stray
from the path of the good or become blind to sin,
but may put his hope ever more fully in God
who is "rich in mercy" (*Eph* 2:4).
May he carry out the good works prepared
by God beforehand (cf. *Eph* 2:10)
and so live completely
"for the praise of his glory" (*Eph* 1:12).

Given in Rome, at Saint Peter's, on the sixth of August, Feast of the Transfiguration of the Lord, in the year 1993, the fifteenth of my pontificate.

✠ JOHN PAUL II

GRATISSIMAM SANE

Letter to Families

Letter of Pope John Paul II,
promulgated February 2, 1994

Dear Families!

The celebration of the Year of the Family gives me a welcome opportunity to knock at the door of your home, eager to greet you with deep affection and to spend time with you. I do so by this Letter, taking as my point of departure the words of the Encyclical *Redemptor Hominis,* published in the first days of my ministry as the Successor of Peter. There I wrote that *man is the way of the Church.*[1]

With these words I wanted first of all to evoke the many paths along which man walks, and at the same time to emphasize how deeply the Church desires to stand at his side as he follows the paths of his earthly life. The Church shares in the joys and hopes, the sorrows and anxieties[2] of people's daily pilgrimage, firmly convinced that it was Christ himself who set her on all these paths. Christ entrusted man to the Church; he entrusted man to her as the "way" of her mission and her ministry.

The Family—Way of the Church

2. Among these many paths, *the family is the first and the most important.* It is a path common to all, yet one which is particular, unique and unrepeatable, just as every individual is unrepeatable; it is a path from which man cannot withdraw.

Indeed, a person normally comes into the world within a family, and can be said to owe to the family the very fact of his existing as an individual. When he has no family, the person coming into the world develops an anguished sense of

---

1.   Cf. Encyclical Letter *Redemptor Hominis* (4 March 1979), 14: *AAS* 71 (1979), 284–85.

2.   Cf. Second Vatican Ecumenical Council, Pastoral Constitution on the Church in the Modern World *Gaudium et Spes,* 1.

pain and loss, one which will subsequently burden his whole life. The Church draws near with loving concern to all who experience situations such as these, for she knows well the fundamental role which the family is called upon to play. Furthermore, she knows that *a person goes forth from the family in order to realize in a new family unit his particular vocation in life.* Even if someone chooses to remain single, the family continues to be, as it were, his existential horizon, that fundamental community in which the whole network of social relations is grounded, from the closest and most immediate to the most distant. Do we not often speak of the "human family" when referring to all the people living in the world?

The family has its origin in that same love with which the Creator embraces the created world, as was already expressed "in the beginning," in the *Book of Genesis* (1:1). In the Gospel Jesus offers a supreme confirmation: "God so loved the world that he gave his only Son" (Jn 3:16). The *only-begotten Son,* of one substance with the Father, "*God from God* and Light from Light," *entered into human history through the family*: "For by his incarnation the Son of God united himself in a certain way with every man. He labored with human hands ... and loved with a human heart. Born of Mary the Virgin, he truly became one of us and, except for sin, was like us in every respect."[3] If in fact Christ "fully discloses man to himself,"[4] he does so beginning with the family in which he chose to be born and to grow up. We know that the Redeemer spent most of his life in the obscurity of Nazareth, "obedient" (Lk 2:51) as the "Son of Man" to Mary his Mother, and to Joseph the carpenter. Is this filial "obedience" of Christ not already the first expression of that obedience to the Father "unto death" (Phil 2:8), whereby he redeemed the world?

The divine mystery of the Incarnation of the Word thus has an intimate connection with the human family. Not only with one family, that of Nazareth, but in some way with every family, analogously to what the Second Vatican Council says about the Son of God, who in the Incarnation "united himself in some sense with every man."[5] Following Christ who "came" into the world "to serve" (Mt 20:28), the Church considers serving the family to be one of her essential duties. In this sense both man and the family constitute "the way of the Church."

The Year of the Family

3. For these very reasons *the Church joyfully welcomes the decision* of the

---

3. Ibid., 22.

4. Ibid.

5. Ibid.

United Nations Organization *to declare 1994 the International Year of the Family.* This initiative makes it clear how fundamental the question of the family is for the member States of the United Nations. If the Church wishes to take part in this initiative, it is because she herself has been sent by Christ to "all nations" (Mt 28:19). Moreover, this is not the first time the Church has made her own an international initiative of the United Nations. We need but recall, for example, the International Year of Youth in 1985. In this way also the Church makes herself present in the world, fulfilling a desire which was dear to Pope John XXIII, and which inspired the Second Vatican Council's Constitution *Gaudium et Spes.*

On the Feast of the Holy Family in 1993 the whole ecclesial community began the "Year of the Family" as one of the important steps along the path of preparation for the Great Jubilee of the Year 2000, which will mark the end of the second and the beginning of the third Millennium of the Birth of Jesus Christ.

This Year ought to direct our thoughts and our hearts towards Nazareth, where it was officially inaugurated this past 26 December at a Solemn Eucharistic Liturgy presided over by the Papal Legate.

Throughout this Year it is important to discover anew the many *signs of the Church's love and concern for the family,* a love and concern expressed from the very beginning of Christianity, when the meaningful term *"domestic church"* was applied to the family. In our own times we have often returned to the phrase "domestic church," which the Council adopted[6] and the sense of which we hope will always remain alive in people's minds. This desire is not lessened by an awareness of the changed conditions of families in today's world. Precisely because of this, there is a continuing relevance to the title chosen by the Council in the Pastoral Constitution *Gaudium et Spes* in order to indicate what the Church should be doing in the present situation: *"Promoting the dignity of marriage and the family."*[7] Another important reference point after the Council is the 1981 Apostolic Exhortation *Familiaris Consortio.* This text takes into account a vast and complex experience with regard to the family, which among different peoples and countries always and everywhere continues to be the "way of the Church." In a certain sense it becomes all the more so precisely in those places where the family is suffering from internal crises or is exposed to adverse cultural, social and economic influences which threaten its inner unity and strength, and even stand in the way of its very formation.

---

6.   Cf. Dogmatic Constitution on the Church *Lumen Gentium,* 11.

7.   Pastoral Constitution on the Church in the Modern World *Gaudium et Spes,* Part II, Chap. 1.

Prayer

4. In this Letter I wish to speak not to families "in the abstract" but *to every particular family in every part of the world,* wherever it is located and whatever the diversity and complexity of its culture and history. The love with which God "loved the world" (Jn 3:16), the love with which Christ loved each and every one "to the end" (Jn 13:1), makes it possible to address this message to each family, as a living "cell" of the great and universal "family" of mankind. The Father, Creator of the Universe, and the Word Incarnate, the Redeemer of man, are the source of this universal openness to all people as brothers and sisters, and they impel *us to embrace them in the prayer* which begins with the tender words: *"Our Father."*

Prayer makes the Son of God present among us: "For where two or three are gathered in my name, I am there among them" (Mt 18:20). This *Letter to Families* wishes in the first place to be a prayer to Christ to remain in every human family; an invitation to him, in and through the small family of parents and children, to dwell in the great family of nations, so that together with him all of us can truly say: "Our Father"! Prayer must become the dominant element of the Year of the Family in the Church: prayer by the family, prayer for the family, and prayer with the family.

It is significant that precisely *in and through prayer, man comes to discover in a very simple and yet profound way his own unique subjectivity:* in prayer the human "I" more easily perceives the depth of what it means to be a person. *This is also true of the family,* which is not only the basic "cell" of society, but also possesses a particular subjectivity of its own. This subjectivity finds its first and fundamental confirmation, and is strengthened, precisely when the members of the family meet in the common invocation: "Our Father." Prayer increases the strength and spiritual unity of the family, helping the family to partake of God's own "strength." In the solemn nuptial blessing during the Rite of Marriage, the celebrant calls upon the Lord in these words: "Pour out upon them [the newlyweds] the grace of the Holy Spirit so that by your love poured into their hearts they will remain faithful in the marriage covenant."[8] This "visitation" of the Holy Spirit gives rise to the inner strength of families, as well as the power capable of uniting them in love and truth.

Love and Concern for All Families

5. May the Year of the Family become a harmonious and universal prayer on the part of all "domestic churches" and of the whole People of God! May this

---

8.   *Rituale Romanum, Ordo Celebrandi Matrimonium,* n. 74, editio typica altera, 1991, p. 26.

prayer also reach families in difficulty or danger, lacking confidence or experiencing division, or in situations which *Familiaris Consortio* describes as "irregular."[9] *May all families be able to feel the loving and caring embrace of their brothers and sisters!*

During the Year of the Family, prayer should first of all be an encouraging witness on the part of those families who live out their human and Christian vocation in the communion of the home. How many of them there are in every nation, diocese and parish! With reason it can be said that these families make up "the norm," even admitting the existence of more than a few "irregular situations." And experience shows what an important role is played by a family living in accordance with the moral norm, so that the individual born and raised in it will be able to set out without hesitation on the road of the good, which is *always written in his heart*. Unfortunately various programs backed by very powerful resources nowadays seem to aim at the breakdown of the family. At times it appears that concerted efforts are being made to present as "normal" and attractive, and even to glamorize, situations which are in fact "irregular."

Indeed, they contradict "the truth and love" which should inspire and guide relationships between men and women, thus causing tensions and divisions in families, with grave consequences particularly for children. The moral conscience becomes darkened; what is true, good and beautiful is deformed; and freedom is replaced by what is actually enslavement. In view of all this, how relevant and thought-provoking are the words of the Apostle Paul about the freedom for which Christ has set us free, and the slavery which is caused by sin (cf. Gal 5:1)!

It is apparent then how timely and even necessary a Year of the Family is for the Church; how indispensable is *the witness of all families* who live their vocation day by day; how urgent it is *for families to pray* and for that prayer to increase and to spread throughout the world, expressing thanksgiving for love in truth, for "the outpouring of the grace of the Holy Spirit,"[10] for the presence among parents and children of Christ the Redeemer and Bridegroom, who "loved us to the end" (cf. Jn 13:1). Let us be deeply convinced that this *love is the greatest of all* (cf. 1 Cor 13:13), and let us believe that it is really capable of triumphing over everything that is not love.

During this year may the prayer of the Church, the prayer of families as "domestic churches," constantly rise up! May it make itself heard first by God and then also by people everywhere, so that they will not succumb to doubt, and all who are wavering because of human weakness will not yield to the tempting glamour of merely apparent goods, like those held out in every temptation.

9.   Cf. Apostolic Exhortation *Familiaris Consortio* (22 November 1981), 79–84: MS 74 (1982), 180–86.

10.   Cf. *Rituale Romanum, Ordo Celebrandi Matrimonium,* n. 74, ed. cit., p. 26.

At Cana in Galilee, where Jesus was invited to a marriage banquet, his Mother, also present, said to the servants: "Do whatever he tells you" (Jn 2:5). Now that we have begun our celebration of the Year of the Family, Mary says the same words to us. What Christ tells us, in this particular moment of history, constitutes a forceful call to a great prayer with families and for families. The Virgin Mother invites us to unite ourselves through this prayer to the sentiments of her Son, who loves each and every family. He expressed this love at the very beginning of his mission as Redeemer, with his sanctifying presence at Cana in Galilee, a presence which still continues.

Let us pray for families throughout the world. Let us pray, through Christ, with him and in him, to the Father "from whom every family in heaven and on earth is named" (Eph 3:15).

I. THE CIVILIZATION OF LOVE

"Male and Female He Created Them"

6. The universe, immense and diverse as it is, the world of all living beings, is *inscribed in God's fatherhood, which is its source* (cf. Eph 3:14–16). This can be said, of course, on the basis of an analogy, thanks to which we can discern, at the very beginning of the Book of Genesis, the reality of fatherhood and motherhood and consequently of the human family. The interpretative key enabling this discernment is provided by the principle of the "image" and "likeness" of God highlighted by the scriptural text (Gen 1:26). God creates by the power of his word: "Let there be …!" (e.g., Gen 1:3). Significantly, in the creation of man this word of God is followed by these other words: "*Let us make man* in our image, after our likeness" (Gen 1:26). Before creating man, the Creator withdraws as it were into himself, in order to seek the pattern and inspiration in the mystery of his Being, which is already here disclosed as the divine "We." From this mystery the human being comes forth by an act of creation: "*God created man in his own image,* in the image of God he created him; male and female he created them" (Gen 1:27).

God speaks to these newly-created beings and he blesses them: "Be fruitful and multiply, and fill the earth and subdue it" (Gen 1:28). The Book of Genesis employs the same expressions used earlier for the creation of other living beings: "multiply." But it is clear that these expressions are being used in an analogous sense. Is there not present here the analogy of begetting and of fatherhood and motherhood, which should be understood in the light of the overall context? No living being on earth except man was created "in the image and likeness of God."

Human fatherhood and motherhood, while remaining *biologically similar* to that of other living beings in nature, contain in an essential and unique way a "likeness" to God which is the basis of the family as a community of human life, as a community of persons united in love (*communio personarum*).

In the light of the New Testament it is possible to discern how *the primordial model of the family is to be sought in God himself,* in the Trinitarian mystery of his life. The divine "We" is the eternal pattern of the human "we," especially of that "we" formed by the man and the woman created in the divine image and likeness. The words of the Book of Genesis contain that truth about man which is confirmed by the very experience of humanity. Man is created "from the very beginning" as male and female: the life of all humanity—whether of small communities or of society as a whole—is marked by this primordial duality. From it there derive the "masculinity" and the "femininity" of individuals, just as from it every community draws its own unique richness in the mutual fulfillment of persons. This is what seems to be meant by the words of the Book of Genesis: "Male and female he created them" (Gen 1:27). Here too we find the first statement of the equal dignity of man and woman: both, in equal measure, are persons.

Their constitution, with the specific dignity which derives from it, defines "from the beginning" the qualities of the common good of humanity, in every dimension and circumstance of life. To this common good both man and woman make their specific contribution. Hence one can discover, at the very origins of human society, the qualities of communion and of complementarity.

The Marital Covenant

7. The family has always been considered as the first and basic expression of man's *social nature.* Even today this way of looking at things remains unchanged. Nowadays, however, emphasis tends to be laid on how much the family, as the smallest and most basic human community, owes to the personal contribution of a man and a woman. The family is in fact a community of persons whose proper way of existing and living together is communion: *communio personarum.* Here too, while always acknowledging the absolute transcendence of the Creator with regard to his creatures, we can see the family's ultimate relationship to the divine "We." *Only persons are capable of living "in communion."* The family originates in a marital communion described by the Second Vatican Council as a "covenant," *in which man and woman "give themselves to each other and accept each other."*[11]

---

11. Pastoral Constitution on the Church in the Modern World *Gaudium et Spes,* 48.

The Book of Genesis helps us to see this truth when it states, in reference to the establishment of the family through marriage, that "a man leaves his father and his mother and cleaves to his wife, and they become one flesh" (Gen 2:24). In the Gospel, Christ, disputing with the Pharisees, quotes these same words and then adds: "So they are no longer two but one flesh. What therefore God has joined together, let not man put asunder" (Mt 19:6). In this way, he reveals anew the binding content of a fact which exists "from the beginning" (Mt 19:8) and which always preserves this content. If the Master confirms it "now," he does so in order to make clear and unmistakable to all, at the dawn of the New Covenant, the *indissoluble character* of marriage as the *basis of the common good of the family*.

When, in union with the Apostle, we bow our knees before the Father from whom all fatherhood and motherhood is named (cf. Eph 3:14–15), we come to realize that parenthood is the event whereby the family, already constituted by the conjugal covenant of marriage, is brought about "in the full and specific sense."[12] *Motherhood necessarily implies fatherhood*, and in turn, *fatherhood necessarily implies motherhood*. This is the result of the duality bestowed by the Creator upon human beings "from the beginning."

I have spoken of two closely related yet not identical concepts: the concept of "communion" and that of "community." "*Communion*" has to do with the personal relationship between the "I" and the "thou." "*Community*" on the other hand transcends this framework and moves towards a "society," a "we."

The family, as a community of persons, is thus the first human "society." It arises whenever there comes into being the conjugal covenant of marriage, which opens the spouses to a lasting communion of love and of life, and it is brought to completion in a full and specific way with the procreation of children: the "communion" of the spouses gives rise to the "community" of the family. The "community" of the family is completely pervaded by the very essence of "communion." On the human level, can there be any other "*communion*" comparable to that *between a mother and a child* whom she has carried in her womb and then brought to birth?

In the family thus constituted there appears a new unity, in which the relationship of "communion" between the parents attains complete fulfillment. Experience teaches that this fulfillment represents both a task and a challenge. The task involves the spouses in living out their original covenant. *The children born to them*—and here is the challenge—*should consolidate that covenant*, enriching and deepening the conjugal communion of the father and mother. When this does not occur, we need to ask if the selfishness which lurks even

---

12. Apostolic Exhortation *Familiaris Consortio* (22 November 1981), 69: *AAS* 74 (1982), 165.

in the love of man and woman as a result of the human inclination to evil is not stronger than this love. Married couples need to be well aware of this. From the outset they need to have their hearts and thoughts turned towards the God "from whom every family is named," *so that their fatherhood and motherhood will draw from that source the power to be continually renewed in love.*

Fatherhood and motherhood are themselves a particular proof of love; they make it possible to discover love's extension and original depth. But this does not take place automatically. Rather, it is a task entrusted to both husband and wife. In the life of husband and wife together, fatherhood and motherhood represent such a sublime "novelty" and richness as can only be approached "on one's knees."

Experience teaches that human love, which naturally tends towards fatherhood and motherhood, is sometimes affected by a profound *crisis* and is thus seriously threatened. In such cases, help can be sought at marriage and family counseling centers, where it is possible, among other things, to obtain the assistance of specifically trained psychologists and psychotherapists. At the same time, however, we cannot forget the perennial validity of the words of the Apostle: "I bow my knees before the Father, from whom every family in heaven and on earth is named." Marriage, the sacrament of matrimony, is a covenant of persons in love. And *love can be deepened and preserved only by Love,* that Love which is "poured into our hearts through the Holy Spirit which has been given to us" (Rom 5:5). During the Year of the Family should our prayer not concentrate on the crucial and decisive moment of the passage from conjugal love to childbearing, and thus to fatherhood and motherhood? Is that not precisely the moment when there is an indispensable need for the "outpouring of the grace of the Holy Spirit" invoked in the liturgical celebration of the sacrament of matrimony?

The Apostle, bowing his knees before the Father, asks that the faithful "be *strengthened* with might *through his Spirit in the inner man*" (Eph 3:16). This "inner strength" is necessary in all family life, especially at its critical moments, when the love which was expressed in the liturgical rite of marital consent with the words, "I promise to be faithful to you always ... all the days of my life," is put to a difficult test.

The Unity of the Two

8. Only "persons" are capable of saying those words; only they are able to live "in communion" on the basis of a mutual choice which is, or ought to be, fully conscious and free. The Book of Genesis, in speaking of a man who leaves father and mother in order to cleave to his wife (cf. Gen 2:24), highlights the *conscious and free choice* which gives rise to marriage, making the son of a family a husband,

and the daughter of a family a wife. How can we adequately understand this mutual choice, unless we take into consideration the full truth about the person, who is a rational and free being? The Second Vatican Council, in speaking of the likeness of God, uses extremely significant terms. It refers not only to the divine image and likeness which every human being as such already possesses, but also and primarily to "a certain similarity between the union of the divine persons and the union of God's children in truth and love."[13]

This rich and meaningful formulation first of all confirms what is central to the identity of every man and every woman. This identity consists in the *capacity to live in truth and love*; even more, it consists in the need of truth and love as an essential dimension of the life of the person. Man's need for truth and love opens him both to God and to creatures: it opens him to other people, to life "in communion," and in particular to marriage and to the family. In the words of the Council, the "communion" of persons is drawn in a certain sense from the mystery of the Trinitarian "We," and therefore "conjugal communion" also refers to this mystery. The family, which originates in the love of man and woman, ultimately derives from the mystery of God. This conforms to the innermost being of man and woman, to their innate and authentic dignity as persons.

In marriage man and woman are so firmly united as to become, to use the words of the Book of Genesis, "one flesh" (Gen 2:24). Male and female in their physical constitution, the two human subjects, even though physically different, *share equally in the capacity to live "in truth and love."* This capacity, characteristic of the human being as a person, has at the same time both a spiritual and a bodily dimension. It is also through the body that man and woman are predisposed to form a "communion of persons" in marriage. When they are united by the conjugal covenant in such a way as to become "*one flesh*" (Gen 2:24), their *union* ought to take place "*in truth and love*," and thus express the maturity proper to persons created in the image and likeness of God.

The family which results from this union draws its inner solidity from the covenant between the spouses, which Christ raised to a sacrament. The family draws its proper character as a community, its traits of "communion," from that fundamental communion of the spouses which is prolonged in their children.

"*Will you accept children lovingly from God, and bring them up according to the law of Christ and his Church?*," the celebrant asks during the Rite of Marriage.[14] The answer given by the spouses reflects the most profound truth of the love which unites them. Their unity, however, rather than closing them up in themselves,

---

13. Pastoral Constitution on the Church in the Modern World *Gaudium et Spes*, 24.

14. *Rituale Romanum, Ordo Celebrandi Matrimonium*, n. 60, ed. cit., p. 17.

opens them towards a new life, towards a new person. As parents, they will be capable of giving life to a being like themselves, not only bone of their bones and flesh of their flesh (cf. Gen 2:23), but an image and likeness of God—a person.

When the Church asks "Are you willing?," she is reminding the bride and bridegroom that they stand *before the creative power of God.* They are called to become parents, to cooperate with the Creator in giving life. Cooperating with God to call new human beings into existence means contributing to the transmission of that divine image and likeness of which everyone "born of a woman" is a bearer.

The Genealogy of the Person

9. Through the communion of persons which occurs in marriage, a man and a woman begin a family. Bound up with the family is the genealogy of every individual: *the genealogy of the person.* Human fatherhood and motherhood are rooted in biology, yet at the same time transcend it. The Apostle, with knees bowed "before the Father from whom all fatherhood [and motherhood] in heaven and on earth is named," in a certain sense asks us to look at the whole world of living creatures, from the spiritual beings in heaven to the corporeal beings on earth. Every act of begetting finds its primordial model in the fatherhood of God. Nonetheless, in the case of man, this "cosmic" dimension of likeness to God is not sufficient to explain adequately the relationship of fatherhood and motherhood. When a new person is born of the conjugal union of the two, he brings with him into the world a particular image and likeness of God himself: *the genealogy of the person is inscribed in the very biology of generation.*

In affirming that the spouses, as parents, cooperate with God the Creator in conceiving and giving birth to a new human being,[15] we are not speaking merely with reference to the laws of biology. Instead, we wish to emphasize that *God himself is present in human fatherhood and motherhood* quite differently than he is present in all other instances of begetting "on earth." Indeed, God alone is the source of that "image and likeness" which is proper to the human being, as it was received at Creation. Begetting is the continuation of Creation.[16]

And so, both in the conception and in the birth of a new child, parents find themselves face to face with a "great mystery" (cf. Eph 5:32). Like his parents, the *new human being is also called* to live as a person; he is called *to a life "in truth and love."* This call is not only open to what exists in time, but in God it is also open to eternity. This is the dimension of the genealogy of the person which has been

---

15. Cf. Apostolic Exhortation *Familiaris Consortio* (22 November 1981), 28: *AAS* 74 (1982), 114.

16. Cf. Plus XII, Encyclical Letter *Humani Generis* (12 August 1950): *AAS* 42 (1950), 574.

revealed definitively by Christ, who casts the light of his Gospel on human life and death and thus on the meaning of the human family.

As the Council affirms, man is "the only creature on earth whom God willed for its own sake."[17] Man's coming into being does not conform to the laws of biology alone, but also, and directly, to God's creative will, which is concerned with the genealogy of the sons and daughters of human families. *God "willed" man from the very beginning, and God "wills" him in every act of conception and every human birth.* God "wills" man as a being similar to himself, as a person. This man, every man, is created by God *"for his own sake."* That is true of all persons, including those born with sicknesses or disabilities. Inscribed in the personal constitution of every human being is the will of God, who wills that man should be, in a certain sense, an end unto himself. God hands man over to himself, entrusting him both to his family and to society as their responsibility. Parents, in contemplating a new human being, are, or ought to be, fully aware of the fact that God "wills" this individual "for his own sake."

This concise expression is profoundly rich in meaning. From the very moment of conception, and then of birth, the new being is meant *to express fully his humanity,* to "find himself" as a person.[18] This is true for absolutely everyone, including the chronically ill and the disabled. "To be human" is his fundamental vocation: "to be human" in accordance with the gift received, in accordance with that "talent" which is humanity itself, and only then in accordance with other talents. In this sense God wills every man "for his own sake." *In God's plan,* however, the vocation of the human person extends beyond the boundaries of time. It encounters the will of the Father revealed in the Incarnate Word: *God's will is to lavish upon man a sharing in his own divine life.* As Christ says: "I came that they may have life and have it abundantly" (Jn 10:10).

Does affirming man's ultimate destiny not conflict with the statement that God wills man "for his own sake"? If he has been created for divine life, can man truly exist "for his own sake"?

This is a critical question, one of great significance both for the beginning of his earthly life and its end: it is important for the whole span of his life. It might appear that in destining man for divine life God definitively takes away man's existing "for his own sake."[19] What then is the relationship between the life of the person and his sharing in the life of the Trinity? Saint Augustine provides us with the answer in his celebrated phrase: "Our heart is restless until it rests

---

17. Pastoral Constitution on the Church in the Modern World *Gaudium et Spes*, 24.

18. Ibid.

19. Ibid.

in you."[20] This "restless heart" serves to point out that between the one finality and the other there is in fact no contradiction, but rather a relationship, a complementarity, a unity. By his very genealogy, the person created in the image and likeness of God, *exists "for his own sake"* and reaches fulfillment precisely *by sharing in God's life.* The content of this self-fulfillment is the fullness of life in God, proclaimed by Christ (cf. Jn 6:37–40), who redeemed us precisely so that we might come to share it (cf. Mk 10:45).

It is for themselves that married couples want children; in children they see the crowning of their own love for each other. They want children for the family, as a *priceless gift.*[21] This is quite understandable. Nonetheless, in conjugal love and in paternal and maternal love we should find inscribed the same truth about man which the Council expressed in a clear and concise way in its statement that God "willed man for his own sake." It is thus necessary that the will of the parents should be in harmony with the will of God. *They must want the new human creature in the same way as the Creator wants him:* "for himself." Our human will is always and inevitably subject to the law of time and change. The divine will, on the other hand, is eternal. As we read in the Book of the Prophet Jeremiah: "Before I formed you in the womb I knew you, and before you were born I consecrated you" (Jer 1:5). The genealogy of the person is thus united with the eternity of God, and only then with human fatherhood and motherhood, which are realized in time. At the moment of conception itself, man is already destined to eternity in God.

The Common Good of Marriage and the Family

10. Marital consent defines and consolidates *the good common to marriage and to the family.* "I, N., take you, N., to be my wife/husband. I promise to be true to you in good times and in bad, in sickness and in health. I will love you and honor you all the days of my life."[22] Marriage is a unique communion of persons, and it is on the basis of this communion that the family is called to become a community of persons. This is a commitment which the bride and bridegroom undertake "before God and his Church," as the celebrant reminds them before they exchange their consent.[23] Those who take part in the rite are witnesses of this commitment, for in a certain sense they represent the Church and society, the settings in which the new family will live and grow.

---

20. *Confessiones,* I, 1: CCL 27,1.

21. Cf. Pastoral Constitution on the Church in the Modern World *Gaudium et Spes,* 50.

22. *Rituale Romanum, Ordo Celebrandi Matrimonium,* n. 62, ed. cit., p. 17.

23. Ibid., n. 61, ed. cit., p. 17.

The words of consent define the common good of the *couple and of the family*. First, the common good of the spouses: love, fidelity, honor, the permanence of their union until death—"all the days of my life." The good of both, which is at the same time the good of each, must then become the good of the children. The common good, by its very nature, both unites individual persons and ensures the true good of each. If the Church (and the State for that matter) receives the consent which the spouses express in the words cited above, she does so because that consent is "written in their hearts" (Rom 2:15). It is the spouses who give their consent to each other by a solemn promise, that is by confirming the truth of that consent in the sight of God. As baptized Christians, they are the ministers of the sacrament of matrimony in the Church. Saint Paul teaches that this mutual commitment of theirs is a "great mystery" (Eph 5:32).

The words of consent, then, express what is essential to the common good of the spouses, and *they indicate what ought to be the common good of the future family*. In order to bring this out, the Church asks the spouses if they are prepared to accept the children God grants them and to raise the children as Christians. This question calls to mind the common good of the future family unit, evoking the genealogy of persons which is part of the constitution of marriage and of the family itself. The question about children and their education is profoundly linked to marital consent, with its solemn promise of love, conjugal respect, and fidelity until death. The acceptance and education of children—two of the primary ends of the family—are conditioned by how that commitment will be fulfilled. Fatherhood and motherhood represent a *responsibility which is not simply physical but spiritual in nature*, indeed, through these realities there passes the genealogy of the person, which has its eternal beginning in God and which must lead back to him.

The Year of the Family, as a year of special prayer on the part of families, ought to renew and deepen each family's awareness of these truths. What a wealth of biblical reflections could nourish that prayer! Together with the words of Sacred Scripture, these prayerful reflections should always include the *personal memories of the spouses-parents*, the children and grandchildren. Through the genealogy of persons, conjugal communion *becomes a communion of generations*. The sacramental union of the two spouses, sealed in the covenant which they enter into before God, endures and grows stronger as the generations pass. It must become a union in prayer. But for all this to become clearly apparent during the Year of the Family, prayer needs to become a regular habit in the daily life of each family. Prayer is thanksgiving, praise of God, asking for forgiveness, supplication and invocation. In all of these forms *the prayer of the family has much to say to God*. It also has much to say to others, beginning with the mutual communion of persons joined together by family ties.

The Psalmist asks: "What is man that you keep him in mind?" (Ps 8:4). Prayer is the place where, in a very simple way, the creative and fatherly remembrance of God is made manifest: not only man's remembrance of God, but also and especially *God's remembrance of man*. In this way, the prayer of the family as a community can become a place of common and mutual remembrance: the family is in fact a community of generations.

In prayer everyone should be present: the living and those who have died, and also those yet to come into the world. Families should pray for all of their members, in view of the good which the family is for each individual and which each individual is for the whole family. Prayer strengthens this good, precisely as the common good of the family. Moreover, it creates this good ever anew. In prayer, the family discovers itself as the first "we," in which each member is "*I*" and "*thou*"; each member is for the others either husband or wife, father or mother, son or daughter, brother or sister, grandparent or grandchild.

Are all the families to which this Letter is addressed like this? Certainly a good number are, but the times in which we are living tend to restrict family units to two generations. Often this is the case because available housing is too limited, especially in large cities. But it is not infrequently due to the belief that having several generations living together interferes with privacy and makes life too difficult. But is this not where the problem really lies? *Families today have too little "human" life.* There is a shortage of people with whom to create and share the common good; and yet that good, by its nature, demands to be created and shared with others: *bonum est diffusivum sui*: "good is diffusive of itself."[24] The more *common* the good, the *more properly one's own* it will also be: mine—yours—ours. This is the logic behind living according to the good, living in truth and charity. If man is able to accept and follow this logic, his life truly becomes a "sincere gift."

The Sincere Gift of Self

11. After affirming that man is the only creature on earth which God willed for itself, the Council immediately goes on to say that he cannot "*fully find himself except through a sincere gift of self*."[25] This might appear to be a contradiction, but in fact it is not. Instead it is the magnificent paradox of human existence: an existence called *to serve the truth in love*. Love causes man to find fulfillment through the sincere gift of self. To love means to give and to receive something which can be neither bought nor sold, but only given freely and mutually.

---

24. *Summa Theologiae* I, q. 5, a. 4, ad 2.

25. Pastoral Constitution on the Church in the Modern World *Gaudium et Spes*, 24.

By its very nature the gift of the person must be lasting and irrevocable. The indissolubility of marriage flows in the first place from the very essence of that gift: *the gift of one person to another person.* This reciprocal giving of self reveals the *spousal nature of love.* In their marital consent the bride and bridegroom call each other by name: "*I ... take you ...* as my wife (as my husband) and I promise to be true to you ... for all the days of my life." A gift such as this involves an obligation much more serious and profound than anything which might be "purchased" in any way and at any price. Kneeling before the Father, from whom all fatherhood and motherhood come, the future parents come to realize that they have been "redeemed." They have been purchased at great cost, *by the price* of the most sincere gift of all, *the blood of Christ* of which they partake through the sacrament. The liturgical crowning of the marriage rite is the Eucharist, the sacrifice of that "Body which has been given up" and that "Blood which has been shed," which in a certain way finds expression in the consent of the spouses.

When a man and woman in marriage mutually give and receive each other in the unity of "one flesh," the logic of the sincere gift of self becomes a part of their life. Without this, marriage would be empty; whereas a communion of persons, built on this logic, becomes a communion of parents. When they transmit *life to the child, a new human "thou" becomes a part of the horizon of the "we" of the spouses,* a person whom they will call by a new name: "our son ...; our daughter ..." "I have gotten a man with the help of the Lord" (Gen 4:1), says Eve, the first woman of history: a human being, first expected for nine months and then "revealed" to parents, brothers and sisters. The process from conception and growth in the mother's womb to birth makes it possible to create a space within which the new creature can be revealed as a "gift": indeed this is what it is from the very beginning. Could this frail and helpless being, totally dependent upon its parents and completely entrusted to them, be seen in any other way? The newborn child gives itself to its parents by the very fact of its coming into existence. *Its existence is already a gift, the first gift of the Creator to the creature.*

In the newborn child is realized the common good of the family. Just as the common good of spouses is fulfilled in conjugal love, ever ready to give and receive new life, so too the common good of the family is fulfilled through that same spousal love, as embodied in the newborn child. Part of the genealogy of the person is the genealogy of the family, preserved for posterity by the annotations in the Church's baptismal registers, even though these are merely the social consequence of the fact that "a man has been born into the world" (cf. Jn 16:21).

But is it really true that the new human being is a gift for his parents? A gift for society? Apparently nothing seems to indicate this. On occasion the birth of a child appears to be a simple statistical fact, registered like so many other data in demographic records. It is true that for the parents the birth of a child means more work, new financial burdens and further inconveniences, all of which can lead to the temptation not to want another birth.[26] In some social and cultural contexts this temptation can become very strong. Does this mean that a child is not a gift? That it comes into the world only to take and not to give? These are some of the disturbing questions which men and women today find hard to escape. *A child comes to take up room, when it seems that there is less and less room in the world.* But is it really true that a child brings nothing to the family and society?

Is not every child a "particle" of that common good without which human communities break down and risk extinction? Could this ever really be denied? The child becomes a gift to its brothers, sisters, parents and entire family. *Its life becomes a gift for the very people who were givers of life* and who cannot help but feel its presence, its sharing in their life and its contribution to their common good and to that of the community of the family.

This truth is obvious in its simplicity and profundity, whatever the complexity and even the possible pathology of the psychological make-up of certain persons. *The common good of the whole of society dwells in man;* he is, as we recalled, "the way of the Church."[27] Man is first of all the "glory of God": *"Gloria Dei vivens homo,"* in the celebrated words of Saint Irenaeus,[28] which might also be translated: "the glory of God is for man to be alive." It could be said that here we encounter the loftiest definition of man: *the glory of God is the common good of all that exists; the common good of the human race.*

Yes! *Man is a common good*—a common good of the family and of humanity, of individual groups and of different communities.

But there are significant distinctions of degree and modality in this regard. Man is a common good, for example, of the Nation to which he belongs and of the State of which he is a citizen; but in a much more concrete, unique and unrepeatable way he is a common good of his family. He is such not only as an individual who is part of the multitude of humanity, but rather as *"this individual."* God the Creator calls him into existence "for himself"; and in coming into the world he begins, in the family, his "great adventure," the adventure of human life. "This man" has, in every instance, *the right to fulfill himself on the basis of his human dignity.* It is precisely this dignity which establishes a person's place among others, and above all, in the family. The family is indeed—more than any other human

---

26. Cf. Encyclical Letter *Sollicitudo Rei Socialis* (30 December 1987), 25: *AAS* 80 (1988), 543–44.

27. Encyclical Letter *Redemptor Hominis* (4 March 1979), 14: *AAS* 71 (1979), 884–85; Cf. Encyclical Letter *Centesimus Annus* (1 May 1991), 53: *AAS* 83 (1991), 859.

28. *Adversus Haereses* IV, 20, 7: PG 7, 1057; SCh 100/2, 648–49.

reality—the place where an individual can exist "for himself" through the sincere gift of self. This is why it remains a social institution which neither can nor should be replaced: it is the "sanctuary of life."[29]

The fact that a child is being born, that "a child is born into the world" (Jn 16:21) is *a paschal sign*. As we read in the Gospel of John, Jesus himself speaks of this to the disciples before his passion and death, comparing their sadness at his departure with the pains of a woman in labor: "*When a woman is in travail she has sorrow* (that is, she suffers), because *her hour* has come; but when she is delivered of the child, she no longer remembers the anguish, for *joy that a child is born into the world*" (Jn 16:21). The "hour" of Christ's death (cf. Jn 13:1) is compared here to the "hour" of the woman in birth-pangs; the birth of a new child fully reflects the victory of life over death brought about by the Lord's resurrection. This comparison can provide us with material for reflection. Just as the resurrection of Christ is the manifestation of *Life* beyond the threshold of death, so too the birth of an infant is a manifestation of life, which is always destined, through Christ, for that "*fullness of life*" *which is in God himself*: "I came that they may have life, and have it abundantly" (Jn 10:10). Here we see revealed the deepest meaning of Saint Irenaeus's expression: "*Gloria Dei vivens homo.*"

It is the Gospel truth concerning the gift of self, without which the person cannot "fully find himself," which makes possible an appreciation of how profoundly this "sincere gift" is rooted in the gift of God, Creator and Redeemer, and in the "grace of the Holy Spirit" which the celebrant during the Rite of Marriage prays will be "poured out" on the spouses. Without such an "outpouring," it would be very difficult to understand all this and to carry it out as man's vocation. Yet how many people understand this intuitively! Many men and women make this truth their own, coming to discern that only in this truth do they encounter "the Truth and the Life" (Jn 14:6). *Without this truth, the life of the spouses and of the family will not succeed in attaining a fully human meaning.*

This is why the Church never tires of teaching and of bearing witness to this truth. While certainly showing maternal understanding for the many complex crisis situations in which families are involved, as well as for the moral frailty of every human being, the Church is convinced that she must remain absolutely faithful to the truth about human love—otherwise she would betray herself. To move away from this saving truth would be to close "the eyes of our hearts" (cf. Eph 1:18), which instead should always stay open to the light which the Gospel sheds on human affairs (cf. 2 Tim 1:10). An awareness of that sincere gift of self whereby man "finds himself" must be constantly renewed and safeguarded in

29.   Encyclical Letter *Centesimus Annus* (1 May 1991) 39: *AAS* 83 (1991), 842.

the face of the serious opposition which the Church meets on the part of those who advocate a false civilization of progress.[30] The family always expresses a new dimension of good for mankind, and it thus creates a new responsibility. We are speaking of the *responsibility for that particular common good* in which is included the good of the person, of every member of the family community. While certainly a "difficult" good (*"bonum arduum"*), it is also an attractive one.

Responsible Fatherhood and Motherhood

12. It is now time, in this Letter to Families, to bring up two closely related questions. The first, more general, concerns the *civilization of love,* the other, more specific, deals with *responsible fatherhood and motherhood.*

We have already said that marriage engenders a particular responsibility for the common good, first of the spouses and then of the family. This common good is constituted by man, by the *worth of the person* and by everything which represents the *measure of his dignity.* This reality is part of man in every social, economic and political system. In the area of marriage and the family, this responsibility becomes, for a variety of reasons, even more "demanding." The Pastoral Constitution *Gaudium et Spes* rightly speaks of *"promoting the dignity of marriage and the family."* The Council sees this "promotion" as a duty incumbent upon both the Church and the State. Nevertheless, in every culture this duty remains primarily that of the persons who, united in marriage, form a particular family. "Responsible fatherhood and motherhood" express a concrete commitment to carry out this duty, which has taken on new characteristics in the contemporary world.

In particular, responsible fatherhood and motherhood directly concern the moment in which a man and a woman, uniting themselves "in one flesh," can become parents. This is a moment of special value both for their interpersonal relationship and for their service to life: they can become parents—father and mother—by communicating life to a new human being. *The two dimensions of conjugal union,* the unitive and the procreative, *cannot be artificially separated* without damaging the deepest truth of the conjugal act itself.[31]

This is the constant teaching of the Church, and the "signs of the times" which we see today are providing new reasons for forcefully reaffirming that teaching. Saint Paul, himself so attentive to the pastoral demands of his day, clearly and

30. Cf. Encyclical Letter *Sollicitudo Rei Socialis* (30 December 1987), 25: *AAS* 80 (1988), 543–44.

31. Cf. Paul VI, Encyclical Letter *Humanae Vitae* (25 July 1968), 12: *AAS* 60 (1968), 488–89; *Catechism of the Catholic Church,* n. 2366.

firmly indicated the need to be "urgent in season and out of season" (cf. 2 Tim 4:2), and not to be daunted by the fact that "sound teaching is no longer endured" (cf. 2 Tim 4:3). His words are well known to those who, with deep insight into the events of the present time, expect that the Church will not only not abandon "sound doctrine," but will proclaim it with renewed vigor, seeking in today's "signs of the times" the incentive and insights which can lead to a deeper understanding of her teaching.

Some of these insights can be taken from the very sciences which have evolved from the earlier study of anthropology into *various specialized sciences such as biology, psychology, sociology and their branches. In some sense all these sciences revolve around medicine,* which is both a science and an art (*ars medica*), at the service of man's life and health. But the insights in question come first of all from human experience, which, in all its complexity, in some sense both precedes science and follows it.

Through their own experience spouses come to learn the meaning of responsible fatherhood and motherhood. They learn it also from the experience of other couples in similar situations and as they become more open to the findings of the various sciences. One could say that "experts" learn in a certain sense from "spouses," so that they in turn will then be in a better position to teach married couples the meaning of responsible procreation and the ways to achieve it.

This subject has been extensively treated in the documents of the Second Vatican Council, the Encyclical *Humanae Vitae,* the "Propositiones" of the 1980 Synod of Bishops, the Apostolic Exhortation *Familiaris Consortio,* and in other statements, up to the Instruction *Donum Vitae* of the Congregation for the Doctrine of the Faith. The Church both teaches the moral truth about responsible fatherhood and motherhood and *protects it from the erroneous views and tendencies which are widespread today.* Why does the Church continue to do this? Is she unaware of the problems raised by those who counsel her to make concessions in this area and who even attempt to persuade her by undue pressures if not even threats? The Church's Magisterium is often chided for being behind the times and closed to the promptings of the spirit of modern times, and for promoting a course of action which is harmful to humanity, and indeed to the Church herself. By obstinately holding to her own positions, it is said, the Church will end up losing popularity, and more and more believers will turn away from her.

But how can it be maintained that *the Church,* especially the College of Bishops in communion with the Pope, is *insensitive to such grave and pressing questions?* It was precisely these extremely important questions which led Pope Paul VI to publish the Encyclical *Humanae Vitae.* The foundations of the Church's doctrine concerning responsible fatherhood and motherhood are exceptionally broad and secure. *The Council demonstrates this above all in its teaching on man,* when it affirms that he is "the only creature on earth which God willed for itself," and that he cannot "fully find himself except through a sincere gift of himself."[32] This is so because he has been created in the image and likeness of God and redeemed by the only-begotten Son of the Father, who became man for us and for our salvation.

The Second Vatican Council, particularly conscious of the problem of man and his calling, states that the conjugal union, the biblical "*una caro,*" can be understood and fully explained *only by recourse to the values of the "person" and of "gift."*

Every man and every woman fully realizes himself or herself through the sincere gift of self. For spouses, the moment of conjugal union constitutes a very particular expression of this. It is then that a man and woman, in the "truth" of their masculinity and femininity, become a mutual gift to each other. All married life is a gift; but this becomes most evident when the spouses, in giving themselves to each other in love, bring about that encounter which makes them "one flesh" (Gen 2:24).

They then experience a moment of special responsibility, which is also the result of the procreative potential linked to the conjugal act. At that moment, the spouses can become father and mother, initiating the process of a new human life, which will then develop in the woman's womb. If the wife is the first to realize that she has become a mother, the husband, to whom she has been united in "one flesh," then learns this when she tells him that he has become a father. Both are responsible for their potential and later actual fatherhood and motherhood. The husband cannot fail to acknowledge and accept the result of a decision which has also been his own. He cannot hide behind expressions such as: "I don't know," "I didn't want it," or "you're the one who wanted it." In every case conjugal union involves *the responsibility of the man and of the woman,* a potential responsibility which becomes actual when the circumstances dictate. This is true especially for the man. Although he too is involved in the beginning of the generative process, he is left biologically distant from it; it is within the woman that the process develops. How can the man fail to assume responsibility? The man and the woman must assume together, before themselves and before others, the responsibility for the new life which they have brought into existence.

This conclusion is shared by the human sciences themselves.

---

32. Pastoral Constitution on the Church in the Modern World *Gaudium et Spes,* 24.

There is however a need for more in-depth study, analyzing the meaning of the conjugal act in view of the values of the "person" and of the "gift" mentioned above. This is what the Church has done in her constant teaching, and in a particular way at the Second Vatican Council.

In the conjugal act, husband and wife are called to confirm in a responsible way *the mutual gift* of self which they have made to each other in the marriage covenant. The logic of the *total gift of self to the other* involves a potential openness to procreation: in this way the marriage is called to even greater fulfillment as a family. Certainly the mutual gift of husband and wife does not have the begetting of children as its only end, but is in itself a mutual communion of love and of life. *The intimate truth of this gift* must always be *safeguarded.* "Intimate" is not here synonymous with "subjective." Rather, it means essentially in conformity with the objective truth of the man and woman who give themselves. The person can never be considered a means to an end; above all never a means of "pleasure." The person is and must be nothing other than the end of every act. Only then does the action correspond to the true dignity of the person.

In concluding our reflection on this important and sensitive subject, I wish to offer special encouragement above all to you, dear married couples, and to all who assist you in understanding and putting into practice the Church's teaching on marriage and on responsible motherhood and fatherhood. I am thinking in particular about pastors and the many scholars, theologians, philosophers, writers and journalists who have resisted the powerful trend to cultural conformity and are courageously ready to "swim against the tide." This encouragement also goes to an increasing number of experts, physicians and educators who are authentic lay apostles for whom the promotion of the dignity of marriage and the family has become an important task in their lives. In the name of the Church I express my gratitude to all!

What would priests, bishops and even the Successor of Peter be able to do without you? From the first years of my priesthood I have become increasingly convinced of this, from when I began to sit in the *confessional* to share the concerns, fears and hopes of many married couples. I met difficult cases of rebellion and refusal, but at the same time so many marvelously responsible and generous persons! In writing this Letter I have all those married couples in mind, and I embrace them with my affection and my prayer.

The Two Civilizations

13. Dear families, the question of responsible fatherhood and motherhood is an integral part of the "civilization of love," which I now wish to discuss with

you. From what has already been said it is clear that *the family is fundamental to what Pope Paul VI called the "civilization of love,"*[33] an expression which has entered the teaching of the Church and by now has become familiar. Today it is difficult to imagine a statement by the Church, or about the Church, which does not mention the civilization of love. The phrase *is linked to the tradition of the "domestic church" in early Christianity,* but it has a particular significance for the present time. Etymologically the word "civilization" is derived from *civis,* "citizen," and it emphasizes the civic or political dimension of the life of every individual. But the most profound meaning of the term "civilization" is not merely political, but rather pertains to human culture. Civilization belongs to human history because it answers man's spiritual and moral needs. Created in the image and likeness of God, man has received the world from the hands of the Creator, together with the task of shaping it in his own image and likeness. The fulfillment of this task gives rise to civilization, which in the final analysis is nothing else than the "humanization of the world."

In a certain sense civilization means the same thing as "culture." And so one could also speak of the *"culture of love,"* even though it is preferable to keep to the now familiar expression.

The civilization of love, in its current meaning, is inspired by the words of the conciliar Constitution *Gaudium et Spes: "Christ ... fully discloses man to himself and unfolds his noble calling."*[34] And so we can say that the civilization of love originates in the revelation of the God who "is love," as John writes (1 Jn 4:8, 16); it is effectively described by Paul in the hymn of charity found in his First Letter to the Corinthians (13:1–13). This civilization is intimately linked to the love "poured into our hearts through the Holy Spirit which has been given to us" (Rom 5:5), and it grows as a result of the *constant cultivation* which the Gospel allegory of the vine and the branches describes in such a direct way: "I am the true vine, and my Father is the vinedresser. Every branch of mine that bears no fruit, he takes away, and every branch that does bear fruit he prunes, that it may bear more fruit" (Jn 15:1–2).

In the light of these and other texts of the New Testament it is possible to understand what is meant by the "civilization of love," and why the *family is organically linked to this civilization.* If the first "way of the Church" is the family, it should also be said that the civilization of love is also the "way of the Church," which journeys through the world and summons families to this way; it summons also other social, national and international institutions, because of families and

---

33. Cf. Homily for the Closing of the Holy Year (25 December 1975): *AAS* 68 (1976), 145.

34. Pastoral Constitution on the Church in the Modern World *Gaudium et Spes,* 22.

through families. *The family in fact depends* for several reasons *on the civilization of love,* and finds therein the reasons for its existence as family. And at the same time *the family is the centre and the heart of the civilization of love.*

Yet there is no true love without an awareness that God "is Love" and that man is the only creature on earth which God has called into existence "for its own sake." Created in the image and likeness of God, man cannot fully "find himself" except through the sincere gift of self. Without such a concept of man, of the person and the "communion of persons" in the family, there can be no civilization of love; similarly, without the civilization of love it is impossible to have *such a concept of person and of the communion of persons.* The family constitutes the fundamental "cell" of society. But Christ—the "vine" from which the "branches" draw nourishment—is needed so that this cell will not be exposed to the threat of a kind of *cultural uprooting* which can come both from within and from without. Indeed, although there is on the one hand the "civilization of love," there continues to exist on the other hand *the possibility of a destructive "anti-civilization,"* as so many present trends and situations confirm.

Who can deny that our age is one marked by a great crisis, which appears above all as a profound *"crisis of truth"*? A crisis of truth means, in the first place, a *crisis of concepts.* Do the words "love," "freedom," "sincere gift," and even "person" and "rights of the person," really convey their essential meaning? This is why the Encyclical on the "splendor of truth" (*Veritatis Splendor*) has proved so meaningful and important for the Church and for the world—especially in the West. Only if the truth about freedom and the communion of persons in marriage and in the family can regain its splendor, will the building of the civilization of love truly begin and will it then be possible to speak concretely—as the Council did— about "promoting the dignity of marriage and the family."[35]

Why is the "splendor of truth" so important? First of all, by way of contrast: the development of contemporary civilization is linked to a scientific and technological progress which is often achieved in a one-sided way, and thus appears purely positivistic. Positivism, as we know, results in agnosticism in theory and utilitarianism in practice and in ethics. In our own day, history is in a way repeating itself. *Utilitarianism* is a civilization of production and of use, a civilization of "things" and not of "persons," a civilization in which persons are used in the same way as things are used. In the context of a civilization of use, woman can become an object for man, children a hindrance to parents, the family an institution obstructing the freedom of its members. To be convinced that this is the case, one need only look at *certain sexual education programs* introduced into the

---

35. Cf. ibid. 47.

schools, often notwithstanding the disagreement and even the protests of many parents; or *pro-abortion tendencies* which vainly try to hide behind the so-called "right to choose" (*"pro-choice"*) on the part of both spouses, and in particular on the part of the woman. These are only two examples; many more could be mentioned.

It is evident that in this sort of cultural situation the family cannot fail to feel threatened, since it is endangered at its very foundations. Everything *contrary to the civilization of love* is contrary to the whole truth about man and becomes a threat to him: it does not allow him to find himself and to feel secure, as spouse, parent, or child. So-called "safe sex," which is touted by the "civilization of technology," is actually, in view of the overall requirements of the person, radically *not safe*, indeed it is extremely dangerous. It endangers both the person and the family. And what is this danger? It is *the loss of the truth about one's own self and about the family*, together with the risk of a loss of freedom and consequently of a loss of *love* itself.

"You will know the truth," Jesus says, "and the truth will make you free" (Jn 8:32): the truth, and only the truth, will prepare you for a love which can be called "fairest love" (cf. Sir 24:24, Vulg.).

The contemporary family, like families in every age, is *searching for "fairest love."* A love which is not "fairest," but reduced only to the satisfaction of concupiscence (cf. 1 Jn 2:16), or to a man's and a woman's mutual "use" of each other, makes persons *slaves to their weaknesses*. Do not certain modern "cultural agendas" lead to this enslavement? There are agendas which "play" on man's weaknesses, and thus make him increasingly weak and defenseless.

The civilization of love evokes joy: joy, among other things, for the fact that a man has come into the world (cf. Jn 16:21), and consequently because spouses have become parents. The civilization of love means "rejoicing in the right" (cf. 1 Cor 13:6).

But a civilization inspired by a consumerist, anti-birth mentality is not and cannot ever be a civilization of love. If the family is so important for the civilization of love, it is because of the particular *closeness and intensity of the bonds* which come to be between persons and generations within the family. However, the family remains *vulnerable* and can easily fall prey to dangers which weaken it or actually destroy its unity and stability. As a result of these dangers families cease to be witnesses of the civilization of love and can even become a negation of it, a kind of *counter-sign*. A broken family can, for its part, consolidate a specific form of "anti-civilization," destroying love in its various expressions, with inevitable consequences for the whole of life in society.

Love is Demanding

14. The love which the Apostle Paul celebrates in the First Letter to the Corinthians—the love which is *"patient and kind,"* and *"endures all things"* (1 Cor 13:4, 7)—is certainly *a demanding love.* But this is precisely the source of its beauty: by the very fact that it is demanding, it builds up the true good of man and allows it to radiate to others. The good, says Saint Thomas, is by its nature "diffusive."[36] Love is true when *it creates the good of persons and of communities;* it creates that good and *gives it* to others. Only the one who is able to be demanding with himself in the name of love can also demand love from others. Love is demanding. It makes demands in all human situations; it is even more demanding in the case of those who are open to the Gospel. Is this not what Christ proclaims in "his" commandment?

Nowadays people need to rediscover this demanding love, for it is the truly firm foundation of the family, a foundation able to "endure all things." According to the Apostle, love is not able to "endure all things" if it yields to "jealousies," or if it is "boastful ... arrogant or rude" (cf. 1 Cor 13:5–6). True love, Saint Paul teaches, is different: "Love believes all things, hopes all things, endures all things" (1 Cor 13:7). This is the very love which "endures all things." At work within it is the power and strength of God himself, who "is love" (1 Jn 4:8, 16). At work within it is also the power and strength of Christ, the Redeemer of man and Savior of the world.

Meditating on the thirteenth chapter of the First Letter of Paul to the Corinthians, we set out on a path which leads us to understand quickly and clearly the full truth about the civilization of love. No other biblical text expresses this truth so simply and so profoundly as the *hymn to love.*

The dangers faced by love are also dangers for the civilization of love, because they promote everything capable of effectively opposing it. Here one thinks first of all of *selfishness,* not only the selfishness of individuals, but also of couples or, even more broadly, of social selfishness, that for example of a class or nation (nationalism). Selfishness in all its forms is directly and radically opposed to the civilization of love. But is love to be defined simply as "anti-selfishness"? This would be a very impoverished and ultimately a purely negative definition, even though it is true that different forms of selfishness must be overcome in order to realize love and the civilization of love. It would be more correct to speak of "altruism," which is the opposite of selfishness. But far richer and more complete is the concept of love illustrated by Saint Paul. The hymn to love in the First

---

36. *Summa Theologiae* I, q. 5, a. 4, ad 2.

Letter to the Corinthians remains the *Magna Charta* of the civilization of love. In this concept, what is important is not so much individual actions (whether self-ish or altruistic), so much as the radical acceptance of the understanding of man as a person who "finds himself" by making a sincere gift of self. A gift is, obviously, "for others": this is *the most important dimension* of the civilization of love.

We thus come to the very heart of the Gospel truth about *freedom.* The person realizes himself by the exercise of freedom in truth. Freedom cannot be understood as a license to do *absolutely anything*: it means a *gift of self.* Even more: it means an *interior discipline of the gift.* The idea of gift contains not only the free initiative of the subject, but also the aspect of *duty.* All this is made real in the "communion of persons." We find ourselves again at the very heart of each family.

Continuing this line of thought, we also *come upon the antithesis between individualism and personalism.* Love, the civilization of love, is bound up with person-alism. Why with personalism? And *why does individualism threaten the civilization of love?* We find a key to answering this in the Council's expression, a "sincere gift." Individualism presupposes a use of freedom in which the subject does what he wants, in which he himself is the one to "establish the truth" of whatever he finds pleasing or useful. He does not tolerate the fact that someone else "wants" or demands something from him in the name of an objective truth. He does not want to "give" to another on the basis of truth; he does not want to become a "sincere gift."

Individualism thus remains egocentric and selfish. The real antithesis between individualism and personalism emerges not only on the level of theory, but even more *on that of "ethos."* The "ethos" of personalism is altruistic: it moves the person to become a gift for others and to discover the joy of giving himself. This is the joy about which Christ speaks (cf. Jn 15:11; 16:20, 22).

What is needed then is for human societies, and the families who live within them, often in a context of struggle between the civilization of love and its oppo-sites, to seek their solid foundation in a correct vision of man and of everything which determines the full "realization" of his humanity. *Opposed to the civilization of love* is certainly the phenomenon of so-called *"free love"*; this is particularly dangerous because it is usually suggested as a way of following one's "real" feelings, but it is in fact destructive of love. How many families have been ruined because of "free love"! To follow in every instance a "real" emotional impulse by invoking a love "liberated" from all conditionings, means nothing more than to make the individual a slave to those human instincts which Saint Thomas calls "passions of the soul."[37] "Free love" exploits human weaknesses; it gives them a certain "veneer" of respectability with the help of seduction and the blessing of public opinion. In

---

37. *Summa Theologiae* I-II, q. 22.

this way there is an attempt to "soothe" consciences by creating a "moral alibi." But not all of the consequences are taken into consideration, especially when the ones who end up paying are, apart from the other spouse, the children, deprived of a father or mother and condemned to be in fact *orphans of living parents.*

As we know, at the foundation of ethical utilitarianism there is the continual quest for "maximum" happiness. But this is a *"utilitarian happiness,"* seen only as pleasure, as immediate gratification for the exclusive benefit of the individual, apart from or opposed to the objective demands of the true good.

The program of utilitarianism, based on an individualistic understanding of freedom—a freedom without responsibilities—is the opposite of love, even as an expression of human civilization considered as a whole. When this concept of freedom is embraced by society, and quickly allies itself with varied forms of human weakness, it soon proves a systematic and permanent threat to the family. In this regard, one could mention many dire consequences, which can be statistically verified, even though a great number of them are hidden in the hearts of men and women like painful, fresh wounds.

The love of spouses and parents has the capacity to cure these kinds of wounds, provided the dangers alluded to do not deprive it of its regenerative force, which is so beneficial and wholesome a thing for human communities. This capacity depends on the divine grace of forgiveness and reconciliation, which always ensures the spiritual energy to begin anew. For this very reason family members need to encounter Christ in the Church through the wonderful sacrament of Penance and Reconciliation.

In this context, we can realize how important *prayer* is with families and for families, in particular for those threatened by division. We need to pray that married couples *will love their vocation,* even when the road becomes difficult, or the paths become narrow, uphill and seemingly insuperable; we need to pray that, even then, they will be faithful to their covenant with God.

"The family is the way of the Church." In this Letter we wish both to profess and to proclaim *this way,* which leads to the kingdom of heaven (cf. Mt 7:14) through conjugal and family life.

It is important that the "communion of persons" in the family should become a preparation for the "communion of Saints." This is why the Church both believes and proclaims the love which "endures all things" (1 Cor 13:7); with Saint Paul she sees in it *"the greatest"* virtue of all (cf. 1 Cor 13:13). The Apostle puts no limits on anyone. Everyone is called to love, including spouses and families. In the Church everyone is called equally to perfect holiness (cf. Mt 5:48).[38]

---

38. Cf. Dogmatic Constitution on the Church *Lumen Gentium,* 11, 40, and 41.

The Fourth Commandment: "Honor Your Father and Your Mother"

15. The fourth commandment of the Decalogue deals with the family and its interior unity—its solidarity, we could say.

In its formulation, the fourth commandment does not explicitly mention the family. In fact, however, this is its real subject matter. In order to bring out the communion between generations, *the divine Legislator could find no more appropriate word than this*: "Honor ..." (Ex 20:12). Here we meet another way of expressing what the family is. This formulation does not exalt the family in some "artificial" way, but emphasizes its subjectivity and the rights flowing from it. The family is a community of particularly intense interpersonal relationships: between spouses, between parents and children, between generations. It is a community which must be safeguarded in a special way. And God cannot find a better safeguard than this: "Honor."

"Honor your father and your mother, that your days may be long in the land which the Lord your God gives to you" (Ex 20:12). This commandment comes after the three basic precepts which concern the relation of the individual and the people of Israel with God: "*Shema, Israel* ...," "Hear, O Israel: the Lord our God is one Lord" (Dt 6:4). "You will have no other gods before me" (Ex 20:3). This is the first and greatest commandment, the commandment of love for God "above all else": God is to be loved "with all your heart, and with all your soul, and with all your might" (Dt 6:5; cf. Mt 22:37). It is significant that the fourth commandment is placed in this particular context. "Honor your father and your mother," because for you they are in a certain sense representatives of the Lord; they are the ones who gave you life, who introduced you to human existence in a particular family line, nation and culture. After God, they are your first benefactors. While God alone is good, indeed the Good itself, parents participate in this supreme goodness in a unique way. And so, honor your parents! *There is a certain analogy* here *with the worship owed to God.*

The fourth commandment is closely linked to the *commandment of love.* The bond between "honor" and "love" is a deep one. Honor, at its very centre, is connected with the virtue of justice, but the latter, for its part, cannot be explained fully without reference to love: the love of God and of one's neighbor. And who is more of a neighbor than one's own family members, parents and children?

Is the system of interpersonal relations indicated by the fourth commandment one-sided? Does it bind us only to honor our parents? Taken literally, it does. But indirectly we can speak of the *"honor" owed to children by their parents.* "To honor" means to acknowledge! We could put it this way: "let yourself be guided by the firm acknowledgment of the person, first of all that of your father and mother, and then that of the other members of the family." Honor is essentially an attitude of unselfishness. It could be said that it is "a sincere gift of person to person," and in that sense honor converges with love. If the fourth commandment demands that honor should be shown to our father and mother, it also makes this demand out of concern for the good of the family. Precisely for this reason, however, it makes demands of the parents themselves. You parents, the divine precept seems to say, should act in such a way that your life *will merit the honor* (and the love) of your children! Do not let the divine command that you be honored fall into a moral vacuum! Ultimately then we are speaking of *mutual honor*. The commandment "honor your father and your mother" indirectly tells parents: Honor your sons and your daughters. They deserve this because they are alive, because they are who they are, and this is true from the first moment of their conception. The fourth commandment then, by expressing the intimate bonds uniting the family, highlights the basis of its inner unity.

The commandment goes on to say: "*that your days may be long in the land* which the Lord your God gives you." The conjunction "that" might give the impression of an almost "utilitarian" calculation: honor them so that you will have a long life. In any event, this does not lessen the fundamental meaning of the imperative "*honor*," which by its nature suggests an *attitude of unselfishness*. To honor never means: "calculate the benefits." It is difficult, on the other hand, not to acknowledge the fact that an attitude of mutual honor among members of the family community also brings certain advantages. "*Honor" is certainly something useful*, just as every true good is "useful."

In the first place, the family achieves the good of "being together." This is the good *par excellence* of marriage (hence its indissolubility) and of the family community. It could also be defined as a good of the subject as such. Just as the person is a subject, so too is the family, since it is made up of persons, who, joined together by a profound bond of communion, form a single *communal subject*. Indeed, the family is more a subject than any other social institution: more so than the nation or the State, more so than society and international organizations. These societies, especially nations, possess a proper subjectivity to the extent that they receive it from persons and their families. Are all these merely "theoretical" observations, formulated for the purpose of "exalting" the family before public opinion? No, but they are another way of expressing what the family is. And this too can be deduced from the fourth commandment.

This truth deserves to be emphasized and more deeply understood: indeed it brings out the importance of the fourth commandment for the modern system of *human rights*. Institutions and legal systems employ juridical language. But God says: "honor." All "human rights" are ultimately fragile and ineffective, if at their root they lack the command to "honor"; in other words, if they lack *an acknowledgment of the individual* simply because he is an individual, "this" individual. *Of themselves, rights are not enough.*

It is not an exaggeration to reaffirm that the life of nations, of states, and of international organizations "passes" through the family and "is based" on the fourth commandment of the Decalogue. The age in which we live, notwithstanding the many juridical Declarations which have been drafted, *is still threatened to a great extent by "alienation."* This is the result of "Enlightenment" premises according to which a man is "more" human if he is "only" human. It is not difficult to notice how alienation from everything belonging in various ways to the full richness of man threatens our times. And this affects the family.

Indeed, *the affirmation of the person* is in great measure to be referred back *to the family* and consequently to the fourth commandment. In God's plan the family is in many ways the first school of how to be human. *Be human!* This is the imperative passed on in the family—human as the son or daughter of one's country, a citizen of the State, and, we would say today, a citizen of the world. The God who gave humanity the fourth commandment is "benevolent" towards man (*philanthropos,* as the Greeks said). The Creator of the universe is *the God of love and of life:* he wants man to have life and have it abundantly, as Christ proclaims (cf. Jn 10:10); that he may have life, first of all thanks to the family.

At this point it seems clear that the "civilization of love" is strictly bound up with the family. *For many people the civilization of love is still a pure utopia.* Indeed, there are those who think that love cannot be demanded from anyone and that it cannot be imposed: love should be a free choice which people can take or leave.

There is some truth in all this. And yet there is always the fact that Jesus Christ left us the commandment of love, just as God on Mount Sinai ordered: "Honor your father and your mother." Love then is not a utopia: it is given to mankind as a task to be carried out with the help of divine grace. It is entrusted to man and woman, in the sacrament of matrimony, as the basic principle of their "duty," and it becomes the foundation of their mutual responsibility: first as spouses, then as father and mother. In the celebration of the sacrament, the spouses give and receive each other, declaring their willingness to welcome children and to educate them. On this hinges human civilization, which cannot be defined as anything other than a "civilization of love." The family is an expression and source of this love. *Through the family passes the primary current of the civilization of love,* which finds therein its "social foundations."

The Fathers of the Church, in the Christian tradition, have spoken of the family as a "domestic church," a "little church." They thus referred to the civilization of love as a possible system of human life and coexistence: "to be together" as a family, to be for one another, to make room in a community for affirming each person as such, for affirming "this" individual person. At times it is a matter of people with physical or psychological handicaps, of whom the so-called "progressive" society would prefer to be free. Even the family can end up like this kind of society. It does so when it hastily rids itself of people who are aged, disabled or sick. This happens when there is a loss of faith in that *God for whom "all live"* (cf. Lk 20:38) and are called to the fullness of Life.

Yes, *the civilization of love is possible; it is not a utopia.* But it is only possible by a constant and ready reference to the "Father from whom all fatherhood [and motherhood] on earth is named" (cf. Eph 3:14–15), from whom every human family comes.

Education

16. *What is involved in rearing children?* In answering this question two fundamental truths should be kept in mind: first, that man is called to live in truth and love; and second, that everyone finds fulfillment through the sincere gift of self. This is true both for the educator and for the one being educated.

Education is thus a unique process for which the mutual communion of persons has immense importance. *The educator* is a person who "*begets*" *in a spiritual sense.* From this point of view, *raising children can be considered a genuine apostolate.* It is a living means of communication, which not only creates a profound relationship between the educator and the one being educated, but also makes them both sharers in truth and love, that final goal to which everyone is called by God the Father, Son, and Holy Spirit.

Fatherhood and motherhood presume the coexistence and interaction of autonomous subjects. This is quite evident in the case of the mother when she conceives a new human being. The first months of the child's presence in the mother's womb bring about a particular bond which already possesses an educational significance of its own. The *mother,* even before giving birth, *does not only give shape to the child's body, but also, in an indirect way, to the child's whole personality.* Even though we are speaking about a process in which the mother primarily affects the child, we should not overlook the unique influence that the unborn child has on its mother. In this *mutual influence* which will be revealed to the outside world following the birth of the child, the father does not have a direct part to play. But he should be responsibly committed to providing attention and support throughout the pregnancy and, if possible, at the moment of birth.

For the "civilization of love" it is essential that *the husband should recognize that the motherhood of his wife is a gift:* this is enormously important for the entire process of raising children. Much will depend on his willingness to take his own part in this first stage of the gift of humanity, and to become willingly involved as a husband and father in the motherhood of his wife.

Education then is before all else *a reciprocal "offering" on the part of both parents:* together they communicate their own mature humanity to the newborn child, who gives them in turn the newness and freshness of the humanity which it has brought into the world. This is the case even when children are born with mental or physical disabilities. Here, the situation of the children can enhance the very special courage needed to raise them.

With good reason, then, the Church asks during the Rite of Marriage: "Will you accept children lovingly from God, and bring them up according to the law of Christ and his Church"?[39] In the raising of children conjugal love is expressed as authentic parental love. The "communion of persons," expressed as conjugal love at the beginning of the family, is thus completed and brought to fulfillment in the raising of children. Every individual born and raised in a family constitutes a potential treasure which must be responsibly accepted, so that it will not be diminished or lost, but will rather come to an ever more mature humanity. This too is a *process of exchange* in which the parents-educators are in turn to a certain degree educated themselves. While they are teachers of humanity for their own children, they learn humanity from them. All this clearly brings out the *organic structure of the family,* and reveals the fundamental meaning of the fourth commandment.

In rearing children, the *"we" of the parents,* of husband and wife, develops into the *"we" of the family,* which is grafted on to earlier generations, and is open to gradual expansion. In this regard both grandparents and grandchildren play their own individual roles.

If it is true that by giving life *parents* share in God's creative work, it is also true that by raising their children they *become sharers in his paternal and at the same time maternal way of teaching.* According to Saint Paul, God's fatherhood is the primordial model of all fatherhood and motherhood in the universe (cf. Eph 3:14–15), and of human motherhood and fatherhood in particular. We have been completely instructed in God's own way of teaching by the eternal Word of the Father who, by becoming man, revealed to man the authentic and integral greatness of his humanity, that is, being a child of God. In this way he also revealed the true meaning of human education.

Through Christ all education, within the family and outside of it, *becomes part of God's own saving pedagogy,* which is addressed to individuals and families

---

39. *Rituale Romanum, Ordo Celebrandi Matrimonium,* n. 60, ed. cit., p. 17.

and culminates in the Paschal Mystery of the Lord's Death and resurrection. The "heart" of our redemption is the starting-point of every process of Christian education, which is likewise always an education to a full humanity.

Parents are *the first and most important educators* of their own children, and they also possess a *fundamental competence* in this area: they are *educators because they are parents.* They share their educational mission with other individuals or institutions, such as the Church and the State. But the mission of education must always be carried out in accordance with a proper application of the *principle of subsidiarity.* This implies the legitimacy and indeed the need of giving assistance to the parents, but finds its intrinsic and absolute limit in their prevailing right and their actual capabilities. The principle of subsidiarity is thus at the service of parental love, meeting the good of the family unit. For parents by themselves are not capable of satisfying every requirement of the whole process of raising children, especially in matters concerning their schooling and the entire gamut of socialization. Subsidiarity thus complements paternal and maternal love and confirms its fundamental nature, inasmuch as all other participants in the process of education are only able to carry out their responsibilities *in the name of the parents, with their consent* and, to a certain degree, *with their authorization.*

The process of education ultimately leads to the phase of *self-education,* which occurs when the individual, after attaining an appropriate level of psycho-physical maturity, *begins to "educate himself on his own."* In time, self-education goes beyond the earlier results achieved by the educational process, in which it continues to be rooted. An adolescent is exposed to new people and new surroundings, particularly teachers and classmates, who exercise an influence over his life which can be either helpful or harmful. At this stage he distances himself somewhat from the education received in the family, assuming at times a critical attitude with regard to his parents. Even so, the process of self-education cannot fail to be marked by the educational influence which the family and school have on children and adolescents. Even when they grow up and set out on their own path, young people remain intimately linked to their *existential roots.*

Against this background, we can see the meaning of the fourth commandment, "*Honor your father and your mother*" (Ex 20:12) in a new way. It is closely linked to the whole process of education. Fatherhood and motherhood, this first and basic fact in the *gift of humanity,* open up before both parents and children new and profound perspectives. To give birth according to the flesh means to set in motion a further "birth," one which is gradual and complex and which continues in the whole process of education. The commandment of the Decalogue calls for a child to honor its father and mother. But, as we saw above, that same commandment enjoins upon parents a kind of corresponding or "symmetrical" duty. Parents are also called to "honor" their children, whether they are young or old. This attitude is needed throughout the process of their education, including the time of their schooling. The *"principle of giving honor,"* the recognition and respect due to man precisely because he is a man, is the basic condition for every authentic educational process.

In the sphere of education *the Church* has a specific role to play. In the light of Tradition and the teaching of the Council, it can be said that it is not only a matter of *entrusting the Church* with the person's religious and moral education, but of promoting the entire process of the person's education *"together with"* the Church. The family is called to carry out its task of education *in the Church,* thus sharing in her life and mission.

The Church wishes to carry out her educational mission above all *through families* who are made capable of undertaking this task by the sacrament of matrimony, through the "grace of state" which follows from it and the specific "charism" proper to the entire family community.

Certainly one area in which the family has an irreplaceable role is that of *religious education,* which enables the family to grow as a "domestic church." Religious education and the catechesis of children make the family a true *subject of evangelization and the apostolate* within the Church. We are speaking of a right intrinsically linked to the *principle of religious liberty.* Families, and more specifically parents, are free to choose for their children a particular kind of religious and moral education consonant with their own convictions. Even when they entrust these responsibilities to ecclesiastical institutions or to schools administered by religious personnel, their educational presence ought to continue to be *constant and active.*

Within the context of education, due attention must be paid to the essential question of *choosing a vocation,* and here in particular that of *preparing for marriage.* The Church has made notable efforts to promote marriage preparation, for example by offering courses for engaged couples. All this is worthwhile and necessary. But it must not be forgotten that preparing for future life as a couple is *above all the task of the family.* To be sure, only spiritually mature families can adequately assume that responsibility. Hence we should point out the need for a special *solidarity among families.* This can be expressed in various practical ways, as for example by associations of families for families. The institution of the family is strengthened by such expressions of solidarity, which bring together not only individuals but also communities, with a commitment to pray together and to seek together the answers to life's essential questions. Is this not an invaluable expression of the *apostolate of families* to one another? It is important that families attempt to build bonds of solidarity among themselves. This allows them to assist each other in the educational enterprise: parents are educated by other parents, and children by other children. Thus a particular tradition of education is created, which draws strength from the character of the "domestic church" proper to the family.

The *gospel of love* is the inexhaustible source of all that nourishes the human family as a "communion of persons." In love the whole educational process finds its support and definitive meaning as the mature fruit of the parents' mutual gift. Through the efforts, sufferings and disappointments which are part of every person's education, love is constantly being put to the test. To pass the test, a source of spiritual strength is necessary. This is only found in the One who "loved to the end" (Jn 13:1). Thus *education is fully a part of the "civilization of love."* It depends on the civilization of love and, in great measure, contributes to its upbuilding.

The Church's constant and trusting prayer during the Year of the Family is *for the education of man,* so that families will persevere in their task of education with courage, trust and hope, in spite of difficulties occasionally so serious as to appear insuperable. The Church prays that the forces of the "civilization of love," which have their source in the love of God, will be triumphant. These are forces which the Church ceaselessly expends for the good of the whole human family.

Family and Society

17. The family is a community of persons and the smallest social unit. As such it is an *institution* fundamental to the life of every society.

What does the family as an institution expect from society? First of all, it expects *a recognition of its identity* and an acceptance of its *status as a subject in society.* This "social subjectivity" is bound up with the proper identity of marriage and the family.

Marriage, which undergirds the institution of the family, is constituted by the covenant whereby "a man and a woman establish between themselves a partnership of their whole life," and which "of its own very nature is ordered to the well-being of the spouses and to the procreation and upbringing of children."[40] Only such a union can be recognized and ratified as a "marriage" in society. Other interpersonal unions which do not fulfill the above conditions cannot be recognized, despite certain growing trends which represent a serious threat to the future of the family and of society itself.

---

40. *Code of Canon Law,* Canon 1055, p. 1; *Catechism of the Catholic Church,* n. 1601.

No human society can run the risk of permissiveness in fundamental issues regarding the nature of marriage and the family! Such moral permissiveness cannot fail to damage the authentic requirements of peace and communion among people. It is thus quite understandable why the Church vigorously defends the identity of the family and encourages responsible individuals and institutions, especially political leaders and international organizations, not to yield to the temptation of a superficial and false modernity.

As a community of love and life, the family is a firmly grounded social reality. It is also, in a way entirely its own, a *sovereign society,* albeit conditioned in certain ways. This affirmation of the family's sovereignty as an institution and the recognition of the various ways in which it is conditioned naturally leads to the subject of *family rights.* In this regard, the Holy See published in 1983 the *Charter of the Rights of the Family;* even today this document has lost none of its relevance.

The rights of the family are closely *linked to the rights of the person:* if in fact the family is a communion of persons, its self-realization will depend in large part on the correct application of the rights of its members. Some of these rights concern the family in an immediate way, such as the right of parents to responsible procreation and the education of children. Other rights however touch the family unit only indirectly: among these, the right to property, especially to what is called family property, and the right to work are of special importance.

But the rights of the family *are not simply the sum total* of the rights of the person, since the family is *much more* than the sum of its individual members. It is a community of parents and children, and at times a community of several generations. For this reason its "status as a subject," which is grounded in God's plan, gives rise to and calls for certain proper and specific rights.

The *Charter of the Rights of the Family,* on the basis of the moral principles mentioned above, consolidates the existence of the institution of the family in the social and juridical order of the "greater" society—those of the nation, of the State and of international communities. Each of these "greater" societies is at least indirectly conditioned by the existence of the family. As a result, the definition of the rights and duties of the "greater" society with regard to the family is an extremely important and even essential issue.

In the first place there is the almost organic link existing between *the family and the nation.* Naturally we cannot speak in all cases about a nation in the proper sense. Ethnic groups still exist which, without being able to be considered true nations, do fulfill to some extent the function of a "greater" society. In both cases, the link of the family with the ethnic group or the nation is founded above all on *a participation in its culture.* In one sense, parents also give birth to children for the nation, so that they can be members of it and can share in its historic and cultural heritage. From the very outset the identity of the family is to some extent shaped by the identity of the nation to which it belongs.

By sharing in the nation's cultural heritage, the family contributes to that *specific sovereignty*, which has its origin in a distinct culture and language. I addressed this subject at the UNESCO Conference meeting in Paris in 1980, and, given its unquestionable importance, I have often returned to it. Not only the nations, but every family realizes its *spiritual sovereignty* through culture and language. Were this not true, it would be very difficult to explain many events in the history of peoples, especially in Europe. From these events, ancient and modern, inspiring and painful, glorious and humiliating, it becomes clear how much the family is an organic part of the nation, and the nation of the family.

In regard to the *State*, the link with the family is somewhat similar and at the same time somewhat dissimilar. The State, in fact, is distinct from the nation; it has a less "family-like" structure, since it is organized in accordance with a political system and in a more "bureaucratic" fashion. Nonetheless, the apparatus of the State also has, in some sense, a "soul" of its own, to the extent that it lives up to its nature as a "political community" juridically ordered towards the common good.[41] Closely linked to this "soul" is the family, which is connected with the State precisely by reason of the *principle of subsidiarity*. Indeed, the family is a social reality which does not have readily available all the means necessary to carry out its proper ends, also in matters regarding schooling and the rearing of children. The State is thus called upon to play a role in accordance with the principle mentioned above. Whenever the family is self-sufficient, it should be left to act on its own; an excessive intrusiveness on the part of the State would prove detrimental, to say nothing of lacking due respect, and would constitute an open violation of the rights of the family. Only in those situations where the family is not really self-sufficient does the State have the authority and duty to intervene.

Beyond child-rearing and schooling at all levels, State assistance, while not excluding private initiatives, can find expression in institutions such as those founded to safeguard the life and health of citizens, and in particular to provide social benefits for workers. *Unemployment* is today one of the most serious threats to family life and a rightful cause of concern to every society. It represents a challenge for the political life of individual States and an area for careful study in the Church's social doctrine. It is urgently necessary, therefore, to come up with courageous solutions capable of looking beyond the confines of one's own

---

41. Cf. Pastoral Constitution on the Church in the Modern World *Gaudium et Spes*, 74.

nation and taking into consideration the many families for whom lack of employment means living in situations of tragic poverty.[42]

While speaking about employment in reference to the family, it is appropriate to emphasize how important and burdensome is *the work women do within the
family unit:*[43] *that work should be acknowledged and deeply appreciated.* The "toil"
of a woman who, having given birth to a child, nourishes and cares for that child
and devotes herself to its upbringing, particularly in the early years, is so great as
to be comparable to any professional work. This ought to be clearly stated and
upheld, no less than any other labor right. Motherhood, because of all the hard
work it entails, should be recognized as giving the right to financial benefits at
least equal to those of other kinds of work undertaken in order to support the
family during such a delicate phase of its life.

Every effort should be made so that the family will be recognized as the
primordial and, in a certain sense "sovereign" *society*! The "sovereignty" of the
family is essential for the good of society. A truly sovereign and spiritually vigorous nation is always made up of strong families who are aware of their vocation
and mission in history. *The family is at the heart* of all these problems and tasks.
To relegate it to a subordinate or secondary role, excluding it from its rightful
position in society, would be to inflict grave harm on the authentic growth of
society as a whole.

II. THE BRIDEGROOM IS WITH YOU

At Cana in Galilee

18. Engaged in conversation with John's disciples one day, Jesus speaks of a
wedding invitation and the presence of the bridegroom among the guests: "the
Bridegroom is with them" (Mt 9:15). In this way he indicated the fulfillment in
his own person of the image of God the Bridegroom, which had already been
used in the Old Testament, in order to reveal fully the mystery of God as the
mystery of Love.

By describing himself as a "Bridegroom," Jesus reveals the essence of God
and confirms his immense love for mankind. But the choice of this image also
throws light indirectly on the profound truth of spousal love. Indeed by using
this image in order to speak about God, Jesus shows to what extent the fatherhood and the love of God are reflected in the love of a man and a woman united

---

42. Cf. Encyclical Letter *Centesimus Annus* (1 May 1991), 57: AAS 83 (1991), 862–63.

43. Cf. Encyclical Letter *Laborem Exercens* (14 September 1981), 19: AAS 73 (1981), 625–29.

in marriage. Hence, at the beginning of his mission, we find Jesus at *Cana in Galilee,* taking part in a wedding banquet, together with Mary and with the first disciples (cf. Jn 2:1–11). He thus wishes to make clear *to what extent the truth about the family is part of God's Revelation and the history of salvation.* In the Old Testament, and particularly in the Prophets, we find many beautiful expressions about the *love of God.* It is a gentle love like that of a mother for her child, a tender love like that of the bridegroom for his bride, but at the same time an equally and intensely jealous love. It is not in the first place a love which chastises but one which forgives; a love which deigns to meet man just as the father does in the case of the prodigal son; a love which raises him up and gives him a share in divine life. It is an amazing love: something entirely new and previously unknown to the whole pagan world.

At Cana in Galilee Jesus is, as it were, the *herald of the divine truth about marriage,* that truth on which the human family can rely, gaining reassurance amid all the trials of life.

Jesus proclaims this truth by his presence at the wedding in Cana and by working his first "sign": water changed into wine.

Jesus proclaims the truth about marriage again when, speaking to the Pharisees, he explains how the love which comes from God, a tender and spousal love, *gives rise to profound and radical demands.* Moses, by allowing a certificate of divorce to be drawn up, had been less demanding. When in their lively argument the Pharisees appealed to Moses, Jesus' answer was categorical: "from the beginning it was not so" (Mt 19:8). And he reminds them that the One who created man created him male and female, and ordained that "a man leaves his father and his mother and cleaves to his wife, and they become one flesh" (Gen 2:24). With logical consistency Jesus concludes: "So they are no longer two but one flesh. What therefore God has joined together, let not man put asunder" (Mt 19:6). To the objection of the Pharisees who vaunt the Law of Moses he replies: "For your hardness of heart Moses allowed you to divorce your wives, but from the beginning it was not so" (Mt 19:8). Jesus appeals to "the beginning," seeing at the very origins of creation God's plan, on which the family is based, and, through the family, the entire history of humanity. What marriage is in nature becomes, by the will of Christ, a true sacrament of the New Covenant, sealed by the blood of Christ the Redeemer.

Spouses and families, remember at what price you have been "bought"! (cf. 1 Cor 6:20). But it is *humanly difficult* to accept and to live this marvelous truth. Should we be surprised that Moses relented before the insistent demands of his fellow Israelites, if the Apostles themselves, upon hearing the words of the Master, reply by saying: "If such is the case of a man with his wife, it is not expedient to marry"

(Mt 19:10)! Nonetheless, in view of the good of man and woman, of the family and the whole of society, Jesus confirms the demand which God laid down from the beginning.

At the same time, however, he takes the opportunity to affirm the value of a decision not to marry for the sake of the Kingdom of God. This choice too enables one to "beget," albeit in a different way. In this choice we find the origin of the consecrated life, of the religious orders and religious congregations of East and West, and also of the discipline of priestly celibacy, as found in the tradition of the Latin Church. Hence it is untrue that "it is not expedient to marry"; however, love for the kingdom of heaven can lead a person to choose not to marry (cf. Mt 19:12).

Marriage however remains the usual human vocation which is embraced by the great majority of the people of God. It is in the family where living stones are formed for that spiritual house spoken of by the Apostle Peter (cf. 1 Pet 2:5). The bodies of the husband and wife are the dwelling-place of the Holy Spirit (cf. 1 Cor 6:19). Because the transmission of divine life presumes the transmission of human life, marriage not only brings about the birth of human children, but also, through the power of baptism, the birth of adopted children of God, who live the new life received from Christ through his Spirit.

Dear brothers and sisters, spouses and parents, this is how the *Bridegroom is with you.* You know that he is the Good Shepherd. You know who he is, and you know his voice. You know where he is leading you, and how he strives to give you pastures where you can find life and find it in abundance. You know how he withstands the marauding wolves, and is ever ready to rescue his sheep: every husband and wife, every son and daughter, every member of your families. You know that he, as the Good Shepherd, is prepared to lay down his own life for his flock (cf. Jn 10:11). He leads you by paths which are not the steep and treacherous paths of many of today's ideologies, and he repeats to today's world the fullness of truth, even as he did in his conversation with the Pharisees or when he announced it to the Apostles, who then proclaimed it to all the ends of the earth and to all the people of their day, to Jews and Greeks alike. The disciples were fully conscious that Christ had made all things new. They knew that man had been made a "new creation": no longer Jew or Greek, no longer slave or free, no longer male or female, but "one" in Christ (cf. Gal 3:28) and endowed with the dignity of an adopted son of God. On the day of Pentecost man received the Spirit, the Comforter, the Spirit of truth. This was the beginning of the new People of God, the Church, the foreshadowing of new heavens and a new earth (cf. Rev 21:1).

The Apostles, overcoming their initial fears even about marriage and the family, grew in courage. They came to understand that marriage and family are a true vocation which comes from God himself and is an apostolate: the apostolate of the laity. Families are meant to contribute to the transformation of the earth and the renewal of the world, of creation and of all humanity.

Dear families, you too should be fearless, ever ready to give witness to the hope that is in you (cf. 1 Pet 3:15), since the Good Shepherd has put that hope in your hearts through the Gospel. You should be ready to follow Christ towards the pastures of life, which he himself has prepared through the Paschal Mystery of his Death and resurrection.

Do not be afraid of the risks! God's strength is always far more powerful than your difficulties! Immeasurably greater than the evil at work in the world is the power of the *sacrament of Reconciliation,* which the Fathers of the Church rightly called a "second baptism." Much more influential than the corruption present in the world is the divine power of the sacrament of *Confirmation,* which brings baptism to its maturity. And incomparably greater than all is the power of the Eucharist.

The *Eucharist* is truly a wondrous sacrament. In it Christ has given us himself as food and drink, as a source of saving power. He has left himself to us that we might have life and have it in abundance (cf. Jn 10:10): the life which is in him and which he has shared with us by the gift of the Spirit in rising from the dead on the third day. The life that comes from Christ is a life for us.

It is for you, dear husbands and wives, parents and families! Did Jesus not institute the Eucharist in a family-like setting during the Last Supper? When you meet for meals and are together in harmony, *Christ is close to you.* And he is Emmanuel, God with us, in an even greater way whenever you approach the table of the Eucharist. It can happen, as it did at Emmaus, that he is recognized only in "the breaking of the bread" (cf. Lk 24:35). It may well be that he is knocking at the door for a long time, waiting for it to be opened so that he can enter and eat with us (cf. Rev 3:20). The Last Supper and the words he spoke there contain all the power and wisdom of the sacrifice of the Cross. No other power and wisdom exist by which we can be saved and through which we can help to save others. There is no other power and no other wisdom by which you, parents, can educate both your children and yourselves. The *educational power of the Eucharist* has been proved down the generations and centuries.

Everywhere the Good Shepherd is with us. Even as he was at Cana in Galilee, *the Bridegroom in the midst of the bride and bridegroom* as they entrusted themselves to each other for their whole life, so the Good Shepherd is also with us today as the reason for our hope, the source of strength for our hearts, the wellspring of ever new enthusiasm and the sign of the triumph of the "civilization of love." Jesus, the Good Shepherd, continues to say to us: *Do not be afraid.*

I am with you. "I am with you always, to the close of the age" (Mt 28:20). What is the source of this strength? What is the reason for our certainty that you are with us, even though they put you to death, O Son of God, and you died like any other human being? What is the reason for this certainty? The Evangelist says: "He loved them to the end" (Jn 13:1). Thus do you love us, you who are the First and the Last, the Living One; you who died and are alive for evermore (cf. Rev 1:17–18).

The Great Mystery

19. Saint Paul uses a concise phrase in referring to family life: it is a *"great mystery"* (Eph 5:32). What he writes in the Letter to the Ephesians about that "great mystery," although deeply rooted in the Book of Genesis and in the whole Old Testament tradition, nonetheless represents a new approach which will later find expression in the Church's Magisterium.

The Church professes that marriage, as the sacrament of the covenant between husband and wife, is a "great mystery," because it expresses *the spousal love of Christ for his Church.* Saint Paul writes: "Husbands, love your wives, as Christ loved the Church and gave himself up for her, that he might sanctify her, having cleansed her by the washing of water with the word" (Eph 5:25–26). The Apostle is speaking here about baptism, which he discusses at length in the Letter to the Romans, where he presents it as a sharing in the death of Christ leading to a sharing in his life (cf. Rom 6:3–4). In this sacrament the believer *is born* as a new man, for baptism has the power to communicate new life, the very life of God. The mystery of the God-man is in some way recapitulated in the event of baptism. As Saint Irenaeus would later say, along with many other Fathers of the Church of both East and West: "Christ Jesus, our Lord, the Son of God, became the son of man so that man could become a son of God."[44]

The Bridegroom then is the very same God who became man. In the Old Covenant Yahweh appears as the Bridegroom of Israel, the chosen people—a Bridegroom who is both affectionate and demanding, jealous and faithful. Israel's moments of betrayal, desertion and idolatry, described in such powerful and evocative terms by the Prophets, can never extinguish the love with which *God, the Bridegroom,* "loves to the end" (cf. Jn 13:1).

The confirmation and fulfillment of the spousal relationship between God and his people are realized in Christ, in the New Covenant. Christ assures us

---

44. Cf. *Adversus Haereses*, III, 10, 2: PG 7, 873; SCh 211, 116–19; Saint Athanasius, *De Incarnatione Verbi*, 54: PG 25, 191–92; Saint Augustine, *Sermo* 185, 3: PL 38, 999; *Sermo* 194, 3, 3: PL 38, 1016.

that the Bridegroom is with us (cf. Mt 9:15). He is with all of us; he is with the Church. *The Church becomes a Bride,* the Bride of Christ. This Bride, of whom the Letter to the Ephesians speaks, is present in each of the baptized and is like one who presents herself before her Bridegroom.

"Christ loved the Church and gave himself up for her ..., that he might present the Church to himself in splendor, without spot or wrinkle or any such thing, that she might be holy and without blemish" (Eph 5:25–27). The love with which the Bridegroom "has loved" the Church "to the end" continuously renews her holiness in her saints, even though she remains a Church of sinners. Even sinners, "tax collectors and harlots," are called to holiness, as Christ himself affirms in the Gospel (cf. Mt 21:31). All are called to become a glorious Church, holy and without blemish. "Be holy," says the Lord, "for I am holy" (Lev 11:44; cf. 1 Pet 1:16).

This is the deepest significance of the "great mystery," the inner meaning of the *sacramental gift* in the Church, the most profound meaning of baptism and the Eucharist. They are fruits of the love with which the Bridegroom has loved us to the end, a love which continually expands and lavishes on people an ever greater sharing in supernatural life.

Saint Paul, after having said: "Husbands, love your wives" (Eph 5:25), emphatically adds: "Even so husbands should love their wives as their own bodies. He who loves his wife loves himself. For no man ever hates his own flesh, but nourishes and cherishes it, as Christ does the Church, because we are members of his body" (Eph 5:28–30). And he encourages spouses with the words: "Be subject to one another out of reverence for Christ" (Eph 5:21).

This is unquestionably a new presentation of the eternal truth about marriage and the family in the light of the New Covenant. Christ has revealed this truth in the Gospel by his presence at Cana in Galilee, by the sacrifice of the Cross and the sacraments of his Church. Husbands and wives thus discover in Christ *the point of reference for their spousal love.* In speaking of Christ as the Bridegroom of the Church, Saint Paul uses the analogy of spousal love, referring back to the Book of Genesis: "A man leaves his father and his mother and cleaves to his wife, and they become one flesh" (Gen 2:24). This is the "great mystery" of that eternal love already present in creation, revealed in Christ and entrusted to the Church. "This mystery is a profound one," the Apostle repeats, "and I am saying that it refers to Christ and the Church" (Eph 5:32). The Church cannot therefore be understood as the Mystical Body of Christ, as the sign of man's Covenant with God in Christ, or as the universal sacrament of salvation, unless we keep in mind the "great mystery" involved in the creation of man as male and female and the vocation of both to conjugal love, to fatherhood and to motherhood. The "great mystery," which is the Church and humanity in Christ, does not exist apart from the "great mystery" expressed in the "one flesh" (cf. Gen 2:24; Eph 5:31–32), that is, in the reality of marriage and the family.

The family itself is the great mystery of God. As the "domestic church," it is the *bride of Christ*. The universal Church, and every particular Church in her, is most immediately revealed as the bride of Christ in the "domestic church" and in its experience of love: conjugal love, paternal and maternal love, fraternal love, the love of a community of persons and of generations. Could we even imagine human love without the Bridegroom and the love with which he first loved to the end? Only if husbands and wives share in that love and in that "great mystery" can they love "to the end." Unless they share in it, they do not know "to the end" what love truly is and how radical are its demands. And this is undoubtedly very dangerous for them.

The teaching of the Letter to the Ephesians amazes us with its depth and the *authority of its ethical teaching*. Pointing to marriage, and indirectly to the family, as the "great mystery" which refers to Christ and the Church, the Apostle Paul is able to reaffirm what he had earlier said to husbands: "Let each one of you love his wife as himself." He goes on to say: "And let the wife see that she respects her husband" (Eph 5:33). Respect, because she loves and knows that she is loved in return. It is because of this love that husband and wife *become a mutual gift*. Love contains the acknowledgment of the personal dignity of the other, and of his or her absolute uniqueness. Indeed, each of the spouses, as a human being, has been willed by God from among all the creatures of the earth for his or her own sake.[45] Each of them, however, by a conscious and responsible act, makes a free gift of self to the other and to the children received from the Lord. It is significant that Saint Paul continues his exhortation by echoing the fourth commandment: "Children, obey your parents in the Lord, for this is right. 'Honor your father and mother' (this is the first commandment with a promise), 'that it may be well with you and that you may live long on the earth'. Fathers, do not provoke your children to anger, but bring them up in the discipline and instruction of the Lord" (Eph 6:1–4). The Apostle thus sees in the fourth commandment the implicit commitment of mutual respect between husband and wife, between parents and children, and he recognizes in it the *principle of family stability*.

Saint Paul's magnificent synthesis concerning the "great mystery" appears as the compendium or *summa*, in some sense, *of the teaching about God and man* which was brought to fulfillment by Christ. Unfortunately, Western thought, with the development of *modern rationalism*, has been gradually moving away from this teaching. The philosopher who formulated the principle of "*Cogito, ergo*

---

45. Cf. Pastoral Constitution on the Church in the Modern World *Gaudium et Spes*, 24.

sum," "I think, therefore I am," also gave the modern concept of man its distinctive dualistic character. It is typical of rationalism to make a radical contrast in man between spirit and body, between body and spirit. But man is a person in the unity of his body and his spirit.[46] The body can never be reduced to mere matter: it is a *spiritualized body*, just as man's spirit is so closely united to the body that he can be described as *an embodied spirit*. The richest source for knowledge of the body is the Word made flesh. *Christ reveals man to himself.*[47] In a certain sense this statement of the Second Vatican Council is the reply, so long awaited, which the Church has given to modern rationalism.

This reply is of fundamental importance for understanding the family, especially against the background of today's civilization, which, as has been said, seems in so many cases to have given up the attempt to be a "civilization of love." The modern age has made great progress in understanding both the material world and human psychology, but with regard to his deepest, metaphysical dimension contemporary man remains to a great extent a *being unknown* to himself. Consequently the family too remains an *unknown reality*. Such is the result of estrangement from that "great mystery" spoken of by the Apostle.

The separation of spirit and body in man has led to a growing tendency to consider the human body, not in accordance with the categories of its specific likeness to God, but rather on the basis of its similarity to all the other bodies present in the world of nature, bodies which man uses as raw material in his efforts to produce goods for consumption. But everyone can immediately realize what enormous dangers lurk behind the application of such criteria to man. When the human body, considered apart from spirit and thought, comes to be used as *raw material* in the same way that the bodies of animals are used—and this actually occurs for example in experimentation on embryos and fetuses—we will inevitably arrive at a dreadful ethical defeat.

Within a similar anthropological perspective, the human family is facing the challenge of a *new Manichaeanism*, in which body and spirit are put in radical opposition; the body does not receive life from the spirit, and the spirit does not give life to the body.

Man thus *ceases to live as a person and a subject*. Regardless of all intentions and declarations to the contrary, he becomes merely an *object*. This neo-Manichaean culture has led, for example, to human sexuality being regarded more as an area *for manipulation and exploitation* than as the basis of that *primordial wonder* which led Adam on the morning of creation to exclaim before Eve: "This

---

46. "Corpore et anima unus," as the Council so clearly and felicitously stated: ibid., 14.

47. Ibid., 22.

at last is bone of my bones and flesh of my flesh" (Gen 2:23). This same wonder is echoed in the words of the Song of Solomon: "You have ravished my heart, my sister, my bride, you have ravished my heart with a glance of your eyes" (Song 4:9). How far removed are some modern ideas from the profound understanding of masculinity and femininity found in Divine Revelation! Revelation leads us to discover in *human sexuality a treasure proper to the person,* who finds true fulfillment in the family but who can likewise express his profound calling in virginity and in celibacy for the sake of the Kingdom of God.

Modern rationalism *does not tolerate mystery.* It does not accept the mystery of man as male and female, nor is it willing to admit that the full truth about man has been revealed in Jesus Christ. In particular, it does not accept the "great mystery" proclaimed in the Letter to the Ephesians, but radically opposes it. It may well acknowledge, in the context of a vague deism, the possibility and even the need for a supreme or divine Being, but it firmly rejects the idea of a God who became man in order to save man. For rationalism it is unthinkable that God should be the Redeemer, much less *that he should be "the Bridegroom,"* the primordial and unique source of the human love between spouses. Rationalism provides a radically different way of looking at creation and the meaning of human existence. But once man begins to lose sight of a God who loves him, a God who calls man through Christ to live in him and with him, and once the family no longer has the possibility of sharing in the "great mystery," what is left except the mere *temporal dimension of life?* Earthly life becomes nothing more than the scenario of a battle for existence, of a desperate search for gain, and financial gain before all else.

The deep-seated roots of the "great mystery," the sacrament of love and life which began with Creation and Redemption and which *has Christ the Bridegroom as its ultimate surety,* have been lost in the modern way of looking at things. The "great mystery" is threatened in us and all around us. May the Church's celebration of the Year of the Family be a fruitful opportunity for husbands and wives to rediscover that mystery and recommit themselves to it with strength, courage and enthusiasm.

Mother of Fairest Love

20. The history of "fairest love" begins at the Annunciation, in those wondrous words which the angel spoke to Mary, called to become the Mother of the Son of God. With Mary's "yes," the One who is "God from God and Light from Light" becomes a son of man. Mary is his Mother, while continuing to be the Virgin who "knows not man" (cf. Lk 1:34). As Mother and Virgin, *Mary*

becomes the *Mother of Fairest Love*. This truth is already revealed in the words of the Archangel Gabriel, but its full significance will gradually become clearer and more evident as Mary follows her Son in the pilgrimage of faith.[48]

The "Mother of Fairest Love" was accepted by the one who, according to Israel's tradition, was already her earthly husband: *Joseph, of the house of David.* Joseph would have had the right to consider his promised bride as his wife and the mother of his children. But God takes it upon himself to intervene in this spousal covenant: "Joseph, son of David, do not fear to take Mary as your wife, for that which is conceived in her is of the Holy Spirit" (Mt 1:20). Joseph is aware, having seen it with his own eyes, that a new life with which he has had nothing to do has been conceived in Mary. Being a just man, and observing the Old Law, which in his situation imposed the obligation of divorce, he wishes to dissolve his marriage in a loving way (cf. Mt 1:19). The angel of the Lord tells him that this would not be consistent with his vocation; indeed it would be contrary to the spousal love uniting him to Mary. This mutual spousal love, to be completely "fairest love," requires that he should take Mary and her Son into his own house in Nazareth. Joseph obeys the divine message and does all that he had been commanded (cf. Mt 1:24). And so, thanks also to Joseph, the *mystery of the Incarnation* and, together with it, the mystery of the Holy Family, *come to be profoundly inscribed in the spousal love of husband and wife* and, in an indirect way, in the genealogy of every human family.

What Saint Paul will call the "great mystery" found its most lofty expression in the Holy Family. Thus the *family* truly takes its place *at the very heart of the New Covenant.*

It can also be said that the history of "fairest love" began, in a certain way, with the first *human couple*: Adam and Eve. Neither the temptation to which they yielded nor the subsequent original sin deprived them completely of the capacity for "fairest love." This becomes clear when we read, for example, in the Book of Tobit that the spouses Tobias and Sarah, in defining the meaning of their union, appealed to their first parents, Adam and Eve (cf. Tob 8:6). In the New Covenant, Saint Paul also bears witness to this, speaking of Christ as a new Adam (cf. 1 Cor 15:45). Christ does not come to condemn the first Adam and the first Eve, but to save them. He comes to renew everything that is God's gift in man, everything in him that is eternally good and beautiful, everything that forms the basis of "fairest love." The *history of "fairest love"* is, in one sense, the *history of man's salvation.*

"Fairest love" always *begins with the self-revelation of the person.* At creation Eve reveals herself to Adam, just as Adam reveals himself to Eve. In the course

---

48. Cf. Dogmatic Constitution on the Church *Lumen Gentium*, 56–59.

of history newly-married couples tell each other: "We shall walk the path of life together."

The family thus begins as a union of the two and, through the sacrament, as a new community in Christ. *For love to be truly "fairest," it must be a gift of God,* grafted by the Holy Spirit on to human hearts and continually nourished in them (cf. Rom 5:5).

Fully conscious of this, the Church in the sacrament of marriage asks the Holy Spirit to visit human hearts. If love is truly to be "fairest love," a gift of one person to another, it must come from the One who is himself a gift and the source of every gift.

Such was the case, as the Gospel recounts, with Mary and Joseph who, at the threshold of the New Covenant, renewed the experience of "fairest love" described in the Song of Solomon. Joseph thinks of Mary in the words: "My sister, my bride" (Song 4:9). Mary, the Mother of God, conceives by the power of the Holy Spirit, who is the origin of the "fairest love," which the Gospel delicately places in the context of the "great mystery."

When we speak about "fairest love," we are also speaking about *beauty:* the beauty of love and the beauty of the human being who, by the power of the Holy Spirit, is capable of such love. We are speaking of the beauty of man and woman: their beauty as brother or sister, as a couple about to be married, as husband and wife. The Gospel sheds light not only on the mystery of "fairest love," but also on the equally profound mystery of beauty, which, like love, is from God. Man and woman are from God, two persons called to become a mutual gift. From the primordial gift of the Spirit, the "giver of life," there arises the reciprocal gift of being husband or wife, no less than that of being brother or sister.

All this is confirmed by the mystery of the Incarnation, a mystery which has been *the source of a new beauty* in the history of humanity and has inspired countless masterpieces of art. After the strict prohibition against portraying the invisible God by graven images (cf. Dt 4:15–20), the Christian era began instead to portray in art the God who became man, Mary his Mother, Saint Joseph, the Saints of the Old and New Covenant and the entire created world redeemed by Christ. In this way it began a new relationship with the world of culture and of art. It can be said that this *new artistic canon*, attentive to the deepest dimension of man and his future, originates in the mystery of Christ's Incarnation and draws inspiration from the mysteries of his life: his birth in Bethlehem, his hidden life in Nazareth, his public ministry, Golgotha, the resurrection and his final return in glory.

The Church is conscious that her presence in the contemporary world, and in particular the contribution and support she offers to the promotion of the dignity of marriage and the family, are intimately linked to the development of culture, and she is rightly concerned for this. This is precisely why the Church is so concerned with the direction taken by the means of social communication, which have the duty of *forming* as well as *informing* their vast audience.[49] Knowing the vast and powerful impact of the media, she never tires of reminding communications workers of the dangers arising from the manipulation of truth. Indeed, what truth can there be in films, shows and radio and television programs dominated by pornography and violence? Do these really serve the *truth about man*? Such questions are unavoidable for those who work in the field of communications and those who have responsibility for creating and marketing media products.

This kind of critical reflection should lead our society, which certainly contains many positive aspects on the material and cultural level, to realize that, from various points of view, it is a *society which is sick* and is creating profound distortions in man. Why is this happening? The reason is that our society has broken away from the full truth about man, from the truth about what man and woman really are as persons. Thus it cannot adequately comprehend the real meaning of the gift of persons in marriage, responsible love at the service of fatherhood and motherhood, and the true grandeur of procreation and education.

Is it an exaggeration to say that the *mass media*, if they are not guided by sound ethical principles, fail to serve the truth in its fundamental dimension? This is the real drama: the modern means of social communication are tempted to manipulate the message, *thereby falsifying the truth about man*. Human beings are not the same thing as the images proposed in advertising and shown by the modern mass media. *They are much more*, in their physical and psychic unity, as composites of soul and body, as persons. They are much more because of their vocation to love, which introduces them as male and female into the realm of the "great mystery."

Mary was the first to enter this realm, and she introduced her husband Joseph into it. Thus they became the *first models* of that "fairest love" which the Church continually implores for young people, husbands and wives and families. Young people, spouses and families themselves should never cease to pray for this. How can we not think about the crowds of pilgrims, old and young, who visit Marian shrines and gaze upon the face of the Mother of God, on the faces of the Holy Family, where they find reflected the full beauty of the love which God has given to mankind?

---

49. Cf. Pontifical Council for Social Communications, Pastoral Instruction *Aetatis Novae* (22 February 1992), 7.

In the Sermon on the Mount, recalling the sixth commandment, Christ proclaims: "You have heard that it was said, 'You shall not commit adultery'. But I say to you that every one who looks at a woman lustfully has already committed adultery with her in his heart" (Mt 5:27–28). With regard to the Decalogue and its purpose of defending the traditional solidity of marriage and the family, these words represent a great step forward. Jesus goes to the very source of the sin of adultery, which dwells in the innermost heart of man and is revealed in a way of looking and thinking dominated by *concupiscence.* Through concupiscence *man tends to treat as his own possession another human being,* one who does not belong to him but to God. In speaking to his contemporaries, Christ is also speaking to men and women in every age and generation. He is speaking in particular to our own generation, living as it is in a society marked by consumerism and hedonism.

Why does Christ speak out in so forceful and demanding a way in the Sermon on the Mount? The reason is quite clear: Christ wants to safeguard *the holiness of marriage and of the family.* He wants to defend the full truth about the human person and his dignity.

Only in the light of this truth can the family be "to the end" the great "revelation," the *first discovery of the other:* the mutual discovery of husband and wife and then of each son and daughter born to them. All that a husband and a wife promise to each other—to be "true in good times and in bad, and to love and honor each other all the days of their life"—is possible only when "fairest love" is present. Man today cannot learn this from what modern mass culture has to say. "Fairest love" is learned above all in prayer. *Prayer,* in fact, always brings with it, to use an expression of Saint Paul, a type of *interior hiddenness with Christ in God, "your life is hid with Christ in God"* (Col 3:3). Only in this hiddenness do we see the workings of the Holy Spirit, the source of "fairest love." He has poured forth this love not only in the hearts of Mary and Joseph but also in the hearts of all married couples who are open to hearing the word of God and keeping it (cf. Lk 8:15). The future of each family unit depends upon this "fairest love": the mutual love of husband and wife, of parents and children, a love embracing all generations. Love is the true *source of the unity and strength of the family.*

Birth and Danger

21. It is significant that the brief account of the infancy of Jesus mentions, practically at the same time, his *birth* and the *danger* which he immediately had to confront. Luke records the prophetic words uttered by the aged Simeon when the Child was presented to the Lord in the Temple forty days after his birth. Simeon speaks of "light" and of a "sign of contradiction." He goes on to predict of Mary:

"And a sword will pierce through your own soul also" (cf. Lk 2:32–35). Matthew, for his part, tells of the plot of Herod against Jesus. Informed by the Magi who came from the East to see the new king who was to be born (cf. Mt 2:2), Herod senses a threat to his power, and after their departure he orders the death of all male children aged two years or under in Bethlehem and the surrounding towns. Jesus escapes from the hands of Herod thanks to a special divine intervention and the fatherly care of Joseph, who takes him with his mother into Egypt, where they remain until Herod's death. The Holy Family then returns to Nazareth, their home town, and begins what for many years would be a hidden life, marked by the carrying out of daily tasks with fidelity and generosity (cf. Mt 2:1–23; Lk 2:39–52).

The fact that Jesus, from his very birth, had to face threats and dangers has a certain *prophetic eloquence*. Even as a Child, Jesus is a "sign of contradiction." Prophetically eloquent also is the tragedy of the innocent children of Bethlehem, slaughtered at Herod's command.[50] According to the Church's ancient liturgy, they shared in the birth and saving passion of Christ. Through their own "passion," they complete "what is lacking in Christ's afflictions for the sake of his body, that is, the Church" (Col 1:24).

In the infancy Gospel, *the proclamation of life*, which comes about in a wondrous way in the birth of the Redeemer, is thus put in sharp contrast with the *threat to life*, a life which embraces the mystery of the Incarnation and of the divine-human reality of Christ in its entirety. The Word was made flesh (cf. Jn 1:14): God became man. The Fathers of the Church frequently call attention to this sublime mystery: "God became man, so that we might become gods."[51] This truth of faith is likewise the truth about the human being. It clearly indicates the gravity of all attempts on the life of a child in the womb of its mother. Precisely in this situation we encounter *everything which is diametrically opposed* to "fairest love." If an individual is exclusively concerned with "use," he can reach the point of killing love by killing the fruit of love. For the culture of use, the "blessed fruit of your womb" (Lk 1:42) becomes in a certain sense an "accursed fruit."

How can we not recall, in this regard, the aberrations that the so-called *constitutional State* has tolerated in so many countries?

The law of God is univocal and categorical with respect to human life. God commands: "You shall not kill" (Ex 20:13). *No human lawgiver can therefore*

---

50. In the liturgy of their Feast, which has its origins in the fifth century, the Church turns to the Holy Innocents, invoking them with the words of the poet Prudentius as "the flowers of the martyrs whom, at the very threshold of their lives, the persecutor of Christ cut down as the whirlwind does to roses still in bud."

51. Saint Athanasius, *De Incarnatione Verbi*, 54: PG 25, 191–92.

assert: it is permissible for you to kill, you have the right to kill, or you should kill. Tragically, in the history of our century, this has actually occurred when certain political forces have come to power, even by democratic means, and have passed laws contrary to the right to life of every human being, in the name of eugenic, ethnic or other reasons, as unfounded as they are mistaken. A no less serious phenomenon, also because it meets with widespread acquiescence or consensus in public opinion, is that of laws which fail to respect the right to life from the moment of conception. How can one morally accept laws that permit the killing of a human being not yet born, but already alive in the mother's womb? The right to life becomes an exclusive prerogative of adults who even manipulate legislatures in order to carry out their own plans and pursue their own interests.

We are facing an immense threat to life: not only to the life of individuals but also to that of civilization itself. The statement that civilization has become, in some areas, a "civilization of death" is being confirmed in disturbing ways. Was it not a *prophetic event* that the birth of Christ was accompanied by danger to his life? Yes, even the life of the One who is at the same time Son of Man and Son of God was threatened. It was endangered from the very beginning, and only by a miracle did he escape death.

Nevertheless, in the last few decades some consoling signs of a *reawakening of conscience* have appeared: both among intellectuals and in public opinion itself. There is a new and growing sense of respect for life from the first moment of conception, especially among young people. "Pro-life" movements are beginning to spread. This is a leaven of hope for the future of the family and of all humanity.

"You Welcomed Me"

22. Married couples and families of all the world: *the Bridegroom is with you!* This is what the Pope wishes to say to you above all else during this Year which the United Nations and the Church have dedicated to the family. "God so loved the world that he gave his only Son, that whoever believes in him should not perish but have eternal life. For God sent his Son into the world, not to condemn the world, but that the world might be saved through him" (Jn 3:16–17). "That which is born of the flesh is flesh, and that which is born of the Spirit is spirit ... You must be born anew" (Jn 3:6–7). You must be born "of water and the Spirit" (Jn 3:5). You yourselves, dear fathers and mothers, are the *first witnesses and servants* of this *rebirth* in the Holy Spirit.

As you beget children on earth, never forget that *you are also begetting them for God.* God wants their birth in the Holy Spirit. He wants them to be adopted children in the Only-begotten Son, who gives us "power to become children of God" (Jn 1:12). The work of salvation continues in the world and is carried out through the Church. All this is the work of the Son of God, the Divine Bridegroom, who has given to us the Kingdom of his Father and who reminds us, his disciples, that "the Kingdom of God is in the midst of you" (Lk 17:21).

Our faith tells us that Jesus Christ, who "is seated at the right hand of the Father," will come to judge the living and the dead. On the other hand, the Gospel of John assures us that Christ was sent "into the world, not to condemn the world, but that the world might be saved through him" (Jn 3:17). In what then does judgment consist? Christ himself gives the answer: "And this is the judgment, that the light has come into the world ... But he who does what is true comes into the light, that it may be clearly seen that his deeds have been wrought by God" (Jn 3:19, 21). Recently, the Encyclical *Veritatis Splendor* also reminded us of this.[52] Is Christ then a judge? *Your own actions will judge you in the light of the truth which you know.* Fathers and mothers, sons and daughters, will be judged by their actions. Each one of us will be judged according to the Commandments, including those we have discussed in this Letter: the Fourth, Fifth, Sixth and Ninth Commandments. But ultimately everyone will be judged *on love,* which is the deepest meaning and the summing-up of the Commandments. As Saint John of the Cross wrote: "In the evening of life we shall be judged on love."[53] Christ, the Redeemer and Bridegroom of mankind, "was born for this and came into the world for this, to bear witness to the truth. Everyone who is of truth hears his voice" (cf. Jn 18:37). Christ will be the judge, but in the way that he himself indicated in speaking of the Last Judgment (cf. Mt 25:31–46). His will be a *judgment on love,* a judgment which will definitively confirm the truth that the Bridegroom was with us, without perhaps our having been aware of it.

The judge is the *Bridegroom of the Church and of humanity.* This is why he says, in passing his sentence: "Come, O blessed of my Father ... for I was hungry and you gave me food, I was thirsty and you gave me drink, I was a stranger and you welcomed me, I was naked and you clothed me" (Mt 25:34–36). This list could of course be lengthened, and countless other problems relevant to married and family life could be added. There we might very well find statements like: "I was an unborn child, and you welcomed me by letting me be born"; "I was an abandoned child, and you became my family"; "I was an orphan, and you adopted me and raised me as one of your own children." Or again: "You helped mothers filled with uncertainty and exposed to wrongful pressure to welcome their unborn child and let it be born"; and "You helped large families and families in difficulty

---

52. Cf. *Veritatis Splendor* (6 August 1993), 84.

53. *Words of Light and Love,* 59.

to look after and educate the children God gave them." We could continue with a long and detailed list, including all those kinds of true moral and human good in which love is expressed. This is *the great harvest* which the Redeemer of the world, to whom the Father has entrusted judgment, will come to reap. It is the *harvest of grace and of good works,* ripened by the breath of the Bridegroom in the Holy Spirit, who is ever at work in the world and in the Church. For all of this, let us give thanks to the Giver of every good gift.

We also know however that according to the Gospel of Matthew the Final Judgment will contain another list, solemn and terrifying: "Depart from me ... for I was hungry and you gave me no food, I was thirsty and you gave me no drink, I was a stranger and you did not welcome me, naked and you did not clothe me" (Mt 25:41–43). To this list also we could add other ways of acting, in which Jesus is present in each case as the *one who has been rejected.* In this way he would identify with the abandoned wife or husband, or with the child conceived and then rejected: "You did not welcome me"! This judgment is also to be found throughout the history of our families; it is to be found throughout the history of our nations and all humanity. Christ's words, "You did not welcome me," also touch social institutions, governments and international organizations.

Pascal wrote that "Jesus will be in agony until the end of the world."[54] The agony of Gethsemane and the agony of Golgotha are *the summit of the revelation of love.* Both scenes reveal the Bridegroom who is with us, who loves us ever anew, and "loves us to the end" (cf. Jn 13:1). The love which is in Christ, and which from him flows beyond the limits of individual or family histories, flows beyond the limits of all human history.

At the end of these reflections, dear Brothers and Sisters, in view of what will be proclaimed from various platforms during the Year of the Family, I would like to renew with you the profession of faith which Peter addressed to Christ: "You have the words of eternal life" (Jn 6:68). Together let us say: "Your words, O Lord, will not pass away"! (cf. Mk 13:31). What then is the Pope's wish for you at the end of this lengthy *meditation on the Year of the Family?* It is his prayer that all of you will be in agreement with these words, which are "spirit and life" (Jn 6:63).

"Strengthened in the Inner Man"

23. I bow my knees before the Father, from whom every fatherhood and motherhood is named, "that he may grant you to be strengthened with might through his Spirit in the inner man" (Eph 3:16). I willingly return to these words

---

54. B. Pascal, *Pensées, Le mystère de Jésus,* 553 (ed. Brunschvicg).

of the Apostle, which I mentioned in the first part of this Letter. In a certain sense they are pivotal words. *The family, fatherhood and motherhood all go together.* The family is the first human setting in which is formed that "inner man" of which the Apostle speaks. The growth of the inner man in strength and vigor is a gift of the Father and the Son in the Holy Spirit.

The Year of the Family sets before us in the Church an immense task, no different from the task which families face every year and every day. In the context of this Year, however, that task takes on particular meaning and importance. We began the Year of the Family in Nazareth on the *Solemnity of the Holy Family*. Throughout this Year we wish to make our pilgrim way towards that place of grace which has become the *Shrine of the Holy Family* in the history of humanity. We want to make this pilgrimage in order to become aware once again of that heritage of truth about the family which from the beginning has been *a treasure for the Church*. It is a treasure which grows out of the rich tradition of the Old Covenant, is completed in the New and finds its fullest symbolic expression in the mystery of the Holy Family in which the divine Bridegroom brings about the redemption of all families. From there Jesus proclaims the *"gospel of the family."* All generations of Christ's disciples have drawn upon this treasure of truth, beginning with the Apostles, on whose teaching we have so frequently drawn in this Letter. In our own times this treasure has been examined in depth in the documents of the Second Vatican Council.[55] Perceptive analyses were developed in the many addresses given by Pope Pius XII to newlyweds,[56] in the Encyclical *Humanae Vitae* of Pope Paul VI, in the speeches delivered at the Synod of Bishops on the Family (1980) and in the Apostolic Exhortation *Familiaris Consortio*. I have already spoken of these statements of the Magisterium. If I return to them now, it is in order to emphasize how vast and rich is the *treasure of Christian truth about the family.*

Written testimonies alone, however, will not suffice. Much more important are *living testimonies*. As Pope Paul VI observed, "contemporary man listens more willingly to witnesses than to teachers, and if he listens to teachers it is because they are witnesses."[57] In the Church, the treasure of the family has been entrusted first and foremost to witnesses: to those fathers and mothers, sons and daughters

---

55. Cf., in particular, Pastoral Constitution on the Church *Gaudium et Spes*, 47–52.

56. Of particular interest is the Address to those taking part in the Convention of the Italian Catholic Union of Midwives (29 October 1951), in *Discorsi e Radiomessaggi*, XIII, 333–353. [The superb addresses of Pius XII recommended here by John Paul II have been collected and are available under the title: *Dear Newlyweds: Pope Pius XII Speaks to Married Couples* (Kansas City, MO: Sarto House, 2001).]

57. Cf. Address to the members of the "Consilium de Laicis" (2 October 1974): *AAS* 66 (1974), 568.

who through the family have discovered the path of their human and Christian vocation, the dimension of the "inner man" (Eph 3:16) of which the Apostle speaks, and thus have attained holiness. *The Holy Family is the beginning of countless other holy families.* The Council recalled that holiness is the vocation of all the baptized.[58] In our age, as in the past, there is no lack of witnesses to the "gospel of the family," even if they are not well known or have not been proclaimed saints by the Church. The Year of the Family is the appropriate occasion to bring about an increased awareness of their existence and their great number.

The history of mankind, the history of salvation, passes by way of the family. In these pages I have tried to show how the family is placed at the centre of the great struggle between good and evil, between life and death, between love and all that is opposed to love. To the family is entrusted the task of striving, first and foremost, *to unleash the forces of good,* the source of which is found in Christ the Redeemer of man. *Every family unit needs to make these forces their own so that,* to use a phrase spoken on the occasion of the Millennium of Christianity in Poland, the family will be *"strong with the strength of God."*[59] This is why the present Letter has sought to draw inspiration from the apostolic exhortations found in the writings of Paul (cf. 1 Cor 7:1- 40; Eph 5:21–6:9; Col 3:25) and the Letters of Peter and John (cf. 1 Pet 3:1–7; 1 Jn 2:12–17). Despite the differences in their historical and cultural contexts, how similar are the experiences of Christians and families then and now!

What I offer, then, is *an invitation:* an invitation addressed especially to you, dearly beloved husbands and wives, fathers and mothers, sons and daughters. It is an invitation to all the particular Churches to remain united in the teaching of the apostolic truth. It is addressed to my Brothers in the Episcopate, and to priests, religious families and consecrated persons, to movements and associations of the lay faithful; to our brothers and sisters united by common faith in Jesus Christ, even while not yet sharing the full communion willed by the Savior[60]; to all who by sharing in the faith of Abraham belong, like us, to the great community of believers in the one God[61]; to those who are the heirs of other spiritual and religious traditions; and to all men and women of good will.

May Christ, who is the same "yesterday and today and for ever" (Heb 13:8), be with us as we bow the knee before the Father, from whom all fatherhood and

---

58. Cf. Dogmatic Constitution on the Church *Lumen Gentium,* 40.

59. Cf. Cardinal Stefan Wyszyński, *Rodzina Bogiem silna,* Homily delivered at Jasna Gora (26 August 1961).

60. Cf. Dogmatic Constitution on the Church *Lumen Gentium,* 15.

61. Cf. ibid., 16.

motherhood and every human family is named (cf. Eph 3:14–15). In the words of the prayer to the Father which Christ himself taught us, may he once again offer testimony of that love with which he loved us "to the end"! (Jn 13:1).

I speak with the power of his truth to all people of our day, so that they will come to appreciate the grandeur of the goods of marriage, family and life; so that they will come to appreciate the great danger which follows when these realities are not respected, or when the supreme values which lie at the foundation of the family and of human dignity are disregarded.

May the Lord Jesus repeat these truths to us *with the power and the wisdom of the Cross,* so that humanity will not yield to the temptation of the "father of lies" (Jn 8:44), who constantly seeks to draw people to broad and easy ways, ways apparently smooth and pleasant, but in reality full of snares and dangers. May we always be enabled to follow the One who is "the way, and the truth, and the life" (Jn 14:6).

Dear Brothers and Sisters: Let all of this be the task of Christian families and the object of the Church's missionary concern throughout this Year, so rich in singular divine graces. May the Holy Family, icon and model of every human family, help each individual to walk in the spirit of Nazareth. May it help each family unit to grow in understanding of its particular mission in society and the Church by hearing the Word of God, by prayer and by a fraternal sharing of life. May Mary, Mother of "Fairest Love," and Joseph, Guardian of the Redeemer, accompany us all with their constant protection.

With these sentiments I bless every family in the name of the Most Holy Trinity: Father, Son and Holy Spirit.

Given in Rome, at Saint Peter's, on the second of February, the Feast of the Presentation of the Lord, in the year 1994, the sixteenth of my Pontificate.

✠ JOHN PAUL II

excerpts[†] from

EVANGELIUM VITAE

On the Value and Inviolability of Human Life

Encyclical Letter of Pope John Paul II,
promulgated March 25, 1995

CHAPTER I
THE VOICE OF YOUR BROTHER'S BLOOD
CRIES TO ME FROM THE GROUND

[...]

"Am I my brother's keeper?" (Gen 4:9)
A perverse idea of freedom

18. The panorama described needs to be understood not only in terms of the phenomena of death which characterize it but also in the *variety of causes* which determine it. The Lord's question: "What have you done?" (Gen. 4:10), seems almost like an invitation addressed to Cain to go beyond the material dimension of his murderous gesture, in order to recognize in it all the gravity of the *motives* which occasioned it and the *consequences* which result from it.

Decisions that go against life sometimes arise from difficult or even tragic situations of profound suffering, loneliness, a total lack of economic prosperity, depression and anxiety about the future. Such circumstances can mitigate even to a notable degree subjective responsibility and the consequent culpability of those who make these choices which in themselves are evil. But today the problem goes far beyond the necessary recognition of these personal situations. It is a problem which exists at the cultural, social, and political level, where it reveals its more sinister and disturbing aspect in the tendency, ever more widely shared,

---

†   [Because these pages present excerpts, footnote numbers do not match those of the original document.]

to interpret the above crimes against life as *legitimate expressions of individual free-dom, to be acknowledged and protected as actual rights.*

In this way, and with tragic consequences, a long historical process is reaching a turning-point. The process which once led to discovering the idea of "human rights"—rights inherent in every person and prior to any Constitution and State legislation—is today marked by a *surprising contradiction.* Precisely in an age when the inviolable rights of the person are solemnly proclaimed and the value of life is publicly affirmed, the very right to life is being denied or trampled upon, especially at the more significant moments of existence: the moment of birth and the moment of death.

On the one hand, the various declarations of human rights and the many initiatives inspired by these declarations show that at the global level there is a growing moral sensitivity, more alert to acknowledging the value and dignity of every individual as a human being, without any distinction of race, nationality, religion, political opinion or social class.

On the other hand, these noble proclamations are unfortunately contra-dicted by a tragic repudiation of them in practice. This denial is still more distress-ing, indeed more scandalous, precisely because it is occurring in a society which makes the affirmation and protection of human rights its primary objective and its boast. How can these repeated affirmations of principle be reconciled with the continual increase and widespread justification of attacks on human life? How can we reconcile these declarations with the refusal to accept those who are weak and needy, or elderly, or those who have just been conceived? These attacks go directly against respect for life and they represent a direct threat to the entire culture of human rights. It is a threat capable, in the end, of jeopardiz-ing the very meaning of democratic existence: rather than societies of "people living together," our cities risk becoming societies of people who are rejected, marginalized, uprooted and oppressed. If we then look at the wider worldwide perspective, how can we fail to think that the very affirmation of the rights of indi-viduals and peoples made in distinguished international assemblies is a merely futile exercise of rhetoric, if we fail to unmask the selfishness of the rich countries which exclude poorer countries from access to development or make such access dependent on arbitrary prohibitions against procreation, setting up an opposi-tion between development and man himself? Should we not question the very economic models often adopted by States which, also as a result of international pressures and forms of conditioning, cause and aggravate situations of injustice and violence in which the life of whole peoples is degraded and trampled upon?

19. What are the roots of this remarkable contradiction? We can find them in an overall assessment of a cultural and moral nature, beginning with the

mentality which *carries the concept of subjectivity to an extreme* and even distorts it, and recognizes as a subject of rights only the person who enjoys full or at least incipient autonomy and who emerges from a state of total dependence on others. But how can we reconcile this approach with the exaltation of man as a being who is "not to be used"?

The theory of human rights is based precisely on the affirmation that the human person, unlike animals and things, cannot be subjected to domination by others. We must also mention the mentality which tends to equate personal dignity with the capacity for verbal and explicit, or at least perceptible, communication. It is clear that on the basis of these presuppositions there is no place in the world for anyone who, like the unborn or the dying, is a weak element in the social structure, or for anyone who appears completely at the mercy of others and radically dependent on them, and can only communicate through the silent language of a profound sharing of affection. In this case it is force which becomes the criterion for choice and action in interpersonal relations and in social life. But this is the exact opposite of what a State ruled by law, as a community in which the "reasons of force" are replaced by the "force of reason," historically intended to affirm.

At another level, the roots of the contradiction between the solemn affirmation of human rights and their tragic denial in practice lies in a *notion of freedom* which exalts the isolated individual in an absolute way, and gives no place to solidarity, to openness to others and service of them. While it is true that the taking of life not yet born or in its final stages is sometimes marked by a mistaken sense of altruism and human compassion, it cannot be denied that such a culture of death, taken as a whole, betrays a completely individualistic concept of freedom, which ends up by becoming the freedom of "the strong" against the weak who have no choice but to submit.

It is precisely in this sense that Cain's answer to the Lord's question: "Where is Abel your brother?" can be interpreted: "I do not know; am I my brother's keeper?" (Gen. 4:9). Yes, every man is his "brother's keeper," because God entrusts us to one another. And it is also in view of this entrusting that God gives everyone freedom, a freedom which possesses an *inherently relational dimension*. This is a great gift of the Creator, placed as it is at the service of the person and of his fulfillment through the gift of self and openness to others; but when freedom is made absolute in an individualistic way, it is emptied of its original content, and its very meaning and dignity are contradicted.

There is an even more profound aspect which needs to be emphasized: freedom negates and destroys itself, and becomes a factor leading to the destruction of others, when it no longer recognizes and respects its essential link with the truth. When freedom, out of a desire to emancipate itself from all forms of tradition and authority, shuts out even the most obvious evidence of an objective and universal truth, which is the foundation of personal and social life, then the person ends up by no longer taking as the sole and indisputable point of reference for his own choices the truth about good and evil, but only his subjective and changeable opinion or, indeed, his selfish interest and whim.

20. This view of freedom leads to a serious distortion of life in society. If the promotion of the self is understood in terms of absolute autonomy, people inevitably reach the point of rejecting one another. Everyone else is considered an enemy from whom one has to defend oneself. Thus society becomes a mass of individuals placed side by side, but without any mutual bonds. Each one wishes to assert himself independently of the other and in fact intends to make his own interests prevail. Still, in the face of other people's analogous interests, some kind of compromise must be found, if one wants a society in which the maximum possible freedom is guaranteed to each individual. In this way, any reference to common values and to a truth absolutely binding on everyone is lost, and social life ventures on to the shifting sands of complete relativism. At that point, everything is negotiable, everything is open to bargaining: even the first of the fundamental rights, the right to life.

This is what is happening also at the level of politics and government: the original and inalienable right to life is questioned or denied on the basis of parliamentary vote or the will of one part of the people—even if it is the majority. This is the sinister result of relativism which reigns unopposed: the "right" ceases to be such, because it is no longer firmly founded on the inviolable dignity of the person, but is made subject to the will of the stronger part. In this way democracy, contradicting its own principles, effectively moves towards a form of totalitarianism. The State is no longer the "common home" where all can live together on the basis of principles of fundamental equality, but is transformed into a *tyrant State*, which arrogates to itself the right to dispose of the life of the weakest and most defenseless members, from the unborn child to the elderly, in the name of a public interest which is really nothing but the interest of one part. The appearance of the strictest respect for legality is maintained, at least when the laws permitting abortion and euthanasia are the result of a ballot in accordance with what are generally seen as the rules of democracy. Really, what we have here is only the tragic caricature of legality; the democratic ideal, which is only truly such when it acknowledges and safeguards the dignity of every human person, *is betrayed in its very foundations.* "How is it still possible to speak of the dignity of every human person when the killing of the weakest and most innocent is permitted? In the name of what justice is the most unjust of discriminations practiced: some individuals are held to be deserving of defense and others are denied that dignity?"[1] When this happens, the process leading to the break-down of a genuinely human co-existence and the disintegration of the State itself has already begun.

To claim the right to abortion, infanticide and euthanasia, and to recognize that right in law, means to attribute to human freedom a *perverse and evil significance:* that of an *absolute power over others and against others.* This is the death of true freedom: "Truly, truly, I say to you, everyone who commits sin is a slave to sin" (Jn. 8:34).

"And from your face I shall be hidden" (Gen 4:14):
The eclipse of the sense of God and of man

21. In seeking the deepest roots of the struggle between the "culture of life" and the "culture of death," we cannot restrict ourselves to the perverse idea of freedom mentioned above. We have to go to the heart of the tragedy being experienced by modern man: *the eclipse of the sense of God and of man,* typical of a social and cultural climate dominated by secularism, which, with its ubiquitous tentacles, succeeds at times in putting Christian communities themselves to the test. Those who allow themselves to be influenced by this climate easily fall into a sad vicious circle: *when the sense of God is lost, there is also a tendency to lose the sense of man,* of his dignity and his life; in turn, the systematic violation of the moral law, especially in the serious matter of respect for human life and its dignity, produces a kind of progressive darkening of the capacity to discern God's living and saving presence.

Once again we can gain insight from the story of Abel's murder by his brother. After the curse imposed on him by God, Cain thus addresses the Lord: "My punishment is greater than I can bear. Behold, you have driven me this day away from the ground; and *from your face I shall be hidden*; and I shall be a fugitive and wanderer on the earth, and whoever finds me will slay me" (Gen 4:13–14). Cain is convinced that his sin will not obtain pardon from the Lord and that his inescapable destiny will be to have to "hide his face" from him. If Cain is capable of confessing that his fault is "greater than he can bear," it is because he is conscious of being in the presence of God and before God's just judgment. It is really only before the Lord that man can admit his sin and recognize its full seriousness. Such was the experience of David who, after "having committed evil in the sight of the Lord," and being rebuked by the Prophet Nathan, exclaimed: "My

---

1. Address to the Participants at the Study Conference on the "Right to Life and Europe," 18 December 1987: *Insegnamenti,* X, 3, 1446–47.

offences truly I know them; my sin is always before me. Against you, you alone, have I sinned; what is evil in your sight I have done" (Ps 51:5–6).

22. Consequently, when the sense of God is lost, the sense of man is also threatened and poisoned, as the Second Vatican Council concisely states: "Without the Creator the creature would disappear ... But when God is forgotten the creature itself grows unintelligible."[2] Man is no longer able to see himself as "mysteriously different" from other earthly creatures; he regards himself merely as one more living being, as an organism which, at most, has reached a very high stage of perfection. Enclosed in the narrow horizon of his physical nature, he is somehow reduced to being "a thing," and no longer grasps the "transcendent" character of his "existence as man." He no longer considers life as a splendid gift of God, something "sacred" entrusted to his responsibility and thus also to his loving care and "veneration." Life itself becomes a mere "thing," which man claims as his exclusive property, completely subject to his control and manipulation.

Thus, in relation to life at birth or at death, man is no longer capable of posing the question of the truest meaning of his own existence, nor can he assimilate with genuine freedom these crucial moments of his own history. He is concerned only with "doing," and, using all kinds of technology, he busies himself with programming, controlling and dominating birth and death. Birth and death, instead of being primary experiences demanding to be "lived," become things to be merely "possessed" or "rejected."

Moreover, once all reference to God has been removed, it is not surprising that *the meaning of everything else becomes profoundly distorted.* Nature itself, from being "mater" (mother), is now reduced to being "matter," and is subjected to every kind of manipulation. This is the direction in which a certain technical and scientific way of thinking, prevalent in present-day culture, appears to be leading when it rejects the very idea that there is a truth of creation which must be acknowledged, or a plan of God for life which must be respected. Something similar happens when concern about the consequences of such a "freedom without law" leads some people to the opposite position of a "law without freedom," as for example ideologies which consider it unlawful to interfere in any way with nature, practically "divinizing" it. Again, this is a misunderstanding of nature's dependence on the plan of the Creator. Thus it is clear that the loss of contact with God's wise design is the deepest root of modern man's confusion, both when this loss leads to a freedom without rules and when it leaves man in "fear" of his freedom. By living "as if God did not exist," man not only loses sight of the mystery of God, but also of the mystery of the world and the mystery of his own being.

---

2.   Pastoral Constitution on the Church in the Modern World *Gaudium et Spes*, 36.

23. The eclipse of the sense of God and of man inevitably leads to a practical materialism, which breeds individualism, utilitarianism and hedonism. Here too we see the permanent validity of the words of the Apostle: "And since they did not see fit to acknowledge God, God gave them up to a base mind and to improper conduct" (Rom. 1:28). The values of *being* are replaced by those of *having*. The only goal which counts is the pursuit of one's own material well-being. The so-called "quality of life" is interpreted primarily or exclusively as economic efficiency, inordinate consumerism, physical beauty and pleasure, to the neglect of the more profound dimensions—interpersonal, spiritual and religious—of existence.

In such a context *suffering*, an inescapable burden of human existence but also a factor of possible personal growth, is "censored," rejected as useless, indeed opposed as an evil, always and in every way to be avoided. When it cannot be avoided and the prospect of even some future well-being vanishes, then life appears to have lost all meaning and the temptation grows in man to claim the right to suppress it.

Within this same cultural climate, the *body* is no longer perceived as a properly personal reality, a sign and place of relations with others, with God and with the world. It is reduced to pure materiality: it is simply a complex of organs, functions and energies to be used according to the sole criteria of pleasure and efficiency. Consequently, *sexuality* too is depersonalized and exploited: from being the sign, place and language of love, that is, of the gift of self and acceptance of another, in all the other's richness as a person, it increasingly becomes the occasion and instrument for self-assertion and the selfish satisfaction of personal desires and instincts. Thus the original import of human sexuality is distorted and falsified, and the two meanings, unitive and procreative, inherent in the very nature of the conjugal act, are artificially separated: in this way the marriage union is betrayed and its fruitfulness is subjected to the caprice of the couple. *Procreation* then becomes the "enemy" to be avoided in sexual activity: if it is welcomed, this is only because it expresses a desire, or indeed the intention, to have a child "at all costs," and not because it signifies the complete acceptance of the other and therefore an openness to the richness of life which the child represents.

In the materialistic perspective described so far, *interpersonal relations are seriously impoverished*. The first to be harmed are women, children, the sick or suffering, and the elderly. The criterion of personal dignity—which demands respect, generosity and service—is replaced by the criterion of efficiency, functionality and usefulness: others are considered not for what they "are," but for what they "have, do and produce." This is the supremacy of the strong over the weak.

24. *It is at the heart of the moral conscience* that the eclipse of the sense of God and of man, with all its various and deadly consequences for life, is taking place. It is a question, above all, of the *individual* conscience, as it stands before God in its singleness and uniqueness.[3] But it is also a question, in a certain sense, of the "moral conscience" *of society*: in a way it too is responsible, not only because it tolerates or fosters behavior contrary to life, but also because it encourages the "culture of death," creating and consolidating actual "structures of sin" which go against life. The moral conscience, both individual and social, is today subjected, also as a result of the penetrating influence of the media, to an *extremely serious and mortal danger*: that of *confusion between good and evil,* precisely in relation to the fundamental right to life. A large part of contemporary society looks sadly like that humanity which Paul describes in his Letter to the Romans. It is composed "of men who by their wickedness suppress the truth" (1:18): having denied God and believing that they can build the earthly city without him, "they became futile in their thinking" so that "their senseless minds were darkened" (1:21); "claiming to be wise, they became fools" (1:22), carrying out works deserving of death, and "they not only do them but approve those who practice them" (1:32). When conscience, this bright lamp of the soul (cf. *Mt* 6:22–23), calls "evil good and good evil" (*Is* 5:20), it is already on the path to the most alarming corruption and the darkest moral blindness.

And yet all the conditioning and efforts to enforce silence fail to stifle the voice of the Lord echoing in the conscience of every individual: it is always from this intimate sanctuary of the conscience that a new journey of love, openness and service to human life can begin.

[...]

CHAPTER III
YOU SHALL NOT KILL

[...]

"We must obey God rather than men" (Acts 5:29):
Civil law and the moral law

68. One of the specific characteristics of present-day attacks on human life— as has already been said several times—consists in the trend to demand a *legal*

---

3.   Cf. *Gaudium et Spes,* 16.

justification for them, as if they were rights which the State, at least under certain conditions, must acknowledge as belonging to citizens. Consequently, there is a tendency to claim that it should be possible to exercise these rights with the safe and free assistance of doctors and medical personnel.

It is often claimed that the life of an unborn child or a seriously disabled person is only a relative good: according to a proportionalist approach, or one of sheer calculation, this good should be compared with and balanced against other goods. It is even maintained that only someone present and personally involved in a concrete situation can correctly judge the goods at stake: consequently, only that person would be able to decide on the morality of his choice. The State therefore, in the interest of civil coexistence and social harmony, should respect this choice, even to the point of permitting abortion and euthanasia.

At other times, it is claimed that civil law cannot demand that all citizens should live according to moral standards higher than what all citizens themselves acknowledge and share. Hence the law should always express the opinion and will of the majority of citizens and recognize that they have, at least in certain extreme cases, the right even to abortion and euthanasia. Moreover the prohibition and the punishment of abortion and euthanasia in these cases would inevitably lead—so it is said—to an increase of illegal practices: and these would not be subject to necessary control by society and would be carried out in a medically unsafe way. The question is also raised whether supporting a law which in practice cannot be enforced would not ultimately undermine the authority of all laws.

Finally, the more radical views go so far as to maintain that in a modern and pluralistic society people should be allowed complete freedom to dispose of their own lives as well as of the lives of the unborn: it is asserted that it is not the task of the law to choose between different moral opinions, and still less can the law claim to impose one particular opinion to the detriment of others.

69. In any case, in the democratic culture of our time it is commonly held that *the legal system of any society should limit itself to taking account of and accepting the convictions of the majority*. It should therefore be based solely upon what the majority itself considers moral and actually practices. Furthermore, if it is believed that an objective truth shared by all is de facto *unattainable*, then respect for the freedom of the citizens—*who in a democratic system are considered the true rulers*—would require that on the legislative level the autonomy of individual consciences be acknowledged. Consequently, when establishing those norms which are absolutely necessary for social coexistence, the only determining factor should be the will of the majority, whatever this may be. Hence [according to this position it follows that] every politician, in his or her activity, should clearly separate the realm of private conscience from that of public conduct.

As a result we have what appear to be two diametrically opposed tendencies. On the one hand, individuals claim for themselves in the moral sphere the most complete freedom of choice and demand that the State should not adopt or impose any ethical position but limit itself to guaranteeing maximum space for the freedom of each individual, with the sole limitation of not infringing on the freedom and rights of any other citizen. On the other hand, it is held that, in the exercise of public and professional duties, respect for other people's freedom of choice requires that each one should set aside his or her own convictions in order to satisfy every demand of the citizens which is recognized and guaranteed by law; in carrying out one's duties the only moral criterion should be what is laid down by the law itself. Individual responsibility is thus turned over to the civil law, with a renouncing of personal conscience, at least in the public sphere.

70. At the basis of all these tendencies lies the *ethical relativism* which characterizes much of present-day culture. There are those who consider such relativism an essential condition of democracy, inasmuch as it alone is held to guarantee tolerance, mutual respect between people and acceptance of the decisions of the majority, whereas moral norms considered to be objective and binding are held to lead to authoritarianism and intolerance. But it is precisely the issue of respect for life which shows what misunderstandings and contradictions, accompanied by terrible practical consequences, are concealed in this position.

It is true that history has known cases where crimes have been committed in the name of "truth." But equally grave crimes and radical denials of freedom have also been committed and are still being committed in the name of "ethical relativism." When a parliamentary or social majority decrees that it is legal, at least under certain conditions, to kill unborn human life, is it not really making a "tyrannical" decision with regard to the weakest and most defenseless of human beings? Everyone's conscience rightly rejects those crimes against humanity of which our century has had such sad experience. But would these crimes cease to be crimes if, instead of being committed by unscrupulous tyrants, they were legitimated by popular consensus?

Democracy cannot be idolized to the point of making it a substitute for morality or a panacea for immorality. Fundamentally, democracy is a "system" and as such is a means and not an end. Its moral value is not automatic, but depends on conformity to the moral law to which it, like every other form of human behavior, must be subject: in other words, its morality depends on the morality of the ends which it pursues and of the means which it employs. If today we see an almost universal consensus with regard to the value of democracy, this is to be considered a positive "sign of the times," as the Church's Magisterium has frequently noted.[4] But the value of democracy stands or falls with the values which it embodies and promotes. Of course, values such as the dignity of every human person, respect for inviolable and inalienable human rights, and the adoption of the "common good" as the end and criterion regulating political life are certainly fundamental and not to be ignored.

The basis of these values cannot be provisional and changeable "majority" opinions, but only the acknowledgment of an objective moral law which, as the "natural law" written in the human heart, is the obligatory point of reference for civil law itself. If, as a result of a tragic obscuring of the collective conscience, an attitude of skepticism were to succeed in bringing into question even the fundamental principles of the moral law, the democratic system itself would be shaken in its foundations, and would be reduced to *a mere mechanism for regulating different and opposing interests on a purely empirical basis.*[5] Some might think that even this function, in the absence of anything better, should be valued for the sake of peace in society. While one acknowledges some element of truth in this point of view, it is easy to see that without an objective moral grounding not even democracy is capable of ensuring a stable peace, especially since peace which is not built on the values of the dignity of every individual and of solidarity between all people frequently proves to be illusory. Even in participatory systems of government, the regulation of interests often occurs to the advantage of the most powerful, since they are the ones most capable not only of maneuvering the levers of power but also of shaping the formation of consensus. In such a situation, democracy easily becomes an empty word.

71. It is therefore urgently necessary, for the future of society and the development of a sound democracy, to rediscover those essential and innate human and moral values which flow from the very truth of the human being and express and safeguard the dignity of the person: values which no individual, no majority and no State can ever create, modify or destroy, but must only acknowledge, respect and promote.

Consequently there is a need to recover the *basic elements of a vision of the relationship between civil law and moral law*, which are put forward by the Church, but which are also part of the patrimony of the great juridical traditions of humanity.

Certainly *the purpose of civil law* is different and more limited in scope than that of the moral law. But "in no sphere of life can the civil law take the place

---

4. Cf. John Paul II, Encyclical Letter *Centesimus Annus* (1 May 1991), 46: *AAS* 83 (1991), 850; Pius XII, Christmas Radio Message (24 December 1944): *AAS* 37 (1945), 10–20.

5. Cf. John Paul II, Encyclical Letter *Veritatis Splendor* (6 August 1993), 97 and 99: *AAS* 85 (1993), 1209–1211.

of conscience or dictate norms concerning things which are outside its competence,"[6] which is that of ensuring the common good of people through the recognition and defense of their fundamental rights, and the promotion of peace and
of public morality.[7] The real purpose of civil law is to guarantee an ordered social
coexistence in true justice, so that all may "lead a quiet and peaceable life, godly
and respectful in every way" (1 *Tim* 2:2). Precisely for this reason, civil law must
ensure that all members of society enjoy respect for certain fundamental rights
which innately belong to the person, rights which every positive law must recognize and guarantee. First and fundamental among these is the inviolable right
to life of every innocent human being. While public authority can sometimes
choose not to put a stop to something which—were it prohibited—would cause
more serious harm,[8] it can never presume to legitimize as a right of individuals—even if they are the majority of the members of society—an offence against
other persons caused by the disregard of so fundamental a right as the right to life.
The legal toleration of abortion or of euthanasia can in no way claim to be based
on respect for the conscience of others, precisely because society has the right
and the duty to protect itself against the abuses which can occur in the name of
conscience and under the pretext of freedom.[9]

In the encyclical *Pacem in Terris*, John XXIII pointed out that "it is generally
accepted today that the common good is best safeguarded when personal rights
and duties are guaranteed. The chief concern of civil authorities must therefore
be to ensure that these rights are recognized, respected, coordinated, defended
and promoted, and that each individual is enabled to perform his duties more
easily. For 'to safeguard the inviolable rights of the human person, and to facilitate the performance of his duties, is the principal duty of every public authority'.
Thus any government which refused to recognize human rights or acted in violation of them, would not only fail in its duty; its decrees would be wholly lacking
in binding force."[10]

---

6. Congregation for the Doctrine of the Faith, Instruction on Respect for Human Life in its Origin
and on the Dignity of Procreation *Donum Vitae* (22 February 1987), III: *AAS* 80 (1988), 98.

7. Cf. Second Vatican Ecumenical Council, Declaration on Religious Freedom *Dignitatis Humanae*, 7.

8. Cf. *Summa Theologiae* I-II, q. 96, a. 2.

9. Cf. Second Vatican Ecumenical Council, Declaration on Religious Freedom *Dignitatis Humanae*, 7.

10. Encyclical Letter *Pacem in Terris* (11 April 1963), II: *AAS* 55 (1963), 273–74. The internal quo-
tation is from Pius XII, Radio Message of Pentecost 1941 (1 June 1941): *AAS* 33 (1941), 200.
On this topic, the encyclical cites: Pius XII, Encyclical Letter *Mit Brennender Sorge* (14 March
1937): *AAS* 29 (1937), 159; Encyclical Letter *Divini Redemptoris* (19 March 1937), III: 79; Pius
XII, Christmas Radio Message (24 December 1942): *AAS* 35 (1943), 9–24.

72. The doctrine on the necessary *conformity of civil law with the moral law* is in continuity with the whole tradition of the Church. This is clear once more from John XXIII's encyclical: "Authority is a postulate of the moral order and derives from God. Consequently, laws and decrees enacted in contravention of the moral order, and hence of the divine will, can have no binding force in conscience …; indeed, the passing of such laws undermines the very nature of authority and results in shameful abuse."[11] This is the clear teaching of Saint Thomas Aquinas, who writes that "human law is law inasmuch as it is in conformity with right reason and thus derives from the eternal law. But when a law is contrary to reason, it is called an unjust law; but in this case it ceases to be a law and becomes instead an act of violence."[12] And again: "Every law made by man can be called a law insofar as it derives from the natural law. But if it is somehow opposed to the natural law, then it is not really a law but rather a corruption of the law."[13]

Now the first and most immediate application of this teaching concerns a human law which disregards the fundamental right and source of all other rights which is the right to life, a right belonging to every individual. Consequently, laws which legitimize the direct killing of innocent human beings through abortion or euthanasia are in complete opposition to the inviolable right to life proper to every individual; they thus deny the equality of everyone before the law. It might be objected that such is not the case in euthanasia, when it is requested with full awareness by the person involved. But any State which made such a request legitimate and authorized it to be carried out would be legalizing a case of suicide-murder, contrary to the fundamental principles of absolute respect for life and of the protection of every innocent life. In this way the State contributes to lessening respect for life and opens the door to ways of acting which are destructive of trust in relations between people. Laws which authorize and promote abortion and euthanasia are therefore radically opposed not only to the good of the individual but also to the common good; as such they are completely lacking in authentic juridical validity. Disregard for the right to life, precisely because it leads to the killing of the person whom society exists to serve, is what most directly conflicts with the possibility of achieving the common good. Consequently, a civil law authorizing abortion or euthanasia ceases by that very fact to be a true, morally binding civil law.

73. Abortion and euthanasia are thus crimes which no human law can claim to legitimize. There is no obligation in conscience to obey such laws; instead

---

11. Encyclical Letter *Pacem in Terris* (11 April 1963), II: *AAS* 55 (1963), 271.

12. *Summa Theologiae* I-II, q. 93, a. 3, ad 2.

13. *Summa Theologiae* I-II, q. 95, a. 2. Aquinas quotes Saint Augustine: "Non videtur esse lex, quae iusta non fuerit," *De Libero Arbitrio*, I, 5, 11: PL 32, 1227.

there is a *grave and clear obligation to oppose them by conscientious objection*. From the very beginnings of the Church, the apostolic preaching reminded Christians of their duty to obey legitimately constituted public authorities (cf. *Rom* 13:1–7; 1 *Pet* 2:13–14), but at the same time it firmly warned that "we must obey God rather than men" (*Acts* 5:29). In the Old Testament, precisely in regard to threats against life, we find a significant example of resistance to the unjust command of those in authority. After Pharaoh ordered the killing of all newborn males, the Hebrew midwives refused. "They did not do as the king of Egypt commanded them, but let the male children live" (*Ex* 1:17). But the ultimate reason for their action should be noted: *"the midwives feared God"* (*ibid.*). It is precisely from obedience to God—to whom alone is due that fear which is acknowledgment of his absolute sovereignty—that the strength and the courage to resist unjust human laws are born. It is the strength and the courage of those prepared even to be imprisoned or put to the sword, in the certainty that this is what makes for "the endurance and faith of the saints" (*Rev* 13:10).

In the case of an intrinsically unjust law, such as a law permitting abortion or euthanasia, it is therefore never licit to obey it, or to "take part in a propaganda campaign in favor of such a law, or vote for it."[14]

A particular problem of conscience can arise in cases where a legislative vote would be decisive for the passage of a more restrictive law, aimed at limiting the number of authorized abortions, in place of a more permissive law already passed or ready to be voted on. Such cases are not infrequent. It is a fact that while in some parts of the world there continue to be campaigns to introduce laws favoring abortion, often supported by powerful international organizations, in other nations—particularly those which have already experienced the bitter fruits of such permissive legislation—there are growing signs of a rethinking in this matter. In a case like the one just mentioned, when it is not possible to overturn or completely abrogate a pro-abortion law, an elected official, whose absolute personal opposition to procured abortion was well known, could licitly support proposals aimed at *limiting the harm* done by such a law and at lessening its negative consequences at the level of general opinion and public morality. This does not in fact represent an illicit cooperation with an unjust law, but rather a legitimate and proper attempt to limit its evil aspects.

74. The passing of unjust laws often raises difficult problems of conscience for morally upright people with regard to the issue of cooperation, since they have a right to demand not to be forced to take part in morally evil actions. Sometimes

---

14. Congregation for the Doctrine of the Faith, *Declaration on Procured Abortion* (18 November 1974), No. 22: *AAS* 66 (1974), 744.

the choices which have to be made are difficult; they may require the sacrifice of prestigious professional positions or the relinquishing of reasonable hopes of career advancement. In other cases, it can happen that carrying out certain actions, which are provided for by legislation that overall is unjust, but which in themselves are indifferent, or even positive, can serve to protect human lives under threat. There may be reason to fear, however, that willingness to carry out such actions will not only cause scandal and weaken the necessary opposition to attacks on life, but will gradually lead to further capitulation to a mentality of permissiveness.

In order to shed light on this difficult question, it is necessary to recall the general principles concerning *cooperation in evil actions*. Christians, like all men of good will, are called upon under grave obligation of conscience not to cooperate formally in practices which, even if permitted by civil legislation, are contrary to God's law. Indeed, from the moral standpoint, it is never licit to cooperate formally in evil. Such cooperation occurs when an action, either by its very nature or by the form it takes in a concrete situation, can be defined as a direct participation in an act against innocent human life or a sharing in the immoral intention of the person committing it. This cooperation can never be justified either by invoking respect for the freedom of others or by appealing to the fact that civil law permits it or requires it. Each individual in fact has moral responsibility for the acts which he personally performs; no one can be exempted from this responsibility, and on the basis of it everyone will be judged by God himself (cf. *Rom* 2:6; 14:12).

[...]

✠ JOHN PAUL II

ON THE PARTICIPATION OF CATHOLICS IN POLITICAL LIFE

Congregation for the Doctrine of the Faith,
promulgated November 24, 2002

The Congregation for the Doctrine of the Faith, having received the opinion of the Pontifical Council for the Laity, has decided that it would be appropriate to publish the present Doctrinal Note on Some Questions Regarding the Participation of Catholics in Political Life. This Note is directed to the Bishops of the Catholic Church and, in a particular way, to Catholic politicians and all lay members of the faithful called to participate in the political life of democratic societies.

To the Bishops, Priests, and Deacons, Men and Women Religious, and All the Lay Faithful:

I. A CONSTANT TEACHING

The commitment of Christians in the world has found a variety of expressions in the course of the past 2,000 years. One such expression has been Christian involvement in political life: Christians, as one Early Church writer stated, "play their full role as citizens."[1] Among the saints, the Church venerates many men and women who served God through their generous commitment to politics and government. Among these, Saint Thomas More, who was proclaimed Patron of Statesmen and Politicians, gave witness by his martyrdom to "the inalienable dignity of the human conscience."[2] Though subjected to various forms of psychological pressure, Saint Thomas More refused to compromise, never forsaking the "constant fidelity to legitimate authority and

---

1. *Letter to Diognetus,* 5, 5; Cf. *Catechism of the Catholic Church,* No. 2240.
2. John Paul II, Apostolic Letter Motu Proprio *Proclaiming Saint Thomas More Patron of Statesmen and Politicians,* 1: *AAS* 93 (2001), 76.

institutions" which distinguished him; he taught by his life and his death that "man cannot be separated from God, nor politics from morality."[3]

It is commendable that in today's democratic societies, in a climate of true freedom, everyone is made a participant in directing the body politic.[4] Such societies call for new and fuller forms of participation in public life by Christian and non-Christian citizens alike. Indeed, all can contribute, by voting in elections for lawmakers and government officials, and in other ways as well, to the development of political solutions and legislative choices which, in their opinion, will benefit the common good.[5] The life of a democracy could not be productive without the active, responsible and generous involvement of everyone, "albeit in a diversity and complementarity of forms, levels, tasks, and responsibilities."[6]

By fulfilling their civic duties, "guided by a Christian conscience,"[7] in conformity with its values, the lay faithful exercise their proper task of infusing the temporal order with Christian values, all the while respecting the nature and rightful autonomy of that order,[8] and cooperating with other citizens according to their particular competence and responsibility.[9] The consequence of this fundamental teaching of the Second Vatican Council is that "the lay faithful are never to relinquish their participation in 'public life', that is, in the many different economic, social, legislative, administrative and cultural areas, which are intended to promote organically and institutionally the common good."[10] This would include the promotion and defense of goods such as public order and peace, freedom and equality, respect for human life and for the environment, justice and solidarity.

The present *Note* does not seek to set out the entire teaching of the Church on this matter, which is summarized in its essentials in the *Catechism of the*

---

3. Ibid., 4.

4. Cf. Second Vatican Council, Pastoral Constitution *Gaudium et Spes*, 31; *Catechism of the Catholic Church*, No. 1915.

5. Cf. Second Vatican Council, Pastoral Constitution *Gaudium et Spes*, 75.

6. John Paul II, Apostolic Exhortation, *Christifideles Laici*, 42: AAS 81 (1989), 472. The present doctrinal *Note* refers to the involvement in political life of lay members of the faithful. The Bishops of the Church have the right and the duty to set out the moral principles relating to the social order; "Nevertheless active participation in political parties is reserved to the lay faithful" (ibid., 60). Cf. Congregation for the Clergy, *Directory for the Ministry and Life of Priests* (March 31, 1994), 33.

7. Second Vatican Council, Pastoral Constitution *Gaudium et Spes*, 76.

8. Cf. Second Vatican Council, Pastoral Constitution *Gaudium et Spes*, 36.

9. Cf. Second Vatican Council, Decree *Apostolicam Actuositatem*, 7; Dogmatic Constitution *Lumen Gentium*, 36; Pastoral Constitution *Gaudium et Spes*, 31 and 43.

10. John Paul II, Apostolic Exhortation *Christifideles Laici*, 42.

Catholic Church, but intends only to recall some principles proper to the Christian conscience, which inspire the social and political involvement of Catholics in democratic societies.[11] The emergence of ambiguities or questionable positions in recent times, often because of the pressure of world events, has made it necessary to clarify some important elements of Church teaching in this area.

II. CENTRAL POINTS IN THE CURRENT CULTURAL AND POLITICAL DEBATE

2. Civil society today is undergoing a complex cultural process as the end of an era brings with it a time of uncertainty in the face of something new. The great strides made in our time give evidence of humanity's progress in attaining conditions of life which are more in keeping with human dignity. The growth in the sense of responsibility towards countries still on the path of development is without doubt an important sign, illustrative of a greater sensitivity to the common good. At the same time, however, one cannot close one's eyes to the real dangers which certain tendencies in society are promoting through legislation, nor can one ignore the effects this will have on future generations.

A kind of cultural relativism exists today, evident in the conceptualization and defense of an ethical pluralism, which sanctions the decadence and disintegration of reason and the principles of the natural moral law. Furthermore, it is not unusual to hear the opinion expressed in the public sphere that such ethical pluralism is the very condition for democracy.[12] As a result, citizens claim complete autonomy with regard to their moral choices, and lawmakers maintain that they are respecting this freedom of choice by enacting laws which ignore the

---

11. In the last two centuries, the Papal Magisterium has spoken on the principal questions regarding the social and political order. Cf. Leo XIII, Encyclical Letter *Diuturnum Illud: ASS* 14 (1881–1882), 4ff.; Encyclical Letter *Immortale Dei: ASS* 18 (1885–1886), 162ff.; Encyclical Letter *Libertas Præstantissimum: ASS* 20 (1887–1888), 593ff.; Encyclical Letter *Rerum Novarum: ASS* 23 (1890–1891), 643ff.; Benedict XV, Encyclical Letter *Pacem Dei Munus Pulcherrimum: AAS* 12 (1920), 209ff.; Pius XI, Encyclical Letter *Quadragesimo Anno: AAS* 23 (1931), 190ff.; Encyclical Letter *Mit Brennender Sorge: AAS* 29 (1937), 145–67; Encyclical Letter *Divini Redemptoris: AAS* 29 (1937), 78ff.; Pius XII, Encyclical Letter *Summi Pontificatus: AAS* 31 (1939), 423ff.; *Radiomessaggi natalizi 1941–1944;* John XXIII, Encyclical Letter *Mater et Magistra: AAS* 53 (1961), 401–64; Encyclical Letter *Pacem in Terris: AAS* 55 (1963), 257–304; Paul VI, Encyclical Letter *Populorum Progressio: AAS* 59 (1967), 257–99; Apostolic Letter *Octogesima Adveniens: AAS* 63 (1971), 401–41.

12. Cf. John Paul II, Encyclical Letter *Centesimus Annus,* 46: *AAS* 83 (1991); Encyclical Letter *Veritatis Splendor,* 101: *AAS* 85 (1993), 1212–13; *Discourse to the Italian Parliament,* 5: *L'Osservatore Romano* (November 15, 2002).

principles of natural ethics and yield to ephemeral cultural and moral trends,[13] as if every possible outlook on life were of equal value. At the same time, the value of tolerance is disingenuously invoked when a large number of citizens, Catholics among them, are asked not to base their contribution to society and political life—through the legitimate means available to everyone in a democracy—on their particular understanding of the human person and the common good. The history of the twentieth century demonstrates that those citizens were right who recognized the falsehood of relativism, and with it, the notion that there is no moral law rooted in the nature of the human person, which must govern our understanding of man, the common good and the state.

3. Such relativism, of course, has nothing to do with the legitimate freedom of Catholic citizens to choose among the various political opinions that are compatible with faith and the natural moral law, and to select, according to their own criteria, what best corresponds to the needs of the common good. Political freedom is not—and cannot be—based upon the relativistic idea that all conceptions of the human person's good have the same value and truth, but rather, on the fact that politics are concerned with very concrete realizations of the true human and social good in given historical, geographic, economic, technological and cultural contexts. From the specificity of the task at hand and the variety of circumstances, a plurality of morally acceptable policies and solutions arises. It is not the Church's task to set forth specific political solutions—and even less to propose a single solution as the acceptable one—to temporal questions that God has left to the free and responsible judgment of each person. It is, however, the Church's right and duty to provide a moral judgment on temporal matters when this is required by faith or the moral law.[14] If Christians must "recognize the legitimacy of differing points of view about the organization of worldly affairs,"[15] they are also called to reject, as injurious to democratic life, a conception of pluralism that reflects moral relativism. Democracy must be based on the true and solid foundation of non-negotiable ethical principles, which are the underpinning of life in society.

On the level of concrete political action, there can generally be a plurality of political parties in which Catholics may exercise—especially through legislative assemblies—their right and duty to contribute to the public life of their country.[16] This arises because of the contingent nature of certain choices regarding

---

13. Cf. John Paul II, Encyclical Letter *Evangelium Vitae*, 22: *AAS* 87 (1995), 425–26.

14. Cf. Second Vatican Council, Pastoral Constitution *Gaudium et Spes*, 76.

15. Ibid., 75.

16. Ibid., 43 and 75.

the ordering of society, the variety of strategies available for accomplishing or guaranteeing the same fundamental value, the possibility of different interpretations of the basic principles of political theory, and the technical complexity of many political problems. It should not be confused, however, with an ambiguous pluralism in the choice of moral principles or essential values. The legitimate plurality of temporal options is at the origin of the commitment of Catholics to politics and relates directly to Christian moral and social teaching. It is in the light of this teaching that lay Catholics must assess their participation in political life so as to be sure that it is marked by a coherent responsibility for temporal reality.

The Church recognizes that while democracy is the best expression of the direct participation of citizens in political choices, it succeeds only to the extent that it is based on a correct understanding of the human *person*.[17] Catholic involvement in political life cannot compromise on this principle, for otherwise the witness of the Christian faith in the world, as well as the unity and interior coherence of the faithful, would be non-existent. The democratic structures on which the modern state is based would be quite fragile were its foundation not the centrality of the human person. It is respect for the person that makes democratic participation possible. As the Second Vatican Council teaches, the protection of "the rights of the person is, indeed, a necessary condition for citizens, individually and collectively, to play an active part in public life and administration."[18]

4. The complex array of today's problems branches out from here, including some never faced by past generations. Scientific progress has resulted in advances that are unsettling for the consciences of men and women and call for solutions that respect ethical principles in a coherent and fundamental way. At the same time, legislative proposals are put forward which, heedless of the consequences for the existence and future of human beings with regard to the formation of culture and social behavior, attack the very inviolability of human life. Catholics, in this difficult situation, have the right and the duty to recall society to a deeper understanding of human life and to the responsibility of everyone in this regard. John Paul II, continuing the constant teaching of the Church, has reiterated many times that those who are directly involved in lawmaking bodies have a "grave and clear obligation to oppose" any law that attacks human life. For them, as for every Catholic, it is impossible to promote such laws or to vote for them.[19] As John

---

17. Ibid., 25.

18. Ibid., 73.

19. Cf. John Paul II, Encyclical Letter *Evangelium Vitae*, 73.

Paul II has taught in his Encyclical Letter *Evangelium vitae* regarding the situation in which it is not possible to overturn or completely repeal a law allowing abortion which is already in force or coming up for a vote, "an elected official, whose absolute personal opposition to procured abortion was well known, could licitly support proposals aimed at *limiting the harm* done by such a law and at lessening its negative consequences at the level of general opinion and public morality."[20]

In this context, it must be noted also that a well-formed Christian conscience does not permit one to vote for a political program or an individual law which contradicts the fundamental contents of faith and morals. The Christian faith is an integral unity, and thus it is incoherent to isolate some particular element to the detriment of the whole of Catholic doctrine. A political commitment to a single isolated aspect of the Church's social doctrine does not exhaust one's responsibility towards the common good. Nor can a Catholic think of delegating his Christian responsibility to others; rather, the Gospel of Jesus Christ gives him this task, so that the truth about man and the world might be proclaimed and put into action.

When political activity comes up against moral principles that do not admit of exception, compromise, or derogation, the Catholic commitment becomes more evident and laden with responsibility. In the face of *fundamental and inalienable ethical demands,* Christians must recognize that what is at stake is the essence of the moral law, which concerns the integral good of the human person. This is the case with laws concerning *abortion* and *euthanasia* (not to be confused with the decision to forgo *extraordinary treatments,* which is morally legitimate). Such laws must defend the basic right to life from conception to natural death. In the same way, it is necessary to recall the duty to respect and protect the rights of the *human embryo.* Analogously, the *family* needs to be safeguarded and promoted, based on monogamous marriage between a man and a woman, and protected in its unity and stability in the face of modern laws on divorce: in no way can other forms of cohabitation be placed on the same level as marriage, nor can they receive legal recognition as such. The same is true for the freedom of parents regarding the *education* of their children; it is an inalienable right recognized also by the Universal Declaration on Human Rights. In the same way, one must consider *society's protection of minors* and freedom from *modern forms of slavery* (drug abuse and prostitution, for example). In addition, there is the right to *religious freedom* and the development of an *economy* that is at the service of the human person and of the common good, with respect for social justice, the principles of human solidarity and subsidiarity, according to which "the rights

---

20. Ibid.

of all individuals, families, and organizations and their practical implementation must be acknowledged."[21] Finally, the question of *peace* must be mentioned. Certain pacifistic and ideological visions tend at times to secularize the value of peace, while, in other cases, there is the problem of summary ethical judgments which forget the complexity of the issues involved. Peace is always "the work of justice and the effect of charity."[22] It demands the absolute and radical rejection of violence and terrorism and requires a constant and vigilant commitment on the part of all political leaders.

III. PRINCIPLES OF CATHOLIC DOCTRINE ON THE AUTONOMY OF THE TEMPORAL ORDER AND ON PLURALISM

5. While a plurality of methodologies reflective of different sensibilities and cultures can be legitimate in approaching such questions, no Catholic can appeal to the principle of pluralism or to the autonomy of lay involvement in political life to support policies affecting the common good which compromise or undermine fundamental ethical requirements. This is not a question of "confessional values" *per se*, because such ethical precepts are rooted in human nature itself and belong to the natural moral law. They do not require from those who defend them the profession of the Christian faith, although the Church's teaching confirms and defends them always and everywhere as part of her service to the truth about man and about the common good of civil society. Moreover, it cannot be denied that politics must refer to principles of absolute value precisely because these are at the service of the dignity of the human person and of true human progress.

6. The appeal often made to *"the rightful autonomy of the participation of lay Catholics"* in politics needs to be clarified. Promoting the common good of society, according to one's conscience, has nothing to do with "confessionalism" or religious intolerance. For Catholic moral doctrine, the rightful autonomy of the political or civil sphere from that of religion and the Church—*but not from that of morality*—is a value that has been attained and recognized by the Catholic Church and belongs to the inheritance of contemporary civilization.[23] John Paul II has warned many times of the dangers which follow from confusion between the religious and political spheres. "Extremely sensitive situations arise when a specifically religious norm becomes or tends to become the law of a state

---

21. Second Vatican Council, Pastoral Constitution *Gaudium et Spes*, 75.
22. *Catechism of the Catholic Church*, No. 2304.
23. Cf. Second Vatican Council, Pastoral Constitution *Gaudium et Spes*, 76.

without due consideration for the distinction between the domains proper to religion and to political society. In practice, the identification of religious law with civil law can stifle religious freedom, even going so far as to restrict or deny other inalienable human rights."[24] All the faithful are well aware that specifically religious activities (such as the profession of faith, worship, administration of sacraments, theological doctrines, interchange between religious authorities and the members of religions) are outside the state's responsibility. The state must not interfere, nor in any way require or prohibit these activities, except when it is a question of public order. The recognition of civil and political rights, as well as the allocation of public services may not be made dependent upon citizens' religious convictions or activities.

The right and duty of Catholics and all citizens to seek the truth with sincerity and to promote and defend, by legitimate means, moral truths concerning society, justice, freedom, respect for human life and the other rights of the person, is something quite different. The fact that some of these truths may also be taught by the Church does not lessen the political legitimacy or the rightful "autonomy" of the contribution of those citizens who are committed to them, irrespective of the role that reasoned inquiry or confirmation by the Christian faith may have played in recognizing such truths. Such "autonomy" refers first of all to the attitude of the person who respects the truths that derive from natural knowledge regarding man's life in society, even if such truths may also be taught by a specific religion, because truth is one. It would be a mistake to confuse the proper *autonomy* exercised by Catholics in political life with the claim of a principle that prescinds from the moral and social teaching of the Church.

By its interventions in this area, the Church's Magisterium does not wish to exercise political power or eliminate the freedom of opinion of Catholics regarding contingent questions. Instead, it intends—as is its proper function—to instruct and illuminate the consciences of the faithful, particularly those involved in political life, so that their actions may always serve the integral promotion of the human person and the common good. The social doctrine of the Church is not an intrusion into the government of individual countries. It is a question of the lay Catholic's duty to be morally coherent, found within one's conscience, which is one and indivisible. "There cannot be two parallel lives in their existence: on the one hand, the so-called 'spiritual life', with its values and demands; and on the other, the so-called 'secular' life, that is, life in a family, at work, in social responsibilities, in the responsibilities of public life and in culture. The branch,

---

24. John Paul II, Message for the 1991 World Day of Peace: "If you want peace, respect the conscience of every person," 4: *AAS* 83 (1991), 414–15.

engrafted to the vine which is Christ, bears its fruit in every sphere of existence and activity. In fact, every area of the lay faithful's lives, as different as they are, enters into the plan of God, who desires that these very areas be the 'places in time' where the love of Christ is revealed and realized for both the glory of the Father and the service of others. Every activity, every situation, every precise responsibility—as, for example, skill and solidarity in work, love and dedication in the family and the education of children, service to society and public life and the promotion of truth in the area of culture—are the occasions ordained by Providence for a 'continuous exercise of faith, hope and charity' (*Apostolicam Actuositatem*, 4)."[25] Living and acting in conformity with one's own conscience on questions of politics is not slavish acceptance of positions alien to politics or some kind of confessionalism, but rather the way in which Christians offer their concrete contribution so that, through political life, society will become more just and more consistent with the dignity of the human person.

In democratic societies, all proposals are freely discussed and examined. Those who, on the basis of respect for individual conscience, would view the moral duty of Christians to act according to their conscience as something that disqualifies them from political life, denying the legitimacy of their political involvement following from their convictions about the common good, would be guilty of a form of intolerant *secularism*. Such a position would seek to deny not only any engagement of Christianity in public or political life, but even the possibility of natural ethics itself. Were this the case, the road would be open to moral anarchy, which would be anything but legitimate pluralism. The oppression of the weak by the strong would be the obvious consequence. The marginalization of Christianity, moreover, would not bode well for the future of society or for consensus among peoples; indeed, it would threaten the very spiritual and cultural foundations of civilization.[26]

IV. CONSIDERATIONS REGARDING PARTICULAR ASPECTS

7. In recent years, there have been cases within some organizations founded on Catholic principles, in which support has been given to political forces or movements with positions contrary to the moral and social teaching of the Church on fundamental ethical questions. Such activities, in contradiction to

---

25.　John Paul II, Apostolic Exhortation *Christifideles Laici*, 59.

26.　Cf. John Paul II, Address to the Diplomatic Corps accredited to the Holy See: *L'Osservatore Romano* (January 11, 2002).

basic principles of Christian conscience, are not compatible with membership in organizations or associations which define themselves as Catholic. Similarly, some Catholic periodicals in certain countries have expressed perspectives on political choices that have been ambiguous or incorrect, by misinterpreting the idea of the political autonomy enjoyed by Catholics and by not taking into consideration the principles mentioned above.

Faith in Jesus Christ, who is "the way, the truth, and the life" (*Jn* 14:6), calls Christians to exert a greater effort in building a culture which, inspired by the Gospel, will reclaim the values and contents of the Catholic Tradition. The presentation of the fruits of the spiritual, intellectual and moral heritage of Catholicism in terms understandable to modern culture is a task of great urgency today, in order to avoid also a kind of Catholic cultural diaspora. Furthermore, the cultural achievements and mature experience of Catholics in political life in various countries, especially since the Second World War, do not permit any kind of "inferiority complex" in comparison with political programs which recent history has revealed to be weak or totally ruinous. It is insufficient and reductive to think that the commitment of Catholics in society can be limited to a simple transformation of structures, because if at the basic level there is no culture capable of receiving, justifying and putting into practice positions deriving from faith and morals, the changes will always rest on a weak foundation.

Christian faith has never presumed to impose a rigid framework on social and political questions, conscious that the historical dimension requires men and women to live in imperfect situations, which are also susceptible to rapid change. For this reason, Christians must reject political positions and activities inspired by a utopian perspective which, turning the tradition of Biblical faith into a kind of prophetic vision without God, makes ill use of religion by directing consciences towards a hope which is merely earthly and which empties or reinterprets the Christian striving towards eternal life.

At the same time, the Church teaches that authentic freedom does not exist without the truth. "Truth and freedom either go together hand in hand or together they perish in misery."[27] In a society in which truth is neither mentioned nor sought, every form of authentic exercise of freedom will be weakened, opening the way to libertine and individualistic distortions and undermining the protection of the good of the human person and of the entire society.

8. In this regard, it is helpful to recall a truth which today is often not perceived or formulated correctly in public opinion: the right to freedom of conscience

---

27.   John Paul II, Encyclical Letter *Fides et Ratio*, 90: *AAS* 91 (1999), 75.

and, in a special way, to religious freedom, taught in the Declaration *Dignitatis Humanae* of the Second Vatican Council, is based on the ontological dignity of the human person and not on a non-existent equality among religions or cultural systems of human creation.[28] Reflecting on this question, Paul VI taught that "in no way does the Council base this right to religious freedom on the fact that all religions and all teachings, including those that are erroneous, would have more or less equal value; it is based rather on the dignity of the human person, which demands that he not be subjected to external limitations which tend to constrain the conscience in its search for the true religion or in adhering to it."[29] The teaching on freedom of conscience and on religious freedom does not therefore contradict the condemnation of indifferentism and religious relativism by Catholic doctrine[30]; on the contrary, it is fully in accord with it.

V. CONCLUSION

9. The principles contained in the present *Note* are intended to shed light on one of the most important aspects of the unity of Christian life: coherence between faith and life, Gospel and culture, as recalled by the Second Vatican Council. The Council exhorted Christians "to fulfill their duties faithfully in the spirit of the Gospel. It is a mistake to think that, because we have here no lasting city, but seek the city which is to come, we are entitled to shirk our earthly responsibilities; this is to forget that by our faith we are bound all the more to fulfill these responsibilities according to the vocation of each. ... May Christians ... be proud of the opportunity to carry out their earthly activity in such a way as to integrate human, domestic, professional, scientific and technical

28. Cf. Second Vatican Council, Declaration *Dignitatis Humanae*, 1: "This Sacred Council begins by professing that God himself has made known to the human race how men by serving him can be saved and reach the state of the blessed. We believe that this one true religion subsists in the Catholic and Apostolic Church." This does not lessen the sincere respect that the Church has for the various religious traditions, recognizing in them "elements of truth and goodness." See also, Second Vatican Council, Dogmatic Constitution *Lumen Gentium*, 16; Decree *Ad Gentes*, 11; Declaration *Nostra Aetate*, 2; John Paul II, Encyclical Letter *Redemptoris Missio*, 55: AAS 83 (1991), 302–304; Congregation for the Doctrine of the Faith, Declaration *Dominus Iesus*, 2, 8, 21: AAS 92 (2000), 742–65.

29. Paul VI, Address to the Sacred College and to the Roman Prelature: *Insegnamenti di Paolo VI*, 14 (1976), 1088–1089.

30. Cf. Pius IX, Encyclical Letter *Quanta Cura*: AAS 3 (1867), 162; Leo XIII, Encyclical Letter *Immortale Dei*: AAS 18 (1885), 170–71; Pius XI, Encyclical Letter *Quas Primas*: AAS 17 (1925), 604–605; *Catechism of the Catholic Church*, No. 2108; Congregation for the Doctrine of the Faith, Declaration *Dominus Iesus*, 22.

enterprises with religious values, under whose supreme direction all things are ordered to the glory of God."[31]

The Sovereign Pontiff John Paul II, in the Audience of November 21, 2002, approved the present Note, adopted in the Plenary Session of this Congregation, and ordered its publication.

Rome, from the Offices of the Congregation for the Doctrine of the Faith, November 24, 2002, the Solemnity of Christ the King.

✠ JOSEPH CARD. RATZINGER
Prefect

✠ TARCISIO BERTONE, S.D.B.
Archbishop Emeritus of Vercelli
Secretary

---

31. Second Vatican Council, Pastoral Constitution *Gaudium et Spes*, 43; see also John Paul II, Apostolic Exhortation *Christifideles Laici*, 59.

DEUS CARITAS EST

On Christian Love

Encyclical Letter of Pope Benedict XVI,
promulgated December 25, 2005

To the Bishops, Priests, and Deacons, Men and Women Religious, and All the Lay
Faithful:

INTRODUCTION

"Good is love, and he who abides in love abides in God, and God abides in
him" (*1 Jn* 4:16). These words from the *First Letter of John* express with
remarkable clarity the heart of the Christian faith: the Christian image
of God and the resulting image of mankind and its destiny. In the same verse,
Saint John also offers a kind of summary of the Christian life: "We have come to
know and to believe in the love God has for us."

We have come to believe in God's love: in these words the Christian can express
the fundamental decision of his life. Being Christian is not the result of an ethical
choice or a lofty idea, but the encounter with an event, a person, which gives life
a new horizon and a decisive direction. Saint John's Gospel describes that event
in these words: "God so loved the world that he gave his only Son, that whoever
believes in him should ... have eternal life" (3:16). In acknowledging the centrality of love, Christian faith has retained the core of Israel's faith, while at the same
time giving it new depth and breadth. The pious Jew prayed daily the words of the
Book of Deuteronomy which expressed the heart of his existence: "Hear, O Israel:
the Lord our God is one Lord, and you shall love the Lord your God with all your
heart, and with all your soul and with all your might" (6:4–5). Jesus united into
a single precept this commandment of love for God and the commandment of
love for neighbor found in the *Book of Leviticus*: "You shall love your neighbor as
yourself" (19:18; cf. *Mk* 12:29-31). Since God has first loved us (cf. *1 Jn* 4:10),
love is now no longer a mere "command"; it is the response to the gift of love with
which God draws near to us.

In a world where the name of God is sometimes associated with vengeance or even a duty of hatred and violence, this message is both timely and significant. For this reason, I wish in my first encyclical to speak of the love which God lavishes upon us and which we in turn must share with others. That, in essence, is what the two main parts of this Letter are about, and they are profoundly interconnected. The first part is more speculative, since I wanted here—at the beginning of my Pontificate—to clarify some essential facts concerning the love which God mysteriously and gratuitously offers to man, together with the intrinsic link between that Love and the reality of human love. The second part is more concrete, since it treats the ecclesial exercise of the commandment of love of neighbor. The argument has vast implications, but a lengthy treatment would go beyond the scope of the present encyclical. I wish to emphasize some basic elements, so as to call forth in the world renewed energy and commitment in the human response to God's love.

PART I
THE UNITY OF LOVE IN CREATION
AND IN SALVATION HISTORY

A problem of language

2. God's love for us is fundamental for our lives, and it raises important questions about who God is and who we are. In considering this, we immediately find ourselves hampered by a problem of language. Today, the term "love" has become one of the most frequently used and misused of words, a word to which we attach quite different meanings. Even though this encyclical will deal primarily with the understanding and practice of love in sacred Scripture and in the Church's Tradition, we cannot simply prescind from the meaning of the word in the different cultures and in present-day usage.

Let us first of all bring to mind the vast semantic range of the word "love": we speak of love of country, love of one's profession, love between friends, love of work, love between parents and children, love between family members, love of neighbor and love of God. Amid this multiplicity of meanings, however, one in particular stands out: love between man and woman, where body and soul are inseparably joined and human beings glimpse an apparently irresistible promise of happiness. This would seem to be the very epitome of love; all other kinds of love immediately seem to fade in comparison. So we need to ask: are all these forms of love basically one, so that love, in its many and varied manifestations, is ultimately a single reality, or are we merely using the same word to designate totally different realities?

"Eros" and "Agape"—difference and unity

3. That love between man and woman which is neither planned nor willed, but somehow imposes itself upon human beings, was called *eros* by the ancient Greeks. Let us note straightaway that the Greek Old Testament uses the word *eros* only twice, while the New Testament does not use it at all: of the three Greek words for love, *eros, philia* (the love of friendship) and *agape*, New Testament writers prefer the last, which occurs rather infrequently in Greek usage. As for the term *philia*, the love of friendship, it is used with added depth of meaning in Saint John's Gospel in order to express the relationship between Jesus and his disciples. The tendency to avoid the word *eros*, together with the new vision of love expressed through the word *agape*, clearly point to something new and distinct about the Christian understanding of love. In the critique of Christianity which began with the Enlightenment and grew progressively more radical, this new element was seen as something thoroughly negative. According to Friedrich Nietzsche, Christianity had poisoned *eros*, which for its part, while not completely succumbing, gradually degenerated into vice.[1] Here the German philosopher was expressing a widely-held perception: doesn't the Church, with all her commandments and prohibitions, turn to bitterness the most precious thing in life? Doesn't she blow the whistle just when the joy which is the Creator's gift offers us a happiness which is itself a certain foretaste of the Divine?

4. But is this the case? Did Christianity really destroy *eros*? Let us take a look at the pre-Christian world. The Greeks—not unlike other cultures—considered *eros* principally as a kind of intoxication, the overpowering of reason by a "divine madness" which tears man away from his finite existence and enables him, in the very process of being overwhelmed by divine power, to experience supreme happiness. All other powers in heaven and on earth thus appear secondary: *"Omnia vincit amor,"* says Virgil in the *Bucolics*—love conquers all—and he adds: *"et nos cedamus amori"*—let us, too, yield to love.[2] In the religions, this attitude found expression in fertility cults, part of which was the "sacred" prostitution which flourished in many temples. *Eros* was thus celebrated as divine power, as fellowship with the Divine.

---

1. Cf. *Jenseits von Gut und Böse*, IV, 168.
2. X, 69.

The Old Testament firmly opposed this form of religion, which represents a powerful temptation against monotheistic faith, combating it as a perversion of religiosity. But it in no way rejected *eros* as such; rather, it declared war on a warped and destructive form of it, because this counterfeit divinization of *eros* actually strips it of its dignity and dehumanizes it. Indeed, the prostitutes in the temple, who had to bestow this divine intoxication, were not treated as human beings and persons, but simply used as a means of arousing "divine madness": far from being goddesses, they were human persons being exploited. An intoxicated and undisciplined *eros*, then, is not an ascent in "ecstasy" towards the Divine, but a fall, a degradation of man. Evidently, *eros* needs to be disciplined and purified if it is to provide not just fleeting pleasure, but a certain foretaste of the pinnacle of our existence, of that beatitude for which our whole being yearns.

5. Two things emerge clearly from this rapid overview of the concept of *eros* past and present. First, there is a certain relationship between love and the Divine: love promises infinity, eternity—a reality far greater and totally other than our everyday existence. Yet we have also seen that the way to attain this goal is not simply by submitting to instinct. Purification and growth in maturity are called for; and these also pass through the path of renunciation. Far from rejecting or "poisoning" *eros*, they heal it and restore its true grandeur.

This is due first and foremost to the fact that man is a being made up of body and soul. Man is truly himself when his body and soul are intimately united; the challenge of *eros* can be said to be truly overcome when this unification is achieved. Should he aspire to be pure spirit and to reject the flesh as pertaining to his animal nature alone, then spirit and body would both lose their dignity. On the other hand, should he deny the spirit and consider matter, the body, as the only reality, he would likewise lose his greatness. The epicure Gassendi used to offer Descartes the humorous greeting: "O Soul!" And Descartes would reply: "O Flesh!"[3] Yet it is neither the spirit alone nor the body alone that loves: it is man, the person, a unified creature composed of body and soul, who loves. Only when both dimensions are truly united, does man attain his full stature. Only thus is love—*eros*—able to mature and attain its authentic grandeur.

Nowadays Christianity of the past is often criticized as having been opposed to the body; and it is quite true that tendencies of this sort have always existed. Yet the contemporary way of exalting the body is deceptive. *Eros*, reduced to pure "sex," has become a commodity, a mere "thing" to be bought and sold, or rather, man himself becomes a commodity. This is hardly man's great "yes" to the body. On the contrary, he now considers his body and his sexuality as the purely

---

3.   Cf. R. Descartes, *Œuvres*, ed. V. Cousin, vol. 12, Paris 1824, pp. 95ff.

material part of himself, to be used and exploited at will. Nor does he see it as an arena for the exercise of his freedom, but as a mere object that he attempts, as he pleases, to make both enjoyable and harmless. Here we are actually dealing with a debasement of the human body: no longer is it integrated into our overall existential freedom; no longer is it a vital expression of our whole being, but it is more or less relegated to the purely biological sphere. The apparent exaltation of the body can quickly turn into a hatred of bodiliness. Christian faith, on the other hand, has always considered man a unity in duality, a reality in which spirit and matter compenetrate, and in which each is brought to a new nobility. True, *eros* tends to rise "in ecstasy" towards the Divine, to lead us beyond ourselves; yet for this very reason it calls for a path of ascent, renunciation, purification and healing.

6. Concretely, what does this path of ascent and purification entail? How might love be experienced so that it can fully realize its human and divine promise? Here we can find a first, important indication in the *Song of Songs*, an Old Testament book well known to the mystics. According to the interpretation generally held today, the poems contained in this book were originally love-songs, perhaps intended for a Jewish wedding feast and meant to exalt conjugal love. In this context it is highly instructive to note that in the course of the book two different Hebrew words are used to indicate "love." First there is the word *dodim*, a plural form suggesting a love that is still insecure, indeterminate and searching. This comes to be replaced by the word *ahabà*, which the Greek version of the Old Testament translates with the similar-sounding *agape*, which, as we have seen, becomes the typical expression for the biblical notion of love. By contrast with an indeterminate, "searching" love, this word expresses the experience of a love which involves a real discovery of the other, moving beyond the selfish character that prevailed earlier. Love now becomes concern and care for the other. No longer is it self-seeking, a sinking in the intoxication of happiness; instead it seeks the good of the beloved: it becomes renunciation and it is ready, and even willing, for sacrifice.

It is part of love's growth towards higher levels and inward purification that it now seeks to become definitive, and it does so in a twofold sense: both in the sense of exclusivity (this particular person alone) and in the sense of being "for ever." Love embraces the whole of existence in each of its dimensions, including the dimension of time. It could hardly be otherwise, since its promise looks towards its definitive goal: love looks to the eternal. Love is indeed "ecstasy," not in the sense of a moment of intoxication, but rather as a journey, an ongoing exodus out of the closed inward-looking self towards its liberation through self-giving, and thus towards authentic self-discovery and indeed the discovery of God: "Whoever seeks to gain his life will lose it, but whoever loses his life will preserve it" (*Lk* 17:33), as Jesus says throughout the Gospels (cf. *Mt* 10:39; 16:25; *Mk* 8:35; *Lk* 9:24; *Jn* 12:25). In these words, Jesus portrays his own path, which leads through the Cross to the resurrection: the path of the grain of wheat that falls to the ground and dies, and in this way bears much fruit. Starting from the depths of his own sacrifice and of the love that reaches fulfillment therein, he also portrays in these words the essence of love and indeed of human life itself.

7. By their own inner logic, these initial, somewhat philosophical reflections on the essence of love have now brought us to the threshold of biblical faith. We began by asking whether the different, or even opposed, meanings of the word "love" point to some profound underlying unity, or whether on the contrary they must remain unconnected, one alongside the other. More significantly, though, we questioned whether the message of love proclaimed to us by the Bible and the Church's Tradition has some points of contact with the common human experience of love, or whether it is opposed to that experience. This in turn led us to consider two fundamental words: *eros*, as a term to indicate "worldly" love and *agape*, referring to love grounded in and shaped by faith. The two notions are often contrasted as "ascending" love and "descending" love. There are other, similar classifications, such as the distinction between possessive love and oblative love (*amor concupiscentiae – amor benevolentiae*), to which is sometimes also added love that seeks its own advantage.

In philosophical and theological debate, these distinctions have often been radicalized to the point of establishing a clear antithesis between them: descending, oblative love (*agape*) would be typically Christian, while on the other hand ascending, possessive or covetous love (*eros*) would be typical of non-Christian, and particularly Greek culture. Were this antithesis to be taken to extremes, the essence of Christianity would be detached from the vital relations fundamental to human existence, and would become a world apart, admirable perhaps, but decisively cut off from the complex fabric of human life. Yet *eros* and *agape*— ascending love and descending love—can never be completely separated. The more the two, in their different aspects, find a proper unity in the one reality of love, the more the true nature of love in general is realized. Even if *eros* is at first mainly covetous and ascending, a fascination for the great promise of happiness, in drawing near to the other, it is less and less concerned with itself, increasingly seeks the happiness of the other, is concerned more and more with the beloved, bestows itself and wants to "be there for" the other. The element of *agape* thus enters into this love, for otherwise *eros* is impoverished and even loses its own nature. On the other hand, man cannot live by oblative, descending love alone. He cannot always give, he must also receive. Anyone who wishes to give love must also receive love as a gift. Certainly, as the Lord tells us, one can become a source from which rivers of living water flow (cf. *Jn* 7:37–38). Yet to become such a source, one must constantly drink anew from the original source, which is Jesus Christ, from whose pierced heart flows the love of God (cf. *Jn* 19:34).

In the account of Jacob's ladder, the Fathers of the Church saw this insepa- rable connection between ascending and descending love, between *eros* which seeks God and *agape* which passes on the gift received, symbolized in various ways. In that biblical passage we read how the Patriarch Jacob saw in a dream, above the stone which was his pillow, a ladder reaching up to heaven, on which the angels of God were ascending and descending (cf. *Gen* 28:12; *Jn* 1:51). A particularly striking interpretation of this vision is presented by Pope Gregory the Great in his *Pastoral Rule*. He tells us that the good pastor must be rooted in contemplation. Only in this way will he be able to take upon himself the needs of others and make them his own: *"per pietatis viscera in se infirmitatem caeterorum transferat."*[4] Saint Gregory speaks in this context of Saint Paul, who was borne aloft to the most exalted mysteries of God, and hence, having descended once more, he was able to become all things to all men (cf. *2 Cor* 12:2–4; *1 Cor* 9:22). He also points to the example of Moses, who entered the tabernacle time and again, remaining in dialogue with God, so that when he emerged he could be at the service of his people. "Within [the tent] he is borne aloft through contempla- tion, while without he is completely engaged in helping those who suffer: *intus in contemplationem rapitur, foris infirmantium negotiis urgetur."*[5]

8. We have thus come to an initial, albeit still somewhat generic response to the two questions raised earlier. Fundamentally, "love" is a single reality, but with different dimensions; at different times, one or the other dimension may emerge more clearly. Yet when the two dimensions are totally cut off from one another, the result is a caricature or at least an impoverished form of love. And we have also seen, synthetically, that biblical faith does not set up a parallel universe, or one opposed to that primordial human phenomenon which is love, but rather accepts the whole man; it intervenes in his search for love in order to purify it and to reveal new dimensions of it. This newness of biblical faith is shown chiefly in two elements which deserve to be highlighted: the image of God and the image of man.

The newness of biblical faith

9. First, the world of the Bible presents us with a new image of God. In surrounding cultures, the image of God and of the gods ultimately remained

4.   II, 5: SCh 381, 196.

5.   Ibid., 198.

unclear and contradictory. In the development of biblical faith, however, the content of the prayer fundamental to Israel, the *Shema*, became increasingly clear and unequivocal: "Hear, O Israel, the Lord our God is one Lord" (*Dt* 6:4). There is only one God, the Creator of heaven and earth, who is thus the God of all. Two facts are significant about this statement: all other gods are not God, and the universe in which we live has its source in God and was created by him. Certainly, the notion of creation is found elsewhere, yet only here does it become absolutely clear that it is not one god among many, but the one true God himself who is the source of all that exists; the whole world comes into existence by the power of his creative Word. Consequently, his creation is dear to him, for it was willed by him and "made" by him. The second important element now emerges: this God loves man. The divine power that Aristotle at the height of Greek philosophy sought to grasp through reflection, is indeed for every being an object of desire and of love —and as the object of love this divinity moves the world[6]—but in itself it lacks nothing and does not love: it is solely the object of love. The one God in whom Israel believes, on the other hand, loves with a personal love. His love, moreover, is an elective love: among all the nations he chooses Israel and loves her—but he does so precisely with a view to healing the whole human race. God loves, and his love may certainly be called *eros*, yet it is also totally *agape*.[7]

The Prophets, particularly Hosea and Ezekiel, described God's passion for his people using boldly erotic images. God's relationship with Israel is described using the metaphors of betrothal and marriage; idolatry is thus adultery and prostitution. Here we find a specific reference—as we have seen—to the fertility cults and their abuse of *eros*, but also a description of the relationship of fidelity between Israel and her God. The history of the love-relationship between God and Israel consists, at the deepest level, in the fact that he gives her the *Torah*, thereby opening Israel's eyes to man's true nature and showing her the path leading to true humanism. It consists in the fact that man, through a life of fidelity to the one God, comes to experience himself as loved by God, and discovers joy in truth and in righteousness—a joy in God which becomes his essential happiness: "Whom do I have in heaven but you? And there is nothing upon earth that I desire besides you … for me it is good to be near God" (*Ps* 73 [72]:25, 28).

10. We have seen that God's *eros* for man is also totally *agape*. This is not only because it is bestowed in a completely gratuitous manner, without any previous merit, but also because it is love which forgives. Hosea above all shows us that

---

6. Cf. *Metaphysics*, XII, 7.

7. Cf. Ps.-Dionysius the Areopagite, who in his treatise *The Divine Names*, IV, 12–14: PG 3, 709–13 calls God both *eros* and *agape*.

this *agape* dimension of God's love for man goes far beyond the aspect of gratuity. Israel has committed "adultery" and has broken the covenant; God should judge and repudiate her. It is precisely at this point that God is revealed to be God and not man: "How can I give you up, O Ephraim! How can I hand you over, O Israel! ... My heart recoils within me, my compassion grows warm and tender. I will not execute my fierce anger, I will not again destroy Ephraim; for I am God and not man, the Holy One in your midst" (*Hos* 11:8–9). God's passionate love for his people—for humanity—is at the same time a forgiving love. It is so great that it turns God against himself, his love against his justice. Here Christians can see a dim prefigurement of the mystery of the Cross: so great is God's love for man that by becoming man he follows him even into death, and so reconciles justice and love.

The philosophical dimension to be noted in this biblical vision, and its importance from the standpoint of the history of religions, lies in the fact that on the one hand we find ourselves before a strictly metaphysical image of God: God is the absolute and ultimate source of all being; but this universal principle of creation—the *Logos*, primordial reason—is at the same time a lover with all the passion of a true love. *Eros* is thus supremely ennobled, yet at the same time it is so purified as to become one with *agape*. We can thus see how the reception of the *Song of Songs* in the canon of sacred Scripture was soon explained by the idea that these love songs ultimately describe God's relation to man and man's relation to God. Thus the *Song of Songs* became, both in Christian and Jewish literature, a source of mystical knowledge and experience, an expression of the essence of biblical faith: that man can indeed enter into union with God—his primordial aspiration. But this union is no mere fusion, a sinking in the nameless ocean of the Divine; it is a unity which creates love, a unity in which both God and man remain themselves and yet become fully one. As Saint Paul says: "He who is united to the Lord becomes one spirit with him" (*1 Cor* 6:17).

11. The first novelty of biblical faith consists, as we have seen, in its image of God. The second, essentially connected to this, is found in the image of man. The biblical account of creation speaks of the solitude of Adam, the first man, and God's decision to give him a helper. Of all other creatures, not one is capable of being the helper that man needs, even though he has assigned a name to all the wild beasts and birds and thus made them fully a part of his life. So God forms woman from the rib of man. Now Adam finds the helper that he needed: "This at last is bone of my bones and flesh of my flesh" (*Gen* 2:23). Here one might detect hints of ideas that are also found, for example, in the myth mentioned by Plato, according to which man was originally spherical, because he was complete in himself and self-sufficient. But as a punishment for pride, he was split in two

by Zeus, so that now he longs for his other half, striving with all his being to possess it and thus regain his integrity.[8] While the biblical narrative does not speak of punishment, the idea is certainly present that man is somehow incomplete, driven by nature to seek in another the part that can make him whole, the idea that only in communion with the opposite sex can he become "complete." The biblical account thus concludes with a prophecy about Adam: "Therefore a man leaves his father and his mother and cleaves to his wife and they become one flesh" (*Gen* 2:24).

Two aspects of this are important. First, *eros* is somehow rooted in man's very nature; Adam is a seeker, who "abandons his mother and father" in order to find woman; only together do the two represent complete humanity and become "one flesh." The second aspect is equally important. From the standpoint of creation, *eros* directs man towards marriage, to a bond which is unique and definitive; thus, and only thus, does it fulfill its deepest purpose. Corresponding to the image of a monotheistic God is monogamous marriage. Marriage based on exclusive and definitive love becomes the icon of the relationship between God and his people and vice versa. God's way of loving becomes the measure of human love. This close connection between *eros* and marriage in the Bible has practically no equivalent in extra-biblical literature.

Jesus Christ—the incarnate love of God

12. Though up to now we have been speaking mainly of the Old Testament, nevertheless the profound compenetration of the two Testaments as the one Scripture of the Christian faith has already become evident. The real novelty of the New Testament lies not so much in new ideas as in the figure of Christ himself, who gives flesh and blood to those concepts—an unprecedented realism. In the Old Testament, the novelty of the Bible did not consist merely in abstract notions but in God's unpredictable and in some sense unprecedented activity. This divine activity now takes on dramatic form when, in Jesus Christ, it is God himself who goes in search of the "stray sheep," a suffering and lost humanity. When Jesus speaks in his parables of the shepherd who goes after the lost sheep, of the woman who looks for the lost coin, of the father who goes to meet and embrace his prodigal son, these are no mere words: they constitute an explanation of his very being and activity. His death on the Cross is the culmination of that turning of God against himself in which he gives himself in order to raise man up and save him. This is love in its most radical form. By contemplating

---

8.　Plato, *Symposium*, XIV–XV, 189c–192d.

the pierced side of Christ (cf. 19:37), we can understand the starting-point of this Encyclical Letter: "God is love" (1 Jn 4:8). It is there that this truth can be contemplated. It is from there that our definition of love must begin. In this contemplation the Christian discovers the path along which his life and love must move.

13. Jesus gave this act of oblation an enduring presence through his institution of the Eucharist at the Last Supper. He anticipated his death and resurrection by giving his disciples, in the bread and wine, his very self, his body and blood as the new manna (cf. Jn 6:31–33). The ancient world had dimly perceived that man's real food—what truly nourishes him as man—is ultimately the *Logos*, eternal wisdom: this same *Logos* now truly becomes food for us—as love. The Eucharist draws us into Jesus' act of self-oblation. More than just statically receiving the incarnate *Logos*, we enter into the very dynamic of his self-giving. The imagery of marriage between God and Israel is now realized in a way previously inconceivable: it had meant standing in God's presence, but now it becomes union with God through sharing in Jesus' self-gift, sharing in his body and blood. The sacramental "mysticism," grounded in God's condescension towards us, operates at a radically different level and lifts us to far greater heights than anything that any human mystical elevation could ever accomplish.

14. Here we need to consider yet another aspect: this sacramental "mysticism" is social in character, for in sacramental communion I become one with the Lord, like all the other communicants. As Saint Paul says, "Because there is one bread, we who are many are one body, for we all partake of the one bread" (1 Cor 10:17). Union with Christ is also union with all those to whom he gives himself. I cannot possess Christ just for myself; I can belong to him only in union with all those who have become, or who will become, his own. Communion draws me out of myself towards him, and thus also towards unity with all Christians. We become "one body," completely joined in a single existence. Love of God and love of neighbor are now truly united: God incarnate draws us all to himself. We can thus understand how *agape* also became a term for the Eucharist: there God's own *agape* comes to us bodily, in order to continue his work in us and through us. Only by keeping in mind this Christological and sacramental basis can we correctly understand Jesus' teaching on love. The transition which he makes from the Law and the Prophets to the twofold commandment of love of God and of neighbor, and his grounding the whole life of faith on this central precept, is not simply a matter of morality—something that could exist apart from and alongside faith in Christ and its sacramental re-actualization. Faith, worship and *ethos* are interwoven as a single reality which takes shape in our encounter with God's *agape*. Here the usual contraposition between worship and ethics simply

falls apart. "Worship" itself, Eucharistic communion, includes the reality both of being loved and of loving others in turn. A Eucharist which does not pass over into the concrete practice of love is intrinsically fragmented. Conversely, as we shall have to consider in greater detail below, the "commandment" of love is only possible because it is more than a requirement. Love can be "commanded" because it has first been given.

15. This principle is the starting-point for understanding the great parables of Jesus. The rich man (cf. *Lk* 16:19–31) begs from his place of torment that his brothers be informed about what happens to those who simply ignore the poor man in need. Jesus takes up this cry for help as a warning to help us return to the right path. The parable of the Good Samaritan (cf. *Lk* 10:25–37) offers two particularly important clarifications. Until that time, the concept of "neighbor" was understood as referring essentially to one's countrymen and to foreigners who had settled in the land of Israel; in other words, to the closely-knit community of a single country or people. This limit is now abolished. Anyone who needs me, and whom I can help, is my neighbor. The concept of "neighbor" is now universalized, yet it remains concrete. Despite being extended to all mankind, it is not reduced to a generic, abstract and undemanding expression of love, but calls for my own practical commitment here and now. The Church has the duty to interpret ever anew this relationship between near and far with regard to the actual daily life of her members. Lastly, we should especially mention the great parable of the Last Judgment (cf. *Mt* 25:31–46), in which love becomes the criterion for the definitive decision about a human life's worth or lack thereof. Jesus identifies himself with those in need, with the hungry, the thirsty, the stranger, the naked, the sick and those in prison. "As you did it to one of the least of these my brethren, you did it to me" (*Mt* 25:40). Love of God and love of neighbor have become one: in the least of the brethren we find Jesus himself, and in Jesus we find God.

Love of God and love of neighbor

16. Having reflected on the nature of love and its meaning in biblical faith, we are left with two questions concerning our own attitude: can we love God without seeing him? And can love be commanded? Against the double commandment of love these questions raise a double objection. No one has ever seen God, so how could we love him? Moreover, love cannot be commanded; it is ultimately a feeling that is either there or not, nor can it be produced by the will. Scripture seems to reinforce the first objection when it states: "If anyone says, 'I love God,' and hates his brother, he is a liar; for he who does not love his brother

whom he has seen, cannot love God whom he has not seen" (*1 Jn* 4:20). But this text hardly excludes the love of God as something impossible. On the contrary, the whole context of the passage quoted from the *First Letter of John* shows that such love is explicitly demanded. The unbreakable bond between love of God and love of neighbor is emphasized. One is so closely connected to the other that to say that we love God becomes a lie if we are closed to our neighbor or hate him altogether. Saint John's words should rather be interpreted to mean that love of neighbor is a path that leads to the encounter with God, and that closing our eyes to our neighbor also blinds us to God.

17. True, no one has ever seen God as he is. And yet God is not totally invisible to us; he does not remain completely inaccessible. God loved us first, says the *Letter of John* quoted above (cf. 4:10), and this love of God has appeared in our midst. He has become visible in as much as he "has sent his only Son into the world, so that we might live through him" (*1 Jn* 4:9). God has made himself visible: in Jesus we are able to see the Father (cf. *Jn* 14:9). Indeed, God is visible in a number of ways. In the love-story recounted by the Bible, he comes towards us, he seeks to win our hearts, all the way to the Last Supper, to the piercing of his heart on the Cross, to his appearances after the resurrection and to the great deeds by which, through the activity of the Apostles, he guided the nascent Church along its path. Nor has the Lord been absent from subsequent Church history: he encounters us ever anew, in the men and women who reflect his presence, in his word, in the sacraments, and especially in the Eucharist. In the Church's Liturgy, in her prayer, in the living community of believers, we experience the love of God, we perceive his presence and we thus learn to recognize that presence in our daily lives. He has loved us first and he continues to do so; we too, then, can respond with love. God does not demand of us a feeling which we ourselves are incapable of producing. He loves us, he makes us see and experience his love, and since he has "loved us first," love can also blossom as a response within us.

In the gradual unfolding of this encounter, it is clearly revealed that love is not merely a sentiment. Sentiments come and go. A sentiment can be a marvelous first spark, but it is not the fullness of love. Earlier we spoke of the process of purification and maturation by which *eros* comes fully into its own, becomes love in the full meaning of the word. It is characteristic of mature love that it calls into play all man's potentialities; it engages the whole man, so to speak. Contact with the visible manifestations of God's love can awaken within us a feeling of joy born of the experience of being loved. But this encounter also engages our will and our intellect. Acknowledgment of the living God is one path towards love, and the "yes" of our will to his will unites our intellect, will and sentiments in the all-embracing act of love. But this process is always open-ended; love is never "finished" and complete; throughout life, it changes and matures, and thus remains faithful to itself. *Idem velle atque idem nolle*[9]—to want the same thing, and to reject the same thing—was recognized by antiquity as the authentic content of love: the one becomes similar to the other, and this leads to a community of will and thought. The love-story between God and man consists in the very fact that this communion of will increases in a communion of thought and sentiment, and thus our will and God's will increasingly coincide: God's will is no longer for me an alien will, something imposed on me from without by the commandments, but it is now my own will, based on the realization that God is in fact more deeply present to me than I am to myself.[10] Then self-abandonment to God increases and God becomes our joy (cf. *Ps* 73 [72]:23–28).

18. Love of neighbor is thus shown to be possible in the way proclaimed by the Bible, by Jesus. It consists in the very fact that, in God and with God, I love even the person whom I do not like or even know. This can only take place on the basis of an intimate encounter with God, an encounter which has become a communion of will, even affecting my feelings. Then I learn to look on this other person not simply with my eyes and my feelings, but from the perspective of Jesus Christ. His friend is my friend. Going beyond exterior appearances, I perceive in others an interior desire for a sign of love, of concern. This I can offer them not only through the organizations intended for such purposes, accepting it perhaps as a political necessity. Seeing with the eyes of Christ, I can give to others much more than their outward necessities; I can give them the look of love which they crave. Here we see the necessary interplay between love of God and love of neighbor which the *First Letter of John* speaks of with such insistence. If I have no contact whatsoever with God in my life, then I cannot see in the other anything more than the other, and I am incapable of seeing in him the image of God. But if in my life I fail completely to heed others, solely out of a desire to be "devout" and to perform my "religious duties," then my relationship with God will also grow arid. It becomes merely "proper," but loveless. Only my readiness to encounter my neighbor and to show him love makes me sensitive to God as well. Only if I serve my neighbor can my eyes be opened to what God does for me and how much he loves me. The saints—consider the example of Blessed Teresa of Calcutta—constantly renewed their capacity for love of neighbor from their encounter with the Eucharistic Lord, and conversely this encounter acquired its realism and depth in their service to others. Love of God and love of neighbor are

---

9. Sallust, *De coniuratione Catilinae*, XX, 4.
10. Cf. Saint Augustine, *Confessions*, III, 6, 11: CCL 27, 32.

thus inseparable, they form a single commandment. But both live from the love of God who has loved us first. No longer is it a question, then, of a "commandment" imposed from without and calling for the impossible, but rather of a freely-bestowed experience of love from within, a love which by its very nature must then be shared with others. Love grows through love. Love is "divine" because it comes from God and unites us to God; through this unifying process it makes us a "we" which transcends our divisions and makes us one, until in the end God is "all in all" (*1 Cor* 15:28).

PART II

CARITAS: THE PRACTICE OF LOVE BY THE CHURCH AS A "COMMUNITY OF LOVE"

*The Church's charitable activity
as a manifestation of Trinitarian love*

19. "If you see charity, you see the Trinity," wrote Saint Augustine.[11] In the foregoing reflections, we have been able to focus our attention on the Pierced One (cf. *Jn* 19:37, *Zech* 12:10), recognizing the plan of the Father who, moved by love (cf. *Jn* 3:16), sent his only-begotten Son into the world to redeem man. By dying on the Cross—as Saint John tells us—Jesus "gave up his spirit" (*Jn* 19:30), anticipating the gift of the Holy Spirit that he would make after his resurrection (cf. *Jn* 20:22). This was to fulfill the promise of "rivers of living water" that would flow out of the hearts of believers, through the outpouring of the Spirit (cf. *Jn* 7:38–39). The Spirit, in fact, is that interior power which harmonizes their hearts with Christ's heart and moves them to love their brethren as Christ loved them, when he bent down to wash the feet of the disciples (cf. *Jn* 13:1–13) and above all when he gave his life for us (cf. *Jn* 13:1, 15:13).

The Spirit is also the energy which transforms the heart of the ecclesial community, so that it becomes a witness before the world to the love of the Father, who wishes to make humanity a single family in his Son. The entire activity of the Church is an expression of a love that seeks the integral good of man: it seeks his evangelization through Word and sacrament, an undertaking that is often heroic in the way it is acted out in history; and it seeks to promote man in the various arenas of life and human activity. Love is therefore the service that the Church carries out in order to attend constantly to man's sufferings and his

---

11. *De Trinitate*, VIII, 8, 12: CCL 50, 287.

needs, including material needs. And this is the aspect, this *service of charity*, on which I want to focus in the second part of the encyclical.

Charity as a responsibility of the Church

20. Love of neighbor, grounded in the love of God, is first and foremost a responsibility for each individual member of the faithful, but it is also a responsibility for the entire ecclesial community at every level: from the local community to the particular Church and to the Church universal in its entirety. As a community, the Church must practice love. Love thus needs to be organized if it is to be an ordered service to the community. The awareness of this responsibility has had a constitutive relevance in the Church from the beginning: "All who believed were together and had all things in common; and they sold their possessions and goods and distributed them to all, as any had need" (*Acts* 2:44–5). In these words, Saint Luke provides a kind of definition of the Church, whose constitutive elements include fidelity to the "teaching of the Apostles," "communion" (*koinonia*), "the breaking of the bread" and "prayer" (cf. *Acts* 2:42). The element of "communion" (*koinonia*) is not initially defined, but appears concretely in the verses quoted above: it consists in the fact that believers hold all things in common and that among them, there is no longer any distinction between rich and poor (cf. also *Acts* 4:32–37). As the Church grew, this radical form of material communion could not in fact be preserved. But its essential core remained: within the community of believers there can never be room for a poverty that denies anyone what is needed for a dignified life.

21. A decisive step in the difficult search for ways of putting this fundamental ecclesial principle into practice is illustrated in the choice of the seven, which marked the origin of the diaconal office (cf. *Acts* 6:5–6). In the early Church, in fact, with regard to the daily distribution to widows, a disparity had arisen between Hebrew speakers and Greek speakers. The Apostles, who had been entrusted primarily with "prayer" (the Eucharist and the liturgy) and the "ministry of the word," felt over-burdened by "serving tables," so they decided to reserve to themselves the principal duty and to designate for the other task, also necessary in the Church, a group of seven persons. Nor was this group to carry out a purely mechanical work of distribution: they were to be men "full of the Spirit and of wisdom" (cf. *Acts* 6:1–6). In other words, the social service which they were meant to provide was absolutely concrete, yet at the same time it was also a spiritual service; theirs was a truly spiritual office which carried out an essential responsibility of the Church, namely a well-ordered love of neighbor. With the formation of this group of seven, "*diaconia*"—the ministry of charity exercised

in a communitarian, orderly way—became part of the fundamental structure of the Church.

22. As the years went by and the Church spread further afield, the exercise of charity became established as one of her essential activities, along with the administration of the sacraments and the proclamation of the word: love for widows and orphans, prisoners, and the sick and needy of every kind, is as essential to her as the ministry of the sacraments and the preaching of the Gospel. The Church cannot neglect the service of charity any more than she can neglect the sacraments and the Word. A few references will suffice to demonstrate this. Justin Martyr († c. 155) in speaking of the Christians' celebration of Sunday, also mentions their charitable activity, linked with the Eucharist as such. Those who are able make offerings in accordance with their means, each as he or she wishes; the bishop in turn makes use of these to support orphans, widows, the sick and those who for other reasons find themselves in need, such as prisoners and foreigners.[12] The great Christian writer Tertullian († after 220) relates how the pagans were struck by the Christians' concern for the needy of every sort.[13] And when Ignatius of Antioch († c. 117) described the Church of Rome as "presiding in charity (*agape*),"[14] we may assume that with this definition he also intended in some sense to express her concrete charitable activity.

23. Here it might be helpful to allude to the earliest legal structures associated with the service of charity in the Church. Towards the middle of the fourth century we see the development in Egypt of the "*diaconia*": the institution within each monastery responsible for all works of relief, that is to say, for the service of charity. By the sixth century this institution had evolved into a corporation with full juridical standing, which the civil authorities themselves entrusted with part of the grain for public distribution. In Egypt not only each monastery, but each individual diocese eventually had its own *diaconia*; this institution then developed in both East and West. Pope Gregory the Great († 604) mentions the *diaconia* of Naples, while in Rome the *diaconiae* are documented from the seventh and eighth centuries. But charitable activity on behalf of the poor and suffering was naturally an essential part of the Church of Rome from the very beginning, based on the principles of Christian life given in the *Acts of the Apostles*. It found a vivid expression in the case of the deacon Lawrence († 258). The dramatic description of Lawrence's martyrdom was known to Saint Ambrose († 397) and it provides a fundamentally authentic picture of the saint. As the one responsible for the

---

12. Cf. *I Apologia*, 67: PG 6, 429.

13. Cf. *Apologeticum*, 39, 7: PL 1, 468.

14. *Ep. ad Rom., Inscr.*, PG 5, 801.

care of the poor in Rome, Lawrence had been given a period of time, after the capture of the Pope and of Lawrence's fellow deacons, to collect the treasures of the Church and hand them over to the civil authorities. He distributed to the poor whatever funds were available and then presented to the authorities the poor themselves as the real treasure of the Church.[15] Whatever historical reliability one attributes to these details, Lawrence has always remained present in the Church's memory as a great exponent of ecclesial charity.

24. A mention of the emperor Julian the Apostate († 363) can also show how essential the early Church considered the organized practice of charity. As a child of six years, Julian witnessed the assassination of his father, brother and other family members by the guards of the imperial palace; rightly or wrongly, he blamed this brutal act on the Emperor Constantius, who passed himself off as an outstanding Christian. The Christian faith was thus definitively discredited in his eyes. Upon becoming emperor, Julian decided to restore paganism, the ancient Roman religion, while reforming it in the hope of making it the driving force behind the empire. In this project he was amply inspired by Christianity. He established a hierarchy of metropolitans and priests who were to foster love of God and neighbor. In one of his letters,[16] he wrote that the sole aspect of Christianity which had impressed him was the Church's charitable activity. He thus considered it essential for his new pagan religion that, alongside the system of the Church's charity, an equivalent activity of its own be established. According to him, this was the reason for the popularity of the "Galileans." They needed now to be imitated and outdone. In this way, then, the Emperor confirmed that charity was a decisive feature of the Christian community, the Church.

25. Thus far, two essential facts have emerged from our reflections:

a) The Church's deepest nature is expressed in her three-fold responsibility: of proclaiming the word of God (*kerygma-martyria*), celebrating the sacraments (*leitourgia*), and exercising the ministry of charity (*diakonia*). These duties presuppose each other and are inseparable. For the Church, charity is not a kind of welfare activity which could equally well be left to others, but is a part of her nature, an indispensable expression of her very being.[17]

b) The Church is God's family in the world. In this family no one ought to go without the necessities of life. Yet at the same time *caritas-agape* extends beyond the frontiers of the Church. The parable of the Good Samaritan remains as a

---

15. Cf. Saint Ambrose, *De officiis ministrorum*, II, 28, 140: PL 16, 141.

16. Cf. *Ep.* 83: J. Bidez, *L'Empereur Julien. Œuvres complètes*, Paris 1960², v. I, 2ª, p. 145.

17. Cf. Congregation for Bishops, Directory for the Pastoral Ministry of Bishops *Apostolorum Successores* (22 February 2004), 194, Vatican City 2004, p. 213.

standard which imposes universal love towards the needy whom we encounter "by chance" (cf. *Lk* 10:31), whoever they may be. Without in any way detracting from this commandment of universal love, the Church also has a specific responsibility: within the ecclesial family no member should suffer through being in need. The teaching of the *Letter to the Galatians* is emphatic: "So then, as we have opportunity, let us do good to all, and especially to those who are of the household of faith" (6:10).

Justice and charity

26. Since the nineteenth century, an objection has been raised to the Church's charitable activity, subsequently developed with particular insistence by Marxism: the poor, it is claimed, do not need charity but justice. Works of charity—almsgiving—are in effect a way for the rich to shirk their obligation to work for justice and a means of soothing their consciences, while preserving their own status and robbing the poor of their rights. Instead of contributing through individual works of charity to maintaining the *status quo*, we need to build a just social order in which all receive their share of the world's goods and no longer have to depend on charity. There is admittedly some truth to this argument, but also much that is mistaken. It is true that the pursuit of justice must be a fundamental norm of the State and that the aim of a just social order is to guarantee to each person, according to the principle of subsidiarity, his share of the community's goods. This has always been emphasized by Christian teaching on the State and by the Church's social doctrine. Historically, the issue of the just ordering of the collectivity had taken a new dimension with the industrialization of society in the nineteenth century. The rise of modern industry caused the old social structures to collapse, while the growth of a class of salaried workers provoked radical changes in the fabric of society. The relationship between capital and labor now became the decisive issue—an issue which in that form was previously unknown. Capital and the means of production were now the new source of power which, concentrated in the hands of a few, led to the suppression of the rights of the working classes, against which they had to rebel.

27. It must be admitted that the Church's leadership was slow to realize that the issue of the just structuring of society needed to be approached in a new way. There were some pioneers, such as Bishop Ketteler of Mainz († 1877), and concrete needs were met by a growing number of groups, associations, leagues, federations and, in particular, by the new religious orders founded in the nineteenth century to combat poverty and disease, and to respond to the need for better education. In 1891, the papal Magisterium intervened with the Encyclical

Rerum Novarum of Leo XIII. This was followed in 1931 by Pius XI's Encyclical *Quadragesimo Anno*. In 1961 Blessed John XXIII published the Encyclical *Mater et Magistra*, while Paul VI, in the Encyclical *Populorum Progressio* (1967) and in the Apostolic Letter *Octogesima Adveniens* (1971), insistently addressed the social problem, which had meanwhile become especially acute in Latin America. My great predecessor John Paul II left us a trilogy of social Encyclicals: *Laborem Exercens* (1981), *Sollicitudo Rei Socialis* (1987) and finally *Centesimus Annus* (1991). Faced with new situations and issues, Catholic social teaching thus gradually developed, and has now found a comprehensive presentation in the *Compendium of the Social Doctrine of the Church* published in 2004 by the Pontifical Council *Iustitia et Pax*. Marxism had seen world revolution and its preliminaries as the panacea for the social problem: revolution and the subsequent collectivization of the means of production, so it was claimed, would immediately change things for the better. This illusion has vanished. In today's complex situation, not least because of the growth of a globalized economy, the Church's social doctrine has become a set of fundamental guidelines offering approaches that are valid even beyond the confines of the Church: in the face of ongoing development these guidelines need to be addressed in the context of dialogue with all those seriously concerned for humanity and for the world in which we live.

28. In order to define more accurately the relationship between the necessary commitment to justice and the ministry of charity, two fundamental situations need to be considered:

a) The just ordering of society and the State is a central responsibility of politics. As Augustine once said, a State which is not governed according to justice would be just a bunch of thieves: *"Remota itaque iustitia quid sunt regna nisi magna latrocinia?"*[18] Fundamental to Christianity is the distinction between what belongs to Caesar and what belongs to God (cf. *Mt* 22:21), in other words, the distinction between Church and State, or, as the Second Vatican Council puts it, the autonomy of the temporal sphere.[19] The State may not impose religion, yet it must guarantee religious freedom and harmony between the followers of different religions. For her part, the Church, as the social expression of Christian faith, has a proper independence and is structured on the basis of her faith as a community which the State must recognize. The two spheres are distinct, yet always interrelated.

Justice is both the aim and the intrinsic criterion of all politics. Politics is more than a mere mechanism for defining the rules of public life: its origin and

---

18. *De Civitate Dei*, IV, 4: CCL 47, 102.

19. Cf. Pastoral Constitution on the Church in the Modern World *Gaudium et Spes*, 36.

its goal are found in justice, which by its very nature has to do with ethics. The State must inevitably face the question of how justice can be achieved here and now. But this presupposes an even more radical question: what is justice? The problem is one of practical reason; but if reason is to be exercised properly, it must undergo constant purification, since it can never be completely free of the danger of a certain ethical blindness caused by the dazzling effect of power and special interests.

Here politics and faith meet. Faith by its specific nature is an encounter with the living God—an encounter opening up new horizons extending beyond the sphere of reason. But it is also a purifying force for reason itself. From God's standpoint, faith liberates reason from its blind spots and therefore helps it to be ever more fully itself. Faith enables reason to do its work more effectively and to see its proper object more clearly. This is where Catholic social doctrine has its place: it has no intention of giving the Church power over the State. Even less is it an attempt to impose on those who do not share the faith ways of thinking and modes of conduct proper to faith. Its aim is simply to help purify reason and to contribute, here and now, to the acknowledgment and attainment of what is just.

The Church's social teaching argues on the basis of reason and natural law, namely, on the basis of what is in accord with the nature of every human being. It recognizes that it is not the Church's responsibility to make this teaching prevail in political life. Rather, the Church wishes to help form consciences in political life and to stimulate greater insight into the authentic requirements of justice as well as greater readiness to act accordingly, even when this might involve conflict with situations of personal interest. Building a just social and civil order, wherein each person receives what is his or her due, is an essential task which every generation must take up anew. As a political task, this cannot be the Church's immediate responsibility. Yet, since it is also a most important human responsibility, the Church is duty-bound to offer, through the purification of reason and through ethical formation, her own specific contribution towards understanding the requirements of justice and achieving them politically.

The Church cannot and must not take upon herself the political battle to bring about the most just society possible. She cannot and must not replace the State. Yet at the same time she cannot and must not remain on the sidelines in the fight for justice. She has to play her part through rational argument and she has to reawaken the spiritual energy without which justice, which always demands sacrifice, cannot prevail and prosper. A just society must be the achievement of politics, not of the Church. Yet the promotion of justice through efforts to bring about openness of mind and will to the demands of the common good is something which concerns the Church deeply.

b) Love—*caritas*—will always prove necessary, even in the most just society. There is no ordering of the State so just that it can eliminate the need for a service of love. Whoever wants to eliminate love is preparing to eliminate man as such. There will always be suffering which cries out for consolation and help. There will always be loneliness. There will always be situations of material need where help in the form of concrete love of neighbor is indispensable.[20] The State which would provide everything, absorbing everything into itself, would ultimately become a mere bureaucracy incapable of guaranteeing the very thing which the suffering person—every person—needs: namely, loving personal concern. We do not need a State which regulates and controls everything, but a State which, in accordance with the principle of subsidiarity, generously acknowledges and supports initiatives arising from the different social forces and which combine spontaneity with closeness to those in need. The Church is one of those living forces: she is alive with the love enkindled by the Spirit of Christ. This love does not simply offer people material help, but refreshment and care for their souls, something which often is even more necessary than material support. In the end, the claim that just social structures would make works of charity superfluous masks a materialist conception of man: the mistaken notion that man can live "by bread alone" (*Mt* 4:4; cf. *Dt* 8:3)—a conviction that demeans man and ultimately disregards all that is specifically human.

29. We can now determine more precisely, in the life of the Church, the relationship between commitment to the just ordering of the State and society on the one hand, and organized charitable activity on the other. We have seen that the formation of just structures is not directly the duty of the Church, but belongs to the world of politics, the sphere of the autonomous use of reason. The Church has an indirect duty here, in that she is called to contribute to the purification of reason and to the reawakening of those moral forces without which just structures are neither established nor prove effective in the long run.

The direct duty to work for a just ordering of society, on the other hand, is proper to the lay faithful. As citizens of the State, they are called to take part in public life in a personal capacity. So they cannot relinquish their participation "in the many different economic, social, legislative, administrative and cultural areas, which are intended to promote organically and institutionally the *common good*."[21] The mission of the lay faithful is therefore to configure social life correctly,

---

20. Cf. Congregation for Bishops, Directory for the Pastoral Ministry of Bishops *Apostolorum Successores* (22 February 2004), 197, Vatican City 2004, p. 217.

21. John Paul II, Post-Synodal Apostolic Exhortation *Christifideles Laici* (30 December 1988), 42: *AAS* 81 (1989), 472.

respecting its legitimate autonomy and cooperating with other citizens according to their respective competences and fulfilling their own responsibility.[22] Even if the specific expressions of ecclesial charity can never be confused with the activity of the State, it still remains true that charity must animate the entire lives of the lay faithful and therefore also their political activity, lived as "social charity."[23] The Church's charitable organizations, on the other hand, constitute an *opus proprium*, a task agreeable to her, in which she does not cooperate collaterally, but acts as a subject with direct responsibility, doing what corresponds to her nature. The Church can never be exempted from practicing charity as an organized activity of believers, and on the other hand, there will never be a situation where the charity of each individual Christian is unnecessary, because in addition to justice man needs, and will always need, love.

The multiple structures of charitable service in the social context of the present day

30. Before attempting to define the specific profile of the Church's activities in the service of man, I now wish to consider the overall situation of the struggle for justice and love in the world of today.

a) Today the means of mass communication have made our planet smaller, rapidly narrowing the distance between different peoples and cultures. This "togetherness" at times gives rise to misunderstandings and tensions, yet our ability to know almost instantly about the needs of others challenges us to share their situation and their difficulties. Despite the great advances made in science and technology, each day we see how much suffering there is in the world on account of different kinds of poverty, both material and spiritual. Our times call for a new readiness to assist our neighbors in need. The Second Vatican Council had made this point very clearly: "Now that, through better means of communication, distances between peoples have been almost eliminated, charitable activity can and should embrace all people and all needs."[24] On the other hand—and here we see one of the challenging yet also positive sides of the process of globalization— we now have at our disposal numerous means for offering humanitarian assistance to our brothers and sisters in need, not least modern systems of distributing

22. Cf. Congregation for the Doctrine of the Faith, *Doctrinal Note on Some Questions Regarding the Participation of Catholics in Political Life* (24 November 2002), 1: *L'Osservatore Romano*, English edition, 22 January 2003, p. 5.

23. *Catechism of the Catholic Church*, 1939.

24. Decree on the Apostolate of the Laity *Apostolicam Actuositatem*, 8.

food and clothing, and of providing housing and care. Concern for our neighbor transcends the confines of national communities and has increasingly broadened its horizon to the whole world. The Second Vatican Council rightly observed that "among the signs of our times, one particularly worthy of note is a growing, inescapable sense of solidarity between all peoples."[25] State agencies and humanitarian associations work to promote this, the former mainly through subsidies or tax relief, the latter by making available considerable resources. The solidarity shown by civil society thus significantly surpasses the action of individuals.

b) This situation has led to the birth and the growth of many forms of cooperation between State and Church agencies, which have borne fruit. Church agencies, with their transparent operation and their faithfulness to the duty of witnessing to love, are able to give a Christian quality to the civil agencies too, favoring a mutual coordination that can only redound to the effectiveness of charitable service.[26] Numerous organizations for charitable or philanthropic purposes have also been established and these are committed to achieving adequate humanitarian solutions to the social and political problems of the day. Significantly, our time has also seen the growth and spread of different kinds of volunteer work, which assume responsibility for providing a variety of services.[27] I wish here to offer a special word of gratitude and appreciation to all those who take part in these activities in whatever way. For young people, this widespread involvement constitutes a school of life which offers them a formation in solidarity and in readiness to offer others not simply material aid but their very selves. The anti-culture of death, which finds expression for example in drug use, is thus countered by an unselfish love which shows itself to be a culture of life by the very willingness to "lose itself" (cf. *Lk* 17:33 *et passim*) for others.

In the Catholic Church, and also in the other churches and ecclesial communities, new forms of charitable activity have arisen, while other, older ones have taken on new life and energy. In these new forms, it is often possible to establish a fruitful link between evangelization and works of charity. Here I would clearly reaffirm what my great predecessor John Paul II wrote in his Encyclical *Sollicitudo Rei Socialis*[28] when he asserted the readiness of the Catholic Church to cooperate with the charitable agencies of these churches and communities, since

25. Ibid., 14.

26. Cf. Congregation for Bishops, Directory for the Pastoral Ministry of Bishops *Apostolorum Successores* (22 February 2004), 195, Vatican City 2004, pp. 214–16.

27. Cf. John Paul II, Post-Synodal Apostolic Exhortation *Christifideles Laici* (30 December 1988), 41: *AAS* 81 (1989), 470–72.

28. Cf. No. 32: *AAS* 80 (1988), 556.

we all have the same fundamental motivation and look towards the same goal: a true humanism, which acknowledges that man is made in the image of God and wants to help him to live in a way consonant with that dignity. His Encyclical *Ut Unum Sint* emphasized that the building of a better world requires Christians to speak with a united voice in working to inculcate "respect for the rights and needs of everyone, especially the poor, the lowly and the defenseless."[29] Here I would like to express my satisfaction that this appeal has found a wide resonance in numerous initiatives throughout the world.

The distinctiveness of the Church's charitable activity

31. The increase in diversified organizations engaged in meeting various human needs is ultimately due to the fact that the command of love of neighbor is inscribed by the Creator in man's very nature. It is also a result of the presence of Christianity in the world, since Christianity constantly revives and acts out this imperative, so often profoundly obscured in the course of time. The reform of paganism attempted by the emperor Julian the Apostate is only an initial example of this effect; here we see how the power of Christianity spread well beyond the frontiers of the Christian faith. For this reason, it is very important that the Church's charitable activity maintains all of its splendor and does not become just another form of social assistance. So what are the essential elements of Christian and ecclesial charity?

a) Following the example given in the parable of the Good Samaritan, Christian charity is first of all the simple response to immediate needs and specific situations: feeding the hungry, clothing the naked, caring for and healing the sick, visiting those in prison, etc. The Church's charitable organizations, beginning with those of *Caritas* (at diocesan, national and international levels), ought to do everything in their power to provide the resources and above all the personnel needed for this work. Individuals who care for those in need must first be professionally competent: they should be properly trained in what to do and how to do it, and committed to continuing care. Yet, while professional competence is a primary, fundamental requirement, it is not of itself sufficient. We are dealing with human beings, and human beings always need something more than technically proper care. They need humanity. They need heartfelt concern. Those who work for the Church's charitable organizations must be distinguished by the fact that they do not merely meet the needs of the moment, but they dedicate themselves to others with heartfelt concern, enabling them to experience

---

29. No. 43: *AAS* 87 (1995), 946.

the richness of their humanity. Consequently, in addition to their necessary professional training, these charity workers need a "formation of the heart": they need to be led to that encounter with God in Christ which awakens their love and opens their spirits to others. As a result, love of neighbor will no longer be for them a commandment imposed, so to speak, from without, but a consequence deriving from their faith, a faith which becomes active through love (cf. *Gal* 5:6).

b) Christian charitable activity must be independent of parties and ideologies. It is not a means of changing the world ideologically, and it is not at the service of worldly stratagems, but it is a way of making present here and now the love which man always needs. The modern age, particularly from the nineteenth century on, has been dominated by various versions of a philosophy of progress whose most radical form is Marxism. Part of Marxist strategy is the theory of impoverishment: in a situation of unjust power, it is claimed, anyone who engages in charitable initiatives is actually serving that unjust system, making it appear at least to some extent tolerable. This in turn slows down a potential revolution and thus blocks the struggle for a better world. Seen in this way, charity is rejected and attacked as a means of preserving the *status quo*. What we have here, though, is really an inhuman philosophy. People of the present are sacrificed to the *moloch* of the future—a future whose effective realization is at best doubtful. One does not make the world more human by refusing to act humanely here and now. We contribute to a better world only by personally doing good now, with full commitment and wherever we have the opportunity, independently of partisan strategies and programs. The Christian's program —the program of the Good Samaritan, the program of Jesus—is "a heart which sees." This heart sees where love is needed and acts accordingly. Obviously when charitable activity is carried out by the Church as a communitarian initiative, the spontaneity of individuals must be combined with planning, foresight and cooperation with other similar institutions.

c) Charity, furthermore, cannot be used as a means of engaging in what is nowadays considered proselytism. Love is free; it is not practiced as a way of achieving other ends.[30] But this does not mean that charitable activity must somehow leave God and Christ aside. For it is always concerned with the whole man. Often the deepest cause of suffering is the very absence of God. Those who practice charity in the Church's name will never seek to impose the Church's faith upon others. They realize that a pure and generous love is the best witness to the God in whom we believe and by whom we are driven to love. A Christian knows

---

30. Cf. Congregation for Bishops, Directory for the Pastoral Ministry of Bishops *Apostolorum Successores* (22 February 2004), 196, Vatican City 2004, p. 216.

when it is time to speak of God and when it is better to say nothing and to let love alone speak. He knows that God is love (cf. *1 Jn* 4:8) and that God's presence is felt at the very time when the only thing we do is to love. He knows—to return to the questions raised earlier—that disdain for love is disdain for God and man alike; it is an attempt to do without God. Consequently, the best defense of God and man consists precisely in love. It is the responsibility of the Church's charitable organizations to reinforce this awareness in their members, so that by their activity—as well as their words, their silence, their example—they may be credible witnesses to Christ.

Those responsible for the Church's charitable activity

32. Finally, we must turn our attention once again to those who are responsible for carrying out the Church's charitable activity. As our preceding reflections have made clear, the true subject of the various Catholic organizations that carry out a ministry of charity is the Church herself—at all levels, from the parishes, through the particular Churches, to the universal Church. For this reason it was most opportune that my venerable predecessor Paul VI established the Pontifical Council *Cor Unum* as the agency of the Holy See responsible for orienting and coordinating the organizations and charitable activities promoted by the Catholic Church. In conformity with the episcopal structure of the Church, the bishops, as successors of the Apostles, are charged with primary responsibility for carrying out in the particular Churches the program set forth in the *Acts of the Apostles* (cf. 2:42–44): today as in the past, the Church as God's family must be a place where help is given and received, and at the same time, a place where people are also prepared to serve those outside her confines who are in need of help. In the rite of episcopal ordination, prior to the act of consecration itself, the candidate must respond to several questions which express the essential elements of his office and recall the duties of his future ministry. He promises expressly to be, in the Lord's name, welcoming and merciful to the poor and to all those in need of consolation and assistance.[31] The *Code of Canon Law*, in the canons on the ministry of the bishop, does not expressly mention charity as a specific sector of episcopal activity, but speaks in general terms of the bishop's responsibility for coordinating the different works of the apostolate with due regard for their proper character.[32] Recently, however, the *Directory for the Pastoral Ministry of Bishops* explored more specifically the duty of charity as a responsibility

31. Cf. Pontificale Romanum, *De Ordinatione Episcopi*, 43.
32. Cf. can. 394; *Code of Canons of the Eastern Churches*, can. 203.

incumbent upon the whole Church and upon each bishop in his diocese,[33] and it emphasized that the exercise of charity is an action of the Church as such, and that, like the ministry of Word and sacrament, it too has been an essential part of her mission from the very beginning.[34]

33. With regard to the personnel who carry out the Church's charitable activity on the practical level, the essential has already been said: they must not be inspired by ideologies aimed at improving the world, but should rather be guided by the faith which works through love (cf. *Gal* 5:6). Consequently, more than anything, they must be persons moved by Christ's love, persons whose hearts Christ has conquered with his love, awakening within them a love of neighbor. The criterion inspiring their activity should be Saint Paul's statement in the *Second Letter to the Corinthians*: "the love of Christ urges us on" (5:14). The consciousness that, in Christ, God has given himself for us, even unto death, must inspire us to live no longer for ourselves but for him, and, with him, for others. Whoever loves Christ loves the Church, and desires the Church to be increasingly the image and instrument of the love which flows from Christ. The personnel of every Catholic charitable organization want to work with the Church and therefore with the bishop, so that the love of God can spread throughout the world. By their sharing in the Church's practice of love, they wish to be witnesses of God and of Christ, and they wish for this very reason freely to do good to all.

34. Interior openness to the Catholic dimension of the Church cannot fail to dispose charity workers to work in harmony with other organizations in serving various forms of need, but in a way that respects what is distinctive about the service which Christ requested of his disciples. Saint Paul, in his hymn to charity (cf. *1 Cor* 13), teaches us that it is always more than activity alone: "If I give away all I have, and if I deliver my body to be burned, but do not have love, I gain nothing" (v. 3). This hymn must be the *Magna Carta* of all ecclesial service; it sums up all the reflections on love which I have offered throughout this Encyclical Letter. Practical activity will always be insufficient, unless it visibly expresses a love for man, a love nourished by an encounter with Christ. My deep personal sharing in the needs and sufferings of others becomes a sharing of my very self with them: if my gift is not to prove a source of humiliation, I must give to others not only something that is my own, but my very self; I must be personally present in my gift.

35. This proper way of serving others also leads to humility. The one who serves does not consider himself superior to the one served, however miserable his situation at the moment may be. Christ took the lowest place in the

---

33. Cf. Nos. 193–98: pp. 212–19.

34. *Ibid.*, 194: pp. 213–14.

world—the Cross—and by this radical humility he redeemed us and constantly comes to our aid. Those who are in a position to help others will realize that in doing so they themselves receive help; being able to help others is no merit or achievement of their own. This duty is a grace. The more we do for others, the more we understand and can appropriate the words of Christ: "We are useless servants" (*Lk* 17:10). We recognize that we are not acting on the basis of any superiority or greater personal efficiency, but because the Lord has graciously enabled us to do so. There are times when the burden of need and our own limitations might tempt us to become discouraged. But precisely then we are helped by the knowledge that, in the end, we are only instruments in the Lord's hands; and this knowledge frees us from the presumption of thinking that we alone are personally responsible for building a better world. In all humility we will do what we can, and in all humility we will entrust the rest to the Lord. It is God who governs the world, not we. We offer him our service only to the extent that we can, and for as long as he grants us the strength. To do all we can with what strength we have, however, is the task which keeps the good servant of Jesus Christ always at work: "The love of Christ urges us on" (*2 Cor* 5:14).

36. When we consider the immensity of others' needs, we can, on the one hand, be driven towards an ideology that would aim at doing what God's governance of the world apparently cannot: fully resolving every problem. Or we can be tempted to give in to inertia, since it would seem that in any event nothing can be accomplished. At such times, a living relationship with Christ is decisive if we are to keep on the right path, without falling into an arrogant contempt for man, something not only unconstructive but actually destructive, or surrendering to a resignation which would prevent us from being guided by love in the service of others. Prayer, as a means of drawing ever new strength from Christ, is concretely and urgently needed. People who pray are not wasting their time, even though the situation appears desperate and seems to call for action alone. Piety does not undermine the struggle against the poverty of our neighbors, however extreme. In the example of Blessed Teresa of Calcutta we have a clear illustration of the fact that time devoted to God in prayer not only does not detract from effective and loving service to our neighbor but is in fact the inexhaustible source of that service. In her letter for Lent 1996, Blessed Teresa wrote to her lay co-workers: "We need this deep connection with God in our daily life. How can we obtain it? By prayer."

37. It is time to reaffirm the importance of prayer in the face of the activism and the growing secularism of many Christians engaged in charitable work. Clearly, the Christian who prays does not claim to be able to change God's plans or correct what he has foreseen. Rather, he seeks an encounter with the Father

of Jesus Christ, asking God to be present with the consolation of the Spirit to him and his work. A personal relationship with God and an abandonment to his will can prevent man from being demeaned and save him from falling prey to the teaching of fanaticism and terrorism. An authentically religious attitude prevents man from presuming to judge God, accusing him of allowing poverty and failing to have compassion for his creatures. When people claim to build a case against God in defense of man, on whom can they depend when human activity proves powerless?

38. Certainly Job could complain before God about the presence of incomprehensible and apparently unjustified suffering in the world. In his pain he cried out: "Oh, that I knew where I might find him, that I might come even to his seat! … I would learn what he would answer me, and understand what he would say to me. Would he contend with me in the greatness of his power? … Therefore I am terrified at his presence; when I consider, I am in dread of him. God has made my heart faint; the Almighty has terrified me" (23:3, 5–6, 15–16). Often we cannot understand why God refrains from intervening. Yet he does not prevent us from crying out, like Jesus on the Cross: "My God, my God, why have you forsaken me?" (*Mt* 27:46). We should continue asking this question in prayerful dialogue before his face: "Lord, holy and true, how long will it be?" (*Rev* 6:10). It is Saint Augustine who gives us faith's answer to our sufferings: "*Si comprehendis, non est Deus*"—"if you understand him, he is not God."[35] Our protest is not meant to challenge God, or to suggest that error, weakness or indifference can be found in him. For the believer, it is impossible to imagine that God is powerless or that "perhaps he is asleep" (cf. *1 Kg* 18:27). Instead, our crying out is, as it was for Jesus on the Cross, the deepest and most radical way of affirming our faith in his sovereign power. Even in their bewilderment and failure to understand the world around them, Christians continue to believe in the "goodness and loving kindness of God" (*Tit* 3:4). Immersed like everyone else in the dramatic complexity of historical events, they remain unshakably certain that God is our Father and loves us, even when his silence remains incomprehensible.

39. Faith, hope and charity go together. Hope is practiced through the virtue of patience, which continues to do good even in the face of apparent failure, and through the virtue of humility, which accepts God's mystery and trusts him even at times of darkness. Faith tells us that God has given his Son for our sakes and gives us the victorious certainty that it is really true: God is love! It thus transforms our impatience and our doubts into the sure hope that God holds the world in his hands and that, as the dramatic imagery of the end of the Book

---

35.   *Sermo* 52, 16: PL 38, 360.

of Revelation points out, in spite of all darkness he ultimately triumphs in glory. Faith, which sees the love of God revealed in the pierced heart of Jesus on the Cross, gives rise to love. Love is the light—and in the end, the only light—that can always illuminate a world grown dim and give us the courage needed to keep living and working. Love is possible, and we are able to practice it because we are created in the image of God. To experience love and in this way to cause the light of God to enter into the world—this is the invitation I would like to extend with the present encyclical.

CONCLUSION

40. Finally, let us consider the saints, who exercised charity in an exemplary way. Our thoughts turn especially to Martin of Tours († 397), the soldier who became a monk and a bishop: he is almost like an icon, illustrating the irreplaceable value of the individual testimony to charity. At the gates of Amiens, Martin gave half of his cloak to a poor man: Jesus himself, that night, appeared to him in a dream wearing that cloak, confirming the permanent validity of the Gospel saying: "I was naked and you clothed me ... as you did it to one of the least of these my brethren, you did it to me" (*Mt* 25:36, 40).[36] Yet in the history of the Church, how many other testimonies to charity could be quoted! In particular, the entire monastic movement, from its origins with Saint Anthony the Abbot († 356), expresses an immense service of charity towards neighbor. In his encounter "face to face" with the God who is Love, the monk senses the impelling need to transform his whole life into service of neighbor, in addition to service of God. This explains the great emphasis on hospitality, refuge and care of the infirm in the vicinity of the monasteries. It also explains the immense initiatives of human welfare and Christian formation, aimed above all at the very poor, who became the object of care firstly for the monastic and mendicant orders, and later for the various male and female religious institutes all through the history of the Church. The figures of saints such as Francis of Assisi, Ignatius of Loyola, John of God, Camillus of Lellis, Vincent de Paul, Louise de Marillac, Giuseppe B. Cottolengo, John Bosco, Luigi Orione, Teresa of Calcutta to name but a few—stand out as lasting models of social charity for all people of good will. The saints are the true bearers of light within history, for they are men and women of faith, hope and love.

41. Outstanding among the saints is Mary, Mother of the Lord and mirror of all holiness. In the *Gospel of Luke* we find her engaged in a service of charity to

---

36. Cf. Sulpicius Severus, *Vita Sancti Martini*, 3, 1–3: SCh 133, 256–58.

her cousin Elizabeth, with whom she remained for "about three months" (1:56) so as to assist her in the final phase of her pregnancy. "*Magnificat anima mea Dominum,*" she says on the occasion of that visit, "My soul magnifies the Lord" (*Lk* 1:46). In these words she expresses her whole program of life: not setting herself at the centre, but leaving space for God, who is encountered both in prayer and in service of neighbor—only then does goodness enter the world. Mary's greatness consists in the fact that she wants to magnify God, not herself. She is lowly: her only desire is to be the handmaid of the Lord (cf. *Lk* 1:38, 48). She knows that she will only contribute to the salvation of the world if, rather than carrying out her own projects, she places herself completely at the disposal of God's initiatives. Mary is a woman of hope: only because she believes in God's promises and awaits the salvation of Israel, can the angel visit her and call her to the decisive service of these promises. Mary is a woman of faith: "Blessed are you who believed," Elizabeth says to her (cf. *Lk* 1:45). The *Magnificat*—a portrait, so to speak, of her soul—is entirely woven from threads of Holy Scripture, threads drawn from the Word of God. Here we see how completely at home Mary is with the Word of God, with ease she moves in and out of it. She speaks and thinks with the Word of God; the Word of God becomes her word, and her word issues from the Word of God. Here we see how her thoughts are attuned to the thoughts of God, how her will is one with the will of God. Since Mary is completely imbued with the Word of God, she is able to become the Mother of the Word Incarnate. Finally, Mary is a woman who loves. How could it be otherwise? As a believer who in faith thinks with God's thoughts and wills with God's will, she cannot fail to be a woman who loves. We sense this in her quiet gestures, as recounted by the infancy narratives in the Gospel. We see it in the delicacy with which she recognizes the need of the spouses at Cana and makes it known to Jesus. We see it in the humility with which she recedes into the background during Jesus' public life, knowing that the Son must establish a new family and that the Mother's hour will come only with the Cross, which will be Jesus' true hour (cf. *Jn* 2:4; 13:1). When the disciples flee, Mary will remain beneath the Cross (cf. *Jn* 19:25-27); later, at the hour of Pentecost, it will be they who gather around her as they wait for the Holy Spirit (cf. *Acts* 1:14).

42. The lives of the saints are not limited to their earthly biographies but also include their being and working in God after death. In the saints one thing becomes clear: those who draw near to God do not withdraw from men, but rather become truly close to them. In no one do we see this more clearly than in Mary. The words addressed by the crucified Lord to his disciple—to John and through him to all disciples of Jesus: "Behold, your mother!" (*Jn* 19:27)—are fulfilled anew in every generation. Mary has truly become the Mother of all

believers. Men and women of every time and place have recourse to her motherly kindness and her virginal purity and grace, in all their needs and aspirations, their joys and sorrows, their moments of loneliness and their common endeavors. They constantly experience the gift of her goodness and the unfailing love which she pours out from the depths of her heart. The testimonials of gratitude, offered to her from every continent and culture, are a recognition of that pure love which is not self- seeking but simply benevolent. At the same time, the devotion of the faithful shows an infallible intuition of how such love is possible: it becomes so as a result of the most intimate union with God, through which the soul is totally pervaded by him—a condition which enables those who have drunk from the fountain of God's love to become in their turn a fountain from which "flow rivers of living water" (*Jn* 7:38). Mary, Virgin and Mother, shows us what love is and whence it draws its origin and its constantly renewed power. To her we entrust the Church and her mission in the service of love:

> Holy Mary, Mother of God,
> you have given the world its true light,
> Jesus, your Son – the Son of God.
> You abandoned yourself completely
> to God's call
> and thus became a wellspring
> of the goodness which flows forth from him.
> Show us Jesus. Lead us to him.
> Teach us to know and love him,
> so that we too can become
> capable of true love
> and be fountains of living water
> in the midst of a thirsting world.

Given in Rome, at Saint Peter's, on the twenty-fifth of December, the Solemnity of the Nativity of the Lord, in the year 2005, the first of my Pontificate.

✠ BENEDICT XVI

www.ingramcontent.com/pod-product-compliance
Lightning Source LLC
Chambersburg PA
CBHW020340100426
42812CB00029B/3195/J